Statham's Abridgment of the law

Nicholas Statham, Margaret
1859-1931 Klingelsmith

STATHAM'S

ABRIDGMENT OF THE LAW

TRANSLATED BY

Margaret Center Klingelsmith, LL B

Librarian of the Biddle Law Library
University of Pennsylvania

I

BOSTON
THE BOSTON BOOK COMPANY
1915

FOREWORD

The work upon this book was done in those hours which could be spared from my duties as Librarian of the Biddle Law Library of the Department of Law of the University of Pennsylvania   In the beginning the inspiration to do the work came from the Dean of the Law Department, William Diaper Lewis, and to him I owe a never-failing encouragement through the years that have followed

To the Faculty of the Law Department I am indebted for a consideration and courtesy which have enabled me to give to the work that detailed attention which it has called for

To the University of Pennsylvania I owe all the acquirements that have enabled me to do the work at all, the defects in the work — many, and more visible to myself than they will ever be to the keenest critic who may scan it — are wholly my own   I had here the opportunity to remedy all those defects of scholarship which I freely acknowledge, if I have not so remedied them, it is, to use the language of "the books," "my own folly "

If I have here failed in giving to the University that which I hoped to give, my regret will be not for myself but for the institution, of which I can say with all my heart,

"I am glad
That here what colleging was mine, I had "

M C K

Quinzime

¶ Si ieo ay terre en vne ville a q̅ ieo ay c̅oeu appendr̅n̅t en auty̅ ville ieo sera taxe pur les bestes sou ils sount conch̅m̅tz z̅ le m̅tz vt pz en teps z̅ c̅ le v̅ a terme dans paiera les quinzimes m̅ b̅ ple p Share z̅ c̅.

¶ Si vn abbe soit seisi des terres des tenpalteez en s̅ mayn demesne il ne paiera .xv. p̅ z̅ c̅ q̅il paia dizimez. donqz si ceo q̅ est en b̅ mayn deuient ville aprez z̅ enhabite oue gentz d̅ z̅ ils paier̅ Et si aprez il dem̅et as maynz labbe q̅re sil paiera xv̅ en b̅ cas labbe de glastonbury b̅n debat̅ z̅ c̅ ceux q̅ sonnt ten̅m̅tz z̅ teign̅ dun baron del plem̅et come de m̅ cel baron p ron de q̅b̅ baronp il vient al plem̅ent ne paiera as ceo pen̅o de ch̅rs m̅ b̅ ple z̅ c̅.

¶ Lou diuers v̅ teign̅ dun abbe ou priory z̅ ils paiount al .xv. p̅ lo' ten̅y Et puis les v̅ deuen̅ as maynz labbe p eschete ou p auty̅ mane en s̅ cas labbe paicra al xv̅. par ceux ten̅tz non obsta̅te q̅ s̅ h̅'ie de m̅z les ten̅tz est ex̅tient p q̅b̅ h̅'ie il paia dizmes z̅ c̅ p oppion c̅m cuy'. z̅ d̅' m̅ b̅ ple q̅ les v̅ en bondage dun abbe ne paicra als̅. xv̅. put c̅ q̅ ceo est en man b̅ tery labbe quar b̅ fee z̅ b̅ frank v̅ b̅ en luy z̅ c̅ n̅ient p̅'s q̅ lou labbe lessa a b̅ tery a terme dans ou a terme de vie z̅ c̅ t̅n il semble q̅ labbe d̅m̅st paier̅ al xv̅. p̅ t toutz ces tenpalteez sicc̅me vne auty̅ home z̅ c̅ Don 33 les ron̅s adc̅r̅n̅t ne baonnt miez a ceux q̅ sonnt ex̅emptz de paier̅ al xv̅. z̅ c̅ q̅re.

Quare incumbrauit

¶ Quare incumbrauit ne gist sinon lou le no abn̅ i̅tas est directe al eues̅qz pen̅d̅ b̅ b̅e z̅ Sion en quare incumbrauit t̅n b̅ natura b̅ i̅uri e contrarie a c̅ io q̅re.

¶ En quare incumbrauit leues̅qz suit troue coup b̅. q̅il au encumby z̅ c̅ as dam̅ z̅ c̅. Thorp p̅ia b̅ dam̅ z̅ q̅ ces tenpalteez soient sh̅iez p̅ c̅ q̅il au encumby enconnty b̅ prohibic̅ sicome suist fa t lauty̅ terme en b̅ cas labbe de M̅ en vne attache' sur prohibic̅ Et p̅ia b̅e al eues̅qz dou̅s̅ty ce' q̅il au encumby et il au r̅ug accordr̅n̅t mez nel q̅ ces tenp alteez suy sensiez z̅ c̅.

¶ Vn home au ree en quare incumbrauit vers leues̅qz z̅ au b̅ie al v̅ie a disty̅ b̅ eues̅qz p̅ d' sacumby z̅ c̅ q̅w .xx. b̅ issuez. Et p̅ie dit q̅il put̅y au p greind̅y issuez z̅ p̅ia b̅e as iustid dau̅s̅ denquerey de ceo z̅ au̅y b̅ie a disty̅ seues̅qz ate̅y z̅ dd̅e icp a cert̅ iou̅y p̅' p̅' p̅ q̅b̅ il au disacumby z̅ huit z̅ c̅ en vn no.

¶ En quare incumbrauit b̅ pb̅ cornb̅ q̅il pb̅ vne prohibic̅ al̅b̅ eues̅qz q̅il ne admitt̅a a nul b̅ clerk pendr̅n̅t vne ple q̅ fuist pend̅ en comen bank nient discusse penty̅ moy z̅ vne h̅ z̅ nient obstante c̅ seues̅qz ad encumby m̅ leglise z̅ c̅ b̅ dc̅s̅ dit q̅ b̅ prohibic̅ fuist d̅l̅.iie a luy z̅ auty̅ io' dem̅it̅q b̅ io' il ad admitt̅a vn T̅ p̅' c̅ q̅il ne sau̅ de nul b̅ ple pend̅ z̅ c̅ s̅m̅z c̅ q̅il au resc̅eu T̅ al̅b̅ es̅gb̅ puis b̅ prohibic̅ et issue suist pris z̅ c̅ z̅ issint semble q̅ home nau̅a quare incumbrauit pend̅ b̅ ple sinon q̅il au ne admitt̅as der̅m̅t z̅ q̅re si seues̅qz resc̅eust vne de lou̅y clerkz aprez les. vi. moys quar il m̅ pr̅es z̅ laps non obstante b̅ prohibic̅ t̅n c̅redo q̅il ne put̅ rec̅euer auty̅ clerk z̅ c̅.

¶ Quare incumbrauit ag̅ boñ lou leues̅qz encumbr̅a infra tempus semesty̅ nient obsta̅te q̅ nul b̅ aco' suist attame der̅m̅t de m̅ leglise.

ABRIDGMENT

OF THE

LAW

By

NICHOLAS STATHAM

Translated by

MARGARET CENTER KLINGELSMITH, LL B.

LIST OF TITLES

TOLLE   VIEWE
TAILLE   VARIANNCE
TOURNE DE VIC   WARREN
                         WITHERNAM
WASTE   VERDIT
VISNEE   VILLENAGE
VOUCHER   UTLARY

PER ME. R PYNSON

INTRODUCTION

I

This Book coming to my hands, which through my own small skill in the Law, perceiving it to be an Ingenious thing, desiring to bring it to the Test, the grave Judgments of such as were profound in the Knowledge of the Law not only approved of it, but highly Commended it, adjudging it a thing worthy to be Published for the good of the whole Nation. Which being done, I represent it to the open View of all men, not doubting that they will find it answer to their desires, to their great Use and Benefit   But knowing on the other side that many will be apt to spurn, if they find the least iota wanting, I crave the favorable construction of all ingenious Persons, and for the Malevilous and Caterpillers of our Age, which will not be content with anything, I leave as I find

The unknown gentleman whose introduction to the book called The Exact Lawgiver I have ventured thus to paraphrase, added one word more to his introduction   I wish I had his courage and could end with *Vale*, after as few words as he felt he needed address to his readers   But while I hope for the "favorable construction of all ingenious persons," I have a great fellow feeling for those "Caterpillers of our Age which will not be content with anything," unless it be well worth their browsing upon it, and it seems that they should be given a little something upon which to feed beyond the solid matter of the translation itself, even though they should be less content with the fore-word than the word itself.

When we have an old friend to introduce to a world which knows of him, honors him so far as its knowledge goes, yet knows him not well enough to do him full honor, we begin to withdraw a little from that friend and make an attempt to regard him with less friendly and more observant eyes   So it is with some of us in regard to our old friend Statham and his book   It is true that one should not need to do this with our author and his book, all know of it   All know that it is the first friend of the bewildered seeker through the maze of precedent pioneer of that long tine of patient digesters of our common law, who have gone on increasing with the increasing years Columbus of the common law, pointing his pinnace straight into the uncharted sea of precedent, he is familiar to us all We have but to look into any bibliography of legal literature to find his name leading all the rest as that of the man who made the "first attempt to methodize our law " But yet it has been for the most part merely a name. He is given credit for being the first to enter the field; for his "originally," for "serving as a model for similar productions " But immediately thereafter we begin to read, "This work had the fate to be of less use than, perhaps, any performance that in the nature of it, assumed to aim at such general utility." [Reeves, Hist. of Eng Law, Vol 4, p 117] And, still worse "His book is much esteemed for the antiquity thereof, for, otherwise, lawyers behold him as soldiers do bows and arrows since the invention of guns, rather for sight than service " [Fuller Worthies, as quoted by Wallace, The Reporters, p 661] Wallace has made this verdict familiar to many who would never have sought it in the "Worthies," and the legal world has accepted it without much thought Indeed we might go further and say that it has accepted it without any thought at all, for had they stopped to think about it they would have found that this work, thus dropped into the limbo of forgotten things, is no archaic engine of a less developed world, fitted only to be thrown aside for the more complete implement of a later day, but that it is indeed the shaped and polished cornerstone of the legal edifice which now shelters us It seems too true that the "ingenious persons" who have written our legal bibliography and the history of our law have been content to repeat the edict of the early and unknown critic who first set the fashion of calling Statham's Abridgment "ancient and outworn " So it has been left for one more of the "Caterpiller" sort, not quite content to rely upon hearsay, and feeding gropingly upon the sources of the law, to come back to this earliest Abridgment of that law with somewhat, it may be, of the feelings of those into whose hands it was first put—a sense of obligation to the maker of the book, and a realization that such work is not done for one generation only, but that its benefits reach out and down into the whole later life of the law This feeling and this realization are what have led to the translation of the work. Others far better fitted to the task might have done it, but it seemed that we might wait a long time before the person perfectly fitted for the task could be found.

None knows better than the present editor how much better it could be done if one were given that unlimited time to strive for perfection which is denied to most workers under modern conditions.

There is apparently an idea among those students who use the older books of the law that Statham has not been very much used since the later abridgments were published, and that such disuse is because of some lack in the book itself, inaccuracies or crudenesses, that it is an older and therefore a ruder piece of work, somewhat carelessly done, and set aside very reasonably when the more skilfully framed and more correct abridgments were offered to the world. With the exception of such remarks as that of Fuller's, which I have just quoted, which seems to hint at the rudeness of the performance, I do not know of any statements to such an effect on the part of the earlier writers. But the impression certainly exists, and must have had some excuse, if not reason, for being   There is one very simple explanation. Statham printed his book (or it was printed) before any of the Year Books had been put into type.   This means that he could give no reference to the folios of the Year Books, such as Fitzherbert could and did give when he printed his Abridgment in 1514   Wherever Fitzherbert gives references to unprinted Year Books, his references are simply to Years and Terms, exactly like those of Statham   This leaves, of course, the entire term to be searched through in order that the case may be identified.   If the term is short this is not so serious a matter, but if the term is long, and many of them are very long, it takes much time and patience to find the desired case.   When the student could turn to Fitzherbert and find his reference completed with the folio number, he would naturally do so, and think it was not worth while to attempt to use the work which required the greater time and patience   In this way there would soon grow up some such feeling about the use of Statham's Abridgment as in our days grows up about a book which may be very good, even very excellent, in many ways, but which has an inadequate index or table of cases.   We know that there is "good matter" there, but we have neither the time nor the patience to search for it when such data are at hand elsewhere.   So the book is cast aside, no new edition appears, and the good matter is lost, or is discredited. This seems a very simple, but is it not a quite adequate, reason for the apparent disuse of the abridgment which bears Statham's name?

Another reason for this real disuse in later times may very easily be the type and the abbreviations used in the printing of Statham.

These presented no difficulties to the scholars of the time when it was printed, indeed they must have seemed a vast improvement upon the manuscripts then in use With a type conforming very beautifully to the better written manuscripts, with the abbreviations very generally expanded, with the clear, perfect printing of the pages, the book must have been a boon to the reader of the latter part of the fourteen hundreds But as printing became more common, as the use of the manuscripts became unusual, as the Year Books expanded the abbreviations and they ceased to be known to the average scholar, the student, when he turned to Statham's Abridgment, would find himself faced with symbols and abbreviations of which he did not know the meaning. Having the cases elsewhere, or thinking that he had them, he would naturally turn to the books he could read with ease, first Fitzherbert, and then Brooke, and gradually the ability to read the abbreviated text became rare, and at last, for a few generations, the ability of the average lawyer to read the crabbed text of the Year Books themselves failed. I know this was only for a short time, and that always there have been "black letter lawyers" ready to give of their stores of knowledge to their less well equipped brothers Yet there was such a period, a period in which the actual readers of the Year Books were comparatively few A period in which we were told that the language of those books was "barbarous", in which it was said (and this by so learned and earnest a student of the Year Books as Mr Luke Owen Pike) that they were "repulsive" [Y. B Rolls Series, 12 & 13 Ed III, Preface, p xiii] During that period those who were repelled from the Year Books would naturally not resort to Statham, although his book is beautiful to look upon, for there they would find not only the barbarous language itself, but its still more uncivilized — or what to them would seem so — abbreviations I believe it to have been very greatly during this period that the use of Statham declined For there are certain facts that show that for many generations Statham as an authority held his own with the other abridgments One of the chief of these facts is that while the earlier editions of the Year Books — one might better speak of printings than editions, perhaps — contain marginal references to "Fitzh." only, later printings add references not only to Brooke but to Statham Had the credit of Statham's work died out between the time of the printing and the date of the Year Books first containing these references, such references would surely not have been added. I have not been able to definitely decide upon the date of the printing of these first marginal references to Statham in the Year Books. There certainly are none in the earliest editions, it seems that some time between 1556 and 1600 citations to both Brooke and Fitzherbert began to find their way into the margins of the Year Books, to be copied into the margins of the 1679 edition. Scattered about among these references we also find notes that "Statham disagrees" or that one is to "see Statham" on a certain point. It is evident from these notes that not only was Statham's Abridgment still in constant use, but that Statham's ideas were still given great credit. And while the Books themselves were in daily use, persons were being constantly referred to the Abridgment by these marginal notes. It would seem, therefore, that only for the comparatively brief period during which the Year Books themselves were less commonly used has Statham's Abridgment been a "curio" merely. For the greater part of four hundred years it has been a necessary part of the equipment of the lawyer as well as the student of the law. And it is evident, now that the revival of the student spirit has brought us back to drink again of the sources of our law, we must naturally turn to this earliest and best of those sources. Again, there are very many who read the Year Books as easily as they do the modern volume, who find no difficulties in the manuscripts themselves, who love the abbreviations of the early print for their very shapeliness. We may then declare, and we believe truly, that there was no long period in which the Abridgment of Statham was either unused or discredited, that our views on this subject have been merely misdirected for a short period by those to whom the early black letter book had become nothing but antiquated law, and that it has in reality been an integral part of the scholar's equipment for the greater part of the time since it appeared in print.

When did it appear in print? The only positive statement to be made is that no bibliographer dares to make any positive statement at all about it. It does not seem worth while to set down here all the guesses on the subject, since at best they are but guesses without any apparent foundation in fact. The guessers range in their dates from 1467 to 1490, and Marvin even says we do not know whether it was printed before or after Fitzherbert's Abridgment. He apparently adopts this idea from Reeves [Reeves, Hist of Eng Law, Vol 4, p 117], but Reeves gives no authority for his statement. For the extreme

on the other side we have the statement in Merewether and Stephens
[Merewether and Stephens, Boroughs and Municipal Corporations,
Vol. 2, pp 686, 691] that Statham's Abridgment was "first published
in 1467, 7th Edward IV." We may, however, offset that statement
by their further statement on page 691 of the same volume, that
Statham was "one of the Barons of the Exchequer in the reign of
Edward IV, ... and his compilation was published at London by
Pynson, in the time of Henry VIII. It has no date or title-page.
But as it has Pynson's mark, it is supposed to have been printed by
William Tailleur, at Rouen, who printed Littleton's Tenures for that
publisher." So we get a very early date and a very late date, and
from the same hand a number of equally well substantiated items.

All that can be said for the various bibliographers or writers about
the book is that they do not pretend to know much, and that they
make no one responsible for their statements In many cases it is
apparent that they have never seen a copy of the book Many of
them speak doubtfully of the colophon of Tailleur, as if it were a mere
supposition that the colophon appeared in the volume, and that the
idea that he printed the book might have arisen from the fact that
he was the printer of Littleton's Tenures Some write as if the
"Printed per me. R. Pynson" might not have actually appeared
on the list of titles, but they think if it were a fact it would show the
book to have been printed somewhere between 1470 and 1490 It
would appear that even those who might very easily have had access
to a copy of the book — like Merewether and Stephens — did not
take the trouble to look at it, but they were not writing bibliographies
and may be forgiven The bibliographers Brooke and Worrall
believe that there were two editions apparently, one a folio, the other
a quarto. I have never been able to trace the authority for this belief,
and I have never seen more than one impression, but the fact that the
volume might class as either a folio or a quarto owing to its size and
shape may very probably have led to its being described by some
one as a quarto, and by some other one as a folio, thus leading to the
belief that it had appeared in both forms

Such facts as we have to base any theories upon are these The book
exists. It is very beautifully printed in a type which does not appear
to have been used in any other English law book, but which closely
resembles a type used in a few other books printed in England at a very
early period It is a small folio, closely approximating a quarto in

shape. It has no title-page, which is a characteristic of the very earliest printed books The folios are not numbered It has a list of titles alphabetically arranged and placed before the subject-matter of the book. There is a colophon, which is not on a folio by itself, but appears on the back of the last folio, which if numbered would be folio 187. The colophon is everywhere recognized as that of Tailleur of Rouen At the end of the list of titles there is printed "Per me R Pynson." This makes Pynson responsible only for the printing of the list of titles. The type, however, is exactly the same as that used in the body of the book These facts leave us in doubt whether the entire book was printed for Pynson or not. It might have been printed — for Statham or another — in Rouen It may never have been actually put on the market until Pynson, having an actually established publishing business, took it up, added the list of titles to make it practically more useful to his patrons, and gave it to the world This, of course, is pure conjecture, but it shows that if Pynson added the list of titles in England, he had the type with which to print it, unless, again, the list was sent to Tailleur If it was done in England it is the only law book of the period which was so well done, the law books of the next century were much cruder performances, typographically speaking.

It has been said, but I do not know that I have ever seen the statement printed, that there is internal evidence that the book was printed much later than 1470 The idea was that the cases cited in the Abridgment ran up to a later date than 1470 I have read with care every word in the book at least twice I have verified so far as has been reasonably possible, every case there cited. I have carefully examined these citations with a view to the testimony as to the date of the book which might be gained from them. The cases run from Edward the Second to the last year of Henry the Sixth (1461). There are only ten cases in this last year of Henry Sixth (39 Hen VI), eight in 38 Hen. VI (1460), while back of that time the various years of Henry VI are represented many times There is an apparent citation to a case in 46 Hen VI (1468), but that is a patent error, as Henry VI only came back to his throne after his 39th year, for that short and troubled period of less than a year, for which year his reign is not counted among the regnal years Had this been a correct citation it would only have brought the latest citation to 1468, which would have left the possible printing of the book in 1470 still clear.

However, the case is patently an error in citation and has no value as evidence whatever   The next apparently late date is that of a citation to 43 Ed IV, and occurs on p 169, b of the Abridgment.   This would of course bring the printing of the book long after the date assigned to it by those who believe in the earlier date, but on investigation the case proves to be a case reported in 43 Ed III, and the addition of the fourth "I" a printer's error.   There is also a "Statute of Primo Ed IV" which brings the date up to the first year of the reign of Edward IV, but as this first year of Edward IV is also the last year of Henry VI's reign, we have no later date in reality, although it sounds later to say that the internal evidence brings us up to the first year of Edward IV than to say that we can trace the cases no later than the last year of Henry VI   After the most careful search I can find no further evidence, even erroneous evidence, which would bring the printing of the book later than 1470, the earliest assigned date   The latest erroneous date would bring the last date given in the book to 1468, the latest correct date is at the latest 1461   This would seem to put to rest all rumors that there is any internal evidence for the later date, and allows nine years between the last date in the book and the earliest assigned date for printing   1470 is an early date for printing done in England   The evidence that it was not done in England, or if done in England was done by French type, strengthens the idea that it is very early printing, or else that it was done in England by English printers who were beginning to print law books just before the end of the fourteen hundreds   Mr. Soule believed that the Year Books began to appear in print about 1480–82, so that the type and the printers would be ready to print such a law book as this of Statham by that time   The fact that it was not so done is very clear proof that it was because it was too early for the work to be handled in England with success, or without the use of the French type, and shows that it must have been before the regular printing of law books in England, which would place the date before 1480   I doubt if the exact date can ever be established; I incline to an early date, *circa* 1470–1475, until some evidence is advanced to show that it was not then published, but I should be very greatly surprised if any evidence should ever be advanced showing it to have been published after 1480

As to the life history of Statham we have but little data, and what we have is of very little authority   The bibliographies list him as

"Statham. Nich Baron of the Exchequer, 7 Ed. IV" But we do not know that "Baron of the Exchequer" has any foundation in fact We have, to be sure, Dugdale's note after the record of his name as reader at Lincoln's Inn, "*postea unus Baronum de Scace*" If Dugdale were infallible this, of course, would be sufficient, but as it is, this is simply evidence that this was thought to be the fact. We are told by Foss [Foss· Biographical Dict. Statham] that on October 30, 1467, Statham received a patent for the grant of the office of Second Baron of the Exchequer [Dugdale, p. 68, says 1468], in reversion on the death of one John Clerke It is not known that the office became vacant while Statham lived, but either he or John Clerke died in 1481, and Thomas Whittington was appointed Baron of the Exchequer [Dugdale Origines, p 249] John Clerke was appointed second Baron of the Exchequer in 1472 [Dugdale, p. 70], but there appears to be no record of his death As there is no record of the patent being granted to Statham, the proof that he was ever a Baron of the Exchequer seems very inadequate It is probable that the reversion to the office did not fall in while he was alive, and that the work we are now considering was made while he was in Lincoln's Inn, either prior to the time he was appointed reader, in 1471, or at that time. It is possible that he may have been appointed reader because of the very fact that it was known that he had prepared the work, and because of the learning and industry which he had shown in thus preparing it It may have been published as an aid to his work as a reader It is just such work as a lecturer of a law school of to-day finds it necessary to do when he takes up any branch of the law which has not been classified in such a way as to make it teachable. No branch of the law was so classified when Statham became a reader There were thousands of Year Book cases still in manuscript—in many cases most excellent manuscript—and collected into volumes in various ways, and usually without arrangement. I say usually, for I have seen manuscripts divided into subjects, a sort of classified arrangement, which yet are catalogued as Year Books These seem to have been the first systematic attempts at the arrangement of our law, but they seem to be neither abridgments nor digests, unless it be in a very elementary way. It is very probable that Statham began by setting down under certain heads the cases he was using, and the scattered points he found in the cases, without at first having any very definite design for the work, and almost certainly without any idea of printing at that early period of the art. But as time went on and he added new subjects, and as he scrutinized the law and verified the statements of his work, finding them useful to himself, and therefore likely to be of use to other students and practisers of the law, it is probable that the idea of publication came to him. But only "probable," for we have no proof that he ever thought of publication or that he lived to know that a book which was to be known by his name was to see the light. There are certain things about the book itself which have led me to believe that the reason that we know so little of Statham, or of his work, is that he died long before 1481, when the reversion to the office of Second Baron of the Exchequer fell in through the death of John Clerke. For the book, careful and complete as it is, with a marvelously small number of errors, yet shows the lack of a master hand in its finish — the sure eye, the fatherly editing, which such a work must surely have secured from a man capable of compiling it. Here is a book, absolutely well done, excellently arranged A book in which the cases are so well digested that it would be very difficult to make them more brief and at the same time convey more of the content of the case. Cases so concisely done that they bear evidence of the intent that nothing extraneous or useless shall be retained, yet also done with great care that nothing essential shall be omitted, and that the law shall be made as clear as possible on every point considered Yet in spite of all this we find little loose threads left, like the citation to "blank Fitz." on page 1, which has been printed solemnly as if it were a finished citation instead of a blank left in the author's manuscript to be filled in later. We also find many careless remarks, evidently not intended for publication, which the compiler himself would have smilingly blue-penciled — if they had the equivalent of the blue pencil in those days — but which the printer, careful though he was (in fact it would seem, through his very carefulness, that nothing should be lost), has conscientiously retained, much to our present day gratification. There is also the evidence of cases thrown into a subject after it was apparently complete. A title will apparently be ended, and a cross-reference given as usual at the end of a subject, and then there will come more cases, generally of a late date, which have apparently been added after the title was finished. It seems quite sure that so careful a compiler, so keen a digester, so thorough a worker, would not have left these blemishes in his work Therefore it seems not too much to assume that Statham was dead when the work was going through the press,

and those who knew the value of the work, and perhaps wished to per-
petuate his name, took the manuscript just as it was and getting Pynson
to take charge of the publication, left it in his hands to be finally shaped
and given to the world. The name of Statham does not appear on the
title-page or in any part of the work itself, there is no attempt at any
introduction or preface, there is no signature at the end. There is
nothing to show the pride or the anxiety of editorship I feel sure
that had Statham lived and had he attained a position equal to his
attainments, as we have them exemplified in this work, we should have
heard much more about him, much more about his book, and that
his book would have shown much surer signs of his workmanship.

It seems that there must have been very great interest in the work
in order that it should get to be printed at all But most of all that
it should get to be printed so well, in such type, and with an evident
idea of making it a beautiful example of the typographical art The
great care and responsibility which must have attended the work,
whether the type was sent over to England, or the book sent to Rouen
to be printed, all go to prove that persons of responsibility and wealth
must have taken the matter in hand Who and what they were
remains a mystery, but we owe a debt of gratitude to those unknown
men who did their work so well, who were content to do it and to
pay for it, yet never to claim any acknowledgment for all that they
did, in title-page, or public statement of any kind

Let us look for a moment at the task which this man, evidently still
young, undertook for the clearing up of the knowledge of the law of
England. Of course he had not all the cases to deal with that we have
in the eleven volumes of the Year Books which make up the collection
of cases of the edition of 1679. The last case with which Statham
deals is, as we have said, in the last year of Henry VI (1461) After
that date we have now the Year Books of Edward IV, and such as
have been printed of Henry VII and VIII Statham made very little
use of the cases decided in the time of Edward II, now printed in the
Maynard, or first volume of the 1679 edition of the Year Books. It
is very probable that the manuscript volume from which these cases
were afterward printed may not have been accessible to Statham, and
he may have taken the few cases he was able to cite from manuscript
notes by another hand This seems to be the more likely, as the
citations to these cases usually appear beside very short abridgments, as
if they be from notes casually jotted down in court. These cases,

when finally traced in the Maynard, have been so traced only after a good deal of time and pains taken, as the points made are hard to identify. It is very probable that some of the Edward II cases which I have apparently identified are in reality not identical, and that I have been in error, a like case may seem identical when looked at from one point of view, and may, even to the same person, seem quite unlike when looked at from another angle. At all events Statham used some cases from the reign of Edward the Second, but not a large number in proportion to those used of the other reigns There are also comparatively few cases cited for the early years of Edward III, although I believe that there are more, and probably better, manuscript reports for that reign than for any other, existent even to-day. The citations to the cases for the latter part of that reign are more abundant and the cases are more easily identified; there is no apparent reason for either fact.

If Statham had any model for the work he set himself, we do not know For all that we know to the contrary he made his own analysis and arranged his cases under that analysis entirely according to his own ideas of what was either the most necessary, the most logical, or the most convenient way. At all events we do know that he proceeded very much as makers of abridgments have been proceeding ever since, that his example has been followed by the early makers of abridgments, who in their turn have been followed by the makers of digests even up to the present day

There are two hundred and fifty-eight titles in Statham's Abridgment At least seventy-six of these are unknown to our modern law, or rather are obsolete as titles in our modern digests. Yet to these unknown and obscure titles our modern law goes back in an unbroken line The Aide de Roy, the Voucher, the Cessavit—all sound somewhat uncouth, a trifle archaic in our ears, yet in tracing these subjects through their early history and later development we find them all giving to our modern law the features and the tendencies which distinguish it The ancestral ruff and farthingale have been discarded, the law no longer wears a robe and wig, but the face and figure are those of the remote ancestors who gave it life and meaning

We find that in these two hundred and fifty-eight titles Statham succeeded in covering the greater part of the law of his day; that his scheme appears to have been comprehensive, and that he had a system of cross-references which, while not exhaustive, yet was intended to do what the cross-reference of to-day does for the modern digest That this system of cross-references was not carried to its intended completeness we may ascribe to the same factor that prevented the complete proofreading of the whole work, the failure of the master hand to hold the reins until the end. As has been noted before, the cross-references often do not come at the end of the title, as it appears in the completed volume The addition of cases at the end of the title probably was by another hand and does not show Statham's own work

The task which Statham set himself was a huge one, as these titles show. That it was completely done in the way of collecting all the cases and printing them in one comprehensive work, we may not claim It would seem that this was not the intention of the compiler Rather it would appear that he intended to show under each head a certain class of cases, and show them in a certain way. It may yet be that some student who cares for the task, and can spare the time for the labor, may be able to trace out the system which Statham used, and find the reason why he eliminated cases which he must have known well, and for putting in cases which are of comparatively little value If the theory be correct that he collected cases for his course as a reader, he would more naturally have collected such cases as bore on his discourse than those on other points, but of this we have no knowledge.

We have said that Statham did not have to digest all the Year Book cases that we now have But he did have some cases that we have now only in manuscript Statham took his cases at first hand, and of course from the manuscript He has references to a good many cases from the reign of Richard II No cases from the reign were ever printed until, in 1914, the twelfth year of that reign was translated and published [Y B 12 Ric II, edited and translated by George Deiser Ames Foundation] To this year I have been able to give citations, where the cases have been identifiable To the other years of the reign no citation can be given, although a good many cases from those years appear in the Abridgment Fitzherbert has printed some of the same cases, looking very much as if they had been copied from Statham. There are other cases which appear in Statham and not in the other Abridgments, and which are not in the printed Year Books In such cases the law given is known to us only as Statham gives it, and we shall have to go to him for it until all the Year Books now in manuscript are given to the world, and perhaps longer, as some of the books to which Statham had access have very probably perished from the earth. He gives us cases from the early years of Edward III. Some of these have been printed in the Rolls Series for those years, and are identifiable, others have not been identified, showing that Statham had access to yet other manuscripts than those from which that series are being printed. There are yet other cases from the later years of Edward III, which have not yet been printed — those between 30 and 38 Edward III. And from the unprinted years of Henry VI we have yet other cases   Brooke does not contain any of these and Fitzherbert rarely has them   All these cases afford what we have every reason to believe are correct digests of cases not elsewhere accessible in any printed book   They are a large addition to our knowledge of the early law, and this added knowledge is surely worth having

Much has been said as to the fascination of the early Year Books, and the light their cases shed upon the period, now so dim to us, in which these litigants come to seek justice — or defeat it — in the courts of England   In some the idea of such fascination evokes amusement, the only amusement they think they will derive from Year Book lore But let them not be deceived! If they are ever enticed into the pleasurable pursuit of Year Book cases, they will find that they will join the ranks of those to whom it is high holiday to put down the last case in the United States Supreme Court report, or the latest arrival in the way of decisions in the Court of Appeal in England, and all their modern tribe, and to plunge into a case where my master Martyn and some of his colleagues are matching wits in a long debate   And why should one who can rejoice in the perusal of Froissart, and his pictures of the light and shade of the life of his day — the jousting and the feasting, and the life of the common road — not enjoy as much the picture by a contemporary pen of those people who appear upon the pages of the Year Book of Henry VI [7 Hen VI p 9, pl 15], where it was asked of the justices why a case was adjourned from Cumberland County to Westminster   And Boynton said that it was a just matter, because the parties in their own counties came with a great rout of armed people, more like coming to battle than to the Assizes, and so for doubt that the power of the King be disturbed, and also because the counsel was in London, they adjourned the Assize   We are back in the times of the strong hand and the armed band, so vividly painted for us by the master hand of Green, the historian   "The violence and anarchy which had always clung like a taint to the baronage had received a new impulse from the war with France   Long before the struggle was over it had done its fatal work on the mood of the English noble   His aim had become little more than a lust for gold, a longing after plunder, after the pillage of farms, the sack of cities, the ransom of captives.   The nobles were as lawless and dissolute at home as they were greedy and cruel abroad."   [Green: Short History of the English People, p 274]   But Green, we believe we may say, did not count the Year Books among the sources from which he drew his knowledge of the period   Had he done so, that paragraph in which he arraigns the brutality of the times, and showed that history, poetry and religion had all gone down together, might have held one gleam of light.   The reign of Henry VI, that dark period which Green is painting in such Stygian colors when seen from the point of view of the Year Books, shows that the courts were doing their work, and doing it well, during this period of darkness and confusion elsewhere.   We get but such small glimpses, as this case which we have just quoted, of the violence and lawlessness of the times   It is characteristic of the placidity of the courts that even this case gives no more time to the episode of the armed men and the rout they made, but the lawyers go on calmly discussing the technical point as to whether the removal of the case was legal, which point went on to be regularly decided   And it is to be noted that many of the foundation cases in our law to-day, cases of Nuisance, Trespass, Contract and Carriers, find their principles first stated in those desolate years of Henry VI.

And one finds touches of human sympathy in the courts of the time also   Take this picture, painted for us in the case found in Michaelmas Term [35 Hen. VI, p 11, pl 18], where a writ of Trespass was brought against an infant   Wangford declared against the defendant, and Billing came and defended and said, "Sir, you see plainly that this defendant is only four years old, so it is clearly proven that he had not discretion to make a trespass, and does not know malice "   Moile said to Wangford "Can you find it in your conscience to declare against this infant of so tender an age?   I think he does not know what malice is, for he is not a person of great strength, and that you can see with your own eyes "   And upon that, Moile lifted up the infant in his hands and put him on the Bar, and said to Wangford, "Here is the very person, and therefore be advised "   Wangford was apparently somewhat confused, but he felt he must do something for his client, so

he said, "I do nothing except what I was told, and here is the party
and the trespass clearly upon him, for by this trespass one of his eyes
was put out." And then Billing asked for the appointment of a
guardian, whom Moile willingly appointed Justice might have been
too blind to see the helplessness of a little child in those days, but not
so the justices themselves, fathers most of them probably, and with
hearts that beat as warmly under judicial robes as they do now. The
case of the Duke of Norfolk against Sir Robert Wingfield shows that
the great men of the time did not always assent to the rough methods
of the armed camp but submitted themselves to the reign of law, and
carried their causes up from lower court to higher court, quite as we
do to-day And this in the midst of that period when, according
to Green, those were years of the deepest gloom, no age of our history
is more sad and sombre! Among the causes of the sombreness was the
most terrible plague the world has ever seen, when we are told half
the population of England was swept away in the course of its repeated
visits to that country. There is a case of waste of this period, not
digested by Statham, in which the trespass is for houses allowed to fall
down for want of repair, and the defence is that on account of the pesti-
lence there was no one to live in them and keep them up, and that therefore they fell down A simple but grim glance into the terrible events
that were making up the history of that time, making law, too, for
it was as a consequence of this devastation of the population that
labor became so scarce and wages so high that the landlord class
found it necessary to pass that famous Statute of Laborers [23 Ed III
(1349-50), Stats at Large, Vol 21, p 26] upon which there are so many
cases in the later years of Ed III and Henry V and VI Of course
there were later cases, but Statham's cases end with the latter reign

The cases on this Statute as given by Statham are interesting, as they
represent many different points of view in regard to the interpretation of
the Statute A case in 47 Ed III [T. 47 Ed. III, Stat tit Laborers, 7]
says that "no servant shall be compelled to serve except in the occupation of husbandman," showing that the idea of the lawmakers in
passing such a Statute was evidently thought to have been the forcing
of the agricultural laborer to do the work of the landlord, and that
it was the general thought that the Statute was not meant to apply
to other occupations As time went on, however, the Statute was
invoked in order to compel other classes of persons to labor whether
they were agreed to do so or not, and in 9 Hen. VI [Paschal, 9 Hen VI,

p. 7, pl 18] we find a case where the action is brought on the Statute to compel a scrivener to serve who has objected to teaching his trade; and no defence is made as to his occupation being outside the Statute, showing how far the law had gone in widening the limits within which the provisions of the Statute were applicable

In 41 Ed III [p. 17, pl. 2], we have a description of the life of the times which is most interesting, as showing the makeshifts to which the people were put when they wished to transfer land so that it should be held, not in the way the law would interpret the ordinary transfer, but as they would have it held. In this case the husband wished to give his wife a share in the property, and the remainder to his daughter in fee, so he "gives" those tenements of his to two priests, who are to re-enfeoff him — the agreement evidently being wholly without witnesses or other formalities — and his wife in tail, the remainder over to his daughter, Agnes, in fee But before the re-enfeoffment is really made, Richard, apparently thinking that there is no hurry, goes off with his wife for four days, perhaps on a visit to that very Agnes for whom he thought he was providing But as they are riding home they come to a mill on their own land, and they very naturally stop, and passing the time of day with the miller, ask "what news?" And the miller has news enough and to spare One of the priests who has been enfeoffed of the property has died Richard is startled enough and says to his wife, "Let us go home, for we have lost all" So they went home and spent the night there, apparently in thinking what they should do to recover what they had lost In the morning Richard goes to the other priest and asks what he shall do The priest apparently does not intend to take advantage of the situation, for he says, "Write a charter and I will seal it" So Richard writes the charter, and puts in all that has been in the feoffment, and the priest sealed it and gave it back to Richard, saying "God give you joy of it," which pious wish was not fulfilled, for although it apparently secured Richard in his lands, he had family troubles apart from his land troubles, and finds after a while that "he loves Kate, his niece, better than Agnes, his daughter." The old feoffment no longer satisfies him and he retakes his lands to himself and his wife in tail, the remainder to Kate, his niece, in fee And having thus provided a very pretty entanglement for those who are to come after him, Richard dies His wife kept the property during her lifetime. but upon her death it was left to Kate, the niece. Agnes, the daughter, had married, and she and her husband at once took possession of the lands, claiming as heirs under the first "tail" Kate then ousted them, and there was nothing left to do but to "go to law." And so we become possessed of the story as it was told in the Bench The justices found it a very interesting case and it was "well debated," and after the matter was throughly threshed out between them, it was decided that Agnes, the daughter, should have the land But through it all we do not hear what was said in regard to the charter written out by Richard and sealed by the priest

Then we have what may be called a vivid description of the way land was held in ancient demesne [40 Ed III, p 22, pl 23] Belknap says "There are in Domesday book different sorts of titles of land which are ancient demesne, that is to say, of lands which were in the hands of St Edward, the title is called *terra Regis Edwardi*, but lands which were in the hands of W Conqueror, the title is *terra Regis*, without more, because men know well at what time the book of Domesday was made, that is to say, in the time of W Conqueror, so in Domesday book it is expressly limited and states certainly the possession of the lords as the possession of the king, so that description is made in this book for all the kingdom, so that all the demesnes which were in the hands of St Edward are ancient demesne, although they were alien and strange lands when the book of Domesday was made, as it happened of the Manor of Tottenham, which was in other hands at the time of the making of Domesday, as it is mentioned in the said books, that it was then in the possession of the Count of Chester, but because the book mentioned in its title that the manor was at one time in the possession of the king, it was acknowledged ancient demesne by the whole counsel and your record, which is before us, makes no mention of *terra Regis Edwardi*, nor of *terra Regis*, so neither title shall be for you, but your title is *terra Sancti Stephani*, which was after the conquest And because they could not show the charters made by St Edward and W Conqueror, they would not adjudge the land to be in ancient demesne, because ancient demesne shall be adjudged by the book of Domesday, which is of record, and not in any other manner "

Britton gives us no clear idea of ancient demesne; Bracton gives us nothing Fitzherbert is very brief, and Blackstone rests what he wrote about entirely upon Fitzherbert I know of no authority which gives so clear an idea of what the thought of the time was in regard to this matter as does this case from 40 Ed III Of course we have the case in the Year Book, but it is the fact of the arrangement here which brings it to our attention.

When Maitland comes to speak of ancient demesne he says [History of English Law, Vol 2 p. 383, 2d ed] "They are that ancient demesne of the Crown which the conqueror held when the great settlement of the conquest was completed and was registered in Domesday Book." He refers to this case we are speaking of, saying, "In the first place the very name of 'Ancient Demesne' shows that the law supposes itself to be conservative It is maintaining the Conquest settlement To decide the question whether a manor be ancient demesne or not, it will go back far beyond all ordinary terms of limitation and prescription, far beyond 'the beginning of legal memory', it will be content with no evidence save that of the great survey Nay, in theory the ancient demesne gained its specific quality before Domesday Book was made The lawyers of the fourteenth century had some doubts as to the exact moment of time at which the manor must have been in the King's hands in order to make it ancient demesne for good and all, and the rule of evidence that they had adopted, namely that no testimony was admissible save that of Domesday Book, must have tended to cause some little confusion, still, on the whole, they think that the privileged manors are 'the manors of St Edward.'" Maitland's comment on this case makes us think that he may have relied on Fitzherbert's report of the case, and may not have gone to the original report, being thrown off the right track by the poor report Fitzherbert gives Certainly he does not make clear what the full report of the case does set forth very plainly

Stubbs says of this period of which we are speaking "There are periods at which the history of its wars is the true history of the people, for they are the description of the national experiences. And this is very much the case with the reign of Edward III If the glories and sufferings be taken out of the picture, little remains but a dull background of administrative business " [Stubbs Constitutional History of England, Vol 2, p 392] Stubbs' attitude is that of the historian exclusively occupied with what seems to be the business of government It has been the attitude of the makers of history for too many years In the light — or darkness — of that attitude we may find the explanation for the blindness of statesmen, for the mistakes in administration of the rulers of national affairs; they can learn of the past only through the accounts of that past given by historians, and the historian hides that past in a mist of wars and cabals, ignoring the fact that the life of the people was flowing on unbrokenly, not in an uninteresting dullness, but in rising and ebbing floods of national morality, happiness, and intelligence, despite wars, despite evil governments, and leaving behind it records of such vital interest, such fascinating romance, such informing incidents, that no one need turn to the history of wars, or of the makers and wagers of wars, for the true history of a nation   One great record for the writers of history, the one record in which the events were set down as they actually occurred, has been ignored by all historians—the case law of the period   All this time while wars, big and little, took up, according to the historian, all that is worthy of the attention of the historical writer, except that which must be given to the dull details of administrative business, there was going on in the courts, without interruption by war or any other cataclysm, the drama that goes on in every country whenever the legal machinery is working, and in the England of the Third Edward it was working with great smoothness   And to its smooth working was added a circumstance unparalleled in any other country at that time   There was being kept and written out for all men to read a detailed account of what was going on   And these detailed contemporary accounts of the legal drama form a vivid picture of the life of the day which the historian has too long ignored. Yet many of the cases then decided and reported in these books have a vital effect on our law to-day, they decided, through the formulation of certain principles which still endure as guiding principles in our law, the cases which are being decided in our courts to-day, while the battles of that far-off time have no effect upon us, they were ephemeral in their effects   France could and did remain France in spite of them, England might win wars on the Continent, she remained insular England and does still   Dynasties might rise to their brief lives and fall, through it all the principles of English life and English government were being formulated, taking firm hold, winning their slow but sure triumphs in the English courts of law   Yet the historians have deliberately preferred the physical contests of the battle-field to the mental conflicts of the courts.

There is not space here to set forth at great length a record of cases which show in detail the facts for which I am contending   Turn at random to any page of Statham, select from that page any case which seems of the slightest interest, and then go to the longer report of the case in the Year Book. It is safe to say that it will prove the contention here made It will show either that the courts were deciding some point of practice or pleading that could only come up in steadily sitting courts of long established usage, that the interests of the land-holding people were being safeguarded, that the humblest people were coming into court and asking for redress against other humble or great people, that contracts were being enforced, agreements being carried out; marriages being entered into; estates being settled and conveyed, children being cared for; and all without so much as a word of war, or pillage, or disturbance of the settled relations of life. The one great matter which disturbs the regular business of the courts seems to be "absence on the service of the King" The King did take the people away from their common life, to the great disturbance of that life, yet the courts looked pretty carefully into the matter and such delays were only allowed in court after due proof But when the husband was away the wife was allowed to answer, and that saved the day when the question was one of an estate, or such like matter.

Further it might seem that in days of such deep gloom and national degradation it is surprising that there is so little criminal law reported in these cases. The subjects and the cases themselves are not on criminal matters We have a few titles like Attaint and Assizes and Corone et Pleas del Corone, but they cover very few pages of the abridgment It is property, lands and chattels, and the matters of contract and covenant Hundreds of case arbitration, questions of church law, matters of annuities and corodies, and money given to use in trade Trespass and replevin and rescous there are, but there seems to be little of the armed band or the disorderly crowd, the cattle are often out in pound, and the legal action is to get them back The process of getting them back, or of getting back anything, may seem at times rather slow, the essoins and protections and pleas of under age, and everything that can be brought in to delay justice, are shown in full flower, but it merely means that justice goes droning along, not with violence or strong-handness, but in the sleepy way of a quiet time, we may know that the times were not quiet, but the courts refused to acknowledge that there was anything of outside consequence enough to keep them from going on straightening out the tangles into which people then as now got themselves So they went on, and so we know that the quiet life of the countryside went on also. It cannot but be felt that the real story of the times is to be found here rather than in the long story of bloodshed and the gloomy tale of courtly diplomacy, which has been the favorite field of the historian

II

It is necessary that some explanation be made of the way in which the annotation of this book has been done; necessary that something be said as to why it was done as it was, and why it was not done in what it might seem was a far better way. It could have been done much better, immensely better, but there were reasons which seemed sufficient for the doing of the thing in just the way it was done   The first question seemed to be the best way to get the book translated, as simply and as strictly in conformance with the original as possible Then the next necessary thing seemed to be to get the citations to the Year Books verified   If a case was not clearly digested, if there were errors in the digest itself, or in the translation of that digest, the best way in which these errors could be clearly traced and set right would be to get the full report of the case as given in the Year Book Statham did not, because he could not, refer to page and placitum It was necessary therefore to take each case, and there are thousands of cases in the entire Abridgment, and trace it in some way to the report in the Year Book   In too many cases this search has been unsuccessful   But these unidentified cases represent an expenditure of more time than the many cases which have been successfully traced. A case which could be followed to Brooke or Fitzherbert, and the citation to the page of the Year Book found there, even though it had to be read in both the abridgment and the Year Book, represented a far smaller expenditure of time and labor than a case which, not being found in either of the abridgments, had to be sought for all through the term of the year for which it was cited, and even through the entire year, for cases are often cited for the wrong term in Statham   Then in identifying the cases there was often occasion for doubt, the case would have to be examined carefully for matter not in the abridgment, or for matter which contradicted the abridgment, and even after a thorough reading there was often room for doubt   Of course in some cases the doubt remains. I have not generally indicated the cases where I am doubtful, I have simply let my identification go for what it is worth. I have had to decide, the case is there for comparison; if I have considered a case identified or identical with the case abridged when it is not so, it seems that the case itself will be a sufficient check on the error, and will do little harm, it will probably remain a matter for the individual judgment, some might think it an exact identification, others might think it folly to deem the case and the abridgment similar. In a very few cases I have noted my doubt in the note which in every instance accompanies the case. Many of the points abridged are almost completely buried in long cases upon diametrically different subjects. The marginal notes in the Year Books are of very little value for finding these points, as they fail to note far the greater number. Sometimes, when the point has been a minor one, I have felt it better to let it go as unidentified rather than to spend hours in a futile search, yet many hours have been spent in just such searches I am sure that had I attempted to make the work perfect on all the points on which an unwearied patience and an absolutely exhaustive search could be brought to bear, it would have been many years before I could have let it go out of my hands. Yet I can truly say that I have spared neither patience nor pains in this part of my work, it required neither great knowledge nor great technical skill, but merely persistence and patience, and these I believe I have given. I have very great hopes that when the book comes into the hands of those with greater knowledge and skill than I can boast, many of these cases which I have had to mark "unidentified" will be identified. I am sure that I shall be able to do some of that identifying myself, there are things which stare at one in print that will not let themselves be seen until it is too late.

At first it was thought that it might be possible to dissect and digest the different abridgments of Statham, Fitzherbert and Brooke, and when there was a disagreement on a point of law, discuss that disagreement, compare them with the case itself, and thus show how the law upon the point stood at that time. That this would have been a most valuable work if done with the ability it would require there can be little doubt, but it would have meant that instead of presenting a complete translation of Statham in the year 1915, in not too bulky a form, there could have been printed in the next few years only a small portion of the book, and the notes would have so far outgrown the text of the translation as to be a commentary upon law of the Year Books rather than merely a translation of a digest thereof

It seems on the whole that the translation itself, with as abundant reference to the cases in the Year Books as could be secured, is the matter of the most moment at the present time   If the book is brought within the reach of the average student, he can then go to the different abridgments and to the Year Books and trace for himself that law to which the Abridgment has been a guide post, and the more such guides we find to follow the more intimate knowledge we shall have of the law they set forth.

There is opportunity for much valuable work in this way to be done in the future, but it seems that it is as well that it should not be made a part of the translation itself.   It has not been a light work, or one for an idle hour, and it will not be adopted as light reading by many as it is, but it may seem less forbidding if it goes on its way into the world untrammeled with a burden of modern notes.

The reason why the two abridgments of Fitzherbert and Brooke are alone used in this system of notation is, of course, plain to all users of the Year Books   They are the two abridgments which are referred to in the Year Books themselves, or, if we count Statham, the three abridgments   I have not been able to decide upon what principle, if any, these citations were made   Some of the Years are thickly annotated, others have very few references of any kind   There are many cases which are abridged in the different abridgments for which there are no citations whatever in the Year Book margins   Sometimes there is a marginal reference to Fitzherbert and none to Brooke or Statham, yet the case will be found to be in both of these abridgments   These references must have been obviously useful to the lawyers of the period, and it is strange that some system of careful annotating was not observed   It was probably another case of getting the work done as well as it could be and not trying for perfection; for the printing of the Year Books as a whole was a great undertaking, and it would have been too much to ask for even usual correctness   We have much to say about the errors and incorrectness of the "vulgate," as Mr Maitland calls it   Without it we may feel quite sure that even the small amount of knowledge of Year Book lore which lingered with us through the nineteenth century would have been almost eliminated

Mention has been made of the marginal references to the subjects supposed to be found in the cases of the Year Books   These are very defective   We may find, for example, marginal references to Trespass in a certain number of cases, and infer from that fact that where there is a case of trespass a marginal reference will be found to it   This is far from being the case, however, and we can form no idea of how many cases there are from running down the marginal indices   Neither do the early abridgments—Brooke and Fitzherbert—cover nearly all the cases of Trespass   In the ten years of Edward III, from 40 to 50 of his reign, neither of these abridgments contain within one hundred cases of a full report of the cases of trespass   Statham has ninety-five cases of trespass in those ten years, of which fifty-seven are not identified in the other abridgments, showing that if one went to the abridgments for a full view of the law of trespass for that period, one would fall very far short of finding all the cases if one relied only on Brooke and Fitzherbert.   Not all of the fifty-seven cases which Statham alone has have been identified in the Year Books   Probably the points are concealed in the long cases upon other points where it has been difficult to identify them   But they are of value just as they stand, and add a large amount of valuable matter to that which has hitherto been easily accessible to the law student   We have seen that Statham is usually correct in his report of a case, and that his abridgments are skillfully made, so that his report may usually stand as correct.

The matter has not been followed up in regard to other subjects treated by the abridgments, but the mass of matter unabridged in other subjects is probably very much the same as for Trespass   We know, at all events, that even when a subject has been traced up through all the abridgments, and through the indices to the Year Books, we cannot assume that we have practically all the cases which are printed in the Year Books   We probably have but a small proportion of it   It is to be hoped that some day we may have the work of collecting these Year Book cases under the proper heads done for us   It is a needed work, and would have been done long since had it been of profit, which it is probable it never will be   As in the case of the translating of Statham, the doing of the work must be the reward of the worker

I shall conclude as I began by borrowing from a modest gentleman of the Middle Temple, who never gave his name to his book, the words in which he presented his translation of the Law Proceedings of the King's Bench and Common Pleas, to the learned in the law of that day:

"I shall think all the Labour and Pains I have taken herein sufficiently rewarded, if it shall be thought by the judicious Part of the Profession, that I have translated but tolerably well . . . yet as my good intentions may not free the whole from some Faults, I hope the Reader will let my good Will to serve my Country plead in their Excuse."

STATHAM'S ABRIDGMENT

STATHAM'S ABRIDGMENT

ACCOMPTE [1]

(1) **In account,** the plaintiff counted upon a receipt in Statham 1 a another county, and for that reason the writ was abated Paschal Contrary, 12 Ed III And both are good law by reason 11 Hen IV. of the Statute

> The case has not been identified in Y B Paschal, 11 Hen IV There Case 1 is a short report of the case referred to as in 12 Ed III, in the Rolls Series 11 & 12 Ed III, p 348 It is not clear that it is "contrary" to this case of 11 Hen IV, the remarks to the effect that in a certain case such a receipt would be good enough, are merely *dicta*

> The Statute is that of 6 Ric II (1382), cap 2 "Action of debt, account, etc, shall be commenced in the counties where the contract was made " Stats at Large, Vol 2, p 253

(2) **In account** against two who were adjudged to account, Hilary *Capias ad Computandum* issued until one was outlawed and 41 Ed III the other came at the exigent, and it was adjudged that he should account for the whole, because it was his own folly to be a receiver with one who was not sufficient, etc

And it was said by FYNCHEDEN, in the same plea, that if at the *Sequatur* against two, one comes and the other does not, the tenant shall be received to say that he who made default had nothing of value, and then the other shall be charged for the whole warranty, etc Query?

> Reported at length in Y B Hilary, 41 Ed III, p 3, pl 8 There are Case 2 further accounts of the case in Y B Paschal, 41 Ed III, p 9, pl 4, and Y B Trinity, 41 Ed III, p 13, pl 2 See also Brooke, Accompt, 10, and Fitzh Accompt, 23

(3) **If a man** delivers certain monies to another upon Paschal conditions which are broken, he who delivers the monies 41 Ed. III shall have a writ of Debt or a writ of Account

> Reported at length in Y B Paschal, 41 Ed III, p 10, pl 5 See Case 3. also Brooke, Accompt, 11, and Fitzh Accompt, 24

Trinity
45 Ed III

(10) In account, the defendant said that he had accounted before the plaintiff himself, in such a place, and it was adjudged a good plea, etc , if he made the plea before the Statute

Case 10

Reported in Y B Mich (not Trinity), 45 Ed III, p 14, pl 13. See also Brooke, Accompt, 16, and Fitzh Accompt, 37.

The Statute referred to is that of Westminster the Second, 13 Ed I, (1285), cap 11, Stats at Large, Vol 1, p 163 (188)

Trinity
47 Ed III

(11) The plaintiff alleged the receipt by the hands of one H BELKNAP This H was your co-monk, not named co-monk, judgment of the writ And for that reason it was the opinion of the COURT that the writ should abate And the law is the same if a man alleges the receipt by the hands of his wife, she should be named his wife, etc

Case 11

Reported in Y B Mich (not Trinity), 47 Ed III, p 16, pl 25 See also Brooke, Accompt, 19, and Fitzh Accompt, 41 The case as reported differs from the abridgment of Statham, and Brooke disagrees with the report, and says the case is badly reported

Paschal
31 Ed III

(12) If, in account, they are at issue whether the receipt was smaller, etc , and it is found for the defendant, can the plaintiff upon his accounting demand more against him than was found by the verdict? But whatever the inquest found, the defendant can discharge himself upon his account, having regard to the inquest, and so it is

Statham 1 b

peremptory in that case for the plaintiff and not for the defendant Query, in that case shall the defendant have attaint, since he can discharge himself upon his account?

And also it was said in the same plea, that notwithstanding it was found by the inquest that it was for a smaller sum, yet the writ should not abate, etc

Case 12

There is no printed year for 31 Ed III Fitzh Accompt, 58, has a very short abridgment of the case, but does not seem to have noted the case in Statham

Hilary
30 Ed III

(13) In account brought by the Prior of St John of Jerusalem, it was counted that he was bailiff of the church of H And the writ was challenged, inasmuch as he named him bailiff of his church, whereas no one can be bailiff of

the church, inasmuch as the church belongs to the parishioners, etc   And also the prior should be named parson,
etc   THORPE   He does not demand anything as parson, etc.
And the writ was adjudged good, etc.

Reported in Y B Hilary, 30 Ed III, p 1, pl 2   The report and Case 13
Statham differ slightly

(14)   **In account** the plaintiff declared his damages, but he Hilary
did not recover damages, etc   Query, if upon the account 30 Ed III
the auditors would award him damages, etc

   And in the same plea, upon the account, the defendant
said that one J was bound to him in a statute merchant for
twenty pounds   The plaintiff and himself were agreed
that the plaintiff should take the twenty pounds from the
said J, in satisfaction, etc   And that was not held a plea,
since for that the plaintiff could not have an action, etc
And for the other part, he said that he had delivered one
tonel of wine to the plaintiff, and the plaintiff said he had
not   Ready to wage his law, etc   Query, if he should
have his law, in that case? etc

Reported in Y B Hilary, 30 Ed III, p 4, pl 19   See also Fitzh Case 14
Accompt, 62   See as to the award of damages in an action of account,
case 23, *infra*

(15)   **An abbot** counted that the defendant was the re- Paschal
ceiver for one such, his predecessor   And the writ was 4 Ed III
adjudged good, etc   Query?

Reported in Y B Paschal, 4 Ed III, p 17, pl 8   Fitzh Accompt, Case 15
97, has a good abridgment of the case

(16)   **In account** it was alleged that the defendant was Paschal
his receiver by the hands of one H   The defendant said, 5 Ed III
"Never his receiver by his hands "   And he was driven
to say, "Never his receiver," generally   Contrary, Trinity,
17, etc   And that is held to be the better law, etc

Reported in Y B Mich (not Paschal), 5 Ed III, p 38, pl 22   See Case 16
also Fitzh Accompt, 99

(17)   **In account** by a woman, the defendant said that Hilary
at the time of the receipt she was a married woman, and 6 Ed III

he had the plea, because the action is given to the executors of the husband, etc

Case 17 Reported in Y B Hilary, 6 Ed III, p 3, pl 5 See also Fitzh Accompt, 101

Hilary
6 Ed III

(18) **The plaintiff** counted that the defendant was his bailiff of his manor of B, from the feast of St Michael, the year, etc, until the feast of Easter next, etc, and had the care and administration of certain goods (and he showed what, etc) And the defendant said that he was his bailiff from the said feast of St. Michael until the feast of Christmas then next ensuing, for which time he was ready to account, and as to the time over, etc, never his bailiff. And the plaintiff showed that he was his bailiff for all the time for which he had counted, etc And the other alleged the contrary And the plaintiff prayed that he should account for that which he had acknowledged, and he could not [have his prayer], because the account could not be taken in parts Query, if it were found for the defendant, should he account for that which he had acknowledged, or would the writ abate?

Case 18 Reported in Y B Mich (not Hilary), 6 Ed III, p 40 pl 18 See also Fitzh Accompt, 104

Michaelis
7 Ed III

(19) **The plaintiff** alleged that the defendant was his bailiff of his house, and his receiver of twenty shillings by the hands of one H, and of twenty shillings by the hands of the plaintiff The defendant said that as to the house he accounted before such auditors, etc, and he was found in arrears for so much, etc And as to the twenty shillings by the hand of H, never his receiver by his hands, and as to the other twenty shillings, always ready to wage his law

Case 19 Reported in Y B Mich 7 Ed III, p 46, pl 13

Michaelis
9 Ed III

(20) **The plaintiff** said that the defendant was his receiver for his house in Dale, and had the care and administration of forty sacks of wool who said, "never his bailiff" And it was found that he was not his bailiff

because the plaintiff had not any such house in Dale.   But
they found that the defendant had received the sacks of
wool from him, to sell and render an account of them
And notwithstanding that part of the plea was found
against the plaintiff, still it was adjudged that the defendant should account for the wool, because the plaintiff
could have no other writ, but to allege him to be his bailiff,
etc   And see that he did not answer as to the wool, yet
the inquest found it

Reported in Mich 9 Ed III, p 36, pl 38   See also Fitzh Accompt, **Case 20**
95, where he gives a very good abridgment of the case

(21) **If a man** receives a certain sum of money from me Hilary
to use in trade, to our common profit, I should have a 10 Ed III
special writ of Account, alleging the receipt to the common
use, and not a general writ, etc   Query?

The case has not been identified in Y B Hilary, 10 Ed III   The **Case 21**
cases of account there reported do not agree with the abridgment of
Statham

(22) **If a stranger** occupies as next friend, of his own Trinity
tort, still the heir shall have a writ of Account against him, 13 Ed III
alleging that he was in his wardship, and counting upon
the Statute, etc

There is no early printed year of 13 Ed III   The case is printed in **Case 22**
the Rolls Series, 12 & 13 Ed III, pp 320–21
The Statute referred to is that of Marlbridge, 52 Hen III (1267),
cap 17, Stats at Large, Vol 1, p 55 (68)

(23) **Auditors** were assigned to one who was adjudged Hilary
to account, and he would not account, wherefore he re- 14 Ed III
mained in the Fleet for two years, and then came the
plaintiff and prayed judgment according to that which he
had counted, and he had it, but he did not recover any of
the profits for the mean time while he was in prison   And
that proves clearly that a man shall not recover damages
in Account at any time

There is no early printed year of 14 Ed III   The case has not been **Case 23**
identified in the Rolls Series for that year and term   Fitzh Accompt,
109, has a short abridgment of the case

Trinity 14 Ed III

(24) **In account,** the defendant came by the exigent, and he traversed the receipt, and found mainprize to attend the inquest; and then he made default, upon which the inquest was taken for his default And it was found that he was his receiver, but not for so much as the plaintiff had alleged And the Court has no regard to the quantity, because it lies in the answer before the auditors, but it was adjudged that the defendant be put to account, and his mainpernors also, etc.

Case 24 There is no early printed year of 14 Ed III The case has not been identified in the Rolls Series, or in the early abridgments

Trinity 14 Ed III.

(25) **In account,** the plaintiff alleged him to be his receiver of twenty shillings As to part, the defendant said, "Never his receiver" As to the other part, he waged his law, and made his law immediately, and the inquest was taken for the remainder, without abating the writ, etc

Case 25 There is no early printed year of 14 Ed III The case has not been positively identified in the Rolls Series, but there is a similar case in that Series, 14 Ed III, p 172

Paschal 16 Ed III.

(26) **In account** against two, one said that at the time of the receipt he was under age, wherefore the other was made to account for all.

Case 26 There is no early printed year of 16 Ed III The case is printed in the Rolls Series, 16 Ed III, pp 190-92

Hilary 15 Ed III.

(27) **In account,** the defendant was outlawed, and had a charter of pardon, and a *Scire Facias* against the plaintiff, to which the sheriff returned that he had nothing, neither could he be found But he came in of his own free will and counted against the other, and was received, etc

Case 27 There is no early printed year of 15 Ed III The case is printed in the Rolls Series, 14 & 15 Ed III, p 280

Trinity 16 Ed III

(28) **The defendant** said that he received the same monies for a debt that the plaintiff owed him, and not to render an account. And the opinion was that he should have the plea Query, since it seems that the plea was

[not] good, because it amounted to no more than "Never his receiver, to render an account," etc

There is no early printed year of 16 Ed III   The case has not been identified in the Rolls Series   But see Fitzh Accompt, 53, where the case seems to accord with the opinion of Statham Case 28

(29) **In account,** the defendant said that he received the money by the hands of one H, and not by the hands of the plaintiff, and the plaintiff was made to answer to that, etc

Trinity 16 Ed III

There is no early printed year for 16 Ed III   The case is probably that printed in the Rolls Series, 16 Ed III, pp 262–63 Case 29

(30) **The plaintiff** alleged that the defendant was his bailiff, etc , and his receiver of twenty pounds   The defendant fully admitted the receipt, but said, "Never his bailiff," and he was adjudged to account immediately, because he had admitted, etc   And so see Account taken by parts (And I believe that the reason is because he had admitted the other things   For if in Account one alleges the defendant to be his receiver of twenty pounds, and the defendant admits part of the receipt, and as to the other part they are at issue, he does not account for any part before the issue is tried   But in the case here he has confessed the receipt of the whole, and said as to the house, "Never his bailiff," which is another thing, etc)   Query?

Michaelis 19 Ed III

Statham 2 a

There is no early printed year of 19 Ed III   The case has not been identified in the Rolls Series Case 30

(31) **In account,** the plaintiff alleged that the defendant was his receiver for so much, etc , from Michaelmas in the Year Eight, etc , until the Michaelmas next ensuing   The defendant said that the plaintiff released to him all actions by the deed, etc , which bore date in the Year Six of the same king, without this that he was ever his receiver after that time   And the plea was adjudged good

Michaelis 19 Ed III

There is no early printed year of 19 Ed III   The case has not been identified in the Rolls Series Case 31

(32) **The defendant** was adjudged to account, and before the auditors he produced a release   And they

Paschal 20 Ed III

would not allow it, because no plea to the action will aid him upon the account, or *e contra* But if the plaintiff had released to the defendant after the award, it seems that the defendant will have the plea, albeit he pleaded as to all actions And the action is ended as well as in a *Scire Facias* to have execution, a release of all actions is a good bar, although executions are not spoken of, etc And then the auditors were two days upon the account And the plaintiff did not come, and the defendant showed that matter to the Court, and he went quit, etc

Case 32 There is no early printed year of 20 Ed III The case has not been identified in the Rolls Series

Hilary
21 Ed III

(33) **The defendant** traversed the account, and it was found, wherefore a *Capias ad Computandum* issued, returnable, etc on which day the plaintiff was nonsuited, wherefore the defendant went quit And the plaintiff had another *Capias*, upon which he was taken, and the plaintiff prayed the account The defendant showed that the plaintiff was nonsuited, as above, and demanded judgment, etc WILLOUGHBY When judgment was given that he should account the original suit was ended, since by no nonsuit afterwards upon the *Capias* after judgment shall the original lose its force And that was the opinion, etc But because the year and the day were passed, the plaintiff was made to sue a *Scire Facias* Which note, etc

Case 33 Reported in Y B Hilary, 21 Ed III, p 7, pl 19 See also Brooke, Accompt, 37, Fitzh Accompt, 65

Hilary
21 Ed III

(34) **If a man** be adjudged to account, and a *Capias* issues against him, he shall not have a writ of Error before he has accounted, because that is part of the judgment, and ought to be fulfilled before they put it upon the record· By SHARSHULL and WILLOUGHBY, in Account

Case 34 Reported in Y B Hilary, 21 Ed III, p 9, pl 25 See also Brooke, Accompt, 39

Hilary
21 Ed III

(35) **In account** against a guardian in socage he said that the land of which he demands the account is ancient

demesne, judgment, etc   And it was the opinion that it was a good plea, because the freehold could come in question, for he can say that he held in Knight's service, etc   It seems that if a man be bailiff of my house in ancient demesne, I shall not have a bill of account in the Court of the lord in ancient demesne, because he cannot award auditors there, then it follows that such a plea to the jurisdiction is of no avail unless I can have an action in ancient demesne, etc   Query?

Reported in Y B Hilary, 21 Ed III, p 10, pl 30   Case 35

(36) **The defendant** was adjudged to account, and then the plaintiff died, and his executors prayed a *Scire Facias* against the defendant for an account with them, and they could not have it, but were estopped and abated by his death, so there was no record by which to award a *Scire Facias* Query? Because the contrary was adjudged, Mich 14 Hen IV, in Account

Michaelis 21 Ed III

Reported in Y B Mich 21 Ed III, p 32, pl 15   The reference is to the case reported in Y B Mich 14 Hen IV, p 1, pl 1   See also Brooke, Accompt, 40

Case 36

(37) **In account** brought by executors, the defendant said that he had accounted before their testator   And upon that they were at issue   And because he came by the *Capias* he found mainprize, and at the day of the *Venire Facias* he made default, wherefore he was adjudged to account without taking the inquest, because by his plea he had confessed the action of the plaintiff, and voided it, and not followed his plea, etc   It is otherwise where his pleading does not confess his action, as where he pleads, "Never his receiver," etc   And the plaintiff had a *Capias* against him and his mainpernors   And then the king died, wherefore the plaintiff came into Court and prayed process against him   HERLE. You cannot have a re-summons, for the original is terminated   and if we awarded a *Venire Facias ad Computandum*, if he did not come then would the distress be long delayed, wherefore he awarded a *Capias ad Computandum*, and a writ against

Hilary I Ed III

his mainpernors. STONORE You cannot award a writ against his mainpernors, for it will not be anything but a fine to the king, for by their default judgment was given against the principal, and they cannot make a fine which was due to the other king, no more than if a man be outlawed in the time of the other king, the king who now is shall not have his goods, but the executors of the other king, etc   Query?

Case 37 Reported in Y B Hilary, 1 Ed III, p 2, pl 10   The abridgment and the report differ in many points

Michaelis
30 Ed III

(38) **In account,** the defendant showed before auditors that he had delivered a statute merchant to the plaintiff, in which one H was bound to him, etc   To which the plaintiff agreed   And he had the plea without showing a tally, or acquittance, etc.   And the plaintiff answered that he had not, etc.

Case 38 Reported in Y B Mich 30 Ed III, p 23, pl 44   See also Fitzh Accompt, 64

Hilary
31 Ed III

(39) **In account** against two, who were adjudged to account   And then one of them died before he had accounted, and the Court was of a mind to abate the whole writ, etc

Case 39 There is no printed Year Book for 31 Ed III   The case has not been identified in the early abridgments

Hilary
1 Hen VI

(40) **In account** because the defendant was his receiver of twenty pounds by the hand of one H PASTON We made a deed to the plaintiff and to this H, witness this receipt, and we demand judgment if, without showing this deed, you should have an action   ROLFF We pray account. PASTON In debt upon a simple contract it is a good plea to say that the plaintiff had an obligation for the same sum MARTYN Not the same, for in your case there are two contracts, but the deed in this case has no other effect save as evidence of the receipt, etc.   And then they demurred in law

Case 40 Reported in Y B Mich (not Hilary), 1 Hen, VI, p 7, pl 31   See also Fitzh Accompt, 1

(41) **In account,** it was alleged that the defendant was Michaelis
bailiff of his house, and had the care and administration of 14 Hen IV
certain goods   The defendant said, "Never his bailiff"
And as to the goods he pleaded the other plea. And the Statham 2 b
opinion was that the first plea went to all   Well debated,
etc   And at last he was driven to hold to the first plea;
and upon that they were at issue, etc.

Reported in Y B Hilary (not Mich), 14 Hen IV, p 20, pl 25. See Case 41
also Brooke, Accompt, 34, and Fitzh Accompt, 22

(42) **In account,** the defendant said that the plaintiff Trinity
assigned auditors to him on such a day, before whom he 32 Ed III
accounted for part   And the auditors took his tallies and
his rolls by which he should account, "and if they would
return them to us we are ready to account"   And that
was adjudged a good plea. Upon which the plaintiff said
that he never took them. Ready   And the other alleged
the contrary

There is no printed year of 32 Ed III   See also Fitzh Accompt, 110. Case 42

(43) **In account** against the guardian in socage, the writ Michaelis
shall specially rehearse the Statute 32 Ed III

There is no printed year of 32 Ed III

The Statute is that of 51 Hen III (1223), cap 27   Stats at Large, Case 43
Vol 1, p 55 (68)

(44) **In account** against one because he had, with Michaelis
another, received certain monies of the plaintiff   And he 28 Ed III
counted that each of them was bound to account for the
whole   And the writ was adjudged good against him,
omitting the other, etc   (It seems that he should show a
specialty for that), etc

The case has not been identified in Y B Mich 28 Ed III, or in the Case 44.
early abridgments

(45) **One brought** a writ of account against his bailiff, Trinity
who counted that he has accounted over to his master, 11 Ric II
etc   And the writ was adjudged good, etc   BELKNAP
One of the vills of which he demands the account is within

the Cinque Ports, judgment, etc   WADE   Then answer
to the other   Which note   Query, if a man be bailiff of
my manor, of which part is in the Cinque Ports or in ancient
demesne, how shall the writ be brought?

Case 45   There is no printed Year Book for 11 Ric II   The case has not
been identified in the early abridgments

**Hilary
11 Ric II**   (46) **In account,** it is a good plea to say that he has
accounted before the plaintiff himself.

Case 46   There is no printed Year Book for 11 Ric II   The case has not
been identified in the early abridgments

**Trinity
2 Ric II**   (47) **The plaintiff** counted that the defendant was bailiff
of his house, and that he delivered to him an obligation to
receive certain monies from a woman who was bound in
the said obligation, and to bail the same obligation to the
woman, of which he demanded an account   HANKFORD
He does not show that we have received the monies, so we
are not his receiver, in which case he shall have an action
of detinue, etc   WADE   That he cannot, for the obligation was not delivered to deliver to the woman, and he has
alleged him to be bailiff of his house, wherefore the writ is
good   Which the Court conceded, etc

Case 47   There is no printed Year Book for 2 Ric II   Fitzh   Accompt,
46, has the case

**Michaelis
18 Hen VI**   (48) **A writ of account** was brought against a woman
FORTESCUE   This writ does not lie   NEWTON   A man
shall have a writ of Account against a woman as guardian
in socage, and a man shall have a writ of Debt upon the
arrears of an Account against a woman   FORTESCUE
So shall a man have against executors, and still he shall not
have an action of account against them   NEWTON   Now
it has passed the Chancery there is no question but it lies
And it has often been adjudged good by bill in the King's
Bench, and in London, wherefore answer   FORTESCUE
Whereas he says that he delivered the twenty pounds to us
for trade and to render an account, we say that he delivered
to us the same sum to deliver to one F   and we have delivered it to him, judgment if action?   PORTYNGTON   That

is no plea unless he says, "Without this that he was our receiver to render an account," for otherwise he does not answer us　And also he cannot have the plea upon the account　ASCOUGH　The plea is good, for she had acknowledged that she was accountable to the plaintiff at one time; for before she had delivered the sum to the said F , she was accountable to the plaintiff, but not afterwards　But it is otherwise where one does not acknowledge that the plaintiff ever had a cause of action　as if in account I say that the plaintiff was indebted to me, and delivered to me the same sum for the debt, that is not a plea without a "without this that," as above　which NEWTON conceded, etc

The case has not been identified in the Y B Mich 18 Hen VI　It is **Case 48** probably the case reported in Y B Mich 19 Hen VI, p 4, pl 10 See also Brooke, Accompt, 43, and Fitzh Accompt, 3

(49) **In account** because the defendant was the bailiff **Michaelis** of his house, and had the care and administration of cer- **27 Hen VI** tain oxen and cows　PRISOT　Judgment of the count, for he does not put in certain how many oxen and how many cows, etc , and the count was adjudged good, etc　And the writ was that he was his bailiff and his receiver, and he counted that he received certain sums of money by the hands of certain persons, and these same persons were tenants of the manor of which he was alleged to be bailiff And yet it was said that the writ had been good against him as bailiff solely, for such receipts are incident to his office, inasmuch as that rent is part of the manor, etc

Reported in Y B Mich 27 Hen VI, p 1, pl 8　See also Brooke, **Case 49** Accompt, 5, and Fitzh Accompt, 5

See as to account, in the title of Process, Paschal, 10 **Note** Hen IV, where process issued against the auditors, where the account was traversed, etc

Statham, title of Process, *infra*, pp 187 b to 141 a　The case does not appear in that title, however

(50) **If a man** be found in arrears before auditors are **Michaelis** assigned in the county, they have no power to commit **27 Hen VI** him to a jail which is in another county, although it be the nearest jail to them, unless it be the jail of the same

county; as in the County of Derby, for the jail of Derby
is in the county of Nottingham For the Statute says,
"to the nearest jail in those parts," which shall be interpreted to mean in the same county.

And it was said in the same plea, that if after a man is found
in arrears he departs from the auditors, and in three or
four days the auditors commit him to prison, that com-
mitment is void, and he shall have a writ of false imprisonment against them, etc.

Case 50   Reported in Y B Hilary (not Mich), 27 Hen VI, p 8, pl 7 See
also Brooke, Accompt, 6

Statute of Westminster the Second, 13 Ed I (1285), cap 11, Stats
at Large, Vol 1, p 117

Hilary
27 Hen VI.

(51) **The Duchess of Somerset** brought a writ of Account
against W Enderby, and counted that he was her receiver
of forty pounds, to use in trade MOILE, for the defendant, acknowledged the receipt, and said that such a day
the defendant came to the plaintiff and brought the said
forty pounds in a bag, and offered the same bag with the
monies to the plaintiff at D, in the county, etc And the
said plaintiff on the same day gave the said bag with the
monies to the defendant, in satisfaction of one hundred
marks, for which she was indebted to him, which matter,
etc POLE· On his own acknowledgment we pray the
account And so to judgment, etc POLE· That matter
does not go in bar of the account, for he can show the same
matter upon the account And if he said that he paid the
monies to another by our commandment, or that he paid
them to us, that is no plea, consequently it is no plea to
say that we gave him the monies, since he has acknowledged the receipt, for the reason above given. And also
he does not say that he has paid the monies to us, but
that he offered them to us, which cannot be good on any
interpretation And even if the plea be good for the sum
that he received, still he should account for the increase,
since we have counted that he received them to use in
trade, wherefore, etc. MOILE *Contra* Sir, if it be a bar
to the principal receipt, it is a bar to all And it was

Statham 3 a

adjudged now lately that in account the defendant said
that for the sum that he had received, and for the profits
arising out of it for all the time since the receipt, he
had made an obligation of one hundred pounds And
that was adjudged a good plea. And the reason is because
the plaintiff was satisfied, in which case he cannot have
the account since it appears that he is satisfied for the
same account. ASSHETON: As to this that if he is barred
of the receipt, still he shall account for the increase, that
is not so, for that is only the form of the writ, for it is no
plea for the defendant to say that he was not his receiver
to trade, wherefore, etc. PORTYNGTON. It is not reasonable that he shall be discharged as to the profits, though
the plea be good for the principal receipt, but if he had said
as above, and that the plaintiff had discharged him as to
all the profits promised from the said sum, that could not
be pleaded in bar of the account, etc And then the defendant was adjudged to account, and immediately the defendant threw a caution in the Court, and a writ of error
And in the King's Bench the opinion of many was that the
plea was good, etc   But yet the judgment was affirmed,
etc

The case has not been identified in Y B Hilary, 27 Hen VI, or in Case 51.
the abridgments

(52) **A bailiff** upon his account prayed an allowance of Hilary
twenty pounds, which he had paid for his master, the lord 41 Ed III
of the fee   THORPE For anything that is contingent you
have no warranty to pay, etc   And then he showed an
acquittance from the lord of the fee for the twenty pounds,
made to his master, and they allowed it, etc   Query?

The case has not been identified in Y B Hilary, 41 Ed III, or in the Case 52.
early abridgments

(53) **In a writ** of *Ex parte talis*, the bailiff denied the Michaelis
tallies shown by the lord, in the Exchequer. And it was 2 Ed III.
found against him by the inquest   And the judgment was
merely that he should account, etc

Case 53   The reference may be to the case in Y B Mich 2 Ed III, p 52, pl 13, but it is not clear   The writ *Ex parte talis* was brought when the auditors would not allow the reasonable expenses of an account, or if they charged the party with more receipts than they ought, then his next friend could sue for him a writ of *Ex parte talis* out of the Chancery, directed to the sheriff, to take four mainpernors to bring his body before the Barons of the Exchequer at a certain day, and to warn the lord to appear there the same day   See Termes de la Ley, Accompt (1721)

Hilary
2 Ed III

(54) **Account** was maintained against the guardian in socage by an infant who was under the age of twenty-one years   And it was adjudged good, etc   And see that such a writ was adjudged good in Hilary Term, in the Year 29 of Edward the Third, in Account, but that was in Gavelkind, etc

Case 54   The case has not been identified in Y B Hilary, 2 Ed III, or in the early abridgments   The case alluded to as in Hilary, 29 Ed III, as in Gavelkind has not been found

Michaelis
32 Ed III

(55) **Account** against a guardian in socage, as a receiver, was of no avail, and that in Account, etc

Case 55   There is no printed year of 32 Ed III   The case has not been found in the early abridgments

Hilary
22 Ed III

(56) **It is a good plea** in Account against a receiver by another hand, to say that he received it to carry, and was robbed of that and of other goods of his, etc.   (But it seems that the plea is not good since he did not say that he was a common carrier, etc.)

Case 56   The case has not been identified in Y B Hilary, 22 Ed III, or in the early abridgments

Michaelis
7 Ed III

(57) **Account** is not maintainable against an infant under age.

Case 57   The case has not been identified in Y B Mich 7 Ed III, or in the early abridgments

Michaelis
27 Ed III

(58) **In account,** it was found that the defendant had paid more, etc   And of that surplusage it was adjudged that he should recover against the plaintiff, but this was a

bailiff, etc. Query, if he should have a *Capias ad Satis-faciendum* in that case? etc (And it seems that they erred, etc)

There is no early printed year of 27 Ed III The case has not Case 58 been elsewhere identified

(59) **An abbot** brought a writ of Account upon a receipt Paschal in the time of his predecessor, and it was adjudged good, 4 Ed III etc

Reported in Y B Paschal, 4 Ed III, p 17, pl 8   Case 59

(60) **In account,** it was alleged that the defendant was Michaelis bailiff of his house, and had administration, etc The 9 Ed III defendant answered both, for although he had no such house, still it might be that the plaintiff could not have any other action And if he brought a writ of Detinue the defendant could wage his law, etc.

Reported in Y B Mich 9 Ed III, p 36, pl 38 See also Fitzh Case 60 Accompt, 95

(61) **In account,** if the plaintiff shows a deed from the Hilary defendant proving the receipt, the defendant cannot wage 16 Ed III his law

And see, in the same plea, that the plaintiff showed a deed proving the receipt, and the defendant said that it was made by duress of imprisonment And the issue was taken upon that (Which is strange, for the action was not conceived upon the deed, etc) Query, if that issue is peremptory?

There is no early printed year of 16 Ed III The case is reported Case 61 in the Rolls Series, 16 Ed III, pp 4–6

(62) **In account,** if the defendant be adjudged to account, Paschal they will not send him to prison, unless he comes by a 29 Ed III *Cepi Corpus* But they will award a *Capias ad Computandum*

The case has not been identified in Y B 29 Ed III, but a case Case 62 which is decided to the contrary is to be found in Y B Paschal, 29 Ed III, p 35, pl 63.

(63) **If, before the auditors,** the defendant alleges pay- Trinity ment to the plaintiff by another hand, the plaintiff shall 29 Ed III

not wage his law   no more than when in a writ of Account
the plaintiff alleges a receipt by another hand, the defendant
shall wage his law

Case 63   Reported in Y B Trinity, 29 Ed III, p 36, pl 1

Trinity
47 Ed III

(64) **In account,** the plaintiff alleged the receipt by the
hands of one J. The defendant tendered his law, and
said that he was the co-monk of the plaintiff   And he
came in by award of the Court, and tendered his law from
the beginning, for otherwise he could not have had the
plea, etc

Case 64   Reported in Y B Mich (not Trinity), 47 Ed III, p 16, pl 25

¹ There would seem to be little necessity for more than a perfunctory
note to the writ of Account, showing the concurrence of the abridged
cases with the well known principles of the writ or action of Account,
or, perhaps, some slight divergence from those principles   We find
ourselves, however, immediately confronted by the fact that the principles do not seem to be well known and that the history of the rise and
subsequent use of that writ never has been adequately written   I
had come to this conclusion before realizing that Mr Luke Owen Pike,
in his learned prefaces to the Rolls Series of Year Books, had twice
touched on this matter, and in an especially illuminating way in his
preface to Y B (R S) 20 Ed III, 2, pp xxviii – xxxvii, where he
shows the importance of the action — contrary to the generally
accepted idea — and the extraordinarily wide area of its activities
But in the necessarily restricted limits of the Year Book prefaces Mr
Pike could not do more than show generally the error into which one
writer on the subject after another had fallen   It has seemed worth
while, in view of these facts, to touch as shortly as possible upon a few
of the facts presented by the cases themselves
    The first question is as to the rise of the action   As usual when we
attempt to trace an action to its source, we find the stream difficult to
follow, at times we lose all trace of its wanderings, and the guides upon
whom we have been taught to depend lead us nowhither   Mr Pike
takes issue, and as it would seem, justly, with Mr Maitland when the
latter says, "the common law action of Account remains at a low level
of development", but before following Mr Pike's guidance let us see
what Mr Maitland, not thinking about Account specifically, had found
to guide us   In his Registry of Original Writs [Harv L Rev 3 97,
167] he has first described a Register of 1227, in which he found no
writ of Account   He then proceeds to analyse a Register of *circa* 1236 –
67, and we find that writ No 83 in his list is a writ of Account   But in

his History of the Common Law [Pollock & Maitland, Hist of the C L Vol 2, 2d ed , p 221] he gives us an example of a still earlier writ which is given in Bracton's Note Book [Bracton Note Book, Vol 2, pl 859] Therefore our first date, so far as present researches go, is 1232 This would be nearly in the middle of the reign of Henry the Third, and probably gave rise to Maitland's remark that "Account appears in Henry III's reign, but it is very rare and seems only used against bailiffs of manors " It is true that the two early writs of which we have any record as yet are both against bailiffs. Maitland's writ 83 is a "Justificies" writ *"Justificies talem quod reddat tali racionabilem compotum suum de tempore quo fuit ballivus suus,"* etc Bracton's writ is *"Theobaldus Hautun petit versus Johannem de Prestona quod reddat ei compotum racionabilem de tempore quo fuit ballivus suus de manerio suo de Mareslet "* [Bracton Note Book, Vol 2, pl 859] The word *"ballivus'* is there in both writs to confirm what Maitland has said above, also another remark of his which has not quite so certain a sound 'We gather that the accountants in question were for the more part 'bailiffs' in the somewhat narrow sense that this word commonly bore, manorial bailiffs " [Pollock & Maitland, Hist of Eng Law, 2d ed , Vol 2, p 221] It would seem that Maitland's thought had already been modified by his longer research into the sources of the older law, and the "only used" of the earlier remark becomes the "for the more part" of the later writings If the action in its earliest beginnings was of so narrow a nature, it must have become rapidly enlarged, for although we have no cases for the later part of the reign of Henry III, or the very early years of Edward I, we come, in 1284, to the Statute of Westminster the Second where we have the provisions "concerning Servants, Bailiffs, Chamberlains, and all manner of Receivers, which are bound to yield Accompt " During these fifty years, which for us are void of case law, there had evidently been great progress made in the action "All manner of Receivers" is a broad statement, and as soon as we get any reported cases we find that they are indeed brought against receivers of all sorts and kinds We discover that Mr Pike is entirely right in his contention as to the wide use of the action [Y B (R S) 20 Ed III, 2 Preface, p xxviii] The action not only did not remain at a low state of development, but it apparently became the "common remedy in mercantile transactions, and in almost all cases where there were dealings and an unliquidated demand " [Reeves, Hist of Eng Law, Vol 3 77, 2d ed , 1787]

It became the most widely used, the most convenient and the most equitable of actions In fact it was in its essence an equitable action, and if we were to follow most of the writers upon the action of Account we should say that it has developed solely on the equitable side, and become the equitable action of Account, because of the greater convenience and adaptability of the equitable remedy [Spence, Eq Jur Vol 1, pp 649–50] Maitland agrees with Spence in the idea that "the common law action of Account remains at a low level of development because of the fact that it was in practice superseded by the equitable jurisdiction of the Chancellor, who in the Bill for Account had a more modern remedy operating under a more favorable and convenient procedure" [Maitland, Equity Forms of Action, 358] "In after times the more powerful and convenient jurisdiction of equity superseded the process of Account at common law" [Pollock & Maitland, Hist of Eng Law, 2d ed, Vol 2, p 222] Then we have quite a chorus of agreement — who would not follow such gracious leaders of legal thought? — "The action of Account eventually proved a failure, not because it was badly or defectively constructed, but because it attempted to accomplish what was beyond the powers of common-law courts" [Langdell Eq Jur, Harv L Rev, Vol 2 257] Holdsworth quotes Maitland both as to the reason for the decrease of the action and as to its having done "little or nothing for the development of the law of contract" [Holdsworth, Hist of Eng Law, Vol 3 323] Holdsworth, however, qualifies his statement by saying, "It was no doubt a useful action before the rise of the action of Assumpsit," which shows that he recognized the true trend of the earlier action, not into equity, but into another common-law action, even though he adds, "and before the growth of the Chancellor's equitable jurisdiction' Mr Pomeroy, resting on all this authority, and also relying on Spence [Spence, Eq Jur 1 650], goes so far as to rise into an almost passionate denunciation of our action "This action was so narrow in its operation, so difficult of application, so dilatory and so expensive, that it seems not to have been brought more than a dozen times within the last two centuries" [Pom, Eq Jur, 3 ed, Vol 6, § 926] It might seem that the action had received its final condemnation and should be remanded to oblivion Yet Mr Jeremy, who is cited in support of his position by Mr Pomeroy, mildly says, "The ground upon which Chancery assumed a concurrent jurisdiction with the courts of law on matters of Account has been said to be that the remedy which it is capable of affording is much more complete than that which may be obtained by action [Jeremy, Eq Jur, p 504] Mr Jeremy's exposition of the reasons for the development of the equitable action are so reasonable, and so little support Mr Pomeroy's contention, and there is so little in common to be found between his clear and calm account and these positive statements of the later writers, that it can only be assumed that not finding the action of Account in common use at a late date, the earlier and calmer statements were first adopted without question, and finally expanded without further research into what may be called the modern attitude on the subject

More and more, as one follows the accepted authorities on Account as an equitable action, one is led — perhaps mistakenly — to suspect that the action of Account at the common law ceased to be commonly used not so much, according to the statements we have cited, "because of the narrow scope and technical rules of the action" [Pomeroy, Vol 6, p 2797], or because of the "difficulty of proceeding to the full extent of justice at the common law," [Mitford, Chan Pleading, pp 120–41] or even because, as Maitland has it, equity had "the more powerful and convenient jurisdiction" [P & M Hist of Eng Law, 2d ed, Vol 2, p 122], but because another legal action, founded upon the same principle as that old action, the equitable principle that one person shall not unjustly enrich himself at the expense of another, which was "the basis of an action of Account, was also the basis of the action of Assumpsit for money had and received " Mr Ames, in his article on the History of Assumpsit [Harv L Rev 2 66] says "The most fruitful manifestations of the doctrine in the early law are to be found in the action of Account One who received money from another to be applied in a particular way was bound to give an account of his stewardship If he fulfilled his commission, a plea to that effect would be a valid discharge If he failed for any reason to apply the money in the mode directed, the auditors would find that the amount received was due to the plaintiff, who would have a judgment for its recovery If, for example, the money was to be applied in payment of a debt erroneously supposed to be due from the plaintiff to the defendant, either because of a mutual mistake, or because of fraudulent representations of the defendant, the intended application of the money being impossible, the plaintiff would recover the money in Account Debt would also lie in such cases, since, at an early period, Debt became concurrent with Account, when the object of the action was to recover the precise amount received by the defendant By means of the fiction of a promise implied in law, *Indebitatus Assumpsit* became concurrent with Debt, and thus was established the familiar action of Assumpsit for money had and received to recover money paid to the defendant by mistake

"Although Assumpsit for money had and received was in its infancy merely a substitute for Account, it gradually outgrew the limits of that action "

We have here the great authority of Mr Ames for the statement that "Assumpsit was in its infancy merely a substitute for Account," which is in effect another way of stating that it is the legal action of Assumpsit rather than the equitable Bill of Account, which took the place of the old action The Bill of Account has indeed fallen heir to the title and to some of the assets of the old legal action, but the legal action of Asumpsit has continued its principles, and continues to enforce the claims which in the old days were enforced only by the legal action of Account — not in a limited and contracted field, but in the wide and generous scope of that old action

The history of the development of the legal action of Account into the action of Assumpsit is an interesting one I do not know that it has been anywhere written from the viewpoint of the history of the action of Account, although it has necessarily become a part of the history of the rise of the action of Assumpsit   Mr Ames has probably done more for that action [History of Assumpsit, Harv L Rev 2 55] than has been done elsewhere, and he has incidentally done something more for the action of Account, but it has been only incidentally and he did not do more than was absolutely necessary for a complete understanding of the rise of the action of Assumpsit   Yet what he did incidentally was far more enlightening than anything anyone else has done when writing upon the action of Account

In the beginning we have the actions of Debt and Account sharing the field together   Reeves [Hist of Eng Law, Vol 4, 388] says "In the old law this action [debt] had held a sort of *divisum imperium* over contracts with the action of Accompt, which also in like manner with the former lost ground as the *Assumpsit* grew more into fashion "   He asserts that the "principal inducement to recur to the *Assumpsit* instead of these writs was to preclude the defendant from his wager of law, when, therefore, a transaction was so circumstanced that the law would not allow this privilege, there was no reason for going out of the ancient track, and if the case was such as to be within the compass of those remedies, it was still usual to bring debt and accompt "   There is nothing here about inconvenient and dilatory procedure, nothing at all about "narrow and limited action," we are merely getting away from the wager of law in any way we can, and no blame to any one or any action for doing so sensible a thing   Here we find Reeves treating our much maligned action of Accompt as a reigning sovereign, sharing its "*dominium*" with the action of Debt   He had already [*Ib*, Vol 2, p 337 *et seq*] spoken of the action of Accompt as having been rendered a "very useful remedy," by the two Statutes of Marlbridge and Westminster the Second, and he there goes on to give a clear exposition of the process upon a writ of Accompt, and incidentally to show that the limitation of the writ to "bailiffs" in "the narrower sense" was incorrect, he, in common with the other writers upon the subject, and following the Year Book cases, states that taking the two statutes together the writ would lie for bailiffs or receivers — that is, the common writ of Accompt, not the writ of *Monstraverunt de Compoto*, which was specially given by the Statute of Westminster the Second — and that the latter term was interpreted so broadly as to include nearly all those persons who had "received" anything under an obligation, express or otherwise, to return the same or account for it.

We have seen that the writ of Account was known and used at the common law against bailiffs   In the face of this well-known fact practically all of the writers upon the action of Account assume that the action against bailiffs was "given" by the Statute of Marlbridge   Many of the Year Book cases would seem to assume this also, and this has probably given rise to the general misstatement, but Coke, in his argument on the seventeenth

chapter of that act, which does give the action to guardians in
socage, says that it was made in declaration or affirmance of the common law" Bacon [Abridgment, title of Accompt, p 32] says "This
statute of Marlbridge is usually recited in the writ as if the writ was
warranted by statute only   but Accompt lay against the guardian
in socage at the common law, and the statute was merely in declaration
or affirmance of it " It seems that Coke's argument upon the seventeenth chapter holds equally well for the twenty-third chapter The
very wording of that chapter puts us on notice that it is meant simply
in affirmance of the already existing law or custom In this connection
it may be interesting to note Maitland's note upon Coke's statement
[P & M Hist of Eng Law, 2d ed , Vol 1, p 323, note] in which he
says "Coke regards the chapter of the Statute of Marlborough touching guardianship in socage as a 'declaration of the common law', but
he did not know the Provisions of Westminster and has no warrant for
his doctrine " But Maitland elsewhere says [P & M Hist of Eng
Law, 2d ed , Vol 1, p 179] "From this time of strain and stress we
have the Provisions of Westminster to which the king gave reluctant
consent in 1259 He did not hold himself bound by them, they never
became a well established part of the law of the land   almost all
of them were re-enacted with the consent of great and small, as the Provisions or Statute of Marlborough " This being so, it would seem
that the Provisions of Westminster, not being accepted as law, had no
effect upon the common law, and the Statute of Marlborough, being
the first statute which was accepted as law, would be declaratory of the
common law, as stated by Coke The matter, perhaps, is a mere
pebble in the mosaic of the old law, but in the end the placing of a
wrong pebble shows in the color scheme, and in the history of the law
of Accompt it seems that nearly every pebble has gotten a wrong tint
in the course of time There is as yet nothing to show that receivers
were bound to account at the common law, yet we have no direct proof
to the contrary The Statute of Westminster the Second brings in "all
manner of receivers" in a very casual way, not at all as if it were opening
wide the action of Account to an entirely new and very large class of
persons — "All manner of receivers which are bound to yield accompt "
(*Quibuscunque receptoribus qui ad compotatum reddendum tenentur*) [West
2, Cap XI] We have no early writ to show that receivers were bound to
accompt in times before the statute There are indications in the cases
that the action was regarded as something new The action is indeed
referred to as new by Bereford, in a case which is not digested by Statham,
and for which we have no printed Year Book, so we know it only in Fitzherbert's Abridgment [Fitzh Abr title Accompt, 127] where he cites
it as having been brought in 30 Ed 1 (1301) Bereford was a justice at
that time, and might well have been sitting in the Eyre for which it is
cited. It is an action against a receiver and Bereford says, "This is a
new writ, and in new causes new remedies " It may be that he refers to

the fact that the Statute of Westminster the Second (1285) first gave
the writ to receivers, but no mention is made of any Statute   In the
few printed Year Books that we have of Ed 1 (Rolls Series), the action
of Account appears in a very fair proportion among the actions   It
seems to be taken as a matter of course, and not as resting upon any
Statute   In the time of Edward the Second cases of Account were
of common occurrence, the marginal references frequently giving the
case as one of *Monstraverunt de Compoto*, showing those cases to be
founded on the Statute of Marlbridge   It might perhaps still be argued
that "for the more part" the action was still against bailiffs, but not
in "the narrower sense," since it may as well be brought for accounts
of "sakes de laine' as "bailiff de mon maison," or of both together.
[Mich 8 Ed III, p 36, pl 38 Fitzh Accompt, 95] Maitland himself
shows that the writ was not of statutory origin, or at all events was not
given by the Statute of Marlbridge, as in his History of Original Writs,
vol 2, p 516, Select Essays in Anglo-American Legal History, he shows
that this writ appears on a very early register, which he places between
1236 and 1267, but believes is not later than 1257   But there is even
earlier authority, as we have the writ given in Bracton [Note Book,
pl 859] as of Michaelmas Term, 16 Hen III (1232)   These are both writs
against bailiffs *"de manerio suo,"* and we have no proof that receivers were
as yet amenable to the writ   This proves but little, however, as before
the discovery of the Note Book, and Maitland's finding of the writ of
Account in the register, we had absolutely no proof that the action of
Account was of so early an origin   We must have assumed that it was,
but the assumption must have been without proof   When the word
"bailiff" began to be used to cover the case of anyone who was bound
to render an account of the property of another, we have no authority
at present to say   Reeves [Hist of Eng Law, 2 338] mentions the writ of
Monstravit de Compoto, as being made use of in this [Ed III] reign "prom-
iscuously with the common capias " [See also Impey, Modern Pleader,
2d ed , 1814, p 120   It is impossible to know to whom the credit of
this statement should belong   The editions of the two books run along
almost simultaneously, and neither gives credit to the other]   It seems
that it was this writ of *Monstravit de Compoto* which caused so
much confusion in the books   The *Monstravit de Compoto* was a new
writ, and it was "given" by the Statute of Marlbridge   The bailiffs
who could be forced to account by the common law were those who
had lands or tenements by which they might be distrained, if they had
no lands or tenements, there was no remedy against them   The new
writ was the *Monstravit de Compoto*, by which they could be "attached
by their bodies " [Reeves, Hist of Eng Law, 348, 1st ed]   The process began with the word by which the writ became known   *"Monstravit "* Fleta gives the usual writ of Account, and then goes on
*"Si autem hujusmodi ballivi se subtraxerint, nec habeant unde dis-
tringantur, tunc succurritur querentibus per tale breve, etc   Rex Vice-*

comiti salutem   Monstravit nobis A   quod cum B   exstitit ballivus suus in N omnium rerum & bonorum suorum habens administrationem, idem B compoto suo non soluto, subrefugia quærens, latitat in ballivia tua, nec poterit inveniri nec distringi ad compotum suum reddendum   Et quia de communi consilio Regni nostri provisum est, quod si ballivi qui dominis suis compotum reddere tenerentur se subtraxerint, & terras & tenemen' non habeant per quae distringi valeant, per eorum corpora attachientur   Ita quod Vicecom' in quorum ballivis inveniantur, eos venire faciant ad compotum suum reddend', tibi praecipimus, quod si praedictus A fecerit te secur' de clamore suo prosequend', tunc praedictum B attachiari fac' ita quod habeas corpus ejus coram Justiciariis nostris, &c, ad reddend' praedicto A compotum suum praedictum   Et habeas ibi," etc   [Fleta, cap 70, p 155, sec 8, ed 1685]   I think we may assume that when the cases say that "this is a new writ," they are alluding to the *Monstravit de Compoto* as a general thing, and not to the usual writ against bailiffs   We may not be able to go as far as to say the usual writ against receivers, for that indeed may have been new in the early days of Ed II, although we do not have to yield that much, since there is no positive evidence on the one side or the other   The writers have not paid much attention to this *Monstravit de Compoto*, but have assumed that it was the usual writ of account, be it either against bailiffs or receivers, that was spoken of as "new "

Beside the *Monstravit* Maitland gives, from a list of writs from the Register, apparently *circa* Ed I (MSS), a *"Breve de compoto super Statutum de Acton Burnel "* This appears to be all that we have to show that writs of Account were ever founded upon that Statute, which, bearing date 11 or 13 Ed I (1283 or 1285), is nearly contemporary with Westminster the Second   The history of the writ or writs of Account for the reign of Edward the First, and indeed for that of Edward the Second, does not appear to have been fully written

When we reach the reign of Edward the Third we find the writ, as Reeves says, "a very useful remedy " [Reeves, Hist of Eng Law, 2 337] He also says that "Receiver   was an universal character that suited every one who had received money or profit to the use of another, for which he ought to account " [Reeves, Hist of Eng Law, 3 78] Reeves is not to be credited with having started the theory that the remedy was inconvenient, he evidently had never heard of that theory He says [Vol 3 77] "This action was the common remedy in mercantile transactions, and in almost all cases where there were dealings and an unliquidated demand " This appears to have been true all through that period with which our abridgment has to deal, and in our cases we have a sufficient number of writs brought against bailiffs and receivers of varied kinds to substantiate the statements of Reeves We have noted that Reeves has said that "in the old law this action [debt] had held a sort of *divisum imperium* over contracts with the action of accompt " [Vol 4 388] For the learning of "the books" on the concurrent jurisdiction of debt and account, *Core's* case [Dyer, 20 28 Hen VIII] with the marginal cases, gives a sort of bird's-eye view, which, being couched in the language of those books and steeped in their atmosphere, better conveys their meaning and content than the later cases But one should also consult *Earl of Leviton* against *Topcliff* [Cro Eliz 644, 1597-8] and the cases there cited These cases would seem sufficient to prove that the two actions were concurrent until at least the time of Charles I (1625–49) We have Pollock's statement to the same effect "The action of account was a remedy (sometimes exclusively, sometimes concurrently with debt) to enforce claims of the kind which in modern times have been the subject of actions of assumpsit for money had and received or the like " [Pollock, Contract Wald's ed , p 153, 1906] But it is in the article on the Early History of Assumpsit by Mr Ames [2 Harv L Rev 53] that we find the most light thrown on the development of the action of Account Nowhere else is the equitable nature of the early action so clearly shown He says "Assumpsit for money had and received was in its infancy merely a substitute for Account" [p 67] In his further outline of the growth of the action of Assumpsit he shows how hard was the struggle for supremacy between the two actions, how assumpsit first became "concurrent with account" [p 69] and finally superseded it All this without showing any of the desire of the writers upon the equitable action of account to throw contempt upon the parent action At first the new remedy was scarcely more liberal than the old, and for a long time the struggle was nearly equal Mr Ames gives us the case of *Bonnel* v *Fowke* [2 Sid 4, 1657] as perhaps the first case where by the fiction of a promise implied in law *Indebitatus assumpsit* became concurrent with debt In 1676, in *Arris* v *Ames* against *Stukely* [2 Mod 260], the encroachment of assumpsit upon account had gone so far as to enable the Court to say, "in disregard of all precedents of account" [Ames, *supra*, 67] that 'an *Indebitatus assumpsit* will lie for rent received by one who pretends a title, for in such case an account will lie Wherever the plaintiff may have an account, an *Indebitatus* will lie" It may have been this case which led Lord Holt to say that "*Indebitatus assumpsit* has been carried too far " [Comb 447, 1697] He proceeds to cite instances where it has been properly allowed, practically all cases where one had received from another money not justly due him, and he continues, "but where there is a bargain, tho' a corrupt one, or where one sells goods that were not his own, I will never allow an *Indebitatus* " [Comb 447, 1697] He was unable to stem the fast flowing tide, the action of Assumpsit was undoubtedly popular, it gave relief in cases in which it could less easily be given by any other action — or at least it apparently seemed to do so — and it checked the tendency to throw all such actions into the Chancery It was a logical outgrowth of the former action of Account, far more so than the equitable action, which has so long boasted of its greater convenience and celerity   In regard to the development of the legal action of Account into the equitable action there was a constant protest going on against turning the "action at law into a suit in equity " [*Tilly* v *Bridges*, 1705, Finch Pre in Chan 252, 1753]

In a case in 1737 [*Morton* v *Frecker* 1 Atk 524], and another in 1749 [*Sayer* v *Pierce*, 1 Ves Sr , 233] the Court refused the equitable action in an apparent attempt to retain the legal action in use   Here and there in the course of time the equitable action of account received from a thoughtful judge or able commentator less honorable mention than we find given it in these latter days   Mr Henry Gwillim, the learned editor of the fifth edition of Bacon's Abridgment (1798), on page 31 of that edition, after citing the usual statement that "proceedings in this action being difficult, dilatory, and expensive, it is now seldom used," says with a gleam of deserved sarcasm   "From the experiment made of this action in the case of *Godfrey* v *Saunders* [3 Wilson, 73], its proceedings seem not to deserve the character here given of them   A matter which had been fruitlessly depending in Chancery upwards of twelve years was thoroughly examined, and finally determined in this form of action in the course of two years "   This action of *Godfrey* v *Saunders* [3 Wils C P Repts 73] seemed to have all the elements which rendered the action of account so "impossible" in a court of law, and yet to have been settled in such a court with comparative ease and celerity   It was in this case that Lord Wilmot said, "I am glad to see this action of account is revived in this Court" [p 117]   In fact, so far as the older cases reveal the action, it seems to have been an action admirably adapted to the ends the litigants had in view, well adapted to doing justice between party and party, elastic in its inclusion of all classes of litigants, and giving relief in a satisfactory way to parties who had afterwards to select an action of Debt, a bill in Chancery — always a dilatory court — or the action of *Indebitatus assumpsit*   As has been suggested, the latter was of all the actions most kindred in spirit, most closely allied in purpose, and best adapted to the purposes for which the legal action of Account had been used in its better days   Impey, in his "Modern Pleader," writing about 1794, quotes this remark of Lord Wilmot [Impey, Modern Pleader, 121] and says further, "And I heard Lord Kenyon say, in a cause before him, wherein *a very long and intricate account was to be gone through* (after the party refused a reference)   '*Why did you not bring an action of account?* We cannot go through this at Nisi Prius ' "

The disuse of this action is laid down to be on account of the great delay in process, which was by "summons, attachment and distress infinite " [2 Inst 280] "But as it may now be brought by Bill of Middlesex, latitat, or capias, in the first instance, I can see no reason why it should not come into use again, especially where the matter is clear, and not very intricate " [Impey, Modern Pleader, pp 121–22] It is evident the writers of a hundred years ago were not convinced that the reasons for the discontinuance of the use of the action were well founded, and the resurrection of something of the old feeling, in the words of Mr Pike, shows a recurrence of the desire that justice be done to the "old common law action of Account " He says our forefathers "were familiar with the Court of Common Pleas, whither they came as plaintiffs in Account when their ventures had not succeeded according to their expectations, just as their descendants are familiar with the Chancery Division, where petitions are made for the winding up of Companies " It is not a new thought to suggest that in this old action are found the beginnings of the law of partnership, many of the actions are really for an accounting between persons who were acting in the relation of partners in mercantile proceedings The money was very often lent "à marchander," and the merchandizing was to be for the mutual benefit, and although we cannot show that the transactions were continuous, there can be little doubt that such transactions, when successful, would be repeated, and would therefore come to be practical and actual joint proceedings over a long period, which would amount to what is now known as a partnership, or what was known as a partnership up to the more modern period of statutory enactments upon such combinations

There is very much of interest in the law of account which has not even been touched upon in this fragmentary note The procedure in the older times has been elaborately set forth in many of the old writers upon Pleading The date of the extension of the action to executors and administrators, to the executor of executors, and against executors and administrators, are all also plainly set forth in the same way The intention of the note has not been so much to repeat all this knowledge which is plainly set forth and findable by all who have access to a library, but to suggest to others better fitted for the task the interest, there is in getting at the real facts and setting forth the true history of the action of Account

AIELL[2]

Statham 3 b
Michaelis
13 Ed II

(1) **In a writ of aiel,** the release of the ancestor himself, although it be with warranty, is no bar.

Case 1

There is but one writ of Aiel in the printed term of Mich 13 Ed II The case does not report the point as given by Statham

Hilary
10 Ed. III

(2) **In a writ of aiel** on the possession of his grandmother, it is no plea to say that the grandfather of the demandant, husband to the grandmother, is alive, and

that it belongs to him to have the land by the curtesy
(I believe the plea is good, etc)   Query?

Reported in Y B Hilary, 10 Ed III, p 10, pl 29   See also Fitzh Case 2.
Aiel, 3

(3)   **In a writ of aiel,** the writ was "Command that he Hilary
render Bastium to the keeping of Pobtis, Abbot of B " 10 Ed III
And it was adjudged good

The case has not been identified in Y B 10 Ed III, or in the early Case 8
abridgments

(4)   **A writ of aiel** brought by two, where he was grand- Michaelis
father to one and great-grandfather to the other   And it 18 Ed II
was adjudged good.   See the Statute

Reported in Y B Mich 18 Ed II, p 560   Case 4

The Statute referred to is that of 6 Ed I (1278), cap 6, Stats at
Large, Vol 1, p 123   The Statute provided that the writ of Mort
d'Ancestor should be used in such cases

ᵃ The Writ of Aiel was one of those writs that were provided to carry
further the action given in the Assize of Mort d'Ancestor, and therefore follows that writ in its nature   The Year Books are full of these
writs, and our Abridgment gives us but a narrow view of what it seems
should have been, at the time of the compilation of the work, an interesting science   Glanville takes no notice of this action   He enlarges
upon the writ of Mort d'Ancestor, which was an ancient action   Maitland in his Registry of Original Writs [Harv L Rev 3 170–75] gives
us two cases of Mort d'Ancestor, none of Aiel, in the Register of
1236–37   One case of Mort d'Ancestor is there given as in an Irish
Register [Ib , p 111] and one apparently of the time of Henry III
[p 114] (the writ de consanguinitate)   Nuper Obiit and Cosinage appear to
come before the writ of Aiel   Maitland makes the birth date of the
writ of Mort d'Ancestor 1176 [P & M Hist of Eng Law, 2 57] and
says, "After a dispute between the justices and the magnates, the former
succeeded in instituting the actions of Aiel, Besaiel, Tresaiel, and Cosinage" (De Avo, de Proavo, de Tritavo, de Consanguinitate), as supplements
for the Assize of Mort d'Ancestor "   This, he says, was "about half
a century later than the beginning of the Mort d'Ancestor," which he
believes to have been instituted by the council held at Northampton in
1176   This would bring the first use of the writ of Aiel about the year
1226   This is a date slightly earlier than that which Maitland gives
to the earliest register he was able to find, but it is to be expected that
still earlier registers may yet be found, and we cannot found too many

theories upon what we now know since they may so easily be over-
turned by newer discoveries.   At all events we find this writ to be an
early one, and that it was in very frequent use by the litigants
whose cases come to us through the Year Book reports

Britton gives a full account of the writ and its use   Later writers
like Reeves and Holdsworth ignore it entirely, although it seems that
it has its clearly defined part in the development of the actions and the
history of the law   Fitzherbert in the *Natura Brevium* sheds no light
upon the history of the writ

ADDICION[1]

Trinity
3 Hen VI

(1) **It is a good addition,** "Command such a one of the
county, etc , yeoman," without naming him as of such a
vill

And it was said in the same plea, that if one be bound
by the name of J of B, of F, in the county of B, it is no
plea to say, "no such vill as F within the same county,"
because he is bound by such a name

Case 1

The point here abridged is found, imbedded, as it were, in a very
long case of debt in Y B Hilary (not Trinity), 3 Hen VI, p 23, pl 2
See also Brooke, Addicions de Hommes et Villes, 3

Paschal
7 Hen IV

(2) **See that the father** does not change his name for
his son, for although his son has the same name, yet the
writ is good against the father, without naming him senior,
but against the son he shall be named junior, or otherwise
the writ shall abate   In Trespass

Case 2

Reported in Y B Paschal, 7 Hen IV, p 11, pl 5   In a writ of
Trespass   See also Brooke, Addicions de Hommes et Villes, 18   See
also Y B Hilary, 21 Hen VI, p 26, pl 9

Michaelis
27 Hen VI

(3) **In trespass** against J de B, of the Parish of S. DANBY.
The defendant, the day the writ was purchased, was
dwelling in the vill of B, within the same parish, the vill
of H is not named, judgment of the writ   ASSHETON
Every parish has a vill, wherefore the writ is good, etc.
PORTYNGTON That is not so, for in the parish of Saint
Clemant there is no vill, and in such a parish which has no
vill within the parish the addition is good, as above; but
if a vill be within the parish and he be of the vill he shall

be named of the vill, for the Statute is that he shall be named of the vill, or a place known to be out of the vill And they adjourned   See the Statute, etc.

The case does not appear in Mich 27 Hen VI, but is found in Case 3 Y B Hilary, 22 Hen VI, p 41, pl 18   See also Brooke, Addicions de Hommes et Villes, 38

The Statute is that of 1 Hen V (1413)   Stats at Large, Vol 3, p 3

(4) **In a recordare,** the defendant demanded judgment Paschal of the writ because it did not state of what vill, nor of what 27 Hen VI. trade, the defendant was, inasmuch as [process of out-lawry does not lie except on the original writ][1] PRISOT: That is not an exception in the county [Court], and the writ should agree with the complaint, and upon the complaint shall the plea be held, wherefore answer, etc   Query?   In Replevin, if, etc

There is no Paschal Term in the printed year of 27 Hen VI, but a Case 4 short report of the case is found in Y B Hilary, 3 Hen VI, p 30, pl 17 See also Brooke, Addicions de Hommes et Villes, 4

(5) **Sawdeour** is a good addition   And yet a knight, an Trinity esquire, and a valet cannot have the same name, etc   27 Hen VI

And it was said in the same plea that "Chopchurch" is a good addition, and "Broggarre," etc , for such occupations are not forbidden by the law   But "thief" or such like thing, which is forbidden by the law, is no addition

The case has not been identified in Y B Hilary, 27 Hen VI Brooke, Case 5 Addicions, etc , 8, and Fitzh Addicions, 4, have a version of the case, as in Hilary, 9 Hen VI, p 65, pl 19   Sawdeour is apparently from the old French Saudoier, a soldier attached to the king. See La Curne de St. Pelaye, Dictionnaire Historique, tome neuvième, 1881   "Chopchurch" is a middle-English word for a man who sold a benefice in a church   The practice was not considered illegal, hence the addition could be upheld, but it was not considered to be morally defensible

(6) **A man** is not allowed to give diversity to a name Hilary except of those who are [not] parties to the writ   And that 7 Ed III in a writ of Intrusion, etc

The point so badly digested here is found in the end of a case on a Case 6 writ of Intrusion, in Y B Hilary, 7 Ed III, p 3, pl 7   The obscure

[1]These words are taken from the report of the case in the Year Book

digest of Statham has had to be reinforced by a word taken from the report of the case, which has been placed within brackets

(7) **"Praecipe** such a one of B, husbandman"; who demanded judgment of the writ because he was a "gentleman, being of the occupation of a husbandman" And it was adjudged a good plea without saying, "not husbandman," etc.

There is no printed Year Book of 15 Hen VI, but the case appears in a very interesting form in Y B 14 Hen VI, p 15, pl 51. See also Brooke, Addicions, etc , 44.

(8) **The writ** was, "Command the aforesaid John F de B, otherwise called J F de C , in the county of Nottingham, gentleman" And because there was no addition to the first name, but [there was] in the "otherwise called," it was reversed by a writ of Error, and that *Coram Rege*, etc.

Probably the case reported in Y B. Mich 28 Hen VI, p 26, pl 10 Brooke, Addicions, 46, has a like case, cited as in 36 Hen VI, 18

[a] Addicion is one of the more ancient titles which have ceased to appear in modern digests It is very easy to see why the "addition" was a most necessary part of the writ in those early times when other means of identification were lacking The cases are innumerable in which the pleas that the writ is void because the vill is named — let us say — Lynn, and "there is no vill in the county without an addition," that is to say, East Lynn, West Lynn, Upper Lynn This Lynn in the writ, therefore, is not identified Writs are frequently abated for this cause Then there is the case of the gentleman who finds himself with the addition of "husbandman" because he occasionally puts his hand to the plough He objects to this addition, and is sustained in the objection. The addition of "Chopchurch" is allowable, because it is a legal, although an objectionable, practice to farm out a benefice, but to say "thief" or such like is not allowable, because that is an illegal occupation The points seem trivial now, but they were sufficiently important in the pleading of the time The fact that many of these apparently smaller points of the pleading of that period are now scarcely alluded to in even the best and most profound of the histories of the English law shows that it is important that these cases such as are found in the Abridgment, unimportant as they seem in themselves, should be brought to the attention of the modern scholar The dryness — the apparent technicality, perhaps one might say the pettiness — of the older pleading has repelled the legal historian from the minuteness necessary to a proper investigation of the subject The law itself is so involved with these technicalities, so wrapped up in the pleadings, that unless we know what

those pleadings meant we are in danger of not knowing what the law itself, which those pleaders are so earnestly striving to get straight, ultimately was decided to be Unimportant indeed it was if we do not rest the law of to-day upon the principles which they were all the time evolving from those seemingly tangled skeins of their endless disputations Most important if we do so rest the law of to-day It is disappointing to go to the histories of the law and find no reference to the very points upon which an awakened interest is awaiting instruction The real history of the old actions would be not a dull and uninteresting one, but one full of a very vivid and real interest to the modern student For these slender links keep the whole chain from breaking, they link together the heavier and more important parts, which would be disconnected without them

ADMINISTRATOURS [4]

(1) **In debt against one as administrator,** he said that he administered to the use of one H, to whom the ordinary, etc , and not in any other manner And the plea was adjudged good

Hilary
50 Ed III

And it was said in the same plea, that in an action against two administrators, who pleaded, "never, etc ," the plaintiff said that [if] one administered in such a place and the other in another place, and the one is found for the plaintiff and the other against him, he against whom the issue is found shall be charged for all, and he shall not have judgment until both issues be tried, etc   But in an action brought against one as administrator when he is not, etc , he should traverse the commission; that is to say, that the ordinary did not commit, etc

Statham 4 a

The case has not been identified in Y B Hilary, 50 Ed III Statham may have had reference to the case in Y B Hilary, 50 Ed III, p 9, pl 18, referred to by Brooke, Administrators, 15, but if so his report of the case was different from that which we have in the printed Year Book See also Fitzh Administrators, 19

Case 1

(2) **In debt,** the plaintiffs showed how one A made his administrators and died, after whose death the will was approved before the ordinary of B, etc. NEWTON Action you should not have, for we say that the metropolitan was

Michaelis
14 Hen VI

assured that the testator had goods in different dioceses, wherefore he discharged the plea, and committed the administration to the defendant by his letters — which he showed — for the reason aforesaid, judgment CHANNT That is no plea, unless he shows what goods, etc And that was not allowed, wherefore he said that the testator made them his executors as they had said, "without this that the said testator had goods in different dioceses at the time of his death[1] Ready " PASTON You could have demurred in law, for where a man dies and has goods in different dioceses, and dies intestate, there it belongs to the metropolitan to commit the administration But when a man has made his executors, and the testament is proved, it is hard to discharge them, etc Query?

Case 2 Reported in Y B Anno 14 Hen VI, p 21, pl 61 The terms are not distinguished from each other in the printed Year Book of 14 Hen VI Statham was probably living at that time, and may have taken the case from his own notes

Michaelis 9 Hen V (3) **In debt** against administrators HULTHORPE He does not show how the administration was committed to all by the ordinary Judgment of the count And it was not allowed, wherefore he said that he was never administrator PASTON Inasmuch as you do not deny that the ordinary committed, etc HANKFORD The ordinary himself will not be charged unless the goods come into his possession For the Statute which gives the action is, "If the goods of the deceased come to the hands of the ordinary to dispose of " Consequently, if the defendant did not get the goods he shall not be charged WESTBOURN The taking of the letters of the ordinary is administration, etc Which COKAYN conceded

Case 3 Reported in Y B Paschal (not Mich), 9 Hen V, p 6, pl 20

The Statute is that of Westminster the Second, 13 Ed I (1285), cap 19, Stats at Large, Vol 1, p 163 (194) The meaning of the words is fairly well given in the text, but the words themselves are misquoted See also Fitzh Administrators, 10

[1] "Vivant" is an error in Statham for "mourant "

(4) **In debt** against a man as administrator, who said that the administration was committed to him and to one B, and because he did not say that the said B administered, the opinion was that it was no plea   And as it seems there is a difference where the administration is committed to two, and where it is committed to one, for where it is committed to one, the acceptance of the letters is administration, but when it is committed to two, although one receives the letters, the other can refuse, wherefore query? etc

And see, in the same plea, that the letters of the ordinary are traversable, that is to say, "he did not commit them," but it is otherwise as to a will   But yet a man shall have the averment that he died intestate, although the testament be approved by the ordinary, etc   Query?

Anno
8 Hen VI

The case has not been identified in Y B Anno 8 Hen VI   Brooke has two cases (Administrators, 24, 27) of Debt against administrators, in 8 Hen VI, but they do not agree with Statham's abridgment

Case 4

(5) **In debt** brought by administrators, who showed the letters of the deputy of the ordinary   And it was adjudged clearly sufficient   But it is otherwise if one alleges excommunication, etc, but it was said that is by Statute (Query?   For I have not seen such a Statute)

Paschal
11 Hen IV

Reported in Y B Paschal, 11 Hen IV, p 64, pl 16   The "Statute' seems, from the report of the case, to have been merely an opinion taken in Parliament   See also Brooke, Administrators, 18, and Fitzh Administrators, 12

Case 5

(6) **In debt** against administrators, the opinion of the COURT was that the plaintiff should show in his count how the administration was committed to the defendant, etc Contrary above

Trinity
11 Hen VI

Reported at great length in Y B Trinity, 11 Hen IV (not Hen VI), p 72, pl 11
"Above" is probably case 3, *supra*

Case 6

(7) **In debt** against the executors of one J   FORTESCUE This J died intestate, and the ordinary committed the administration to us.   Judgment of the writ   ASCOUGH

Trinity
18 Hen VI

If they are administrators by their own tort, the commission lies against them as executors NEWTON If the administration was committed to them, it shall have relation and shall be understood to be [of the time of] the death of the intestate, etc Query, if it be committed to them pending the writ?

Case 7   Reported in Y B Hilary (not Trinity), 18 Hen VI, p 29, pl 1

Trinity
18 Hen VI

(8) **Administrators** shall have an action of trespass for a trespass made before the administration was committed to them, and after the death of the testator, although the ordinary has released the action, for no action is given to the ordinary, and consequently he can [not] release any action. And that was well argued.

And it was said in the same plea, that if a villein brings a writ of Trespass for goods carried away, or a writ of Debt, the release of his lord is a good bar (Which I do not believe, inasmuch as no property is in the lord before he is seised, etc But peradventure he can take them, etc)

Case 8   Reported in Y B Mich 18 Hen VI, p 22, pl. 7 See also Fitzh Administrators, 2

Michaelis
18 Hen VI

(9) **In debt** against one J, as executor of B, who said that the said B made him his executor, and that he refused before the ordinary And a long time afterwards the ordinary committed the administration to us, etc, in which case, etc, judgment of the writ PORTYNGTON To that we say that after the death of the testator, and before the administration was committed to him, that he administered MARKHAM He does not say that he administered before the ordinary discharged him, etc NEWTON· If he administered at any time before the administration was committed to him, the action lies against him as executor and the commission is void MARKHAM Emparle Query? etc

Case 9   The case has not been identified in Y B Mich 18 Hen VI, or in the early abridgments.

Note   **See as to administrators,** in the title of Executors Statham, title of Executors, *infra*, pp 86 a, to 87 b

Statham gives us no early cases of Administration, and therefore does not reach the interesting questions which arise in regard to the use of the terms executor and administrator in the discussions of the earlier law   That these terms were used exchangeably seems certain, although the case that Maitland gives [Hist of Eng Law, Vol 2, p 361, note 2] as in Y B 38 Ed III [21] does not seem as exactly on that point as the note would indicate   The Statute of Ed III [Stat 1, cap 3, Stats at Large, Vol 2, p 108 (113)] may possibly deserve, as he has said, the distinction of having introduced the name administrator as a technical term into our law   That takes us back to 1357, none of our cases go back as far as that case of 38 Ed III   For some reason, never to be known by us in all probability, all our cases of Administrators save one are in the reign of Henry the Sixth, and the one case not in his reign is in the fiftieth year of Edward the Third   Thus our most satisfactory period in the development of this law is not illustrated by these cases

Our first case is evidently under the Statute passed only thirteen years before, but no reference is made to it   A reference is made to a statute in case 3, but it is to the Statute of Westminster the Second, in which the creditor of the testator was given the right to claim his debt   The king's court had begun to give the creditor of the testator rights against the executor, the Statute gives an action against the ordinary   Jenks [Hist of Eng Law, p 64] calls the executor a "new person" to the English law of the early thirteenth century, that is to say, a person introduced by no less an instrument than *Magna Charta* [Magna Charta of 1215, cap 26]   It can hardly be supposed, however, that Magna Charta invented the executor, it must have found him ready and waiting to be used   However this may be, the theory that it was the desire of the Church to be represented in the distribution of the goods of the deceased, which led to the legislation which invented first the executor and then the administrator, with the powers which we find them exercising in the reported cases, has some force   Jenks — and he seems to have been the first to do so — traces through the provisions of these statutes the rise of the distinction between real and personal property in that the land goes to the heir, the personal property to the executor

Of course we have nothing to do with all that in these cases of the Abridgment, but they do bring out the points in regard to the statutes, and, as in so many other cases, we find that the principle which controlled the law of the executor and the administrator has never been thoroughly worked out   Most of the learning on the point seems to rest on Selden's statement   [Selden's Collected Works, Vol 3, p 1677 On the Disposition of Intestates' Goods]   He thinks that up to the time of Henry First all administration of an intestate's goods was by the friends or kindred, and he seems to be the first to claim that it was after the Statute of 31 Ed III that the "name of administrator was as

common as their office ' What we seem to need is an independent examination of the early cases in order to determine just how much of that
Statute was a new departure, and just how far it was declaratory of the
common law The statements made by the best and most responsible
of our writers — Reeves, Maitland, Holdsworth, and Jenks — are supported by the statutes, of course, and Maitland gives us one case,
elsewhere we have none There is another case which supports Maitland's in 43 Ed III, 1 [Fitzh Abr Administrators, 14.] But it does
not appear that administrator, even as a "technical term," was unknown
to our law before the Statute of 31 Ed III, as it is used frequently in the
earlier cases, unless Maitland means more by the word "technical" than
appears on the surface There is one case in 4 Ed III [Y B Mich 4 Ed
III, p 43, pl 19] where the administrator and the administration is
spoken of, although the term there seems to be interchangeable with that
of executor The earliest use seems to be in very much that way, the
phrase is "executor and administrator" or "executor or administrator "
In Y B Mich 17 Ed II, 502, 503, it is "administered as ordinary "
"Those who have administration " [Y B Paschal, 18 Ed II, 607] "To
have the administration of all the goods " [Y B Mich 10 Ed II, 303]
The administrator as we know him to-day may be argued out of all these
cases, yet administrator he is, and known to the law as such, there may
be a will, and he seems to have rights under a will as a modern administrator has not, but neither was the executor of the day an exact dupli-
cate of our modern executor The administrator was known, the
question is just what his duties were and his powers, and how was he
differentiated from the executor Was he at first the same, and how, if
so, did they gradually get to be two persons? The answer is as yet not
known

The figure of the administrator, his rise and progress through the
early years, in spite of the thin threads of learning about him running
through all the books, and to be traced through Glanville, Britton,
Lyndhurst, Perkins, Selden and the modern writers, seems still dim,
vague, unformed The Year Books hold his portrait in fragments,
some time, it is to be hoped, to be pieced together and made a complete
figure in the perfected portraiture of the time in which he now moves
only as a shadow

AGE [5]

atham 4 b
dary
Hen IV

(1) **A man** shall not have his age in a *Contra Formam
Collationis* at the *Scire Facias*, etc. By the opinion of the
COURT, etc

ise 1

Reported at length in Y B Hilary, 2 Hen IV, p 16, pl 24 See also
Brooke, Age, 11

The *Contra Formam Collationis* was a writ granted when a man had given alms to any of the House to support the poor, or to do some religious service, if they alienated the lands the donor or his heir had the rent

(2) **If a man** enfeoffs his heir, who is under age, of land in fee simple, and dies, the issue shall have his age, and the paramount warranty And this by FYNCHEDEN, in a Formedon

Michaelis 40 Ed III

Reported in Mich 40 Ed III, p 43, pl 27 And see Y B Mich 43 Ed III, p 23, pl 17 See also Brooke, Age, 56, and Fitzh Age, 31

Case 2

(3) **The father** and the son, under age, purchase lands to them and to the heirs of the father, then the father dies and the son is empleaded, he shall have his age, because the action lies against him by reason of the freehold which he had in the lifetime of his father, etc By FYNCHEDEN, in a *Dum fuit infra Ætatem*, etc

Paschal 43 Ed III

Reported in Y B Mich (not Paschal), 30 (not 43), Ed III, p 17, pl 20 Fitzh Age, 58

Case 3

(4) **In a praecipe quod reddat,** the tenant said that his father died seised and he was in as heir, under age, and he prayed his age BELKNAP Your father did not die seised. Ready, etc FYNCHEDEN That is no plea, for it may be that his father was disseised and that the heir entered after his death, etc Upon which it was adjudged that he should have his age, etc

Trinity 43 Ed III

Reported in Y B Trinity, 43 Ed III, p 18, pl 2 See also Brooke, Age, 7, and Fitzh Age, 35

Case 4

(5) **In a quod ei deforceat,** the tenant vouched one under age to warranty, upon which the plea was stayed, etc FYNCHEDEN The writ is that she claims to hold in dower, in which case the woman should be in the same condition in which she would be in a writ of Dower Which THORPE conceded. Query, if he shall show cause for the voucher, as he shall, in a writ of Dower?

Michaelis 44 Ed. III

Reported in Y B Mich 44 Ed III, p 42, pl 49 The report of the case omits the claim of the woman to hold in dower, but in the margin "Statham 5" is cited See also Fitzh Age, 38

Case 5

**Trinity
47 Ed III**

(6) **In a writ of error** against two, one was under age and prayed his age, and because he was not tenant and the other was tenant, he was ousted of his age, etc

Case 6

Reported at great length in Y B Mich (not Trinity), 47 Ed III, p 7, pl 4 The report refers to "Statham, Age, 6" See also Brooke, Age, 9, and Fitzh Age, 43 The latter gives a very long digest of the case.

**Hilary
50 Ed III**

(7) **In formedon,** for default of the tenant one prayed to be received, and he said that he was under age, and that the reversion descended to him, and he prayed his age And the opinion of WILLOUGHBY was that he should not have it, etc

Case 7

The case has not been identified in Y B. Hilary, 50 Ed III, or in the early abridgments.

**Paschal
31½Ed III**

(8) **In a per que servicia,** or in a *Quid Juris Clamat,* the tenant shall not have his age, because the land is demanded against him But yet, query as to the *Quid Juris Clamat,* inasmuch as he can claim a fee and so lose the land.

And it was said in the same plea that a man shall not have his age in *Cessavit* of his own cesser, nor in a writ of Admeasurement of Dower. And that well debated in a *Per que Servicia,* etc

Case 8

There is no printed year for 31 Ed III The case has not been identified in the early abridgments

**Hilary
6 Ed III**

(9) **In a writ of entry** in which he had no entry except by one H, who disseised the father of the demandant, the tenant said that the demandant was under age, and demanded judgment if, during the nonage, he shall be received to this writ, which is in the right And it was adjudged that the plea should stay, for the Statute is not intended to apply except to the entry of the heir of the disseisor, and the heir of the disseisee

Case 9

Reported in Y B Hilary, 6 Ed III, p 3, pl 4 See also Fitzh Age, 62

The Statute is that of 13 Ed. I (1275), cap 49, Westminster the First, Stats at Large, Vol 1, p 74 (105)

(10) **In a cui in vita,** the tenant vouched the heir of the husband of the demandant to warranty   And because he was under age, etc , it was adjudged that the plea should stay, because the Statute is, "Let the purchaser tarry," which is only to be understood as for the alienee of the husband, and he who now holds was the heir of the alienee; so out of the purview of the Statute

Michaelis 6 Ed III

Reported in Y B Mich 6 Ed III, p 46, pl 36   See also Fitzh Age, 46

The Statute is that of Westminster the Second, 13 Ed I (1285), cap 40, Stats at Large, Vol 1, p 163, (218)

Case 10

(11) **In a nuper obiit** on the seisin of one A, grandfather of the demandant, and mother of the tenant, the tenant was ousted of his age, for HERLE said that in this writ the tenant shall not have his age, nor bind the voucher to warranty, etc.   Query?

Paschal 7 Ed III

Reported in Y B Paschal, 7 Ed III, p 13, pl 6   See also Fitzh Age, 111

Case 11

(12) **In a writ** of *Particione Facienda*, the tenant shall have his age   By HERLE, because when he makes partition by judgment that will bind him   It is otherwise if it be by agreement without judgment, etc.

Paschal 8 Ed III

Reported in Y B Paschal, 8 Ed III, p 24, pl 17

Case 12

(13) **In a scire facias** out of a recovery limited against the father of the tenant, for rent, the tenant was ousted of his age, etc

Michaelis 9 Ed III

Reported in Y B Mich 9 Ed III, p 30, pl 21

Case 13

(14) **In a writ of entry** against a woman, she said that she was tenant in dower of the heritage of one J, who is under age, of whom she prayed aid, and that the case be stayed   The demandant said that the land was in Gavelkind, where a man can alienate at the age of fifteen years, and we say that the heir is fifteen years, etc   But notwithstanding it was adjudged that the case be stayed, since a custom shall be taken strictly, and he did not say that

Michaelis 9 Ed III

the custom was that a man shall not have his age if he be past fifteen years

Case 14 Reported in Y B Mich 9 Ed III, p 38, pl 44

(15) **In a cessavit,** the tenant bound seisin in his ancestor The tenant said that the demandant was under age, and prayed that the cause be stayed HERLE This writ is in lieu of an avowry, therefore, etc The tenant passed over of his own free will.

Case 15 Reported at length in Y B Paschal, 10 Ed III, p 18, pl 13

(16) **In a writ of entry** upon a disseisin against a woman, by the heir of the disseisee, the woman prayed the disseisor in aid, because she was tenant in dower of his heritage And because he was under age it was adjudged that he should have his age, for the Statute is not applicable except where the writ is brought against the heir of the disseisor

Case 16 Reported in Y B Trinity, 10 Ed III, p 31, pl 8 See also Fitzh Age, 92

The Statute is that of 3 Ed I (1275), cap 47, Westminster the First, Stats at Large, Vol 1, p 105

(17) **In a scire facias** out of a recognisance against the heir of the recognisor, he shall have his age, by award of the Court The contrary was seen in a *Scire Facias* out of a recognisance, wherefore, query as to the difference? The law seems to be the same in debt against the heir who is under age, since he shall not have his age, etc., for by the recognisance his right is disproved. But for the recognisor in a Statute Merchant by which his land shall be put in execution, the heir cannot make a recognisance while under age, as to what land is liable and what is not

Case 17 There is no early printed year of 11 Ed III It may be the case reported in the Rolls Series, 11–12 Ed III, p 48 It begins, "In a note," and is a case of a *Scire Facias* A man died leaving an infant heir against whom the *Scire Facias* was brought The heir claimed his age and had it Nothing of the remaining matter which is in Statham appears in this report of the case See also Fitzh Age, 4

(18) **In a writ of entry** on a disseisin made on the Michaelis 10 Ed III
grandfather of the demandant, the tenant said that the
demandant was under age. STONORE (for the demandant)
Our grandfather brought an Assize against you for the
same land and died while pleading, and our father brought
a writ of Entry, and died while pleading, wherefore, etc. And
for that reason the tenant was put to answer immediately,
etc Query?

Reported in Y B Mich 10 Ed III, p 58, pl 58 See also Fitzh Case 18
Age, 94

(19) **In an assize** the plaintiff appeared by guardian. Michaelis 12 Ed III.
The tenant said that the plaintiff was of full age the day
the writ was purchased, and prayed that he be viewed
To which the justices said that the plaintiff should not be
delayed by such an allegation, unless he showed matter that
would bind him [if he were of full age][1], wherefore the
tenant pleaded the release of the plaintiff, of all actions,
and prayed that he might be viewed SHARSHULL It is
of record that we were guardian And it was not allowed,
but a day was given for him to be viewed

There is no early printed year of 12 Ed III The case is to be found Case 19
in the Rolls Series, Y B 12 Ed III, pp 21–25 The judge there
appears as Shardelowe, not Sharshull

(20) **In a juris utrum** against one under age, who said Paschal 16 Ed III
that one A, who was a bastard, held certain lands (which
were put in view) of his father, whose heir he is, and that
the seignory descended to him, and that he was seised of Statham 5 a.
the services by the hand of the said A, and then A died
without issue, wherefore he entered as in his escheat, by
reason of the seignory which had descended to him, and
he prayed his age To which the demandant said that he
did not claim anything in the services,[2] but he prayed a
jury for the demesne which your ancestor never had,
etc And it was adjudged that the defendant should have
his age, because the land had come in lieu of the services
which had come to him by descent, etc

[1] Words not in Statham, taken from the report of the case
[2] Seignory, in Statham See also Fitzh Age, 46

Case 20

There is no early printed year of 16 Ed III   The case is printed in the Rolls Series, 16 Ed III, Pt 1, pp 245–49   As usual it would appear that Statham had access to some report of the case not known to the editors of this series

Hilary
19 Ed III

(21) In a cui in vita, the tenant vouched one J, who was the feoffee of the husband, who entered into the warranty and vouched the heir of the husband, who was under age, and he prayed that the case be stayed   And the demandant prayed seisin of the land, but he could not have it, because the Statute only extends to cases where the tenant in demesne vouches the heir

And in the same term, in a writ of Entry brought by the heir of the disseisee against one A, who vouched to warranty the heir of the disseisor, he prayed that the case be stayed because he was under age, and so it was adjudged, since the Statute extends only to cases where the writ is brought against the heir of the disseisor by the heir of the disseisee, etc   And so see that these statutes are taken strictly   (And I believe that the reason is because they are in restraint of the common law, etc.)

Case 21

There is no early printed year of 19 Ed III   The case has not been identified in the Rolls Series

The Statute is that of Westminster the First, 1 Ed I (1275), cap 47, Stats at Large, Vol 1, p 105

Trinity
15 Ed III

(22) In a scire facias against one under age, out of a recovery limited against his father, he was ousted of his age, because by the recovery the right of his father was defeated and disproved   But it is otherwise as to a fine or recognisance. By WILLOUGHBY and SHARSHULL, etc.

Case 22

There is no early printed year of 15 Ed III   What appears to be a long report of the case, from which this very short abridgment of Statham's is taken, appears in the Rolls Series, Trinity, 15 Ed III, pp 236–42   See also Fitzh Age, 95, where a long report of the case is given

Trinity
19 Ed III

(23) In a cui in vita against the alienee of the husband of the heir, the husband was under age, and he prayed that the case be stayed   And the demandant had judgment to recover immediately. Which note   THORPE

How shall we get to our warranty when the heir comes of age? STONORE The tenant shall have a *Scire Facias* against the vouchee when he comes to his age, and the vouchee shall show such matter to the tenant as he should against the demandant if the demandant were in Court And if the Court sees that he shows sufficient matter to bar the demandant, a *Scire Facias* shall issue against the demandant, and he shall answer to the bar; and if he is not able to do that, the tenant shall recover his land, etc THORPE said, "That is marvelous!"

There is no early printed year of 19 Ed III No case of a *Cui in Vita* appears in that year and term in the Rolls Series — Case 23

(24) **In a writ** of Entry *in consimili casu,* the tenant said that the demandant was under age, etc And it was not allowed, and yet the lease was made by his father, etc. (I believe that was because of the Statute, etc) — Trinity 18 Ed III

Reported in Y B Hilary, 18 Ed III, p 2, pl 9 See also Fitzh Age, 10 — Case 24
The Statute is apparently that of 6 Ed I (1278), Stats at Large, Vol 1, p 120

(25) **A woman** was received to bring a writ of Mesne, with her husband, during his nonage, although that is a writ of right, etc. — Trinity 18 Ed III

See report of the case in Y. B. Hilary (not Trinity), 18 Ed III, p 2, pl 9 Case 24, *supra* This point appears on p 3 of the report of the case — Case 25

(26) **In formedon** in the descender, the tenant said that the plaintiff was under age, judgment, etc SHARSHULL This writ is given in place of the Assize of Mort d'Ancestor, wherefore answer Wherefore he pleaded a recovery against a stranger and a mesne gift The demandant answered that the gift was before the title of the writ, wherefore the tenant should answer Ready, etc THORPE now prayed that the case be stayed, inasmuch as the plaintiff could not acknowledge, etc. SHARSHULL· That plea comes from his part, but if the deed of his ancestor had been pleaded in bar, then the case would be stayed; wherefore answer, etc — Trinity 16 Ed III

Case 26.   There is no early printed year of 16 Ed III   The case has not been identified in the Rolls Series   Fitzh   Age, 45, has what may be an abridgment of the case

Paschal
24 Ed III

(27) **If a writ of entry** upon a disseisin be brought by the heir of the disseisee against the heir of the disseisor, under age, the opinion is that he shall have his age, because the demandant did not make fresh suit, but suffered him to continue in possession years and days, for the Statute is that by the nonage of the one nor the other shall the plea be delayed, but as much as a man can without offending the law, the plea shall be hastened by fresh suit after the disseisin, etc.

Case 27   Reported in Y B Paschal, 24 Ed III, p 25, pl 12   The last part of the case is a quotation from the Statute of 3 Ed I, cap 47, Westminster the First (1275), Stats at Large, Vol 1, p 105   The case as reported in the Year Book, and the digests as given by Fitzherbert, Age, 101, and Brooke, Age, 22, do not sustain Statham's abridgment of the case   The age is distinctly refused   Fitzherbert gives the case as in Trinity Term, Brooke makes an error in the chapter of the Statute, making it chapter 46

Trinity
24 Ed III

(28) **One H** recovered damages against one F, in a suit of intrusion of wardship   And the executors of H sued a *Scire Facias* against F, and the sheriff returned that he was dead, wherefore he had a *Scire Facias* against one M, who was terre-tenant, who said that one S, his father, died seised of the same land, and he was his heir, and under age, and he prayed his age and had it, because his father was a stranger to the recovery   But if the recovery had been tailed against his ancestor it had been otherwise. WIL-LOUGHBY   The reason is, as it seems, inasmuch as the recovery was for another thing, etc   Query also, if the land be executory in this case, for it seems that he shall not have execution except of the goods and chattels of F, etc., or by *elegit?*

Case 28   What appears to be a very poor report of this case is found in Y B Trinity, 24 Ed III, p 28, pl 11   The same report appears to have been used by Fitzh   Age, 102, and Brooke, Age, 24   See also Y B Trinity, 24 Ed III, p 56, pl 43, where there is a longer report of the case

(29) **In formedon,** the tenant made default after default Came one F, and said that one H was seised and leased to the tenant for life, remainder to the father of F, and his heirs in fee, and F is dead, and he prays to be received as his heir   And because he was under age, etc.   NEWTON He is in as purchaser, for he has shown the gift which is his title, and his father never had possession, wherefore he is a purchaser, etc   THORPE   He is seised of the same thing by descent, wherefore he prays to be received, that is to say, of the reversion and of the right, etc.   And they adjourned, etc.   Query?

The reports of this case as printed in the Year Books are long and confused   See Y B Mich 24 Ed III, p 32, pl 16, and Y B Mich 24 Ed III, p 76, pl 101   No decision was come to in either case, but there was apparently a further report in 25 Ed III, which is not found in the printed Year Books

(30) **In a scire facias** one prayed to be received upon default of the tenant, and he prayed his age, and was ousted, etc   (And I believe that that was because of the Statute which ousts delays in a *Scire Facias.   Distinguendum est*, etc)

There is no early printed year of 19 Ed III   The case has not been identified in the Rolls Series for that year, or in the early abridgments.

The Statute is probably that of Westminster the First, 3 Ed I (1275), cap 45, Stats at Large, Vol 1, p 104.

(31) **In attaint** against the heir of the tenant he shall not have his age, because before he comes to his age all the jurors might be dead, in which case he will lose the attaint, etc   But it is otherwise in a writ of Error   And yet, all the same, if a writ of Error is brought against him who is a party he shall not have his age, and in deceit against the heir of the tenant, he shall not have his age, because the garnishers or summoners may be dead before he comes to his age, etc   By WILLOUGHBY and SHARSHULL.

The case has not been identified in Y B Mich 24 Ed III, or in the early abridgments.

Trinity
24 Ed III

(32) **Land descends** to a woman was under age, who takes a husband of full age; they are empleaded; she shall not have her age, by the opinion of SHARSHULL, in a *Præcipe quod Reddat.*

Case 32

The case has not been identified in Y B Trinity 24 Ed III Fitzh Age, 134, has practically the same abridgment of the case, but an incomplete citation He gives Hilary as the Term

Hilary
43 Ed III

(33) **In a quid juris clamat** by one under age, against one who said that the ancestor of the plaintiff leased the land to him for life, without impeachment of waste, by this deed (which he showed), and, saving the advantage to him, he is Ready. And because the plaintiff could not acknowledge the deed of his ancestor during, etc , it was adjudged that the case stay, etc. But yet, query? And inasmuch as he demanded only an attornment [he should answer] And also it seems that in that case he should answer to the deed of his ancestor, for if it was the deed of a stranger he should answer in that case, etc

Case 33

Reported in Y B Hilary, 43 Ed III, p 5, pl 11 A short case. See also Brooke, Age, 57, and Fitzh Age, 34

Paschal
50 Ed III

Statham 5 b

(34) **The youngest son** in Borough English shall not have his age By THORPE And the law is the same for the youngest son in Gavelkind, etc In Formedon, etc Then, query? If the action be brought against him and his elder brother, who is heir at the common law?

Case 34

The case has not been identified in Y B. Paschal, 50 Ed III There is no Paschal Term for 50 Ed II in the printed years, and the case has not been identified in Brooke or Fitzherbert

Hilary
8 Ed III

(35) **If one under** age makes a recognisance, if he wishes to avoid it by a plea, when he comes to his age, or while he is under age, and he cannot, etc , shall he have a writ of Error while he is under age, as he would have on a fine? See [this case] for it was well debated, in an *Audita Querela,* etc Query, if the recognisance was in the Chancery, how would the error be sued, etc ?

Case 35

The case has not been identified in Y B Hilary, 8 Ed III, or in the early abridgments.

(36) **Shall one under age** be forced to make partition? ^{Paschal} See the title of Partition   Well debated   And see also in the same term, as to those who are under age, in the title of Laborers

Paschal 9 Hen VI

The point abridged by Statham appears at the end of a very long ^{Case 36} case which is printed in Y B Paschal, 9 Hen VI, pp 5-7, pl 13   The point in question is printed on page 7

(37) **Where the remainder** is limited to the right heirs ^{Trinity} of one B, which B is dead at the time of the grant, so that the remainder can take effect, the heir of B shall not have his age, for he is a purchaser (as if it came to him in his own name)   But where land is given to one for the term of his life, the remainder over in tail, and the remainder to the right heirs of the tenant for life, and then the tenant for life dies, and the tenant in tail dies without issue, the issue of the tenant for life shall have his age, by the possession which his father had at one time.   Query? etc   And, by the opinion of HANKFORD, where his father might have had possession by any possibility, he shall have his age, as if land be given for life, the remainder to one D and his heirs   D dies and the tenant for life dies, and the issue of B enters under age, he shall have his age, because it is possible his father could have had [possession]   And his father also had the fee and the reversion, for he could have had an action of waste and a writ of Intrusion   And see the year 40 Ed III, in the case the *Provost of Beulay*

Trinity 11 Hen IV

Case of a *Scire Facias*   Printed in Y B Trinity, 11 Hen IV, p 74, ^{Case 37} pl 14   See also Brooke, Age, 15, and Fitzh Age, 25   They vary much in their matter

(38) **In a writ of entry** in the Per, it was alleged that ^{Michaelis} the tenant had no entry except by one H, who disseised the ^{27 Hen VI} father of the demandant   DANBY — by way of protestation — said that the said H did not disseise your father, but we say that the said H had us as issue, and then he enfeoffed us of this same land in tail, and died, so we vouch ourselves as heir of this H to save the tail   And because we are under age we pray that the case be stayed   MOILE   That cannot be, for you are yourself the

person against whom the writ is brought, and by your own confession you are heir of the disseisor, wherefore you are within the purview of the Statute   NEWTON   That is not so, for although he be his heir the writ is brought against him as purchaser, and inasmuch as he has vouched himself as heir, he is now in as tenant by the warranty, and the Statute does not apply except where the writ is brought against him as tenant of the land and heir to the disseisor at the commencement, etc   For if in such a writ the tenant vouches to warranty the heir of the disseisor, who is under age, the case will stay, for the above reason   so here   And they adjourned, etc

Case 38

The case has not been identified in Y B Mich 27 Hen VI, or in the early abridgments

The Statute is that of Westminster the First, 3 Ed I (1275), Stats at Large, Vol 1, p 105

Paschal
42 Ed III

(39) **In formedon** by one under age, the case will not stay by reason of nonage, because the action is given in lieu of an Assize of Mort d'Ancestor   But if the deed of his ancestor be pleaded in bar, the case will stay, although the deed be enrolled

Case 39

Reported in Y B Paschal, 42 Ed III, p 13, pl 23, where a reference is given to this case in Statham   The *placita* in Statham are not numbered, but the Year Book cites the case as "Statham, 39," which is correct   See also Fitzh   Age, 32

Trinity
47 Ed III

(40) **In a writ of dower,** the case will not stay because of the nonage of any person, for if so she might die before the [coming of] age, etc

Case 40

The case has not been identified in Y B Trinity, 47 Ed III, or in the early abridgments

Hilary
24 Ed III

(41) **In a scire facias** by one under age, a deed of the ancestor was pleaded in bar, and "assets by descent "   The demandant said that "nothing, etc "   The defendant prayed that the case be stayed   NOTTINGHAM   You come too late, for you should have said that in your plea, but now that you have suffered the plaintiff to reply to you, it will be in his election whether, etc.

And it was said in the same plea, that in a writ of Mort d'Ancestor or of Cosinage, if the deed of another ancestor be produced the case will stay, notwithstanding the Statute, etc   Query?   etc

The case has not been identified in Y B. Hilary, 24 Ed III   Fitzh Age, 100, reports a similar case as in Y B Mich 23 Ed. III, p 22, pl 16, but the two abridgments and the case as reported all differ in essential points   Case 41

(42)   **If an idiot** be vouched, and bound by the deed of his ancestor, and his lands are seised into the hands of the king, the case will stay until, etc   Query, if he shall answer without the king, in that case?   And if so, shall he answer by his next friend, to whom the land is committed, etc? See as to this matter in a note   Michaelis 9 Ed III

The case has not been identified in Y B Mich 9 Ed III, or in the early abridgments   Case 42

(43)   **Two brought** a *Dum fuit infra Ætatem*   And because one was under age it was adjudged that the case should stay against both   and WILLOUGHBY gave as his reason that if the release of their ancestor were pleaded in bar, he who was under age could not answer that, and consequently the other could not, because the deed was entire, etc.   Query?   Trinity 30 Ed III

A short report of the case is printed in Y B Trinity, 30 Ed III, p 7, pl 2   See also Fitzh Age, 82   Neither the reports of Fitzherbert mention WILLOUGHBY   Case 43

(44)   **The heir** of the disseisee brought a writ of Entry upon a disseisin against the wife of the disseisor, who was tenant in dower of the inheritance of the heir   She vouched the heir and the case was stayed, because it is not within the purview of the Statute, unless the action be brought against the heir, etc   Hilary 34 Ed III

There is no printed Year for 34 Ed III   The case has not been identified in the early abridgments   Case 44

The Statute is that of Westminster the First, 3 Ed I (1275), Stats at Large, Vol 1, p 105

Michaelis
11 Hen IV

(45) **In a scire facias,** the tenant prayed aid of one J, as son and heir of one B, and because he was under age he prayed that the case should stay and so it was adjudged. But that was a *Scire Facias* out of a fine, etc   And the law seems to be the same in a *Scire Facias* out of a recognisance, inasmuch as it is not brought against the heir of him against whom the recovery was made   But if the heir of him against whom the recovery was limited be prayed in aid, and is under age, query if the case would stay, inasmuch as the action is not brought against him?

Case 45

The case has not been identified in Y B Mich 11 Hen IV, or in the early abridgments

Note

Query, if the king brought an action against one who was under age, should he have his age in any case?

Michaelis
13 Hen VI

(46) **In a writ of annuity** against a parson of a church, who prayed in aid the heir of his patron, who was under age, and that the case should stay   And he could not have it, etc

Case 46

The case has not been identified in Y B Mich 13 Hen VI, or in the early abridgments

Anno
1 Ed II

(47) **In an assize** of Mort d'Ancestor, the tenant shall have his age.   In an Iter of Northampton.

Case 47

The case has not been identified in the Year Book of Ed II, or in the early abridgments

Paschal
8 Ed III

(48) **In a writ** of *Particione Facienda*, the tenant shall have his age

Case 48

This appears to be a second abridgment of Paschal, 8 Ed III, p 24, pl 17   See case 12, *supra*

Michaelis
3 Ed II

(49) **In waste** against a tenant *pro indiviso*, for waste made by his father, he was ousted of his age   See the Statute

Case 49

Reported in Y B Mich 3 Ed II, p 54, pl 1

The Statute is that of Westminster the Second, 13 Ed I (1285), cap 22, Stats at Large, Vol 1, p 196

(50) **In a writ of entry** upon a disseisin, by the heir of
the disseisee, albeit he was not the immediate heir, but
was heir to another who was heir to the disseisee and
under age, still the case will not stay, for he is in the case of
the Statute, if he makes himself heir to the disseisee.

The case has not been identified in Y B Mich 12 Ed II

The Statute is that of Westminster the First, 3 Ed I (1275), cap 47,
Stats at Large, Vol 1, p 105

⁵ This is another title which has dropped out of our abridgments and
digests   Necessarily the matter treated of is as much a part of the law
as ever   The minor is still protected and still used as a shield in our
modern law, even as he was of old   The particular kind of "age" we
have in these cases is the "age prier," in which an infant shows to the
Court that he is under the legal age and prays that the action may stay —
the parole may demur — until he comes of age   This is the reason
why some authorities say that the plea is called "parole demur '   The
difficulty lies in the translation of "parole" which means plea, cause, or
action, yet which is a little different from any one of them   The word
has split up into remnants of meaning, none of which cover the whole
content of the old word

And we are to "note well" that there are many diversities of ages
"For the lord shall have aid of his tenant in socage to marry his daughter
when the daughter is of the age of seven years, and aid to make his son
and heir a knight when he is of the age of seven years   also that
is the age of male and female to sue and be sued for lands which they
have or claim by descent," which is the chief point of all these cases here
collected   The idea, of course, was to protect the infant, in too many
cases it is evident that the plea was made to delay justice   The infant
is often "demanded" and "viewed," and sometimes seen clearly to be of
age, and sometimes not   That the plea was often used for delay is
shown by the fact that it was not allowed to be made in writs of dower
to keep the widow out of her portion   But Bracton gives an exception to
this [Bracton, 422, b] in the special case "where the grandfather of a
minor has endowed his wife, and she after the death of her husband has
not claimed dower for a long time, to wit, ten, twenty, or thirty years, in
the lifetime of the heir of her husband, and upon the death of that heir
before the assignment of dower, his heir having been left a minor, if the
wife can then claim on account of dower, such an heir shall not answer
to her before he is of age "   "Likewise he shall answer under age sometimes if the answer touches the king " [Twiss Bracton VI, 335, f 422, b]
It was not allowed in an Assize   In our case 11 the aid prayer is refused
in the case of a *nuper obiit*   The age is also refused in case 31, in an
attaint, "because before he comes to his age all the jurors might be dead,
in which case he will lose the attaint, etc "   This reason — that all the

jurors or the widow might be dead before the heir can reach his full age — is often given where the Statute cannot be made to apply Through all the cases the fact that this had come to be a plea for delay becomes more and more plain, and that the Statute was made to "oust delays" as our case 30 has it   The youngest son in borough English is denied his age in our case 34, but of course this is the special customary law of Kent   The plea was not allowed in a Formedon, since this writ was in the place of a Mort d'Ancestor, and the exception was not allowed in that writ   However, our case 47 is contrary to this   Bracton treats of this plea as one of the exceptions which are available to the tenant against the person of the claimant, and which were dilatory and temporary   [Bracton, f 421]   The exception did not abate the writ but delayed it until the heir reached his majority   Our case 32, where the woman under age marrying a man of full age is denied the exception, is directly contrary to Bracton [Bracton, f 423, b   Twiss, Brac VI, pp 341–42], who says   "Likewise a person may have an exception by reason of an adjunct person, which he would have of himself, as between husband and wife, as if the husband, being of full age, should take to wife someone with an inheritance who was under age, and they should be impleaded concerning a tenement of the wife's, on account of the minority of the wife the trial shall be stayed without day, until the wife, whose right should be at stake, has attained full age "

Bracton [ff 424, b, 425, a] goes very elaborately into the manner of proving age.   The detail with which he treats the subject is in itself sufficient to show its importance at that time, and, as a matter of that older procedure out of which has grown our own procedure, is a matter of interest to us to-day

AIDE

Statham 6 a
Hilary
2 Hen IV

(1) **A man shall have aid** in a *Scire Facias* out of a *Contra Formam Collationis*. By the opinion of the COURT, etc   Tenant in tail after possibility [of issue extinct] was ousted of the aid in the same term

Case I

The case of the *Scire Facias* has not been identified in Y B Hilary, 2 Hen IV   The case of a tenant in tail after possibility, etc, is reported in Y B Paschal, 2 Hen. IV, p 17, pl 2   See also Brooke, Aide, 37

Hilary
40 Ed III

(2) **In debt** upon a penal sum granted by the predecessor of the defendant upon an annuity which was ratified by the patron and the ordinary, the defendant prayed aid,

etc. BELKNAP This is only a penal sum, etc , wherefore, etc. CANNDISH The plaintiff has a writ of Annuity for the same annuity pending against us in the Court Christian, in which it might be that he will be barred, and so this action would not lie, etc And by this action our church is to be charged, wherefore, etc. THORPE It is reasonable that you have the aid, or else that the plaintiff demur on his action until the writ of Annuity be ended. And they adjourned, etc

Reported in Y B. Hilary, 40 Ed III, p 3, pl 8 See also Brooke, Aide, 18, and Fitzh Aide, 109 **Case 2**

(3) **In a praecipe quod reddat,** the tenant said that one J was seised and leased to him for the term of his life, the remainder to K in tail, the remainder to H and S, his wife, in the tail; and he prayed aid of K, and of H and S, and of this same S, because she is heir to the donor and under age, and he prayed that the case be stayed The aid was granted, as above, but it was adjudged that he sue a summons immediately because of the mesne estate, etc. Well debated. **Hilary 40 Ed III**

Reported in Y B Hilary, 40 Ed III, p 13, pl 29 See also Brooke, Aide, 19 **Case 3**

(4) **In a scire facias** out of a fine, the tenant showed how she was tenant in dower of other lands, and that these lands in demand were given to her in exchange for the other, by one W, and she prayed aid of the said W, and had it **Paschal 40 Ed III**

And see in the same plea, a protection was allowed to the party, etc , for which see the Statute of *his quæ recordata sunt*

Reported in Y B Hilary (not Paschal), 40 Ed III, p 18, pl 9 See also Brooke, Aide, 20 **Case 4**

The Statute is that of Westminster the Second, see case 49, *supra* The words are the first words of chapter 45, p 224, "*Quia de his quæ recordata sunt*"

(5) **A man** shall have aid in a *Scire Facias*, but he shall not vouch **Michaelis 41 Ed III**

Reported in Y B Trinity (not Mich), 41 Ed III, p 16, pl 10 See also Brooke, Aide, 23, and Fitzh Aide, 111 **Case 5**

Michaelis
41 Ed III

(6) **In a scire facias** against a parson on a judgment limited against his predecessor, in a writ of Annuity, he shall have aid of the patron and of the ordinary, notwithstanding he had had the aid in the writ of Annuity, etc

Case 6

Reported in Y B Mich 41 Ed III, p 20, pl 5   See also Brooke, Aide, 24, who says "Contrarium, Ed 3, titel de *Scire Facias* in Fitzh. 152"   See also Fitzh   Aide, 112

Paschal
42 Ed III.

(7) **The aid** was granted in a writ of Attaint, notwithstanding it was on a judgment given in an Assize, in which none shall have the aid, except he who is named in the Assize. And consequently not in an Attaint.

Case 7

Reported in Y B Mich (not Paschal), 42 Ed III, p 26, pl 13   See also Brooke, Aide, 25

Paschal
42 Ed III

(8) **Land** was given to one G for the term of his life, the remainder to H in tail, the remainder to the right heirs of G, and G had aid of H, notwithstanding the fee was in himself, but it was not executed, etc.   And some said that he should have prayed aid of H and of himself by a feigned name, because one should have aid of all in the remainder, etc.

Case 8

Reported in Y. B Paschal, 42 Ed III, p 8, pl. 4   See also Fitzh Aide, 113

Paschal
43 Ed III

(9) **In replevin,** the tenant avowed upon the plaintiff as tenant by the curtesy, who prayed aid and had it.

Case 9

Reported in Y B Paschal, 43 Ed III, p 13, pl 5   See also Brooke, Aide, 26

Paschal
43 Ed III

(10) **In trespass** where the plea of the defendant amounts to no more in substance than "not guilty," although they are at issue, he shall have the aid

Case 10

The case has not been identified in Y B Paschal, 43 Ed III, or in the early abridgments

Paschal
44 Ed III

(11) **A master** of a hospital, if there is no common seal, shall have aid, as well as a parson of a church   In a *Jure d'Utrum* also.

Case 11

Reported in Y B Paschal, 44 Ed III, p 11, pl 13   See also Brooke, Aide del Roy, 15, and Fitzh   Ayde de Roy, 54

(12) **In trespass** against two, one said that the plaintiff
was villein regardant to the manor of D, which the defendant held for the term of his life of the lease of one H   The
plaintiff said "free," etc , and the defendant had the aid
The other defendant said that he came in aid of the other
as bailiff, and the plaintiff said "free," and the defendant
prayed aid of his master. FYNCHEDEN   The other, of whom
he prays aid, is named in the writ, and he has pleaded with
the plaintiff, etc   And if in Replevin against two, *i e* ,
the master and his bailiff, if the master makes an avowry,
the other is discharged. so here. Wherefore he was
ousted of the aid, and had the same day until the inquest
was passed between the plaintiff and the other, because
that shall make an end of all, etc.

Reported in Y B Hilary, 45 Ed III, p 46, pl 1   See also Brooke,
Aide, 32, and Fitzh   Ayde, 116, where the citation is incorrect

(13) **In a scire facias** upon a recovery in a writ of
Annuity against a parson, he was ousted of the aid because
his predecessor had the aid in the writ of Annuity, etc
Contrary 39, in the case of *Lira*.

Reported in Y B Hilary, 46 Ed III, p. 6, pl 19   See also Fitzh
Ayde de Roy, 57   See also case 6, *supra*

(14) **A man** shall have aid in a writ of Error, of one who
was named in the writ   Query, if he shall have aid of a
stranger, etc ?

The point is embedded in the very long case found in Y B Mich
(not Trinity), 47 Ed III, p 7, pl 4

(15) **In a writ of annuity** brought by an abbot against
a vicar, demanding one hundred pounds of wax, on an
annual rent of twenty pounds of wax, and he prescribed,
etc   BURCH   The abbot who is plaintiff is parson of the
same church, and holds it to his own use, and that of
the bishop and the ordinary, and he found his church
discharged, and he prayed aid of them and had it   Notwithstanding the abbot was plaintiff, and notwithstanding
the plaintiff alleged the seisin by the hand of the defend-

ant As to which, query? For in a *Cessavit* against a
tenant for life, of his own cesser, he shall not have the aid,
etc And so see in that case he shall have the aid of the
plaintiff, for otherwise he cannot have the aid of the ordinary But of the plaintiff alone it is wrong to have the
aid And one can also vouch the demandant with another,
but not alone, etc.

Case 15 The case has not been identified in Y B Hilary, 50 Ed III, or in
the early abridgments

**Hilary
50 Ed III** (16) **In trespass** against two, one justified as "estray,"
etc, and the other said that he came in aid of him as his
servant. The plaintiff said, "Of their tort," etc The
servant prayed aid of his master, and could not have it,
because his master had justified that he might make an
end of all But if his master had pleaded "not guilty,"
etc, and the servant had justified, then he should have had
the aid, notwithstanding his master was named And
the law is the same in Replevin

Case 16 The case has not been identified in Y B Hilary, 50 Ed III, or in the
early abridgments

**Trinity
7 Ed III** (17) **A chaplain** of a chantry shall have aid of the
patron and the bishop, in Avowry, etc

Case 17 The case has not been identified in Y B Trinity, 7 Ed III, or in the
early abridgments

**Michaelis
30 Ed III** (18) **One R. Gillibrond** brought a *Scire Facias* against
one H and one Alice, out of a fine to execute a remainder
And he showed how one R was seised And for the fine
it was recited that whereas one T held the same lands
for the term of his life, the reversion regardant to R,
with remainder to this G, now demandant PULTON One
R was seised of these same tenements, to him and to the
heirs of his body begotten, and he had issue K and M,
and died, after whose death the reversion descended to
them because their father had leased these same lands
to one T for the term of his life, and T died and they
entered. And K married H, against whom this writ is
brought, and had issue one P And M took for a hus-

band one J, and had issue the said A, against whom, etc   And then K, M and J died, so H holds by the law of England, the reversion regardant to P, of whom he prays aid.   And because he was under age he prayed that the Statham 6 b case be stayed.   And Alice said that she held in parcenry with H, tenant by the curtesy, and prayed aid of P, as above, and that the case be stayed, etc   SKIPWITH You see clearly that they never could have had any partition, wherefore, etc   WILLOUGHBY The tenant by the curtesy *de mero jure* should have the aid of his issue, then that is in a manner a partition, for he has put another to answer for his portion, then it is reasonable that Alice shall have the aid for the severance aforesaid, wherefore the aid will be granted if you will not say anything else   SKIPWITH This R is the same person who granted us the reversion of T, and we brought our action to defeat the descent from R to them, in which case we hold that the aid is not grantable   WILLOUGHBY If K and M had been in, etc, peradventure they would not have the aid, because by your suit you are to defeat the same reversion which descended, etc   But when K married H, and they had issue, then H is in by another title, that is to say, by the law, etc   And also Alice, who is issue of M, is in by another descent, wherefore it is reasonable that they have the aid   SKIPWITH We say that the wife of H had nothing in the land after the marriage, in demesne or in reversion   Ready   And inasmuch as Alice tells us that M, her mother, had nothing at the time of her death, in demesne or in reversion, etc   PULTON Inasmuch as you do not deny the disseisin in common at one time, judgment, etc, for although M had nothing at the time, etc., it may be that she was disseised, and that after her death, Alice entered, in which case she is adjudged in by descent. And the law is the same as to the tenant by the curtesy, etc, wherefore your counterplea of is no value   And such was the opinion of the COURT, wherefore he said that K nor M never had anything   Ready   And the others alleged the contrary   Well debated [by] HERLE, etc

The citation should be Paschal, 21 Ed III, p 14, pl 17   See also Case 18   Brooke, Aide, 65, and Fitzh   Ayde, 21

Trinity
7 Ed III

(19) **Herle said** that when a bailiff makes a conusance and has aid of his master he can amend his conusance, etc. Query?

And in the same plea [it was said] that he shall have the aid of his master before the issue is joined (which note) on the part of the defendant in Replevin. And the bailiff shall also have aid of his master where he makes a conusance in his own right, before the issue is joined. Paschal, 21.

Case 19

The case has not been identified in Y B Trinity, 7 Ed III

Paschal
21 Ed III

(20) **In a scire facias** where his father gave to one H, saving the reversion   And the gift to H was in the tail, etc , and H died without issue, and he brought *Scire Facias* out of the fine, etc   Which query? For it was executed, etc   The tenant said that she was the wife of this same H, and after his death one J, his son, endowed her, and that the reversion is in one F, of whom she prayed aid   FYNCHEDEN · You should show how the reversion is to F. DARR If the reversion be granted to him by a fine, we are a stranger to it, and we show you how we came to the land   Wherefore SHARSHULL said, if it be a fine that is matter of record, of which you should take notice   And if it be by deed nothing passed, unless you attorned, which you should show, etc   And they adjourned. Query, if the plaintiff were granted the aid in that case, if he were precluded afterward, inasmuch as the matter of his aid prayer goes in bar of the action, etc?

Case 20

Reported in Y B Paschal, 21 Ed III, p 12, pl 6   See also Brooke, Aide, 64, and Fitzh Ayde, 46

Trinity
21 Ed III

(21) **In a writ of ejectment** from wardship, the defendant said that the ancestor of the infant held for the term of his life, of the lease of one H, the remainder to one F, and that after his decease he entered as bailiff of F, etc   And the plaintiff said that he had a fee Ready, etc   The defendant prayed aid of F, and because nothing was to be tried except whether the tenant had a fee or not, which

trial would not be prejudicial to the right of F, it was moved that he should not have the aid; but yet the aid was granted, etc. Contrary 46, in the case of *Dassing-bourne*, etc

Reported in Y B Trinity, 21 Ed III, p 22, pl 13 See also Brooke, Aide, 66 — *Case 21*

(22) **In trespass** for trees cut, the defendant said that one H was seised of a house in the same vill, to which he had a common of estovers appendant in the place where, etc. And he leased us the same house for a term of six years, which still lasts, and we cut, for our reasonable estovers, etc And the plaintiff said "of his own tort, without such cause Ready," etc. And the other alleged the contrary. The defendant prayed aid of H. SHARSHULL If the right to the estovers were to be tried you should have the aid, but since the issue is taken on your tort it is otherwise, wherefore answer without the aid. And the law is the same if the plaintiff traverses the aid of the lessee, inasmuch as it is all one issue, since the lease will be tried But in this case the right of the lessor does not come in question, for the plaintiff had not denied the title of the lessor, wherefore, etc — *Michaelis 21 Ed III*

Reported briefly at end of case in Y B Mich 21 Ed III, p 40, pl 43. — *Case 22*

(23) **One shall have aid** by reason of a lease made to him pending the writ By SHARSHULL And also if one purchases a reversion pending the writ, he will be received And that in a *Præcipe quod Reddat*, etc — *Michaelis 21 Ed III*

The case has not been identified in Y B Mich 21 Ed III, or in the early abridgments — *Case 23*

(24) **In an avowry** the plaintiff, who was a stranger to the avowry, prayed aid of another than him upon whom the avowry was made, and he was ousted, etc. And he pleaded "out of his fee", and the other said "within," etc. And then he prayed aid, as above, and was ousted, etc. — *Hilary 18 Ed III*

Reported briefly in Y B Hilary, 18 Ed III, p 7, pl 22 See also Fitzh Ayde, 139 — *Case 24*

Hilary
18 Ed III

(25) **In a writ of annuity** against the Bishop of D, for an annuity granted by his predecessor to the defendant, he showed a confirmation of the chapter to the bishop, and he prayed aid of the chapter. SHARSHULL He is their sovereign, and he can traverse the confirmation without them KELSAY That annuity was granted by his predecessor, which is of no value without the confirmation of the chapter after his death Wherefore the aid was granted, etc.

Case 25   Reported in Y B Hilary 18 Ed III, p 7, pl 23 See also Fitzh Ayde, 138 It has not been identified in the early abridgments

Paschal
24 Ed III

(26) **One made a conusance** as bailiff to his master upon the plaintiff, who said that the master of the bailiff, who made the conusance, had leased his seignory to one D for a term of ten years, which still lasts, judgment, etc And the other prayed aid of his master WILLOUGHBY Where one pleads "out of his fee," the bailiff shall not have the aid, etc , and this plea amounts to no more, wherefore stand ousted of the aid, etc Query, if he shall have the aid after issue joined, where he pleaded "out of his fee," etc ?

Case 26   The case has not been identified in Y B Paschal, 24 Ed III, or in the early abridgments

Trinity
14 Hen VI

(27) **In a writ of entry** in the nature of an Assize, the tenant prayed aid NEWTON He shall not have aid of another who is not named in the writ no more than in an Assize MARTYN One who is a stranger to the writ shall be received to defend his right, wherefore let him have the aid, etc

Case 27   Reported briefly in Y B 14 Hen VI, p 22, pl 65 See also Brooke, Aide, 100

Hilary
6 Ric II

(28) **In a cui in vita**, the tenant was ousted of the aid of the heir of the husband of the demandant, because he could vouch him, etc Query, as to the reason? And see in Hilary Term, 11 of the same king, in Dower, the aid was granted conditionally, that is that he would not

vouch afterwards, but the aid was prayed of one who was in the wardship of the king.

There is no printed Year Book for Ric II   The case has not been Case 28 identified in the early abridgments

(29) **In a writ** of Admeasurement of Pasture, against a Michaelis parson of a church, he shall have the aid of the patron and 10 Ed II of the ordinary, before any plea pleaded, although the sur- Statham 7a charge were of his own tort. And the reason is because the admeasurement shall be for all time.

The case has not been identified in Y B Mich 10 Ed II, or in the Case 29 early abridgments, which contain very few cases of the reign of Ed II, as the years of that reign were not printed until after Brooke and Fitzherbert had made their compilations

(30) **In a dum fuit infra aetatem,** in the per and que, Hilary the tenant prayed aid out of the line, and had it, and yet 34 Ed III that is contrary to the writ, for he prayed aid of another than of him by whom his entry was alleged. But the Court granted the aid, etc   And the Statute speaks only of a voucher.

There is no printed year for 34 Ed III   The case has not been Case 30 identified in the early abridgments

The Statute may be that of 3 Ed. I, Westminster the First (1275), cap 40 "None shall vouch out of the line" Stats at Large, Vol 1, p 100

(31) **A man** shall [not] have aid in Avowry for a part, Michaelis unless he agrees with the avowant, or it is consistent with 15 Hen VI the avowry: as if a man avows that a stranger holds twenty acres of land of him, and the plaintiff says that the stranger leased a part of it to him; then he shall have the aid, but otherwise not, for he cannot admit the avowry to be good in part, and show anything as to the other part contrary to that, etc

There is no printed year of 15 Hen VI. The case has not been iden- Case 31 tified in the early abridgments

(32) **Tenant** at will was ousted of the aid in Trespass, Trinity etc. And see that HANKFORD held in the same plea, that 11 Hen IV

in a writ of false imprisonment brought against me, if I justify because the plaintiff was villein to my wife, and he would not be justified, but said, "free," upon which we were at issue, although I had no issue by my wife and my wife was dead, still I shall have aid of her heir, etc   Query?

Case 32   Reported in Y B Trinity, 11 Hen IV, p 90, pl 46   See also Brooke, Aide, 53, and Fitzh Ayde, 105   The errors in the text of the abridgment have been corrected by the aid of the reported case

Trinity
32 Ed III

(33) **In replevin,** the plaintiff prayed aid of one H   And because this H was a stranger to the avowry the opinion was that he should not have the aid, unless he were ready to join.

Case 33   There is no printed year of 32 Ed III   The case has not been identified in the early abridgments

Trinity
38 Ed III

(34) **In formedon,** the tenant showed how the land descended to him and to one K, which K enfeoffed one H, of that which belonged to her, so in law a partition was made, and we pray aid of K.   FYNCHEDEN   There was no partition in fact   And where you cannot have the aid you can have the paramount warranty only   And also she had nothing that could be recovered *pro rata*, wherefore the aid is not grantable, etc.   And that was the opinion of the COURT, etc   Query, if they were coparceners by descent, and an action was brought against one of them, if she could have the aid?   For otherwise she could not recover *pro rata*   And the action does not lie against them jointly, because they are in by separate titles, etc   Query?

Case 34   Reported in Y B Trinity, 38 Ed. III, p 20, pl 39   See also Brooke, Aide, 61, and Fitzh Ayde, 107.

Hilary
II Ric II

(35) **In trespass,** the defendant said that the plaintiff was villein regardant to the manor of which the defendant is seised, as in right of his wife, etc.   And the plaintiff said, "free," etc.   The defendant prayed aid of his wife and had it.   And it was said that if he had prayed in aid of his wife, although the plaintiff had been found free, that would not have concluded the wife.   And yet when she

came in aid she could not vary from the plea of her husband. Query, if she shall have Attaint?

There is no printed Year Book for 11 Ric. II. The case has not been identified in the early abridgments Case 35

(36) **In trespass,** if the defendant justifies as his freehold, and the plaintiff entitles himself to the freehold, and they are at issue, he shall not have aid of him in the reversion, as he shall have in case he justifies in another's right, or by reason of a lease for a term of years   By RIKHILL, etc Trinity 12 Ric II

There is no early printed Year Book for the reign of Ric II   It is probable that the case is that printed in Y B Trinity, 12 Ric II, pp 29–30   Ames Foundation, ed Deiser Case 36

(37) **In a writ of entry** for rent, the tenant prayed aid because one H leased him of lands of which, etc HANKFORD   He prays aid of another thing than that which is in demand   and it is not like a voucher, where one is to charge the land   CHARLTON   If the plaintiff recovers the rent, he in whom the reversion is is discharged forever, wherefore have the aid, etc Hilary 12 Ric II

There is no early printed Year Book for the reign of Ric II   The case is printed in Y B Hilary, 12 Ric II, pp 127–8 Case 37

(38) **J. G., executor** of the will of a parson of the church of D, brought a writ of Debt upon the arrears of an annuity, and he counted that his predecessor was parson of the church of D, and that he and his predecessors had been seised of the same annuity time, etc , and for so much in arrear, in the lifetime of their testator, he brought this action. The defendant, who was parson of the church of F, prayed aid of the patron, and of the ordinary. ROLFF. By this action for the arrears, the church shall not be charged   And if I lease land for a term of life, rendering a certain rent, and die, and my executors bring a writ of Debt for the arrears, against the tenant for life, he shall not have aid of my heir, etc. And then the aid was granted, etc. And, query, if that action lies for the executor? For it seems that he shall not have the arrear- Paschal 12 Hen VI

ages of an annuity, when the annuity is granted in fee: no more than executors shall have arrears of a rent service, etc. But yet some say that executors shall have an action for a rent service accruing in the lifetime of their testator, for otherwise no one shall have it, etc.

Case 38   Reported in Y B Paschal, 12 Hen VI, p 8, pl 4   See also Brooke, Aide, 4, and Fitzh Ayde, 48

Trinity
9, Hen VI

(39) **In replevin,** the defendant who has a seignory for a term of life, or for years, if he makes an avowry, shall pray aid of his lessor upon the avowry, and shall have it   And the law is the same if one avows upon the husband and his wife, as in right of the wife, upon the showing of the avowant, the plaintiff shall have aid of his wife, etc

Case 39.   Reported in Y. B Trinity, 9 Hen VI, p 27, pl 29

Michaelis
11 Hen IV

(40) **If between two parceners** there is a partition, and afterward one alienates her part, and retakes an estate, she shall not have aid of the other, because it is not in the course of the parcenry. But if she took an estate for the term of her life, and was empleaded and prayed aid of her feoffor, who came and vouched her to warranty; now, inasmuch as she had entered into the warranty, she shall have aid, because she has come in the same course in which she was before she made the alienation But if one coparcener alienates, still the other coparcener shall have aid of her, for her deed does not injure her coparcener. Query, if, in that case, she should recover other lands *pro rata?* Or if the same lands are liable into whatsoever hands they have come, etc ? Well argued, in a *Cui in Vita.*

Case 40   The case may be that reported in Y B Mich 11 Hen IV, p 22, pl 45   If it is the case the parceners were in Gavelkind, and were not women as Statham has them   See also Brooke, Aide, 46

Paschal
11 Hen IV

(41) **In replevin,** the defendant avowed upon one H The plaintiff said that the said H leased the same lands to one D, for a term of ten years, which still lasts   Which D made us and F his executors, and we pray aid of F.

HANKFORD: You have an equal estate, for which the aid Statham 7 b
does not lie SKRENE· Otherwise we can not have the
aid of the lessor of our testator. Wherefore the aid was
granted, etc.

Reported in Y B Paschal, 11 Hen IV, p 63, pl 15 See also Brooke, Case 41
Aide, 49, and Fitzh· Ayde, 104

(42) **A prior** who is presentable, if he is conventual[1] and Trinity
has a convent and a common seal, shall not have aid, for 11 Hen IV
his founder shall have a *Contra Formam Collationis* against
him. And his successor shall have the *Sine Assensu Capitalis*, albeit he has not come in by election but by presentment. But where a parsonage is appropriated to an abbot
he shall have a *Jure d' Utrum* as a parson, etc Query, if he
shall have aid of the ordinary, inasmuch as he himself
is a patron? Trinity 11, in a *Scire Facias* brought against
the Prior of Delburrough, which is a monastery of the Abbey
of Saint Osa; and on every vacancy the abbot names one
of his canons to the patron, and he presents him to the
ordinary And this same prior could charge his church
without the assent of the abbot of Saint Osa, and without
the assent of the patron or of the ordinary, and that
charge will bind his successor, as appeared in the same
plea But yet it shall be under the common seal, etc

Reported at very great length in Y B Paschal, 11 Hen IV, p 68, Case 42
pl 3 See also Brooke, Aide, 50.

(43) **In trespass** a tenant at will had aid, after issue Paschal
[joined], of the Archbishop of Canterbury And on another 21 Hen VI
day he showed how the Archbishop had died after the
last continuance, and that such a one was created, etc
And he prayed aid of him. And because there was no
privity between him and the successor of the lessor, he
was ousted of the aid See as to this, for it is contrary
to the opinion of many that a tenant at will shall have
aid, etc

Reported in Y. B Paschal, 21 Hen VI, pp 36–39, pl 4 The dis- Case 43.
cussion is very long and learned See also Brooke, Aide, 82

[1] "Perpetual," in the report of the case

(44) **In replevin,** the defendant avowed upon one W.
The plaintiff said that one H was seised and leased to
him for his life, and he prayed aid of him TYRWHIT:
He shall not have aid of any other than upon him whom
our avowry is made HANKFORD It is not so, for peradventure this H can force you to avow upon him Wherefore the aid was granted, etc.

Reported in Y B Trinity 7 Hen IV, p 18, pl 21 See also Brooke,
Aide, 42

(45) **In a scire facias,** the tenant showed how one W
gave the land to one A and E, his wife, in tail, and A
died without issue, which estate of E we have, and we
pray aid of W DANBY He cannot have aid, for he is but
the tenant after possibility, etc , who could not have had
aid And also he does not show how he had his estate,
for if he disseised him he had a fee. And also he cannot
have his estate, because it is an estate tail And if I lease
land to a man for the term of his life, without impeachment of waste, who leases his estate to another, his lessee
shall not be impeached for waste, for he shall be of the same
condition, as he through whom he claims ASCOUGH Your
case of waste is not law, unless the grant be to him and to
his assignees. And even if it be so, still I doubt MOILE.
If I grant the reversion of my tenant after possibility,
who has leased over his estate, and a *Quid Juris Clamat* is
brought against the lessee to the use, he shall be forced to
attourn, for he is in another course, etc. And if I grant
the services of my tenant in tail, he shall be forced to
attourn PRISOT So shall your tenant in fee simple,
for it is for another thing, etc. And as to that, query?
For if I grant the reversion of my tenant in tail, he shall
not be forced to attourn, and yet my services pass with
the reversion, etc (Query, as to the diversity?) POLE
(for the plaintiff). Sir, we will deliver him And we say
that he was seised in his demesne as of fee DANBY
That is no plea unless you say, "without this that we held,"
as above PORTYNGTON. He has said enough, and you

should answer him DANBY: I will not answer him.
PORTYNGTON: Then respond without the aid, etc

The case has not been identified in Y. B Mich 27 Hen VI, or in Case 45
the early abridgments

See as to aid, in the title of Voucher, Trinity, 21 Ed Note
III. In the title of Dower, Trinity, 15 Hen VI.

See Statham, title of Voucher, p 182 b, case 20, *infra*, and title of
Dower, *infra*, 73 a to 75 b   No case of Trinity, 15 Hen VI, appears
there, however.

(46) **A parson** shall have aid of the patron and of the Trinity
ordinary, on a grant by himself. And that in Annuity. 2 Hen VI

Reported in Y. B Trinity, 2 Hen VI, p 12, pl 3   See also Fitzh Case 46
Ayde, 52, and Brooke, Aide, 5

(47) **In annuity** against a parson on a deed made by Michaelis
himself, the patron and the ordinary, he shall have aid of 25 Ed III
the patron and of the ordinary, notwithstanding he was a
party to the deed

Probably this is the short case reported in Y B Trinity (not Mich), Case 47
25 Ed III, p 82, pl 23   See also Fitzh   Ayde, 7

(48) **In a writ against an abbot** who was parson Hilary
imparsoné, he shall have aid of himself as patron, and of 25 Ed III
the ordinary

Reported in Y. B Mich (not Hilary), 25 Ed III, p 97, pl 19. Case 48.
See also Fitzh   Ayde, 10

(49) **Tenant** by the curtesy was ousted of the aid of the Paschal
parcener of his wife 19 Ed III

There is no early printed year of 19 Ed. III   The point appears in a Case 49
long case in the Rolls Series, 19 Ed III, pp 50–56

(50) **Aid** was granted to the husband and his wife on a Michaelis
lease made to them by a deed *in pais*, in a *Scire Facias*. 19 Ed III

There is no early printed year of 19 Ed III   The case is printed in Case 50
the Rolls Series, 19 Ed III, p 304

Trinity
21 Ed III.

(51) **Aid was** granted after issue, in a writ of Ejectment of Wardship, contrary Michaelis, 16 Ed. III

Case 51.

Reported in Y B. Trinity, 21 Ed III, p. 22, pl 13   See also Brooke, Aide, 68, and Fitzh Ayde, 54

Trinity
12 Hen IV

(52) **A man** shall not have aid of him who is in the remainder, unless he shows a deed, but it is otherwise if the reversion be granted, because the deed does not belong to him

Case 52

The case has not been identified in Y B Trinity, 12 Hen IV, or in the early abridgments

Trinity
3 Ed III

(53) **Aid shall** not be granted upon a plea in abatement of the writ, and that in Dower.

Case 53

The case has not been identified in Y B Trinity, 3 Ed III, or in the early abridgments

Trinity
5 Ed III

(54) **The defendant** shall have aid of his wife in Trespass, before issue joined, where the deed of the ancestor of the same woman was pleaded by the plaintiff in his replication.

Case 54

The case has not been identified in Y B Trinity, 5 Ed III, or in the early abridgments

Michaelis
22 Ed III

(55) **In a praecipe quod reddat,** the tenant was ousted of the aid of him who had purchased the reversion pending the writ, etc

Case 55

The case has not been identified in Y B Mich 22 Ed III, or in the early abridgments

Trinity
13 Ric II

(56) **Aid shall not be granted** for services, and that in a *Scire Facias*.   Query, if he prays aid of the tenant? etc.

Case 56

There is no printed Year Book for the reign of Ric II   The case has not been identified in the early abridgments

Michaelis
13 Hen VI.

(57) **An abbess** brought a writ of Annuity against a vicar and he made his title by prescription   And the vicar prayed aid of the abbot, who was plaintiff, and of the ordinary, and had it, notwithstanding the abbot was plaintiff. See the judgment in the case of the *Prioress of Sheen*

Case 57

There is no printed year for 13 Hen VI   There is a similar case reported in Y B Mich 21 Hen VI, p 2, pl. 3   See also Brooke, Aide, 29

AIDE DE ROY [6]

(1) **In a formedon in London,** the tenant vouched a foreigner to warranty, wherefore the record came into the Bench, and process was awarded against the vouchee And at the summons the tenant said that while the process was pending against the vouchee, it was found before the Mayor of London, that one J, in the time of the grandfather of the king who now is, and a long time before the gift, died seised of these same tenements, and held them of the king, wherefore he was seised, and committed to us, etc. And we pray aid of the king. And the justices recorded his prayer, and sent back the plea, etc

Reported in Y B Hilary, 44 Ed III, p 2, pl 10

Statham 8 a
Hilary
44 Ed. III.

Case 1.

(2) **In a writ of entry,** the tenant said that the king leased to him for the term of his life, and he prayed aid and produced a patent which told how one H was indebted to the king, wherefore he was seised of these same lands under a distress, until, etc , and he committed these same lands to the defendant until, etc PERSHAY Now, judgment, inasmuch as he has affirmed the plea to be good against him as tenant of the freehold, and now shows the contrary But yet the aid was granted, etc Query? For the king had not lost in that case, although the land were recovered

There is no printed year of 31 Ed III The case has not been identified in the early abridgments

Trinity
31 Ed. III

Case 2

(3) **The Prior of M** brought a writ of Trespass upon the Case against the mayor of Windsor, and other burgesses of the same town, reciting that whereas there had been a leet within the said town, time, etc , and he put one H there to hold his leet three days, etc , and they disturbed him and beat him To which they said that the town of W is an ancient borough of which the King Edward the First was seised, and had the view of Frankpledge for all the inhabitants of this same town, time, etc , and by his

Trinity
18 Hen VI.

letters-patent he granted to all the men of this same town, this same town with the appurtenances, rendering to him a fee farm, etc , judgment, if without the counsel of the king, etc FORTESCUE They are seised of the town of their demesne and not in the right of the king, and although a fee farm be reserved to the king he cannot lose, for we claim the leet from time, etc. And it may be that we had a leet and the king also, and if the tenant of the king came to our leet, still it does not pass with such words as "with the appurtenances, etc " But yet the aid was granted   And this case was well argued

Case 3

Reported in Y B Trinity, 18 Hen VI, pp 11–13, pl 1   The case as it appears in Statham is confused, probably by the attempt to put into a few lines the gist of a long case   The last two lines attempt to outline a discussion as to whether the rights passed by the words *"cum pertinences"* or *"Burgum cum pertinences,"* or *"Burgum et visum "*

Trinity
48 Ed III

(4) **The mayor** and commonalty of Lincoln brought a writ of Covenant against the bailiffs and commonalty of Derby, and they showed a composition made between their predecessors, that they of Lincoln should not pay toll, etc   And they told how one such and one such of D had taken, etc. The defendants said that the king H had granted to them this same vill for a certain fee farm, so they could not charge this vill without the king, and they prayed aid of him   And because the composition was after the charter, it was their own deed, and they were ousted of the aid.

Case 4

Reported in Y B Trinity, 48 Ed III, p 17, pl 2   See also Fitzh· Ayde de Roy, 59

Hilary
50 Ed III

(5) **Where the king** had seised by force of an office and committed the patent to one J, came one who was ousted from the office and traversed it, and had a *Scire Facias* against J, and prayed aid of the king, and had it, although the king was a party to the trespass, etc

Case 5

The case has not been identified in Y B Hilary, 50 Ed III, or in the early abridgments.

(6) **In a scire facias,** the tenant said that he was tenant Hilary 24 Ed III for life of the lease of the king, and he prayed aid of him And he did not show any deed of the lease THORPE One cannot say that he did not lease, wherefore you must show your deed WILLOUGHBY If he does not show a deed, one shall not have anything on the lease, as it seems And then a writ came from the Chancery witnessing the lease, then the aid was granted

And it was said in the same plea, that one shall have aid of the king in a *Scire Facias* where his aid is prayed in place of a voucher, albeit he cannot vouch anyone else In a *Scire Facias*

There is a very short report of this case in Y B Hilary, 24 Ed III, Case 6. p 23, pl 6 See also Brooke, Aide del Roy, 48, and Fitzh Ayde de Roy, 58

(7) **In trespass,** the defendant justified as servant of the Hilary 4 Hen VI patent of the king, and prayed aid of the king, and was ousted, because he was a stranger.

Reported in Y B Hilary, 4 Hen VI, p 10, pl 4 See also Brooke, Case 7 Aide del Roy, 55, and Fitzh Ayde de Roy, 9

(8) **In trespass** for a close broken, the defendant said Paschal 4 Hen VI that the king was seised and leased to him for the term of his life, and he showed how the plaintiff had lands adjoining And the plaintiff alleged that part of the land leased to us was part of his land, etc , and he entered, upon whom we entered and made the trespass, and we pray aid of the king MARTYN After a *procedendo*, if he shall have the aid in this case he can plead not guilty, and also no damage to the king, for he did not demand anything which was leased for it is not like the case which was just put, to wit where the defendant justified because such a one who held of the king died, his heir under age, and the king seised and committed the guardianship to us during, etc And the plaintiff claimed to have a common there and there put in his cattle, and we took them, etc., for there the king remained tenant, and livery shall be sued at the full age of the heir And if the patentee be ousted he shall have an action in

the name of the king, because he has intruded upon the possession of the king. But it is otherwise where a man is tenant for life of the lease of the king, for if one says that the king leased to him for the term of his life, and prays aid, it is not to the purpose, for nothing is taken away from the king Wherefore the Court would not grant the aid until the issue was taken upon the freehold, so that the Court could understand that the king was [not] to lose, etc. Wherefore it was adjudged that he be ousted of the aid, etc

Case 8 Reported in Y B Hilary (not Paschal), 4 Hen VI, p 12, pl 8 See also Brooke, Aide del Roy, 57, and Fitzh Ayde de Roy, 11

Michaelis 32 Ed III (9) **In a writ of entry** upon a disseisin, the tenant said that the king by his charter enfeoffed one H, who enfeoffed us, and we pray aid of the king, and because he was a stranger to the charter he was ousted. But yet some say that any one who is tenant immediate to the king shall have aid of him, etc

Case 9 There is no printed year for 32 Ed III The case has not been identified in the early abridgments

Trinity 38 Ed III (10) **If one prays** aid of the king because of a warranty and the king be adjudged to warrant him in the Chancery, the tenant shall plead to the action in the Chancery, because no fraud shall be done to the king, to wit. between the demandant and the tenant And when they are at issue they shall be sent into the Bench to be tried, etc Query, how shall the demandant have a day in that case? For no day is given to the demandant when the Court tells the tenant that he shall have the aid, etc

Case 10 Reported in Y B Trinity, 38 Ed III, p 18, pl 32

Hilary 9 Hen VI. (11) **In a quare impedit,** the tenant showed how the king granted to him by his patent a manor to whom, etc, in recompense, and he alleged possession in the king by his title, and he prayed aid of the king.

Statham 8 b PASTON This is only a personal action, for in this action one does not recover the advowson, and he has also shown a feoffment in fee from the king, so by reason of the reversion he cannot have the aid, but his aid prayer is in place of a voucher, and in this action he shall not vouch another person, wherefore, etc.   But in a writ of right of an advowson one shall vouch, etc.   And here he has also made a title which is in place of a declaration, so he has become an actor, in which case he can vouch, etc.   MARTYN   He cannot have warranty of charter against another person, but it is not so against the king, wherefore it is reasonable that he have the aid.   And to this that he is an actor, so is the avowant in Replevin, and yet after avowry he shall have the aid   PASTON· That is when he avows in the right of another, but it is not so here, etc

And it was said in the same plea, that if in an Assize the tenant acknowledges the disseisin, and says that he enfeoffed the king and the king re-enfeoffed him, and he prays aid of the king, he shall have the aid, because it may be that the king had a release from the plaintiff, or some other bar, etc   COTTINGHAM   To this that is said that he does not recover the possession, I say that when he recovered and had a writ, etc.   Which was conceded.   ROLFF   Yet he does not recover the advowson, for his heir shall not have a writ of Execution   BABYNGTON Sue to the king.   Which note, etc   And then the incumbent pleaded the same plea   Well debated, etc

Reported in Y. B Hilary, 9 Hen VI, p 56, pl 1   See also Brooke, **Case 11** Aide del Roy, 6, and Fitzh Ayde de Roy, 15   The case and the three abridgments all differ from each other   Statham's account is again much confused by reason of a desire to shorten the abridgment too much   It is difficult to translate the case intelligently without importing into it much which is not in the abridgment, but which is in the case itself

(12) **In an action** upon the case against an escheator, Hilary because he returned a false office, he prayed aid of the 9 Hen VI king and was ousted, etc

Reported in Y B Hilary, 9 Hen VI, p 60, pl 9   See also Fitzh **Case 12** Ayde de Roy, 16

(13) **In trespass** for cattle taken   CANNDISH   One A Hilary was seised of the manor of B, and held it of the king. 9 Hen VI

And one B was seised of an acre of land in the place where,
etc, and held it of the said A, as of the said manor by
one penny of rent. A died, and the manor and the penny
of rent descended to one C, within age, and the king seized
and committed it to us by his patents until, etc And for
one penny rent after the grant was made to us, we took the
beasts, etc, and we pray the aid of the king. (Query, if
the plea be good, for it does not say that the infant was
under age at the taking of possession, and he did not show
the letters patent, etc) FULTHORPE We say that the
trespass was made in another place within the same vill,
which is not part of the manor, etc. PASTON. That is
not to the purpose in ousting him of the aid, for "part"
and "not part" shall not be in issue, inasmuch as he alleges
the charter of the king in witness that the lands in this
vill were in his hands, and the "not comprised" is not to
the purpose But if the tenant in an Assize says that the
tenements are seised into the hands of the king, and does
not show any charter which witnesses that, the plaintiff
can say that they are not seised Ready, and upon that
the escheator shall inquire if they are present, and if they
are not there it shall be tried by the Assize To which
the Court agreed (See a similar matter well debated,
Anno 21 and Anno 28 *Liber Assisarum*) FULTHORPE
We say that C had livery out of the hand of the king,
and was of full age, judgment And we pray that he
be ousted, etc. Query, if that be a plea? For he did not
say that he had sued livery before the possession And
since the defendant could not deny that no rent was
reserved upon the patent to the king, so nothing would
injure the king, and he was ousted of the aid

Case 13   Reported in Y B Hilary, 9 Hen VI, p 61, pl 15   See also Brooke,
Aide del Roy, 7, and Fitzh Counterplea del Ayde, 9

Trinity
9 Hen VI

(14) **An under collector** shall not have aid of the
king because a collector has a commission and cannot
lease his estate, etc   But the committee of the king
shall have aid of the king because the committee

of the king can lease his estate, etc · By MARTYN, in Trespass, etc.

Reported in Y B Trinity, 9 Hen. VI, p 20, pl 15   See also Brooke, Case 14 Aide del Roy, 4, and Fitzh Ayde de Roy, 17.

(15) **See as to trespass,** by MARTYN, where one prayed Michaelis 3 Hen VI aid of the king for a certain cause, and the Court put him over, etc , he could pray aid for another cause, but if it be adjourned until another term it is otherwise, etc See [this case] for it was well debated.

Reported in Y. B Mich 3 Hen VI, p 5, pl 5   See also Fitzh Ayde Case 15 de Roy, 8

(16) **In debt,** the plaintiff counted that the defendant Michaelis 11 [Hen] IV was clerk of the works of the king, and bought of us certain gravel, etc., and for ten shillings, which the defendant was allowed in the Exchequer. SKRENE We pray aid of the king upon this matter shown, etc   HANKFORD It is on your own contract, and you were also allowed [on account] so the king cannot lose. HORTON A purveyor shall have aid where the action is brought against him in such a case HANKFORD Not the same, for in your case he can take cattle for the king, against his will, by his commission, and not so here, etc   SKRENE: We were not paid by the king Ready, etc., and we pray the aid. THIRNING It may be that the plaintiff has released to the king, wherefore when he avers that he is not paid by the king it is reasonable that he should have the aid   And then the aid was granted

The citation in Statham is defective, the name of the king being Case 16 left blank The case is reported in Y B Mich 11 Hen IV, p 28, pl 53 See also Brooke, Aide del Roy, 29, and Fitzh Ayde de Roy, 44

(17) **In trespass** for cattle taken, the defendant justified Michaelis 9 Hen IV because he was a collector, and that the plaintiff was assessed for a certain sum, etc. And the plaintiff said that he was assessed for his cattle in another vill, and not there, etc. And the defendant prayed aid of the king In that case he shall be ousted of the aid, because it shall be under-

stood that he took them of his own wrong. (See this case,
for many good cases of aid prayer are put in the same
plea)

Case 17   The citation to this case in Statham is evidently an error   The case
is reported in Y B Mich 11 Hen IV, pp 34–37, pl 66   It is a very
long case, and as Statham says there are "many good cases of aid
prayer" in it   See also Brooke, Aide del Roy, 30, and Fitzh Ayde de
Roy, 45

Trinity   (18) **In an assize,** the tenant said that he held for the
11 Hen IV   term of his life, the reversion regardant to the king, and
he prayed aid of the king   And it was held a good plea to
secure the aid without showing how the reversion was
to the king, because immediately through his prayer the
reversion came to the king. (But yet, query, etc)
And the plaintiff, to oust him of the aid, said that he himself was seised in his demesne as of fee, of this same land,
and the defendant put in his cattle, claiming pasture, and
because of that he had brought the Assize   HANKFORD.
You should say, "And so he was disseised," according to
the form of the Statute. But yet the aid was granted.
(And I believe that the reason was that the tenant was a
disseisor in fact, inasmuch as he took the tenancy upon
him, for he could have said that the freehold was in the
plaintiff, and have demanded judgment of the writ, etc.
Query?) And then in the Chancery, the plaintiff prayed
a *procedendo*   And it was shown, for the king, that the
land was held of the manor of K, which manor is ancient
demesne of the king, as of his Duchy of Lancaster   And
he showed the record of Domesday, proving that the said
manor was ancient demesne, etc   SKRENE   Although
the said manor be ancient demesne, still it does not prove
that the land is held of the manor, and the king shall not
have that averment upon us, for if it be so he could have an
action of deceit   And also the tenant who has prayed
aid of the king has affirmed the jurisdiction, wherefore
Statham 9 a.   the king cannot disaffirm   THIRNING   The king is not
like another person, but it seems that you should have
the *procedendo*, for it is said by the tenant for the king

that the land is of the Duchy of Lancaster, in which case
the king shall answer like any other person. For if anyone prays aid of the king, and shows a patent of the Duchy
of Lancaster, he shall not have aid, no more than he would
have it of the Duke if he were alive   Which HANKFORD
denied.   And so, inasmuch as the defendant has not
shown how the reversion was in the king, we think that
it is not in the king, unless by his aid prayer.   And if I
bring a writ against one who enfeoffs the king while my
writ is pending, my writ shall not abate, consequently
not when any matter is in question.   And if we were
informed immediately afterwards, we could be advised
to grant a *procedendo ad judicium.*   And also since he
has not shown how the reversion is in the king, we shall
not have any basis for making a search for the king, but
if it was of record here in the Chancery that the reversion was in the king, then he should not have a *procedendo,*
etc   (Query as to that?)   And if the reversion is in the
king, if they plead in the Chancery, and if they are at
issue there, it shall be tried by the Assize in Court   Otherwise when the king has made a search, if he informed the
tenant of such matter as he had to bar the demandant,
and upon that to take the *procedendo,* then the plaintiff
would sue by petition to the king.   HANKFORD   It would
be bad pleading to pray aid of the king and not show how
the reversion was in him, for if the king was seised of the
land and leased to him, etc , then the land is a free fee
And afterwards all the justices were agreed that the allegation of ancient demesne was not to the purpose, inasmuch as the king could have a writ of Deceit, etc   Query
as to this matter?

Reported in Y B Trinity, 11 Hen IV, p 85, pl 36   See also Brooke, Case 18
Aide del Roy, 32, and Fitzh   Counterplea del Ayde, 16

(19) **In annuity** against a parson of a church   He prayed   Michaelis
aid of the king as patron, and he also prayed aid of the   48 Hen VI
ordinary and had it, wherefore it was said to him that
he should sue to the king   MARKHAM   We pray a summons *ad auxiliandum* against the ordinary.   NEWTON   It

seems that he can have it, for there is no difference between an aid prayer and "the king not counseled," for the entry of the king not counseled is, *"et petit judicium si rege inconsulto ulterius procedere debet"* And so he cannot restrain the procedure But the entry in the other case is *"petit auxilium de rege,"* in which case our power cannot be restrained, but we can make a process against another, etc (And this has been done in Trespass, etc) Ascough It may well be in Trespass, etc, for there pleas are several, but in this case I do not know to what effect process shall issue against the ordinary, for although the ordinary came, he could not do any thing before the *procedendo* came And it may be that the plaintiff had released to the king, in which case no *procedendo* shall issue Newton Although he had released to the king, that does not come into question in a debate in the Chancery, for they do not plead upon this aid prayer there, etc But it is otherwise where the aid prayer is in place of a voucher to have recompense, for they do not plead in the Chancery, except where the king was to have lost, and in this case he is not to have lost, wherefore, etc Query as to that, etc ? Broun said that if the defendant wished that, the entry in the aid prayer shall be *"et petit judicium si rege inconsulto,"* etc. And they adjourned See the plea, for it was well argued

Case 19 The citation in Statham is an obvious error The case has not been identified in either of the early abridgments

Michaelis 7 Hen IV. (20) **In trespass** for the king against the bailiffs of Nottingham. And he counted that he was Lord of Leicester, and that those of Leicester should not pay toll, etc., and that they had taken toll, etc The bailiffs said that they held the vill of Nottingham of the King by a fee farm, and they prayed aid of him Thirning The king is plaintiff in this action, how can you have the aid? Frisby We do not know how to plead without him And they adjourned, etc

Hankford said in the same plea, that if a man who is in ancient demesne brings such an action, it is hard for the bailiffs to have aid of the king, because it is the inheritance of the king that his tenant in ancient demesne shall not pay toll, etc

Reported in Y B Mich 7 Hen IV, p 2, pl 13   See also Brooke, Case 20 Aide del Roy, 24

(21) **If land** be given to a man for the term of his life, ^{Trinity} the remainder over in tail, the remainder over to the king ^{7 Hen. IV} in fee, the tenant for life shall not have aid of him in the remainder, and of the king also, as if the remainder was in another person, but he shall have aid of him in the remainder, and *he* shall have aid over, because the processes do not agree, etc   But yet, query?   For the Court was in doubt, etc

The case seems to be that reported in Y B Trinity, 7 Hen IV, p 18, Case 21 pl 23   But the case as abridged in Statham differs considerably from the report in the Year Book, and also from the abridgment of the case by Brooke   See Brooke, Aide del Roy, 27

(22) **In an assize** against two, one answered as tenant, ^{Hilary} and showed how such a one leased to him for the term of ^{12 Hen IV} his life, the remainder to the king, and he prayed aid of the king   The other said that he was tenant, without this that the other had anything, and he pleaded a like plea   And the plaintiff said that one of them was tenant and to the plea pleaded by the other, or no law, etc JUYN   We cannot award the Assize upon that point, for their tenancy cannot be tried without the king   Wherefore, for the advantage of the king, the aid was granted to both, etc   Query, if the justices would give a day to the parties when they granted the aid of the king, where the tenant said that the tenements were seised in the hand of the king   And if they adjudged that the plaintiff sue to the king, they will not give a day to the parties, but the plaintiff shall sue by a *procedendo*, etc.   Query?

And see in the same plea, that an Assize may be awarded three times, for where one of the defendants said that the tenements were seised into the hand of the king, and because the escheator was not present, they awarded an

Assize to inquire into it, which found it was so, etc   And then the *procedendo* came, and one of the defendants said that he was tenant, and pleaded a plea in bar; and the other said that he was tenant, without this that, etc., and pleaded a foreign release, then the Assize shall be awarded to inquire which of them is tenant.   And if it be found that he who pleaded a foreign release is tenant, the Assize shall be adjourned to try it, and if it be found not the deed of the plaintiff, the Assize shall be remanded and adjudged to inquire as to the seisin and disseisin, etc. Query, in that case, when one of the defendants said that the tenements were seised into the hands of the king or prayed aid of the king for another reason, if the other could plead any plea in bar before the *procedendo* came? etc

Case 22   The case has not been identified in Y B Hilary, 12 Hen. IV, or in the early abridgments

Michaelis 22 Hen VI Statham 9 b   (23)   **If one** prays aid of the king in an Assize, the justices will give a day to the parties at the next sessions   But if the *procedendo* does not come on that day, then it is discontinued, and the plaintiff shall have an attachment or another day afterward   By NEWTON, etc

Note   **See as to aid of the king,** in the title of Petition, Mich 21 Ed III, in the title of Monstrans, Mich. 11 Hen IV, and in the title of Error, Mich 8 Hen. IV, and in the title of *Procedendo,* etc

Case 23   The case has not been identified in Y B Mich 22 Hen VI, or in the early abridgments   For the references to the other titles see Statham, title of Peticion, *infra,* p 137 b, case 1, title of Monstranz de Faitz, etc , *infra,* p 126 b, case 33, title of Errour, *infra,* p 93 a, case 34, title of Procedendo, *infra,* p 136 b

Trinity 7 Hen IV   (24)   **In a scire facias,** the tenant for life shall have aid of the king, where the reversion is to the king by way of forfeiture

Case 24   Briefly reported in Y B Trinity, 7 Hen IV, p 18, pl 23   See also Brooke, Aide del Roy, 27   See *supra,* case 21

(25) **In formedon,** the tenant shall have aid of the $\quad$ Michaelis
king by reason of a confirmation made by the king with- $\quad$ 9 Ed III
out warranty, to the grantee of the queen   And see a like
case Hilary, 15 Ed. III, in a note, etc

> The case has not been identified in Y B Mich 9 Ed III, or in the $\quad$ Case 25
> early abridgments

(26) **Aid was granted** by the king by reason of a feoff- $\quad$ Paschal
ment in fee simple without warranty   In a note $\quad\quad\quad$ 10 Ed II

> The citation in Statham is an error, the case is briefly reported in $\quad$ Case 26
> Y B Paschal, 10 Ed III, p 26, pl 47   As Statham says, it is merely
> a note

(27) **In right of an advowson,** the tenant shall have $\quad$ Trinity
aid of the king, because he gave the same advowson to the $\quad$ 7 Ed III
abbot of B, his predecessor, in free alms, without war-
ranty, etc

> The case has not been identified in Y B Trinity, 7 Ed III, or in the $\quad$ Case 27
> early abridgments

(28) **In a scire facias,** the tenant shall have aid of the $\quad$ Hilary
king by reason of a lease made to him by the king   And $\quad$ 24 Ed III
he did not show the lease, but a writ came to the justices
witnessing the lease.

> Briefly reported in Y B Hilary, 24 Ed III, p 23, pl 6, and at $\quad$ Case 28
> much greater length in the "*Residuum*" of the same year and term,
> p 39, pl 18   See also Fitzh Ayde de Roy, 58

(29) **The plaintiff** was ousted of the aid of the king $\quad$ Michaelis
by a collector of fifteenths, who avowed the taking in $\quad$ 7 Hen IV.
another place than was counted in the plea   And they
were at issue as to the place   And that in Replevin

> Briefly reported in Y B Mich 7 Hen IV, p 6, pl 35   See also $\quad$ Case 29
> Brooke, Aide del Roy, 25, and Fitzh Ayde de Roy, 42

(30) **If the king** grants a patent of a thing to a man, and $\quad$ Paschal
then he grants the same thing to another by another $\quad$ 35 Hen VI.
patent, and the first patentee brings a *Scire Facias* against
the second patentee in the Chancery, to revoke it, and
they interplead in the Chancery, neither of them shall

have aid of the king, for the king is to suffer no loss. By the opinion of the COURT, clearly. In Trespass *Coram Rege.*

Case 30   Reported in Y B Paschal, 35 Hen VI, p 56, pl 2   See also Brooke, Aide de Roy, 13, and Fitzh   Ayde del Roy, 28, both at much greater length than Statham

Trinity **(31) An escheator** shall not have aid of the king in
35 Hen VI Trespass, as a collector shall have, because he is not charged by matter of record certified, as the collector is, etc   By YELVERTON, in Trespass *Coram Rege.* But yet that may be distinguished, etc

Case 31   The case has not been identified in Y B Trinity, 35 Hen VI, or in the early abridgments

Anno **(32) Query** as to the case of the Lord of Grammont,
36 Hen VI where a *Scire Facias* was brought against him by the Duke of York, to repeal letters patent made to him by the king for the term of his life. And the said Lord of Grammont showed how the king leased to him for a term of years which still lasts, rendering to him more rent than the duke paid, and he prayed aid of the king   And that was in the Chancery.

Case 32   The case has not been identified in Y B Anno 36 Hen VI, or in the early abridgments

⁶ It is almost as necessary to add to this title of Aide the word "Prier," as it is in the title of Age, since the aid which is still familiar to us in our own law is that aid which was given to the king or other lord to marry their daughters, make their sons knights, and the like   This word, as applied to subsidies of various kinds, has survived, while we find nothing whatever as to this praying of aid in the later historians of our law   Pollock and Maitland, Holdsworth or Jenks, give us nothing, although the first two both mention the aid prayer once   Reeves, however, does give us something valuable   [Reeves, Hist of Eng Law, 3 443]   He says it "bears some affinity with vouching to warranty, and probably was first suggested by it   When an action was brought against a person who, though in possession of the thing in question, had not the complete and entire property, and if judgment passed against him another person who had a right would be injured, the tenant or defendant might pray to have the aid of such person to defend the suit "   What is a more simple and probably a better definition is

given us by the Termes de la Ley [Ed 1721, p 34] "Aid pryer is the justification of a Title by the Assistance of others in joining with him " It is better, for as we read the cases we find it difficult to limit and define the instances where it may be called for, doubtless there are definite limitations, but our modern knowledge of the old pleading is not sufficient to enable us to draw any very strict lines of limitation Reeves gives us the entry of the Aid Prier *"Et praedictus tenens per attornatum suum venit, et dicit quod, &c* (Then the cause of aid prayer was alleged) *Et sic praedictus tenens dicit quod ipse tenet, et die impetrationis brevis originalis praedicti querentis tenuit tenementum praedictum pro termino vitae suae remanere cuidem praefato B, et haeredibus masculis de corpore suo exeuntibus, sine quo idem tenens non potest tenementum praedictum cum pertinentiis in placitum deducere, neque praefato querenti inde respondere Et petit Auxilium de ipso B Et ei conceditur, &c Ideo Praeceptum est vicecomiti quod summoneat per bonos summonitores praedictum B, quod sic a die Paschae, &c ad jungendum cum praefato tenente simul, &c in respondendo praefato querenti de praefato placito si, &c idem dies datus est partibus praedictis, &c "* This is taken from Rastall's Entries, Aid Prier When the aid was granted, the tenant sued out a judicial writ called a summons *ad auxiliandum,* and if the person did not essoin himself, or appear on the return of the writ, or if he defaulted afterward, judgment was entered against him So that it was a very important matter for the person in interest that he should appear or give some sufficient reason for not doing so

But it was not only in real actions that the aid was granted, although there seems to be an impression that this was the case Even in our not over long list of cases we find many personal actions in which the aid was asked, for example, in Attaint, Replevin, Trespass, many cases of *Scire Facias* and Annuity, Ejectment from a Wardship, and Debt Reeves cites several of our cases, our case 12 apparently being contrary to his comment on it The difference is merely that the Abridgment leaves out the later steps of the case which led to the final decision that a parson shall have aid of the patron and of the ordinary on a grant by himself The production of the deeds finally led to a grant of the aid which was denied until they produced the deeds, as Reeves says

Yet we have cases like that in the ninth year of Henry Sixth [Y B. 9 Hen VI, 56, pl I] where PASTON says, "He shall not have aid of the king, for this is merely a personal action, and every aid is by reason of some title in reversion of which the king shall be disinherited if he be not made patron, or else the aid is to such an effect as to have recompense and to be in place of a voucher COTT In many cases one shall have aid in personal actions, as has been adjudged here lately in debt brought for the payment of an annuity ' The argument in this case is long and involved and the point for which we have here cited it remains undecided It had been decided, however, in other cases Reeves [Eng

Law, 3 445] states that it was granted in Ravishment of Ward as well as
in the actions given above, and so far as I have been able to trace it the
action was personal as well as real   [See the cases in Fitzh   Ayde, 178,
32 Ed I, 179; 30 Ed I, 180, 29 Ed I, 184, 34 Ed I] These are cases
of *Cui in Vita*, Admeasurement of Pasture, Formedon, and Wardship of
the Body.   Also a case of *Quod Permittat* [Y B (R S) 32 – 33 Ed I,
116], Escheat [*Ib* , 30], Formedon [*Ib* , 124], Replevin [*Ib* , 182], *Quare
Impedit* [*Ib* , 243] and many others   An examination of these cases
seems to make it plain that there was no question as to the granting of the
aid in personal actions   Just what was the aide prier which looks at us
with its thousand eyes through the Year Book cases? Does anybody
tell us?   If Reeves [Hist of Eng Law, 2 143] is right the "aid prier was
       the name now given [period of Ed I] to the cause mentioned
by Bracton [Bracton, f 382] as a substitution for vouching   Later he
says [Reeves, Hist of E Law, 3 443] that it bears some affinity with
vouching to warranty, and probably was first suggested by it "   No one
else has anything of importance to say about it, everyone knows that
it exists and gives cases when it was or when it was not allowed, but no
one has anything to say as to when or where it first appeared, or how
it grew to be of so much importance, or to what branch of the law it
belongs   Crabbe [Hist of E Law, 407] says "Praying aid is an old
piece of law, mentioned by Bracton, and commonly known in this day
by the name of *Aide prier*   It is spoken of by that author in the case
where the tenant, instead of vouching the king to warranty, which by
law he could not do, prayed aid of the king in this form '*Sine rege respondere non potest, eo quod habet chartam suam de donatione, per quam
si amitteret, rex et teneretur ad excambium* '   In this day *aide prier* was
a frequent proceeding between common persons   Thus a tenant for
life by the curtesy, and the like, might pray aid of him in reversion or
remainder, to plead for him and defend his inheritance "
As a matter of fact there seems to have been very little similarity
between vouching to warranty and praying in aid   As the books which
touch on it at all (and they are few) give us very little light on the subject, we may with profit, perhaps, give a cursory examination of some
of the cases in which an aid prayer occurs and see if they throw any
light upon the proceeding   The cases abridged by Fitzherbert, and
which are in the reign of Ed. I, are the earliest, but except for one case
of a Formedon they are very short   This case [Fitzh Aide, 180] is fairly
long, but sheds little light upon the proceeding   The earliest reported
cases which have been printed we find in the Rolls Series, and of these
the first is in the Year Book of 32 Ed I [R S 24]   It is a writ of Escheat
against a woman, one Margaret, who asks aid of one T, in whom the
right "reposes, without whom she cannot answer, and she prays aid of
him " The Statute is invoked [West 2, c 3] by HULL who shows that the
provisions of the statute apply to the prayer to be received and not to the
"*prier eyde q'est a la comune ley, e chief en avoyment de delays* " [*Ib* , p 31]

So we get here the thought that the proceeding was of the common law
and the Statute intended to avoid delays   There does not seem to be
any trace of vouching to warranty here   The next case [30 Ed I, p 58,
R S] is one of trespass   The defendant acknowledges the cutting and
carrying away of the trees, as bailiff of one E de C, and by his orders
He cannot bring this matter to judgment without her, and he prays aid
of her   It was objected that the writ of Trespass must be pleaded as a
personal matter   Apparently the pleading is held to turn the plea into
a real plea   But we do not know if the plea was granted on that ground
The case shows, however, that the objection was made to the grant of
aid in personal matters, and it would seem as if such an objection must
have been upheld at an earlier time, and thus became a decided point
in law or we should not have it occurring and re-curring in these later
cases   The next case is in Easter Term [Y B 32 – 33 Ed I, R S
p 116] and is a *Quod Permittat* by a parson   Aid is not asked in the
report of the case, but HENGHAM says,"He shall have aid of the patron
and of the bishop "   We get nothing here except that a parson in such
cases was granted the aid   A writ of Formedon comes next   [Y B 32–
33 Ed I, R S p 124]   Tenements are demanded against a chaplain who
asks aid of the patron   It is granted and he comes into Court, and joins
with John in answering, and says that the tenements were aliened
before the Statute [*De Donis*]   The patron thus becomes a witness and
gives evidence (as we should say now) on a most important point   In
the same term and year [*supra*, p 182], "one avowed for damage in
his property," and the defendant said, "Not his separate property "
The aid of the wife was asked "in whose right the soil is," and was
granted, but as she did not come we cannot tell if she was joined and
gave her evidence or aid   A writ of *Quare Impedit* was brought in the
same year and term [*supra*, p 200] against a widow who asked aid of her
husband's heir   She, having only a freehold, and the right reposing in
the person who has prayed in aid, the aid was granted   Here again the
aid is most important evidence   In a case in Trinity Term [Y B 32
Ed I, p 228, R S] we have a writ of Admeasurement of Pasture against
Robert de R and others, who said that he held the tenement by a lease,
and asked aid of the reversioner and had it   BEAUFORD later seemed to
think that there was not sufficient privity shown and denied the aid
Still later in the case, the aid was claimed for tenant in tail of the heir
BEAUFORD said, "Robert and Eve, to whom the tenements were given in
tail, are still alive, so it is impossible to know who will be their heir,
therefore answer, you shall not have aid of him "   [*Ib* , p 236]   This
estate being uncertain, the aid was refused   In a writ of Wardship the
aid of a parcener was prayed. [*Ib* , p 244]   "SCROPE You ought not to
have aid, for this is a plea of trespass where we are demanding only a
chattel, and there is nothing savoring of the realty, and it concludes in
damages, judgment, etc.   HULL declared that it was a writ of Right of
Wardship, and that in this writ one may vouch to warranty '"   After

securing testimony to show that he was a parcener, the aid was granted.
Here we have the assumption that aid must only be granted in a writ
"savoring of the realty," and that if one can vouch to warranty one can
have aid, but there is no argument on these points, in fact no notice at
all is taken of them, and the aid is granted without question   The aid
of the reversioner was granted [*supra*, p 316] to a tenant for a life term,
in a writ of right   They said he should not have it because he could
vouch, and yet the aid was granted   Evidently here it was not granted
because of the lack of power to vouch   The next case, one of replevin,
[*supra*, p 366] finds the defendant praying aid of his wife and two
others, which was granted, the wife came and asked aid of the other
two, but they having been summoned did not come and she was ousted
of their aid, so we get little from the case   The remaining cases in
the Year Book of 32 Edward I yield us too little to be worth repeating
and we may pass on to the Year Book of 33–34 Ed I, p 568 (of course of
the Rolls Series)   Here we find but one case that appears to be useful
for our purpose   This is an entry sur disseisin in which the aid is asked
of the reversioner   STAUNTON wished that it might be refused and
TOUDEBY said, "And if we plead without him in whose person the fee
and the right are, to his disinheritance, he will perchance oust us, and
that is all our doubt" [p 570]   HENGHAM "If you doubt of that, go to
the Chancery and purchase for yourself against them a writ of warranty
of charter   And he was ousted of the aid "   This shows why the aid was
asked in many cases, and also that it was, as was said by HERLE in
Y B 32 Ed I [R S 24], "*chief in avoyment de delays* " [p 30] It was a
swift and valuable method of producing the evidence not to be obtained
otherwise than by suing a writ out of the Chancery   One point comes
clearly to light as we plod through the dimness of the cases, if they
could get the aid it was a great gain   It cannot be claimed that these
cases throw any great light upon the point as to whether the aid could
be granted in personal actions or not, we can only infer that it could
be so used, as the arguments against its use are passed by without
remark, and the aid is also granted in such cases without remark
The argument against its use seems to be treated as some remnant
of an older law, which survived in the mouths of those not as yet learned
enough in the law to be aware that the theory had been long over-
turned   The point cannot be resolved by the later cases, as it had
already been settled by the time we have reached the period of Ed III.
The cases cited by the authorities are nearly all of the reign of Hen VI,
too late for our purpose — too late even to be authority for the points
for which they are cited, as the cases which settled the law were a
hundred or more years behind, and the later cases do not cite them
Although we often meet the statement in the later cases that "this is
a personal action, and therefore you should not have the aid," the
number of cases in which aid was granted in personal actions is
nearly as great as those in which it is granted in real actions   Trespass

follows closely on replevin, and annuity has nearly as many as the writ of entry, in Fitzherbert   He gives many cases of *Scire Facias,* some of attaint and debt   The cases of aid in the Maynard [Ed II] show very little deviation from the few in the time of Ed I   The points regarding the granting of the aid are generally concealed in the midst of the cases, which are often very long   Many points must necessarily be missed in running over the nearly seven hundred pages of the Maynard   I believe they have never been examined for these points, there are no marginal references to aid, and therefore the matter is bound up in a great mass of pleading, through which it has to be carefully sought

Of course when we come to the reign of Ed III we have more aid from the notes and marginal references, but the law on the subject becomes no clearer   Aid is granted or not granted for reasons which in many cases rest on grounds which had been argued and settled long before we have any printed decisions   We do find, as time goes on, that it is more often asked for and granted in personal actions than in real   Fitzherbert has 136 cases, 84 of which are personal

The question of what aid is, and to what branch of the law it properly belongs, presents itself as we read of the prolonged struggle of counsel to gain the aid of A or B, or to prevent the opposing counsel from securing it   Frequently it is granted "because of the feebleness of the estate," or "case" of the client   When we read such pleas, as when we read over and over again the plea made by counsel that if they are not admitted to plead in this, that, or the other way, "it will be a great mischief, for we have no other remedy," we get a side-light on the pleading of that day   Technical it might be, an art it certainly was, but it was not a ruthless mechanism crushing indiscriminately all that came in its way, as we might think from the criticisms constantly leveled against it   On the whole we gather that justice was greatly favored, and intended to be done   Not exactly our modern justice, perhaps, but if the rules, interpreted too strictly, made for injustice, why, let down the bars a little and let in the needed proof — aid, evidence, and the like   For, after all, was it not evidence that they asked for in the aid prayer?   What is calling in a witness to attest the truth of a certain state of facts, but securing evidence?   The aid prayer is evidently a part of the pleadings, but pleading and evidence at this period had not been differentiated   The law of evidence is old   The law of evidence, as thought of by twentieth century minds, is new   Thayer tells us so   "Sir James Stephen, writing in 1888 (Nuncomar and Impey 1, 121, n) remarks, 'After much study of the law of evidence, my opinion is that the greater part of the present law came into definite existence, after being for an unascertainable period the practice of the courts (differing by the way to some extent on different circuits), just about one hundred years ago ' "   "To be sure we find Lord Kenyon saying in 1790 [*R* v *Emswell*, 3 T R 707] that "the rules of evidence   have been matured by the wisdom of the ages, and are now revered from their antiquity " [Thayer, Evidence, p 493, note] But in comparing that statement with Stephen's, made a century later, we find that all depends upon what is meant when you speak of the rules, or law, of evidence   Lord Kenyon doubtless included those numerous exclusions of evidence running far back into the Year Books, which "go upon grounds of substantive law and Pleading " He also quotes Finch's "Nomotechnia" [Thayer, Ev p 181] *"L'evidence al jurie, est quecunque chose que serve le partie a prover lissue per luy "* [Finch Nomotechnia, 61, b] The only possible way the "partie' could "prover lissue per luy" was by calling in the other party in issue to join him in the action   It was pleading, but it seems, if the history of evidence is to be taken back into the Year Books, where it most assuredly had its being along with the remainder of our law, we shall have to seek it, not under the name of evidence, where we equally assuredly will not find it, but under the various technical terms not now known to our law, and spoken of as the aide prier is now spoken of by our text writers, as "an old piece of the law " Hidden in these old pieces of the law are the germs of whatever in our law seems new

I grant that the case for this specific "old piece" is not completely made out, there is much room for argument left   Nevertheless there would seem to be a leading and a dim light, which, if followed, might bring a clearer conception of some points now left, if not in darkness, at least in an exceeding great dimness

ACCIONS SUR LEZ ESTATUTZ [7]

Statham 10 a
Paschal
41 Ed III

(1) **See actions** upon the Statutes of Jurors and Embracers, brought against the jurors and against the embracers all in one writ, etc.

Case 1

Reported in Y B Paschal, 41 Ed III, p 9, pl 3   See also Brooke, Decies Tantum, 5, in which he says that the Year Book report is bad   See also Fitzh Decies Tantum, 9   See also the Statutes of Jurors, 34 Ed III, cap 8, Stats at Large, Vol 2, p 139, and the Statute of Jurors and Embracers, 38 Ed III, Stat 1, cap 12   Stats at Large, Vol 2, p 172

Paschal
42 Ed III

(2) **A man shall have** an action of debt against the warden of the Fleet by a bill, where he let the prisoner go, albeit the Statute gives the action by writ   And *simile*, 7 Hen. VI, in the case of *H Somerset*

Case 2

Reported in Y B Paschal, 42 Ed III, p 13, pl 20   See also Brooke, Bills, 3, and Fitzh Bills, 10

The Statute Merchant for the recovery of debts, is that of 11 or 13 Ed I (Statute of Acton Burnel), Stats at Large, Vol 1, p 141

(3) **In a writ** against the husband and his wife, etc Paschal
43 Ed III
The husband and his wife brought an action upon the
Statute of Jurors and Embracers, and because it should
have been brought in the name of the husband alone, it
was abated

Very briefly reported in Y B Paschal, 43 Ed III, p 16, pl 18 See Case 3
also Brooke, Baron and Feme, 17, and Fitzh Joynder in Action, 21
For the Statute of Jurors, see *supra*, case 1

(4) **Trespass was** brought against the Abbot of W, Hilary
30 Ed III
because by the same Statute of Marlborough it is not
allowed to anyone to drive the cattle which he took in one
county into another county And the defendant said
that the place where, etc , was held of the manor of F,
which is in another county, and that he, for rent in arrears,
etc But yet it was adjudged that the plaintiff should recover his damages And it is against the opinion of many
that he should recover damages, for the Statute does not
give any other remedy against the sheriff, except that he
shall be amerced, etc

Reported in the *Liber Assisarum*, Anno 30 Ed III, p 179, pl 38, Case 4
See also Brooke, Actions sur le Statute, 42 Statute of Marlbridge,
52 Hen III (1267), cap IV "A distress shall not be driven out of
the county" Stats at Large, Vol 1, p 58

(5) **If a lord of court,** or a bailiff, procures any man to Trinity
11 Hen IV
certify any complaint against another, although his plea
be true, yet he shall have an action upon the Statute
because of the procurement, which was conceded by all
the Court. And that in Trespass But the action is a
replevin by the Statute And if the defendant justifies
by reason of such a plaint he shall have the [plea of fraud],
etc

The case has not been identified in Y B Trinity, 11 Hen IV The Case 5
Statute appears to be that of 28 Ed I, cap II Stats. at Large, Vol 1,
p. 298

(6) **One sued** a writ upon the Statute that [whereas] Michaelis
7 Hen VI.
none should be impleaded in the Marshalsea unless one
party be of the household of the king, etc , that the

defendant had, etc., and the action was maintained, etc
And that was reasonable, because in the Marshalsea they
will not admit such an exception, etc.

Case 6   Reported in Y B Paschal (not Mich), 7 Hen VI, p 30, pl 23 The
Statute is that of 28 Ed III (1300), cap 3 Stats. at Large, Vol I,
p 294

**Paschal
11 Hen IV**

(7) **A writ** upon the Statute of Liveries was brought
against him who gave the robes, and against him who
took them, etc SKRENE They should have had separate
writs, for the tort of one is not the tort of the other And
the writ was adjudged good, etc Query, if it could be
brought against several, alleging that they had separately
given livery? etc.

Case 7   Reported in Y B Paschal, 11 Hen IV, p 65, pl 23 See also
Brooke, Joinder in Action, 27, and Fitzh Briefe, 238
The Statute is that of 1 Hen IV (1399), cap 7, Stats at Large, Vol
2, p 391

Note

See as to actions upon the Statutes, in the title of *Decies
Tantum*, and in the title of Laborers, and in the title of
Provisors, in the title of Maintenance, and in the title of
Champerty

Statham, title of Decies Tantum, *infra*, p 63a, title of Labourers,
infra, pp 117b to 122a, title of Provisors, *infra*, p 144a, title of
Mayntenannce, *infra*, pp 124a to 125a, title of Champertie, *infra*, p 40a.

**Michaelis
44 Ed III**

(8) **In a decies tantum** it was alleged that they took
from both parties, and so it was found KIRTON demanded
judgment against them both, and also according to the
Statute, etc. FYNCHEDEN The Statute of "ambidextrous"
was intended to apply where they are indicted for this at
the suit of the king, wherefore as to that we do not wish
to do anything. Wherefore as to that of which they were
attainted, it was adjudged that the king should recover
the half, and the party the other half

Case 8   Reported in Y B Mich 44 Ed III, p 36, pl 28 See also Brooke,
Decies Tantum, 8
The Statute is 5 Ed I (1331), cap 10, Stats at Large, Vol 1, p 445,
and is entitled, "The punishment of a juror that is ambidexter " It
is known in the Year Books as the "Statute of Ambidexter "

(9) **In an action** upon the Statute the defendant said, Hilary 7 Ed III "No such Statute," and he had the plea, etc. Query, how shall it be tried? etc (That is not the law, unless the action be brought upon a special act, etc The reason appears, etc.)

The case has not been identified in Y B Hilary, 7 Ed III The Case 9 Statute is necessarily left unidentified, it is apparently meant to be applicable as a general plea against any Statute which cannot be proved

Forestalling nor Regrating, as it appears in an Iter of Note London In a note

This appears to be a mere fragment, left among the notes by accident, probably a note that was to have been looked up further

(10) **One brought an action** upon the Statute which Anno 20 Ed II says that no forester shall arrest any man in the forest unless he found him with the stolen goods, or that he was trespassing within the forest; or that he be indicted for a trespass made within the forest, whereas the defendant took and imprisoned one A, servant to the plaintiff at such a place, etc YOUNG It does not appear by his bill that the place where he was taken was within the forest, for if it be out he shall have his action at the common law, and not recover the double damages which are given by the Statute And the Statute also provides that the parties damaged by this arrest shall recover, by which is not meant the master of him who was damaged, etc And upon these two points they demurred in law And that was in the King's Bench, etc

There is no printed Year Book for the very short last year of Ed II Case 10 The Maynard, or Year Book of Ed II, only contains years 1–19

The Statute may be that of 3 Ed I (1278), cap 20 Stats at Large, Vol 1, p 90

---

[7] This title, so short in Statham, was afterwards expanded by Fitzherbert and Brooke, but after that period seems to have been abandoned as a title in the abridgments Rolle has left it out entirely The title does not fall in readily with the plans of the later abridgments or commentaries which were founded upon the writs, probably as the easier or the more practicable plan Where there are no writs the learning of the law is apt to fail us Under this head we get in Statham a miscellaneous assortment of cases, none of them apparently of great

importance, yet every one of them was of value in the pleading of
the day That they were held to be so is evidenced by the
expansion we find in the abridgments following Statham This value
evidently grew less as time passed and the formal pleadings under the
Statutes became crystallized, so that there was no longer any doubt as
to the manner of proceeding Naturally, as the Statutes covered diverse subjects, the decisions upon them would fall under many classifica-
tions, and the classification under this separate head would not be used
after many cases had been brought together in an abridgment The
labor of hunting up the cases under such a broad classification would
be too much, and it would then cease to be useful, as it evidently did
Yet these cases, not especially those in the abridgment before us, but
the many which we find throughout the Year Books, could be made very
useful in any exhaustive or critical study of the old pleading that might
be made — indeed that some day will doubtless be made They speak to
us out of the old pages, but we do not know their language, they have
much meaning, but we cannot as yet translate it into modern terms
Yet to do so would doubtless solve many questions now without an
answer

ACCIONS SUR LE CAS [8]

Statham 10 b
Michaelis
2 Hen IV

(1) **One brought** an action upon the case, and the writ
told how he stood seised of a road over the land of the
defendant as far as his meadow, etc , and the defendant
had ploughed his road there wrongfully, and to the damage, etc And it was adjudged that he should take nothing
by his writ, because he could have an Assize, etc. But if he
claimed the road to his fish pond it would be otherwise, etc.

Case 1

Reported in Y B Mich 2 Hen IV, p 11, pl 48 See also Brooke,
Action sur le Case, 29, and Fitzh Accion sur le Cas, 24 As to the
remark of Statham at the end of the case, SKRENE says, "That way
still remains, but it is not so easy as it was before "

Hilary
2 Hen IV

(2) **A man** brought an action upon the case, because
the common custom of the realm was that every one
should carefully guard his fire, and how by the negligence
of the defendant in guarding his fire, his house was burned.
And they were at issue that the house was not burned by
his fire, etc

And it was said in the same plea, that if my servant
burns my house, so that the house of my neighbor is burned,
I shall answer for it, etc   (Which I do not believe)

Reported in Y B Paschal (not Hilary), 2 Hen IV, p 18, pl 6   A Case 2
much quoted and well-known early case in the law of negligence   See
also Brooke, Action sur le Case, 30, and Fitzh   Accion sur le Cas, 25

(3) **One brought an action** against a miller because he Michaelis
and his ancestors had been used to mill without toll, 41 Ed III
whereas the defendant took a bushel of grain, etc , *vi et
armis*   THORPE   You shall not have anything against
the miller except a general writ of Trespass, and a *Quod
Permittat* against the tenant of the soil, etc   Which FYNCH-
EDEN conceded   *Simile*, Trinity 44, in Trespass, well
debated, and there the writ was adjudged good

Reported in Y B Mich 41 Ed III, p 24, pl 17   See also Brooke, Case 3
Action sur le Case, 14, and Fitzh   Accion sur le Cas, 31

(4) **One brought** a writ of Conspiracy against one T Trinity
and W, alleging that they had procured the said W to 42 Ed III
oust the plaintiff from certain lands, and to enfeoff one B,
against whom the said T brought a *Scire Facias* to have
execution of an elder title, so that the plaintiff lost his
warranty   And the writ was challenged because he
alleged that the defendants "procured" the said W, whereas
W could not "procure" himself   And then the defendants
pleaded "not guilty," etc

Reported in Y B Hilary (not Trinity), 42 Ed III, p 1, pl 2   The Case 4.
report of the case is continued in Y B Hilary, 43 Ed III, p 10, pl 29,
where they are at issue on "not guilty '   See also Brooke, Conspiracy, 5

(5) **One brought** a writ of Arrest, alleging that the Hilary
defendant had arrested his wools and detained them, and 42 Ed III
would not permit them to be delivered according to the
agreement, etc   And the opinion was that the writ could
not be maintained upon such an allegation, etc

The case has not been identified in Y B Hilary, 42 Ed III, or in the Case 5
early abridgments

(6) **One brought** an action against an innkeeper, and Paschal
he counted the common custom, etc , that every inn- 42 Ed III
keeper should keep [safely], etc   And he had a writ upon
all his matter, etc   The defendant demanded judgment

inasmuch as he did not count upon any delivery made to him, but that he left the goods in the chamber, etc   And it was adjudged that the plaintiff should recover his damages, etc.

Case 6   Reported in Y B Paschal, 42 Ed III, p 11, pl 13   See also Brooke, Action sur le Case, 15

Paschal 42 Ed III

(7) **A writ** of Conspiracy upon the Case was brought against an abbot and others   And the abbot died, and they brought a new writ against his successor and the others, comprising the same matter, which matter was debated for a long time.   Which see, etc

Case 7   Reported in Y B Paschal, 42 Ed III, p 14, pl 27   See also Brooke, Action sur le Case, 16

Hilary 43 Ed III

(8) **One brought** a writ of Trespass because the defendant had taken toll of his tenants of the manor of B, who have been used of time, etc , to go to every market and ferry, etc , which usage the king had confirmed, etc   And because the defendant could not deny this, the plaintiff had judgment to recover his franchise and his damages, etc

Case 8   Reported in Y B Mich (not Hilary), 43 Ed III, p 29, pl 14, under the head of "Certaine cases prises hors d'un veil written copy de 43 nient imprimé devant "   A quaint mixture of French and English

Hilary 48 Ed III

(9) **A woman** brought a writ of Trespass against one B, surgeon of London, and the writ said that her right hand was wounded by one F, and the defendant undertook to cure her, whereas by the negligence of the defendant her hand was injured so that it was lost, to the wrong and to the damage, etc   (And note that no place where he undertook was put in the writ, but he declared it in his count, to wit at Strand Cross) HASTY He did not take upon himself to save it Ready to wage his law   PERSHAY This is an action of Trespass which lies in the notice of the country, so the law does not lie   FYNCHEDEN But it is not law to answer, "*ne contra pacem,*" wherefore it seems the law lies   But it seems that the action does not lie, for

she was not maimed by the defendant, but by him who
hurt her, and if she recovers damages now against us she
will recover another time against him who maimed her,
and so twice, etc. But yet, Ready, etc And the other
alleged the contrary HASTY Now, judgment of the
writ, because the place is not made certain PERSHAY
You affirm the writ to be good by the tender of the issue
But yet the writ was abated, etc.

Reported in Y B Hilary, 48 Ed III, p 6, pl 11, where it is said to Case 9
have been a man who brought the writ See also Brooke, Action sur
le Case, 24

(10) **One made** his complaint to the king by bill, that Hilary
in a plea for the taking of cattle by himself and one H, 24 Ed III
a *Nisi Prius* was granted in Essex before KELSHULL, on
which day the inquest was charged, and because they
could not agree on that same day, the inquest was delivered
to the sheriff to keep safely, etc And the next day KEL-
SHULL could have taken the verdict, but because of the
procurement of certain people of the vill (whom he named),
he suffered them to go at large and eat and drink, etc ,
for which reason KELSHULL would not take the inquest, so
it was delayed, to the damage· and we prayed a remedy, and
the king endorsed a certain bill, and sent it to the justices
of the Bench, commanding them to do right to him, etc
Wherefore they awarded a *Venire Facias* against the jurors
and the procurors, who came and were at issue upon the
matter, upon which a *Venire Facias* was issued to the
coroners

Reported in Y B Hilary, 24 Ed III, p 24, pl 10   Case 10

(11) **One brought** an action of Trespass on the Case Trinity
because the defendant had bargained with him to enfeoff 14 Hen VI
him of certain lands, and that the same defendant before
such a day, etc., should make one H release to him all
his right in the same land, and that he did not make
the release. NEWTON That sounds merely in covenant,
wherefore, etc PASTON It seems that the action well
lies, for if a blacksmith makes a covenant with me to shoe

my horse, and he does it negligently, so that the horse is hurt by a nail, I shall have an action on the case   And I say that if he will not shoe my horse, that still I have an action on the case, for by his default peradventure his horse is injured by lack of a shoe, so that both cases are dependent upon covenant   Which JUYN conceded, etc

Case 11

Reported in Y B Anno 14 Hen VI, p 18, pl 58   A very good case for the example it contains   See also Brooke, Action sur le Case, 69, and Fitzh   Accion sur le Cas, 8

Trinity
14 Hen VI

(12) **One brought** a writ of Trespass on the Case because the defendant sold him certain wood at F for twenty pounds, and he showed him a certain portion of the wood which was good and marketable, and he warranted the remainder of the wood to be as good, etc , and he [showed] that the remainder was defective, etc   NEWTON said that he sold

Statham 11 a

him certain wood for the same sum at G, which was good and marketable, without this that he sold it at F, as he has alleged, etc   And it was held a good plea   So note that in this action the place shall be made a part of the issue   Query, if the place be in another county? etc

Case 12

Reported in Y B Anno 14 Hen VI, p 22, pl 66

Hilary
1 Hen VI

(13) **If a man** recovers by default against me in a *Præcipe quod Reddat* and the summoners and the viewers are dead, I shall have an action on the case against the sheriff   By JUYN   Which was conceded, etc

Case 13

Reported in Y B Mich (not Hilary), 1 Hen VI, p 1, pl 4   See also Brooke, Action sur le Case, 73, and Fitzh   Accion sur le Cas, 1

Trinity
39 Ed III

(14) **One brought** a writ on the case because the defendant had forged a release, and put it in evidence in an inquest between the plaintiff and one B, in a writ of Wardship, which passed against him by reason of that release   THORPE   You cannot have an action for that, for it is not in evidence that any judgment was given upon it, and you can have an Attaint, wherefore you will not take anything by your writ, etc

Case 14

Reported in Y B Paschal (not Trinity), 39 Ed III, p 13, pl 23 (writ of Conspiracy)   See also Brooke, Action sur le Cas, 68

(15) **One brought an action** because the defendant sold him a horse and warranted the horse to be sound and well and that the defendant knew the horse to be sick, and that the horse died within a week afterwards   And the defendant said that he sold him the horse sound and well, without this that he warranted him, etc   Ready   And the other side alleged the contrary   (It seems that the action is double)

There is no printed Year Book for 11 Ric II   The case has not been identified in the early abridgments

(16) **One brought an action** because the defendant undertook to cure the plaintiff of a certain sickness, in London, in such a ward, and he [told] how he came to the plaintiff in the Strand, and there gave him the wrong medicine for his infirmity (and he told what the infirmity was), and the writ was brought in London   RIKHILL He alleges the tort to be done in another county than the writ does, and also the action sounds in covenant, which should be brought in the same county, etc   And the writ was adjudged good, etc

There is no printed Year Book for 11 Ric II   The case, however, is abridged in Fitzh   Accion sur le Cas, 37   He give a much longer digest than that of Statham

(17) **The wardens** of a church brought an action against one A for certain things belonging to the church, which were carried out of their keeping   The defendant said that he was one of the parishioners of the said church and the plaintiff also, so the goods are in them in common, judgment if such an action lies against us   And it was the opinion that the action would well lie, etc

Reported in Y B Mich 11 (not 10) Hen IV, p 12, pl 25

(18) **If I buy** a horse of a man, and the horse is in another place at the time of the purchase, so that I cannot see him, and he warrants me that the horse is sound and well, and the horse has a visible malady like "splint and spalen," I shall have an action upon the case, etc   By THIRNING

It is otherwise if I see the horse at the time of the purchase, etc

Case 18 The case has not been identified in Y B Hilary, 13 Hen IV, or in the early abridgments

Hilary 9 Hen VI (19) **One brought** an action against an escheator because he had taken an office by an inquest, and returned other names, etc , and other things which were not found, and the action was good   And the law is the same against a sheriff, if he returns "four actions" when there are five

Case 19 Reported in Y B Hilary, 9 Hen VI, p 60, pl 9   See *supra*, title Aide de Roy, case 12   See also Brooke, Action sur le Case, 9, and Fitzh   Accion sur le Cas, 6

Michaelis 3 Hen VI (20) **One brought** an action against one because the defendant undertook to make a mill by a certain day, and he did not do it, etc   The defendant answered that, but not "*rigore juris*," for MARTYN said clearly that the action does not lie, because it sounds in covenant   And it was also said that the writ was not good because it did not state that the defendant should have anything for the making of it; for it should be for a certain sum, etc (And it is good enough without putting how much in certain, etc)

Case 20 Reported in Y B Hilary (not Mich), 3 Hen VI, p 36, pl. 33   See also Brooke, Action sur le Case, 7

Hilary 11 Hen IV (21) **In trespass** against a common innkeeper, etc , the defendant said that he went to the sheriff to be at the hundred the same day, etc., and he loaned the key of the house to the plaintiff, who took it at his peril, etc , and before he returned, the horse of the plaintiff was stolen, etc , judgment if action?   And the opinion was that the plaintiff should recover his damages.   NORTON   He does not say in his count that we were a common innkeeper. SKRENE   We have rehearsed the custom by which it is to be understood that he is a common innkeeper   And also you have passed that matter   THIRNING   It appeared [of record], wherefore take nothing by your writ, etc

Case 21 Reported in Y B Hilary, 11 Hen IV, p 45, pl 18   See also Brooke, Action sur le Case, 41

(22) **A schoolmaster** brought an action on the case [showing] how the collation to the school of B belonged to the Prior of B, from time, etc., and that he was in by his collation, and that the defendant had set up a school, so that where I was accustomed to take twenty pence every quarter for scholars, I have only twelve pence, etc HANKFORD One can have *Damnum absque Injuria*, wherefore you take nothing by your writ

Reported in Y. B Hilary, 11 Hen IV, p 47, pl 21 A well-known and much cited case See also Brooke, Action sur le Case, 42, and Fitzh Accion sur le Cas, 28

(23) **Pelham brought** a writ of Trespass against the Prior of B, inasmuch as the said prior, by reason of his water mill in S, should repair a bridge over the water which ran to the said mill, by which bridge the plaintiff, by reason of his manor of F, and all those whose estate, etc , were accustomed to pass with their provisions and their cattle, etc And he showed how the said prior and his predecessors, and all those whose estate they had in the said mill, had repaired the same bridge for time, etc , and that the said defendant suffered the said bridge to be out of repair, so that the plaintiff could not pass for a long time, to the damage, etc SKRENE Judgment of the writ, for the plaintiff has claimed the road appendant to the manor of F, and he has not claimed the road to go to his freehold, and no place, etc And that was not allowed SKRENE Still you should have an assize of nuisance, and not this action HANKFORD That cannot be, for nothing was raised as a nuisance, or torn down, but he has suffered the bridge to fall, wherefore answer

Reported in Y B Trinity (not Hilary), 11 Hen IV, p 82, pl 28 See also Brooke, Action sur le Case, 44, and Fitzh Accion sur le Cas, 30

(24) **One brought** an action of deceit on the case, and he counted that he brought a writ of Entry against the defendant And he produced a protection "*quia moriatur,*" which was allowed. And the case was put without day, and he remained in B, in the county of E, to the

damage, etc   And the writ was brought in the county of E, etc.   FORTESCUE   The writ should be brought in the county of Middlesex, where the protection was thrown, etc , for that is the cause of his action   NEWTON   The writ is good, for it shall be tried whether he remained there or not   FULTHORPE   On a protection, *"quia profecturus,"* no such action lies, for he who throws the protection can go when he will, but in this case the action lies, and it is because of the throwing of the protection, which was

Statham 11 b brought in Middlesex   NEWTON   Answer   FORTESCUE He did not say in his writ by what writ we are impleaded   PORTYNGTON   We have said it in our count   FORTESCUE This is a special writ in which all the matter should be comprehended   NEWTON   Answer, etc

Case 24   The case has not been identified in Y B Trinity, 19 Hen VI, or in the early abridgments

Trinity (25) **One brought** an action upon the case because he
27 Hen VI delivered to the defendant nine sacks of wool, to take care of, and the defendant, for six shillings, which the plaintiff paid him, took upon himself to keep them safely   And because the defendant [did not] keep them safely they were taken and carried away   DANBY   This action does not lie, for it appears clearly that he could have a writ of Detinue, and also in his count he does not show by whom they were carried away   PORTYNGTON   If he said that they were carried away by one unknown it were enough, but it seems that the action does not lie, for the above reason   PRISOT   The action well lies, to my mind   (But he did not say why)   And then DANBY answered to the action.   And I believe the reason the action lies is because the defendant took six shillings to take care of them, which six shillings could not be recovered by a writ of Detinue, etc.   Query?

Case 25   The case has not been identified in Y B Trinity, 27 Hen VI, or in the early abridgments

Note   **See as to actions on the case,** in the title of Deceit, and in the title of Justification, Hilary, 19 Hen VI, and also in the title of Conspiracy

Statham, title of Disceipte, *infra*, pp 69 a to 69 b, title of Justificacion, *infra*, p 116 a, case 1, title of Conspiracy, *infra*, pp 48 a to 48 b   The only case appearing in this title after this note is a case in 36 Hen VI, one of the very latest cases in the book   It may be that the case was added just before the book went to press, and not by Statham

(26) **One brought** an action on the case because the defendant sold him a horse at Southwark, knowing him to be infirm in body through various diseases, and warranting him to be a sound horse   And it was challenged for doubleness, and it was adjudged good, for it was said that the action does not lie in this case unless there had been a warranty, also he cannot have an action on that warranty unless he shows the deceit, for upon the warranty by itself the action does not lie without a specialty, because it sounds in covenant, and therefore it is necessary that he show a deceit precedent, etc   MOILE We sold him a horse in such a place in London, which was sound and well, for this same sum, without this that we sold him any horse at Southwark in the manner, etc   POLE That is no plea, for it amounts to no more than that he did not sell to you the horse at Southwark MOILE In Detinue it is a good plea to say that the plaintiff bailed him the same thing in another county upon condition, without this, etc   And if we had pleaded that we sold the horse to him in another county upon condition, etc , it had been a good plea, consequently, since he has pleaded without conditions, the plea is good, for in neither case can it be understood to be the same contract, etc , for nothing will be tried except whether we sold the horse in Southwark in either case   PORTYNGTON It seems to me that one shall not have the plea in either case   ASSHETON There are such pleas in London, where they can have a venue of two parishes   But when such a condition is pleaded in another county it is wrong, etc   But in London there are many venues, and yet there is but one county, and the law is the same, it seems, in each county, [so] that defendant can allege such a matter in another venue within the same county

Michaelis
31 Hen VI

The case has not been identified in Y B Mich 31 Hen VI, or in the early abridgments

Case 26

[8] This action, being a favorite of legal writers of the present day, has had a most adequate treatment, so that it is not necessary here to go into the difficulties of the early litigants and eulogize the benefits that came to them through the Statute of Westminster the Second The immortal case of the overloaded boat on the Humber [Y B 22 Ed III, *Liber Assisarum*, p 94, pl 41] and the drowning of the horse "*a tort et a damage*," has come down through all the ages, and one might well stop to pity — not the poor horse thus cut short in his career, — but the long ranks of burden bearers who have become overladen with the learning of actions *in consimili casu* Statham, however, was not so overwhelmed with cases on the subject, we have in the Abridgment only twenty-six cases, Fitzherbert has only fifty-two Naturally many of these cases are in the reigns of the two Henrys, and comparatively few in the time of Edward the Third We have one case in 24 Ed III [10] which is very early for *Accion sur le cas*, being only two years after the cases in the *Liber Assisarum* It is noticeable that this case, unlike the other cases cited by Statham, begins "One brought his complaint to the king by bill," whereas all our other cases are "One brought an action of trespass" or "Trespass on the Case," or "an Action on the Case," or "A writ of Conspiracy" or "A writ of Arrest' It is evident that the form of the action at this period was as yet unevolved and that they were feeling after the best method of framing the action However full the books may be of learning about the action on the case, they are very chary of that learning when it comes to speak of the bill We are told that "actions were brought in this way during all the reign [Ed III] and the books are full of them" [Reeves, Hist of Eng Law, 3 93] Crabb paraphrases Reeves This bill is not the bill in equity, as action was commenced in either of the three courts, King's Bench, Common Pleas and Exchequer More will be said as to the bill under that title It is enough to note it here

AMESUREMENT [9]

Paschal, 44 Ed III

(1) **In a writ** of Admeasurement of Dower against a woman, who came in and said that she was ready to be admeasured And the demandant counted that she had received more than her dower, etc , by twenty pounds And then a writ issued to the sheriff, for him to admeasure, who returned that he had admeasured and that she had more than, etc., by forty shillings And because he did not return the extent for the two parts, and for each part, etc , he was amerced, and a *Sicut Alias* issued And then there was an argument on the Statute,

to wit if the admeasurement should be before justices or before the sheriff And it should not be made before the sheriff unless it is viscontiel But in this case, although it was sent to the sheriff it was before justices, etc

Reported in Y B Paschal, 44 Ed III, p 10, pl 12 The Statute upon which there was an argument is that of Westminster the Second, 13 Ed I (1285), caps 7 and 8 Stats at Large, Vol 1, p 115 (180, 181) Case 1

(2) **If a man** has common in two vills by reason of his freehold in one of the vills, a writ of Admeasurement should be brought against him in the two vills, for otherwise he will be admeasured in the one vill according to his freehold, so he will lose his common in the other vill And that in Admeasurement *Michaelis 11 Ed II*

Reported in Y B Mich 11 Ed II (Maynard), p 330, pl 1 Case 2

(3) **In a writ** of Admeasurement of Dower, all the lands which she had in dower within the same county shall be admeasured, to wit all the lands that she had in her endowment as of the endowment of the heir when the guardian brought the action, etc And although she be endowed in the Chancery before the heir sues livery, yet the heir shall have a writ of Admeasurement (In the same plea) *Trinity 7 Ric II*

There is no printed Year Book for 7 Ric II The case has not been identified in the early abridgments Case 3

(4) **A writ** of Admeasurement of Dower is maintainable against a woman who is endowed in the Chancery, as appeared in the case of the *Count of Devonshire.* *Anno 12 Hen VI*

The case has not been identified in Y B 12 Hen VI Fitzh Admeasurement, 9, has a very short abridgment of the case, which he may very well have taken from Statham

⁹ Under this title we have three cases of admeasurement of dower and one of admeasurement of pasture These were both viscontiel, directed to the sheriff [Fitzherbert, *Nat Brevium*, 125, 148] The writ of admeasurement of dower lay where the heir when under age had endowed the widow with more than her lawful share, or the guardian had endowed her with more than the third part of the land, then the heir at his Case 4.

coming of age could have the writ The admeasurement of pasture was a writ between tenants in common, where common was appendant to their freeholds, and one of the commoners "surcharged" the common, that is, put in more cattle than he was entitled to The "admeasurement" seems to have been made sometimes by the sheriff, sometimes before the justices. [Reeves, Hist of Eng Law, 2d ed , Vol 1, p 343] The process is given by Fleta [Book 4, cap 23, *De Admensur Pasturæ*] The writ, probably in a somewhat more ancient form, figures in Maitland's Register of Original Writs, as No 107 He attributes this Register to the middle part of the reign of Henry III (1236–37) [Sel Essays in Anglo-American Legal History, Vol 2, p 572] He gives the writ there as "Surcharge of Pasture, *summone*   B, *quod sit   quod sit astensuras quare super honerat pasturum*" [*Supra*, p 377] Bohun [Eng Lawyer, p 130] says, "This writ was formed to bring those to equity and moderation who usurp more than their shares or part, and to that end it formerly lay in divers cases, though the Precedents of the Register and Fitz , *Nat Brev* , have given us the forms thereof only of two kinds, viz Writs of Admeasurement of Dower [and] of Pasture " We should like to know what were the "divers cases" Bohun had in mind He was apparently unprepared to give these instances which we should like so much to have It might be that a patient search of the cases with this object in mind might show us some traces of these lost precedents I have, however, been unable to make the exhaustive search necessary for the purpose

AMERCIAMENT [10]

Paschal
48 Ed III

(1) In a scire facias, *Quid Juris Clamat,* and such like actions, which are founded upon a record, unless the plaintiff be named he shall not be amerced

Case 1

The case has not been identified in Y B Paschal, 48 Ed III Brooke and Fitzherbert have one case of Amercement in 48 Ed III (Mich 48 Ed III, p 22, pl 4), Brooke, Amerciament, 12, and Fitzherbert, Amerciament, 13, but it does not appear to be the case here abridged by Statham, unless the latter had access to a different report of the case

Hilary
28 Ed III

(2) In replevin, the issue was taken that the place where, etc , was out of his fee, and it was found for the plaintiff, and yet the avowant was not amerced, because the action was not founded upon the Statute which says that a man shall not distrain out [of his fee, or place where he has jurisdiction]

The case has not been identified in Y B Hilary, 28 Ed III Fitz- *Case 2*
herbert apparently took the case from Statham, as he gives the same
citation without the folio number See Fitzh Amerciament, 24 The
Statute is that of Marlbridge, 52 Hen III (1267), cap 2 Stats at
Large, Vol 1, p 57

See as to amercement, in the title of Return   *Note*

See Statham, title of Retourne, p 157 a to 158 b, *infra*

(3) **In a writ** of Aiel, one was summoned and severed and *Hilary*
died, and the other was amerced   Query, why?   *5 Ed III*

The case has not been identified in Y B Hilary, 5 Ed III, or in the *Case 3*
early abridgments

(4) **The sheriff** returned, upon a *Fieri Facias*, that he had *Trinity*
delivered the monies to the party   And for that reason he *2 Ed III*
was amerced   In Debt, etc

The case has not been identified in Y B Trinity, 2 Ed III, or in the *Case 4*
early abridgments

(5) **The sheriff** was amerced because he returned people *Anno 38*
who were not sufficient, upon an indictment of felony, etc. *Liber Assis-*
arum, In
Indictment.

The case has not been identified in Y B 38 *Liber Assisarum*, or in *Case 5*
the early abridgments

(6) **If the jurors** in an Assize make default on the first *Paschal*
day, they shall not be amerced, etc   (But yet the contrary *Anno*
has been adjudged since that time, etc) But at the *Venire* *13 Ed III*
Facias they shall not be amerced, etc., because the defendant can be essoined or make default, and because they did
not use to demand the tenant on that day, etc   But in a
Scire Facias if the jurors do not appear at the *Venire Facias*
they shall be amerced, because such delays for the defendant are ousted by the Statute, etc   Query?

There is no early printed Year Book for 13 Ed III The case has *Case 6*
not been identified in that year and term in the Rolls Series

The Statute is 13 Ed III (1285), cap 28, Stats at Large, Vol 1,
p 163 (202)

[10] Here we have a fragmentary title, expanded to somewhat greater
lengths in the later digests or abridgments The collected cases wherever found could scarcely be representative of the whole subject, for
the penalty of the unsuccessful suitor was to be amerced, and the

amerciament was, as Coke called it, "*Miserecordia*, for that it ought to be assessed mercifully " [Coke, 1st Inst , 126, b] Those familiar with the cases may judge for themselves if this were always remembered. Reeves says that in the reign of Henry III, "It was endeavored, by declaring the law more fully on that subject, to prevent all abuse of the *miserecordia*, or amerciament " Magna Charta — the Magna Charta of the English Statutes at Large, "made in the ninth year of King Henry the Third" — used the following language as an effort toward securing this object "A free man shall not be amerced for a small fault, but after the manner of the fault, and for a great fault after the greatness thereof, saving to him his contenement (*contenemento suo*), and a merchant likewise, saving to him his merchandise, and any other villain than ours shall be likewise amerced, saving his wainage, if he fall into our mercy And none of the said amerciaments shall be assessed, but by the oath of honest and lawful men of the vicinage Earls and barons shall not be amerced but by their peers, and after the manner of their offense No man of the church shall be amerced after the quantity of his spiritual benefice but after his lay tenement, and after the quantity of his offense " [Magna Charta, chap 14, Stats at Large, Vol 1, p 6] But it seems that this did not have the required effect, for there arose a writ founded upon the unmerciful mercies of the *miserecordia*, or the writ of *Moderata miserecordia*, which was given for "a case where a man is amerced in a Court Baron, or other Court which is not a court of record, outrageously for Trespass or other offense " [Fitzh *Nat Brev , Moderata Miserecordia*, 75] This appears, however, to have been available only in cases of trespass, as a matter of fact But trespass in the thirteenth century and even somewhat later "will cover all or almost all wrongful acts and defaults " [P & M Hist of Eng Law, 2d ed , Vol 2, p 512] "Thousands of amerciaments are being inflicted (note the word!) by courts of all kinds " [*Supra*, p 513] The amerciament was imposed in civil actions as in criminal "Every tort, nay, every cause of civil action, was a punishable offense Every vanquished defendant, even though the action was 'real,' or was contractual, had earned punishment Every defeated plaintiff could be amerced for a false claim Then again, every default in appearance brought an amerciament on the defaulter and his pledges Every mistake in pleading, every miskenning or *stultiloquium*, brought an amerciament on the pleader if the suit was to be retrieved A litigant who hoped to get to the end of his suit without an amerciament must have been a sanguine man " [*Supra*, p 519] The Note Book [Bracton Note Book, pl 187, 206, 342, note 3] is given by Maitland as his authority for all this, and the cases cited bear him out But the Year Books are filled with cases showing the infinite variety of ways in which the litigant found himself to be in mercy, sometimes, to the satisfaction of the reader, when he was evidently planning to throw the burden on the other party in the case There is a case in the Ancien Coutumier, given by Maitland in a note, which illuminates this side of the

matter. "the person against whom the jury is demanded is represented
as some *comes vel baro vel aliquis potens homo*,' who desires to grab land
from his tenants, or neighbors, while the plaintiff is an *impotens homo* '"
"*Potens vero   in miserecordia remanebit et impotens suam habebit
terram*" So justice appears to be done   Bracton in his Note Book
gives a number of cases in which one of the litigants was in *miserecordia*, the earliest being in 1219 [Bracton N B 213]   There is one
case [*supra*, 214] in 1224, one in 1228 [*supra*, 120]   In 1229 we have
one where both litigants were in mercy [*supra*, 360]   In 1230 Thomas,
Bishop of Norwich, prays for the amerciaments throughout his liberty,
in the County as well as in the Eyres.   He claims to have them by a
royal charter [*supra*, 391]   There is but one case given as in 1230, the
case of an advowson [*supra*, 427]   In 1231 we have the case of the upper
chamber, decided by all the hustings [*supra*, 489]   In 1233 we have
one case of trespass [*supra*, 770] and one of an advowson [*supra*, 981]
In 1235 there are three cases [*supra*, 1149, 1159, 1170]   In 1236 there
is but one [*supra*, 1191]   In 1238 we have two [*supra*, 1239, 1249]
There is more to be said of the "Amerciament in a plea real" as is said
by Coke   He also notes a relation of the Amerciament to the Saxon
"bote"   [Coke, 1st Inst , 127, a]

ANNUITE

(1) **In a writ of annuity,** the defendant said that he had   Michaelis
been at all times ready to pay, etc., and still is   GAS-   2 Hen IV
COIGNE. You now come in by distress, wherefore it was
adjudged that the plaintiff should recover, etc , and his
damages were taxed by the Court

Reported in Y B Mich 2 Hen IV, p 3, pl 8   This was the year   Case 1
in which Gascoigne was appointed judge of the Common Pleas   He
appears in the report, however, as counsel   See also Brooke, Annuitie, 12

(2) **"Nothing in arrears"** is no plea in a suit of Annuity,   Trinity
by the opinion of the COURT in a *Scire Facias*.   And the   44 Ed III
same law was adjudged in a *Scire Facias* on the arrears of
an annuity, Hilary, 46 Ed III   And in the same plea it
was the opinion of the COURT that it is no plea to say that
the money to him, unless he shows an acquittance, etc ,
for it is not under his distress, etc

Reported in Y B Trinity, 44 Ed III, p 18, pl 9   See also Brooke,   Case 2.
Annuitie, 9.

(3) **In a writ of annuity** against one H, as heir to his father, he said that he had nothing by descent, and it was found that he had ten shillings by descent, and because the issue was found against him the plaintiff had judgment to recover all the annuity, that is to say, twenty pounds, etc THORPE said that he should have pleaded "nothing by descent, except so much," etc. Query, all the same, as to this matter, for the plaintiff had no land in execution which had descended, and consequently the action did not lie against the heir, etc

Case 3

There is no early printed year of 19 Ed III The case has not been identified in the Rolls Series

(4) **In a writ of annuity**, if the defendant shows an acquittance for the arrears, still the plaintiff shall have judgment to recover the annuity, as in a writ of Mesne, where the defendant says that he was never disturbed by his default, the plaintiff shall not have an acquittance immediately And this in Mesne, etc.

Case 4

Reported in Y B Mich 30 Ed III, p 21, pl 37

(5) **Executors brought** a writ of Debt for the arrears of an annuity accrued in the life of their testator, and showed how their testator and all his predecessors had been seised of this same annuity, from time, etc No exception was taken to the writ Query, if the action lies, for it seems that it should not, no more than for the arrears of a rent service, etc And see the *Registrum*, for it seems that this action of debt for the arrears of an annuity does not lie, except where the annuity is recovered, and for those arrears the action lies and not for the arrears accrued after the recovery, and the plaintiff should declare upon the recovery, etc Query?

Case 5

Reported in Y B Paschal, 2 Hen VI, p 8, pl 4 The "*Registrum*," "Register of Writs," a register of writs originally written in the reign of Henry II Statham probably had a manuscript copy of this book, to which he often refers It is said to have contained the original writs "long before the Conquest" It was printed as early as 1531, and has passed into four editions, 1531, 1634, 1681, 1687 It is in Latin and has never been translated

(6) **One A brought a writ** of Annuity for ten pounds Michaelis
9 Hen VI
against the queen, and he showed the letters-patent from the
same queen, showing the Abbot of Bury paid annually to
the king, Henry the Fifth, forty pounds, which he assigned
to the queen in lieu of dower, and how she had granted
to the said plaintiff an annuity of ten pounds to receive
of the said abbot   And the opinion was that the queen
would be charged with the said annuity, inasmuch as she,
etc, granted it.   And though it was uncertain yet it
charged the person, etc.   As if I grant an annuity to the
parceners of the manor of B, although I have no such
manor, still my person is charged   And although I have
such a manor and grant the annuity with distress, still it
is in his election if he will charge my person or the land
And if I say that such a one held of me for twenty shillings
of rent, and I grant to you twelve pence of this rent, that
is not an annuity, for that grant was to no purpose unless
the tenant attorned to him in whom this rent was before
But if I say (as above) when I have not any such rent,
then that charges my person for the annuity   And if I
recite that such a one held of me by twenty shillings of
rent and I have granted to you twelve pence of the said
twenty shillings, my person is charged, for in that case the
twelve pence are not part of the twenty shillings,   and
also rent cannot issue from a rent   And they adjourned, etc

Reported in Y B Mich 9 Hen VI, p 53, pl 36   See also Brooke, Case 6
Annuitie, 3, and Fitzh Annuitie, 4

(7) **And afterwards** in Trinity Term one Margery Trinity
9 Hen VI
Parker brought a writ of Annuity against the same queen,
and showed the letters-patent of the same queen for an
annual rent of twenty pounds, which sum was assigned
to her in dower, according to the great custom of London,
to be received by the hands of the collectors of this same Statham 12 b
custom   And it was adjudged that she should recover the
annuity for the above reason, and still the custom is not
a thing certain   But yet, query, etc ?

Reported in Y B Trinity, 9 Hen VI, p 12, pl 1   See also Brooke, Case 7
Annuitie, 3, and Fitzh Annuitie, 5

Michaelis 9 Hen VI

(8) **See** by PASTON, that generally a writ of right does not lie upon the arrears of an annuity, no more than for a rent service, unless the freehold be ended, etc.

Case 8

The words of PASTON have not been identified in the cases of Annuity in 9 Hen VI

See of annuity, in the title of Grant.

See reference to the title of Grannte, *infra*, Grannte, 3 (Mich 2 Hen IV)

Paschal 7 Hen IV

(9) **If a parson** of a church has a license from the patron and from the ordinary to grant an annuity, that grant of an annuity with such a license shall charge his successor forever, without any other grant or confirmation from the patron or from the ordinary, for in that case the grant of the annuity shows the license, etc.

Case 9

The case has not been identified in Y. B Paschal, 7 Hen IV, or in the later abridgments

Paschal 12 Hen IV.

(10) **If one** brought a writ of Annuity against an abbot, and upon this the abbot levied a fine, that will bind his successor, for it shall be understood that this was the same annuity as before, and this fine shall have no other effect, etc Query? But see in the same plea that it is clearly held that if one recovers an annuity against an abbot for default, this will bind his house forever, etc

Case 10

This may be the case reported in Y B Paschal, 12 Hen IV, p 21, pl. 13, but the identification is not clear It has not been identified elsewhere

Paschal 27 Hen VI.

(11) **W. Rous** brought a writ of Annuity against an abbot, and showed a deed for the annuity made by the predecessor of this same abbot, and sealed with the seal of the convent, which annuity was for certain bread, and ale, and robes, and other things, etc. POLE· The Statute of Carlisle says that Cistercienses and Premonstratenses and others who have a convent and a common seal, that the common seal shall be in the keeping of the prior, who is under the abbot, etc., and four others, the wisest of the house, and that any deed sealed with the common seal which is not thus in their keeping shall be void And we say that at the time this deed was sealed the seal was out of their keeping And the opinion of the COURT was that

the Statute was void, since it is impossible to be observed, for when the seal was in their keeping the abbot could not seal anything with it, for when it was in the hands of the abbot it would be out of their keeping, *ipso facto* And if the Statute shall be observed every common seal will be defeated by a simple allegation which cannot be tried, etc See [the case] for it was well debated, and many exceptions were taken to the plea, etc

Those who have not access to the manuscripts cannot take the advice Case 11
of Statham and "See this case," for we have no printed Paschal Term for 27 Hen VI   The "Statute of Carlisle" would seem to be "*Asportatis Religiosum*," Anno 35 Ed I, Stat 1, cap IV, Stats at Large, Vol 1, p 329, which has the provisions quoted by Statham

(12) **In [a writ] of annuity** (title of Prescription), releas- Paschal
ing all actions, real and personal, *ratione debiti compoti seu* ^12 Ric II
ratione alterius contractus, is not a bar against the plaintiff's recovery, etc

There is no early printed Year Book for 12 Ric II   The con- Case 12
fused text of Statham is, however, made clear by the abridgment of the case in Brooke, Annuitie, 42, and in Fitzh Reless, 29, where there is a clear abridgment of the case from the report   There is also a report of this, or a similar case, in Y B 12 Ric II, in Hilary Term, p 135 Ames Foundation, ed Deiser

(13) **If a man** grants an annuity for him and his heirs Hilary
to another in fee, although it be with warranty, it will not ^2 Hen IV
bind his heir, etc   Query, if he had assets by descent, if then, etc ? But that was not decided in the opinion of the COURT, in Annuity.

Reported in Y B Mich (not Hilary), 2 Hen IV, p 13, pl 54   The Case 13
case as there reported seems scarcely to justify Statham's statement See also Brooke, Annuitie, 13, and Fitzh Annuitie, 16

(14) **If an annuity** be granted to a man until he be Trinity
advanced to a benefice of holy church, and the grantee ^5 Ed III
marries, the annuity is extinguished

The case has not been identified in Y B Trinity, 5 Ed III, but the Case 14
same facts and decision appear in Y B Trinity, 7 Hen IV, p 16, pl 4

In a writ, the plaintiff recovered the arrears as well pend- Note
ing the writ as before, etc [1]

[1] This statement is found in the same case

(15) **[An] annuity** granted to man of religion without a license is good, although it be forever and ever

Case 15   Reported in Y B Trinity, 7 Hen IV, p 15, pl 3   See also Fitzh Annuitie, 17

Hilary
45 Ed III

(16) **An annuity** granted *pro consilio suo, impenso et impendende,* the grantee is not bound to go to the grantor, but may advise him where he is, etc

Case 16   The case has not been identified in Y B 45 Ed III, but it is found reported at length in Y B Hilary, 41 Ed III, p 6, pl 14, and continued in Y B Mich 41 Ed III, p 19, pl 3   See also Brooke, Annuitie, 7

Paschal
19 Ed III

(17) **Annuity** lies against the heir, if he had assets by descent, and this in Annuity

Case 17   There is no early printed Year Book for 19 Ed III   The case is to be found in the Rolls Series, Y B Paschal, 19 Ed III, p 107, sec 37 See also Fitzh Annuitie, 26

Michaelis
16 Ed III

(18) **A man** shall have a writ of Annuity in whatever county he will   That is, where the writ bears date, etc (But yet it seems that it follows the person, etc.)

Case 18   There is no early printed Year Book for 16 Ed III   The case has not been identified in the Rolls Series, or in the later abridgments

Michaelis
16 Ed III

(19) **A parson** can grant an annuity without the ordinary, and this will bind his successor, if he had *"quid pro quo"*   (But this is not the law, as I believe)

Case 19   There is no early printed Year Book for 16 Ed III   The case has not been identified in the Rolls Series, Y B Mich 16 Ed III, pp 586–87, sec 90   See also Fitzh Annuitie, 24   Statham seems to have misunderstood the case, the ordinary gave his assent, but there was nothing to show the consent of the *patron*

ARBITREMENT [11]

Statham 13 a

Trinity
46 Ed III

(1) **In trespass,** the defendant said that they put themselves upon an arbitration, etc., which awarded that "if we should wage our law, that we were not guilty, etc , that then we should go quit, etc   We waged our law by our

oath, etc , wherefore they adjudged that we should go quit, etc " This was not held a plea because they did not award anything to be paid, etc. Query?

Reported in Y B Trinity, 46 Ed III, p 17, pl 14   See also Brooke, Case 1 Arbitrement, 8, and Fitzh Arbitrement, 21

(2) **If the parties** put themselves into an arbitration Hilary without a deed, they can discharge the arbitrators without 49 Ed III a deed before the day, etc., or they can put off the day by the assent of both, without a deed   But if the submission be by deed it is otherwise by FYNCHEDEN, in Debt, etc., for he should be discharged by both parties by deed, etc Query?

Reported in Y B Hilary, 49 Ed III, p 8, pl 14   See also Fitzh Case 2 Arbitrement, 22

(3) **In debt** upon arrears of an account, the defendant Paschal told how he and the plaintiff put themselves into an arbi- 1 Hen IV tration as to this debt and other transactions, etc , which awarded, etc   NEWTON   That is no plea, for our action is founded upon matter of record, etc   COTESMORE   It is not so, for the auditors are not judges except by the Statute, and that is not in point, to wit   that they could commit him to prison, and now they have not committed him to prison, and albeit the defendant cannot wage his law, still he shall plead an arbitration as well as in debt on the arrears of a lease   MARTYN   In debt on arrears on a lease it is a good plea, as you say, because that is not founded on any specialty, but in every case where the action is founded upon a specialty, as in debt on an obliga- tion, or upon matter of record as it is here, it is otherwise, etc.   Wherefore it was adjudged that the plaintiff should recover, etc.   Query, if in debt upon an obligation the defendant pleaded an arbitration and showed a deed of the plaintiff of the submission?   For that is as strong as an acquittance

The citation in Statham is probably a misprint for Paschal, 11 Hen Case 3 IV, where the first part of the case is printed on p 64, pl 17   The continuation of the case is on p 91, pl 48, in Trinity Term of the same year   The other abridgments have the same case under other heads, but not under that of arbitration

The Statute referred to is that of 5 Hen IV, cap 8. Stats at Large, Vol 2, p 449 (1403)

**Trinity
18 Hen VI**

(4) **If one pleads** an arbitrement, and shows that because of certain controversies they had put themselves into an arbitration, he should show the cause of the controversy; as to say that "the defendant was indebted to us, etc And for this reason and for other reasons there was a controversy between us," etc   By the opinion of NEWTON, in Debt, etc

Case 4

The case has not been identified in Y B Trinity, 18 Hen VI, or in the later abridgments

**Michaelis
14 Hen IV**

(5) **A man** may plead an arbitrement in bar, in an Assize of Novel Disseisin, although he show no deed of the submission; by the opinion of HANKFORD, etc., as to say that they put themselves upon the arbitration of certain persons who awarded that the plaintiff should surrender to us certain lands, etc , by force of which he surrendered, etc   But yet in that case the surrender is a good bar by itself, whether he made it by force of the arbitrement or not, etc.   In Ravishment of Wardship.

Case 5

The case has not been identified in Y B Mich 14 Hen IV, but the matter is rather meagerly stated in the last part of a case in Y B Hilary, 14 Hen IV, p 24, pl 31   It may have been taken from the original case known to Statham, as the report we have seems to refer to another case   See also Brooke, Arbitrement, 16, and Fitzh Arbitrement, 18

**Paschal
2 Hen V**

(6) **In account,** the defendant pleaded an arbitration in bar, and by advice of the justices the plea was adjudged good   And because it was uncertain, to wit. the increase, for in Debt where the demand is certain, an arbitration of that same thing by itself is no plea, unless he says that as to the debt and the other trespasses, "we put it into arbitration," that is good   Query if it be not "for trade" but only to render an account?

Case 6

The case has not been identified in Y B Paschal, 2 Hen V, or in the later abridgments

**Hilary
13 Hen IV**

(7) **In trespass,** the defendant pleaded an arbitrement, and the plaintiff said that at the time of the submission he was under age.   HANKFORD.   Inasmuch as you do not

deny that you were of full age at the time the arbitrement was made, judgment   And so to judgment, etc   And it seems that the plaintiff shall be barred because he could have discharged the said arbitrators when he came to his age.

The case has not been identified in Y B Hilary, 13 Hen IV   Brooke, **Case 7**
Arbitrement, 43, and Fitzh   Arbitrement, 4, have a case to the same
effect taken from Y B Mich 10 Hen VI, p 14, pl 46, but do not
abridge the case cited by Statham

(8)   **In detinue** for a charter concerning land in fee simple, **Hilary**
the defendant pleaded an arbitrement as to that and other **9 Hen VI.**
disputes, etc , as it would appear, inasmuch as the demand
[does not lie in] certain actions   BABYNGTON   That is no
plea in this case, for it is in a manner real   And in a writ
of Annuity arbitrement is no plea.   PASTON   A man shall
have an action of trespass on such a deed, wherefore, etc
COTESMORE   There is a difference between a deed concerning land in fee simple, and a deed concerning land in tail,
for if I have a deed concerning land in fee simple, I can give
it, and my heir shall have no action of detinue for it, it
is otherwise if it concerns land in tail

Reported in Y B Hilary, 9 Hen VI, p 60, pl 10   See also Brooke, **Case 8**
Arbitrement, 2, and Fitzh   Arbitrement, 3

See by HANKFORD that if the tenant in an assize shows **Note**
a deed indented which the plaintiff and himself have put **Michaelis**
themselves in arbitration, etc , that is a good bar in Debt, etc **11. Hen IV**

(9)   **In a writ** of Forgery of Deeds, they were at issue **Trinity**
MARKHAM. After the last continuance the plaintiff and **19 Hen VI**
defendant put themselves in the arbitrement of D and B
for all trespasses, etc , who, because the defendant had an
assize pending against the plaintiff, awarded that he should
be nonsuited in the assize, and that the plaintiff should not
sue his action further, etc , which award the defendant should
be ready to perform at the next assize, etc.   FORTESCUE
demurred to this plea and said   That is no plea, since
they have awarded that the defendant shall have a thing
for which the plaintiff cannot have an action; nor can the
arbitrators themselves, or the plaintiff, compel him to do it,

for it is for the Court to award a nonsuit, so there is no
satisfaction to the plaintiff   And also, although he be nonsuited, still he can bring a new assize, etc   NEWTON, to
the same effect   If MARKHAM owes me twenty pounds on
an obligation, and I owe him twenty pounds by contract,
and we put ourselves on an arbitration, etc , which awards
that one shall go quit as against the other, etc , that is
good, because the annulling of the debt of one is the satisfaction of the other   But when one demands a debt and
the other land, it is not so, for although he awards that
one shall enfeoff the other of the lands, and that he shall
pay him a certain sum of money, that arbitration is of no
value, because such an arbitration does not give an estate
in the land, nor can they force him to make a feoffment,
nor can I myself any more   So here   And then by
advice, etc , it was adjudged that the plaintiff should have
a writ to inquire as to the damages, etc

Case 9   Reported at length in Y B Mich (not Trinity), 19 Hen VI, p 36,
pl 80   See also Brooke, Arbitrement, 21, and Fitz Arbitrement, 6

Hilary   (10) **In trespass,** the defendant said by PORTYNGTON
20 Hen VI   That they had put themselves into the arbitration of certain persons, who awarded that the plaintiff should pay
to the defendant twenty marks, and also release to him all
actions of trespass   And afterwards the defendant should
release to the plaintiff all trespasses, which sum the
plaintiff had not paid, nor had he released, which if he
will perform we are ready to release, etc   FORTESCUE
That is no plea, for although the plaintiff shall have paid
Statham 13 b   to him [the sum awarded]. and also released, still he cannot
force the defendant to release, for he cannot have an
action to compel him, etc   In which case when he has
paid to you, you can have an action on the first trespass,
and yet he be barred of his action   Then this arbitration
is of no value, no more than if the arbitrators awarded
that the one party shall be quit against the other, and
say nothing at all as to the other being quit as to him, etc.
But yet it has been adjudged a good arbitrement that
the one shall go quit against the other, without anything
adjudged to be paid, wherefore, etc.   But, Sir, our matter

is clear, wherefore we say that "no such arbitrement,"
Ready   And the other alleged the contrary, etc

Reported in Y B Hilary, 20 Hen VI, p 18, pl 12   See also Brooke, Case 10
Arbitrement, 3, and Fitzh Arbitrement, 8

(11) **The Duke of Norfolk** brought a writ of Account Michaelis 30 Hen VI
against Sir Robert Wingfield, because he was his receiver,
etc   Who said that they put themselves into the arbitrement of certain persons for the sum aforesaid, and of all
other trespasses, providing that their award should
be given before a certain day, etc   The arbitrators
before the said day awarded that the said Sir Robert should
account for the same receipt, before such auditors as the
said arbitrators should assign, and that if it be found in
arrears before them that he should pay the same arrears
to the said duke, and *ipso facto* each of them should be
acquitted as to the other of all quarrels, etc   And that
in the meanwhile neither should implead the other for
any matter occurring before the aforesaid day of the arbitration, etc , which award he is and at all times has been
ready to perform, judgment, etc   And the duke demurred
upon the plea, and then in the Exchequer chamber, DANBY
[said] that is no plea for various reasons   For, first, that
cannot be a sufficient award, inasmuch as he does not
prove any satisfaction to him, for they have awarded
nothing to him but that which was due to him before
As, perchance, the arbitrators might say that whereas you
owe me twenty pounds, you shall pay me the same twenty
pounds, that is nothing to the purpose, for the above
reason   And also the award is uncertain, for it provides
that the defendant shall account before such auditors as
they shall assign, and it might happen that they would
never assign them   And when they are assigned, it does
not follow that he will be found in arrear, so by this award
no action is given to the duke.   And as to this that each
shall go quit against the other, that is not a good award
unless it be recited what offense one had done to the
other, and upon that it be adjudged that one shall go quit
against the other, as above   And also it appears that
this award is void, for the submission is, "provided that the

award shall be given," etc , which day is now passed, so their power to assign auditors has expired, etc POLE *Contra* As to this that you say, that there was no satisfaction, that is not so, for he was satisfied in various ways, one, that he shall pay such things as to which he was found in arrears, which was the chief cause of the controversy, etc., another, that each shall go quit against the other, for it may be that the duke has done many trespasses to him, and although they are not rehearsed, the award is not harmed And to this that you say that their power is ended, inasmuch as the day is passed, that is not so, for they may have given the same power to other persons to have auditors assigned them, consequently to themselves, etc PORTYNGTON, to the same effect For if you and I put ourselves into an arbitrement before MOILE, and when we are before him, I say that you took my horse worth one hundred shillings, and you say that he is worth only twenty shillings, and MOILE awards that if CHOKE can say that the horse is worth one hundred shillings then he will award that I shall pay you one hundred shillings, and if he says that he is worth only twenty shillings, then he will award that I shall pay you twenty shillings, that is a good award   And yet it puts the power of the award in another person, who can make an end of it after the day which is limited in the proviso, for that is only to execute the first award, and not a new award, etc FORTESCUE, to the same effect To that which is said, that it is uncertain because it may be that they will never assign auditors, suppose that they have assigned the names of the auditors immediately, still it may be that the auditors will never hear the account which is also uncertain, and yet such an award is good, and many awards are made conditionally, and yet they are good enough, etc

Case 11   Not identified in Mich 30 Hen VI   This is a very short term in the printed Year Book, with very few cases   Statham doubtless had access to a longer manuscript Year Book

Note   **See of arbitrement,** in the title of Trial, etc , Mich. 30 Hen VI

The note apparently has reference to the title of Triall in Statham's own book, but he has there no reference to any case in 30 Hen VI

(12) **Arbitrement** is a good plea in an action upon the Statute of Laborers.

Michaelis
12 Ric II

Case 12

There is no early printed Year Book for 12 Ric II The case is printed in Y B Mich 12 Ric II, p 37, Ames Foundation, ed Deiser Fitzh Arbitrement, 24, has apparently copied from Statham

(13) **Arbitrement** was held a good plea in a writ of Annuity if the submission be made by deed, etc

Michaelis
14 Hen IV

Case 13

Reported in Y B Hilary (not Mich), 14 Hen IV, p 18, pl 20 See also Brooke, Arbitrement, 15, and Fitzh Arbitrement, 25

(14) **It is a good plea** that they have put themselves upon an arbitration which is not yet made, and this in Trespass

Hilary
13 Ric II

Case 14

There is no printed Year Book for 13 Ric II Fitzh Arbitrement, 26, has nearly the same abridgment of the case

[11] That there was an early custom for litigants, or prospective litigants, to agree to arbitrate the matters in dispute between them, is shown by some very early cases Bracton [Note Book, f 649] has a case of a very early date (1231), another in 1233 [732], and another in 1224 [983], all rather uninteresting cases, which in no way indicate that there was anything novel about the proceeding These cases show us nothing in regard to the procedure at that time It was probably entirely informal, and yet it was necessary to prove the "conventione" or whatever it was by which they "put themselves upon an arbitrement " In the second case in Bracton [N B 732] (1233), one "*profert quoddam scriptum quod hoc testatur,*" and his opponent also offered another writing which showed a later agreement, changing the conditons, and the latter writing was apparently accepted The first case in Bracton [N B 649] (1231), shows both parties producing their *secta*, which proves sufficient, but the defendant produces also "*literas petentes*", they do not seem to have any effect upon his cause, however The third case is an entirely different proceeding [N B 984] in which the final agreement seems to be put into the hands of arbitrators, two of whom were justices sitting on the case

West [Symbolography, title Compromise and Arbitration, Pt 2, p 164, §21] says that an "Arbitration is an extraordinary judge, which is chosen, and hath power to judge given to him by thonly mutual consent to the end they may decide their controversies "

Kyd [Awards, p 2, 2d ed , 1799] says, "After the multiplied concerns, and the complicated rights of men, had rendered the exercise of the law a distinct profession, and courts with a regular course of proceeding were established, many reasons concurred, in many cases, to induce contending parties still to have recourse to the original mode of reference to a domestic judge chosen by their mutual consent, . accordingly we find that the title of award makes no inconsiderable figure in almost every system of law with which we are acquainted " [3, 4] The submission to an arbitrator could be without deed, as see our case 2 Bacon [Abridgment, Arbitration and Award, 204] says that at first there was no remedy to force the party to perform the award, but in the later cases an action was sustained [*Supra*, p 204, and cases there cited] The "deed" was probably the mutual bond which afterwards became usual, given by the parties to each other on conditions, to be void when the award was performed [Kyd Award, p 12] The early cases in the Note Book show us nothing of the process, except that it seemed to be a well established method of settling disputes between two persons The early history of the law of arbitrations does not seem to have greatly troubled anyone Kyd, our earliest writer on the subject, after crediting the principles of the English law to the influence of Roman law, says that it is not "easy to say at what precise period they were adopted here, or whether they were admitted at once, or by degrees, as a component part of our practical system In the most ancient repositories of the decisions of our courts [the Year Books] the greater part of them are mentioned as known and uncontroverted vested law" [*Ib* , pp 3, 4] Here is a tool of the law, a convenient and much used tool, one which in various altered forms has come down to, and become a part of, our modern law, but we have no history of its rise, its growth, its permutations and re-incarnations It is in the "most ancient repositories of our law" full-grown and attired in correct costume Of what nature was the form within the costume at the time of these our adjudged cases and earlier? It would seem that it behooves to us to know

ASSIZES [12]

Statham 14 a
Hilary
41 Ed III
(1) **In an assize** for tenements in Gloucester, the complaint was for rent The tenant pleaded "out," etc The plaintiff said "within," etc The tenant said, "To that he shall never come, for all the tenements in Gloucester are held of the king in chief," and he produced a record proving it, to wit a charter which said so And notwithstanding, the assise was awarded to inquire into it, etc

Case 1
 The case has not been identified in Y B Hilary, 41 Ed III, or in the later abridgments

Michaelis
41 Ed III
(2) **John and Alice,** his wife, brought an assize against K And it was found by verdict that one R was seised and

gave the same lands to two priests to re-enfeoff him and
A his wife in tail, the remainder to Alice, his daughter,
who is plaintiff   And then R went out of the village, and
came back four days after, by a mill which was part, etc
And he asked of the miller, "What news?"   Who said
that one of the priests was dead   And R said to his wife,
' Let us go to our own house."   And so they went there and
remained there all the night, and the next day R wrote a
charter to himself and to his wife in the tail, with the
remainder to Alice, his daughter, as above   And he went
to the other priest, who sealed it, and said, "God give you
joy of this "   And then R enfeoffed other persons in this
same land, and re-took an estate to him and to his wife in
tail, the remainder to his niece, who is now tenant in fee
And then R died and his wife remained in, and then by a
deed — which was put in evidence — she told how the
reversion was to K, and by the same deed she surrendered
her estate to her, and then died   And the plaintiff claimed
by force of the first entry, and K ousted them, and we
pray your counsel   BELKNAP   It seems that they shall be
barred, for when the miller told him that one of the priests
was dead, and he said, "Let us go," as above, and they
stayed there, that was an entry which should be understood one of two ways, one, that he entered, because
one of the priests was dead, so the other could not fulfill
the conditions, etc , or else that he entered of his own tort
And whether it be one way or the other he shall have a
fee simple, then the deed made in his possession is but a
confirmation which cannot change his estate, then the
feoffment and the retaking of the second estate was good,
and consequently the remainder is to K, who is tenant
and not to the plaintiff, etc , wherefore, etc   THORPE
Contra   For inasmuch as he came to the priest with the
deed of feoffment it proves clearly that he claimed no
estate, but renounced all estates   And it is not found
that he claimed any estate, etc   Then, when the
priest sealed the deed and he entered by force of it, that
is a good feoffment since that is found by verdict   Then
when R made the second feoffment and took an estate,

as before, the remainder to K, and then he died and his wife survived him, she shall be adjudged immediately in her better estate, and the remainder to Alice who is the plaintiff Then his surrender after to K did not change the first remainder which was once vested, wherefore we award that the plaintiff shall recover seisin of the lands, etc. (See, because it was well argued, etc) And the plaintiff prayed her damages for the issues after verdict given, inasmuch as by their verdict they said, "To the value of the land," and it is now a year since the verdict was given, etc. THORPE We will take counsel, etc.

Case 2

Reported in Y B Mich 41 Ed III, p 17, pl 2 It is a long and interesting case which is not made over-clear in the abridgment

Trinity 43 Ed III

(3) **In an assize** against several, one undertook the tenancy for all, and pleaded that such a one died seised and the lands descended to him as cousin and heir, and he showed how And the plaintiff claimed the same lands as son and heir, whereas he was a bastard, and he entered and he ousted him And the plaintiff said that he was legitimate, etc And all the others pleaded to the assise And on the next day no justice came, and on the next day after that the bishop certified that he was legitimate THORPE The writ that issued to the bishop for certification was returned on the next day, after which day no justices came, wherefore he comes now without a warranty, etc. But yet it was adjudged good And because the tenant had confessed an ouster, the plaintiff prayed seisin of the land, and release of his damages against the other FYNCHEDEN The others have pleaded to the assize and it may be that they are tenants, in which case this recovery will bind them THORPE If they are tenants and are ousted by this judgment they shall have the assize, wherefore it was adjudged that the plaintiff should recover, etc

Case 3

The case has not been identified in Y B Trinity, 43 Ed III, or in the later abridgments

Trinity 43 Ed III

(4) **In an assize** after the verdict had passed for the plaintiff, LUDDINGTON demanded the tenant BELKNAP: He is not demandable. LUDDINGTON He is so, for he

can plead the release of the plaintiff made after the verdict
BELKNAP That is not so, for if it were so his plea would
be tried by the assize, who are discharged, etc And if
the plaintiff sues execution against such a release, the
tenant shall have an assize   Query, etc ?

The case has not been identified in Y B 43 Ed III, or in the later Case 4
abridgments

(5) **In an assize** the tenant said that the panel was not Michaelis
arraigned for four days before the assize as the Statute
says. THORPE That is only a penalty for the sheriff
which shall be levied by suit, wherefore he had the assize
sworn, etc.

The case has not been identified in Y B Mich 43 Ed III, or in the Case 5.
later abridgments

The Statute is that of 13 Ed III (1285), cap 30, Stats at Large,
Vol 1, p 203 (4)

(6) **In an assize** for lands in S, the tenant said that he Hilary
brought the assize against the plaintiff for tenements in B, 44 Ed III.
within the same county, and he showed that the lands which
were now put in view were then put in view, and he recovered judgment, etc And the plaintiff demanded judgment because they were in another vill And it was not
allowed Wherefore he said, "Not put in view, so not
comprised," and the other alleged the contrary And the
plaintiff prayed a process against the first jurors and had
it, notwithstanding he had a process against them in
another assize for this same land, to which the sheriff
returned that they were dead But in that case he was
nonsuited; thus nothing done pending the writ should
conclude him

Reported in Y B Mich (not Hilary), 44 Ed III, p 45, pl 60 See Case 6
also Brooke, Assize, 28, and Fitzh Assize, 55 The references to
Fitzherbert in Brooke appear to be erroneous Statham's abridgment
of this case is not complete

(7) **A prior** brought an assize and made complaint as to Hilary
profits à *prendre*, that is tithes parted from all kinds of 44 Ed III
growing grain in ten acres of meadow mowed, and this
after the tithes were assigned to the parson and delivered.

And judgment was asked inasmuch as the plaintiff was a man of religion, so the law assumes tithes, judgment if the Court will take jurisdiction   And the plaintiff said that one B was parson, etc , and he was seised of the tithes, and we and our predecessors have been seised of the tithes parted as above, that is, after the tithes are delivered to the parson   And then the assize was awarded

Case 7

The case has not been identified in Y B Hilary, 44 Ed III, but may be the case reported in Y B Mich 42 Ed III, p 25, pl 9, although some points in the reported case and the abridgment are not identical This, however, is often the case when the report is fully identified

Paschal 43 Ed III

(8) **If the** tenant pleads a plea in bar and the plaintiff makes title to himself, traversing the bar, although it be that the title of the plaintiff was false, still the tenant shall not have the advantage of praying the assize upon the title, but he will be driven to maintain his bar, etc It is otherwise where the plaintiff himself makes title to himself and does not answer the bar   And this in an Assize, etc

Case 8

The case has not been identified in Y B Paschal, 43 Ed III, or in the later abridgments

Statham 14 b
Paschal 44 Ed III

(9) **See an assize** against one under age, who pleaded a plea upon which they were adjourned, and after the adjournment he would have enforced his bar.   And the opinion clearly was that he could not get to that   But the opinion of THORPE and FYNCHEDEN was that the Assize should inquire as to that matter by which he would have enforced his bar, because he was under age.

Case 9

Reported in Y B Paschal, 44 Ed III, p 10, pl 11. See also Brooke, Assize, 21, and Fitzh Assize, 56

Trinity 44 Ed III

(10) **In an assize** against two, one pleaded a release of the plaintiff, and the other pleaded joint tenancy of him who pleaded the release with one who was not named, etc. The assize was taken, which said that he held jointly as above, and that the release was not the deed of the plaintiff, for the plaintiff said that it was not his deed   And then the plaintiff prayed seisin of the land for the part, etc , but could not have it. But the whole writ was

abated because one who was tenant *"per me et per tout"* was not named, etc

Reported in Y B Trinity, 44 Ed III, p 22, pl 28   See also Brooke, Case 10. Assize, 23

(11) **In an assize** against a husband and his wife, who pleaded a plea in bar and confessed an ouster, the plaintiff traversed the bar, and then the husband made default, and the wife was received and pleaded the same plea, and it was found for the plaintiff   But it was found that there was no disseisor named in the writ, and the opinion was that the writ should abate because the husband was out of Court and a *feme covert* could not be a disseissor by her plea, albeit she was received as a *feme sole*, etc

Trinity 44 Ed III

Reported in Y B Trinity, 44 Ed III, p 23, pl 29   See also Brooke, Case 11 Assize, 24, and Fitzh   Assize, 58

(12) **In an assize** against two, one pleaded joint tenure by deed with a stranger, the other pleaded in bar   And the plaintiff said that he who pleaded in bar was tenant And to the plea pleaded by the other "no law" [compelled him to answer]   And the assize was taken and said that he who pleaded joint tenure was tenant, without inquiring anything as to the joint tenure   THORPE: It seems that the writ should abate, because the plaintiff has badly chosen his tenant, so the joint tenancy is not denied by the plaintiff   FYNCHEDEN   It seems not, since such a dilatory plea is not so peremptory as if he had pleaded a plea in bar to which the tenant must answer   But it seems that process shall issue by the Statute, etc   Upon which it was asked of the plaintiff if he would reply to the joint tenure, who said "no," whereupon the writ was abated But formerly they would have awarded process upon the Statute, etc., in which case the assize would have been twice awarded, etc

Trinity 44 Ed III

Reported in Y B Trinity, 44 Ed III, p 23, pl 30   See also Brooke, Case 12 Assize, 25, and Fitzh   Assize, 59

The Statute is that of *De Conjunctim Feoffatis*, 34 Ed I, Stat 1, Stats at Large, Vol 1, p 313 (1306)

(13) **In an assize upon a rent charge** it is a good plea to say that the tenant of part of the land of which, etc , is not named, but it is no plea in a rent service, etc   But in neither case is it a plea if he be parcener of the rent named in the writ, for a parcener shall plead in bar for both rents, and not the tenant, although the tenant be named, etc   And the law is the same in an assize for estovers, and other profits à *prendre,* if parceners of the same profits are named they shall plead in bar and not the tenant of the soil.

And see in the same plea, that if a man plead in bar in an assize of rent and gives color to the plaintiff by the grant of a reversion where the tenant did not attorn, and that after the death of the tenant the plaintiff came upon the land and took distress as above, etc.   Query, if it be color to say that the plaintiff claimed by deed or grant of the reversion, where nothing passed by the deed, etc ?

Case 13   The case has not been identified in Y. B Trinity, 44 Ed III, or in the early abridgments

(14) **Assize** against one A and others, and it was found that A was tenant although he had named no disseisor, etc , wherefore the writ was abated, and then he brought another writ against A and others, and A pleaded in bar because he was formerly acquitted of the disseisin, and upon that they adjourned, etc

Case 14   The case has not been identified in Y B Mich 46 Ed III, or in the early abridgments

(15) **In an assize** for estovers the plaintiff made his complaint, and rehearsed the substance of the deed by which he had the estovers, in his complaint, as he ought, etc   And the defendant asked what he had to show for the estovers   And because the assize was brought against two it was the opinion he should not have the plea, unless he answered as tenant, for a disseisor shall not have this plea, no more than he shall plead "out of his fee," etc   Wherefore he took the tenancy, and said (as above), etc   And the plaintiff showed a deed.   And then the tenant would have pleaded in abatement of the writ and could

not, because that plea that he had pleaded before was a plea in bar, etc , wherefore it was said that he should not plead anything to the writ, except such matter as appeared, etc   And see this [case] for the plaintiff showed a deed of the Bishop of Coventry and Lichfield, predecessor of the defendant, for his title, and he showed a ratification by the Prior and Chapter of Coventry.   And because the bishop was chosen by the Dean and Chapter of Coventry as well as by the Dean and Chapter of Lichfield, it was the opinion that his title was of no value, etc

The case has not been identified in Y B Hilary, 50 Ed III, or in Case 15 the early abridgments

(16) **In an assize** the tenant pleaded a release from the Trinity plaintiff of all his right, etc   The plaintiff showed a 30 Ed III defeasance that, if he would pay certain monies on a certain day and certain place to the defendant, then, etc And he showed how he paid the monies to the defendant at another place where the defendant received them, etc And the defendant demurred upon the plea, inasmuch as the payment was at another place   And because the tenant had received them, be it at one place or another, that would not change the case, wherefore the assize was awarded in right of the damages   And query as to this, inasmuch as no ouster was confessed in the bar, etc And SHARSHULL also noted a difference where the plaintiff demurs on the plea at bar, and where the tenant demurs upon the title (which I do not understand, etc)

Unless this is the case in Y B Mich 30 Ed III, p 12, pl 10, abridged Case 16 by Fitzherbert, Assize, 100, it has not been identified   It is a very poorly reported case in the printed Year Book of 30 Ed III

(17) **In an assize** the tenant pleaded the deed of the Trinity ancestor of the plaintiff, with warranty, in bar   The 31 Ed III plaintiff said that he was a bastard, and the next day the tenant pleaded to the assize by bailiff, and to this he was received, etc

There is no printed Year Book for 31 Ed III   There is a case very Case 17 like the case abridged in the Rolls Series, 14 Ed III, Easter Term, pp 48–62

Paschal
14 Ed III

(18) **In an assize** it is no plea to say that the plaintiff has another assize pending against him for the same lands, unless he has appeared [in that assize], and the plaintiff has made his complaint etc

Case 18

There is no early printed Year Book for 14 Ed III   The case has not been identified in the Rolls Series

Trinity
19 Ed III

(19) **A man can** distrain the tenant for rent for his disseisin, because he raised the rent of his tenants by coercion of distress   But if the tenant pays him the rent of his free will, that shall not be understood to be the rent which I should have had, but another rent, for by such a payment I shall have the assize, etc.

Case 19

There is no early printed year for 19 Ed III   The case has not been identified in the Rolls Series

Statham 15 a

Paschal
21 Ed III

(20) **In an assize** certain persons were summoned who were not empanelled, and they showed this to the Court, upon which the sheriff was amerced, but yet the Court empanelled them and had them sworn, etc.

Case 20

The case has not been identified in Year Book 21 Ed III, or in the early abridgments.

Paschal
18 Ed III

(21) **In an assize** the tenant pleaded the deed of the ancestor of the plaintiff, with warranty   The plaintiff said that a long time after this, etc , this same ancestor was seised and died seised, and the tenant demurred upon the plea, inasmuch as he did not show how this ancestor came to the land after the release, etc   THORPE awarded the assize, but he said that if the title had been traversed, and the assize found the title to be true, they should not inquire as to the disseisin, as they would where the bar is traversed, etc   With which WILLOUGHBY concurred (But yet the law is not so, as I believe, for if the bar or the title be traversed on any point, if no ouster be in the bar, they shall not inquire as to the disseisin, etc)

Case 21

Reported in Y B Paschal, 18 Ed III, p 13, pl 8.

Michaelis
24 Ed III

(22) **In replevin** the defendant had returned, "irrepleviable," and the opinion of WILLOUGHBY and SHARSHULL was that he should not have the assize by reason of that return unless he had possession of the rent in fact

Case 22

Reported in Y. B Mich. 24 Ed III, p 33, pl 22.

(23) **In an assize** against an infant under age and two Paschal
others of full age, each one took the tenancy severally and 3 Hen IV
pleaded in bar   The plaintiff said that he who was under
age was his tenant, and he made title to himself and traversed his bar, and as to the pleas pleaded by the others,
"no law"   And the justices commanded the jurors first
to inquire which of them was tenant, who said that the
infant was tenant the day the writ was purchased, and
besides this they found the title for the plaintiff   And the
justices inquired who were the disseisors, and they said
that the two disseised the plaintiff, to the use of him who
was under age, and that he was, at the time of the disseisin, of the age of two years, and that he was still under
age   And upon this the justices awarded that the plaintiff should recover seisin of the land   And in this they
erred, inasmuch as they should have barred the plaintiff,
because the disseisin by the two to his use could not
give him possession or title while he was under age, etc
But yet it was said that they should inquire as far as
necessary upon this point, etc   Well debated, etc   Query?

Reported in Y B Paschal, 3 Hen IV, p 16, pl 12   See also Brooke, Case 23
Assize, 46

(24) **"Never attached"** is no plea where the franchise Trinity
was granted, etc   In an assize, etc   6 Ric II

There is no printed Year Book for Ric II   The case has not been Case 24
identified in the early abridgments

(25) **"Never attached** for fifteen days"** was tried by the Trinity
bailiff who made the attachment, by examination, etc   6 Ric II
And it was found against the tenant, and yet the tenant
pleaded in bar, etc   But where "never attached" is tried
by the *assize* and found against the tenant it is otherwise,
etc   And where the tenant says "never attached," the
plaintiff should show by whom the attachment was made,
in the same plea, etc   (And all the same "never attached"
generally is no plea, because it is contrary to the return of
the sheriff, etc.)

There is no printed Year Book for Ric II   The case is abridged by Case 25
Fitzh Assize, 452

Paschal
49 Ed III

(26) **If rent** descend to me after the death of my father, and before the day for the payment of the rent the tenant puts me in seisin by [payment of] an ox, that seisin is not sufficient to have the assize   But if he pays me one penny as part of my rent, although it be before the day the rent is due, on that possession I shall have the assize.   But if I recover rent, and before the day of payment the sheriff puts me in seisin of the rent by an ox, for that possession I shall have the assize   By THORPE, in the same plea, etc   And it was said that if he held of me by fealty and rent, and although he performs the fealty, that does not put me in possession so that I can have the assize for the rent, nor enable me to make an avowry, etc.   Well debated, etc   But in all the cases before mentioned such seisin is sufficient to enable me to maintain an avowry, etc.   Query?

Case 26

The case may be that in Paschal, 49 Ed III, p 15, pl 9   The same matters are discussed in the long debate, but they are not put as Statham puts them   They come as *dicta* and could hardly substantiate the points made by Statham

Note

(27) **Note that a good point** in an assize for rent is to compel the plaintiff to make title and not to plead "out of his fee," for then the plaintiff will say "within his fee," and not show title, but he shall have the assize, and he will say in that, that the land of which, etc , was one carucate of land for which he answers as tenant, and that he granted to the plaintiff an annual rent issuing from it for the term of the life of one A, which A is dead, and he can show such a one, who is dead in fact, in which case the plaintiff shall be entitled to all.   Note well, for this case is of great value

Case 27.

This is apparently merely a note from the notebook of the reporter   Whoever he may have been he is noting a valuable point in practice

Trinity
8 Ed III.

(28) **If he who is in** the reversion is received in an assize because he was named, etc , he can plead that the plaintiff had a writ of a higher nature pending against his tenant for life, who made default, albeit he was a stranger to that. And because the plaintiff recovered by the first writ, his right is gone.

And it was said by HERLE, in the same plea, that if he who is in the reversion be named in the assize, that if the tenant for life will plead to the assize, or another plea which is not good, he who is in the reversion may plead in bar well enough, etc. Yet I believe that this is not law, for then the Statute of Richard, which gave the recovery upon a feigned plea, did not need to be made, and yet this case of an assize differs from other writs in regard to that evil, therefore, query, etc., for if the law be so there is no need that he who is in the reversion shall be received upon a feigned plea, where he is not named, etc. Query, if he will be received upon a feigned plea where he is not named, when he would not have been received upon default of his tenant for life, in an assize, unless he be named in the assize?

The case has not been identified in Y B 8 Ed III, or in the early abridgments   Case 28

(29) **In an assize** for a rent service, if the tenant for part of the land be not named, that shall not abate the writ, except for the part. It is otherwise in a rent charge, unless parceners of the rent are named And it was said in the same plea, that if there are no takers of the rent who are not named, the writ shall abate for so much Query, if such an exception lies in the mouth of him who is not tenant, etc And it was said in the same plea that the assize is properly brought against the parcener, leaving out the tenant, as well for a rent charge as for a rent service Query, if the law be thus for a rent seck? etc   Trinity 33 Ed III

And it was said by SHARSHULL, in the same plea, if the husband and his wife purchase jointly, and the husband alienates all and dies, she shall have the assize for all, etc (which I do not believe, etc.).

There is no printed Year Book for 33 Ed III   Case 29

(30) **In an assize** against one who pleaded "nul tort," the assize found that he disseised the plaintiff, but he said that he held the land jointly with one who was not named, wherefore it was adjudged that the writ should abate, etc.   Hilary 33 Ed III

From this it follows that the assize can inquire *ex officio* of such matters, etc.

Case 30   There is no printed Year Book for 33 of Ed III

Hilary
1 Hen VI

(31) **An assize** was brought in the King's Bench; and it was returnable "15 of the same," and because no certain day was given the writ was abated, etc.

Case 31   The case has not been identified in the short report of Y B Mich 1 Hen VI   There is no other term in the printed Year Book

Hilary
1 Hen VI

(32) **In an assize** the tenant pleaded joint tenure with one A, of the feoffment of one B   ROLFF   We were seised until disseised by the tenant, upon whom B entered and enfeoffed them, and we entered and were seised until disseised by you alone.   ASKAM   To the plea pleaded in the

Statham 15 b   manner   And so to judgment   CHEYNE   The plea is good   And if we award the assize it will be awarded in right of the damages, because the plaintiff has alleged an ouster in fact of the tenant, which he has not denied, etc. With which the COURT concurred

And so see where the tenant traversed the title, or demurred in law upon the title, and it was found, or adjudged, for the plaintiff, that he shall have the assize in right of the damages, etc., because when it is found for the plaintiff, it shall be held as admitted by the defendant, etc

Case 32   The case has not been identified in Y. B 1 Hen VI

Hilary
10 Hen IV

(33) **A man** was seised of land in the right of his wife, and the land was recovered against him alone.   And it was said that after his death his wife should have the assize. by HANKFORD, in an Assize, etc   But yet this is a hard case [to depend on] for the reason that her husband was never disseised. therefore the wife was not, no more than if the husband had made a feoffment, etc

Case 33   The case has not been identified in the short Hilary Term of Y B 10 Hen IV

Paschal
33 Ed III

(34) **In an assize** the patent shall be awarded to the plaintiff, but as soon as the record is engrossed he shall deliver his patent to the clerk of the assize, for otherwise he will have no warranty, etc

Case 34.   There is no printed Year of 33 Ed III

(35) **In an assize** the tenant said that he was not attached for fifteen days. And the bailiff who made the attachment was not present, wherefore WILLOUGHBY awarded the assize to inquire of it (And so see that an assize can be twice awarded)

And see in the title of Aide de Roy, Hilary, 12 Hen VI, an assize can be three or four times awarded, and *contra* in the [title of] Trial, Hilary, 50 Ed III Query as to this?

Statham gives no citation for this case, neither is there any citation Case 35 of Hilary, 12 Hen VI, in his title of Aide de Roy, or to 50 Ed III, in the title of Triall Apparently the compiler had notes not incorporated in the printed text

(36) **In an assize** if the tenant pleads a plea in bar that Michaelis is triable by the assize, he shall not say "which matter he 30 Hen VI is ready to aver," etc But if he pleads a foreign plea, or matter of record which is not traversable by the assize, it is otherwise, as I believe, etc By FORTESCUE, in the assize of Wenlock

The case has not been identified in the very short term of Michaelmas Case 36 in the printed Year Book of 30 Hen VI, or in the later abridgments There is but one case of an assize reported for this year and term Brooke and Fitzherbert both cite that case, but do not cite the case abridged by Statham

(37) **In an assize** against three, one pleaded to the assize, Michaelis and two pleaded a release of all actions The plaintiff 1 Hen V said he was seised until disseised by the three, to the use of him who had pleaded to the assize, and he took the profits of this land And many feoffments had been made which he did not acknowledge, and as to the plea pleaded by them, "no law," etc. And upon this the assize was adjourned, and it was adjudged that the plaintiff should not take anything by his writ, for HULS said that if there was anyone within the writ who pleaded in bar, or to the writ, the plaintiff ought to answer him, he was not in the case of the Statute when there was a tenant in the writ who pleaded in bar, etc (I believe that it was his folly to name the two in the writ, unless he would aver that all three were parceners of the profits, for the third, to whose use the disseisin was made, was a disseisor, and

the writ had been well brought against him, etc.) And see also that a disseisor can plead such a release of all actions to excuse himself from damages

And it was said in the same plea that the Statute is to be understood as well as applying to joint as non-tenancy, etc And also, since neither of the two pleaded in abatement of the writ, as to say that there was no tenant of the freehold named in the writ, it seems he should not take advantage of the Statute, since the Statute is not meant to apply except where he cannot have a good writ, because he does not acknowledge his tenant, etc   Query?

Case 37   Reported in Y B Paschal (not Mich), 1 Hen V, p 4, pl 4   See also Brooke, Assize, 403, and Fitzh Assize, 41   The Statute is West II, 13 Ed III, cap 25 (1285)   Stats at Large, vol. 1, p 163 (198)

Michaelis 8 Hen VI   (38) **In an assize** for tenements in Dale and Dover, etc , the tenant said that the tenements were in Dover, etc   And upon that plea the assize was adjourned   RADFORD · It seems that the plea is of no value, for although none of the tenements are in Dale, yet he should answer over for the tenements in Dover, so his plea does not go to the assize as to any tenements in Dale, but if he will say that part of the tenements are in another vill that will go in abatement of the writ, for then the writ does not give any warrant to the Court to hold the plea in another vill which is not named, etc , but in this case it is only a safeguarding, wherefore, etc.   MARTYN   In an assize for tenements in two vills and the plaintiff abridged his complaint for all that which was in one vill, the writ was abated   So here   And then the plaintiff was nonsuited.   Query, if it be a plea if the plaintiff shall be forced to answer it?   Or if it does not go to the assize, etc?   And it seems it shall be inquired into, for if all the tenements are in the one vill it is not reasonable that the people of the other vill, which shall be understood to have another venue, shall try this, but the writ should abate, for otherwise the plaintiff could put many vills in the writ with the intent to have the venue at his will, which is not reasonable.

Case 38   Reported in Y B Mich 8 Hen VI, p 12, pl 31   The principal case is given by the citators as on p 9, pl 17, but only a few lines are

there reported   See Fitzh   Assize, 4   "Dale and Dover   become
magna and *parva* Dunmore in the report   These changes of proper
names are very frequent   It seems of no use to note them in each case
as they are of value as to the point of law   The names would doubtless be changed again in the Rolls

(39) **In an assize** the tenant said that one A was seised,   Hilary
etc , and held of him, etc , and A was outlawed for felony,   11 Hen II
and after the year the defendant entered as in his escheat,
and the plaintiff, claiming as sister and heir, entered, upon
which, etc   And the [plaintiff] demurred upon the plea
inasmuch as the plaintiff had no color of claim during the
natural life of A, etc

 The case has not been identified   The citation in Statham is to   Case 39
Hilary, 11 Hen II, which is probably a misprint, possibly for 11 Hen
IV, or VI, but the case has not been found in Hilary Term for the year
eleven of either of those reigns

(40) **In an assize** by a man and his wife, the tenant said   Michaelis
that the uncle of his wife enfeoffed one B, and died, and   11 Hen IV
you, alleging that this uncle had died seised, entered and B
ousted you and enfeoffed us   CHEYNE   He does not give
any color to the plaintiff, for his ancestor could not enter
against his feoffment   HANKFORD   He has admitted possession in your ancestor, and it is a good plea to say that the
ancestor of the plaintiff disseised the tenant, upon whom
a stranger entered, upon whom the tenant entered, and
the plaintiff as heir entered, and the tenant ousted him.
TYRWHIT   There the possession of the ancestor was not
defeated by his deed   GASCOIGNE and HULS held the
plea good, and the others did not   But yet the plaintiff
made title, etc.   But if the tenant had shown that the
feoffee had suffered the ancestor of the plaintiff to occupy
at his will and died, and the plaintiff had alleged [it], the
plea had been good without question, etc.   And so see
here that this plea is a bar against both the plaintiffs,
because it will be understood *prima facie* that the land
is in right of the woman plaintiff, etc.

 Reported in Y B Mich 11 Hen IV, p 2, pl 6   See Fitzh   Assize,   Case 40
46. A very poor abridgment of the case

Michaelis
9 Hen IV

(41) In an assize if the tenant says that he was not attached for fifteen days, if the bailiff who made the attachment is not present they will not inquire into it, for they will not award the assize upon that point, etc

Case 41

The point abridged is to be found at the end of the case reported in Y B Mich 9 Hen IV, p 1, pl 6   See also Brooke, Assize, 53

Anno
26 Hen VI

(42) In an assize held in York, the bailiffs of a franchise asked as to their jurisdiction, and the plaintiff said that the land was out of their franchise, etc   And the justices said to the tenant that he should keep to one part or the other, and so he did, and he pleaded in bar immediately, and when they were at the assize they inquired first if the lands were within the franchise, etc   Query, if the plaintiff had demurred in law upon the bar, etc , and if the tenant had demurred upon the title, etc , what would have been done?

And in the same year, in an assize in Southwark, the jurors were examined as to the view, and they had not had the view, wherefore a day was given to have the view, but the tenant was driven to plead in bar immediately. And the law is the same where the assize remains for default of the jurors, etc , and the tenant appears by guardian, and they will not admit his appearance unless he comes in his own person   It is otherwise in other actions than an assize

Case 42

The case has not been identified in Anno 26 Hen VI, or in the early abridgments

Note

See as to assize, in the title of Repleader, Mich 30 Hen VI [1]   In the assize of Wenlock, how there could be a jeofail in an assize, etc   And see of assize in the title of Plaint and also in the title of Title, many matters

Statham 16 a
Paschal
9 Ed III

(43) The bailiff said that the lands were ancient demesne, and he had the plea, but not to such an effect that the plaintiff should answer it, but to the effect that the assize should inquire as to it, etc   (But yet it seems that it is not triable by the assize)

Case 43

Reported in Y B Paschal, 9 Ed III, p 13, pl 14.

[1] See *infra*, Repleder, p 153 b, Case 6   Title of Pleynt, p 143 a   Title of Title, *infra*, pp 174 a to 175 b

(44) **An assize** of rent was taken by default, and the
assize said that the plaintiff was seised and disseised; for
they said that the plaintiff distrained and the defendant
sued a replevin, and it was a rent charge   And upon that
the plaintiff recovered before COKAYN and STRANGE, at
Warwick, etc.

There is no printed Year Book for 6 Hen VI   Case 44

(45) **A man** shall have an assize for a rent charge *in*
confinis comitatus, but he shall [not] distrain, for the assize
in confinis comitatus is not given except at common law
As appeared in an assize, by the opinion of the COURT
(But yet it is given by the Statute of Ric Anno VII)

The case has not been identified in Y B 22 Ed III, or in the early Case 45
abridgments, although Paschal, 22 Ed III, p 4, pl 7, or Mich 22
Ed III, p 12, pl 20, might, if we had a better report, prove to be the
case abridged here

The note is apparently made by a reporter — Statham or another —
who forgets that the case was decided before the date of the Statute of
7 Ric II   See Stats at Large, Vol 2, p 267, cap 10 (1383)

(46) **If the king** grants my land by patent to another who
enters by force of that grant, I shall have an assize against
him   By the opinion of the COURT in an assize in the
Common Bench, etc.

There is no printed Year Book for 20 Ric II   See Fitzh Assize, Case 46
467, where much there is the same abridgment of the case   He
refers to the "Statute of Hen IV " See 1 Hen IV, cap 8, Stats
at Large, Vol 2, p 391 (1399), which covers the point in the case,
but is later than the case digested

(47) **If the plaintiff** cannot show his patent, in an assize,
still the justices will call the jurors, and if it remains
for default of the jurors, they will give a day to them until
the next assize, for if he brings his patent before the assize
be awarded it is time enough   And so HANKFORD said
twice at Exeter, etc

The case may be that in Y B Mich 13 Hen IV, p 10, pl 31, Case 47
although it cannot be fully identified Fitzh Assize, 155, has a long
abridgment of the case

(48) **In an assize** against several, if one answers as tenant
and pleads a plea in bar, and the others plead in abate-

ment of the writ, the pleas in abatement of the writ shall
not be inquired into   By the opinion of HANKFORD, at
the assizes at Southwark, etc

Case 48   The case has not been identified in Y B 8 Hen VI, or in the later
abridgments

Anno
26 Hen VI   (49) **The tenant** in an assize said, "Not attached for
fifteen days " And the Court demanded of the plaintiff
who made the attachment   And the plaintiff replied, one
such, his servant   And he was demanded and he did not
come, whereupon a new attachment was awarded, without
any inquiry into this by the assize, because it was the folly
of the plaintiff that he did not bring him with him   But
it were otherwise if the bailiff had wrongly made the attachment, and had been demanded and had not come, the
assize should have inquired as to that   By the opinion of
NEWTON, in the same plea, and this he took for a diversity,
etc , at the assizes at Exeter   And he also said that if
the servant of the plaintiff, who made the attachment, had
been present he would have examined the sheriff as to
whether he gave him a warrant to make the attachment or
not

Case 49   There is no 26 Hen VI in the printed Year Books   Brooke, Attachment in Assize, 1, gives the case as in 27 Hen VI (Mich 27 Hen VI, p 2
pl 18), although the facts are different from those given by Statham
See also Fitzh Assize, 14, who gives both citations

[12] To speak of the Assize generally, even in the manner of a digest,
would be an absurdity in a short note   The learning in regard to the
Assize is voluminous and accessible in the books on the history of the
English law   To say that it is all to be found within the compass of
any one work would be greatly to exaggerate, that comprehensive
task is yet to be undertaken   Our abridgment, in its reported cases,
does not in any way cover the field, does not even give us what might be
called representative cases   Statham abridges twenty-nine cases,
Fitzherbert, finding the title ready made, expanded the twenty-nine
cases into four hundred and seventy-two, and might have gone on and
on   Brooke went a little further with an exact five hundred cases,
probably because he found it time to stop, not because he had exhausted
his cases   Exactly why Statham chose the cases he did from the super-
abundant material at his command does not clearly appear in the cases
themselves   They appear to be of the ordinary type, and there are
hundreds like them in the books   We have in case 2, however, one of

the most picturesque and interesting cases within the whole compass
of the Year Books   As an example of the Assize, or as authority upon
the law of the Assize, it does not appear remarkable, but as a picture
of the period it is invaluable   It is probable that Statham had very
little to do with Assizes, his own career appears to have been that
of the student and of the scholar, first the acquiring of the law,
and then the imparting of that which he had acquired, all within the
cloistered spaces of the Inns of Court   One almost feels sure that it
was the story of this case that appealed to him, the vivid human
nature of it, even perhaps the literary quality of it.   Yet this may be
an entire misjudgment, it may be that the legal principles involved
were in some way peculiarly those which he wished to inculcate, to
set before those who would use his book   Some day it may be that we
shall be able to take his book and find from it just what were the most
needed doctrines in the practice and the teaching of the law of his time
It would be a most interesting task

ASSIGNE [13]

(1)   **A man** vouched one to warranty as assignee, without Paschal
40 Ed III
showing what he had for the assignment, for it could be
assigned without a deed, but he ought to show the first
deed in the warranty was to be taken for all   And this by
the opinion of THORPE and FYNCHEDEN   And he who
vouched in this case was the heir of the assignee   (So
see that the [heir of the assignee] shall have the voucher.)

Reported in Y B Paschal, 40 Ed III, p 22, pl 22   There is an Case 1
apparent misprint in the case which makes BELKNAP show a deed,
and the index gives the point in that way, thus making the case contradict Statham   The error in the text is obvious, however

(2)   **A man** brought a writ of Annuity as assignee, and Michaelis
41 Ed III
this was adjudged good, which note.

Reported in Y B Mich 41 Ed III, p 27, pl 24 Case 2

(3)   **It was found** at Exeter, before NEWTON, that one Anno
26 Hen VI
had leased land for a term of life, rendering a certain rent,
and for default of payment it well belonged to him and

to his heirs and assigns to enter; and that afterwards
the feoffor granted the reversion to one B, and the tenant
attorned And for the rent in arrear after the attornment, B entered, and the other brought the assize And
the opinion of NEWTON clearly was that his entry was not
lawful, etc.

Case 3   The case has not been identified in Y B 26 Hen VI

Hilary
36 Ed III   (4) **A man** shall have Warranty of Charter By the
opinion of THORPE and FYNCHEDEN, as assignee, if he has
a deed, etc In a writ of Warranty of Charter, etc, by
NEWTON, the contrary was held, and by ASCOUGH in a
writ of Covenant Hilary, 26 Hen VI

Case 4   There is no printed Year Book for the year 36 Ed III

[13] Little as we have in regard to the assignee in this collection, it had
very recently become possible to make a gift to a donee and his heirs
and assigns [P & M Hist of Eng Law, 2d ed, Vol 2, p 14.]

Bracton speaks of assignments [Bracton, f 176] of lands *De Legibus
Ang* Maitland gives the appearance of the word in the charters as
soon after the year 1200 [P & M Hist of Eng Law, 2d ed, Vol 2, p 14]
From that time forward it seems to have had its settled place in the law
Britton [f 122] says that it "was in favor of bastards that the word
assigns was first devised to be inserted in feoffments," and Cowell adds
[Cowell Assigne] "because they cannot pass under the name of heirs,
and therefore were and are comprised under the name of assignees"

ATTACHEMENT

Michaelis
21 Hen VI   (1) **A man** shall be attached for goods which are in his
possession, albeit the property in them is in another person By the opinion of NEWTON, in Trespass Query?
For if he did not come on the day of the attachment,
the attachment would be forfeited And if one borrows
my horse and he is arrested for his debt, it is not reasonable that I lose my horse.

Case 1   The case has not been identified in Y B Mich 21 Hen VI

(2) **A feme covert** shall be attached for the goods of Hilary 7 Hen VI her husband. And this in an Assize, etc.

Reported in Y B Mich (not Hilary), 7 Hen VI, p 9, pl 15 See Case 2 also Brooke, Attachment in Assize, 4

See of Attachment, in the title of Assizes [1]   Note

(3) **Attachment** upon a prohibition or attachment which Michaelis 30 Hen VI issues upon an action for contempt, shall be always for the body, etc., upon which no distress follows, but attachment *infinite* And there is such process in the Exchequer in debt, etc Yet in any attachment upon a rescous, it is by the body, etc

The case has not been identified in Y B Mich 30 Hen VI Fitzh Statham 16 b. has not the title, or Brooke the case

ATTEINT [14]

(1) **An attaint was maintained** where the greater Hilary 2 Hen IV part of the petty jury were dead

Reported in Y B Paschal (not Hilary), 2 Hen IV, p 18, pl. 5 The Case 1 case gives a citation to 6 Ric II, *contra* See also Brooke, Attaint, 23

(2) **Attaint** was brought by two, one appeared by guar- Hilary 41 Ed III dian, who said that he would not sue, wherefore he was non-suited, and the other put to sue alone, etc And because he who would not sue was under age he was not imprisoned, etc. Query, if the jury were attainted would the infant be restored, for when he came of age he could not have the attaint, for the jury cannot be twice attainted

The case has not been identified in Y B Hilary, 41 Ed III, or in the Case 2 later abridgments

(3) **The king** brought attaint and the writ was adjudged Hilary 42 Ed III good

Very short report in Y B Mich (not Hilary), 42 Ed III, p 26, Case 3 pl 14 See also Brooke, Attaint, 15, and Fitzh Attaint, 18

[1] Note to case 2

Paschal
42 Ed III

(4) **See** the judgment and the execution in attaint, and that well expressed, in Attaint

Case 4

Reported in Y B Mich (not Paschal), 42 Ed III, p 26, pl 13

Hilary
19 Ed III

(5) **An attaint** was brought in between the day of *Nisi Prius* and the day in the Bench, and for this reason it was abated, etc

Case 5

There is no early printed year of 19 Ed III   The case has not been identified in Y B Hilary, 19 Ed III, of the Rolls Series

Hilary
21 Ed III

(6) **Attaint** was brought for a false oath given in the Court at Oxford in an assize of fresh force, and the plaintiff had caused the record to be brought into the Common Bench by a writ out of the Chancery, and it was challenged because an attaint should be brought in the same place as that where the verdict passed, etc   SHARSHULL. Inasmuch as the record is here you shall sue the attaint here And then the tenant said that he was not tenant of the part, etc.   FYNCHEDEN: We pray a jury for the remainder DARR   That exception goes to the whole, wherefore answer, etc   Whereupon he said that he was tenant of the whole, etc   And this was tried by twelve at the *Nisi Prius*

Case 6

Reported in Y B Hilary, 21 Ed III, p 10, pl 32   See also Brooke, Attaint, 32

Anno
21 *Liber Assisarum*

(7) **In attaint** in a personal action the sheriff returned "*nihil*" to the summons, and the plaintiff prayed a jury, for one shall not have a re-summons unless the first be sued.   STONORE   You shall not have the jury, for you can have a summons in another county upon a *testatum est.* And so he had it, etc.   Query?

Case 7

Reported in the *Liber Assisarum*, 21 Ed III, p 76, pl 5

Michaelis
21 Ed III.

(8) **In attaint,** if the Grand Jury remain for want of jurors, a writ shall be directed to the sheriff that he shall take twelve of the best men, or eighteen, or as many, etc, where any of them were ousted by challenge

Case 8

Reported in Y B Mich 21 Ed III, p 41, pl 45

(9) **In attaint** against A and B, the writ was "Summon Michaelis
A and B, *'qui tenet'* the aforesaid lands " And the writ 21 Ed III
was challenged because it was not *"tenant "* And A
was not tenant, but she was party to the first recovery,
wherefore she was named, and the other was sole tenant,
and for this reason the writ was adjudged good, etc See
the *Registrum*

The case has not been identified in Y B Mich 21 Ed III, or in the Case 9
later abridgments The index to the Year Book cites this case as on
p 23 of 21 Ed III, but the case is not found there

(10) **In attaint,** the tenant pleaded non-tenure, and so it Paschal
was found, etc And the petty twelve said that they had 20 Hen VI
made a good oath, and the plaintiff said that the tenant
had made a feoffment to persons unknown, etc , according to the Statute PASTON That shall be tried by another
inquest than by the Grand Jury NEWTON. That is not so,
for inasmuch as the issue is not on the point of false swearing, it is not peremptory, but the party can have an attaint,
as when in a writ of Right the tenant pleads a collateral
warranty in bar, that shall be tried by the Grand Jury,
for the above reason, etc Query, if it be tried by the
Grand Jury on the attaint, if it shall be tried by all or by
twelve of them? etc And see the Statute of Westminster
the Second, which says that no one shall be put on the
jury, unless they were summoned to the, same etc

The case has not been identified in Y B Paschal, 20 Hen VI The Case 10
Statute is that of West II, 13 Ed I, Stats at Large, Vol 1, p 203, cap 3

(11) **A man** shall not have attaint in an appeal of mayhem, Hilary
or of felony, because this is not warranted by the Statute 10 Hen IV
Hilary, 10 Hen IV by TYRWHIT, etc , and at the common
law there was no attaint, etc

What may be a report of this case appears in Y B Mich 11 Hen IV, Case 11
p 7, pl 18 It is not clearly identified, however

The Statute is 3 Ed I (1275) cap 38 (West I) Stats at Large,
Vol 1, p 74 (99)

(12) **In mort d'ancestor** the tenant vouched one who Michaelis
entered into the warranty and barred the demandant 38 Ed III

And then the demandant brought an attaint against the heir of the vouchee and the tenant   And the writ ran "*inter quos certis de causa,*" the assize passed, and the writ was adjudged good, etc.

Case 12

The case has not been identified in Y B Mich 38 Ed III, or in the later abridgments

Michaelis
9 Hen VI

(13) **In detinue,** the plaintiff and the garnishee were at issue, and it was found for the garnishee, wherefore the plaintiff brought attaint against the garnishee, and the writ ran "*falsum fecerunt sacramentum in loquela,*" which was between the plaintiff and the garnishee, and did not mention the defendant, against whom the writ was brought [1] MARTYN   The writ is of no value, for the above reason ROLFF: It is not the same as a *Præcipe quod Reddat,* for when an attaint is brought against a vouchee or the tenant on the receipt, it is reasonable that the tenant of the land who lost be named, because he is to have back the land; but in this case the defendant shall not have the deed, etc PASTON   If two plaintiffs interplead upon two original writs, and one recovers against the other by a tried action, shall not the action mention both the originals? BABYNG-TON   No, sir, but of the original on which they agreed to interplead, etc   (Query?) PASTON. The garnishee shall have oyer of the first declaration, and if it is of no value it will be abated, so the plea is held upon the original, consequently the defendant shall be named, etc   BABYNG-TON   The original writ will not be abated for any matter, except for such matter as appears [to the Court] [2]   To my mind the plea is held upon the *Scire Facias* which is in effect between the plaintiff and the garnishee, albeit it is awarded at the prayer of the defendant. (And see the plea, where it was well argued), etc

Case 13

Reported in Y B Mich 9 Hen VI, p 38, pl 13

Paschal
10 Hen IV

(14) **A man** who is indicted for trespass and found guilty by another inquest, shall not have an attaint, or a petition

---

[1] Words from the report of the case

[2] Words from the report of the case   The text in Statham is obscure

in the nature of an attaint, because the twenty-four in a manner have given the verdict, since both verdicts agree. But if he is acquitted the king clearly shall have an attaint, etc By THIRNING, in Trespass But if the defendant be attainted in an appeal of felony, although he be attainted they will not omit in that account to do execution, for execution does not cease by reason of an attaint in any case But if he be put in prison and the judgment respited for certain reasons, or be delivered to the ordinary, it seems that he shall have an attaint, etc Query?

The case has not been identified in Y B Paschal, 10 Hen IV   Case 14

(15) **Where a writ** issues to the sheriff through the Hilary default of the defendant, to inquire as to waste, the party 3 Hen VI. shall have an attaint [for this is greater and higher] [1] than an inquest of office, for where the sheriff returns damages taxed by the inquest, the justices can choose to give judgment according to that return or not, for they could have given judgment before, but it is otherwise in the other case, etc And also the other party shall have his challenge, and if they find no waste the plaintiff shall be barred, and thus the judgment is given on the verdict, etc For it is not the same as where a man acknowledges the waste, and a suit issues to inquire as to the waste, for there they ought all to find the waste, for this writ does not issue by the Statute, but by the common law to affirm the judgment of waste and the damages, and thus there is a distinction, etc

Reported in Y B Hilary, 3 Hen VI, p 28, pl 13 See also Brooke, Case 15 Attaint, 105

The Statutes are 52 Hen. III (1267) c 23 (Marlb), and 6 Ed I, (1278) c 5 (Glouc), Stats at Large, Vol 1, pp 55 and 117

(16) **Assize** was brought against two, and one pleaded a Statham 17 a release of the plaintiff in bar, which was denied, and the Michaelis other pleaded a misnomer of the plaintiff, "and if it be so II Hen IV. found," etc And it was found that the plaintiff was well

_____
[1] Words from the case

named, and they acquitted him who pleaded of the disseisin, and it was found that the release was not the deed of
the plaintiff, and that he who pleaded the release disseised
him, etc, wherefore he recovered   And then he who
pleaded the release brought an attaint and assigned as a
false oath that they found that the release was not his
deed, and also because that they found that the plaintiff
was well named   SKRENE   As to the release, they swore
a good oath, Ready   And as to the other, you see clearly
that he assigns a false oath for that which another pleaded,
and that he is a stranger [to that].   And also the other
was acquitted of the disseisin, in which case no attaint is
given to him   NORTON: Yes, sir, if he were tenant   For
the land was lost, and also if the misnomer had been found
the writ had been abated   HANKFORD   As to the misnomer, you shall have no advantage for that, for the above
reason, wherefore we will discharge you of that.   NORTON:
Judgment of the writ, for it runs *"ad recognoscendum"*;
he who is now plaintiff disseised him who is now tenant,
or not   And he has assigned a false oath on another
point which is not comprised in the writ.   THIRNING
Upon a writ which is general the party can assign all the
false oaths he wants to, to wit   *"quod juris falsum fecerunt
sacramentum,"* etc   But this is a special writ, wherefore
he cannot pass his writ   Which was conceded   WAKE-
FIELD.   The course is, when an assize is taken, except upon
seisin and disseisin, that he shall have a special writ,
such as is here.   But when an issue is taken out of the
point of the assize, and besides that the seisin is found, he
shall have a general writ, and so he shall where the assize
is taken out of the point of the assize and the tenant confesses an ouster, etc.

Case 16   The case has not been identified in Y B Mich 11 Hen IV, or in the
early abridgments

Hilary   (17) **In an assize** against the husband and his wife, who
11 Hen IV.   pleaded a record in bar, and on the day, etc, they failed
of the record, wherefore the woman was received and
pleaded different pleas out of the point of the assize, upon

which the assize was awarded, and it was found for the
plaintiff, and then the husband and his wife brought an
attaint which was general, without mentioning the receipt
of the wife. HORTON. By the default the husband was
out of Court, and upon such a general writ they could not
assign a false oath, except upon the disseisin solely. GAS-
COIGNE They could assign the false oath upon this writ
on any point, for "*reddendo singula singulis*" the husband
was not out of Court, for by the receipt of his wife his
default was saved   And it is not like a *Præcipe quod Reddat*,
where judgment shall be given upon the default, for in this
case, notwithstanding the default, they should inquire
as to the disseisin, and judgment will be given upon the
verdict, consequently he is a party, wherefore, etc. TYR-
WHIT. If the woman, after she was received, had pleaded
in bar and had admitted an ouster, and the plea had been
found against her, the plaintiff would have had seisin of
the land without inquiring as to the seisin and disseisin,
because the wife had confessed an ouster, and her husband
was disseised by the failure of the record, which GAS-
COIGNE and HANKFORD denied wholly, etc , and with this
the Book of the Assizes agrees   And if in an assize the
tenant vouches, and he is out of Court, and pays his fees
immediately, still [they] shall inquire if he disseised the
plaintiff, and if it be so found the plaintiff shall recover
his damages against him, since he is a party, etc   And
then the justices were agreed that they would assign upon
this a writ of false swearing on every point   And so they
did, and they would have had the false oath of the pleas
pleaded by others, etc , and it was not allowed, etc

Reported in Y B Hilary, 11 Hen IV, p 50, pl 28   See also Brooke, Case 17
Attaint, 28, and Fitzh Attaint, 16

(18) **In an assize,** the tenant said that one H enfeoffed Paschal
him, and they suffered the said H to hold the same land 8 Hen IV
at his will. And then H died, and the plaintiff alleged
that he had died seised, etc , in fee, etc , and he entered
as son and heir, upon whom one F entered, upon whom
the tenant entered   The plaintiff said that H died in his

estate as of fee, etc , and the assize was taken and said
that he did not die seised in fee, wherefore it was adjudged
that he was barred   And then he brought an attaint
and assigned the false oath on this point, etc , that they
found that they made a false oath   HULS   They should
inquire as to the seisin and disseisin, or else the plaintiff
cannot have seisin of the land, for if in the assize the issue
had been found for the plaintiff they should have inquired
as to the seisin and disseisin, inasmuch as no ouster was
admitted in bar, consequently they should inquire now,
etc   GASCOIGNE   This attaint is only to inquire of the
false oath, wherefore, etc   HANKFORD   In the plea in
bar, he acknowledged that a stranger ousted the plaintiff,
which is sufficiently strong etc , for although in an assize the
tenant confesses an ouster in a stranger and it is found
for the plaintiff, it is not *de rigore juris* that they shall
inquire as to the seisin and disseisin, but it is the courtesy
of the law   And then by advice it was adjudged that the
plaintiff should recover seisin of the land, and the damages
that he lost   And so note that he had judgment to recover
seisin of the land, etc , although many said that he should
be put to a new assize, etc   Query, if he shall be restored
to the profits in the meantime, etc ?

Case 18   Reported in Y B Paschal, 8 Hen IV, p 23, pl 10   See also Brooke,
Attaint, 26, and Fitzh Attaint, 14

Michaelis   (19) **If the party,** etc , the other shall not have attaint,
21 Hen VI   by NEWTON   And this in Debt   And the law is the same
in all personal actions
    And he said in the same plea that if the jurors be attainted
they could make a fine for their goods and lands

Case 19   The case has not been identified in Y B Mich 21 Hen VI, or in the
early abridgments

Michaelis   (20) **In attaint,** one of the petty twelve said that the
12 Hen VI   writ was purchased pending the writ of Assize, and he
demanded judgment of the writ   And the opinion was
that he should have the plea, and also that he should plead
the release of the plaintiff, etc.   The contrary was held in

the Book of the Assizes, *ibid.*, that he should plead no plea except to excuse himself of the false oath.

And in the same plea it was said that if in an attaint an issue be taken which is not of the false oath, as upon a release or something of that sort, the Grand Jury will not try it, but it will be tried by another inquest in the nature of a *Nisi Prius* But it is otherwise in a writ of Right, for although the writ of Right be arrayed by four knights still there are no more in the inquest than twelve, therefore although a collateral issue be taken which is not tried, that right will be tried by the same inquest, but final judgment will not be given unless the right be put in issue, etc

See in the same plea, if the jurors do not come, or some of them come and the others do not at the second distress the Grand Jury shall be awarded for their default, and against the Grand Jury the process is as in an assize, etc

The case has not been identified in the printed Year Book of Mich Case 20
12 Hen VI, or in the early abridgments

(21) **In an attaint** for a false oath given in the franchise Statham 17 b
of the Archbishop of Canterbury, the plaintiff prayed a Michaelis
Certiorari out of the Common Pleas to the bailiffs of the 27 Hen VI
franchise to certify the record PORTYNGTON You should
have a *Certiorari* out of the Chancery, because it is confessed by the plaintiff that the writ was not his, since it
was returned that he did not find pledges to prosecute
And therefore PORTYNGTON said that you should have a
Certiorari from the Chancery and that then they would
come here by a *Mittimus*, and that before the writ comes
in before us, that is not to the purpose, for we cannot do
anything before the record has come here And they
adjourned, etc.

There is no printed Year Book for 27 Hen VI   Case 21

(22) **See a good** distinction between a writ of Error and Paschal
an attaint, in the title of Error, 29 Hen VI   29 Hen VI.

There is no printed Year Book for 29 Hen VI   Case 22

Paschal
44 Ed III

(23) **In trespass** against two, one came and was found guilty by one inquest, and the other by another inquest He who was found guilty by the last inquest shall have an attaint, although he is a stranger to it, because he is damaged because the first inquest taxed the damages and not the second inquest, etc   And for these damages he shall have the attaint, as appeared in Trespass   Well debated, etc.

Case 23

This is apparently an abridgment of the very short case in Y B. Paschal, 44 Ed III, p 7, pl 4   See also Fitzh Attaint, 21

Michaelis
4 Ed III

(24) **It was** claimed that he who is in the reversion shall have an attaint after the death of his tenant for life, and it was adjudged good   And the Statute of Richard gave an attaint to him while the tenant was living, etc.

Case 24

Reported in Y B Mich 4 Ed III, p 54, pl 59   See also Brooke, Attaint, 49

The Statute is that of 9 Ric II, cap 3   Stats at Large, Vol 2, p 277 (1385)

Anno
8 Ed III

(25) **A man** shall have an attaint. (Out of the rolls of the justices in the Eyre of Northampton)

Case 25

This appears to be merely a fragment of a note, possibly from some passing remark   It cannot have been meant to be inserted in the printed book as it stands

Michaelis
18 Ed II

(26) **Attaint** was maintained against a juror of London.

Case 26

The point is found in the case reported in Y B Mich 18 Ed. II (Maynard), on page 570

Hilary
16 Ed II

(27) **If a man** be named in an attaint, it is peremptory, etc   Query, if it is before appearance, etc.?

Case 27

There is no early printed Year Book for the year sixteen of Ed. II The case, or rather the point, has not been identified in the Rolls Series for that year

Paschal
23 Ed III

(28) **Attaint** will not be maintained for a concealment, as appeared in an attaint, etc.

Case 28

There is but one short term — that of Michaelmas — in the printed year of 23 Ed III   The point has not been identified there

(29) **Attaint** was maintained by the vouchee, and yet Paschal
the writ did not state that he who entered into the 25 Ed III.
warranty, etc., was dead or alive.

The case has not been identified in Y B 25 Ed III, or in the early Case 29
abridgments.

(30) **In trespass** against several who pleaded not guilty, Paschal
if a general judgment is given for the damages, a general 18 Ed III
attaint or a several attaint lies.   But if it is several on the
judgment for damages then the attaint is several, etc
And although the judgment be general, still as to the
principal, to wit   that of which they are found guilty,
a several attaint lies, as it seems, etc

The case has not been identified in Y B Paschal, 18 Ed III, or in Case 30
the early abridgments.

(31) **Attaint** was adjudged good for him who had pleaded Michaelis
non-tenure, but he showed how he was injured, because 22 Ed III
he had the land by a remainder, etc

The case has not been identified in Y B Mich 22 Ed III, or in the Case 31
early abridgments.

(32) **Attaint** against the tenant and the vouchee was Michaelis
adjudged good 4 Ed III

The case has not been identified in Y B Mich 4 Ed III, or in the Case 32
later abridgments

(33) **Attaint** was brought by the tenant for a receipt, Trinity
and it was adjudged good, notwithstanding the writ did 3 Ed II
not say whether the tenant for life was dead or alive

The point in the case has not been identified in Y B Trinity, 3 Ed Case 33
II, but is found as given by Brooke, Attaint, 49, in Y B Mich 4 Ed II,
p 58, at the end of the case beginning on page 54   See also Fitzh
Attaint, 47   He gives the same citation as Brooke

(34) **A man** had issue two daughters, and he leased his Hilary
land to one of them for the term of his life, and died, and 43 Ed III

the other sister granted the reversion of the half by a fine
In this case the opinion clearly was that she should attorn,
because the reversion was severed by course of law   (But
yet a man cannot grant a half of a reversion, etc   Nor
where two have a reversion jointly, one cannot grant his
part, etc)

Case 34   The case has not been identified in Y B Hilary, 43 Ed III   There
are cases that are similar in many ways, but it cannot be asserted with
any authority that Statham did not have some unprinted case in his
mind or on his notebook which is the authority for this point

[14] The attaint may be said to be an early form of an appeal   Thayer
says, "The attaint   long held its place as the only way of remedying
a false verdict " [Thayer Evidence, p 137] The jury were supposed
or alleged to have rendered a false verdict, and a new jury—a grand
jury, or jury of twenty-four — are to pass upon the question whether
they had sufficient evidence to justify their verdict or not   Although
Maitland thinks the penalties given against the petty juries were often
small and not so onerous as they might seem [P & M Hist of Eng
Law, 2d ed , Vol 2, p 542], they "are to be imprisoned and to lose their
chattels," also they "lose the law of the land," that is, they cease to be
"oath worthy " He cites a case in Bracton's Note Book [pl 917] in
which the "moderate fine" seems severe enough, as they have to pay
fifty marks
      It was a cumbersome and on the whole not an over-just procedure
There was ample time between the first and second actions for the more
powerful litigant to influence the grand jury   Mr Thayer gives us a
vivid example from the Paston Letters [Thayer Evidence, p 138]
"In 1451 the inhabitants of Swaffham asked Parliament to annul a verdict and judgment in Novel Disseisin, alleging perjury in the jurors
by 'reason of menaces,' and setting forth that the said inhabitants,
for pity and remorse of their consciences, were loth to use a writ
of attaint, since the 'said assize durst not, for dread of the horrible menaces of the said Sir Thomas, otherwise do but be forsworn in giving the
verdict in the same assize ' "   But this is the view of a later time than
that of Maitland   By 1451 we are getting away from the cases in our
abridgment   Year Book law will go on for a hundred years, but by
the end of that time attaints will have gone practically out of use
[Smith, Commonwealth of England, Bk 3, chap 2, p 207] Much of the
learning on the subject of attaints is to be found in Thayer's great work
on Evidence, where it is set forth in a very wonderful way in the fourth
chapter   With that chapter to refer to no student need lack
enlightenment

ATTOURNEMENT [15]

(1) **In a quid juris clamat,** the tenant would not attorn Statham 18 a
because the conusor held the same lands of the king in Paschal
chief, because then he would be charged to the king by the 45 Ed III
fine, etc , wherefore the demandant showed a license for
the purchase and for the alienation, and then he attorned,
etc

Probably the case reported in Y B Paschal, 45 Ed III, p 6, pl 3, Case 1
although the refusal of attornment is eliminated from the printed text

(2) **If the king** grants me the services of his tenant I can Michaelis
avow without attornment, for I cannot have a *Per que* 21 Ed III
Servicia, nor a *Quid Juris Clamat*, etc , by SHARSHULL in
Wardship

The case has not been identified in Y B Mich 21 Ed III, or in the Case 2
early abridgments

(3) **If I grant** a manor to a man, which is part in demesne Hilary
and part in service, and deliver seisin to him, he can avow 21 Ed III
upon the other lands which I hold of the manor, without
attornment, because he is seised of the principal [part],
and this by WILLOUGHBY   But yet, query?

The case has not been identified in Y B Hilary, 21 Ed III, or in the Case 3
early abridgments.

(4) **Land was leased** to one A for life, the remainder Michaelis
to B, if he survived A, for life, the remainder to the right 24 Ed III
heirs of A   And A, by his deed, granted to B that he
should not be impeached for waste when the land came
to him   A died, and C, who was his son and heir, granted
the reversion of B, by a fine, to one D, and he brought a
Quid Juris Clamat against B, who said that A, who was
the father of the grantor, has granted to him that he
should not be impeached for this, and saving to him the
advantage of that, he is ready, etc   NOTTINGHAM   This
A, at the time of the grant, had nothing but a term for

life, for there was no reversion to him, but to his heirs, for he could not have had an action for waste, consequently his grant was void. And B also had nothing in the land at the time of the grant, therefore we pray that he may attorn generally. THORPE· If A had alienated, the fee had passed from his heirs, granting he had a fee, and he could have charged the reversion forever, and the grantor could not claim except as heir to him, wherefore, etc , for it is not the same where there was no possession in the father, and where he had possession, wherefore will you say anything else? PERSHAY We pray that our protestation be entered, to wit that we do not acknowledge the deed, for otherwise we could not deny the deed afterward, etc. And so it was. But yet, query as to what effect, because he could have answered to the deed then, and it seems that he could not deny the deed afterward, etc

Case 4   The case has not been identified in Y B Mich 24 Ed III, or in the early abridgments

Hilary 31 Ed III   (5) **In a quid juris clamat** against a woman, she said that whereas the note alleged that she held for the term of her life, the reversion regardant to the conusor, she said that she held in dower, the reversion regardant to the conusor, and she demanded judgment if upon such a note she should attorn And because she did not claim a better estate than a term for life, it was adjudged that she should attorn

Case 5   There is no printed Year Book for the Year 31 Ed III

Trinity 5 Hen V   (6) **If I give** land to one in tail reserving a rent, and I grant this rent by a fine, the tenant shall be forced to attorn, etc It is otherwise if I grant the reversion, etc Still by such a grant the rent will pass, etc

Case 6   The case has not been identified in Y B 5 Hen V, or in the early abridgments

Michaelis 10 Hen IV   (7) **If the reversion** of the tenant in dower be granted, and she grants over her estate, and afterwards she attorns,

it was the opinion of THIRNING, that the attornment was
good   In an Assize, etc.

The case has not been identified in Y B Mich 10 Hen IV, or in the   Case 7.
early abridgments

(8) **In a quid juris clamat** a woman prayed to be   Michaelis
received upon the default of her husband   HULS· That   2 Hen V.
cannot be, for no land is in demand against you   STRANGE
If she shows cause it is reasonable that she shall be received,
and we say that she is tenant after possibility of issue, etc
in which case, if she be not received, she will be impeached
for waste   SKRENE   If your husband attorned, that will
not bind you after his death   HANKFORD   Yes, sir, for
she is a party to the writ.   But it seems that the husband
cannot attorn without his wife, etc.   Query?

Reported in Y B Paschal (not Mich), 2 Hen V, p 1, pl 4   Case 8

(9) **In a quid juris clamat** against one A, out of a note   Paschal
by which the reversion of certain lands, which the said A   32 Ed III.
held for the term of twelve years, was granted, etc   SADLER
One R was seised of the same lands in fee and leased to one
W for the term of his life and twelve years over, which W
was our husband, and the said W devised to us, etc , six
years of the said twelve years, and made us and one H
his executors, and so this H and we are executors for six
years   The said H is not named in the note, judgment
if upon such a note, etc   SKIPWITH   Since you are tenant
for the entire term and we cannot have another note, judgment, etc.   NOTTINGHAM   If there are two joint tenants
for life, and the note alleges one to be tenant, he should not
attorn, etc.   FYNCHEDEN   In your case where the estates
are equal — not so here   THORPE   The attornment of
an executor is good for all, wherefore he should attorn,
and his protestation will be so entered that he shall not be
impeached of waste, etc , unless because it belonged to
him, etc   And so it was done, etc.

There is no printed Year Book for 32 Ed III.   Case 9

Trinity
11 Ric II

(10) In a quid juris clamat, the tenant attorned for part, etc.

Case 10   There is no printed Year Book for 11 Ric II

Trinity
11 Ric II

(11) A woman granted the reversion of her tenant for life, and before the attornment she married the grantee, and the tenant attorned, and it was adjudged good, etc Query? In a *Præcipe quod Reddat.*

Case 11   There is no printed Year Book for 11 Ric II

Paschal
11 Hen IV

(12) In a quid juris clamat, the tenant as to part claimed a fee, and upon that they were at issue, and as to the remainder he said that he was ready to attorn. HANK-FORD He cannot attorn for part THIRNING· Yes, sir, he shall in this case, for as to that in which he has claimed a fee, it is clear he shall never attorn, for if the issue be found against him he has lost the land, etc Wherefore it was adjudged that he should attorn immediately [for the part]

Case 12   Reported in Y B Paschal, 11 Hen IV, p 57, pl 6 There is some confusion in the case as abridged, but the printed report clears up the case It is not easy to clear up the errors in these cases without re-writing them entirely The best plan seems to be to follow the case as closely as may be, writing in a few words in brackets, and then referring the reader to the case itself

Note   **See as to attornment,** in the title of Receipt,[1] Hilary, 21 Ed. III, and in the title of *Per que Servicia,* and in the title of *Quid Juris Clamat,* and also in the title of Avowry, Mich 19 Hen VI [2]

Michaelis
22 Ed III

(13) Attornment for part by the tenant can pass all As appears in a note. Query, etc

Case 13   The case has not been identified in Y B Mich 22 Ed III, or in the early abridgments

Statham 18 b

Trinity
16 Ed III

(14) Attornment after the death of the grantor was adjudged good (The contrary is held to be law)

Case 14   There is no early printed Year Book for 16 Ed III The case is reported in the Rolls Series, Y B Trinity, 16 Ed III, p 220

[1] See *infra,* title of Resceipte, p 153 a, pl 11
[2] See *infra,* title of Avower

(15) **The tenant** for life grants over his estate, the Anno
8 Hen VI tenant in fact should attorn   But yet this should be distinguished, for if he grants over his estate after the grant of the reversion, it seems that the attornment of either of them is good   And this in a note, etc

The case has not been identified in Y B 8 Hen VI   Case 15

(16) **The tenant** in dower attorned to the heir of the Hilary
24 Ed I grantee of the reversion, after the death of the grantee, and it was adjudged good where the grant was by a deed, etc.   But yet, query?

There are no early printed Year Books for the reign of Ed I   The Case 16 Rolls Series began printing what were supposed to be the earliest known manuscript years, 20 and 21 Ed I   There are, however, it has been stated, some earlier years still in manuscript   No year 24 has been put into print

(17) **After the fine is engrossed** and the parts deliv- Trinity
1 Ed III ered to the parties, the tenant will not be forced to attorn, nor will they grant a *Quid Juris Clamat*, etc , for the law considers it to be finished   As appears in a note, etc

The case has not been identified   These allusions to "notes" are Case 17 probably to manuscript notes in the margins of the Year Books used by Statham   The notes are frequent and he probably used such as he thought of interest   Or, it may be that these notes were made by Statham himself on the margin, or in the body, of his own manuscript, and that they were inserted by the person or persons who finally edited and published his manuscript   It is, of course, all conjecture

(18) **When** the husband and his wife attorn, the husband Hilary
18 Ed III has the plea   As appears in a note, etc

The note to case 17 will apply as well here   Case 18

[15] The tenant, by what means we know not, had a certain power over the lands he occupied   If the tenant does not acknowledge the new lord or "attorn" to him, "he that buyeth any lands and tenements which are in the occupation of a third cannot get the possession   [Cowell Law Dictionary]   Maitland says [P & M Hist of Eng Law, 2d ed , Vol 1, p 349, note 2] "But the tenant who will not attorn can be sent to jail " [Y B 33-35 Ed I, 317 R S] But the case there reported seems only to show that the

tenants were sent to jail for keeping silent on "what right they had " If the tenant could have been sent to jail for a refusal to attorn, it would seem that so perfunctory a right as this of the attornment would have fallen into disuse long years before it did

Our first case shows a refusal of a tenant to attorn, in which refusal he was upheld by the Court   Our case 6 says, "the tenant shall be forced to attorn," but it would seem that the forcing was a legal procedure, as by the *Per que Servicia,* to show cause why he had not so attorned or a *Quem Redditum Reddit* [Coke, sec 569, p 316, b] or a *Distringas ad attornandum* [Fitzh *Nat Brev* 147], if he is adjudged to attorn Again the matter has to be left at loose ends.   From the history of the times one would take it for granted that the tenant would necessarily attorn, from a reading of the Year Book cases one would say that he — and she — was constantly refusing to do so, and that the courts upheld them in that refusal

We have several cases which raise a point upon which Coke says there was great authority against Littleton   Littleton says [Sec 566] "Also, if there be many jointenants which hold by certain services, and the lord grant to another the services, and one of the joyntenants attourne to the grantee, this is as good as if all had attourned, for that the seignory is entire, etc "   Coke observes [Inst Pt 1, p 314], "And albeit there is a great authority against Littleton, yet the law hath been adjudged according to Littleton's opinion, as it hath been in other of his cases when they have come in question," so we take it that although Coke may have had his private doubts on the matter, that we have his authority as well as Littleton's for the statement of case 13, "Attournment for part by the tenant shall pass all "   In case 12 Hankford did not think so, but only because one part needed no attornment and therefore was practically no part at all   Are these things of no moment?   If so, how is a history of English law ever to be written?   If we do not know the parts we must fail in a knowledge of the whole

There is also a case which is reported in Y B 20 Ed III, R S Pt. 2, p 550   It is a case of a *Quid Juris Clamat,* in which the argument for and against the attornment shows no sign of knowledge that there is any force which it is possible to use   This case was cited by Coke and has stood so cited in his Institute ever since it was published in 1628, but it was not until the year 1911 that those in search of knowledge, and finding that case cited, have been able to go back of the citation to the report and find the case there printed, for it was not until the publication of the Rolls Series of the Year Book of 20 Ed III, that the case could be consulted by anyone who had not access to the manuscript Year Books

ATTOURNEY [16]

(1) **An attorney** can acknowledge that his master is a villein And this in Trespass, etc _{Hilary 44 Ed III}

Reported in Y B Hilary, 44 Ed III, p 2, pl 9 See also Brooke, Attorney, 19, and Fitzh Attourne, 45 _{Case 1}

(2) **The king brought** a *Quare Impedit* against a prior, and his attorney said that he was a monk of the Abbey of C, and that he had no convent or common seal; and he had the plea, notwithstanding that this was in disability of the law, etc And then the plaintiff alleged the records in the same place in which the defendant had named him prior, and the defendant could not deny it, wherefore the writ was adjudged good, etc. _{Michaelis 44 Ed III}

Reported in Y B Mich 44 Ed III, p 32, pl 15 See also Fitzh Attourne, 46 _{Case 2}

(3) **In a writ of waste** brought by the heir, who was under age, against his guardian, he was received to sue by attorney, and the guardian made protestation that he was under age and pleaded over, for if he had admitted him to be of full age he would have been estopped afterwards to claim the wardship, etc _{Paschal 48 Ed III}

Reported in Y B Paschal, 48 Ed III, p 10, pl 1 Abridged by Brooke on other points, but not on any point of Attorneys _{Case 3}

(4) **In a writ of entry,** the tenant appeared by attorney, who said that his master was under age and attorney, etc And the demandant said that he was of full age, wherefore a day was given for him to be viewed So see that he had the plea notwithstanding that he had a warrant of attorney as of full age, etc. _{Paschal 6 Ed III}

The case has not been identified in Y B Paschal, 6 Ed III, or in the early abridgments _{Case 4}

(5) **In a per que servicia** the plaintiff could not make an attorney in any manner because he should attorn in his _{Michaelis 48 Ed III}

own person, and he shall not do any other thing, etc. But in a *Quid Juris Clamat* if he claims a fee, or pleads a plea by which the land may be lost, he shall have an attorney, by FYNCHEDEN, in a *Per que Servicia*, etc.

Case 5   Reported in Y B Mich 48 Ed III, p 23, pl 7   The point is to be found in the midst of the very long case, on p 24   See also Brooke, Attorney, 23

Paschal 21 Ed III   (6) **In a writ of wardship** brought by the husband and his wife who sued by attorney, and then the writ came by which the wife had removed her attorney. It was challenged because she was covert, and it was not allowed Query as to the cause, etc , for it seems that inasmuch as the warrant of attorney was joint, one of them could not remove him without the other, etc

Case 6   Reported in Y B Paschal, 21 Ed III, p 12, pl 3   See also Brooke, Attorney, 34, and Fitzh   Attourne 91

Paschal 22 Ed III   (7) **Whenever** a man is indicted for trespass he shall have his attorney

Case 7   The case has not been identified in Y B Paschal, 22 Ed III, or in the early abridgments

Paschal 18 Ed III   (8) **One prayed to be received** and the plaintiff demurred in law by reason of a receipt   And he who prayed to be received made an attorney before he was received, etc. In a *Præcipe quod Reddat*, etc

Case 8   The case has not been identified in Y B Paschal, 18 Ed III, or in the early abridgments

Paschal 24 Ed III   (9) **In any case** where one is received to defend his right, and pleads a plea, he can make an attorney   In a *Præcipe quod Reddat*, etc.

Case 9   Reported in Y B Paschal, 24 Ed III, p 51, pl 41   See also Brooke, Attorney, 50

Hilary 14 Hen VI   (10) **One brought a writ of detinue** for a chest, with charters   And he declared one charter in special concerning certain lands   The defendant, as to all except the charter, waged his law. And as to that he made no denial, and the defendant prayed that he might make an attorney. NEWTON He comes by the exigent, wherefore, etc PASTON The reason the exigent was awarded was because of the chest, which is determined since he has made his law as to that Wherefore the opinion clearly was that he should have his attorney, etc And so note that he declared on a charter in special because the defendant could not have his law, but yet many say that he could not accept notice of any charter in special, when he demanded a chest or a bag sealed, etc And it also seems in that case that his declaration would abate his writ, for it was contrary to the process which was awarded, etc

Reported in Y B Anno 14 Hen VI, p 1, pl 1 See also Brooke, Case 10 Attorney, 57 and the reference to 51 And Fitzh Attourne, 7, and the references there given The digest in Statham is obscure, but the case as reported is fairly clear

(11) **In trespass, a capias** was awarded and the defend- Michaelis ant came into Court and found mainprise and had a *Super-* 3 Hen IV *sedeas* And the sheriff returned *non est inventus*, on which day the defendant appeared by attorney, etc HANKFORD It cannot be by attorney, inasmuch as the *Capias* was awarded, but after he had pleaded a plea it could, etc. THIRNING He has appeared once, wherefore count against the attorney, etc Query, how the mainprise were found in that case, for if it were to have him in his own person, then it could not be by attorney, etc Query, if at the *Capias* the sheriff returned as above, where he does not render himself, shall he have an attorney, etc , and where he comes *gratis*, etc

Reported in Y B Mich 3 Hen IV, p 2, pl 10 See also Brooke, Case 11 Attorney, 98, and Fitzh Attourne, 31 The queries in the case appear to be by Statham

(12) **A man cannot** join in aid nor join the plaintiff in Statham 19 a Replevin, nor enter into the warranty, by attorney, before Hilary they come in by process, but they can in their own person, 1 Hen VI but at the return of the summons they can enter and join

by attorney in all the cases aforesaid. **Which** was conceded by all the justices in a *Recordare*

Case 12.

Reported in Y B Mich (not Hilary), in the printed Year Book 1 Hen VI, p 4, pl 18   There is no printed Hilary Term for 1 Hen VI   The manuscript may show that this case was really in Hilary Term as reported by Statham   See also Brooke, Attorney, 59

Michaelis
4 Hen VI

(13) **If a man** comes in by a *Capias Cepi Corpus*, and another has an action against him, he can make an attorney against the other and against all except him at whose suit he is imprisoned   And the law is the same in the King's Bench where I sue a bill[1] against one in the custody of the marshal, and although he is imprisoned at my suit, in an action, still he shall have an attorney against me in another action   Query, if a man who is imprisoned at another's suit will be put to reply to me, where I have a writ against him in the same place?   It seems not, because he did not come in at my suit, etc   And also the plaintiff is not harmed, for he can have the process against him, etc   But yet if he be outlawed upon such a process he can sue again, for the above reason, etc.   Query, if a man can have a bill of debt against one in the custody of the Warden of the Fleet?   By the Justices in an Eyre

Case 13

Reported in Y B Mich 4 Hen VI, p 5, pl 13   See also Fitzh Attourne, 3   Statham's digest differs from that of Fitzherbert, and the case, as printed seems rather slender authority for the point as it is given in the abridgment

Michaelis
21 Hen VI.

(14) **When the appellee** is acquitted by the inquest, and they inquire as to the abettors, and the abettors are found, and the justices will be advised as to the judgment, the appellee shall have an attorney because all the matters of the appeal are tried   And this in an Appeal

Case 14

The case has not been identified in Y B Mich 21 Hen VI, or in the later abridgments

Michaelis
23 Hen VI.

(15) **An attorney** shall not say that his master dwells in another vill than the writ alleges.   And this in Debt.

Case 15.

There is no printed Year Book for 23 Hen VI   There is a gap of four years between the printed year of 22 Hen VI, and 27 Hen VI

[1] "Vill" in the text

(16) **In a writ** *de nativo habendo,* the defendant shall Hilary
not have an attorney
19 Ed II

The case has not been identified in Y B Hilary, 19 Ed II   Case 16

(17) **After the law** is waged by attorney in a plea of Michaelis
land, to wit on the day of the law, the attorney can
2 Ed III
plead the release of the demandant, if he has a new warranty, otherwise not. Query? etc In Dower   Query,
if the release was made before the last continuance?

The only case in Y B Mich 2 Ed III, upon which this digest could Case 17
be based is that of Mich 2 Ed III, p 18, pl 24, a case of Detinue
If this is the case, Statham's report must have been fuller than that of
"the vulgate "

(18) **In debt,** the defendant was outlawed and sued a Trinity
charter of pardon, and had a *Scire Facias,* and the plaintiff
7 Ric. II
counted against him, and he prayed that he might make
his attorney, and could not, but found mainprise, etc

There are no printed Year Books for the reign of Ric II Fitzh Case 18
Attourne, 60, has a longer digest of the case

(19) **An attorney** can plead a misnomer of his master Paschal
which stands with his warrant, as if the warrant be "J atte
2 Hen VI
Style *pro loco suo,*" etc , he can say that he was made a
knight And this in Waste, etc And he can say that
his master is dead, as appears Hilary, VI Ric , in
Replevin

The case has not been identified in Y B Paschal, 2 Hen VI, or in Case 19
the early abridgments

(20) **In a per que servicia** and a *Quid Juris Clamat,* the Michaelis
tenant should appear in his own person, but when he
11 Hen IV
pleads a plea he can make an attorney, as when a man
comes in freely by a capias, and if he be adjudged to attorn
a distress to attorn shall issue against him By HANKFORD
Contrary elsewhere, etc.

Reported in Y B Mich 11 Hen IV, p 28, pl 54 The point is Case 20
brought up in the midst of a long case See also Fitzh Attourne, 35

Paschal
19 Ed II

(21) **An attorney** cannot be received in a writ of Account, etc (But yet the contrary has been the custom, etc)

Case 21

The case has not been identified in Y B Paschal, 19 Ed II, or in the early abridgments

Hilary
5 Hen IV

(22) **After the exigent** is awarded, the defendant shall have an attorney if the process is not well continued, by the opinion of HANKFORD. And this in Trespass, etc

Case 22

Reported in Y B Hilary, 5 Hen IV, p 3, pl 12, which refers the reader to 3 Hen IV, folio 5, and that in turn refers to folio 2 of the same year See also Brooke, Attorney, 25, and Fitzh Attourne, 32

Michaelis
33 Ed III

(23) **The tenant** made an attorney in a *Per que Servicia,* etc And it is reasonable as well there as in Account *Simile* Mich 39 Ed. III, in a *Per que Servicia,* etc

Case 23

There is no printed Year Book for the year 33 Ed III, there being an hiatus in the printed years from 31 to 37 inclusive of the years of that reign The case has not been identified in the later digests

Trinity
8 Ed II

(24) **In an appeal** of Mayhem the defendant cannot make an attorney.

Case 24

The case has not been identified in Y B Trinity, 8 Ed II Fitzh Attourne, 93, has "Note, it is said that in an appeal of mayhem the defendant cannot make an attorney " He gives the same citation as Statham but no folio or placitum He apparently copied from Statham, adding the "it is said," as he could give no complete citation

Hilary
18 Ed. III

(25) **In detinue**, the attorney against the defendant was attorney against the garnishee without any other warrant

Case 25

The case has not been identified in Y B Hilary, 18 Ed III, or in the later abridgments

Trinity
1 Ed I

(26) **None of** the petty twelve shall have an attorney In Attaint

Case 26

There are no Year Books for the reign of Ed I except those of the Rolls Series, which do not contain the first year Fitzh Attourne, 85, has the case in the same form as that in Statham

Michaelis
22 Hen VI

(27) **He who** comes in by a *supersedeas* shall have an attorney, notwithstanding the sheriff returns *"ante adven-*

tum supersedeas" he had taken him But if he had
returned that *"ante datum* of the *supersedeas"* he had taken
him it would be otherwise, by the opinion of NEWTON,
etc

Reported in Y B Hilary (not Mich) 22 Hen VI, p 46, pl 34 See Case 27
also Brooke, Attorney, 47

[16] By the time of the earliest Year Book the practice of making
an attorney had become fully established We have one very
short case in the reign of Ed I, our case 26 If the citation is
correct it is an interesting one, showing that Year Books were in existence in the first year of Ed I Statutes had begun to be made about
attorneys, to punish their misconduct, for unhappily they were not
always incorrupt In the Statute of Westminster the First [West I,
cap 29] they are called "Count" and they are known as counters through
all the earlier period Apparently the counter was the father of the
modern counsel in England, and the attorney was the parallel to the
modern barrister there   [P & M Hist of Eng Law, 2d ed , Vol
1, p 216] All the authorities, and noticeably and of course most inter-
estingly Maitland, touch upon the subject of attorneys, it is not necessary
to repeat their learning here, yet if one were to have to argue the point
as to the power to make an attorney in a certain case, under certain
circumstances, it is not clear that our present knowledge of the law
would be sufficient to solve the point involved In all these cases we
have been skimming lightly and pleasantly over these various subjects,
and in so doing we are but following our guides and teachers The
history of the law is too voluminous, too intricate and technical, to be
more than skimmed over by even the deepest and most wonderful of
all those who have written upon it Almost any one of these titles
in this abridgment would furnish valuable, even necessary, matter
enough to fill an ordinary volume, how, then, expect the two or three
volume histories of our law to cover exhaustively even a small part of
it? It is when we go to our histories of the law to find answers to questions upon just such subjects and find little or nothing upon them —
a real Mother Hubbard's emptiness — that we realize how much there
is yet to be done

AUNCIEN DEMESNE [17]

(1) **In replevin,** the defendant said that the place where, Statham 19 b
etc , was ancient demesne, and the plaintiff told how one Hilary
J rendered these tenements by a fine to one B, so it became 40 Ed III
a free fee, and so it was challenged because it was not

shown that the fine was executed, so there was no transmutation of possession And it was not allowed, for THORPE said that immediately upon the levying of the fine it became a free fee

Case 1

Reported in Y B Hilary, 40 Ed III, p 4, pl 9 See also Brooke, Auncien Demesne, 4, and Fitzh Auncien Demesne, 8 There are a number of references to other cases on Ancient Demesne at the end of the reported case

Michaelis
41 Ed III

(2) **If the lord** in ancient demesne brings a *Præcipe quod Reddat* against another, who says that it is ancient demesne, etc , it is a good plea for the demandant to say that he is lord of the same manor of which this is a part, or of which manor this is held, etc , because it defeats the estate of the tenant to make a free fee

And see in the same plea that the tenant said that the land was part of the manor of D, which manor is ancient demesne (But I believe that that is no plea, for the land which is held of the manor is not part of the manor, but the rent by which it is held is part of the manor, for that which is part of the manor is pleadable at the common law, wherefore it is a better plea to say that is held, as above)

Case 2

Reported in Y B Mich 41 Ed III, p 22, p 13 See also Brooke, Auncien Demesne, 6, and Fitzh Auncien Demesne, 9 Both give long digests of the case

Michaelis
31 Ed III

(3) **In replevin,** the defendant said that the place where, etc , was ancient demesne SADLER One H, lord of the same manor, of which, etc , by his deed granted and confirmed to one B, then tenant of the land of which, etc , that he and his heirs and assigns should hold the said land for ten shillings for all services, free of other customs except the enclosing of a park, and suit to his court, and saving tallage when, etc. FYNCHEDEN It seems that it is a free fee by this confirmation, for by this same deed he shall have a *Contra Formam Feoffmenti*; which was conceded. But THORPE said that it did not yet appear why the distress was taken, and also there was not by this confirmation

any transmutation of possession, for if a tenant in ancient
demesne acknowledges all his right by a fine, to be in
you as, etc , if there was no render in that fine it remained
ancient demesne, for the above reason, so here, etc

There is no printed Year Book for 31 Ed III   The case has not been Case 3
identified in either of the early abridgments

(4) **A plea** was removed out of ancient demesne by a Michaelis
pone, because he held the same land at the common law, 21 Ed III
and thus by prescription, etc   And then in the Bench he
showed how the lord of the manor by a deed had confirmed
his estate to hold by certain services, and so it became a
free fee   And this was challenged because he showed other
reasons which were not in the writ   THORPE   He can
perfectly well show any reason to prove the free fee, if he
wishes to show twenty reasons   Which was conceded.
And the demandant said that this action which was in
ancient demesne was a *Nuper Obiit*, which was brought
before the confirmation, so that by use of this action he
was to make these same tenements as in ancient demesne.
And it was not allowed, etc   (And I believe the reason is
because there is no damage to any one except to the lord
of the manor, who can have his remedy if a fine be levied
by one of these tenants   But when he himself by his
confirmation has made it a free fee, it shall be a free fee
forever, etc , wherefore the demandant said that the deed
of confirmation was only for the term of his life, and also
upon condition, and if it be once a free fee it is always
a free fee, etc , which is against the will of the lord who
made the confirmation, etc)   SHARSHULL   It shall not be a
fee any longer than the confirmation lasts, no more than
where the lord of another court remits *curam suam regi
hac vice*, etc   Which was conceded, etc

Reported in Y B Mich 21 Ed III, p 32, pl 17   See also Brooke, Case 4
Auncien Demesne, 18

(5) **If a man** sues a pone to remove the plea out of Hilary
ancient demesne, and the sheriff returns that the suitors 18 Ed III
will not give him the record, to wit· the writ of right, he

shall have a writ to distrain the suitors, as appears Hilary, 18, in a *Recordare*

Case 5   Reported in Y B Hilary, 18 Ed III, p 3, pl 10

Michaelis
30 Ed III

(6) If the lord paramount distrains the tenant in ancient demesne he shall have a writ of Mesne against his lord in the court of his lord of ancient demesne. And the writ of Warranty of Charter is also maintainable against him in his Court, and against another tenant who holds of the same manor also, for he cannot vouch, for if he recovers in value the sheriff will put him in execution, and then, by the judgment in the King's Court, the land will become a free fee And this by THORPE, in Replevin, etc

Case 6   Reported in Y B Mich 30 Ed III, p 12, pl 12   See also Fitzh Auncien Demesne, 30

Paschal
32 Ed III

(7) If the king grants to a man a manor in ancient demesne, in an ancient borough, that the grantee of the king shall not have tallage of them as the king shall have, but that the king shall have it, for it belonged to him by his prerogative, etc. (And yet it seems that the [grantee of the] king shall have it inasmuch as he demised the manor) But yet GRENE held that the grantee shall not have it, but he said that it should be levied by a writ out of the Chancery, and not by distraint, etc

Case 7   There is no printed Year Book for the year 32 Ed III, nor does the case appear in Brooke or Fitzherbert   The case is obscure and needs correction, but there is no printed case by which to correct it   It seems always unprofitable to correct by inference, where the inference may very likely be wrong

Trinity
3 Hen VI

(8) In an assize the tenant said that the land was held of the manor of D, which manor is ancient demesne, and had been pleaded, etc. (But yet that is no plea, for he should say that all the lands held of the said manor are pleadable, etc) The plaintiff said that he did not admit that it was held of the manor of D, but we say that the said land is and always has been pleadable at the common law, without this that it has been pleaded within the said manor   ROLFF Inasmuch as you do not deny that the land is held of the manor, judgment   And so to judgment, etc. GRENE It is no plea, for it is not denied by the plaintiff that the land is held of that manor, then to say that it is pleadable at the common law, without saying how by special matter, is not to the purpose. PASTON It is not a good plea to say that it is held of the manor of D, which is ancient demesne, without saying more Which was denied BABYNGTON Suppose that before time of memory and before the Statute "Quia," [1] etc , the lord of the manor had enfeoffed him to hold of him as of the manor, now the land is held of the manor and still it is a free fee And if our case be such we cannot plead otherwise And, Sir, to my thinking, it is a good plea to say that it is a free fee Ready, etc , without saying more And the opinion was that it was not a plea without showing how it had become a free fee, etc

And see in the same plea that copyhold is not ancient demesne, but is pleadable by a bill in the same Court, according to the custom, etc

Reported in Y B Trinity, 3 Hen VI, p 47, pl 4 A long, rambling Case 8 case See also Brooke, Auncien Demesne, 2, where the abridgment differs much from that in Statham

(9) **If the tenant** in ancient demesne vouches a foreigner Hilary to warranty, the tenant shall have a *supersedeas* out of 19 Hen. VI the Chancery directed to the king to surcease in the bill Statham 20 a until the voucher be tried and to have another bill to the justices of the common bench to try the warranty, then to remand it back again By NEWTON and ASCOUGH, in Debt, etc

The case has not been identified in Y B Hilary, 19 Hen VI, or in Case 9 the early abridgments

(10) **See by** THIRNING, that where jurisdiction of the Michaelis plea is granted to the commonalty of a vill who have 8 Hen. IV been accustomed time, etc., to be empleaded by the little writ of right close, if they use the franchise by force of the jurisdiction, that they have lost the liberty that they had

[1] Statute of West the Third (*Quia emptores terrarum*), 16 Ed I, Stat 1, Stats at Large, Vol 1, p 255 (1290)

before, etc   In a writ of Error   Query, as to the city of London, for they are in the same case, and still they use both, etc   But yet they do not demand jurisdiction, etc

Case 10

The case has not been identified in Y B Mich. 8 Hen IV, or in the early abridgments.

**Anno
7 Ed II**

(11) **In an assize,** the tenant said that the land was ancient demesne, and it was tried by the Assize, etc.   In the Eyre of Nottingham.   *Simile* in the Eyre of Northumberland, in a writ of Entry, etc.   (But I believe that they would not try it now, unless by Domesday Book.)

Case 11

The case has not been identified   There are very few cases from the Eyres in the printed Year Books   The Selden Society has now printed one volume of the Eyres, and it is to be hoped that we shall have a continuation of these hitherto unprinted records of the Courts

**Hilary
7 Ed III**

(12) **In a juris d'utrum,** it is no plea to say that the land is ancient demesne because he cannot have a writ of right close, but such a writ as the Statute gives   And also they say that it cannot be free alms and ancient demesne, etc   Query?

Case 12

The case has not been identified in Y B. Hilary, 7 Ed. III, or in the early abridgments

[1] In our first case we find that ancient demesne is contrasted with a freehold   Through the rendering by A of a tenement in ancient demesne to B, "immediately upon the levying of the fine it became a free fee [case 1]   As the tenants in ancient demesne were more or less privileged they usually did not care to lose those privileges   All through the cases here adjudged we find the tenants struggling to maintain this tenancy   This struggle is well set forth in the vigorous phrases of the Statute of Ric II, cap 6, "that in many seignories and parts of the realm of England the villains and tenements in villainage, who owe services and customs to their said lords, have now late withdrawn, and do daily withdraw their services and customs due to their said lords, by consent and procurement of their counsellors, maintainers and abettors in the country, which have taken hire and profit of the said villains and land tenants, by colour of certain exemplifications made out of the book of doomsday of the manors and towns where they have been dwelling, and by virtue of the same exemplifications, and their evil interpretations of the same, they affirm them to be quite and utterly discharged of all manner servage, due as well of their body as of their said tenures, and will not suffer any distress or other justice to be made upon them, but do menace the ministers of

their lords of life and member, and (which is more) gather themselves together in great routs, and agree by such confederacy that every one shall aid other to resist their lords with strong hand " I Ric II, cap 6, (1377) Does not the history of ancient demesne sound like the editorial of a modern newspaper denouncing the trades-unions? Has it not a most familiar sound even to the ultra-modern ear? The "exemplifications made out of the Book of Domesday," the just claims arising therefrom, and the variety and increasing value and force of the claims made by virtue of these exemplifications, apparently excited the ire of the privileged classes of that day, much as the anger of those of to-day is aroused by the increasing claims of the hitherto unprivileged We hear in these words the angry voice of the landlord and a certain vigor in the expression of such anger voiced in the bitter phrases It sounds as if the tenants for the moment were getting the best of the prolonged struggle One may perhaps be permitted to wonder how the history of land tenure or landlordism in England would have worked out if the Parliament had not been a parliament of landlords

Most of the cases in our Abridgment are prior to the statute One of them (case 11) brings up the question as to whether Domesday Book was the only evidence in such cases Many writers state this simply as a fact Maitland [P & M Hist of Eng Law, 2d ed , Vol 1, p 399] is inclined to doubt that this was the rule in the fourteenth century He did not cite our case, but gives another one from the reign of Ed II, and two from Ed III In our case they were evidently getting evidence from the vicinage and were not resting upon the authority of Domesday, and it does seem that this is as yet an open question

For further examination into the history of Ancient Demesne we have Vinogradoff Villeinage 87–129, P & M Hist of Eng Law, 2d ed , Vol 1, pp 383–406, Holdsworth, Hist of Eng Law, Vol 3, pp 229–234 An exhaustive study of the Year Book cases seems to be the only real hope of gaining further light upon what the pleading in ancient demesne really was

AUDITA QUERELA [18]

Statham 20 b

(1) **In an audita querela** against two executors, one Hilary made default, and the other was put to answer, etc Query, 2 Hen IV if it was in the first writ, etc.?

Reported in Y B Hilary, 2 Hen IV, p 17, pl 28   Case 1

(2) **One brought an audita querela** against one J, Michaelis and he showed in his writ and his declaration how he made 43 Ed III a statute merchant to the said J, in ten shillings, and by assent of them the statute was delivered to one B, upon

condition that if they should stand at the arbitrement of
the said B, etc , that then the statute should be re-delivered
to the said A   And he showed how the said B made an
award, which he had performed, etc   And that the said B,
by [collusion] [1] had delivered the statute to the said J,
and he did not show anything as to the conditions, etc ,
and for that reason the defendant demurred upon him, etc.
CANNDISH   If I am bound to you in a statute merchant,
and you deliver [it] to me in place of an acquittance, and
afterwards retake it, I shall have an *Audita Querela*   So
here   FYNCHEDEN   I grant it freely, because in that case
the statute has lost its force when it is delivered in place
of an acquittance, but here the statute remains in force,
wherefore it is not the same.   CANNDISH   In a writ of
Detinue I show that it was delivered by a stranger and the
plaintiff upon conditions, and pray a *Scire Facias*, etc ,
and show nothing of the conditions, and that is for the
advantage of the third person.   So here   THORPE   To this
that you say, that it is for the advantage of the third person,
that is not so, but the reason that he shall so plead in your
case is because his action of detinue is not founded upon
a specialty, but upon a bailment, and that is the reason
that a man shall plead a condition without showing anything of them   And so shall a man in every personal action
which is not founded upon a specialty nor upon a record.
But do you think that it is a good plea in a writ of debt
brought upon an obligation to say that the obligation
was delivered into his own hands upon condition — as above
— without showing the conditions in writing?   I say no
Neither here, for now it is founded upon an action upon
the statute, which is matter of record, etc , wherefore your
case is not proved, etc   And you are not injured for you
can have a writ of Detinue   BELKNAP. He to whom the
bailment was made died intestate, so our action fails.
THORPE   You could have an action against whomever
got the deed, as executor, etc , and if you withdraw your
action it will be your own folly, etc.

Case 2   Reported in Y B Mich 43 Ed III, p 27, pl 11   See also Brooke,
Audita Querela, 1, and Fitzh   *Audita Querela*, 16

[1] Words from the report of the case.

(3) **One sued** an *Audita Querela* because the conusor
sued an execution on a statute merchant against certain
conditions [broken] and also the plaintiff had released to
him, etc.   The defendant challenged the writ because of the
doubleness and the plaintiff confined himself to the release,
and that was received, as well as [where] a man pleads a
double plea, he can confine himself to one matter, etc.

   The case has not been identified in Y B Mich 46 Ed III, or in the Case 3
early abridgments

(4) **An audita querela** was sued comprising such matter.
that whereas the conusor had certain lands the day the
recognizance was made, of which part was in the hands
of one H, the conusee had sued execution of the lands of
the conusor and not of the lands of H, wherefore he had a
Venire Facias against the conusee and the terre-tenant, on
which day the terre-tenant put forward an acquittance of
the conusee.   THORPE   The *Venire Facias* should have
issued against the conusee only, if he knew anything to say
wherefore he should recover his land, for we cannot try
the plea of the terre-tenant and the conusee until this
matter is discussed between them.   Which was conceded,
wherefore the writ was awarded against the conusee, etc.
But yet, query?   For it seems that an *Audita Querela* does
not lie in that case for him who made the conusance, for by
the conusance he could have execution of all his lands and of
his body, etc   But if he sued execution of that land which
is in the hand of another person for such land as was in the
conusor the day, etc , for that man who had purchased
that part an *Audita Querela* well lies, etc   Query?

   Reported in Y B Trinity (not Mich), 45 Ed III, p. 17, pl 9   See Case 4
also Brooke, *Audita Querela*, 2, and Fitzh, *Audita Querela*, 19   The case
as reported in the Year Book and as abridged in the two abridgments
is different from the abridgment of the cases by Statham   It is evidently
the same case, but the abridgers all insert matter not in the case or in
each other   The case as abridged by Statham is confused, owing
probably to over-condensation

(5) **One sued** an *Audita Querela* because the plaintiff
sued an execution against certain conditions [broken]

The plaintiff said that the conditions were such that if the conusee held certain lands in peace without damage or loss by default of warranty of the defendant, that then the statute would be void.   And he said that one such brought a writ of Dower against him and he vouched the reconusor as heir, who entered as he who had nothing by descent, and lost, and so we put to lose.   HANKFORD: The writ which you sued to have execution was purchased before the loss of which you speak, judgment, etc   FYNCHEDEN. It seems that the writ should abate, for at the time of the purchase of the writ he had no cause to sue execution, and also, although the vouchee had nothing by descent, still he might have had it afterwards   And this well debated, etc.

Case 5   Reported in Y B Mich 46 Ed III, p. 27, pl. 20   See also Brooke, *Audita Querela*, 4

Michaelis
46 Ed III
(6) **One sued** an *Audita Querela* as heir of the conusor   The defendant said   After the death of your ancestor you yourself enfeoffed one H of the same lands which we have in execution, whose estate we have, and the opinion was that the plea was good   Query?   For he did not show that the plaintiff was seised, etc , nor that he ousted him, nor that he attorned, in which case it seems that nothing passed, etc.

Case 6   Reported in Y B Mich 46 Ed III, p 30, pl. 30   See also Brooke, *Audita Querela*, 5

Michaelis
47 Ed III
(7) **One sued** an *Audita Querela* because the defendant had sued execution of a statute merchant against an indenture, etc   And that he had taken the indenture from him by force, etc.   And he prayed a *Venire Facias* against the party and had it out of the Common Bench, etc., who came and demanded judgment inasmuch as he did not show the conditions   And so to judgment   And so see that they granted the writ in the Chancery without seeing [anything] of the conditions, etc

Case 7   Reported in Y B Mich 47 Ed III, p 25, pl 69   See also Brooke, *Audita Querela*, 9

Hilary
47 Ed III
(8) **In an audita querela,** the defendant did not come at the distress and the plaintiff went quit   And so note the process is, *"Venire Facias distringus "*   But it seems he

should have distress *"infinite,"* for if he has execution of the lands he cannot take the lands without answer, etc.

Reported in Y B Trinity (not Hilary), 47 Ed III, p 34 (1), pl 1   Case 8
See also Brooke, *Audita Querela,* 7, and Fitzh   *Audita Querela,* 2

(9)   **In an audita querela,** a *Venire Facias* was awarded   Paschal
to the party, and the sheriff returned that he had nothing   31 Ed III
within the bailiwick of which to be attached, nor that he
was found, etc , wherefore the plaintiff prayed to go quit,
and it was not allowed, wherefore he prayed a *Venire Facias
Sicut Alias*, and could not have it, but was put to sue a new
Audita Querela in the Chancery, etc   And I believe that
this was against the law, for they should have awarded a
distress, etc , or a *Venire Sicut Alias*, etc.

There is no printed Year Book for the year 31 Ed III   Case 9

(10)   **Executors** sued a *Scire Facias* for the damages recov-   Statham 21 a
ered by their testator, and the sheriff returned that the   Paschal
21 Ed III
defendant had nothing by which to be garnished, wherefore they awarded execution on the first day   (Which is
strange, that they should have execution before he was
garnished, etc)   And then the defendant came into Court
and showed a release of one of the executors made before
execution was sued, and he prayed an *Audita Querela.*
WILLOUGHBY   You have had your day in Court by the
Scire Facias, wherefore no remedy is given you, etc   DANBY
Although we have had a day by the *Scire Facias*, when the
sheriff returned that we had nothing, etc , we never had a
day for garnishment   And then the writ was adjudged
good for him   And so see *Audita Querela* adjudged good
in the Common Bench, etc   Contrary Hilary, 18 Ed III,
where one sued execution out of a recognizance made in
the Common Bench, and the other came into the Bench
and showed an acquittance and prayed an *Audita Querela*,
and could not [have it] but was put to sue in the Chancery

Reported in Y B Paschal, 21 Ed III, p 13, pl 14   See also Brooke, Case 10
Audita Querela, 18, and Fitzh   *Audita Querela*, 25

(11)   **If I am bound** to one in a statute merchant, and   Michaelis
he purchases the land which I have the day, etc , and then   34 Ed III

I come to the land, and he sues execution, I shall not have an *Audita Querela*, for against me the Statute is executory; for the Statute is that he shall have execution of the lands which I had the day, etc , or ever afterwards, etc.   But if a stranger comes to the land after the possession of the conusee and the conusee sues execution, the stranger shall have an *Audita Querela*, and so it was adjudged here, etc And so note that a man shall have an *Audita Querela* upon a surmise without a specialty, etc

And see in the same plea that the process is *Venire Facias* and distress *infinite*

Case 11

There is no printed Year Book for the year 34 Ed III   The case has not been identified in the early abridgments

The Statute is the Statute of Merchants, 13 Ed I (1285), cap 1, Stats at Large, Vol. 1, p 236 (240)

Hilary
3 Hen IV

(12) **One made a suggestion** that the conusor was imprisoned by force of a statute merchant, and he showed an acquittance made to him by the conusee   And he prayed an *Audita Querela* and had it, and he prayed a writ to the mayor of S, where he was imprisoned to deliver him, and he was ready to find surety, and he had it

Case 12

Reported in Y B Hilary, 3 Hen IV, p 12, pl 16   See also Fitzh *Audita Querela*, 14

Hilary
39 Ed III

(13) **A man shall have** an *Audita Querela* because the reconusee had sued execution, etc   And yet the writ of execution was not returned, etc

Case 13

This case appears to be the case reported in Y B Mich (not Hilary), 39 Ed III, p 30, pl 32   See also Brooke, *Audita Querela*, 26

Hilary
11 Ric II

(14) **An audita querela** against two, they were at issue upon a deed, and then FYNCHEDEN Sir, after the *Nisi Prius* one of the defendants died, and we pray that the writ may abate, etc   RIKHILL. This writ is in a manner a trespass, wherefore the death of one does not abate the writ   CHARLTON In an *Audita Querela* against two, if one dies the other shall have execution by the survivorship, as where two recover and one dies the other shall have execution by the survivorship, wherefore the writ shall not abate   BELKNAP: At least he should sue a new *Venire*

Facias And I have seen that in an *Audita Querela* against several, one came and pleaded his plea without his companion, etc SKIPWITH We will continue the process against him, as in a trespass, if one dies after the issue, the process shall be continued in reciting that one is dead, etc Query of that matter, etc ?

There is no printed Year Book for 11 Ric II The case has not been identified in the early abridgments Case 14

(15) **If one has** execution of my lands by force of a statute merchant against certain defeasances, and then he alienates the land, I shall have an *Audita Querela* against his alienee By THIRNING and HANKFORD, etc , notwithstanding that he is a stranger to the statute. And that in an *Audita Querela*, etc Hilary
12 Hen IV

The case has not been identified in Y B Hilary, 12 Hen IV, or in the early abridgments Case 15

(16) **Although the plaintiff be** non-suited in an *Audita Querela*, still he shall have another *Audita Querela* Paschal
22 Ed III

Reported in Y B Paschal, 22 Ed III, p 4, pl 12 See also Fitzh *Audita Querela*, 11 Case 16

(17) **An audita querela** was sued against the lessee of the reconusor, by the opinion, etc. Query? Paschal
22 Ed III

The case has not been identified in Y B Paschal, 22 Ed III, or in the early abridgments Case 17

(18) **If an assize** be brought against a man of a city or borough and he names the mayor and the commonalty of the same borough, because it shall not be tried against him if he be sole tenant, he shall have an *Audita Querela* before judgment, directed to the justices of the Assize before whom the Assize is arraigned As appeared by the Register, which see, etc. Hilary
12 Hen IV

The case has not been identified in Y B Hilary, 12 Hen IV, or in the early abridgments Case 18

(19) **If I am bound** in a statute merchant and then he delivers the statute to me in place of an acquittance, and then he takes it, or assigns the statute and sues execution, I shall have an *Audita Querela* on that matter As appeared, etc. Anno
43 *Liber
Assisarum*

Case 19   Probably the case reported in Y B *Liber Assisarum*, 43 Ed III, p 270, pl 18

[18] That this was a most important writ for a long period in our law is shown by the space given to it in the old *Natura Brevium*, Fitzherbert's *Natura Brevium*, and the books on pleading up to the later seventeen hundreds. Originally a writ directed to the justices of the King's Bench or Common Pleas [Fitzh *Nat Brev*, 293] by the Chancellor, it gradually took upon itself the nature of an equitable action, and could be brought either by writ in the nature of a bill in Chancery, or by such a bill [Crompton Pleading, Vol 2, p 416–24, 3 ed, 1716] It is in its nature an equitable action, since it is a suit for relief against a judgment, or, in the modern phraseology of some of our jurisdictions, is a request to the court for a "rule to set aside a judgment" "upon suggestion of some just cause " The motion for a rule to set aside a judgment is in fact the modern form of the *Audita Querela*

AVERREMENT [19]

Statham 21 b
Michaelis
40 Ed III

(1) **In a praecipe quod reddat,** the sheriff returned that the tenant was dead   The tenant averred that he was alive, against the return of the sheriff, and the sheriff maintained that he was dead   BELKNAP   To that you shall not be received, for the Statute allows you at the first day to say that the vouchee is dead.   FYNCHEDEN He can have the averment on any day, for if the tenant vouches one who vouches over another, the demandant can say that the first vouchee is dead, and pray a resummons, because that cannot come in by the return of the sheriff   And also when you say that the vouchee is alive you give him the averment to say that he is dead, wherefore say something else, etc

And it was said in the same plea that if the sheriff returns at the summons that the vouchee had nothing, if the vouchee comes freely he shall not answer, because he had no day, etc   But if he comes at the time of the voucher or at the *sequatur* it is otherwise, for the mischief, etc

Case 1   Reported in Y B Mich 40 Ed III, p. 36, pl 8   See also Brooke, Averrement, 59, and Fitzh Averrement, 22

(2) **A man** shall not have the averment against a fine upon a conusance of right which alleges a gift executed in himself, to say that he did not give, etc., be he a privy or a stranger, because it is contrary to the fine, for it is not like a plea which goes in voidance of the fine, etc *Simile* Hilary, 50 Ed III, in a fine upon a grant and render, etc.

Paschal 42 Ed III

Reported in Y B Paschal, 42 Ed III, p 9, pl 8

Case 2

(3) **In a quid juris clamat,** the tenant showed how he was tenant after possibility, etc., and showed it especially by a fine, etc. The demandant offered to aver that he was tenant for a term of life as the note alleged, and had the averment, although his conusor could not have had the averment, inasmuch as he was a party to the first fine

Hilary 43 Ed III

Reported in Y B Hilary, 43 Ed III, p 1, pl 1

Case 3

(4) **In a writ of intrusion,** the tenant said that he whom the demandant alleged held for term of life, etc , had a fee simple at the time of the death, etc. And he had the averment without alleging the lease which the demandant alleged in his count, etc

Hilary 43 Ed III

Reported in Y B Hilary, 43 Ed III, p 5, pl 9

Case 4.

(5) **A man** shall have the averment to say that a man died intestate albeit a will approved by the ordinary be shown, etc In Debt

Trinity 44 Ed III

Reported in Y B Trinity, 44 Ed III, p 16, pl. 1. See also Brooke, Averrement, 48

Case 5

(6) **In a quid juris clamat** against a tenant for term of life, who said that your conusor [re]leased to us by this deed, etc., before the note was levied. BELKNAP He held for a life term as the note alleged Ready FYNCHEDEN You shall not have the averment generally, but you must answer to the release, because you claim by him who made the release; as in a rent charge the tenant can say that

Michaelis 44 Ed III

your grantee released before the grant, etc.   And so it was adjudged   Which note well as above

Case 6   Reported in Y B Mich 44 Ed III, p 34, pl 20   See also Brooke, Averrement, 50

Paschal
45 Ed III.

(7) **A man** shall have the averment against things presented in a leet; to wit. such things as touch the freehold or inheritance; but of things which are of sudden adventure in the personalty, as bloodshed and outbreaks against the Assize, against such things a man shall not have the averment, etc

And it was said in the same plea that if it be presented in a leet that I have built a house to the nuisance of the highway and it is torn down by force, of that I shall have an Assize

Case 7   The case has not been identified in Y B Paschal, 45 Ed III, or in the early abridgments

Hilary
50 Ed III.

(8) **One prayed** to be received for default of his tenant for term of life, and he gave as a reason that H, who was tenant for term of life, admitted all the right, etc , to be in one B, who granted and rendered to H, for the term of his life, the remainder to him in fee   And the demandant said that before the fine was levied, and still, etc., the said H was and is seised, and that the said B did not render, etc.   And he was ousted of the averment, because it was contrary to the fine, etc   And also it seemed that his plea was double; and also he should answer whether he who prayed to be received had anything in the reversion or not, since he showed matter which is triable by *pais*   But if he would say, "no such record," that is a good plea without saying further what he had in the reversion, for that is triable by the record, etc., for that plea is not contrary to the fine, which is a fine upon a render, etc

Case 8   Not identified in Y B Hilary, 50 Ed III, or in the early abridgments

Paschal
49 Ed III.

(9) **It was found** in an office by virtue of a writ which issued out of the King's Bench, that one H was outlawed

for felony and had certain lands of which one J was tenant, wherefore a *Scire Facias* issued against him, who said that H had nothing in the said land at the time the felony was done nor ever after. And it was the opinion that he should have the averment, etc. THORPE said in the same plea that he could have the averment to say that he was not guilty of the felony, for otherwise it would follow that for a false indictment bearing date before his purchase of the land that he would lose his lands, etc. Query? For the lands would not be lost because he was guilty, but for the contumacy, etc

The case has not been identified in Y B Paschal, 49 Ed III, or in the early abridgments   Case 9

(10) **Where a return** is made by two coroners or by the sheriff of London, the party shall have the averment to say that one of them died before the return By HANK-FORD For at the common law [if] the sheriff had returned that the vouchee was summoned, the party could not have said that the vouchee was dead, etc And for that reason the Statute was made And that in a writ of ejectment from a wardship.   Michaelis 14 Hen. IV

The case has not been identified in Y B Mich 14 Hen IV, or in the early abridgments.   Case 10

The Statute referred to is 3 Ed I (1275), cap 40, (West I), Stats at Large, Vol I, p. 79 (100)

(11) **In a quid juris clamat,** the tenant said that one W, ancestor of the conusor, granted to him in the tail And he put forward the deed, etc. CHARLTON He held for a life term as the note alleges. Ready And he could not have the averment, but was put to answer the deed, therefore he said as above, without this that he gave by the deed, etc   Trinity 38 Ed III

Reported in Y B Trinity, 38 Ed III, p 20, pl 37   Case 11

(12) **See by** FYNCHEDEN, that where a writ is brought against a tenant for term of life, who makes default after default, and he in the reversion is received to traverse the action of the demandant, and then the tenant for term of life brings a *Quod ei Deforceat,* and he shall traverse the same   Michaelis 38 Ed III

point that was formerly tried, because he is a stranger to that, etc   In a *Quare Impedit*. Query, if he shall have the *Quod ei Deforceat* in that case?   For from that it would follow that the judgment is given upon his default and not against him who was received, etc.

Case 12

The case has not been identified in Y B Mich 38 Ed III, or in the early abridgments

Trinity
6 Hen V

Statham 22 a

(13) **In a scire facias** which issued against certain mainpernors of one who had found surety of the peace, and afterwards was attainted of felony for the killing of a man and was hung, and the mainpernors would aver that he was not guilty of that felony, the opinion was that they should not have the averment, inasmuch as they were strangers to that, etc.   Query, if my tenant be attainted of felony shall his heir have the averment, inasmuch as he is privy in blood? etc

Case 13

There is no printed year of 6 Hen V   Fitzh. Averrement, 46, has the case

Michaelis
11 Hen IV

(14) **If a man** enfeoffs me of lands and then admits a felony before the coroner for a felony made before the feoffment, wherefore he abjured the kingdom, I shall have the averment, and say that that he was not guilty of the felony.   And this in a note

Case 14

The case has not been identified in Y B Mich 11 Hen IV, or in the early abridgments   The note may have been merely a marginal note not reproduced in the printed years.

Paschal
20 Hen VI

(15) **A man** shall have the averment against a writ of privilege from the Chancery, to say that he was not his menial servant, notwithstanding the contrary was certified by the writ.   And this in a note

Case 15

Reported in Y B Paschal, 20 Hen VI, p 26, pl 14   This is a printed note   See also Fitzh   Averrement, 3

Note

See averment in defeasance of a record in the title of *Scire Facias*, Hilary, 20 Hen. VI   And in the title of Trespass, and in the title of Issue.

This is merely a note   The case of a *Scire Facias* referred to is to be found in Y B Hilary, 20 Hen VI   The first part of the case is on p 24, pl 5, and the continuation on p 25, pl 13

(16) **An averment** against the return of the sheriff lies for "too small issues" returned as to the jurors, as well as to the party, etc Michaelis 2 Ric II

There is no printed Year Book for 2 Ric II The sheriff returns the jurors to be worth less a year than the amount specified by the Statute See the Statute of West Second, cap 31, Stats at Large, Vol 1 (1285), pp 216–17 Case 16

(17) **An averment** against the return of the sheriff upon the *Statute de Militibus* was received, to wit where the sheriff returned that he could expend forty pounds, he said only ten pounds, etc. Trinity 7 Ed III

The case has not been identified in Y B 7 Ed III Fitzherbert, Averrement, 37, has a longer digest of the case, but no reference to the folio of 7 Ed III, where it should be found The "Statute de Militibus" is apparently the Statute for Knights, 1 Ed II, Stat 1, Stats at Large, Vol 1, p 333 (1307) Case 17

(18) **An averment** was received against the record of the coroner, who recorded that he who was at the bar was himself the person who made the abjuration, and the party said that this was not in the arraignment, etc Contrary Paschal, 12 Hen IV, in the King's Bench, etc Hilary 2 Ed III

The case has not been identified in Y B Hilary, 2 Ed III, or in the early abridgments Case 18

(19) **If the justices** of jail delivery command the sheriff to bring before them a prisoner in his keeping, who says that he died in prison, query if he shall have the averment without saying that the coroner sat on him? For COKAYN adjourned such a matter, etc Anno 4 Hen V

There is no printed year of 4 Hen V The abridgments do not appear to have the case Case 19

(20) **In dower** against the husband alone, who said that he had nothing except in the right of his wife, and that his wife was enfeoffed by a deed, which he showed, the demandant could not have the averment that he was sole Hilary 18 Ed III

tenant, against the deed, etc. (And yet it is not like a
joint tenancy alleged by a deed), etc.

Case 20   The case has not been identified in Y B Hilary, 18 Ed III, or in the early digests

[19] In spite of the learning of the commentators, the subject of averment remains obscure We have Coke and his comments upon Littleton, we have later digests of Comyns and Bacon and Viner But these writers cite the later cases rather than those of the older law, very much as the modern writer prefers for his authority the later rather than the earlier case One would not dare to estimate how many times the litigant in the Year Book cases offers to aver instead of going to the country Over and over and over again we read of it, and it takes a very profound student of the early pleading to be able to foresee that the offer will or will not be accepted Our selection of cases in the abridgment seems to have been made on no general principle which we may recognize, nor do these cases shed any very special light upon that history of the averment which has not as yet emerged into the clear light of definite statement We have not been shown by any collection of cases, or any outline of the growth of the practice, how the averment of the old books became the averment of the new — two very different things We have been content to speak slightingly of the old practice and its pettiness and pitfalls, but even the best of our leaders and teachers do not give us any complete outline of what that old pleading was It is plain enough what it is to aver It is plain enough what the averment of the later pleading was, but it is not plain enough what the older averment was in the whole effect of its use If we could have Bereford, or Hankford, or Newton tell us what the real uses and abuses of the averment were, and why it could sometimes be used and why it could not be used in what appear to us parallel cases, we should have a lecture on pleading worth listening to, and it is not wholly unlikely that we should have to revise some of our contemptuous views of that old pleading they knew — really knew — something about

AVOWER

Statham 22 b
Hilary
40 Ed III

(1) **When** a man has pleaded to the action of the avowry he cannot resort to a plea in abatement of the avowry, as appeared in the case of *Ravenshire*, etc. Likewise in matter apparent he shall have the advantage at all times

Case 1   Reported in Y B Hilary, 40 Ed III, p 9, pl 18 The point abridged appears in the midst of a very long case The Year Book of 1679 has

"Statham, Avowrie, 1," as a reference in the margin   See also Fitzh
Avowrie, 63

(2) **The defendant** avowed for damage feasant   The
plaintiff prescribed as having common appendant in the
same place, where, etc   The defendant said, "One of
those whose estate you have never had common there," etc.
FYNCHEDEN   You cannot traverse the title by prescription in this action, for the right to the common cannot
be tried in an avowry, but in a *quo jure*, etc , wherefore
the defendant said that this was his several pasture, without this that the plaintiff had common appendant there,
etc.

Hilary
40 Ed. III

Reported in Y B Hilary, 40 Ed III, p 10, pl 20   The marginal
note refers only to Statham

Case 2

(3) **One J brought** replevin   The defendant avowed
upon one E because one F was seised and held, etc , of one
G by two pence, etc , which G granted to us the services,
and F attorned, and he bound the seisin of the two pence
in G, and then F enfeoffed H and E, his wife, in tail, the
remainder to his right heirs, and we say that H is dead
and therefore we have avowed upon E. CANNDISH: E
could have nothing in the life of H, except as a *feme covert*,
but H was seised in his demesne as of fee and enfeoffed us,
and we have paid the services to your bailiff, who accepted
them to your use, judgment if this avowry, etc   BELKNAP
He is a stranger to the avowry, he cannot claim by him
upon which we have avowed, besides this he has alleged a
payment to our bailiff, which should be understood as to
the bailiff of E.   He paid to our bailiff the services which
our bailiff had no warrant to charge our tenant, etc
THORPE The amount of this plea is that you have accepted
the services from him and he has also traversed the gift,
etc   And they adjourned, etc   (It seems that this traverse
was not good for it was only an argument)

Michaelis
41 Ed. III

Reported in Y B Mich 41 Ed III, p 25, pl 22   See also Brooke,
Avowrie, 19, and Fitzh Avowrie, 65   It is difficult to render the digest
comprehensible without a reading of the case, or putting too much of
the case into the digest

Case 3

Michaelis
41 Ed III.

(4) **One** avowed because he had the view of frankpledge, etc , and that the plaintiff was amerced there because it was recited that he had received one A for a year and a day who was not put in the dozen, wherefore he was amerced six pence   [And we say] that he found the cattle in the possession of the plaintiff, and on his soil, etc

And so note that he did not avow upon the person or upon the land, but by the manner, etc.

And see by Thorpe in the same plea, that he could not take other cattle on the land of the plaintiff for this amerciament, except the cattle of him who was so amerced, etc (But I believe that the law is the other way)

Case 4

Reported in Y B Mich 41 Ed III, p 26, pl. 23   See also Brooke, Avowrie, 20, and Fitzh Avowrie, 65   Fitzh 264, is also cited in an abridgment of the case on pp 25–26 of the Year Book

Hilary
42 Ed III

(5) **The defendant** took it as bailiff of the sheriff of S, because there is a hundred in the same county which is called W, within which hundred there are certain people in a vill called H, who have paid to the sheriff at every tourn held in that place a horse or one half mark from time, etc , which is a gift for an easement that the sheriff should do for them, and he and all sheriffs of the same county have been seised for time, etc , and because, etc , he avowed, etc.   And because the sheriff could not allege a prescription in his predecessor, nor did he show that it was chargeable upon his account, and also because it was only a gift which was chargeable at the will of the donor, it was adjudged that the plaintiff recover his damages, etc.   And see that the avowry was not good for another reason, for he did not allege any prescription in the distress, etc., and he did not show what people paid it, nor by reason of any tenure, etc

Case 5

Reported in Y B Hilary, 42 Ed III, p 4, pl 16   See also Fitzh Avowrie, 66

Hilary
43 Ed III

(6) **A man** avowed because the land where, etc , is land held in the vill of our manor of F, of which we were seised, etc., within which manor there has been a custom time of,

etc , that everyone who holds in villeinage of the said manor, when he marries himself, his son or his daughter, [without a license from the lord] [1] that he shall be fined, etc And for two shillings he avows in the place where, etc , as land held of us in villeinage (And so see that he avowed upon the land, albeit the custom was his title, etc Query?) CANNDISH It is clearly against the law that a man should put himself into servitude by his marriage BELKNAP: You speak truly, but when you took the land of us by such a service, you were bound by way of a covenant, etc. Which the Court conceded, wherefore he said that he did not hold the land of him by that custom KYRTON That is not so, for he is not tenant of the land [1] so he cannot hold [the land by such customs, etc] Wherefore he said that there was no such custom as to the land in the vill. Ready, etc.

(This seems a negative pregnant, etc.)

Reported in Y B Hilary, 43 Ed III, p 5, pl 13 See also Fitzh **Case 6** Avowrie, 68

(7) **In replevin,** the defendant avowed upon the plaintiff **Paschal** and one A, his wife, and showed that they had issue, and **43 Ed III** avowed, as above upon the plaintiff and his wife, as in right of the wife, with the other co-heirs of the wife, for homage, etc And judgment was demanded inasmuch as by the issue had between them he had become tenant to the lord, in which case he should have avowed upon him by himself, without the co-heirs of his wife And the opinion was that the avowry was good, etc Query? Wherefore he prayed aid of his wife and had it, etc. Query, to what effect? For he could not plead anything without her coparceners, and she shall not have aid of them, etc

Reported in Y B Paschal, 43 Ed III, p 13, pl 5 See also Brooke, **Case 7** Avowrie, 22, and Fitzh Avowrie, 70. But the abridgment of Fitz-herbert seems to be incomplete

(8) **Where one** avowed the taking of an ox because the **Paschal** custom, etc , had been from time, etc , that the tenants of **44 Ed III** the manor, etc , should annually choose one to be their

[1] Words from the report of the case

beadle, to collect the rents and amercements, and if he was not sufficient that they should answer for him, and because of the insufficiency of one who was chosen beadle, he avowed for the rents and amercements, etc CANNDISH As to the rent, no such custom, and as to the amercement, he was sufficient Ready THORPE The plea is for one and the same ox, and he has pleaded two pleas, so one might be found for him and the other against him, which could not be executed on one and the same ox. FYNCHEDEN. Well enough Which the Court conceded, etc. Well debated, but it seems one plea went to all, etc

Case 8   Reported in Y B 44 Ed III, p 13, pl 25 See also Brooke, Avowrie, 25, and Fitzh Avowrie, 73

Trinity
44 Ed III

(9) **In replevin,** the defendant avowed because there was a meeting among the parishioners, in order to repair their church and they, by the assent, etc , taxed each one a certain sum according to their chattels. And the defendant was made collector of this, and they agreed further that they could distrain, etc , and for so much, etc , for which the plaintiff was taxed, he made the distraint. And he said, to further enforce his plea, that there was such a custom in the county time, etc. THORPE· There might well be such a custom, for there is a custom in some counties called a by-law, that the people, as above, can make a tax to make a bridge, and for that one can have an avowry, etc But it seems the avowry is double, for he has shown that by assent of the parishioners they fix the tax, in which case the assent binds the plaintiff so far as he was a party to it, etc FYNCHEDEN He has rested upon the assent, for that is the strength of his plea, etc Wherefore the plaintiff said that he did not assent, etc It seems that the avowry is not double although he relies upon all, for such an assent is not good unless the custom be such, etc.

Case 9   Reported in Y B Trinity, 44 Ed III, p 18, pl 13 See also Fitzh. Avowrie, 74

Statham 23 a
Trinity
46 Ed III

(10) **One avowed** upon an abbot, who said that he held in free alms. And the opinion was that that plea was no

plea without showing how, and also he did not reply to
the seisin

Reported in Y B Trinity, 46 Ed III, p. 19, pl 18   The case and Case 10
the short abridgment do not wholly agree, or rather the abridgment
takes a very slight point in the case for its subject-matter

(11) **One avowed** upon the plaintiff because he held of Hilary
him by homage, fealty, and ten shillings rent   And for the 48 Ed III
homage he avowed, etc   To which the plaintiff said that
he was never seised of the homage   KELSHULL. You
cannot plead as privy for you should admit you held of
him by some service, for he alleged many services and
avowed for one in arrear, etc

Reported in Mich (not Hilary), 48 Ed III, p 25, pl 12   See also Case 11
Brooke, Avowrie, 32, and Fitzh Avowrie, 84   Case and digests
differ greatly

(12) **If my tenant** in tail of my gift alienates in fee, still Hilary
I shall avow upon the said tenant in tail, and not upon the 48 Ed III
alienee, albeit the alienee gives me notice, for otherwise I
have lost my reversion, since the avowry upon the alienee
shall be as upon my very tenant; albeit the alienee be my
tenant in fact, the other is my tenant in law   For by
FYNCHEDEN I shall have *Cessavit* against the alienee
(Which query? etc)   And if I grant the services of my tenant where he is disseised at the time of the grant, the services of the disseisor shall pass, *ergo* he is not my tenant in
fact, etc   And I shall not be coerced to avow upon the
alienee for another reason, for then after the Statute *"Quia"*
etc , I shall have a seignory in fee simple, which cannot be
   And it was said in the same plea that if I grant the services
of my tenant in the tail, he shall not be driven to attorn
(But yet, query?)   But if my tenant in tail for rent grants the
rent, the tenant will be forced to attorn   But if I grant
the reversion of my tenant in tail he shall not be forced to
attorn   And if my tenant in tail alienates, in that case
the reversion is discontinued, and not the rent, for I shall
have avowry for the rent, etc   And in that case the
avowry is made upon the alienee   And the tenant in tail

who sued a replevin pleaded this matter in abatement of the avowry, and it was argued that he should not have the plea for two reasons one, because he was a stranger to the avowry, the other, because he had admitted that he himself made the feoffment And also it might be that the alienee had a collateral warranty to bar the issue in tail, etc And also this avowry was made by the guardian who had the heir of the donor in wardship (Query, how the avowry was made by the guardian, etc?) And it was said that the avowry would not injure the heir, but he would avow upon the tenant in tail at his full age (Query as to that, etc) And it was said that if the avowry be adjudged good he shall not have a return, but the plaintiff shall have an answer to it, to wit in bar of the avowry. As if in a *Præcipe quod Reddat* the tenant pleads in abatement of the writ a plea which is adjudged against him, he has no answer, so here

And it was said in the same plea, that a stranger to the avowry can plead in abatement of the avowry a thing which appeared in the avowry, as well as he can demur in law upon the avowry.

Case 12   Reported in Y B Hilary, 48 Ed. III, p 8, pl 18 See also Brooke, Avowrie, 33, and Fitzh Avowrie, 18. A long and complicated case upon which each digester has exercised his ingenuity.

Hilary
7 Ed III

(13) **If there is** a mesne lord and a tenant, the lord can avow upon the tenant for the arrears incurred by the mesne before the forejudgment, etc. And this in Release

Case 13   The case has not been identified in Y B Hilary, 7 Ed III, or in the early abridgments

Paschal
10 Ed III

(14) **A man** cannot avow for the taking of cattle for rent in arrear, which cattle were taken at night, but he can for damage feasant, etc In Trespass

Case 14   The case has not been identified in Paschal, 10 Ed III, or in the early abridgments

Michaelis
12 Ed III

(15) **An avowry** should be made in a vill or hamlet, and if it be for a rent service it should be made in a vill, because when the lord has to bring a writ of right upon a disclaimer

it should be brought in a vill, and should be warranted by the record. (But yet it is not a judicial writ, etc) *Simile* Hilary, 3 Ed III

Case 15 There is no early printed Year Book for 12 Ed III   The case has not been identified in the Rolls Series, 12–13 Ed III, or in the later abridgments

(16) **The plaintiff** counted of his sheep taken, and the defendant avowed, because he himself as guardian (and he showed how, etc), assigned dower to the plaintiff, and because the dower amounted to more than the third part of the husband, the plaintiff and she herself, by this deed, granted to us four shillings of rent with distress, etc   And the woman demanded judgment because she was *covert* at the time, etc   And for this reason she recovered her damages   Which note   Hilary 17 Ed III

Case 16 Reported in Y B Hilary, 17 Ed III, p 9, pl 33   See also Fitzh Avowrie, 95

(17) **If my tenant** gives land in tail to hold of the lord, still I shall avow upon the feoffor, etc   By SHARSHULL and HERLE, etc   Hilary 16 Ed III

Case 17 There is no early printed Year Book for 16 Ed III   The case has not been identified in the Rolls Series, Y B 16 Ed III, or in the early abridgments

(18) **A man** shall not avow for relief if he has accepted the homage of the same person   By HERLE   (All the same, that does not seem to be law.)   Paschal 15 Ed III

Case 18 There is no early printed Year Book for 15 Ed III   The case is to be found in the Rolls Series, 15 Ed III, p 107   The point abridged appears on p 108   It is simply noted in the text as the opinion of the Court, and is accompanied by a query, so that it does not stand as a decision of the Court

(19) **If a man** takes my sow, and afterwards she has pigs in the pound, I shall have a general replevin for the sow and pigs, and maintain it by special matter, etc   And so it was adjudged, etc.   Michaelis 18 Ed III

Case 19 The case has not been identified in Y B Mich 18 Ed III, or in the early abridgments

Trinity
19 Ed III

(20) **The Abbot of S** avowed for ten shillings, and bound the seisin by the hand of the plaintiff, who said that one H, whose estate the abbot had in his seignory, enfeoffed him by this deed, rendering one penny for all services. Judgment if for many services, etc. And the abbot was made to answer it, notwithstanding he bound the seisin by his own hand, and notwithstanding the abbot was a stranger to the deed.

Case 20

There is no early printed Year Book for 19 Ed III The case is printed in the Rolls Series, 19 Ed III, p 198

Hilary
18 Ed III

(21) The defendant avowed because the plaintiff held an acre of land of him for one penny, etc. Who said that he held the same acre and another acre by the same services, etc , judgment of this avowry SETON He can take it by protestation. STONORE. Answer him, etc

Case 21

The case has not been identified in Y B Hilary, 18 Ed III, or in the later abridgments

Statham, 23 b
Hilary
20 Ed III

(22) **The alienee** of the tenant shall not drive the lord to avow upon him unless he tenders him all the arrears But yet he can avow upon him for all the arrears before any tender, etc

Case 22

There is no early printed Year Book for 20 Ed III The case has not been identified in the Rolls Series, 20 Ed III, or in the early abridgments

Hilary
4 Ed III

(23) The defendant avowed because one H granted the rent to him, and the tenant attorned The plaintiff said that he who attorned had only a free marriage, of the gift, etc And the avowant would have driven him to disclaim, and could not, but was made to answer him, etc. It seems that the attornment was good during his life, etc.

Case 23

The case has not been identified in Y B Hilary, 4 Ed III, or in the early abridgments

Michaelis
4 Ed III

(24) **One avowed** for homage and escuage and rent [upon the defendant who] said that as to the escuage, never seised And the opinion of SETON was that this was a

good plea   And yet it might be that escuage was not
granted after time of memory, etc

And it was said in the same plea, that if my villein purchases certain lands and leases them to another for the
term of his life, rendering to him a certain rent, that I
cannot claim the services after the avowry for the rent,
etc. (But yet some say that he should claim it in a
Court of record as, for instance to bring a writ of Waste)

The case has not been identified in Y B Mich 4 Ed III, or in the Case 24
early abridgments

(25) **One avowed** for a heriot, and the plaintiff demanded Hilary
payment because he did not bind seisin in the heriot, etc 4 Ed III
WILLOUGHBY   This is a customary heriot, wherefore he
does not need to bind seisin   But it is otherwise of a heriot
service, etc

~ ~ Reported in Y B Hilary, 4 Ed III, p 8, pl 13   Case 25.

(26) **One avowed** upon an abbot for three shillings of Hilary
rent, and bound seisin by the same abbot   SCROPE   Your 3 Ed III
ancestor enfeoffed our predecessor in free alms by this
deed, judgment if against, etc   And it was the opinion
he should not have the plea against such a seisin, but
should be put to the *ne injuste vexes* or a *contra formam
feoffmenti*, etc   (But yet such actions do not lie here,
as it seems, for he alleged that he distrained for many
services   And he who holds in free alms does not hold by
any services.   Therefore, query as to this, etc)

The case has not been identified in Hilary, 3 Ed III, or in the early Case 26
abridgments

(27) **If the guardian** in socage makes a conusance in Michaelis
right of the heir for ten shillings rent, of which the father 7 Ed III
of the infant was seised, etc , and the plaintiff says that
the land of which, etc , is in gavelkind, and is partible,
etc , and he had a brother, etc   And because he did not
show that the rent was divisible the conusance was adjudged
good for the land may be partible and not the rent, and a

custom shall be taken strictly, etc   And so note that he did not avow as guardian in chivalry, but made a conusance, etc

Case 27

The case has not been identified in Y B Mich 7 Ed III, or in the early abridgments

Michaelis 4 Ed III

(28) **If there be** several mesne tenants and the lord paramount distrains the tenant for the services of the mesne, who is a purchaser of the lord paramount, in that case the tenant shall plead "nothing in arrear" albeit he is a stranger to the avowry, because he cannot have a writ of mesne against him upon whom the avowry was made, and he cannot join him for he is the immediate lord to him, etc   So to avoid evil he shall have the plea But yet some say that he shall have a writ of Mesne against his next lord, and so each one against the other   But it seems that that is not so, for he can say that he was not distrained for his default, which is true   And this in Replevin   Query?

Case 28

The case has not been identified in Y B Mich 4 Ed III, or in the early abridgments

Trinity 5 Ed III

(29) **One avowed** for homage, fealty, suit, and rent, and he made an entire avowry for the whole, etc, to wit the taking of six oxen, etc   And it was challenged because one could be found for him and the other against him, then it is not reasonable that he have an answer for all   HERLE   The same reason can be given if he avows for rent alone, for part may be in arrear and part not, wherefore answer   And one J came and said that he upon whom the avowry was made was seised and enfeoffed him, and whereas the avowry was that R held of him for twenty shillings a year, he held it on four shillings only, etc   And as for this that he alleged the rent to be in arrear for seven years, it was only in arrear for two years, and for these he offers the arrears   And as to many services, "never seised," etc   PERNANT   We were seised of twenty shillings Ready, etc   THIRNING· You should answer as well if he were in arrears for only two years or

not HERLE That he should not, for you have pleaded
in abatement of the avowry, wherefore the avowry should
be made upon you, and you have offered the services contrary to his avowry, in which case if it be found that he
was seised of twenty shillings he shall have a return,
because you have not offered in accordance. And if it be
found for you, the avowry will abate, so the issue cannot
be taken except upon the seisin of the twenty shillings
And see that he did not say that he gave him notice after
the feoffment, in which case the plea is not good, etc.

The case has not been identified in Y B Trinity, 5 Ed III, or in the Case 29
early abridgments

(30) **In avowry** upon a stranger, the plaintiff said that Hilary
he upon whom the avowry was made held by lesser services, 10 Hen IV
and that he enfeoffed him, and he paid the services, in which
case he should have avowed upon him, judgment of the
avowry This is a good plea by THIRNING, in Replevin.

The case has not been identified in Y B Hilary, 10 Hen IV, or in Case 30
the early abridgments

(31) **He who** is a stranger to the avowry may say that Trinity
the avowant is seised of part of the lands or of all, by 15 Ed III
HERLE, etc. And he said in the same plea that he who
is a stranger to the avowry, where the avowry is made
upon the mesne, shall plead "nothing in arrear" And
the reason is because if rent be in arrear, and he brings
a writ of Mesne against the mesne, he can say that he did
not distrain in his default And it is true, in which case
he will recover no damages against him, so if he could not
have the plea he would be vexed without reason, etc.
But if the avowry be made upon the plaintiff, and he says
that he has enfeoffed a stranger in fee and retaken an
estate for the term of his life, he shall not plead "nothing
in arrear." And yet he is not privy, but if he wishes to
plead "nothing in arrear" he should admit the tenure as
he had avowed. And this in Replevin.

There is no early printed year of 15 Ed III The case has not been Case 31
identified in the Rolls Series for that year and term

Paschal
18 Ed III

(32) **He who** is a stranger to the avowry shall force the avowant to avow upon him, albeit he does not claim by him upon whom the avowry is made, if he can bind seisin by the plaintiff by his hands, for if the avowant accepted him for his tenant, whether he came in by disseisin or otherwise, he can avow upon him.

And it was said in the same plea, if the bailiff makes a conusance and the lord joins himself to him, the plaintiff shall recover damages solely against the lord. And if the lord avows for the same reason, the bailiff is immediately out of court (It seems the law is the same if he avows for other reasons)

Case 32

Reported in Y B Hilary (not Paschal), 18 Ed III, p 7, pl 22

Statham 24 a
Michaelis
18 Ed III

(33) **A stranger** to the avowry shall not say that the one upon whom the avowry is made is covert of a husband, or that he is dead, or that none such is *in rerum natura* And this by HERLE, in Replevin, etc

Case 33

The case has not been identified in Y B Mich 18 Ed III, or in the early abridgments

Trinity
5 Ed III

(34) **If a man avows** for suit at a leet or a thing of that sort, which belongs to a view of frankpledge, or to a franchise, etc , he shall not be driven to show his title of right or charter, but that he was seised of such a manor to which the view of frankpledge, etc But in a *quo warranto* at the suit of the king it is otherwise, etc

Case 34

The case has not been identified in Y B Trinity, 5 Ed III, or in the early abridgments

Michaelis
6 Ed III

(35) **If a man** avows for a heriot, although it be a heriot service, he shall not avow upon the person, for he can take it out of his fee Query then, if every stranger who has his beast taken can plead in bar of the avowry

And see in the same case that [the reason] he did not avow upon the person was because he did not avow for any services which any man who was alive could do, etc (But yet he should bind seisin for services, etc) And if he avows for a heriot custom he shall recite the custom in his avowry, etc.

The case has not been identified in Y B Mich 6 Ed III, or in the early abridgments Case 35

(36) **One avowed** upon his tenant in dower because one H, his grandfather, held the manor of C by twenty shillings of rent of one F, of whose services, etc , and that his grandfather died, after whose death S, his father, entered and endowed the wife of the present plaintiff, of the third part of the manor, rendering to him the third part of the services of which he is charged over, etc   And for so much in arrear he avowed upon him as upon his tenant in dower And it was challenged because he did not show that he had paid the services over, etc   And it was not allowed, for it is sufficient to show that he is charged over, to wit that he held over, etc.   And he ought to show that fully, etc Hilary 3 Ed III

Reported in Y B Hilary, 3 Ed III, p 6, pl 20   See also Fitzh Avowrie, 173 Case 36

(37) **See an avowry** made for divers services, etc , as of any other avowry Michaelis 5 Ed III

The case has not been identified in Y B Mich 5 Ed III, or in the early abridgments Case 37

(38) **If a man** avows for waste he can plead that he who stole the beast was attainted for felony for stealing that same beast. Michealis 5 Ed III

Not identified in Y B Mich 5 Ed III, or in the early abridgments Case 38

(39) **If a man** be amerced in the sheriff's tourn the sheriff can distrain him for all the county, and a lord of a leet for all the precinct, and he shall not plead "out of his fee," but he shall say that he took the distress out of the precinct of his leet, etc Hilary 8 Ric II

There is no Year Book for Ric II   The case has not been identified in the early abridgments Case 39

(40) **If I give land** to a man in the tail to hold of me, and then I release to him all my right, now the tenant shall Michaelis 24 Ed III

avow upon him as upon his very tenant, etc   And consequently, after such an avowry, if he commits a felony for which he is attainted the lord shall have the escheat, etc. (But this was argument, not proof)

The case has not been identified in Y B 24 Ed III, or in the early abridgments

(41) **If a man** avows for a heriot and says that he and his ancestors have been seised for time, etc   Still he shall bind a special seisin in him, or in one of his ancestors, and say by whose hand, etc   And this in Replevin

The case has not been identified in Mich 24 Ed III, or in the early abridgments

(42) **If one grants** a rent to another and to me, and my companion releases to me, I shall have an entire avowry for all the rent, and yet I am in by a several title, but it is necessary for me to show the lease in my avowry.

There is no printed Year Book for 33 Ed III   Fitzherbert, in Avowrie, 195, has apparently copied the case from Statham

(43) **In a recordare,** the defendant said that one H held one acre of land of the king as of his manor of D, by two pence of rent, and by the services that at every alienation he should pay four shillings to the king in the name of relief; which manor the king granted to us for a term of years which still endures, by his letters-patent, etc   And the said H alienated to one B, and for four shillings, etc., we avowed, etc , upon the said B as upon the very tenant of the king, in the manner, and this avowry was admitted for good   But yet, query as to this, etc , for he avowed in his own right, then to say that he avowed upon the tenant of the king, he is a stranger, etc.   And also this cannot be a service, but is a fine, in which case the avowry should not be made upon the person, etc.   Query, if a man leases his seignory to one for a term of years, how shall I avow? To wit as upon my very tenant, or as upon my tenant in the manner, etc.?

There is no printed Year Book for 15 Hen VI.

(44) **The avowant** showed that he was seised of the manor of F, of which he had waif, etc , and he said that the defendant had carried away certain sheep which came to the same vill, and hue and cry was made upon him, where-fore he waived the beasts, and he took them, etc And the plaintiff said that he did not waive them, and it was not allowed without answering the averment that he waived them, etc Query, if it be a plea to say that he did not waive them, and not to answer the charges that he carried them away? etc And it seems that it is only a justification, etc

Paschal 29 Ed III

There is no early printed Year Book of 29 Ed III Case 44

(45) **In a recordare** against an abbot who said that one A, his predecessor, before the Statute gave an acre of land to one B, to hold of him and his successors for twelve pence, of which services, etc , and at the same time the said B was seised of a furlong of land, etc , and by this deed indented granted to the said A and his successors that they could distrain in the said land for the said twelve pence in the said furlong of land, and for so much in arrear, etc , he avowed the taking etc , as upon the land charged with this distress FULTHORPE One T was seised of the same acre in fee and leased to us the same acre for a term of years which still endures, and we pray aid of him NEWTON We have avowed for a rent charge, in which case, although he be a stranger to the avowry, he can plead every plea in bar of your avowry, in which case the aid is not grantable JUYN Although you avow as for a rent charge, still it is a rent service, in which case it is reasonable that he have the aid, for it is the same rent which was reserved and no other rent, in which case if he have not the aid he will have no plea except "out of his fee," etc NEWTON Inasmuch as the avowry is not made upon any person, how can he have the aid? And he also prayed aid of other lands than those on which our avowry was made, etc And afterwards the aid was granted And he came in aid and disclaimed that he held of him, etc (It was wonderful that he should disclaim inasmuch as no avowry was made upon him, etc Although a man avows upon a rent charge still it seems that

Trinity 15 Hen VI

the plaintiff can have aid because of the feebleness of his estate, but peradventure not before the issue is joined, etc. Study this avowry, for it seems that he cannot afterwards avow for this rent upon the person, etc. Query?)

Case 45

There is no printed Year Book of 15 Hen VI The Statute is that of Westminster the Third, *Quia Emptores Terrarum*, 18 Ed I, Stat 1, Stats at Large, Vol 1, p 255

Hilary
4 Hen VI

(46) **Where** one avowed because one H was seised and granted the rent to him, etc, it is a good plea to say that at the time, etc, H had nothing in the land, without saying more, for every stranger who has his beasts taken, although he did not have the land, could plead in bar of the avowry, etc.

Case 46

Reported in Y. B Hilary, 4 Hen VI, p 9, pl 1 See also Fitzh Avowrie, 5

Statham 24 b

Trinity
50 Ed III

(47) **If I give** land to a man after the Statute, in fee, rendering to me one penny of rent, and saving to him the forinsic services, I shall have such services of him as I held over before the feoffment And this by HILARY and THORPE in an avowry, etc (Which was strange, for from this it seems I can commence a seignory after the Statute, for the land was never held of me before And I cannot have such services as I held over unless I remain tenant to the lord paramount, etc Wherefore, query as to this)

Case 47

The case has not been identified in Y B Trinity, 50 Ed III The early abridgments do not abridge any cases in 50 Ed III under the title of Avowry

The Statute of West the Third, *Quia Emptores Terrarum*, 18 Ed I, Stat 1, Stats at Large, Vol 1, p 255

Hilary
13 Hen IV

(48) **In avowry** for a relief, it is no plea to say "never seised of the escuage," for the seisin of the homage is sufficient, etc

And see in the same plea, that a man can hold by homage for all services which are in socage And so it is when he holds by homage, fealty, and rent, which is only socage

Case 48

Reported in Y B Mich (not Hilary), 13 Hen IV, p 5, pl 11 See also Fitzh Avowrie, 197

(49) **In a recordare,** one, as bailiff of his master, made Michaelis 14 Hen IV
a conusance upon one H, and showed how one G was seised
of the honor of Gloucester. And he made the descent
of this same honor to his master, and that the custom there
was that every tenant who held of this honor should pay
at every alienation that he made a certain sum by way of
fine, and he showed how one W, his ancestor, was seised
of such a fine, and showed how one J held certain lands
of the same honor, and alienated without a license, and
for that made the conusance. To which the plaintiff
said, by way of protestation, he did not admit the custom,
but he said that this same G was seised as above, and
that he was seised of this same land as part of the honor
in demesne and was so seised before the Statute, and afterwards in time of memory, by this deed gave the same lands
to one B to hold of him by fealty and a certain rent for all
services, which estate he had, judgment, etc NORTON
And we judgment And so to judgment SKRENE It
seems that we should have a return for one reason because
the custom was always incident to the land into whatever
hands, etc. And another reason is that he is a stranger to
the avowry, so that he cannot plead anything except "Out,"
etc HORTON As to that he is a stranger, etc, there is a
difference when the avowry is made upon the person and
when it is not, for when a man avows for a rent charge, or
upon some such custom, every stranger can plead what he
will, if he be a party to the writ, etc Which was conceded
And as to the other point there is a difference between a
custom which runs through a whole country, as a heriot,
for there unity of possession is not to the purpose, but in this
case the custom is only a private customary right of that
honor, in which case the law is different, etc And also the
avowry is not good because he has not shown the quantity
of the land which was alienated, [and thus he cannot show]
the certainty of the fine, in which case if the return be
adjudged good, they would not know what fine to adjudge,
etc SKRENE In that case it would be adjudged according
to our discretion, as if I distrain for a suit, and he wishes
to offer me amends, it will be according to my discretion;

and the law is the same in a *Cessavit* for divine services, where a man tenders the arrears, etc., and also for damage feasant, etc   HANKFORD   There is a difference between this custom and one where a man has a prerogative of the king by a grant, as the Bishop of Durham and the Prior of Chester, who have from their tenants a fine at each alienation, for there, although the land comes to the lord by escheat, or he alienates part of the demesne, yet they shall have the fine as well as the king, for if the land escheats to the king, and he gives the same land to one who alienates without a license, the king shall have a fine, etc.   And then it was adjudged that the plaintiff should recover his damages And this was well debated, etc

Case 49

Reported at very great length in Y B Mich 14 Hen IV, p 2, pl 6 It was "debated" at leisure by the Court and counsel   It is difficult, as is usually the case in regard to these long reports, to make the digest clear enough to convey the sense of the arguments without importing into the digest of the case more of the case itself than is desirable See also Brooke, 46, and Fitzh Avowrie, 60   The latter gives a very long abridgment, being apparently unable to condense the case to his satisfaction.

Trinity
12 Ric II

(50)   **One made a conusance** as servant to one A, executor of the will of one B, and by his conusance, etc.   RIKHILL. He had another executor, etc   HULS· For anything, etc. And so to judgment.   Query?

Case 50

There is no early printed Year Book for 12 Ric II   Fitzh Avowrie, 88, has a longer and somewhat different abridgment of the case.

The case has not been identified in Y B Trinity, 12 Ric II, Ames Foundation, ed Deiser

Paschal
2 Hen VI

(51)   **If a rent charge** descends to two daughters, and one of the two has issue and dies, the issue shall avow for half of the rent, in the half of the land, etc

Case 51

Reported in Y B Paschal, 2 Hen VI, p 7, pl 2. See also Fitzh Avowrie, 2

Trinity
2 Hen VI

(52)   **She** who had an estate with a coparcener avowed upon a rent charge and a grant upon the purpart without a deed   And she showed the matter in her avowry — what estate she had, etc

Case 52

Reported in Y B Trinity, 2 Hen VI, p 14, pl 14   See also Fitzh Avowrie, 3

(53) **One avowed** because one H held of him by homage, etc , and that he was seised by the hand of H, which H enfeoffed the plaintiff The plaintiff demanded judgment of the avowry, for H never had anything except in right of one K, his wife, of whom no mention was made in your avowry, etc. SKRENE He does not deny that he is in by the feoffment of H, by whose hand we were seised of the homage, so he will be estopped to say, "Although H was seised in his own right" HANKFORD You say well. Wherefore, NORTON amended his plea and said (as above), and that A died, after whose death one F, as heir of K, entered and enfeoffed us Judgment of the avowry THIRNING This avowry is not made upon H, but upon you, so that which he alleges of the seisin of H is only a convenience, etc , in which case you should traverse the seisin or answer the avowry, for if I am seised of the services by a disseisor that will bind the disseisee HANKFORD. The plea is good Which the Court conceded Wherefore the avowant said that H was seised, etc., without this that the woman had anything, etc And see in this plea that afterward the plaintiff prayed in aid one who was joined to him, and then he pleaded in abatement of the avowry

Reported in Y B Mich 11 Hen IV, p 28, pl 54 See also Brooke, Avownie, 43, and Fitzh Avownie, 54

Michaelis
11 Hen IV

Case 53

(54) **One avowed** for ten shillings rent, upon one H, and he showed that the said H held of one J as of his manor of F, one acre of land for the said ten shillings, of which the said J was seised, etc , as part of the same manor And afterwards this same J, by a fine, granted this same manor to one B, for the term of his life, remainder to us in tail, and B was seised of the rent and died, after whose death we entered and were seised of the rent And for the said ten shillings in arrear, etc. PORTYNGTON This plea is double, for the seisin of his tenant for life, or his own seisin, had been good enough MARKHAM Our seisin is only a redundancy, but the seisin of the tenant for life ought to be all, for if he were not seised the remainder would not pass, and so no seisin is traversable except that, etc. NEWTON

Michaelis
19 Hen VI

Statham 25a If the grant had been made by deed the law would be as you say, but when it is by a fine the remainder passes, although the tenant for life was never seised for if I grant the services of my tenant to you for the term of your life, the remainder over in fee, by a fine, and you die before any attornment, he who is in the remainder shall have the *per que servicia*, wherefore it is double. FORTESCUE No attornment is needed in the case here, for if I enfeoff you of a manor which is partly in demesne and partly in service, there is no need that you have attornment of the tenants, for the principal passes by livery, etc., wherefore the action shall be in the same condition, for an advowson or rent by itself cannot pass without a deed, but as part of a manor it can, wherefore, etc NEWTON He should have the attornment of the tenant in your case, which PASTON conceded FORTESCUE In many cases one shall avow for rent without attornment, as if one has execution of my manor which is part in demesne and part in service, by force of a statute merchant, he shall avow upon the tenants without attornment And the law is the same when I lease the manor for a term of years, etc And suppose that I lease such a manor to you for the term of your life, and the tenants who hold of the manor attorn to you, and afterwards I grant the reversion of the same manor to MARKHAM in fee, and you attorn to him and die, now MARKHAM shall avow without any attornment of the tenants, and yet they have never attorned to him And then MARKHAM of his own accord amended the doubleness, etc

Case 54   The case has not been identified in Y B Mich 19 Hen VI, or in the early abridgments

Michaelis
19 Hen VI   (55) **If my very** tenant gives certain lands to a man in tail, the remainder over in fee, I shall avow upon the tenant in tail as upon my very tenant by the manner, etc. But if my tenant gives the land in tail to hold of him, he shall avow upon him as upon his tenant in the manner, etc , and not upon his very tenant, etc , by NEWTON.

And he said in the same plea that if my tenant be

disseised and the disseisor dies, and his heir is in by descent, that it is in my election to avow upon him or upon the disseisee, for he said that I shall not be forced to avow upon a stranger, except where the land goes legally out of the possession of my tenant. (But yet I believe that this is not the law, and that because the law throws the possession upon him)

The case has not been identified in Y B Mich 19 Hen VI, or in the early abridgments **Case 55**

(56) **If I lease** at will, rendering a certain rent, I shall avow upon the land, etc , by MARKHAM. (But I believe he should avow upon the lease, etc.) **Paschal 21 Hen VI**

The case has not been identified in Y B. Paschal, 21 Hen VI, or in the early abridgments **Case 56**

(57) **If the defendant** avows upon one B for homage and four pence of rent — HILARY. This B held of you by fealty and one penny for all services, whose estate we have, and we say that we paid you, judgment if you should maintain this avowry. SKRENE: The land is held by homage and four pence rent, as we have alleged. Ready And the other alleged the contrary. Query as to this, for it seems double; one, that he avowed upon him, and not upon B, another, that he held by lesser services, which goes in bar And see also that he traversed the tenure, whereas the tenure is not traversable in avowry But he should have said that he held of him by one penny, and as to more services, "never seised," etc. Query? **Hilary 7 Hen IV**

Reported in Y B Hilary, 7 Hen IV, p. 10, pl 17. See also Brooke, Avowrie, 37, and Fitzh Avowrie, 50 **Case 57**

(58) **If the mesne** be forejudged, the lord shall avow upon the tenant for the arrears incurred in the time of the mesne before he was forejudged, etc., for he cannot avow upon the mesne, since the mesnalty is extinct. **Hilary 7 Ed III**

Reported in Y. B Hilary, 7 Ed III, p. 8, pl 17. See also Fitzh· Avowrie, 143 **Case 58**

(59) **In replevin** against a prior, he said that one H held of him by twenty shillings of rent, of which services, etc., the said H enfeoffed the plaintiff, and for the rent in arrear for four years he avowed upon the plaintiff   TYL· He has not shown whether the rent was in arrear in the time of the said H, or in the time of the plaintiff, wherefore, etc. And it was not allowed   (But it is otherwise on the part of the lord where he purchases the lordship, etc.)   Wherefore he said H enfeoffed him to hold of the predecessor of the defendant, by the services of four pence which he tendered to the predecessor of the defendant and he received them, judgment if for more services, etc.   THIRNING   It is hard to preclude his successor by such an acceptance of his predecessor, etc , but it is otherwise as to an heir, etc And they adjourned

Reported in Y B Paschal, 7 Hen IV, p 14, pl 12   See also Brooke, Avowrie, 38, and Fitzh Avowrie, 51

(60) **In replevin,** the defendant said that the beasts belonged to one D, and not to the plaintiff, and to have the return he had avowed upon the plaintiff, for rent in arrears TYRWHIT   True it is that they belong to the said D, and because B held the land of us we took them out of the pound and put in our beasts in pledge, etc   And this was adjudged good   But see that he did not answer the avowry, and it seems that he should have pleaded immediately to the avowry, for his plea is not contrary to the plea of the plaintiff, etc

And it was said in the same plea that the lord paramount could act in the same manner, and if he did not the mesne could have a writ of Mesne against him, and still he is not tenant of the land, which was conceded by the Court

Reported in Y B Trinity, 7 Hen IV, p 18, pl 20

(61) **He upon whom** the avowry was made was received to plead "out of his fee," etc   But yet the contrary has been the custom heretofore, inasmuch as he could disclaim, and that amounts to no more

The case has not been identified in Y B Mich 27 Hen VI, or in the early abridgments.

(62) **One avowed** for fealty and rent, and he made an Hilary
27 Hen VI
entire avowry, etc , for all was but one service, but if he
had avowed for homage and rent it had been otherwise, etc

The case has not been identified in Y B Hilary, 27 Hen VI, or in the Case 62
early abridgments

(63) **He who had** an estate in the seignory had only an Michaelis
26 Hen VI
estate tail, and the tenant of the land had a fee, in the lands;
he shall avow upon him as upon his very tenant in the
manner, and not as upon his very tenant, for if he does
so the tenant can disclaim, in which case he shall have a
writ of right upon a disclaimer, where he had only an estate
tail in the seignory, which cannot be   And he should show
in his avowry how the rent was given to him in tail, and
he should not bind the seisin generally, etc   But yet it
seems that he does not need to bind seisin, etc., for the
apparent reason, etc.

There is no printed Year Book for 26 Hen VI   The case does not Case 63
appear in the early abridgments under the title of Avowrie

See of avowry, in the title of Joinder, Mich 2 Hen VI Note
(The reference to this title seems incorrect)

(64) **The conusance** of a bailiff can be amended after the Statham 25 b
aid prayer, when his master comes, etc. As appeared in Trinity
7 Ed III
Replevin

Reported in Y B Paschal (not Trinity), 7 Ed III, p 19, pl 25 Case 64

(65) **Where the husband** and his wife [hold] in the right Michaelis
9 Ed III
of the wife, and replevin is sued against the husband, he
cannot avow as in right of his wife, because she is not named,
and if he makes a conusance it is hard to make it good, for
he shall have it in his name and in the name of his wife, and
the rent will be paid to him, so in a manner he makes the
recognizance for himself, etc   Query?

The case has not been identified in Y B Mich 9 Ed III, or in the Case 65
early abridgments

(66) **If a man** avows for homage, it is no plea to say that Hilary
20 Ed III
he tendered it and it was refused, judgment if for other

times, but he shall say that he is ready to do it, and then not speak to any other effect except to excuse him from the damages, etc.

Case 66   There is no early printed Year Book for Hilary Term, 20 Ed III The case is reported in the Rolls Series, Y B Hilary, 20 Ed. III, p 44.

Paschal 13 Hen IV   (67) **A man** shall not make a conusance for rent in arrear as bailiff for a man and his wife in right of the wife, but only as bailiff of the husband, for a *feme covert* cannot have a bailiff, etc But he shall say as bailiff of the husband, who has the rent in right of his wife; and so it was decided by HANKFORD, etc

Case 67   There is no printed Paschal Term for 13 Hen IV The case has not been identified elsewhere

Hilary 7 Ed III.   (68) **If a man** drives over my corn I cannot take the horse damage feasant and the law is the same if a man brings nets and gins into my warren, I cannot take them from his hands for "damage feasant" And this by HERLE in Replevin, etc.

Case 68   The case has not been identified in Hilary, 7 Ed III, but it is abridged by Fitzherbert in Avowrie, 199, in practically the same words as those used by Statham

Trinity 19 Ed III   (69) **If a man** avows for brewing against the assize, he cannot plead that his avowant or his ancestor enfeoffed him by his deed to hold by one penny for all services and customs, etc., and because he did not pay by reason of such tenure but by reason of his residency, etc[1] And then avowant shall show in such a case that he had had time, etc , for every gallon brewed two gallons of beer, and that he had been used to distrain for that, time, etc And in that case he should bind the seisin of the plaintiff, or of such a one whose estate he has, in the same house in which he brews, etc.

Case 69   There is no early printed Year Book of 19 Ed III. The case has not been identified in the Rolls Series for that year

[1] See the word "receant" in La Curne de St. Pelaye.

ADJOURNMENT

(1) **When** the parties are adjourned upon a plea which
is adjudged void in law, he who pleaded the plea can plead
other matter which is relevant to the first plea, but no
other matter. As appeared in a Mort d'Ancestor, which
see. Well [debated], etc

Paschal
42 Ed III

Reported in Y B Paschal, 42 Ed III, p 11, pl 16   See also Brooke,
Adjournment, 1.

Case I

(2) **See good** matter as to Adjournment in the title of
Certification, etc , where HANKFORD held that the justices
in a certification could not adjourn the matter   As appeared in a Mort d'Ancestor, which look at carefully, etc

Michaelis
12 Hen IV

Reported in Y B Mich 12 Hen IV, p 9, pl 18   See also Brooke,
Adjournment, 3, and Fitzh Adjournment, 3

Case 2

(3) **One was** associated with a justice of the assize *in pais*,
and the association was *"hac vice"* And because of the
difficulty they adjourned the assize before them to Westminster, on which day HANKFORD said that they had not
power to adjourn the assize, inasmuch as the association
was *"hac vice,"* in which case their power was ended the
same day, etc   And the opinion of the Court was that
the adjournment was good, and that these words *"hac vice"*
had relation to all the time that the assize was pending, etc
Well debated, etc

Hilary
12 Hen IV

Reported in Y B Paschal (not Hilary), 12 Hen IV, p 20, pl 5
And see also a long residuum in the same year in Trinity Term, p 22,
pl 1   See also Brooke, Adjournment, 4, and Fitzh Adjournment, 4

Case 3

(4) **In an assize** for rent the tenant pleaded "out," etc
The plaintiff said that one H was seised of certain land,
and granted the rent to one B, who granted the rent to
him, and he did not show the first deed   And upon that
they were adjourned. And then in the Bench they showed
the deed FYNCHEDEN This is too late now THORPE
No, sir, since it is to avoid the title, but it is otherwise when

Michaelis
38 Ed III

it is to avoid the bar, etc   And so it was adjudged   Query as to the difference?

Case 4.   Not identified in Y B Mich 38 Ed III, or in the early abridgments

AMENDMENTZ

Statham 26 a
Michaelis
2 Hen IV

(1) **A nisi prius** was sent to the justices of *Nisi Prius* as to the damages of one hundred shillings in a writ of Trespass   And the jurors found for the plaintiff to the damage of twenty pounds   And the principal record in the Bench was one hundred pounds   And all the matter was shown here in the Bench, and by advice, etc , the record of the *Nisi Prius* was amended and made accordant, etc , because it was an error of the clerk   And it was adjudged that the plaintiff should recover twenty pounds. (Which note, for the party made a bill of exception to this, and one of the justices sealed it)

Case 1   Reported in Y B Mich 2 Hen IV, p 6, pl 23   See also Fitzh: Amendment, 8

Hilary
2 Hen IV

(2) **A bill** can be amended in the Exchequer for an error of the clerk, as well after the exceptions as before, etc

Case 2   Reported in Y B Mich (not Hilary), 2 Hen IV, p 4, pl 10   See also Fitzh   Amendment, 7

Paschal
40 Ed III

(3) **If the process** be wrongly continued, the judges will return to the commencement of the same process, and where it was bad they will amend it, etc

Case 3   Reported in Y B Paschal, 40 Ed III, p 15, pl 5, and Trinity, 40 Ed III, p 30, pl 9   See also Brooke, Amendment, 16, and Fitzh Amendment, 12

(4) **If a grand cape** be awarded instead of the petty cape, the justices can amend it   But if the writ be brought against me in the name of J, and the process is continued against B, that cannot be amended, etc   By FYNCHEDEN, in a *Præcipe quod Reddat.*

Case 4   Statham gives no citation for this case   It has not been identified in the year books or the early abridgments.

(5) **If there be error** in a process, the judges can amend it after judgment, ıf ıt be ın the same term, although ıt be entered ın the roll, for all the term the record is ın them and not in the roll. And although a wrıt of Error comes to them, in such case they wıll not put ıt in the record, but wıll amend ıt. And thıs ın the case of Hallywell

The case has not been ıdentıfıed ın Y B Mıch 7 Hen VI   The poınt ıs ın a manner contaıned ın a number of cases ın 7 Hen VI, though not ın Mıchaelmas term   Brooke and Fıtzherbert also have a number of cases on the poınt, but none whıch can be saıd to be posı-tıvely ıdentıcal wıth thıs case

(6) **If a writ** of re-summons be ın dısagreement wıth the orıgınal, ıt cannot be amended, notwıthstandıng it is a judıcıal writ, because ıt is in a manner original, as a *Scıre Facıas* out of a fine it cannot vary, etc.   And the law ıs the same ın a re-attachment, by the opınıon of the COURT ın Detinue, etc

The case has not been ıdentıfıed ın Y B Paschal, 4 Hen VI, or ın the early abrıdgments

(7) **In debt** the ınquest found for the plaıntiff   YELVER- TON   You should not go to judgment, for in the orıgınal the defendant ıs named of Eston and ın all the process after, etc , of Weston, etc , and so a dıscontinuance, etc.   NEW-TON   The Sıre de Lowell once for one put ın a warrant of attorney, to wıt. that the said lord *pro loco suo* in a *Scıre Facıas*, whereas there was no such wrıt pendıng, but a Formedon, and yet the warrant was amended accordıng to the fact   And also in a wrıt agaınst a husband and hıs wıfe, the wıfe had been left out, and yet ıt had been amended. Wherefore ıt was amended, etc

The case has not been ıdentıfied ın Y B Mıch 18 Hen VI, or ın the early abrıdgments

(8) **If the process** does not agree with the baptismal name, ıt cannot be amended, and thıs ın Debt   Query, if the judges can amend the orıgınal wrıts in any case, etc., ınasmuch as they are made in another Court, etc.?

Reported ın Y B Hılary, 20 Hen. VI, p 18, pl 7

Trinity
22 Hen VI.

(9) **The judges** allowed the sheriff to amend the name, where in a *Venire Facias* it was Robert and in the distraint Richard, although the sheriff had returned the issues upon Robert, and he lost the issues if he made a default, etc In the case of *Fitzwilliam*

Case 9

The case has not been identified in Y. B Trinity, 22 Hen VI, or in the early abridgments

Trinity
22 Hen VI

(10) **A writ of debt** was brought by J. Hull, where the obligation was J Hill, and it was amended notwithstanding it was an original [bill] etc But they said it is otherwise when it is on the part of the defendant.

Case 10

Reported in Y B Hilary (not Trinity), 22 Hen VI, p 43, pl 26 See also Brooke, Amendment, 40, and Fitzh Amendment, 31

Michaelis
22 Hen VI

(11) **In debt,** a release by the plaintiff was pleaded in bar The plaintiff said "not his deed," and as to this he put himself upon the country, and this was questioned and it was amended after verdict.

Case 11

The case has not been identified in Y B Mich 22 Hen VI, or in the early abridgments

Anno
11 Hen VI.

(12) **A writ of forgery** of deeds was amended notwithstanding the writ was an original. And the writ ran "ygmaginavit" where there is no such Latin, but it should be *imaginatus est*, etc

Case 12

Reported in Y B Mich 11 Hen VI, p 2, pl 5 See also Brooke, Amendment, 81, and Fitzh Amendment, 24

Statham 26 b

ATTACHMENT SUR PROHIBICION

Michaelis
44 Ed III

(1) **In an attachment** upon a prohibition, because the defendant had summoned the plaintiff at Canterbury to appear in Lincoln before, etc , to answer for hay, timber, and other things which had nothing to do with matrimony or wills, the process was continued until he was excommunicated. BELKNAP challenged the writ because it was brought in the county of K, and the grievance was in the

county of L. THORPE He was summoned to Canterbury
because the grievance was there. And suppose he was
summoned to Rome shall he not have an action for that
where he was summoned? (As if he said he would)
Wherefore answer, etc   And the defendant said it was for
tithes, Ready. And the other alleged the contrary And
the jury came from the county of K, etc   It seems that
it should have been tried by a certification of the Court
Christian

Reported in Y B Mich 44 Ed III, p 32, pl. 14   See also Brooke, Case 1
Attachment upon Prohibition, 3, and Fitzh Attachment upon Prohibition, 6

(2) **Three sued** an attachment upon a prohibition Hilary
against one H, because he had sued a plea in a Court 50 Ed III
Christian for great trees, etc , until they were put out of
the church,[1] etc. FENCOT Judgment of the writ brought
by them in common, for the grievance of one cannot be the
grievance of the others. HANKFORD The woods were
in us in common, wherefore, etc   And for this reason the
writ was adjudged good etc

Reported in Y B Hilary, 50 Ed III, p 10, pl 21   See also Brooke, Case 2
Attachment upon Prohibition, 5, and Fitzh Attachment upon Prohibition, 7. The two abridgments and the report of the case are singularly
diverse in many points, yet there can be little doubt that both abridgments refer to this case

(3) **In an attachment** upon a prohibition because the Michaelis
defendant was in the Court Christian against the plaintiff 46 Ed III
for things which belonged to the King's Court, and he
showed what things, etc   The defendant said that he took
the turkeys, to wit, those same things which were devised
to him by the testator of the plaintiff   And the plaintiff
showed a deed in the same Court Christian, by which the
goods were given to him by the testator himself and he
set forth the proof, etc   And after we were concluded in
the case the prohibition was delivered, etc   HAM The
goods were given to us, without this that we were executor
or administrator, etc. FYNCHEDEN That is not at all to the

[1] Into the Chancery

purpose, whether you were executor or not, since the cause will not be tried here, to wit whether this action were false or true, wherefore you shall take nothing by your writ, etc See the Statute, Anno 18 Ed. III

Reported in Y. B Mich 46 Ed III, p 32, pl 37 See also Brooke, Att upon Pro 4. The Statute is that of 18 Ed III, Stat 3, cap 6, (Statute of the Clergy), Stats at Large, Vol 2, p 16

(4) **One sued** an attachment upon a prohibition because the defendant sued in the Court Christian, a thing, etc SHARSHULL He did not sue after the prohibition was delivered to him WILLOUGHBY That is no plea, for he should not have any answer to the delivery of the prohibition, albeit there was never any prohibition delivered, for the Statute is a prohibition in itself. Wherefore he said that he had not sued any plea in the Court Christian on a lay fee, Ready. Query, how could that be tried? etc

Reported in Y B Mich 21 Ed III, p 29, pl 5 See also Brooke, Att upon Pro 9, and Fitzh Att upon Pro 13 For the Statute see case 3, *supra*

(5) **One sued** an attachment upon a prohibition because the defendant sued to the Court of Rome for something which belonged to the Court of the King, to wit. for a mare The defendant showed how he was vicar of B, and after the death of any one of his parishioners he should have his best beast in the name of a mortuary, and how one J, who was his parishioner, died, and this mare was his best beast, and the plaintiff disturbed him from taking it, wherefore he sued in the Court of Rome, as well he might, etc BELKNAP He had possession of the beast before he sued THIRNING Still he sued in right of the mortuary and he did well, which HANKFORD conceded

The case does not appear in the short printed year of 9 Hen IV, but what appears to be the same case is found in Y B Mich 10 Hen IV, p 1, pl 2, 1 *Præmunire Facias* See also Fitzh Att upon Pro 12.

(6) **The Abbot of E** came in by an attachment upon a prohibition And the plaintiff counted that he made an appointment with him to be before the ordinary such a day, year, and place, etc, to answer for the tithes of great

trees, to wit *"silva cedua"* FULTHORPE We ask you to record that he does not plead any Statute, and we say that no prohibition was delivered to us, Ready, etc MARTYN That is not to the purpose, a prohibition is in itself, etc FULTHORPE Justified as having tithes for great trees, to wit *"silva cedua,"* by prescription and binds seisin in him as it would seem NEWTON To the plea pleaded by the manner, etc And so to judgment, etc Query as to this matter, for it does not appear by his declaration whether the action was brought upon the Statute or at the common law, for he should not recite the Statute because there was such an action at the common law But whether it be one or the other it seems that the prescription is of no value, etc , for a private person cannot prescribe in a thing which is prohibited by the law, etc

The case has not been identified in Year Book 9 Hen VI, or in the **Case 6** early abridgments The Statute (if any definite Statute is here meant) is probably that of 46 Ed III, Cap 3, Stats at Large, Vol 2, p 190 "A prohibition shall be granted where a suit shall be commenced in a spiritual court for *Sylva Cædua* "

(7) **In an attachment** upon a prohibition the plaintiff **Hilary** should count that he delivered the prohibition to the **9 Hen VI** defendant such a day, year, and place, in the presence of such a one and such a one; albeit the party shall not have an answer to the delivery, etc. Query, if the attachment be founded on the prohibition at the common law, of which no Statute speaks, etc , if the defendant shall have an answer to the delivery, etc ?

Reported in Y B Hilary, 9 Hen VI, p 61, pl 12 See also Fitzh **Case 7** Attachment upon Prohibition, 2

(8) **One had a prohibition** to the steward of the Court **Hilary** of the manor of B, commanding him that he should not **19 Hen VI** proceed in a plea before him, which amounted to the sum of forty shillings, and because he would not cease, he sued an attachment against him, and also against the plaintiff in the said suit PORTYNGTON It appears by the writ that he should have had several writs, to wit a writ

against the steward and another against the plaintiff
NEWTON   No, sir, for it is but one entire tort   But it
seems that the writ is not good for another reason, for
the attachment relates that one had sued against the
prohibition and the other against the law of England, for
the prohibition was only directed to the steward, so to
join them together in one writ was wrong, etc   Query?

Case 8   Reported in Y B. Hilary, 19 Hen VI, p 54, pl 17   See also Brooke,
Attachment upon Prohibition, 11, and Fitzh   Attachment upon
Prohibition, 3

Statham 27 a.   ASSETZ PAR DISCENT

Hilary   (1) **In a scire facias** to have execution out of a fine
43 Ed III   by which the land was rendered to one B for life, the remainder to one C in tail. And the demandant as heir to C
demanded execution. BELKNAP   Your father confirmed
our estate for the term of our life, with warranty, and you
have assets by descent, judgment, etc   CANNDISH   Our
father was indebted to the king, who seised this same land
which you allege descended to us, and committed this same
land to us until the debt should be raised, which debt never
was raised, without this that we have any other land by
descent   BELKNAP. And we, judgment, since you are
seised of the freehold, and of the fee, etc   And so to judgment.   (He did not say that the king was seised in the life
of his father, so the descent was not denied, etc)

Case 1   Reported in Y B Hilary, 43 Ed III, p 9, pl 27   See also Brooke,
Assets by Descent, 9

Paschal   (2) **Although nothing descends** to the heir except
7 Hen IV   lands in ancient demesne, still he shall be charged by that
descent by a writ of Debt, as heir to his father, by HANK-
FORD and HILARY   But the plaintiff shall not have execution
of that land, for the sheriff cannot put him in execution
of it, for then it would be a free fee   Query, how then
should he have execution?   For it is not reasonable that
any other thing be put in execution, except the land which

descended, etc   Query, if he shall have execution of land which descended afterwards, as in Formedon, etc , by a *Scire Facias*, etc ? And query, if such assets in ancient demesne are a bar in Formedon, etc ?

Reported very briefly in Y B Paschal, 7 Hen IV, p 14, pl 11   Case 2
The abridgment is longer than the reported case. See also Brooke, Assets by Descent, 11

(3) **Where assets** by descent are pleaded in Formedon,   Michaelis
the demandant can say that the same ancestor had nothing   35 Hen VI
in the same land which descended to him, except by a disseisin made on another who had entered. Or else he can say that after the death of his ancestor he waived the possession, for the above reason   by HALTOSTE in Debt, in the Exchequer, etc

The case has not been identified in Y B Mich 35 Hen VI, or in the   Case 3
early abridgments

ACCORDE

(1) **If I plead** an accord in bar, in a writ of Trespass, or   Michaelis
other action in which such a plea lies, it is necessary for me   30 Hen VI
to allege in fact that the plaintiff was satisfied, to wit that an agreement was made between the plaintiff and the defendant that the defendant should pay him for all in debate, etc , which he has paid , and not to say, "which he is ready to pay" as in an arbitration, etc. For upon an arbitrement the plaintiff can have an action of debt, but not upon an accord, etc

And it was said in the same plea that there cannot be an accord except between the parties, for if another man be a party to it, it is an arbitration and not an accord, because when he pleads the accord he shall not say that "by the mediation of their friends" this accord was taken, etc In Trespass in the King's Bench, etc   Query, if an accord can be pleaded in an action of debt, etc , since such an accord cannot be pleaded except where it appears by the action that a wrong was done by the defendant to the plaintiff, etc   And if in debt a man can say that as to this debt and all trespasses an accord was taken, as one pleads in an arbitration, etc ?

Case 1   Reported in Y B Paschal (not Mich), 30 Hen VI, p 4, pl 6   See also Fitzh Accord, 5

Hilary
36 Hen VI

(2) **In trespass** it is a good plea that one H gave to the plaintiff two shillings in satisfaction of a trespass, which he received, judgment, etc. And the opinion was that it was a good plea notwithstanding the said H was not a party to the trespass

Case 2   The case has not been identified, but in Y B Mich 36 Hen VI, p 8, pl 5, there is a very long case where the law of accord is "well debated "

AMERALTIE

Statham 27 b   (1) **See the power** of the Court of Admiralty well dis-
Michaelis   cussed in the title of Replication; and that in Michaelis 18
18 Hen VI   Hen VI [1]

Case 1   The citation has not been identified in Y B Mich 18 Hen VI

AD QUOD DAMPNUM

Hilary
2 Ed III

(1) **Ad quod dampnum** shall not be as to anything which belongs to the crown and dignity of the king   As if the king grants to me to have return of writs and like things, etc , by the opinion, etc , in an *Ad Quod Dampnum*, etc Query?

Case 1   The case has not been identified in Y B Hilary, 2 Ed III

ABBE

Hilary
22 Hen VI.

(1) **An abbot** shall not be charged by his co-monk for anything done after his entry into religion, if it be not to the

[1] The reference is to Statham, title of Replicacion and Rejoynder, p 151 b, case 1, *infra*

use of the house, by FORTESCUE in the case of the *Abbot of Westminster*

Reported in Y B Mich (not Hilary), 22 Hen VI, p 4, pl 4   See also Brooke, Abbe and Prior, 8, and Fitzh Abbe, 20   Case 1

(2) **An abbot** shall be charged for a contract made by an officer of the house to the use of the house   And this in Debt, etc   Trinity 25 Ed III

Reported in Y B Mich (not Trinity), 25 Ed III, p 48, pl 2   (In the edition of 1679 there is a confusion in the pagination of the years 24 and 25 Ed III   The paging is continuous, and so p 48 of Ed III, becomes p 91 in the "vulgate" as Maitland called it   Mich 25 Ed III, p 91, pl 2)   See also Fitzh Abbe, 19   Case 2

(3) **If the abbot and the convent** seal a deed with my seal the successor shall be charged, etc.   Michaelis 22 Ed III

The case has not been identified in Y B Mich. 22 Ed III   Fitzh Abbe, 21, has a very short abridgment   He has it "a" seal, not "my" seal   Case 3

(4) **An abbot** without a convent can by a fine bind his successor, to wit   acknowledge for himself and his successors, but not by a deed enrolled, etc. (Note the distinction)   And this in an Iter of Cornwall, folio primo (And so can the bishop, as it seems, etc)   In Iter Cornub fo p⁰

We have not the printed Eyre of Cornwall which is cited   Fitzh Abbe, 21, has the case   Case 4

(5) **If an abbot** acknowledges a deed, in an action brought against him, that will bind his successor, as was held in Debt, in the King's Bench   Anno 20 Hen VI

Reported in Y B Trinity, 20 Hen VI, p 45, pl 36   See also Fitzh Abbe, 22   Case 5

(6) **An abbot was charged** by a deed made by his predecessor and the convent, by the words *"Sigillum nostrum apposuimus"*, and it did not say, *"Sigillum nostrum commune"* or *"conventuale,"* etc   In Debt   Trinity 22 Hen VI

Reported in Y B Mich (not Trinity), 22 Hen VI, p 4, pl 6   See also Fitzh Abbe, 24   Case 6

Hilary
20 Hen VI
(7) **See in the title of debt** an action was brought against an abbot on a contract made by his predecessor. Good matter. Hilary 20 Henry VI.

Case 7   Reported in Y B Hilary, 20 Hen VI, p 45, pl 36

Hilary
25 Ed. III
(8) **If an abbot** who is a parson emparsoné by appropriation can charge without his ordinary, inasmuch as he is patron, and shall he have aid of the ordinary, and has the bishop correction of him as of other persons? Since from that it would follow that he should examine every abbot as to his ability, etc. And it seems that he shall have aid of himself and of the ordinary, and so it was adjudged, Hilary, 25 Ed III, in Annuity

Case 8   The case has not been identified in Y B Hilary, 25 Ed III, or in the early abridgments.

BASTARDIE

Statham 28 a

Trinity
43 Ed III
(1) **In an assize,** the bishop certified that the plaintiff was legitimate, and this by special matter. And it was adjudged good, etc And there was also a writ which issued to the bishop for certification, which was returnable at their next session; on which day no justices came, wherefore the assize was re-attached to another day, on which day the bishop certified, and it was admitted, etc. See the Statute of Bastardy and the proclamation, etc

Case 1   The case has not been identified in Y B Trinity, 43 Ed III, or in the early abridgments   Statute of Bastardy   See 20 Hen III, cap 9, Stats at Large, Vol 1, p 31

Paschal
44 Ed III
(2) **If a man** marries a woman who is *enceinte* by another man at the time of the marriage, that issue will be a bastard. But it is otherwise if she be *enceinte* by himself, etc   But the issue as to legitimacy shall be tried as to whether she was first *enceinte* by him or another at the time of the marriage. And this in a *Scire Facias*, etc.   See as to Bastardy in the Book of Assizes, etc

Case 2   Reported in Y B Paschal, 44 Ed III, p 12, pl 21

(3) **If the defendant** alleges bastardy generally, and the plaintiff shows that such a one, his father, took his mother to wife, within which espousals he was born and was legitimate, the defendant shall have no answer to that special matter, but should maintain his issue (But yet it seems that this shall be tried by the country; and therefore it is good for the defendant to show special matter at the commencement) Query as to this?

Statham omits the citation to this case, which is, therefore, unidenti- Case 3
fied

(4) **One brought a scire facias** to execute a remainder Hilary
as heir, etc, and he showed how one H married one K, 1 Hen VI
his mother, between whom he was the issue Huls
Execution, etc., for a long time before the marriage, etc ,
this K was *enceinte* by one P, of this same demandant, and
afterwards she was married as [was said] before and then
she eloped from her husband and went to the said P, and
lived with him for a quarter of a year, within which time the
demandant was born, judgment if he shall be received as
heir, etc Rolff· That is no plea And, first the elope-
ment is not to the purpose, but the strength of the plea is that
she was *enceinte* And sir, "*enceinte*" and "not *enceinte*" is a
good issue, and shall be tried by women, but he said that she
was *enceinte* by one P, and that cannot be tried, for if it be
so he is a bastard, and the son of no one, etc And also a
woman has been *enceinte* for four years, etc Strange
If he had said that the demandant was the son of one who
was her first husband and he was born after the marriage
between H and herself, that had been a good plea to bastardize him by such special matter, as to say that her husband
was of the age of eight years And then by advice execution
was awarded, etc

Reported in Y B Mich (not Hilary), 1 Hen VI, p 3, pl 8 See also Case 4
Brooke, Bastardy, 26, and Fitzh Bastardy, 1

(5) **See by Thorpe** in an assize, that a divorce can be Michaelis
made after the death of both [of those] who were married, 39 Ed III.
etc And by the divorce their issue shall be bastardized,

but FYNCHEDEN [said] that this cannot be except the issue be made a party to it. And when this matter is taken before the ordinary, the **ordinary** should make process against the issue, etc

And see in the same plea, the tenant alleged a general bastardy, and the plaintiff showed special matter which was triable by the country to which the tenant was made to answer

Case 5   Reported in Y B Mich 39 Ed III, p 31, pl 35   See also Brooke, Bastardy, 23

Trinity
11 Hen IV   (6) **General bastardy** certified by the Bishop will preclude strangers as well as privies   But where the bishop certifies that one is legitimate, still a man can allege special bastardy in him, for that is not contrary to the certification of the bishop, for he may be legitimate by the law of the church and a bastard by our law.   But if he be a bastard by the law of Holy Church he is wholly bastard in our law and the bishop cannot certify twice, wherefore, etc

Case 6.   Reported in Y B Trinity, 11 Hen IV, p 84, pl 32   See also Brooke, Bastardy, 12, and Fitzh Bastardy, 6

Hilary
7 Hen IV   (7) **If a man** pleads special bastardy in me, I may choose to answer to the special matter, or else to say "legitimate and not bastard" and not answer the special matter, for all the special matter amounts to nothing more than to bastardize him, by THIRNING in a *Scire Facias*.

And *simile* Anno 6 Ric II   (But yet I believe that this is not the law, for he should answer to the special matter as it seems)

Case 7   Reported in Y B Hilary, 7 Hen IV, p 9, pl 13   See also Brooke, Bastardy, 8, and Fitzh Bastardy, 4

Hilary
18 Hen VI.   (8) **Bastardy** alleged in Trespass shall be tried by the county and not by the Bishop, by the opinion of the COURT in Trespass.

Case 8   The case has not been identified in Y B Hilary, 18 Hen VI, or in the early abridgments

(9) **Bastardy** shall be tried by the bishop where the land Hilary
is, notwithstanding the marriage is alleged to have been 7 Hen IV
in another diocese   And this in a *Cui in Vita*, etc

The case has not been identified in Y B Hilary, 7 Hen IV, or in the Case 9
early abridgments

(10) **If a bastard** enters as heir and dies seised, his issue Hilary
shall hold the land, and the lawful issue shall be estopped 2 Ed III
from bastardizing him in an assize of Mort d'Ancestor
brought by the legal issue for the land, but for other lands
he can bastardize him   This is also understood where the
bastard is the oldest son, and this in a Mort d'Ancestor,
etc   *Simile* in the time of King Edward the First, in
different places, etc   (But yet it is strange law!)

The case has not been identified in Y B Hilary, 2 Ed III, or in the Case 10
early abridgments.

(11) **Divorce** because of kinship between the parents Anno
shall not bastardize, by the opinion of the COURT   And 29 Ed I
this in a note, etc. [folio ultimo]

There are no early printed Year Books for 29 Ed I   The citation Case 11
seems to be to some Eyre

(12) **Although** the bastard continues in possession, as Michaelis
above, still, for other lands which descend to his issue after- 14 Ed II
wards, the lawful issue can enter, and his entry is legal
And it was said in the same plea that where he died
seised, without claiming, and without issue, the lord shall
not have the land by escheat against the legal issue   And
this in an assize of Novel Disseisin   Query, if the lawful
issue brought a writ of right against the issue of the bastard,
if such a continuance would cause him to have a right
against the lawful issue   It seems not, etc

The case has not been identified in Y B Mich 14 Ed II, or in the Case 12
early abridgments.

BRIEFE[20]

Statham 28 b

(1) **In debt against** a husband and his wife the woman Michaelis
was called M, at Stile, which was the name of her father, 2 Hen. IV

and by this name she was bound   But yet, because by the taking of a husband she had lost her name, the writ was abated.   Query, how shall the writ be in that case, etc?

Case 1 Reported in Y. B Mich 2 Hen IV, p 1, pl. 5. See also Brooke, Briefe, 52, and Fitzh Briefe, 207.

Michaelis 2 Hen IV (2) **In trespass,** the defendant justified for rent in arrear to his master, and asked judgment of the writ *vi et armis*, and the opinion was the servant was not in the purview of the Statute, to wit *non ideo puniatur dominus.*

Case 2 Reported in Y B Mich 2 Hen IV, p 4, pl 11 See also Fitzh Trespass, 399

The Statute is that of 52 Hen IV, Marlbridge, cap 111   Stats. at Large, Vol 1, p 57

Michaelis 2 Hen IV (3) **The Bishop of Winchester** brought a writ of Trespass against several   And in the pone one was mis-named, and notwithstanding that they could have answered separately in that writ, the writ was abated against all. But it is otherwise if there are several pones or several *præcipes*

Case 3 Reported in Y B Mich 2 Hen IV, p 8, pl 40 See also Fitzh Briefe, 209

Paschal 2 Hen IV (4) **The Bishop of Winchester** brought a quod permittat against the abbot of Hyde "*Quod Permittat episcopum redunde cursum cujusdam aquæ in Hyde, quem W, predecessorum prædicti abbatis duxit ad nocumentum sibi tenementum sui* " And the writ was abated.   That he permitted

Case 4 Reported in Y B Mich (not Paschal), 2 Hen IV, p 13, pl 55 See also Brooke, Briefe, 529   (That he permitted his bishop to destroy the course of his water in Hyde, which W, the predecessor of the aforesaid abbot had cut, to the damage of his free tenement)

Paschal 2 Hen IV (5) **In a formedon,** the tenant prayed aid of the king and had it. And then the *procedendo* came and the tenant said that the demandant had made an omission of the descent, etc , and he asked judgment of the writ RIKHIL He has prayed aid, wherefore, etc. HANKFORD

We have seen that the reversion is in the king, who should
not lose through your false writ, wherefore answer him, etc

Reported in Y B Paschal, 2 Hen IV, p 19, pl 15   See also Brooke, Case 5
Briefe 97, and Fitzh Briefe, 212

(6) **If a man** recovers against me pending another writ Hilary
40 Ed III
against me, if he does not sue execution the first writ stands
good, etc. In Wardship.

Reported in Y B Hilary, 40 Ed III, p 7, pl 16   See also Brooke, Case 6
Briefe, 39, and Fitzh Briefe, 520

(7) **A bishop** brought a writ of Wardship alleging that Hilary
40 Ed III
the ancestor of the infant held of him   The defendant said
that the same ancestor died in the time of your predecessor
And the writ was abated, for it may be that the ancestor
held of his predecessor, and it seems that it belongs to his
executor, etc

Reported in Y B Hilary, 40 Ed III, p 14, pl 31   See also Brooke, Case 7
Briefe, 502, and Fitzh Briefe, 521

(8) **A writ** against a master of a college, leaving out his Paschal
40 Ed III
soholars,[1] is good, by the opinion   And [see the] contrary,
for their possession is not the same as that of a dean and
chapter   And this in Debt

Reported in Y B Paschal, 40 Ed III, p 23, pl 23   Case 8

(9) That which is nugatory does not abate the writ, and
this in a Formedon.

Statham has no citation for this case, which is reported in Y B Case 9
Paschal, 40 Ed III, p 25, pl 29   See also Brooke, Briefe, 41, and Fitzh
Briefe, 525

(10) **In debt,** the writ was *"Præcipe Priori de T,"* And Paschal
40 Ed III
the obligation was *"Priore Monasterii de T"* And because
of the disaccordance the writ was abated, etc

Reported in Y B Paschal, 40 Ed III, p 25, pl 30   Case 10

[1] The printed report of the case gives "his chapter" intead of his
"scholars"

Trinity
40 Ed III

(11) In a praecipe quod reddat, the tenant said that the demandant had another writ pending against him for the same land, in which he had the view, etc.   And for this reason the writ was abated.

Case 11

Reported in Y. B. Mich (not Trinity), 40 Ed III, p 35, pl. 3   See also Brooke, Briefe, 43, and Fitzh   Briefe, 528

The Year Book margin gives Statham, case 10, which would be correct if we did not include the case of "nugacion"

Michaelis
40 Ed III

(12) In dower, the demandant was nonsuited at the *Nisi Prius*   And after this, and before the day in the Bench, she purchased another writ.   And although the day in the Bench and the day in the *Nisi Prius* were all one day [in law] the second writ was abated, since it was purchased before the other writ was abated by judgment, etc

Case 12

Reported in Y B. Mich 40 Ed III, p 38, pl 12   See also Brooke Briefe, 44, Fitzh· Briefe, 530

Michaelis
40 Ed III

(13) If a writ be brought against a woman who takes a husband pending the writ, the writ shall not abate because that was her own deed.   And this in *Scire Facias*, where the writ was brought as above, and she took a husband, and the demandant brought another writ against the husband and the wife, which was abated, etc   (But yet it was reasonable in that case, because the first writ was not abated by a judgment)

Case 13

Reported in Y. B Mich 40 Ed III, p 44, pl 28   See also Brooke, Briefe, 45, and Fitzh   Briefe, 531   The margin of the Y B refers to this case as Statham 12   See *supra*, case 11

Michaelis
41 Ed III

(14) The writ was brought in H and W, and because W was a hamlet of H, and he thus demanded one thing twice, the writ was abated.

Case 14

Reported in Y B Mich 41 Ed III, p 22, pl 12   See also Brooke, Briefe, 50, and Fitzh Briefe, 536   The margin of the Y B gives Statham 13, Fitzh   546, and Brooke, 51

(15) **In a writ of waste** against the tenant for term of Michaelis 41 Ed III
life, after he who was in the reversion entered, by reason
that he alienated in fee, the writ was "*quod tenet*" and it
was adjudged good, etc.

This is apparently the case reported in Y B Mich 41 Ed III, p. 23, Case 15
pl 15 The report and the abridgment, however, are quite "*disaccor-
dant*" See also Fitzh Briefe, 540, but Fitzherbert has lost his page

(16) **In a scire facias** brought by two, one was sum- Hilary 42 Ed III
moned and severed, and died; and yet the writ stood good,
since by the severance he was out of court.

Reported in Y B Hilary, 42 Ed III, p 2, pl. 9. See also Brooke, Case 16
Briefe, 53; and Fitzh Briefe, 551 The margin of the Year Book is
right for Statham, but gives Brooke, 54, and Fitzh 531

(17) **At the return of the great cape** the tenant abated Hilary 42 Ed III
the writ for matter apparent, etc

Reported in Y B Hilary, 42 Ed III, p 3, pl 10. See also Brooke, Case 17
Briefe, 54 The margin of the Year Book gives Statham 16

(18) **In a praecipe quod reddat** against two who Paschal 43 Ed III
vouched one J, who vouched one who said that one of the
tenants was dead, the writ was abated, etc.

The case has not been identified in Y B Paschal, 43 Ed III, or in the Case 18
early abridgments

(19) **If, pending** the writ against the tenant, another Trinity 43 Ed III
recovers against him, and pending the writ he sues execution and the tenant returns to the land, the first writ stands
good, for he shall say that he was tenant the day, etc. And
yet, etc   In Cosinage, etc.

Reported in Y B. Trinity, 43 Ed. III, p 21, pl. 9 See also Brooke, Case 19
Briefe, 61.

(20) **A man shall have** a *Quare Impedit* for a prebend Michaelis 43 Ed III
in the county, where the body of the prebendary is, notwithstanding the cathedral church, in which, etc , is in
another county. And the writ was good.

Reported in Y B Mich 43 Ed III, p 33, pl 42 See also Fitzh Case 20
Briefe, 566 Margin of Y B gives Statham, 19

**Paschal
44 Ed III**

(21) **In formedon** the writ was *"præcipe quod reddat B, manerium, etc F juxta K"* BELKNAP: Part of the manor of F is in K, judgment of the writ. And the opinion was that the writ should abate, although it was known by the same name And from this it follows that as to a manor which extends into different vills, every vill shall be in the writ, or else he shall demand the manor, except, etc

Case 21

Reported in Y B Paschal, 44 Ed III, p 12, pl. 23 See also Brooke, Briefe, 67, and Fitzh Briefe, 574 The margin of the Y B gives Brooke, 68, Statham, 20

**Trinity
46 Ed III**

(22) **In trespass** for goods carried away, it is no plea to say that there was another writ pending for the same trespass, unless the names of the vills agree, etc Query, for if a man should recover I should bar him by such matter and aver that it was the same trespass, etc But in a battery one shall abate the writ by such a plea, because it can be continued

Case 22

Reported in Y B Trinity, 46 Ed III, p 16, pl 12 See also Fitzh Briefe, 602 The text of the abridgment in Statham is very corrupt

**Statham 29 a
Trinity
44 Ed III**

(23) **In trespass** *"quare bona et cattalla cepit,"* etc. The declaration was for barley taken. HANKFORD Judgment of the writ, for he should have a writ *"quare tot quarteria argei,"* etc And the writ was adjudged good But he could not declare for so much silver, etc, taken, for that which was taken must be certain, etc

Case 23

Reported in Y. B Trinity, 44 Ed III, p 20, pl 17. The margin of the Y B gives Statham 20

**Hilary
48 Ed III**

(24) **In a cui in vita,** the writ was *"qua clamat tenere sibi et haeredibus de corpora suo exeunt"* And it did not mention by whose gift, and for this reason the writ was abated, etc It is otherwise in a *Quod ei Deforceat*, etc.

Case 24

The case has not been identified in Y B Hilary, 48 Ed III, or in the early abridgments

**Hilary
30 Ed III**

(25) **In a praecipe quod reddat** the tenant said that on the day, etc, he had nothing in the land, but before

the writ was purchased he bought the reversion, and pending the writ the tenant died, so we became tenant while the writ was pending   Judgment, etc

Reported in Y B Hilary, 30 Ed III, p 3, pl 11   See also Fitzh   Case 25
Briefe, 297

(26) **One made** a statute merchant to the husband and   Paschal
his wife, who made a defeasance, and against this sued   48 Ed III
execution, wherefore he sued an *Audita Querela* against
them   And the writ was challenged because it should
have been against the husband alone   And the opinion
was that this was good   And this well debated, etc

Reported in Y B Paschal, 48 Ed III, p 12, pl 4   See also Brooke, Case 26
Briefe, 80

(27) **If an abbot,** prior, or bishop, brings an action, he   Michaelis
does not need to have this clause in the writ, to wit   "if   26 Hen VI
the plaintiff makes you secure," etc., for the law will con-
sider that they are sufficient, etc   And the law is the same
for a Mort d'Ancestor by one under age, to wit   various
clauses may be left out.   By the opinion of NEWTON in
the Exchequer Chamber

There is no printed Year Book for 26 Hen VI.   Case 27

See as to brief, in the title of Formedon, many matters   Note
And also in the title of Misnomer

(28) **In formedon** for a manor with the appurtenances,   Paschal
the tenant said that part of the manor extended into   4 Ed III
another county, etc , and he was forced to show how
And for this reason the writ was abated

Reported in Y B Paschal, 4 Ed. III, p 23, pl 16   Case 28

(29) **In a writ** of *sur cui in vita* for land and rent, as   Trinity
to the land the tenant alleged joint tenure, and as to the   5 Ed III
rent he said that the very land in demand was put in view,
so he demanded lands and rent issuing out of the same
land   DARR   He has pleaded two pleas to abate our writ
we pray that he be kept to one   SETON   If we pleaded

the joint tenure you would force us to answer to the rent,
wherefore, etc   And then the plaintiff was forced to answer,
who said that he put other land in view within the same
vill   HERLE   You ought to traverse generally, that he
cannot be tenant of the rent.   And so he did   And the
demandant said he was tenant of the other land, so tenant
of the rent, etc

Case 29

Reported in Y B Trinity, 5 Ed III, p 21, pl 9   See also Fitzh
Briefe, 721

Hilary
7 Ed III

(30) **If I have a writ** pending on the quindene of Michaelmas, and then it is abated, and in the meantime, between
the said fifteenth day and the day the writ was abated, the
plaintiff purchases another writ, it is a good purchase, if
it be in the same term, for the abatement of the writ shall
relate to the said fifteenth, because all the term, in effect,
is only one and the same day   And this in a Ravishment
of Wardship, etc

Case 30

Reported in Y B Hilary, 7 Ed III, p 11, pl 23   See also Fitzh
Briefe, 433

Hilary
7 Ed III

(31) **A writ of dower** was abated because it was brought
against the guardian not named guardian, etc   And the
same day another writ of Dower was abated because it was
brought against the heir, whereas he had a guardian in
chivalry for the same land, etc

Case 31

Reported in Y. B Hilary, 7 Ed III, p 10, pl 21

Hilary
8 Ed III

(32) **In a cessavit** against two, one made default after
default, the other said he was tenant of the entirety, without this, etc   Wherefore the demandant counted against
him   (Query, for it seems that he should maintain his
writ, etc)   And the tenant said that he held the same lands
for the term of his life, of the lease of him who made default,
and vouched him to warranty.   To which the demandant
said that the vouchee nor any of his ancestors, ever
had, etc , after the title, etc , up to the day the writ was
purchased   The tenant demanded judgment since, as

he had brought this writ against him, so he had admitted
the contrary of his writ.   But yet the writ was adjudged
good, because it might be that he had nothing before the
writ was purchased, but he might have had it afterwards,
in which case the writ is good, and the admission of a
man shall not abate his writ, except where it is an express
admission, etc

The case has not been identified in Y B 8 Ed III, or in the early Case 32
abridgments

(33) **In dower** against one as guardian, he said that he Hilary
had nothing except for a term of six years of the lease of 8 Ed III
one A who was guardian in law   And the writ was abated
because he was not guardian in law, nor guardian in fact,
because he did not have all the estate of a guardian

Reported in Y B Hilary, 8 Ed III, p 15, pl 46   See also Fitzh Case 33
Briefe, 446

(34) **In a praecipe quod reddat** for a rent charge Hilary
against two tenants in common, one *præcipe* is good enough, 9 Ed III
although they are in by separate titles; but it is otherwise
of a rent service, because it can be severed

Reported in Y B Paschal (not Hilary), 9 Ed III, p 13, pl 13 See Case 34
also Fitzh Briefe, 458

(35) **An abbot** brought a *Cessavit*, and the writ was Hilary
challenged because it was not "which he claimed to be 10 Ed III
the right of his church," but he declared [it] in his count,
and the writ was adjudged good, etc

The case has not been identified in Y B Hilary, 10 Ed III   Fitzh Case 35
Briefe, 690, has the case, but there is no citation to page or placitum

(36) **If a man** pleads in abatement of the writ, because Michaelis
of the form he should give the plaintiff a better writ, but 10 Ed III
it is otherwise if he pleaded to the matter of the writ   And
this by HERLE, in Waste

The case has not been identified in Y B Mich 10 Ed III, or in the Case 36
early abridgments

Michaelis
6 Ed III

(37) **The vouchee** shall plead in abatement of the writ for the form of the writ, but not to the matter, etc , since the tenant has committed, etc.

Case 37

The case has not been identified in Y B Mich 6 Ed III, or in the early abridgments   The text is apparently corrupt   I give it literally

Paschal
13 Ed III

(38) **In trespass** brought by the abbot and his co-monks, for a battery made on the co-monk it was *"ad damnum ipsorum,"* and it was adjudged good

Case 38

There is no early printed year of 13 Ed III   The case is printed in the Rolls Series, 12 & 13 Ed III, pp 248-49

Trinity
16 Ed III

(39) **In formedon** against one J, who said that this same demandant brought Formedon for this same land against one F, who vouched us to warranty, and that the writ still pends, judgment, etc   And because he did not say that he entered into the warranty, in which case he was not a party to the first writ, the writ was adjudged good, etc (It seems that he could have estopped the demandant, because, etc)

Case 39

There is no early printed year of 16 Ed III   The case has not been identified in the Rolls Series for that year

Michaelis
18 Ed III

(40) **In trespass** against the parson of the church of E, the process continued until he was outlawed, and he had his charter of pardon, and sued a *Scire Facias*, and the plaintiff counted against him   And he demanded judgment of the writ because he was parson of only half the church, etc   DARR   To that you shall not be received, inasmuch as you sued your *Scire Facias* as parson of the entirety   And this was not allowed because he could not do anything but that which was in accordance with the record, etc. (But yet it seems the contrary [was right] and that he was not outlawed, etc)

Reported in Y B Mich 18 Ed III, p 33, pl 11

Statham 29 b
Michaelis
18 Ed III.

(41) **In dower** against the guardian of the scholars of C RIKHILL   He is the master, and he produced the letters of the king as to his foundation, etc   SETON   He is known by both names   But yet the writ was abated   But it

is wonderful that he who was a stranger could take notice of the name of his foundation, when it was known by different names, etc

The case has not been identified in Y B Mich 18 Ed. III, or in the early abridgments

Case 41

(42) **In debt** the writ was, "Distrain M, who was the wife of A de B, of F, husbandman" ROLFF. Judgment of the writ, for he did not name the wife as of any vill, for F refers only to the husband, and not to the wife, etc Query?

Michaelis 4 Hen VI

Fitzh Briefe, 25, gives this case as reported in Mich 4 Hen VI, p 4, pl 9 It has not been identified in any of the editions to which I have had access

Case 42

(43) **Detinue** against the husband and his wife for a bailment made to them after the coverture And the writ was abated because it should have been brought against the husband alone, etc Query, if the bailment had been made to the woman before the coverture? Or if the woman had them as executrix?

Hilary 38 Ed III

Reported in Y B Hilary, 38 Ed III, p 1, pl 1

Case 43

(44) **In a writ** of annuity against one J, as co-canon of the Priory of B, and perpetual custodian of B, the defendant alleged a variance between the writ and the deed, etc And on another day he said he was under the obedience of the said prior, not named, etc FYNCHEDEN· To that you shall not get, inasmuch as you have alleged a variance, etc SHARSHULL· He shall have this plea notwithstanding that, etc , inasmuch as this plea goes to the action, wherefore answer, etc

Michaelis 21 Ed III

Reported in Y B Mich 21 Ed III, p 35, pl 26

Case 44

(45) **If one be bailiff** of my manor which extends into different vills, all the vills shall be named And if any of the vills be within a franchise I shall have my action for that which is within the franchise, notwithstanding he is bailiff of the entire manor, etc., by SHARSHULL, etc

Trinity 24 Ed III

The case has not been identified in Y B Trinity, 24 Ed III, or in the early abridgments

Case 45

Trinity
34 Ed III

(46) **In a quare impedit** the writ was, "*Præcipe* the chaplain, etc , and if not, etc , then summon the aforesaid A " And because it was not "then summon the aforesaid bishop" the writ was abated, for he shall be summoned by his name of dignity, etc.

Case 46

There is no early printed Year Book for 34 Ed III The case has not been identified in the Rolls Series for that year

Paschal
14 Hen VI

(47) **In a writ of entry** by the husband and his wife, the writ was "Of which he disseised them." NEWTON. Judgment of the writ, for at the time of the alleged disseisin the woman was sole seised, and after that this her husband espoused her, in which case it should be "disseised her " FULTHORPE That is no plea, for no time for the disseisin is alleged in our writ nor in our declaration. And also he does not answer us, for he ought to answer "without this that he disseised them both, without this that the husband had anything at the time of the disseisin. PASTON I believe that he cannot have any other writ in the Chancery But yet he said that it was not a good plea to confess the disseisin. Query, How could he plead it? etc

Reported in Y B Anno 14 Hen VI (this year fourteen is not divided into terms in the printed Year Books), p 13, pl 46

Trinity
16 Ed III

(48) **It is no plea** to say that the plaintiff has another writ pending against him, etc., unless he says that the plaintiff had appeared, for it might be that a stranger of the same name brought the writ, in which case he would not be precluded, etc And this in Formedon

Case 48

There is no early printed year of 16 Ed. III The case has not been identified in the Rolls Series for that year

Michaelis
18 Ed III

(49) **In formedon** in the descender the tenant said that formerly the demandant brought a writ of Formedon in the remainder against him for the same gift and lands, etc , to which he appeared And the demandant said that "in the first writ you waged your law of not summoned, upon which the writ was abated, and we purchased this

writ," etc And the writ was adjudged good, etc But see that this was no plea in abatement of the writ, etc , on that day, for he shall plead the whole record, or else the plaintiff shall say "no such record "

The case has not been identified in Y B Mich 18 Ed. III, or in the early abridgments   Case 49

(50) **If the tenant** by the curtesy surrenders to him in the reversion, pending a writ against him in the reversion, the writ shall not abate, for the agreement to surrender was his deed. Well debated. And with this agrees the Book of the Assizes, in the case of *Quyntyn*, upon a fine, where the tenant said that he had recovered the lands against a stranger pending the writ, and the writ was adjudged good because it was his deed, as above, etc   And from this it follows that where land comes to a man pending the writ, that this shall not abate the writ in any case except only where it comes to him by descent, and the reason there is because he cannot do otherwise, for the law throws the possession upon him in spite of himself, etc   Hilary 1 Hen VI

The case has not been identified in Y B Hilary 1 Hen VI   The only term for this year in the printed books is that of Michaelmas   Case 50

(51) **In account** for a receipt in the county of H, the defendant said that the receipt was in another county, in which case he should have brought his action there, etc , according to the Statute BABYNGTON   It seems that he shall not have this plea, but he shall have his remedy by way of an action [on the Statute], as if a man distrains in the high road, etc. MARTYN Not the same, for in your case the Statute is made for the plaintiff, and in this case for the defendant, therefore it is reasonable that he have it by way of a plea, etc. And this was the opinion of the COURT, etc.   Michaelis 4 Hen VI

Reported in Y B Mich 4 Hen VI, p 2, pl 4   See also Brooke, Briefe, 205, and Fitzh Briefe, 23   Case 51

The Statutes are those of 6 Ric II, Stat 1, cap 2, Stats at Large, Vol 2, p 253 (1382), and Marlbridge, 52 Hen III, Stat 1, cap 15 Stats at Large, Vol 1, p 67 (1267)

(52) **In trespass** for a close broken, brought by two, the defendant said that one of the plaintiffs had nothing in the said land on the day of the alleged recognizance, except jointly with one H, who is alive, and not named, etc   DANBY What do you say against the other plaintiff? POLE That goes to all   MOILE. That is not so, for if a man pleads in abatement of the writ, he shall give the plaintiff a better writ, and it may be that the other plaintiff held jointly with other persons, wherefore, etc   POLE If one plaintiff has nothing, not even a cause of action, and the other held jointly, how should we plead? ASSHTON You will plead as above as to one, and as to the other that he never had anything, etc   POLE That is no plea, for it amounts to nothing more than "not guilty," wherefore I shall be forced to take the general issue   And if I plead "not guilty" against him that is contrary to the other plea, for then I shall admit that he was seised at the time of the alleged trespass. PORTYNGTON You can take that by protestation   PRISOT· That cannot be, for even if it is taken by protestation, still he has admitted that he has a cause of action, etc   DANBY If two bring an action against me, and I say that one of them is my villein, I shall plead over to the other, to wit   "and inasmuch as he has conceived this action with one who is not responsible, judgment, etc "

FULTHORPE. Not the same   And it may be that one of the plaintiffs holds jointly, as he has alleged, and that the other holds in common, wherefore if the defendant will say that both of the plaintiffs hold jointly, or in common, that will be found against him, wherefore it seems that he has pleaded well   ASCOUGH Still it seems to me that he should answer to the other plea, and the plea that goes in abatement of the writ shall be first tried   PRISOT If he should say, as Danby has said in the case of the villein, to wit. "inasmuch as he has conceived, etc," that plea is double, for he pleads two pleas in abatement of the writ   And in a *Præcipe quod Reddat* brought by two, where one had no cause of action, I cannot see how he shall plead in abatement of the writ, unless the plea goes to the action, etc   But if he had matter in abatement of the writ,

as misnomer of one of the plaintiffs, and that the other
held jointly, peradventure he could have both the pleas,
for there none of them goes to the action, etc   Query, if
it had been a plea to say that one of the plaintiffs held
jointly, etc , without this that the other had anything, etc ?
And it seems not, for the above reason, etc

And it was said in [the same plea] if tenants in common
bring trespass, where one of the two is tenant of one part,
and another of two parts, and another of three parts, that
it shall be asked of how much each of them is tenant, and
their damages shall be severed accordingly, etc.   Query?

The case has not been identified in Y B Mich 27 Hen VI, or in   Case 52.
the early abridgments.

(53) **If one demands** judgment of the writ because he   Michaelis
is a co-monk, it is no plea unless he says that he is under   14 Hen IV.
the obedience of one such, etc , for an abbot is a co-monk.
And this in Debt, etc

The case is not easily identified   A discussion of the point may be   Case 53
found in Y B Mich 14 Hen IV, p 10, pl 8

(54) **In a monstraverunt,** the defendant said that one   Paschal
of the plaintiffs died pending the writ, judgment of the writ   2 Hen V
STRANGE. The writ should have been brought against three
or two of them, for there is no need that all be named,
any more than in a writ of Error brought by a number, the
death of one of them shall not abate the writ, for one of
them can have a writ of Error, leaving out the others
HULS   It is brought for an injury done to them, as
in Trespass, wherefore it seems that the writ shall not abate
And also the action is merely personal, for it is not like
a *ne injute vexes*, etc , which is in the right, wherefore, etc
Well argued.

The case has not been identified in Y B Paschal, 2 Hen V, or in   Case 54
the early abridgments.

(55) **In debt** by a prior against one J, who demanded   Michaelis
judgment of the writ because since the last continuance he   9 Hen V
was deposed. STRANGE   That is no plea, without saying,

"So not Prior," for it might be that he was restored, etc
And a plea in abatement of the writ ought to be good, to
all ordinary intents   And this well argued, etc

Case 55   Reported in Y B Paschal (not Mich), 9 Hen V, p 11, pl 1   See
also Brooke, Briefe, 134

Trinity
32 Ed III

(56) **In a scire facias** brought by two coparceners, one
was severed   BARTON· She who was severed had taken
a husband pending the writ. FYNCHEDEN   That is no
plea, for it does not appear whether she took a husband
before the severance or after   THORPE   Either way the
writ is abated.   And so it was adjudged, etc.

Case 56   There is no printed year for 32 Ed III   The case has not been identified in the early abridgments

Hilary
38 Ed III

(57) **In debt** by executors, one was severed and died,
and the writ was abated   The law is the same where an
executor comes by distraint, and is made to reply alone,
and afterwards his companion dies, the writ will abate, etc
Simile Mich. 28 Hen. VI, in a Formedon against two, one
disclaimed and died, and it was the opinion that the writ
should abate

Case 57   Reported in Y B Paschal (not Hilary), 38 Ed III, p 11, pl 19
The report is very brief   See also Brooke, Briefe, 136, and Fitzh
Briefe, 498

Michaelis
38 Ed III.

(58) **In a quare impedit** by two parceners, the death of
one does not abate the writ   The law is the same if one
of the two be named, etc , and because of the harm done
by the lapse

And it was said in the same plea that if a husband and
his wife be disturbed in an advowson which is in right of
the wife, and the wife dies, the husband shall not have a
Quare impedit because he cannot make title, unless he be
tenant by the curtesy, etc.   Then query, who shall have
the presentation?

Case 58   Reported in Mich 38 Ed. III, p 35, pl 51   See also Brooke, Briefe,
136

(59) **In a praecipe quod reddat** against two by several *præcipes*, he was non-suited against one, and the writ stood good against the other, etc.   Contrary *ex quo*, etc Michaelis 38 Ed III

The case has not been identified in Mich 38 Ed III, or in the early abridgments Case 59

(60) **In debt** by the husband on an obligation made to him and his wife, the writ was adjudged good in his own name, etc   Well argued. But yet, query? Trinity 12 Ric II

There is no early printed Year Book for 12 Ric II   Fitzh Briefe, 639 has an abridgment of the case   It has not been identified in Y B Trinity, 12 Ric II, Ames Foundation, ed Deiser Case 60

(61) **Debt** was brought in London upon a recognizance made in the Chancery at Westminster   And because the writ was not brought in Middlesex, it was abated Hilary 13 Ric II

There is no printed Year Book for the reign for 13 Ric II   Fitzh Briefe, 649, has the case Case 61

(62) **In debt** by the husband and his wife, on an obligation made to the wife when she was sole, the writ was, "*præcipe T. quod juste, etc , reddat B, et A, uxori ejus alias dicit Aspold*"   ROLFF She cannot have two names   And the writ was adjudged good, for "*alias*" in that case shall be "*alias tempore*" and not "*aliter*," etc   Query? Michaelis 2 Hen VI

Reported in Y B Mich 2 Hen VI, p 4, pl 2   See also Brooke, Briefe, 4, and Fitzh Briefe, 5   The Latin of the writ is given differently in the report of the case, and in each abridgment, and the arguments differ accordingly Case 62

(63) **In trespass** against four who pleaded "not guilty" at the *Nisi Prius*. And then in the Bench ROLFF said that one of the defendants had died since the inquest passed, and he prayed that the whole writ should abate, for the death of one of them   For in a former case [1] after the plea, and before the inquest was taken, all the writ was abated , so here, for there was only one *Venire Facias* awarded, etc   And it was adjudged that the plaintiff should recover Michaelis 2 Hen VI

---

[1] The text is corrupt and has been slightly changed in translation, in accordance with the text of the reported case

against the three, and that he should take nothing as to the fourth   Query, for it seems that the defendant had no day to plead that plea, etc   Well debated, etc.

Case 63   Reported in Y B Trinity (not Mich), 2 Hen VI, p 12, pl 5   See also Fitzh Briefe, 9

Paschal
2 Hen VI

(64) **In waste.** ROLFF. Judgment of the writ, for whereas he has alleged the waste to have been made in seven vills, as to three of the vills (and he named their names), we say that there are no such vills or hamlets or place known, etc , within that county, judgment of the writ. MARTYN   What do you say to the remainder? ROLFF   That goes to the entire writ   And that was the opinion of the COURT, etc

Case 64   The case has not been identified in Y B Paschal, 2 Hen VI, or in the early abridgments

Michaelis
9 Hen VI

(65) **If a man** brings a writ for two things where he could not have an action for one of them, as appeared by the writst, ill the writ is good for the remainder   But it is otherwise where he can have a writ for each of them by itself   As if a woman demands dower of lands and common for a great number of cattle, as to the land, the writ is good, because she could not have an action for such a common, but where a man brings an assize for lands and

Statham 30 b   for common, it shall abate for all, because he could have had separate writs   And this in a fine pleaded by the Prior of Saint Bartholomew, etc   And from this it follows that if I vouch two to warranty, and I show the lien of only one of them, still I shall not fail of my voucher against him who made the lien since I have no cause for a lien against the other, nor reason for a voucher   But yet it is not like the other case, for it does not appear but that I can bind him by another deed, or another cause, etc

Case 65   The case has not been identified in Y B Mich 9 Hen VI, or in the early abridgments

Hilary
9 Hen VI

(66) **In a writ of entry** in the nature of an assize, CHANNT asked judgment of the writ because it was purchased pend-

ing an assize against us by the plaintiff, for this same land
And he made it all certain, etc   MARTYN If two assizes,
or two actions, of the same nature, are returned on one and
the same day and the plaintiff appears in both, both shall
abate   But if they are returnable on different days, the
second assize shall abate and not the first   But if a man
had a writ pending and purchased a writ of a higher nature,
that would stand good, and the writ of a lower nature
would abate, because of its greater dignity, etc , in which
many concurred.   STRANGE If a man has a bill of
debt in the Exchequer it is a good plea to say that the
plaintiff has a writ for this same debt pending against him
in the King's Bench, or in the Common Bench, to which he
has appeared, judgment, etc   But it is otherwise in Trespass, etc   And it was also said that if a man purchases a
writ of Trespass pending another writ for the same Trespass, the last writ shall not abate   Query as to the cause
of this difference, etc.

Reported in Y B Mich (not Hilary), 9 Hen VI, p 50, pl 34 See Case 66
also Brooke, Briefe, 17

(67) **A man shall not have a writ** *de herede rapto*, Paschal
unless it be for his heir apparent, for if it be a younger son 22 Ed III
or daughter, it does not lie for them   And this by WIL-
LOUGHBY

The case has not been identified in Y B Paschal, 22 Ed III, or in Case 67
the early abridgments

(68) **"Præcipe A, pannar London."** That writ is not Michaelis
good, for he might be a baker in London, and live in another 7 Hen VI
county, but "præcipe" one such, a baker of London, is
good without saying of what county, because it is a county
in itself.   And this in Debt

Reported in Y B Mich (not Paschal), 7 Hen VI, p 1, pl 4   The Case 68
case of the baker is written "the case of a pointmaker" and the town
Bristol See also Fitzh Briefe, 30

(69) **One B** brought a writ of Debt and counted that the Paschal
defendant was the receiver of one C, his testator, and that 9 Hen VI
the plaintiff, as executor of the said C, assigned auditors

for him, and that he was found in arrears of the sum in demand, etc The defendant demanded judgment of the writ inasmuch as he was not named executor PASTON It seems the writ is good. As if I make an obligation to an executor for the debts of his testator, he shall have an action without naming himself executor. MARTYN It is not the same, for even if an executor assigned auditors to him, that is in the name of all, so all shall be named, and consequently, since there is but one executor, he will be named, and the release of one of them is a bar against all But in the case which PASTON has put it [does not] appear whether the debt was to his testator or not, wherefore, etc. And the opinion was that the writ should abate. [PASTON dissenting]

Case 69

Reported in Y B Paschal, 9 Hen VI, p 11, pl 33 See also Fitzh Briefe, 57

Hilary
7 Hen VI

(70) **In a quare impedit,** the defendant said that after the last continuance the plaintiff was made a knight at B, in the county, etc Judgment of the writ And the opinion was that the writ should abate. And this well argued The contrary was adjudged Anno 3 Hen. V.

Case 70

Reported in Y B Mich (not Hilary), 7 Hen VI, p. 14, pl 24 See also Brooke, Briefe, 158, and Fitzh Briefe, 35

Hilary
3 Hen VI

(71) **In debt** upon an obligation, ROLFF asked judgment of the writ, for by the Statute of Ric , Anno VI, it is decreed that all the actions of debt, detinue, and covenant shall be brought in the same county where the contract is made, and we say that this contract was made in the county of Lincoln, in which case, etc. And the plaintiff was obliged to answer this, and he said that the deed was delivered[1] to B in the county where the writ was brought, etc Contrary elsewhere, etc

Case 71

Reported in Y B Hilary, 3 Hen VI, p 29, pl 14 See also Fitzh Briefe, 18

The Statute is that of 6 Ric II, cap 2, Stats at Large, Vol 2, p 253 (1382)

[1]"Made" in the report of the case

(72) **Executors** brought a writ of Trespass for goods carried away in the life of their testator, and for his close broken SKRENE Such an action for the close of their testator broken is not given by the Statute, wherefore judgment of all the writ. THIRNING. Answer to the remainder (And I think the reason was because as to the close broken they could not have an action, etc, which would accord with the re-summons) (MARTYN From the other side of this page, next placitum, etc) Michaelis 11 Hen IV.

Reported in Y B Mich 11 Hen IV, p 3, pl 8 See also Brooke, Briefe, 118, and Fitzh Briefe, 229 Case 72.

The Statute is that of 4 Ed III, cap 7, Stats at Large, Vol 1, p 434 (1330)

(73) **A woman** brought a *quid juris clamat*, leaving out her husband because the note was levied on him before the coverture, and she could not vary from the note But yet the writ was abated, etc. Michaelis 11 Hen IV.

Reported in Y B Mich 11 Hen IV, p 7, pl 16 See also Brooke, Briefe, 522, and Fitzh Briefe, 230 Case 73

(74) **In trespass** the writ was "*Contra pacem Richardi nuper Regis Angliæ et contra pacem nostram*" And the plaintiff counted that part of the trespass was made in the time of the other king, and part in the time of this king SKRENE Judgment of the writ, for the whole writ is against the peace of two kings, etc NORTON But I have made the writ good by my count, etc Which the Court conceded, etc. Michaelis 11 Hen IV

Reported in Y B Mich 11 Hen IV, p 15, pl 33 See also Brooke, Briefe, 519, and Fitzh Briefe, 232. Case 74

(75) **Two brought** an assize, and one was severed after appearance. SKRENE Judgment of the writ, for he who was severed is an alien, and born out of the allegiance of the king, and never made a denizen HANKFORD The writ is good for the other, for this plea goes to the action for the denizen For if an alien and I purchase jointly, Michaelis 11 Hen IV

the king shall be seised of only the half, for an alien can purchase well enough, and the king shall be seised, for it is not the same as where a monk and I purchase jointly, there all shall vest in me, etc   And then the writ was adjudged good, but the reason was that he who was severed had nothing except in right of his wife, and so clearly, etc

Case 75   The case has not been identified in Y. B Mich 11 Hen IV, or in the early abridgments

Trinity
18 Hen VI   (76)   **A writ** of debt was brought and it ran, *"Præcipe Societate Lumbardorum "*   And the writ was good enough, etc.   (In the case of *Enderby*, etc)

Case 76   The case has not been identified in Y B Trinity, 18 Hen VI, or in the early abridgments

Paschal
19 Hen VI   (77)   **In debt** against A de B, of Skene, in the county of Middlesex, formerly of Abington PORTYNGTON: The writ is not good, for my matter is such that I do not know how to plead in abatement of the writ, for the defendant was never of Skene nor of Abington.   And if I plead the one in abatement of the writ he will counter upon me because I do not deny the other; and if I plead both the plea is double.   MARKHAM It seems that the "formerly" is void, unless the action is brought upon a specialty which is made accordingly, etc   NEWTON We will be advised, etc

Case 77   Reported in Y B Paschal 19 Hen VI, p 66, pl 6   See also Brooke, Briefe, 436

Michaelis
19 Hen VI

Statham 31 a.   (78)   **In debt** by executors, they counted that the defendant had accounted before auditors, assigned by them for a receipt of their testator   The defendant demanded judgment of the writ because it was *"detinet"* solely, whereas it should be *"debet et detinet,"* inasmuch as he was never indebted to their testator   MARKHAM   Where it is not necessary that two be named executors, but they are named, so for the redundancy the writ shall be as you say   As where executors brought a writ of Trespass for goods taken out of their possession and recovered, and they brought a writ of Debt for those damages, and named them executors,

the writ shall be "*debet et detinet*" for the above reason.
But in the case here it is quite necessary that they be named
executors   Wherefore the writ was adjudged good, etc

The case has not been identified in Y B Mich 19 Hen VI, or in *Case 78*
the early abridgments

(79) **In trespass** against A and B, A said that there was *Paschal 20 Hen VI*
no such B alive   YELVERTON   You shall not have this plea
PASTON: Yes, sir, as well as he shall say that the said B was
dead before the writ was purchased, which the Court conceded, etc   But he did not plead a misnomer of his companion, etc

Reported in Y B Paschal, 20 Hen VI, p 30, pl 29   See also Fitzh *Case 79*
Briefe, 85

(80) **Where he** who prayed in aid died after he was *Paschal 21 Hen VI*
joined in aid and had pleaded with the demandant, still
the writ shall not abate, for he is only a stranger to the writ
in law, for the plea that he pleaded is wholly the plea of
the tenant, and no judgment will be given against him
And the law is the same where he upon whom the avowry
is made dies, etc   But query, if he joins himself to the
tenant, and then dies, then it seems that the writ shall
abate.   And this in a Replication, etc.

The case has not been identified in Y B Paschal, 21 Hen VI, or in *Case 80*
the early abridgments

(81) **In debt** against one J, who said that after the last *Michaelis 4 Hen VI*
continuance he was consecrated Bishop of S, judgment of
this writ   And it was not allowed, for it was his own deed
etc   Query, if he be made duke, or count, or knight? etc

Reported in Y B Mich 4 Hen VI, p 2, pl. 8   See also Fitzh *Case 81*
Briefe, 893

(82) **In trespass,** the writ was that the defendant, together *Hilary 8 Hen. V*
with others, made the trespass; and the writ was abated,
inasmuch as it appeared by the writ that the trespass was
made with others not named, etc., for it is not the same as

an Oyer and Termmer, which is issued to inquire upon a suggestion, etc

Case 82 Reported in Y B Hilary, 8 Hen V, p 5, pl 20 See also Fitzh Briefe, 786

Michaelis
12 Hen IV

(83) **In a writ** of Ejectment from Wardship, against two, the death of one, pending the writ, shall not abate the writ because it is only a trespass, etc., but it is otherwise on the part of the plaintiff, etc

Case 83 Reported in Y B Mich 12 Hen IV, p 10, pl 20 See also Fitzh Briefe, 482

Hilary
12 Hen IV

(84) **In a writ de herede rapto,** the writ was challenged because it was "whose marriage belonged to him," because it is to recover damages to the value of the marriage. And the opinion was that the writ was good But yet query, if he shall recover for the value, etc ?

Case 84 Reported in Y B Hilary, 12 Hen. IV, p 16, pl 9 See also Fitzh. Briefe, 483

Trinity
27 Hen VI

(85) **In trespass** because a certain obligation in which the defendant was bound to the plaintiff, at such a place, he found, took and tore up POLE This writ comprehends double matter, to wit one, the taking and the other the [tearing up] PORTYNGTON The taking is nothing except to connect the action with the other, to wit, the [tearing up] wherefore answer, etc.

Case 85 The case has not been identified in Y B Trinity, 27 Hen VI, or in the early abridgments

Michaelis
26 Hen VI

(86) **In debt** by executors, or against executors, the death of one of them shall abate the writ

Case 86 There is no printed year for 26 Hen VI The case has not been identified in the early abridgments

Michaelis
28 Hen VI

(87) **In formedon** against two, one disclaimed, the other vouched to warranty, and afterward he who disclaimed died And the opinion was that the writ should abate

Case 87 The case has not been identified in Y B Mich 28 Hen VI, or in the early abridgments

See as to brief, in the title of Formedon, in the title of View, in the title of Misnomer; in the title of Prescription, Mich 18 Hen VI, and in the title of Maintenance of Writs, and also in the titles of Nontenure, Joint Tenancy, Several Tenancy, and in the title of Addition, etc.[1]

(88) **In a writt** brought against a parson for lands in his glebe, and he resigns, pending the writ, the writ shall abate Anno
15 Ed III

There is no early printed year for 15 Ed III The case has not been identified in the Rolls Series for that year Case 88

(89) **A writt brought** in the Common Bench for land in Wales, which was not in the franchise, was held good in a *Quare Impedit*, etc Query, to whom should the writ be directed? Paschal
6 Ric II

There is no printed Year Book for 6 Ric II The case has not been identified in the early abridgments Case 89

(90) **A writt** shall abate in all where the demandant is seised of part And this in a *Dum Fuit infra Ætatem* Hilary
16 Ed III

There is no early printed year for 16 Ed III The case has not been identified in the Rolls Series for that year. Case 90

(91) **A writt** of Trespass "*quare talum nativum*, etc , *et servientem suum ou* [*apprenticiam suum*"] was adjudged good, as in the case of *Hungerford*, etc Michaelis
22 Hen VI

Reported in Y. B Mich 22 Hen VI, p 30, pl 49 A very long drawn-out case, where the learning of the period is "debated" with great solemnity Case 91

(92) **A writt of assize** which was brought for lands, part within the franchise and part without, was abated because the panel could not be arraigned by those of the franchise, nor by the sheriff, etc. Query? Michaelis
18 Ed II

---

[1] This is one of the instances in which the cross-references, which would naturally come at the end of the title, have been placed in the midst of the case It forms one part of the proof showing that Statham did not correct his own proof, or make any final arrangement of the cases he had so carefully collected

The one title which carries a reference is that of the title Prescription, and the case there referred to is to be found *supra*, Statham, Prescription, 133 a, case 7

Case 92   The case has not been identified in Mich 18 Ed II, or in the early abridgments   There is a similar case in Hilary, 18 Ed III, p 86, pl 1, but the decision differs from that of the abridged case

Michaelis
20 Hen VI   **(93) In a praecipe quod reddat** against two, they waged their law, and on the day, etc , one of them said that the other had died after the last continuance. And he had the plea, etc

Case 93   The case has not been identified in Y. B Mich 20 Hen VI, or in the early abridgments

Trinity
16 Ed III   **(94) Debt was brought** by executors, and one was severed   The defendant demanded judgment of the writ because he who was severed was dead   And the writ was adjudged good, because the executors of him who was dead could not join in an action with the other executors, etc

Case 94   There is no early printed year for 16 Ed III   The case is printed in the Rolls Series, 16 Ed II, 2, p 178

Michaelis
4 Hen V   **(95) In trespass,** the writ was that the defendant "together with others" made the trespass, and because the word "*ignotus*" was left out, the writ was abated, because the intention is that the plaintiff shall give notice to them, in which case he should have named them in the writ, etc   *Coram Rege*   It is otherwise as to a bill, as was said

Case 95   There is no printed year for 4 Hen V   The case has not been identified in the early abridgments

It may be further noticed here that the cases inserted after the note (see *supra*, note to case 87) are nearly all from manuscript cases, that they are very poorly done, and would seem to be of very little authority, the whole evidence seems to point to the absence of the master hand in the work

[20] The all-important matter of the writ seems too limitless to attempt to confine within the bounds of the title in an abridgment   Yet the maker of this earliest of the abridgments apparently did not feel hampered by the great bulk of cases which could even then have come logically under this head   When he found a case which to his mind answered a question as to the proper treatment of a writ by the Court, he put it in his title, not bothering whether or not it could logically go somewhere else just as well or better   Any one of us to-day would probably put most of the cases which he has put under this title elsewhere, but that only means that not one of us knows our old pleading as he did

He, in common with those about him, wanted to know just these things about the writ, these things that come up in everyday practice, so here we have them — points of practice set down for the practising lawyer of the late fourteen hundreds

The first case abridged here is important as throwing light on the ideas of the time as to the right of a woman to the name to which she was born Rikhill says, "Although she still remains daughter to her father, nevertheless she has lost her surname" Times change, and a judge in a case decided in Wisconsin [*Lane* v *Duchac*, 73 Wis 646, 1889] knows of "no law which will invalidate obligations or conveyances executed by her and to her in her baptismal name, if she chooses to give them or take them in that form" He gives no authority for his statement, and had evidently never heard of "mon maistre Rikhil" and his equally unsupported decision It has also been said [Greene Woman's Manual of Law, p 72, sec 85] "The law does not compel any wife to take her husband's surname when she marries It is merely a custom not having the force of law"

The early law seems to form itself upon and be formed by the writ The Abridgments, treatises, compendiums of all kinds, all that we have in print that treats of the early English law, are based upon the writ Bracton, Britton, Fleta, the *Natura Breviums* old and new, follow the names of the writs for the formulation of their compilations or treatises A subject which has not been formulated into a writ has small chance of getting much attention, but let it once become the subject of a writ and it comes into its own, or more than its own We know when a writ for any certain object first got into the register, we know its first form, we know its later evolutions We can trace it through the courts, and know how the judges treated it and when it would be sustained and when not We have at least something well known and tangible to base further knowledge on, but if a subject never came to be formed into a writ, then we may seek in vain for anything but the most perfunctory knowledge or data upon it, we must in the greater number of cases trace the meanderings of our topic painfully through the byways of the books, for the guide posts will be wanting The great places to which the highways of learning run, filled with crowds of facts, filled with light and crowded with information, are the writs, all else is but vill and hamlet or even *terra incognita*, lonely and isolated places where one may not even find a single habitant to answer the simplest query

It is not strange, perhaps, that we find the title of Briefe a sort of refuge for a motley collection of writs, such a collection as might well be labelled "miscellaneous" to-day in a collection where the author or compiler has a lot of information or matter left which he has not been able to include under any specific head, but has not wished or dared to utterly discard It would be safe to include the greater portion of the Year Book cases under this title, but although we have a goodly number of cases our compiler has been merciful, and the title has not been swollen unduly

BRIEFE AL EVESQUE

Statham 31 b.
Paschal
41 Ed III

(1) **In a praecipe quod reddat,** the parties were at issue upon "profession" and the writ was awarded to the bishop And the defendant brought a writ to the justices, testifying that the bishop was out of the realm, and he prayed a writ to his vicar, and had it, notwithstanding the other writ was not returned, but it was returnable a long time afterward, etc

Case 1

Reported in Y B Paschal, 41 Ed III, p 10, pl 6

Hilary
50 Ed III

(2) **In dower** against the bishop of S, and another, by different *præcipes*, the plea was "never married," etc And because the bishop was tenant a writ issued to the metropolitan, and because the other was tenant a writ issued to the same bishop, etc (They erred, as it seems)

Case 2

The case has not been identified in Y B Hilary, 50 Ed III, or in the early abridgments

Michaelis
24 Ed III

(3) **The king** brought a *Quare Impedit* against two, and against one it was adjudged that he should have a writ to the bishop, but the writ was not to issue until the plea between the king and the other should be argued, to wit when they were at issue, or at law Query, shall a man have a writ to the bishop in a writ of right for an advowson, etc ?

Case 3

The case has not been identified in Y B Mich 24 Ed III, or in the early abridgments

Hilary
13 Hen IV

(4) **In a quare impedit,** if the defendant pleads that he did not disturb him, the plaintiff shall have a writ to the bishop immediately, because the defendant does not claim anything in the patronage.

Case 4

The case has not been identified in Y B Hilary, 13 Hen IV, or in the early abridgments

Hilary
13 Hen IV

(5) **The defendant** shall have a writ to the bishop where the writ was abated for false Latin, for it is not like nonsuit, etc By HANKFORD, etc

Case 5

The case has not been identified in Y B Hilary, 13 Hen IV, or in the early abridgments

(6) **If bastardy** be alleged in Trespass, a writ shall issue to the bishop to certify it   By the opinion of THIRNING, etc , in Trespass Michaelis 14 Hen IV

The case has not been identified in Y B Mich 14 Hen IV, or in the early abridgments Case 6

See as to Writ to the Bishop in the title of *Quare Impedit*, and in the title of Trial Note

(7) **A writ** to the bishop shall be awarded on every appearance, if the defendant makes default, in a *Quare Impedit* Michaelis 10 Ed II

Reported in Y B Mich 10 Ed II, p 305, pl 1 Case 7

(8) **If the defendant** in a *Quare Impedit* wishes to have a writ to the bishop upon the nonsuit of the plaintiff, he shall make a sufficient title to have a writ to the bishop, etc. Hilary 2 Hen VI

Reported in Y B Mich (not Hilary), 2 Hen VI, p 8, pl 13   See also Brooke, Briefe al Evesque, 25, and Fitzh Briefe al Evesque, 5 Case 8

(9) **The king** brought a *Quare Impedit*, and on the return of the summons the sheriff returned "*nihil*," and upon the attachment "*nihil*," and to the distress "*nihil*"   And now the question is whether the king shall have a writ to the bishop or not?   MARTYN It seems that he shall not have a writ to the bishop, for by the common law a man shall have no other process in a *Quare Impedit* except distress *ad infinitum*   Thus, if he shall have a writ to the bishop it shall be by the Statute of Marlbridge, which abridged the process in a *Quare Impedit*   And it seems that he is not within the purview of the Statute, for the Statute is, "*Et in placito vero quare impedit, si ad primum diem ad quem summonitus fuerit non venerit nec essonium miserit impeditor, tunc attachietur ad alium diem quo die si non venerit, nec essonium miserit, distringatur, et si tunc non venerit, scribatur episcopo loci,*" and so it appears by the words of the Statute that the writ should be sued   And now he has returned "*nihil*" to all three writs, so none of them is served, wherefore, COTTINGHAM It seems that the sheriff should be amerced, for he could have summoned him upon the glebe of the Anno 11 Hen VI

parsonage, etc. BABYNGTON That is not so, for nothing is in demand in this *Quare Impedit,* but in a writ of right for an advowson it should be as you say. MARTYN If in [a writ of] right of an advowson the tenant makes default upon which the Grand Cape is awarded, what shall be taken into the hand of the king? BABYNGTON The glebe. PASTON That is not so, for the patron shall never have the glebe, for on trespass made while the church is vacant the patron shall not have an action, for the glebe does not belong to him but to the ordinary   But at the Grand Cape the church shall be taken into the hand of the king   And this can be clearly proven, for an advowson can pass by livery, and that shall be at the door of the church, for a sign that the advowson, which is only a novation, passes, etc. MARTYN That does not show how it can pass by livery, etc NEWTON: The king shall have a writ to the bishop in that case   And since the Statute says, *"ad quem diem"* etc., that proves that he should be summoned   At the common law there was only a distress "in infinite," and the plaintiff lost his issues   Then at the common law he would much rather appear since he loses his issues "in infinite" where there are any issues to lose.   And when a *"nihil"* is returned upon him, in which case he loses nothing, then that is a greater evil than it was at the common law.   And when there are two evils in one action and the lesser evil is remedied by express words in a Statute, it seems that the greater shall be included in the same remedy, although nothing is said about it.   So here   PASTON (to the same effect) Although the Statute is *"ad quem diem,"* etc , it shall not be understood by those words that he was summoned in fact, for there are no actions of debt in that place   Wherefore the defendant was outlawed upon the *"nihil"* returned to the summons   And yet the entry is that such a one was summoned to answer, etc   And yet in fact he was not summoned, then that entry is nothing but to prove that a summons issued here, wherefore, etc   And they adjourned.

Case 9   Reported in Y B Mich 11 Hen VI, p 3, pl 8

The Statute is that of Marlborough, 52 Hen III (1267), cap 12 Stats at Large, Vol 1, p 65   See also Brooke, Briefe al Evesque, 24, and Fitzh   Briefe al Evesque, 4

BILLE [21]

(1) **A man shall have a bill** of trespass in the King's Statham 32 a
Bench, or in the Common Bench, for trespass made in any Trinity
county in England, although there be an action pending 31 Ed II
against him, if a man assaults him on the way going to
court, and he shall be attached in the hall by a crier, or
by an officer of the place, for when a man pleads or is empleaded, he is immediately under the protection of the king

There is no printed Year Book for 31 Ed II   Case 1

(2) **See by the opinion** of MARTYN in a *Scire Facias*, if a Hilary
man be imprisoned in the Common Bench, and in the keeping 3 Hen VI
of the warden of the Fleet, that a man can have a bill of debt
against him, as a man shall have in the King's Bench, in the
custody of the marshal, etc   (But it is not the custom, etc)

Reported in Y B Hilary, 3 Hen VI, p 25, pl 6   (The point is to Case 2
be found on p 26)   It is obscure even there.   See also Fitzh Bylle, 18

(3) **A man shall not have** a bill against one of the clerks Michaelis
of the Bench, except for trespass, or on a contract made 7 Hen IV
in the same [county][1] where the Bench is, but he shall
sue by writ, and this in a bill, etc
    And it was said in the same plea that a man shall not have
process of outlawry in any case where the original suit
commenced by a bill, etc   Query, if he shall have a *Capias
ad Satisfaciendum*, where he recovers upon a bill, etc

Reported in Y B 7 Mich Hen IV, p 5, pl 34 (point on p 6)   See Case 3
also Brooke, Bille, 4, and Fitzh Bylle, 17

(4) **One brought a bill** in the King's Bench for a deceit Anno
made in the Hall of Westminster   And the marshal of 7 Hen V
the place took the panel of the people who were in the Hall
    And see, by HANKFORD, in the same plea, that an essoin
does not lie in any plea which commences by a bill, and no
more does it in the Oyer and Terminer, etc

The case has not been identified in Y B 7 Hen V, or in the early Case 4.
abridgments

[1] Word from the report of the case   Statham has it "Contract"

[11] The first attempt to clear up the story of the Bill as we find it in the early Year Books, and consequently in our abridgment, resulted only in the conviction that the bill as it was known in these early times had been respectfully neglected by all our writers upon the early law Crabb alone [Crabb, Hist of Eng Law] seems to have had some idea of the ancient bill, for he says [p 282] that the "bill seems to be of more ancient date than the writ" His reason for this statement makes one suspect that he had seen some of the old bills in manuscript, for he says that they were better adapted to the extraordinary jurisdiction exercised by the earlier kings than the writ Later knowledge seems to prove this contention, but no one else pays much attention to the point thus brought forward Reeves [Hist Eng Law, Vol 3, p 93] feels that the knowledge of the subject had become lost in the mists of time! The origin of the practice of making use of the bill rather than the writ is only conjectural The use of it in the three courts is sufficiently attested by the Year Books of Ed III, these courts being the King's Bench, Common Pleas and Exchequer He says further, "It is beyond all question that actions were brought in this way during all this reign, and the books are full of them" [Ib, p 93] Reeves was influenced, as everyone seems to have been, by the idea which grew up around the subject that the proceeding by bill might have arisen through the jurisdiction of the marshal He found cases in which the jurisdiction of the marshal was not mentioned, but he thought that might be explained by the fact of the custody being understood without necessity of mention No one else seems to have thought much about the matter Either they had not the insight which led Crabb to doubt the accuracy of the inference that the bill grew from that in which the defendant was *in custodia marescalli*, and from that into the bill of Middlesex, or they had too much respect for the depth of the dust overlying the subject to care to disturb it At all events they one and all, the greatest as well as the least, left it where they found it There it was found when, coming to the subject of bills in the Abridgment, it became apparent that Crabb was right —that the bill was a very ancient method of procedure, concurrent with the writ, and that it had nothing whatever to do with the custody of the marshal, and therefore, nothing to do with the bill of Middlesex Yet the evidence was not wholly complete, the truth was not fully cleared by such evidence as was at hand All that could be said was that taking it all together the actual evidence as to the history of the bill was not complete We might read through the lines of the cases where nothing is shown in regard to the custody of the marshal and infer from the cases where it is mentioned that it was to be read in by inference to the other cases There was no actual proof that the contrary was true, although the atmosphere of the cases was convincingly the other way The only thing to say was the somewhat futile sentence, "The cases do not let in sufficient light for us to decide as yet, but the cases have not given us all the light they contain" It

seemed hard to let it go at that, better say nothing and let the law remain undisturbed in its dusty hiding place   And then, upon that decision, came the proof that was needed   Mr W C Bolland had met and — thanks to his possession of the evidence so long shut away from us — had conquered the difficulty   In his introduction to Volume Twenty-seven of the Selden Society Publications [Y B Series, Vol 7, Fyre of Kent, 6-7, Vol 2, Ed II, 1313-14, p xxi] he says   "The Year Books and Rolls of the general Eyres reveal to us a procedure which has been so long extinct and which continued for so comparatively short a time that all memory of it seems to have been lost for centuries past   Not a single authority, ancient or modern, that I have consulted — and I have searched wherever I thought instruction might be found — tells us anything of it   I refer to the procedure, in certain cases, by bill instead of by writ "   He goes on to say that they were not the bills mentioned in the Roll recording the Trials of the Judges and other ministers of the King before the Commission instituted by Ed I   Neither did he find that they had "any connection with the ancient bills mentioned by the Lord Chief Justice Hale in his Discourse Concerning the Courts of King's Bench and Common Pleas "   [Hargrave's Law Tracts (1787), p 363]   "Neither have they anything to do with that special kind of bill which came to be known by the generic title of 'bill of Middlesex ' "   [p xxii]   At last light had come!   The bill which had been so puzzling was not any relation to that bill of Middlesex which was so constantly laying claim to it as a relative, yet which had been seen to show no trace of kinship   Nor does Mr Bolland stop with assertion, he goes on to give us proof of the matter, and in so doing gives a description of the bills themselves   It was this description which led to the remark above made about Crabb apparently having seen some of the bills themselves   Here is Mr Bolland's description   "They are formed of strips of parchment varying in size with what had to be written upon them   Some of them are barely as wide as a man's little finger   They are almost invariably written in Anglo-French   A very few are in Latin   They are largely used by very poor people   No rules as to form affect them, so that no expert knowledge being necessary, they can be framed and presented by any one who can write or who can get another to write for him   There is no evidence that any fee was payable on the presentation of a bill, as it was on the purchasing of a writ, but there is conclusive evidence that the way of the very poor man to the ear of the King's Justices was made easy for him   Now to what does all this point?   Surely to the immemorial belief that inherent in the King are the right and the power to remedy all wrongs independently of common law or statute law, and even in the teeth of these   I think that there can be no doubt that these bills are the very beginning of the equitable jurisdiction "   [Ib , Pref xxviii] Crabb was right, it appears, this bill was a proceeding "better adapted to the extraordinary jurisdiction exercised by the earlier kings," than the

writ   Was it insight on his part, or had he indeed seen these "strips of
parchment" so variable in size and so utterly without form that all the
usual defences in regard to form fail?   For there is a case given us by
Mr Bolland, in the Eyre of London of 15 Ed II [p. xxvi] in which one
Agnes de Warr was unjustly thrown into prison and brought her bill
She leaves out all statements as to how long she was confined in the dun-
geon, and as to how and when the money was taken from her, and what
her damages were.   The judge himself learns all these matters by
questioning her, and makes the defendant answer fully   Here we
find ourselves freed from all quibbles, all webs to catch the unwary
The poor man and the poor woman make out their complaint or bill, as
it is known, in the simple and unlearned language of the poorer people,
and send it in without formal address, even "Sire" being sufficient
[p xxii], to one of the king's justices, and he, apparently, hears the complaint much as the lord of a manor might have heard it, and decides in
a dispute between two tenants or servants

Mr Bolland's account is so full of interest, so illuminating historically, that no one interested in the subject can fail to read and re-read it
with profit and interest   Were it not accessible to every student it
would seem almost necessary to reprint it here, as it contains the only
certain knowledge of the subject in print to-day   His earlier cases are
long before those in this abridgment   Indeed they appear to range
from Ed I to Ed III   Mr Bolland was editing an Eyre, he believes
that only justices in Eyre had jurisdiction of these bills, and apparently he would call them "Bills in Eyre"   An examination of the
printed years of Ed II and Ed III appear to give additional evidence
that this is so, since we find but two cases in the Maynard in which we
are told that a bill was brought   The first is Y B 14 Ed II [p 425],
and is a bill of debt, brought in an eyre in London   The second is a
bill of trespass [Y B 14 Ed II, p 425] brought against an abbot
Here there is nothing to show where the bill was brought, and the
case stands without giving any testimony for or against the theory of
the bill in eyre   The first case in Y B Ed III [18 Ed III, 28, 31]
shows that a bill for goods carried away was brought in the Common
Pleas, while a writ for the same trespass was pending in the King's
Bench   The case presents us with no argument upon the subject of the
differences or likenesses as to bills — plain or in eyre — and writs, in
fact the bill and the writ are spoken of as if they were practically the
same thing   There is no symptom of the doctrine of *custodia marescalli* or bill of Middlesex   Taken by itself we might infer from the
case that a bill and a writ were exactly the same   The case seems to
stand by itself among the printed cases, and so standing it is not sufficient as a basis for a new theory as to the status of writs at this period

In 21 Ed III [p 46, pl 65] a bill of fresh force was brought, in which it
was alleged that it was pleadable by the common law and not by way of
bill   This idea would show the bill to be a sort of equitable bill,

which the bill in eyre seems to have been in a way, although we have seen already one case in the Common Pleas Our next case of a bill brings us into the region of the bill of Middlesex, and does not belong to the bill we are considering [Y B 27 Ed III, p 4, pl 1] Another case in 27 Ed III [Y B 27 Ed III, p 6, pl 25] shows us a bill in the King's Bench "alleging divers things," but there is nothing to show how the bill was treated by the Court The only other case of a bill [Y B 42 Ed III, p 13, pl 20] is against the warden of the Fleet and is probably a bill of Middlesex

Perhaps we should look at the four cases in our abridgment in which the bill is used instead of the writ The first case is only known to us through the abridgment itself, for we have no printed Year Book for the year 31 Ed III It is rather a note than a case, but it states boldly that a bill of trespass may be brought in either the King's Bench or Common Bench, it seems as if it narrowed the bringing of a bill down, however, to the case where a man has an action pending against him, and he is therefore in the protection of the king This being the case, it would again be the extraordinary jurisdiction of the king which makes the proceeding by bill the proper proceeding The second case is again a case of bill of Middlesex

We get little, if anything, on our special point from the next two cases, they are points of pleading on the bill rather than cases which show us anything about the bill itself, and it is interesting to learn from our case four that an essoin did not lie in a case which began by a bill, evidently the shifts which were used to gain time in the writs were not allowed in the more equitable proceeding by bill

On the whole we have made one step and but one in the discovery of the history of the procedure by bill in the early cases We know that these bills were brought in the eyres We have some cases to show that they were also brought in the King's Bench and the Common Pleas in the common course The evidence necessary to prove that these bills were not simply bills in eyre but bills in opposition, or in an alternative procedure to the writ, is as yet but slight, but is sufficient for hope that now that the attention of the patient legal searcher for historical fact has been called to the matter, we shall soon be able to trace the history of the bill, and the signs are that we shall find it, not a forerunner of the bill of Middlesex, not even a bill in eyre simply, but an alternative procedure to the writ, of an equitable nature, but in many ways unlike the bill in equity

BARRE [22]

(1) **In trespass,** the defendant said that the plaintiff formerly. etc , affirmed a complaint for the same trespass against the same defendant, in London, etc , and he pleaded Statham 32 b
Paschal
40 Ed III

all the record, etc , and had judgment to recover forty shillings for the damages, which we have been ready at all times to pay, and still are   And he offered the money. UFFLETE   He pleads a record in a lower Court, and also he does not show that we have sued execution, wherefore it is no plea   And afterwards it was adjudged that the plaintiff was barred, etc

Case I   Reported in Y B Trinity (not Paschal), 40 Ed III, p 27, pl 3 See also Fitzh   Barre, 194

Michaelis
40 Ed III

(2) **In a writ** of *rationabili parte bonorum*, the defendant showed that the plaintiff had a reversion descending through his father, so she was estopped as she had had an advancement   And the opinion was that it was a good bar notwithstanding the reversion had not fallen in, because she could sell it, etc.

Case 2   Reported in Y. B Mich 40 Ed III, p 38, pl 13   Statham and the report differ as to the words of the case

Paschal
41 Ed III

(3) **In formedon,** it was alleged that one A gave to his father   CANNDISH   This A, who gave, is the same person who is tenant   And he said that this gift was by force of imprisonment, and it was adjudged a good bar, etc

Case 3   Reported in Y B Paschal, 41 Ed. III, p 9, pl 2

Trinity
42 Ed III

(4) **In formedon** in the descender, on a gift made by one F to G and C, his wife, in tail, and to the demandant as son and heir to them, etc   FENCOT   One F, your grandfather, whose heir you are, gave these same lands to the said G and C, in fee, with warranty, by his deed, etc   G survived C, whose estate we have   Judgment if, against the warranty, etc   BELKNAP   This F, and F, the donor, are all one and the same person   And inasmuch as your plea is contrary to your writ, judgment, etc   THORPE This plea is good enough, for he relies upon the warranty, wherefore answer him if you will, etc

Case 4   Reported in Y B Trinity, 42 Ed III, p 19, pl. 1

(5) **In a writ of entry,** it was alleged that the tenant had no entry except by one A, who disseised the father of the demandant. FENCOT. Your grandfather, whose heir you are, enfeoffed us with warranty, judgment, etc And it was adjudged a good bar And so is warranty of every ancestor a good bar, or of the demandant, notwithstanding it is contrary to the writ But yet the feoffment without warranty is not to the purpose, without traversing the point of the writ, etc.

Hilary 43 Ed III

The case has not been identified in Y B Hilary, 43 Ed III, or in the early abridgments.

Case 5

(6) **In trespass,** the plaintiff counted that this bailiff took certain cattle within his fee, etc , in such a place, for rent in arrear, and the defendant made a rescue on him. The defendant said that he took them in another place within the same vill, which is out of his fee, and he made the rescue, etc. BELKNAP He does not answer us, wherefore, etc. FYNCHEDEN. It is enough for him to arrest[1] you for a distress, wherefore answer him, etc Query as to this, for it seems that it is no plea, for various reasons, etc

Paschal 43 Ed III

The case has not been identified in Y B Paschal, 43 Ed III, or in the early abridgments

Case 6

(7) **In detinue** against the husband and his wife, the plaintiff counted for twenty sheep bailed to the wife before coverture BELKNAP He bailed them to our wife to fertilize his land and afterwards we married her; and we commanded you to take your sheep, and you would not And then we found them damage feasant on our soil, and we took them. Judgment if action (etc) And it was adjudged a good bar. Which note

Trinity 43 Ed III

Reported in Y B Trinity, 43 Ed III, p 21, pl 10

Case 7

(8) **In trespass,** the defendant said that the plaintiff had an action of detinue pending against him for the same thing, and that he had appeared Judgment if action (etc.). And it was not allowed, because this action was of a different

Trinity 43 Ed III

[1] The writ *"Arristandis bonis ne disipentur."*

nature   Which note, for it might be that he had cause for both actions

Case 8   Reported in Y B Mich (not Trinity), 43 Ed III, p 23, pl 15

Michaelis   (9) **In a writ of entry** on a disseisin made on his grand-
46 Ed III   father, the tenant [said] that one H was seised and gave
the same tenements to your grandfather, and A his wife, and the heirs of his wife; and your grandfather died and his wife remained in, whose estate we have   And this is a bar   But yet query, for it did not give him color for an action, etc.   See the plea, etc

Case 9   Reported in Y B Mich 46 Ed III, p 30, pl 26

Trinity   (10) **In trespass** for a close broken, the defendant said
47 Ed III   that the plaintiff had leased the same close before the alleged trespass to one B, for a term of ten years, which still lasts, judgment if action (etc).   Query, if it be a plea, since he did not say what estate he had, etc

Case 10   The case has not been identified in Y B Trinity, 47 Ed III, or in the early abridgments

Hilary   (11) **In trespass** for a close broken, the defendant said
48 Ed III   that he was amerced in the court of the plaintiff at D for two shillings for the same trespass, which he had paid to him at such a place   And it was adjudged a good bar But this amercement was not legal, as it seems, then neither is the plea good, unless it be by way of accord, etc.

Case 11   Reported in Y B Hilary, 48 Ed III, p 8, pl 16   See also Fitzh Barre, 222

Hilary   (12) **In a writ of annuity** by a prior against a parson,
31 Ed III   he counted that the predecessor of the prior had leased to the predecessor of the parson certain tithes, for which the said predecessor of the parson, with the assent of the patron and of the ordinary, granted to our predecessor the annuity, etc   FULTHORPE He did not lease it   And the opinion was that this was not a bar, for he had declared according to the specialty   And although there was no

such lease, still, to end the dispute, the annuity was granted, etc

There is no printed year for 31 Ed III   Case 12

(13) **One avowed** upon the tenant because he leased Paschal certain lands to him for the term of his life, rendering a 30 Ed III certain rent, and for so much in arrear, etc , The tenant said that the avowant entered upon him and enfeoffed one H in fee, judgment, etc Query if it be a bar, since he did not say what estate he had, etc ? But yet the plea seems good, for it amounts to "out of his fee," etc It seems double, etc

There is no printed Paschal Term for 30 Ed III   Case 13

(14) **In debt** upon an obligation, the defendant said that Hilary he said to one F, if the plaintiff would make an in- 13 Hen VI denture and deliver it to him, then he would make an obligation in the name of the defendant And he said that the plaintiff had not performed the conditions, so not his deed (And so see that he admitted no livery, etc , for if he admitted a livery and pleaded as above, the opinion of many is that the plea was not good, etc.)

There is no printed year for 13 Hen VI   Case 14

(15) **In formedon** on a rent service, it is no plea that the Paschal lands are not held of him, because by the presumption of 19 Ed III this action he is out of the possession of the rent, in which case he does not hold of him, etc And also it is no answer to the writ, which alleges a gift, etc. And if it be a plea it amounts to no more than that the land is out of his fee, which is no plea in a formedon for rent, because the title is comprised in the writ But yet it does not appear by the writ what rent it is Query, should he put it in his count? etc And if he showed in his count that it was a rent service, shall he say, "out" etc ? And it seems not, Statham 33 a but that he shall answer to the gift, etc

The case has not been identified in Y B Paschal, 19 Ed III in the Case 15 Rolls Series, or in the early abridgments

Michaelis
24 Ed III

(16) **In a writ of intrusion,** the tenant said that he enfeoffed this same [person] whom you allege to be tenant for life, in the tail, and he died without issue, and we entered, without this that he died your tenant for life. And the plea was adjudged good. But yet, query, etc

Case 16

Reported in Y B Mich 24 Ed III, p 74, pl 95

Hilary
14 Hen VI

(17) **In maintenance,** the defendant said that he was his cousin, and he showed how as appears [in the case]. And he said he was his mainpernor, which was the alleged maintenance, etc (The plea seems double, etc And also he did not say, "without this that he maintained in any other manner ") But yet the plea was adjudged good, etc

Case 17

Reported in Y B Anno 14 Hen VI, p 6, pl 30 See also Fitzh Barre, 15

Trinity
3 Hen IV

(18) **In debt** upon an obligation, the defendant said that formerly the plaintiff sued a bill of debt for this same obligation before the sheriff of London, against this same defendant, who pleaded a release of the plaintiff, bearing date at Windsor And the plaintiff demurred upon the plea, inasmuch as the custom is that no such foreign plea is sufficient, etc Wherefore, inasmuch as that was a good plea, it was adjudged that the plaintiff should have a *sequatur* at the common law, and that the defendant should go without day. And we demand judgment, inasmuch as you were once barred REDE Since the force of the judgment was of no other effect than that we were put to sue at the common law, and inasmuch as the plea that was pleaded went to the jurisdiction, judgment, etc HANKFORD· It seems that the plea shall be barred, for when the defendant pleaded that plea, it was a good plea *prima facie*, for the plaintiff could have admitted it, and said that it was made through duress in London, in which case the Court would have had jurisdiction, or if he had said, "not his deed," then they would have adjudged that it was at the common law, but when he demurred in judgment generally, it was his own folly And to this that is said, that the judgment contains two kinds of judgment, to wit that the

plaintiff sue at the common law, and the defendant go
without day, that shall be taken according to the matter
And the reason for the judgment, which was that he should
be barred, [is] as in a *Quare Impedit* brought by the king
if the defendant bars the king, the judgment is that he go
without day, and if he abates the writ of the king, judgment is in the same manner, so it does not appear by the
judgment whether the king shall have another action or
not, but that it shall be taken according to the plea of the
defendant   So here   And they adjourned, etc

Reported in Y B Trinity, 3 Hen IV, p 18, pl 3   Case 18

(19) **In debt** upon an obligation, the defendant said Michaelis
the obligation was endorsed upon the condition that if he 14 Hen VI
obeyed the award and arbitrement of one G, then, etc ,
which G adjudged that I should pay to you at the feast
of Nowel last past, ten pounds, on which day I offered
you the money, and you refused it, judgment if action, etc
NEWTON   That is no plea, for he does not say that he has
been at all times ready, etc   Nor does he offer the money
to the Court, etc   MARTYN   There is a difference when
a man pleads an arbitration in bar and when he pleads
a condition, for if the obligation be endorsed that I shall
pay ten pounds on such a day, I shall plead as you say,
for there it is all the time a debt owed by me, for which the
plaintiff can have an action   But in the other case I shall
be forced to pay only according to the form of the arbitration   And if it appears by his plea that he has performed
the award, then the plaintiff can have an action for that,
wherefore answer, etc

Reported in Y B Anno 14 Hen VI, p 23, pl 68   The year 14 Case 19
Hen VI is not divided into terms in the printed Year Book

(20) **In a writ** *de herede rapto*, the plaintiff said that he Hilary
was grandfather to the infant, and had one hundred pounds 31 Ed III.
of land, and that the infant was his next heir for this same
land, and that he took him by reason of nurture, judgment
if wrongfully —without this that he would aver that the
mother of the infant who brought the action never had any

lands which could descend to him   WILLOUGHBY Whether she has lands or not the nurture belongs to the mother, wherefore your plea avails not   Which was conceded by the Court

Case 20   There is no printed Year Book for 31 Ed III

Hilary
31 Ed III   **(21) If a woman** brings a writ of Dower against the heir and is barred, and then she brings another writ of Dower against his guardian, he shall plead this matter in bar, etc   And the law is the same for an advowson recovered by the heir, and if he against whom the recovery was limited brings a *Quare Impedit* against the guardian in chivalry, or in socage, he can bar him by such matter, because he claims in right of the heir   And this in a *Quare Impedit*, etc.

Case 21   There is no printed Year Book for 31 Ed III

Paschal
49 Ed III   **(22) In detinue** upon an obligation, the defendant said that the obligation was delivered to him by the plaintiff and one A, who was bound to the plaintiff in the same deed, etc , and he prayed a *Scire Facias*, etc   [A] came and pleaded the release of the plaintiff for all matters in dispute.   And the opinion was that he should not be barred in that action because if he recovered and brought a writ of Debt upon that, then he would be barred   (And yet *"frustra sit per plura "*)

Case 22   Reported in Y B Paschal, 49 Ed III, p 13, pl 6

Paschal
49 Ed III   **(23) "Never joined,"** etc , is no plea in a *Cui in Vita*, because she does not claim anything of the possession of her husband, nor by him, etc   By THORPE, in an Assize, etc

Case 23   The case has not been identified in Y B Paschal, 49 Ed III, or in the early abridgments

Trinity
49 Ed III   **(24) In a cui in vita,** in which she claimed to hold to herself and the heirs of her body issuing, etc.   BABYNGTON He did not give it   THORPE That is no plea, for the point of her writ is the feoffment of her husband, which ought to be received, and although he did not give it, still if

another gave it she shall have an action   And albeit
no gift was made by anyone, but it came to her by descent,
still she shall have an action, wherefore you can have it
in abatement of the writ, and not by way of bar, since the
writs are of different forms, etc

Reported in Y B Trinity, 49 Ed III, p 22, pl 6   Case 24

(25) **In waste,** the defendant said that he did not sur- Michaelis
render to the plaintiff before the purchase of the writ; to ^{15 Hen VI}
which he agreed   GOODREDE   That is well, for if the plain-
tiff said that he did not surrender, the tenant will say that
he surrendered at such a place, etc   And in the same way
in regard to money, if the issue is taken upon that, as
where a man pleads a release in bar, who says "not his
deed "   Then the defendant shows the place in sufficient
time, and he shall say, "Your deed made at such a place "
Query, could he have alleged that place in another county,
etc ?   I think he could not, etc

There is no printed year book for 15 Hen VI   Case 25

(26) **In debt** upon the arrears of a lease for a term of Michaelis
years, it is a good plea to say, "levied by distress," without ^{4 Hen VI}
answering to the *debet*, etc., for it is a special declaration, Statham 33 b
in which case each point is traversable, etc

Reported in Y B Mich 4 Hen VI, p 5, pl 12   Case 26

(27) **If a man** pleads an accord in bar, he should show Hilary
in his plea in what place the accord was taken, etc , and not ^{15 Hen VI}
plead generally as in a release   And this in Trespass,
etc

There is no printed Year Book for 15 Hen VI   Case 27

(28) **In a writ of entry,** it was alleged that the tenant Hilary
had no entry except by one J, who disseised the demandant ^{4 Hen VI}
COTESMORE   One H, your father, was seised, etc , and
gave these same lands to the said J, our father, in tail,
and then your father died, and you, alleging that he had
leased for the term of his own life solely, entered, etc , and

our father ousted you and died, etc., judgment, etc   And it
was held a good bar.   And so see that in every writ of Entry a
man can give "color of action," as in an assize on a specialty,
where the disseisin is made on the demandant himself, etc

Case 28   Reported in Y B Hilary, 4 Hen VI, p 10, pl 3

Hilary
35 Ed III

(29) **In a writ of entry** in the post, on a disseisin made
on the father of the demandant, it is a good bar to plead
the feoffment of the said father, without warranty, for the
writ does not allege with certainty any entry, etc

Case 29   There is no printed Year Book for 35 Ed. III

Paschal
18 Hen VI

(30) **In debt,** the plaintiff counted upon an obligation
made by the defendant to the plaintiff, bearing date the
first day of May, in the first year of the present king, and
that this same deed was first delivered to the plaintiff the
first day of July in the same year. FORTESCUE said
that the plaintiff and the defendant put themselves upon
the arbitrement of A, B and C, the first day of April in the
same year, as to all trespasses and disputes, etc , who
awarded that the defendant should make this same obligation and deliver it to the wife of the plaintiff, to the use
of the plaintiff, and that he made the obligation and
delivered it to the wife, as above, the same first day of May
And then, the first day of July, the said wife first delivered
the said obligation to her husband, who is now plaintiff
And the said plaintiff, by his deed, which is here, bearing
date the last day of May, released to us all actions   Judgment if against this release, action, etc   PORTYNGTON
To the plea pleaded by the manner, etc. Sir, that is no
plea, for he does not answer us unless he says, "Without
this that it was first delivered the first day of July," for
two affirmatives cannot make an issue, and that plea refers
to this that was delivered to our wife the first day of
May, which delivery is of the date of the deed, and
not of the other delivery, etc   FORTESCUE   No, sir, for
the delivery to the wife to your use is not good until you
have agreed, etc. And we have shown that the wife first
delivered the deed to you the first day of July, and it shall

be understood that if you did not agree before that, then you agreed with us as to the days, etc , wherefore it is not necessary for us to traverse you, etc   And this was truly well debated   And it was adjudged that the plaintiff should recover his debt and his damages.

The case has not been identified in Y B Paschal, 18 Hen VI, or in the early abridgments.   Case 30

(31) **In an action** upon the Statute of Laborers against the master, the servant of the master said that whereas you have counted that he was retained by you on Candlemas Day, the year 18 of the present king, until Candlemas next following, we say that on the first day of March, in the year 16 of the same king, we retained him to serve us for one year next ensuing, and he on the twentieth day afterward departed from our service, and the same day made a covenant to serve you for one year next ensuing And then we found him in your service, and required him to come to us, and he came back, without this that you retained him at the feast of Candlemas, etc   FORTESCUE That is no plea, for it may be that the plaintiff retained him on another day before or after, which is good enough For it may happen that he came to the plaintiff at the Candlemas which the plaintiff has alleged, at which time your term was ended, wherefore, etc   And this was the opinion of the COURT, wherefore he said as above, "without this that he was retained to serve him from Candlemas to Candlemas," etc.

Trinity 18 Hen VI

Reported in Y B. Trinity, 18 Hen VI, p 13, pl 2   Case 31
Statute of Laborers, 23 Ed III (1349), Stats at Large, Vol 1, p 26

(32) **In trespass** for a servant beaten MARKHAM Action, etc , for we [say by way of] protestation that we did not beat him   But we say that at the time of the alleged trespass he was not your servant   Ready. PORTYNGTON. That is no plea, no more than in trespass for goods carried away it is a plea to say that at the time, etc , the property of the same goods was in another, for it amounts to "not guilty" NEWTON   It is not the same, for in the

Trinity 18 Hen VI

case here the plea is good   (But he did not give the reason, etc) Query as to the difference? But he could have made a good plea of this matter if he had said that he was a common tailor, or suitmaker, and made robes for the plaintiff and others, without this that he was his servant in any other manner. and he would then have given color to the plaintiff to have an action, etc. *Simile*, Mich 11 Hen. IV, placitum one.

Case 32   Reported in Y B. Trinity, 18 Hen VI, p. 16, pl 5   See also Fitzh Barre, 18

Trinity
18 Hen VI   (33) **In debt** upon the arrears of a lease for a term of years, the plaintiff counted upon the lease, which was by deed indented   MARKHAM: Nothing owing him, Ready, etc   FORTESCUE   That is no plea against the specialty   NEWTON   A levy by distress is a good plea, and it is reasonable, for he cannot constrain the lessor to make him an acquittance; but he should say further, "and so nothing owing him, and so nothing in arrears." PASTON   Although the plaintiff has declared by a deed indented, that does not alter the case to my mind, for the action is founded upon the lease.   And such a plea has often been admitted. And also in debt upon the arrears of an account, the plea is good.   And they adjourned.   Query as to that conclusion, to wit "And so nothing in arrears," for if he pleaded thus he would not reply to the point of the writ, to wit   to the *debet*, etc

Case 33   Reported in Y B Trinity, 18 Hen VI, p 17, pl 8   See also Fitzh. Barre, 19

Michaelis
30 Hen VI   (34) **Where one** is bound in a recognizance to be in the Chancery on a certain day, or to have another man there on a certain day, on which day he does not come, wherefore a *Scire Facias* is issued against him to have execution, it was the opinion of many of the judges that he should say that on the day, etc , he was imprisoned at such a place at the suit of such a one, wherefore no default was in him And also he could not have an action against him at whose suit he was imprisoned, for the imprisonment was legal

by force of a suit. It is otherwise where a man imprisons
him by his own tort, in which case he would not make a
plea [of that sort]   But yet it seems hard for him to have
his plea, for it was his own folly to be bound by such Statham 34 a
a recognizance so strictly, as appeared in the year 40 Ed
III, where a man bound himself by his deed that he would
be excused for anything which came by sudden adventure,
which is an act of God. *À fortiori* he could not excuse
himself in that case, except for that for which he was [not]
bound, to wit if he be dead, because death dissolves all things

The case has not been identified in Y B Mich 30 Hen VI, or in the Case 34
early abridgments

(35) **In debt** upon an obligation for twenty pounds, the Michaelis
defendant said that it was endorsed upon the condition 30 Hen VI
that if he paid to the plaintiff ten pounds on a certain day
and place, that then, etc., on which day he offered the
money to him and he refused it, judgment if action   And
the opinion of FORTESCUE was that this was no plea, because
for the sum of ten pounds the plaintiff could not have an
action   And it clearly appeared that it was a debt, and
so he ought to show that he had been at all times ready,
etc., for it is not the same as where the condition is that
they will submit to the award of certain persons, who
award that they shall pay to the plaintiff ten pounds on
such a day and [at such a] place, which they offered him
and he refused, for on that the plaintiff can have an action,
and therefore it is sufficient   But it is otherwise in this
case, etc   And they adjourned   (Query, all the same, in
the case of the arbitrement), etc

The case has not been identified in Y B Mich 30 Hen VI, or in the Case 35
early abridgments

(36) **In formedon** for rent, the warranty of the same Hilary
ancestor, with assets by descent, is a good bar, although 33 Ed III
the rent cannot be discontinued except at the will of the
issue   But it is the folly of the issue to bring such an action,
which proves him to be out of possession of the rent, etc ,
for he could have distrained, etc

There is no printed Year Book for 33 Ed III   Case 36

Paschal
34 Ed III.

(37) **In an assize,** the tenant said that one such rendered to me the same land by a fine, and the estate of the plaintiff is mesne. SHARSHULL That is no plea, for it is not like a recovery, which disproves the right of the plaintiff and every right *prima facie.* To which the COURT agreed, etc In that case there was not any mesne [at the] time

Case 37

There is no printed Year of 34 Ed III The text seems corrupt, but I give it as it stands, not being able to correct it without changing the text more than seems best

Michaelis
21 Hen VI

(38) **In a scire facias** to recover damages, the plaintiff[1] said that within the year the plaintiff sued a *Fieri Facias* to the sheriff, who had levied for the same sum,[2] judgment if another time, etc And it was adjudged a good plea, etc See such matter well debated, Anno 11 Hen IV

Case 38

Reported in Y B Mich 21 Hen VI, p 5, pl 13

Trinity
21 Hen VI

(39) **In a writ of entry** in the nature of an assize, the tenant said that the plaintiff enfeoffed such a one, "whose estate I have " And the opinion was that this was not a bar Query as to the reason, for it is a good bar in an Assize.

Case 39

Reported in Y B Mich (not Trinity), 21 Hen VI, p 12, pl 26

Michaelis
21 Hen VI

(40) **In debt** against a collector, he declared that the king had given him the sum by a patent, and that there was a liberate delivered to the same collector. The defendant said that he had paid all that was in his hands by force of a tally delivered to him, and he did not say that the tally was delivered to him before the liberate and for this reason the plaintiff demurred upon him FRAY When a man brings an assize of Novel Disseisin or an action which is uncertain, the defendant can plead a release or a feoffment which is also uncertain, and this is sufficient to stay the plaintiff from any possession, but where the day and the year are declared in certain, the law is otherwise, wherefore it was adjudged that the plaintiff should recover, etc

Case 40

The case has not been identified in Y B Mich 21 Hen VI, or in the early abridgments.

[1] Defendant   [2] Words from the report of the case

(41) **In debt** upon an obligation against two, one pleaded
a release by the plaintiff, the other denied the deed   And
it was found that the plaintiff had released, and that the
obligation was the deed of the other   And the opinion was
that the plaintiff should recover against him, because he
could take no advantage by the release, etc

The case has not been identified in Y B 21 Hen VI, or in the early
abridgments

(42) **In debt** upon a lease for a term of years, it is no plea
to say that the plaintiff commanded him to make repairs
unless he shows a deed for the command, by HANKFORD
But in Trespass it is a good plea to say that the plaintiff
gave him a license to cut the same trees, and he need not
show the license   Query, if in debt upon a lease for a term
of years it is a plea to say that the plaintiff gave him the
same arrears without showing a deed?

Reported in Y B Hilary (not Mich), 14 Hen IV, p 27, pl 35   See
also Fitzh   Barre, 192

(43) **In detinue,** the plaintiff counted of a box with muniments, and especially of a charter concerning the manor
of B, of which one H was seised, and he conveyed the
descent of this same manor down to himself, etc   And the
defendant said that this same H, by whom you claim, was
never seised, etc   And he had the plea   And so see the
difference, for if he had admitted the bailment, the bailment
had then been traversed generally, etc

Not identified in Y B. Mich 14 Hen IV, or in the early abridgments

(44) **In replevin,** the defendant made a conusance as
bailiff of his master, for rent in arrear   STRANGE   Of
your own wrong, without such cause   And the opinion
clearly was that this was no plea in that case

Reported in Y B Paschal, 2 Hen. V, p 14, pl 1

(45) **In debt** upon a lease for a term of years, the defendant said that he paid the money in another county,

judgment, etc STRANGE That amounts to no more than "nothing due him," therefore he should then conclude so, etc HULS Then he shall not have the advantage of that, for it shall be tried where the writ is brought Wherefore the plea was adjudged good, etc Query?

Case 45   The case has not been identified in Y B Mich 9 Hen V, or in the early abridgments

Michaelis 9 Hen V   **(46) In a scire facias** out of a judgment in a writ of annuity, the defendant pleaded "nothing in arrear " And the opinion of all the COURT was that this was no plea without showing an acquittance The law is the same in debt for the arrears of an annuity, where the annuity was recovered before, etc

Case 46   The case has not been identified in Y B Mich 9 Hen V, or in the early abridgments

Hilary 32 Ed III   **(47) In waste,** the tenant said that the plaintiff was seised of part, etc , the day the writ was purchased And he had the plea And he was forced to answer over for the other part.

Case 47   There is no printed Year Book for the year 32 Ed III

Trinity 32 Ed III   **(48) A woman** brought a writ of *de rationabili parte bonorum* against the executors of her husband, who said that the goods of their testator were so much As to one portion, they said that they had paid certain moneys for which their testator was indebted, etc And as to another part, they said that they had paid a certain sum to the king, for which their testator was indebted And as to another part, they said that their testator had made legacies of certain goods to different persons, whom they had paid, and as to that which remained, they were ready

Statham 34 b. to render, etc BIRT demurred upon the first plea, because they did not show that their testator was bound by a writing, etc , in which case no action lay against them, etc And upon the second, because they did not show any process issued against them by the king And upon the third plea, because the legacies would not take effect until he was dead, and her title to have her reasonable part came from the marriage, so her title was the elder, etc   And they adjourned, etc   Query?

There is no printed year of 32 Ed III   Case 48

(49) **In debt,** the plaintiff declared upon a loan   The Trinity defendant said that at the time, etc , he was under age   39 Ed III And it was adjudged a good plea, etc

Reported in Y B Mich (not Trinity), 39 Ed III, p 20, pl 5   Case 49

(50) **In debt,** the plaintiff counted upon an arbitrement   Michaelis ROLFF   They did not put themselves into an arbitrement   8 Hen VI Ready   MARTYN   Do you think you can have that plea? to wit   to traverse the propriety of the action, since you can wage your law?   ROLFF   Yes, truly   And they adjourned, etc

Reported in Y B Mich 8 Hen VI, p 5, pl 13   Case 50

(51) **In debt** upon an obligation   RIKHIL   The obligation Trinity is endorsed that if the defendant delivers certain goods   12 Ric II to one A, before such a day, that then, etc   And we say that at the time of the making of this obligation, the property in these goods was in this same A, who before that day released to us, by this deed, all actions and all that he had in these goods, judgment if action, etc   And the plaintiff demurred upon the plea

There is no early printed Year Book for the reign of Ric II   The Case 51 case has not been identified in Y B Trinity, 12 Ric II   Ames Foundation, ed Deiser

(52) **In a writ of entry** [where it was] alleged that the Michaelis tenant had no entry except by one A, who disseised the father   9 Hen VI of the demandant, it is no plea to say that the father enfeoffed the said A, etc , unless he traverses the disseisin, for it is contrary to the writ   But it is a good plea to say that this same father enfeoffed a stranger, whose estate the tenant has, etc , as in an assize   But yet, query?   For this amounts to nothing more than that he did not enter by A, etc   And if that be a plea, it is a good plea to say

that same father enfeoffed the tenant, etc , in which case the point of the writ is not taken. (But yet with warranty the plea is good) And this in Trespass, etc

Case 52   Reported in Y B 9 Hen VI, p 55, pl 41

Michaelis
9 Hen VI

(53) **In ravishment of wardship,** it is no plea to say that the father of the infant enfeoffed him, unless he entitles himself to the wardship, for that feoffment is not a title, since the plaintiff was in possession of the wardship, wherefore he pleaded as above   And he made his title as next friend. And he also made protestation that the lands were held in socage, and not in chivalry.   And the COURT said that such a plea is no plea in right of the wardship   But he should say, "Without this that he died in his homage," etc. Query as to that protestation, for it does not seem good, etc   But such a plea has often been pleaded in a writ in right of the wardship, to wit   the feoffment of the ancestor of the infant, without saying more, etc

Case 53   Reported in Y B Hilary, 9 Hen VI, p 61, pl 13

Paschal
9 Hen VI

(54) **In detinue** for a charter, it is a good plea that the defendant delivered the same charter to the plaintiff in another county, without answering to the detinue   And the reason is that he cannot wage his law, etc , for in detinue on an obligation he shall not have such a plea.   From this it follows that in debt upon the arrears of an account, it is a good plea to allege a payment in another county, for the above reason   Query, etc.

Case 54   Reported in Y B Paschal, 9 Hen VI, p 9, pl 24

Trinity
9 Hen VI

(55) **If one demands** a charter touching lands tailed to him by a remainder, the opinion is that it is no plea to plead a release of his ancestor with warranty, for the right to the land shall not be tried in that case, etc.   Query?

Case 55   Reported in Y B Trinity, 9 Hen. VI, p 15, pl 5

Michaelis
3 Hen VI

(56) **In trespass** for hunting in his warren, it is a good plea to say that it is the freehold of the defendant, judgment if without showing how you have a warren you can

have an action, etc   From this it follows that it is a good plea to say, "What have you [to show] for the warren?" as in an assize for a common in gross, etc   But yet that is no plea unless he can show the freehold is in himself, as it seems, etc

Reported in Y B Mich 3 Hen VI, p 12, pl 15 Case 56

(57) **In debt** against executors, they told how their testator was outlawed at the time of his death, etc   PASTON That is no bar for they do not deny it although they have administered, and although they are chargeable to the king, still they are chargeable to us, and this by their own act, inasmuch as they administered, for they could have pleaded as above, and that they had not administered except to the use of the king   And also they could not disable their testator, no more than could their testator himself, for their testator could not allege outlawry in himself, consequently neither could they, etc   And they adjourned, etc. Well argued, etc Michaelis 3 Hen VI

The case has not been identified in Y B Mich 3 Hen VI, or in the early abridgments Case 57

(58) **In trespass** for a close broken and grass cut, it is a good plea to plead the feoffment of the ancestor of the plaintiff to the defendant by a fine, or to such a one whose estate he has, and demand judgment, if without showing special matter action, etc   And the law is the same on a recovery against his ancestor, and it seems that this is by way of an estoppel   And it also seems that the feoffment of the ancestor of the plaintiff with warranty is a good bar, etc. Query, etc. Hilary 3 Hen VI

Reported in Y B Hilary, 3 Hen VI, p 27, pl 9 Case 58

(59) **In a writ of wardship,** it is a good plea to say that the ancestor of the infant enfeoffed him, without answering to the averment that he died in his homage, and still he shall not have the wardship of the infant, for he is not his tenant in law, but as to making an avowry he is his tenant, where- Hilary 3 Hen VI

fore, etc   Query if it be a plea as to the [wardship] of the body, etc?

Case 59   Reported in Y B Hilary, 3 Hen VI, p 32, pl 23

Hilary
3 Hen VI

(60) **In a scire facias** against one A, to have execution out of a recovery tailed by the plaintiff against one B, in Formedon, the tenant said that one H was seised and enfeoffed him, so he was seised until disseised by this B, and he entered pending the writ of Formedon, judgment, etc MARTYN   That is no plea unless you make a title of an elder time than that of the gift, or else show that B disseised you by fraud between the demandant and himself And they adjourned, etc   But yet the plea is good enough, for by his entry pending the writ of Formedon, the writ of Formedon was abated, so he could not falsify the recovery nor make an elder title, but the demandant should answer to the disseisin, etc   But if he showed that his entry was after the judgment, then it would be otherwise, etc

Case 60   Reported in Y B Hilary, 3 Hen VI, p 34, pl 28

Hilary
3 Hen VI

Statham 35 a

(61) **In a scire facias** upon an annuity, ROLFF   After the judgment in a writ of Annuity, and before the purchase of the *Scire Facias*, you yourself delivered the same deed by which the annuity was granted, instead of an acquittance Judgment if action, etc.   PASTON demurred upon the plea, and said   It does not seem to be a plea, for it is not like a release or an acquittance in fact, to which the plaintiff could say, "not his deed," etc

Case 61   Reported in Y B Paschal, 3 Hen VI, p 40, pl 7

(62) **In debt,** the plaintiff counted that the defendant bought of him thirty pounds of tallow, for the sum in demand, to wit   forty shillings   NEWTON   We bought the said tallow for ten shillings only, without this that we bought it for forty shillings, which ten shillings we are ready to pay, and we offer the money   And as to the remainder, "Nothing owing him," etc   (Study this plea well for divers reasons)

Case 62   The citation to this case is missing in Statham, it has not been identified elsewhere

(63) **In trespass** for goods carried away and his servants Michaelis 11 Hen IV
beaten ROLFF. Judgment of the writ, for the plaintiff
is the villein of the bishop of W, regardant, etc , and he
and his predecessors, etc , are seised, and we say that
the bishop, by one B, his seneschal, etc , seized the same
goods, and afterwards delivered them to the plaintiff, to
the use of the bishop, so that at the time, etc , the goods
belonged to the bishop, judgment, etc And as to the
servant we say that she was your daughter, and lived in
your house, and was a common laundress to us and to you[1]
and others, without this that she ever was retained in your
service CHEYNE As to the first plea, the seneschal
made a general seisin, without this that he made such a
special seisin, etc ROLFF And as to the other plea, she
was retained, etc. Ready And they were at issue It
seems that the first plea is good, inasmuch as the plaintiff
is not chargeable over to his lord, by way of an action
for if the lord brought an action against him, he is enfranchised. But if he was chargeable over, although he were
not retained, it is not legal for any one to take him out
of my service without cause. And he has not shown any
cause or justification to take him, wherefore, etc Query?
For it seems that such a common servant, during the time
that he is a common servant, cannot be a special servant,
and such an action does not lie for a special servant, etc.

Reported in Y B Mich 11 Hen IV, p 1, pl 2 Case 63

(64) **In trespass** for goods carried away in the life of Michaelis 11 Hen IV
their testator, brought by executors HORTON Your
testator gave the goods to D, in another county, etc
HANKFORD You do not answer him as to the trespass made
in this county, etc (But yet, if he said, as above, "by
force of which he came to the place where the trespass
was alleged, and took them," that is a good plea, for otherwise it would follow that a man could not give any goods
but the goods that he had in the same county, etc)

The case has not been identified in Y B Mich 11 Hen IV, or in the Case 64
early abridgments

[1] Words from the report of the case

Michaelis
11 Hen IV

(65) **Waste** was assigned in a house that the defendant held for life, of the lease of the plaintiff The defendant said that the father of the plaintiff was seised before the lease, and sold the same house to one B who, after the death of your father, and after the lease, came and tore down the said house, judgment, etc HANKFORD After the death of your father it was not legal to tear it down, because it was not [annexed][1] to the freehold in the life of the father HILARY Yes sir, when the land is in fee simple, but it is otherwise as to land in tail Which was conceded, etc

Case 65

Reported in Y B Mich 11 Hen IV, p 32, pl 59 See also Fitzh Barre, 180

Hilary
11 Hen IV

(66) **In a writ** upon the Statute of Laborers, the defendant said that he was retained upon condition that if he was pleased with his service at the end of one month next ensuing, etc., then he would serve him for the whole year, and if not, that he should depart And he said that he was not pleased at the end of the month, and he departed, judgment, etc And it was adjudged a good plea

Case 66

Reported in Y B Hilary, 11 Hen IV, p 43, pl 15

The Statute is the Statute of Laborers, 23 Ed III (1349) Stats at Large, Vol 2, p 26

Hilary
11 Hen IV

(67) **In detinue** for charters, the defendant showed a redelivery in another county, and the opinion was that it was a good plea, since he could not wage his law, etc.

Case 67

Reported in Y B Hilary, 11 Hen IV, p 50, pl 27

Trinity
11 Hen IV

(68) **In debt** upon the arrears of a lease, it is no plea to say that the plaintiff had an obligation for the same sum, because the defendant cannot wage his law, for he shall have no such plea except where he can wage his law. By HANKFORD and HULS. (But yet that is not the case, etc)

Case 68

The case has not been identified in Y B Trinity, 11 Hen IV, or in the early abridgments

[1] From the report of the case "Examine" in the abridgment

(69) **In trespass** for his park broken, the plaintiff counted according to the Statute MARKHAM What have you of the park? FULTHORPE What is that to you? It is necessary that you excuse yourself of the tort, etc MARKHAM I shall not have imprisonment unless it be a park by the grant of the king, or by prescription, for the Statute relates to a park and not to a close PASTON Plead at your peril MARKHAM He has not had a park there for time, etc , nor by grant of the king, judgment if without a specialty shown, etc NEWTON That goes to the action PASTON This plea is worse than the other, for you have traversed something that is not alleged by the plaintiff. ASCOUGH If the plaintiff had no park, as above, you can make a justification of the entry in the close of the plaintiff, "without this that it was a park in any other manner" MARKHAM We say by protestation that you have no park, but we say that we rode by the palings and let our dogs run at a doe in the high road nearby, and the dogs followed it over the palings, and we did that which was in our power to prevent them, without this that he is guilty in any other manner. And as to the taking and carrying away, etc , not guilty And it was adjudged a good justification

And it was said in the same plea that in a trespass made in a warren the defendant shall say that the place where, etc , was his freehold, and was so at the time, etc And he shall demand of the plaintiff what he has of the warren, etc

Reported in Y B Mich (not Trinity), 18 Hen VI, p 21, pl 6   Case 69
The Statute is that of 3 Ed III (1275), cap 20, Stats at Large, Vol 1, p 90, "Offences Committed in Parks and Ponds"

(70) **In debt** upon an obligation, the obligation was en- dorsed upon the condition that if one A abided by the arbitrement of one F, on the death of one G, her husband, providing that the award be made before such a day, then, etc. And we say that the said A died before any award was made FORTESCUE That is no plea, for it might accord with that that an award was made, and that she died

before, etc   Also that she died and the award was made, wherefore it is necessary for you to state definitely the day on which the award was made, or else say no award was made   Which the Court conceded, etc

Case 70   The case has not been identified in Y B Trinity, 18 Hen VI, or in the early abridgments

Trinity 18 Hen VI

Statham 35 b.

(71) **In trespass,** the plaintiff alleged that the defendant entered in his warren and took coneys, etc., and also that he fished in his several fishery at such a place, etc   YEL-VERTON   As to all except the fishery, "not guilty", and as to that action, etc., for we say that the place where, etc , is a water running from S to F, and as to part of the same water (and he made the boundaries certain), that at the time, etc , the soil upon which that part ran was our free-hold, and we took fish there, as well we might, judgment, etc   And as to the fishery in all the remainder, we say that we and all our ancestors have had common of fishery there, from time, etc , and we fished, etc   FULTHORPE The first plea is no plea.   NEWTON   It is good enough, for if the soil where the water runs is his freehold, you shall have no fishery there without special matter shown   And this was the opinion of the COURT, etc   Wherefore he emparled, etc

Case 71   Reported in Y B Hilary (not Trinity), 18 Hen VI, p 29, pl 2   See also Fitzh Barre, 20

Michaelis 18 Hen VI

(72) **In forgery of deeds,** MARKHAM [by way of] protestation [said] he did not forge them   But he said that he gave the plaintiff a gallon of good wine in satis-faction of the same trespass, to which he agreed.   Judg-ment if action   FORTESCUE   That is no plea unless you say that an agreement was made between them   NEWTON The plea is good   FORTESCUE   We did not receive the gallon of wine in satisfaction of the trespass   Ready And they were at issue.   It seems that he should say for what cause he received the wine, etc

Case 72   Reported in Y B Mi ch 19 Her VI, p 29, pl 52   See also Fitz Barre, 26

(73) **In debt upon an** obligation, the defendant said that he delivered the same obligation to one B, to deliver to the plaintiff when the plaintiff had delivered to him a release to our use, and otherwise that he should hold it as an escrow, and he delivered the obligation and did not take the release, and so not his deed And it was adjudged a good plea

Hilary 19 Hen VI

Reported in Y B Hilary, 19 Hen VI, p 58, pl 22

Case 73

(74) **In trespass** for fish taken in his several fishery MARKHAM The place where, etc , contains ten perches in length, and four in width, and the soil upon which, etc , was my freehold at the time, etc Judgment if action FORTESCUE That is no plea for you should reply, "Judgment, if without special matter shown," etc Wherefore MARKHAM concluded so, etc. NEWTON said that both pleas were good enough, etc Query?

Trinity 19 Hen VI

Reported in Y B Mich (not Trinity) 20 Hen VI, p 4, pl 12 See also Fitzh Barre, 27

Case 74

(75) **In replevin,** the defendant said that at the time of the taking the property in the cattle was in one A, and not in the plaintiff, etc , and he had the plea, etc But yet it is no plea in trespass Query as to the difference, etc ? (It seems that the difference is because in replevin, to the common understanding, the taking is legal, and that he does not claim property, so he does not need to excuse himself of the tort But trespass is not to be considered legal in any event, etc) (Study well, my son)

Hilary 19 Hen VI

The case has not been identified in Y B Hilary, 19 Hen VI, or in the early abridgments The note at the end can hardly have been meant to appear in a serious digest of cases, however refreshing such notes may be to us now

Case 75

(76) **In debt** upon the arrears of an account, the defendant alleged payment in another county FORTESCUE That is no plea, unless you conclude, "So nothing owing him." MARKHAM Then our special matter is not to the purpose,

Hilary 20 Hen VI

for then it shall be tried where the writ is brought, where they will have no notice of this   And it is reasonable for two reasons that we have this plea   One reason is, because as soon as we were found in arrears, it is a debt to the plaintiff, which he can demand in every county, in which case unless we pay him we shall be charged with the damage to him; then, if we pay him in one county, and he demands it by an action of debt in another county, and we have not this plea, we are injured   For the other reason, it is the law, to my thinking, that where a man cannot wage his law he can have such a special answer, as well as where he cannot wage his law he can have a traverse to the jurisdiction of the action, as in debt upon the arrears of a lease, I shall say that he did not lease, and I allege payment in another county   FORTESCUE   There it is reasonable that you allege payment in another county, for you are charged against him by distress, so in avoiding the distress you can pay him where he demands it   But in this case you are not in such danger   And they adjourned, etc   But it seems that is no plea, for if it is founded upon matter of record, or a specialty, the defendant shall not have such a plea, for in debt upon an obligation, or in debt founded upon a record, such a plea is of no avail, and yet in those cases the defendant cannot wage his law   But that reason, to wit   that where a man cannot wage his law he shall have his answer to the necessity of the action, or else allege such special matter, is where the action is not brought upon a matter of record or a specialty, and yet the defendant cannot wage his law, as in debt upon the arrears of a lease, although the lease be a deed, still the action is founded upon the lease and not upon the specialty, for although the lease be without a deed the defendant shall not wage his law   And the law is the same in detinue for charters; the defendant can allege a release in another county, for the above reason, but not so here   (Study this matter well)

Case 76   Reported in Y B Hilary, 20 Hen VI, p 16, pl 3   The remarks after the adjournment are those of the author of the abridgment   They are not in the Year Book case

(77) **In debt** upon the arrears of a lease for life, the defend- Hilary
20 Hen VI
ant said that the plaintiff disseised one W, and leased to
him for life, and W entered before he entered, so nothing
in arrear. And it was not allowed, because he did not
answer to the *debet*, wherefore he said as above, "at which
time he owed him nothing," etc   NEWTON It seems that
he can plead it in bar of all the rent, for he is charged against
the disseisee for the trespass at the same time   PASTON
I do not know that, and although it be so, yet a man can
charge it to two persons for one and the same thing in
different cases, etc And they adjourned, etc Query,
for it seems that the action of debt does not lie in such a
case, since it appeared by the declaration of the plaintiff
that the term still lasted, still in that case it were hard to
have an action of debt unless he shows the matter in his
declaration, to wit that the term is ended.

Reported in Y B Hilary, 20 Hen VI, p 20, pl 15   Case 77

(78) **In a scire facias** to have execution of a certain debt, Michaelis
20 Hen VI
the defendant said that the plaintiff sued a *Scire Facias* to
the same sheriff who had raised the money, etc FORTESCUE·
That is no plea unless he says that the sheriff returned
his writ, for such judicial writs are not of record before
they are returned, etc   Query? (In a note, etc)

Reported in Y B Mich 20 Hen VI, p 4, pl 13   Case 78

(79) **In trespass** for an obligation taken out of the Paschal
20 Hen VI
possession of the plaintiff MARKHAM You delivered
the obligation to one B, to deliver to us, and he delivered
the obligation to us, and we took it, which is the same
taking And it was held a good plea, etc Query?

Reported in Y B Paschal, 20 Hen VI, p 24, pl 9   Case 79

(80) **In debt** upon an obligation MARKHAM The Statham 36 a
Paschal
20 Hen VI
obligation is endorsed upon condition that if we paid four
pounds to the plaintiff annually, for a farm which we had
of him, etc , that then etc , and we say that the plaintiff
never had anything in the said lands which we have of him

to farm, except by a disseisin made by one who entered upon us before any day of payment, etc Judgment if action And the opinion was that this was no plea against the obligation, but in debt upon the lease it is otherwise.

Reported in Y B Paschal, 20 Hen VI, p 23, pl 2

(81) **In debt** upon an obligation, the defendant said that the obligation was made in Paris, in the Kingdom of France, and not, etc , judgment of the writ PORTYNGTON That is no plea MARKHAM If the obligation bore date in Paris you could not maintain an action upon that, consequently when there is no date in the deed we shall have the averment NEWTON That goes to the action, wherefore be advised And MARKHAM dared nor demur, but emparled

Reported in Y B Paschal, 20 Hen VI, p 28, pl 21

(82) **In debt** upon arrears of an account, brought by administrators for a woman who died intestate, and who assigned auditors, etc MARKHAM At the time she assigned auditors she was covert of one B, judgment if action, etc YELVERTON demurred upon the plea, etc It seems that it is no plea unless he says, as above, and also "at the time of the account," etc Query?

The case has not been identified in Y B Paschal, 21 Hen VI, or in the early abridgments

(83) **In trespass** for his apprentice taken with force and arms at London, etc (Query if this be good without showing at what place in London he was taken, etc.) YELVERTON Such a day, year and place before the alleged trespass the plaintiff discharged this apprentice from his service, judgment, etc NEWTON An apprentice cannot be retained without a specialty, wherefore that discharge cannot be pleaded unless you show a specialty for it Wherefore it was adjudged that the plaintiff recover his damages, etc

Reported in Y B Hilary (not Paschal), 21 Hen VI, p 31, pl 18

(84) **In detinue,** the defendant said that the plaintiff gave him the same goods, without this that he bailed them to

him to rebail to the plaintiff, etc   And it was the opinion
of NEWTON and PASTON that it was a good plea to traverse
the bailment by such a special matter, etc.   It seems that
the gift is a good plea for him, etc.

The case has not been identified in Y B Paschal, 21 Hen VI, or in   Case 84
the early abridgments

(85) **In debt** upon an obligation, the defendant said that   Hilary
the plaintiff delivered to him the obligation in lieu of an   5 Hen VI
acquittance, and then he took it back from us, judgment
if action HANKFORD For this retaking you can have
an action of trespass.   And if a man could avoid an obligation by such a plea, an obligation will be of little value.
Wherefore it was adjudged that the plaintiff should recover,
etc

There is no printed year of 5 Hen VI   The citation is an error, and   Case 85
should be Y B Hilary 5 Hen IV, p 2, pl 6

(86) **In a writ of waste,** it was alleged that he had done   Hilary
waste in lands leased to him by the plaintiff for life.   And   6 Hen IV
he assigned the waste as of the cutting of trees.   HILARY
(for the tenant): Sir, you yourself, who are plaintiff, cut
the trees, and we demand judgment if, for this cutting,
action, etc.   HORN. We are much injured if we cannot
have this action, for otherwise he can bring a writ of Trespass
against us for this same cutting, and recover his damages
HANKFORD · If he has the plea now, to bar you of the waste,
he shall not have an action of trespass afterwards.   Wherefore it was adjudged that the plaintiff was barred

Reported in Y. B Hilary, 5 Hen IV, p 6, pl 8, or in the early   Case 86
abridgments   See also Fitzh Barre, 238

(87) **In debt** at the distress, the plaintiff said that he had   Hilary
been at all times ready, etc.   And he had the plea, etc.   7 Hen IV
(But if the other writs were served, I believe that he should
not have the plea, etc)

Reported in Y B Hilary, 7 Hen IV, p 9, pl 15.   Case 87

(88) **In detinue,** the plaintiff showed that the deeds were   Paschal
concerning certain lands, which were given to his ancestor   7 Hen IV

in tail   The defendant showed that the land was given to his ancestor, and traversed the gift   And the opinion of THIRNING was that he should answer to the detinue, etc

Case 88   The case has not been identified unless it is the case in Y B Paschal, 7 Hen IV, p 14, pl 14   This case, however, differs in many points from the case in the abridgment

Paschal 7 Hen IV.   (89) **In account,** it is a good plea to say that he has accounted before the plaintiff himself

Case 89   Reported in Y B Paschal, 7 Hen IV, p 14, pl 17.

Paschal 7 Hen IV   (90) **In trespass** for goods carried away, it is a good plea to say that the plaintiff had sued a replevin for these same cattle, etc.   (*Distinguendum*, etc.)

Case 90   The case has not been identified in Y B Paschal, 7 Hen IV, or in the early abridgments

Trinity 7 Hen IV   (91) **In debt** upon an obligation   RIKHILL   The obligation is endorsed that if we pay a lesser sum on such a day, etc , then, etc , on which day we tendered it to him, and he refused it, judgment if action   And the plea was adjudged good   And the law is the same in replevin — to say that he tendered the rent to the plaintiff, etc , upon the land, and he refused it, without showing the money to the Court, for he shall not pay it except on the land   In which case the defendant shall be put to a new distress, etc   And if he avows for homage, it is a good plea to say that it was offered and refused, judgment if another time   And albeit the tender was in another county, for he refused the homage and he shall not have the homage at any time afterwards, etc.

Case 91   Reported in Y B Trinity, 7 Hen IV, p 18, pl 17

Trinity 7 Hen IV   (92) **In a juris d'utrum,** the tenant pleaded a recovery against the demandant in bar by a writ of *Cessavit*, and the opinion of HANKFORD was that it was no bar, because the right is to be tried by the writ, but he should conclude, "And so it is his lay fee, etc."   Query, etc.?

Case 92   Reported in Y B Trinity, 7 Hen. IV, p 20, pl 30

(93) **In detinue,** the plaintiff counted on a bailment
made by himself to the defendant in London, in a certain
ward and parish. The defendant said by protestation,
not admitting the bailment as the plaintiff had alleged,
but he said that the plaintiff bailed them to the defendant
in another place, in another ward, within the same city,
upon certain conditions, and he made the conditions in certain etc , which he had fulfilled, and he showed how, etc ,
judgment if action   HULS   That is no plea unless you say,
"Without this that he gave them in the place where he has
declared "   PASTON   In battery I shall say that in another
place within the same county the plaintiff had assaulted
me, and did the evil, etc , and I shall not say, "Without
this."   LODYNGTON   I grant your case, because the battery
could be continuous, but take the case of a horse carried
away, and you shall not have the plea   And the opinion
was that he should not have the plea, etc   But in London
it is usually pleaded, and then the venue will come from both
parishes, etc.

Reported in Y B Hilary, 8 Hen. V, p 3, pl 11   See also Fitzh
Barre, 311

*Hilary
8 Hen V*

Case 93

See as to Barre, in the title of Actions upon the Case,
Michaelis, 31 Hen VI. Good matter

The reference is to Statham, Accions sur le Cas, p 11 b, case 26, *supra*

Note

(94) **Debt upon the arrears** of an account   The defendant pleaded an arbitration for the same arrears, and other
trespasses   And the opinion was that that it was not a bar,
no more than against the obligation, etc   But yet the
contrary was held elsewhere, etc

Reported in Y B Hilary, 8 Hen V, p 3, pl. 13

*Statham 36 b
Hilary
8 Hen V*

Case 94

(95) **In a writ** of Entry in the nature of an assize, the
tenant said that he was seised until disseised by one H,
who enfeoffed the plaintiff, upon whom one L entered,
upon whom the tenant entered   And the opinion was that
that was no bar, but that it went only in abatement of
the writ, since it admitted the ouster in one who was a

*Michaelis
12 Hen VI*

stranger to the writ, in which case the plea proves that the plaintiff should have a writ of entry in the per, etc   But yet this is a good plea in an assize   And yet it seems that it amounts to no more in an assize although there was no disseisor named in the writ.   (But I think that the reason it is good in an assize is because in an assize the nature of the writ is to inquire as to the disseisin, in which case the conveyance of the tenant of the tenancy is not to the purpose, for there shall be an inquiry as to the disseisin, although that bar be found or adjudged against him, unless he acknowledge an ouster in fact, etc.   As in the assize the tenant says that the plaintiff was never seised so that he could be disseised, that is a plea in bar, and although it be found that he was seised, still they could inquire as to the disseisin, albeit the tenant did not plead over to the assize, to wit   "And if it be found," etc , because that is the nature of the action   But it is otherwise in any writ of Entry which is a *Præcipe quod Reddat* and not a *Juris Utrum.*)

Case 95   The case has not been identified in Y B 12 Hen VI, or in the early abridgments

Michaelis   (96) **In debt** upon an obligation by one J of F, against
12 Hen VI   one H   NEWTON We made this obligation and delivered it to another J of F, and not to the plaintiff, Ready, etc   CHAUNT   Then you shall not say, "Not your deed." COTESMORE. He cannot do that, but he may well plead, etc   And the plaintiff was made to answer to this plea And he said that it was delivered to him, Ready, etc

Case 96   Reported in Y B Mich 12 Hen VI, p 7, pl 7

Michaelis   (97) **In debt** upon an obligation for twenty pounds, the
27 Hen VI   defendant said that the obligation was endorsed, upon the condition that if he paid ten pounds to the plaintiff, etc., then, etc , and he said that he paid the ten pounds to one B, by command of the plaintiff, judgment, etc.   PORT-YNGTON· That is no plea, for it does not agree with the conditions, etc   Which the Court conceded, wherefore he said that he paid the ten pounds to the plaintiff by

the hands of this said B, Ready   And the other alleged
the contrary   And so note, etc

Reported in Y. B Hilary (not Mich), 27 Hen VI, p 6, pl 1   See Case 97
also Fitzh Barre, 43

(98) **In a writ of entry,** it was alleged that he had no Paschal
27 Hen VI
entry except by one H, to whom B demised, who disseised
the ancestor of the demandant   POLE The same ancestor released all the right he had in the land to one B, then
tenant, whose estate you have, judgment if action   DANBY
That is no plea, for the writ alleges that you entered
by H, and your plea proves the contrary. PORTYNGTON
This plea is good, for it may be that he who disseised your
ancestor enfeoffed the said G, in whose possession your
ancestor released, and then G re-enfeoffed the disseisor,
and he made the demise as the writ alleges, in which case
the writ lies, as it is brought either in the post or at the
election of the demandant, wherefore, etc   In which the
COURT concurred, etc

The case has not been identified in Y B 27 Hen VI   There is no Case 98
printed Paschal Term for that year

(99) **In detinue,** the plaintiff counted that he bailed to Michaelis
27 Hen VI
the defendant a barrel of tar to rebail to him, etc   POLE
A long time before the plaintiff had anything, etc , one J
was in possession of this same barrel and bailed it to us,
upon condition that if one A paid to us ten shillings at
the feast of Easter next ensuing, we would bail the said
barrel to him, and the said A sold the said barrel to the
plaintiff for a certain sum, by force of which the plaintiff came and took the barrel, and we took it back, without this that he bailed the said barrel to us to rebail to
him ASCOUGH It is hard for you to traverse the bailment, unless you admit the delivery POLE We have
acknowledged the property to be in him   And the opinion
was that the plea was good   But yet it seems that he
should say that A did not pay the said ten shillings

The case has not been identified in Y B Mich 27 Hen VI, or in the Case 99
early abridgments

Michaelis
27 Hen VI

(100) **In trespass** for a horse, the defendant showed how formerly the plaintiff brought a writ of Trespass against him for the same horse, and the same taking, and recovered his damages, judgment, etc   DANBY   He does not say that we issued an execution, wherefore it is no plea   And the opinion was that the plea was good, because he could sue execution when he would   And so see, etc

Case 100

The case has not been identified in Y B Mich 27 Hen VI, or in the early abridgments

Michaelis
30 Hen VI

(101) **In the assize** of Wenlock, the tenant said that one H was seised and enfeoffed him by force of which he was seised until one H entered upon him and enfeoffed the plaintiff, upon which, etc   Query if it be a bar?   For it seems that he should say that the said H disseised him, and to this the plaintiff could have replied   And also it seems that the plea is double.

Case 101

The case has not been identified in Y B Mich 30 Hen VI, or in the early abridgments

Michaelis
30 Hen VI

(102) **An assize was** brought by the Duchess of Suffolk and others against J Wenlock and others, and one of the defendants pleaded the release by one of the plaintiffs of all actions real and personal, and relied upon the doubleness of the actions, etc.   And they demurred in judgment as to whether that should be a bar against all the plaintiffs, or only against him who made the release   And then in the Exchequer Chamber DANBY [said]   It seems to me that this shall be no bar, except against him who made it, for in an assize severance lies, and although one of them will say that he will not sue further, still the other shall sue further, for his deed shall not injure his companion, and he shall also recover the freehold, etc   And in detinue for charters this action is personal, and yet the release of one plaintiff does not bar both, for severance lies when the action is for charters   (As if he said the reason is the same, etc)   POLE (to the same effect)   For if this shall be a bar against all, it may be that they are without a remedy, and yet it appears that their title and right

remain in them, for it may be that their entry is tolled by the discharge of the tenant   And it may be that they cannot join in a writ of right because peradventure they have separate estates   And it may be that they cannot join in a writ of entry in the nature of an assize, as if lands be given to a man for life, the remainder to two in fee, and they have the lands in execution by virtue of a statute merchant made to them by the tenant for life, and they are ousted by a stranger, who enfeoffs another, now a writ of entry upon a disseisin would fail them, and yet an assize lies.   So it may be that they have no action but an assize, for they cannot have any action to execute this Statham 37 a remedy, in which there is a mischief to you if it shall be a bar against them all   And the plea will be taken to better effect for him against whom it is pleaded, wherefore, etc And in a writ of annuity by two, the release of one will not bar both, because they cannot have any other action, and yet the action is personal, etc.   MOILE. Which nobody will deny   But if an action be brought by one, and a release of all actions personal be pleaded in bar, that will bar him wholly, wherefore, etc   BITELTON (to the same effect).   And if twenty men have cause to have the assize against me, if one of them be agreed with me they will never have an assize, for if they bring an assize and make their plea for the land, he who has agreed with me shall say that the plea is for rent, and the others will allege the contrary, and then the Court cannot proceed   And, sir, it is not apparent to the Court [how] they could have another action, wherefore, etc   LACON *Contra*   Albeit that *prima facie* the action is personal, still the action is more in the realty than the personalty, for the judgment will be that he recover seisin of the land and his damages, which judgment is real.   And if two bring a writ of descent against me, the release of all actions personal by one of them will not bind both, and yet *prima facie* the action is personal.   But the nature of the action is that he may be restored to the land   And the law is the same for a writ of covenant brought by two heirs to found a singing chaplain, etc.   ILLINGWORTH: *Contra.*   To that which is said

that in a *Quare Impedit* and in a writ of wardship the release
of one will not bar both, that is not so, for they sound merely
in the personalty, and this can well be proved, for one
who has but a term of years in a manor to which an advowson is appendant shall have a *Quare Impedit* and a writ
of wardship also   And a fermor cannot have any action
which is in the realty, and yet these actions sound in the
realty as well as an assize   And, sir, that this release bars
every one of the plaintiffs I shall prove, for I understand that
where several bring an action and the defendant disables
one of them of his action, and yet, notwithstanding, their
title and rights remain jointly to them, in that case all
will be disabled. As if one of the defendants says that
one of the plaintiffs is outlawed in a personal action or
that he is excommunicated, now all shall be disabled, for
their title remains to them jointly and it cannot be disproved
by that   So here they can have a writ of right, on a writ of
entry upon disseisin, for anything which is yet shown, etc.
HENKSTON *Contra*. It seems to me that it shall be a bar
against none of the plaintiffs   And FORTESCUE said to him
not to argue any more on that point, for we will not change
the law which has been in use for so long a time, to wit   that
that shall be a bar against him who made it, etc. HENKSTON
Well, sir, then it seems to me that it shall not be a bar
against the other plaintiffs, for in an assize against a man
who pleads a plea in bar, and admits an ouster, and I demur
upon the plea, and it is adjudged no plea, now I can release
my damages and pray seisin of the land   And still, for the
reason that ILLINGWORTH gave, that the assize was brought
wholly on the wrong done, to wit   for the disseisin, inasmuch as he demands no lands, it follows that if he released
his damages, he would be barred from the land, which
cannot be, for it is the common course in an assize.
CHOKKE It is not the same, for in your case he can clearly
release his damages, but if he wishes to release his action,
then he shall be barred, for a man shall plead a release of
all personal in an assize made after the last continuance,
wherefore, to my mind, your case is not proved   NEDE-
HAM· *Contra*   To my mind the action is real, for it shall
be brought against the tenant of the freehold, or else it

shall abate, and a joint tenancy is a good plea, and the tenant shall vouch and shall pray in aid, and he shall be received, so it is real, and this is clearly proved, for of this same disseisin his heir shall have a writ of entry, and so the disseisin is not only a personal tort, for then it would have died with his person WANGFORD The damages are merely the issues of the land in the meantime, and that is the reason that a man shall recover damages in an assize at the common law, for in no other action by which a man recovered land were there damages at the common law, and although the heir shall have an action for the same disseisin, still he does not recover damages for that disseisin, for he does not recover damages except for the time [since] the death of his ancestor. And it appears here that the plaintiffs could join in another action, as has been well said Then the law compels them to be joined, for if they were now severed and the other recovered, still he would hold in common with them, which is not reasonable And then it may be they bring an action for the half of the other half, and it will be severed, and so on *ad infinitum* until all is recovered, and damages for all, which is against reason And it has been adjudged where a husband and his wife and a third purchased jointly and lost by default, and the husband died, then the wife should not have a *Cui in Vita* for that, because she and the third could join in a writ of right, or in a *Quod ei Deforceat*, and if they could not join in a writ of right for their several estates, then peradventure the law would suffer them to have separate actions, but otherwise not, etc. PRISOT This action is not merely personal, nor merely real, and whoever calls it an action personal or an action real abuses his terms And yet in an assize a release of all actions personal is a good bar, and so is a release of all actions real, for when the action is personal and real and a man releases the personalty or else the realty, then his action is gone, for it cannot be divided. Then it is to be seen in this case, where the action is thus mixed, whether the release made by one of them shall be a bar against all And it seems to me that it shall be a bar but against him who made it, for when his action is so mixed it shall rather be adjudged according to the realty than according to the personalty, and the realty shall be more favored because of its greater dignity, etc   And in a real action the release of one of the plaintiffs is no bar except as to him who made it, consequently not here, wherefore, etc   FORTESCUE (to the same effect)   And this is clearly proved, for in a *Quare Impedit* by two, where one of the plaintiffs is nonsuited, the other shall have a writ to the bishop for the whole advowson because the deed of one of them shall not hurt the other, in such an action which is mixed, but rather shall it give him standing, as in a writ of wardship for the body brought by two, the release of one of them shall not hurt the other, but gives

Statham 37 b

him standing, for he should recover the entire wardship, and hold his companion out of that which he had released, as it seems, etc   And the law is the same in all like cases   And afterwards it was adjudged that it should be no bar, except against him who had made it, etc   Which note

Case 102

The case has not been identified in Y B Mich 30 Hen VI   Fitzh Barre, 256, has a very short digest of the case

Note

See as to Barre in the title of Arbitrement, in the title of Account, in the title of Assizes, and in the title of Ley, Hilary, 31 Ed III   In the title of Entry, in the title of Debt, many matters   And in the title of Justification, and in the title of Trespass, and others, etc

Paschal 34 Ed III

(103) **In an assize** for a common, the release of the ancestor of the plaintiff, with warranty, is no plea, because it is for another thing   (But I believe that it is no bar for another reason also, for the law cannot defeat the warranty of his ancestor by entry on the land, for his entry on the land cannot be legal, so to bar him by the deed of his ancestor when there can be no laches or default directly in him is wrong, etc)

Case 103

There is no printed year of 34 Ed III

Michaelis 3 Ed III

(104) **In ravishment of ward,** the defendant said that at the time of the alleged ravishment the infant was of full age   And the Court said that the plea would not avail, for the day was not traversable unless he justified, etc. And it might be that he stole him some other day when he was under age, wherefore he said that he was not stolen

under age, Ready   And the other alleged the contrary
(It seems that this is a negative pregnant)

The case has not been identified in Y B Mich 3 Ed III, or in the early abridgments   Case 104

(105)   **In debt** upon an obligation, the defendant said that the plaintiff recovered the same debt at Kingston by a plea affirmed on the same obligation   And it was not allowed, because it was his folly that the obligation was not cancelled, etc   Paschal 17 Ed III

Reported in Y B Paschal, 17 Ed III, p 24, pl 11   See also Fitzh Barre, 246   Case 105

(106)   **It is a good plea** in bar, in debt against executors, to say that such a one sued a writ of Debt against them, upon the obligation of their testator, of an elder date, and had judgment to recover, and they had nothing in their hands except so much on which he could sue execution at his will, etc   Query, if it be of a later date?   It seems it is all one, etc   Michaelis 20 Ed III

There is no early printed year for Mich 20 Ed III   The case is printed in Y B Mich 20 Ed III, Pt 2 (R S.), p 418   Case 106

(107)   **In trespass** for a close broken, the defendant said that he was seised of the place, etc., until disseised by one A, who enfeoffed the plaintiff, to maintain for him the title to the same land, without this that he ever had any other possession.   LITTLETON   The Statute says that if the disseisor makes such a feoffment in the way of maintenance, such a feoffment is void, and it is reasonable that the disseisee shall have the advantage of that, as well in a writ of Trespass brought against him, as where he brings the assize, etc   FORTESCUE   The Statute of Westminster the Second, cap 1, says, "*Et si finis inde levetur ipso jure sit nullus,*" and yet it is a discontinuance, and is good until it be defeated   So here it is good until it be defeated by an action or retrogression of the seisin, etc   And they adjourned, etc   *Coram Rege*   Michaelis 31 Hen VI

The case has not been identified in Y B Mich 31 Hen VI, or in the early abridgments.   Case 107

The Statute is West Second, 13 Ed I (1285), cap 1, Stats at Large, Vol 1, p 163.

(108) **A man** found sureties of the peace, to wit two men were bound for him in twenty pounds to keep the peace and also to be at the King's Court on such a day, on which day he did not come, wherefore a *Scire Facias* issued against his sureties [to show] why the king should not have execution for the twenty pounds These said that on the day, etc , the person they should have brought to the Court was imprisoned at Dale in the custody of such a one and such a one, the bailiff, etc. Judgment, etc. And upon this the attorney for the king demurred in law YELVERTON It was his act to be so bound, wherefore it is no plea to excuse him, for it is not like the Petty Cape where a man shall say that he was imprisoned, etc , for there he was not bound by his deed but by the law, wherefore he cannot excuse himself by such an averment, unless he will say that he was dead, for if he was dead he could not have his body there, etc But yet in some cases death does not excuse him, as if I be bound to a man that J at Stile shall make a house by such a day, it is no plea for me to say that before the day J at Stile died, for another man could have made it for him, no more than where a man is bound in twenty pounds that J at Stile shall pay twenty pounds on such a day, it is a plea to say that he was dead before the day, for the above reason. FORTESCUE If he had said that he was imprisoned at the suit of the king, the plea were good, but [not] to say that he was imprisoned at the suit of another man, for if he be imprisoned wrongfully, he could have his remedy against him who imprisoned him, etc. As in a writ of waste it is no plea to say that a stranger made the waste, for the above reason, but it is a good plea to say that the plaintiff made the waste So here. Wherefore it is well to see the record, etc   And the record was examined, and it was that he for whom they were bound was detained in prison under the custody of such a one and such a one, bailiffs of Dale, without more, etc. YELVERTON. It may be that he was a cutpurse, and that he was imprisoned for that reason, in which case the plea were of no value, etc But my master FORTESCUE has informed you how you shall plead in order to save the twenty pounds, etc   Which note

The case has not been identified in Y B Mich 31 Hen VI, or in the **Case 108** early abridgements

22 To take up the subject of the old pleading so far as it relates to the plea in bar is a task which is outside the limits of these notes   Coke says of the plea in bar [Coke, 1st Inst f 372] "Barre is a word common as well to the English as to the French, of which cometh the noun, *a Bar*, Barra   It signifieth legally a destruction forever, or taking away for a time of the action of him that right hath   And Barra is an Italian word, and signifieth Bar, as we use it, and it is called a Plea in Bar when such a Bar is pleaded"   The later writers simply copy or paraphrase Coke

It is easily to be seen that the plea is capable of an infinity of variations, and that in our one hundred examples in the abridgment we shall find many kinds of writs, yet there seems to be a preponderance of writs of debt and trespass   Why these cases were chosen by the compiler, and if there were any reason why the plea in bar was more useful or less settled in the writs of debt or trespass, we do not know, to solve the problem would take such a knowledge of the old pleading as Littleton inculcates [Coke, 1st Inst sec 534, f 302]   We might then be able to state why this case was rejected and that accepted   As it is we can take the maxim of Littleton to heart   "*Et saches, mon fils, que est un des plus honorables, laudables, et profitables choses in nostre ley, de aver le science de bien pleder en actions real et personals, et pur ceo jeo toy counsaile especialment de mitter ton courage et cure d'ceo apprender*"   For if it is necessary to know the old law in order to apprehend the underlying principles of the new, then it is also necessary to understand this "bien pleder" which was indeed a science, a mold into which went that crude law which came out a perfected and skilfully shaped system

CONNTE 23

(1) **In a writ of annuity,** the plaintiff counted upon an annuity which was granted by a composition for a dispute as to tithes between their predecessors, and he counted the year of grace one thousand, and there was nothing said as to any king.   And the opinion of WILLOUGHBY was that the count was good, etc. — Statham 38 a Paschal 24 Ed III

Reported in Y B Trinity (not Paschal), 24 Ed III, p 53, pl 35 **Case I** See also Brooke, Count, 41, and Fitzh Count, 40   Brooke has the date twelve hundred, which is probably nearer right.

(2) **In a scire facias** a man shall [not] count upon that matter which is comprised within the writ, no more shall — Michaelis 30 Hen VI

he in a distraint, where he has judgment to recover an acquittance by the statute, and so in other judicial writs, etc

And it was said in the same plea, that in a writ of Mesne a man shall count that the defendant should acquit him generally. But yet it does not acquit him except against the chief lord, but the form is such, etc   And also in a writ of Dower, there is no count, but a demand   And the law is the same in a writ *de Tale Quale*

Case 2   The case has not been identified in Y B Mich 30 Hen VI, or in the early abridgments

Michaelis   (3) **A woman** brought a writ of Detinue against executors,
30 Ed III and she counted that by the common custom of the king-
dom, women have, after the death of their husbands, the half of their goods, if they have no issue, etc , and then only the third part   And she showed that her husband was dead without issue between them   SETON   Judgment of the count, for she declares on a common custom, and if there were such a custom through all the kingdom, then it is the common law, and I never knew a man rehearse the common law in his count, for if, in a writ of Dower, I wish to rehearse in my count that women shall be endowed of the third part, that is of no avail.   And if I would say "no such custom" that could not be tried by the inquest, for it is common law   WILLOUGHBY: A writ of Dower is general, and yet a woman shall have her special demand, and she shall say that by license of gavelkind she shall have the half, etc   THORPE   That is only a private custom which is contrary to the common law   WILLOUGHBY   I shall count against one as a common hosteler, and I shall recite the custom   SETON   It is reasonable in that case, because the writ is special, and rehearses the custom, so the count should be accordant, etc   THORPE   Answer   SETON   Still, judgment of the count, for she counts that her husband died without issue between them, and it may be that he had issue by another wife   WILLOUGHBY   Then you can show that, and although you do show it, still it is no plea unless you say that they were never advanced,

etc. And then the count was adjudged good, etc (All the same, query? For I think that this is not the common custom through all the kingdom, etc) SETON We tell you that we were charged and impleaded before the ordinary for various things touching the testament, and we do not think that before the testament be proved as to this action the Court will take jurisdiction WILLOUGHBY. You have taken exception to the count, and to the writ, so you have affirmed the jurisdiction SETON I have taken no exception except such as appeared in the writ and the count THORPE Shall not a man have a writ of debt against you, notwithstanding that? SETON Yes, sir, but not this action. WILLOUGHBY. If what you say is true, I do not know how it shall be tried here. And they adjourned, etc.

Reported in Y B Mich 30 Ed III, p 25, pl 51   Case 3

(4) **If a man** declares upon an obligation [which is] with- out date, he shall show in his declaration where it was made But if the defendant pleads an acquittance [which is] without date, he does not need to put any place where, etc , but only the day, etc. But if the plaintiff denies it, then there is time enough [to do it] And this in Debt, etc

Michaelis 3 Hen IV

Reported in Y B Mich 3 Hen IV, p 4, pl 15   Case 4

(5) **In debt,** the plaintiff counted that he leased, by a deed indented, certain lands to the defendant, to do certain covenants, and to fulfill the covenants the defendant by the same deed bound himself to the plaintiff in one hundred pounds And the plaintiff counted that the covenants were broken, so accrued, etc And note that he did not declare on any covenant, Ready, etc *Simile*, Mich 3 Hen VI, in Debt.

Hilary 3 Hen IV

The case has not been identified in Y B Hilary, 3 Hen IV   Case 5

(6) **In detinue,** the plaintiff counted upon a bailment to rebail to him, and the defendant had a *Scire Facias* against one who came and said that the plaintiff delivered

Michaelis 15 Hen VI

them upon certain conditions; and the plaintiff showed that the conditions were different And the opinion of PASTON was that the count should abate, inasmuch as he had shown conditions contrary to the declaration, etc.

Case 6   There is no printed Year Book for 15 Hen VI

Paschal 15 Hen VI   (7) **If I lease** land for a term of life, the remainder over in fee, the tenant for life shall have a writ of Mesne, and count that he holds of me, etc , for which services as by the hands of his very tenant And although the matter be disclosed the count shall not abate, for the seisin is not traversable in that case, etc

Case 7   There is no printed Year Book for 15 Hen VI

Hilary 34 Ed III   (8) **In all writs** of entry founded upon a disseisin, a man shall count, "After the first passage," for they claim by the disseisin, in which case they shall have the same limitation But in other writs of entry, a man shall count upon a seisin after the coronation of the same king, according to the Statute of Westminster the First By WILLOUGHBY, in a writ of entry *in consimili casu*, etc

Case 8.   There is no printed Year Book for 34 Ed III Fitzh Count, 39, has the case

Michaelis 30 Hen VI   (9) **In a quare impedit,** the plaintiff counted that one H was seised of the manor of D, to which, etc , and he presented, etc , and enfeoffed him, and the church was vacant so it belonged to him [to present]. DANBY Judgment of the count, because he does not show that he was seised of the manor at the time of the vacancy. And it was not allowed, because it shall be understood so, until the reversion be shown, etc.

And it was said in the same plea, that if I am disseised of a manor to which an advowson is appendant, that I can present to the advowson before I enter into the manor, etc

Case 9.   The case has not been identified in Y B Mich 30 Hen VI, or in the early abridgments

(10) **In trespass** for his apprentice wrongfully taken Hilary
MARKHAM Judgment of the count, for he does not declare 21 Hen VI
for what time he was his apprentice NEWTON If the
action had been brought against the apprentice for his
departure, then that had been a good exception, by which
he would recover his term And the law is the same for
a servant taken, etc , but against a stranger the count is
good, wherefore answer, etc

Reported in Y B Hilary, 21 Hen VI, p 31, pl 18 See also Fitzh Case 10
Count, 33

(11) **In debt** against one B, the plaintiff counted that Statham 38 b
one H was his apprentice, and this H and the defendant Michaelis
were bound in twenty pounds, in an indenture (which he 14 Hen. IV.
produced) that the said H would serve him well, and that
the conditions were broken, etc So note that in every
case where a man cannot have an action, except by reason
of a broken covenant, he should show how the covenant
was broken in his declaration, for it is not like an obligation
which has a condition, for the condition being fulfilled
defeats the obligation, which cannot be shown by the plea,
etc And see also that the plaintiff in his count showed
that the other who made the indenture was under age at
the time of the making, etc , for otherwise he varied from
his specialty, for the writ was brought against B alone

The case has not been identified in Y B Mich 14 Hen IV, or in the Case 11
early abridgments

(12) **In an attachment** upon a prohibition, the plaintiff Hilary
counted that he delivered the prohibition to the defendant, 9 Hen VI.
such a day, year, and place, in the presence of such a one,
and such a one, although the party had nothing to show
[for] the livery Query if attachment be founded upon
prohibition at the common law? etc

Reported in Y B Hilary, 9 Hen VI, p 61, pl 12 See also Brooke, Case 12
Count, 11

(13) **In debt** upon an obligation made to B, in the county Michaelis
of N ROLFF. Judgment of the count, for the vill of B 3 Hen VI

extends into divers counties (and he showed which), and he does not say in which county the deed was made MARTYN· It shall be understood to be in the same county where the writ is brought, wherefore answer, etc

Case 13.   Reported in Y B Hilary (not Mich), 3 Hen VI, p 35, pl 30   See also Brooke, Count, 6, and Fitzh   Count, 6

Paschal
3 Hen VI

(14) **In formedon** against the husband and his wife, who made default after appearance, etc   At the Petty Cape the husband made default and the wife was received and asked judgment of the count because he counted on a gift, etc , and said "by force of which their donor was seised," where it should be the donee. ROLFF We are ready to count anew against you, for the first count is gone through the default, etc BABYNGTON So it seems, for he shall count anew as well in this case as against the tenant by the warranty, or against him who is received because of a reversion, etc PASTON It is reasonable there, for they are strangers to the first count, but the woman is a party, etc ROLFF Still she is now in another course And this was well debated   And then it was adjudged that he should count anew

And it was said in the same plea, if after the declaration the tenant makes default at the Petty Cape, the demandant can choose to release the default or to hold to the default, and if he releases the default, then he shall count anew, because by the default the first count is gone, as if the case be put without day after a declaration, by protestation, at the resummons the plaintiff shall count anew, and if he holds to the default the tenant cannot save it, [so]¹ if the count be not good the justices will not give judgment upon it if it seems bad, etc   And it was said on this account it seemed to them here that the demandant held himself to the default when he suffered the woman to be received   But he could not do otherwise for he had no choice in this case, since the receipt is given by the Statute, as it seems, etc

¹ "Issuit" in the Year Books

Reported in Y B Paschal, 3 Hen VI, p 41, pl 10   See also Brooke, Case 14
Count, 7, and Fitzh   Count, 4

The Statute is Westminster the First, 13 Ed I, cap 4 (1285),
Stats at Large, Vol 1, p 163 (171)

(15) **In detinue** for a writing, against a man as executor Michaelis
of one B, he counted that the father of the plaintiff bailed 18 Hen VI
this same deed to his testator, in which it was set forth
that one A gave to the father of the plaintiff, and to E,
his wife, all the lands which he had in the county of Middlesex, in tail, to rebail to the said father and mother and their
heirs aforesaid.   And that after the death of your testator
the deed reverted, etc   FORTESCUE   Judgment of the
count, for the plaintiff has [not] shown in what vill the land
is.   MARKHAM: There is no land in demand, except the
deed, wherefore he should entitle himself according to the
deed   FORTESCUE· You say truly, where a man has
demanded as heir general, but here he entitles himself as
heir in tail.   NEWTON   The declaration is double, for he
demands as heir to the land, and also because of a bailment given   One would suffice, but you have pleaded in
abatement of the writ, wherefore you have passed the point
of taking exception to the count, wherefore answer, etc
(But yet that matter appeared, wherefore he shall have
the advantage which, etc ?)

The case has not been identified in Y B Mich 18 Hen VI, or in Case 15
the early abridgments

(16) **In wardship** the demandant was driven to show in Hilary
his count that the heir was under age, and yet the writ did 12 Hen IV
not mention it.   Which note, for the *tales* are not so, etc

Reported in Y B Hilary, 12 Hen IV, p 16, pl 10   Case 16

(17) **In ravishment of ward.**   DANBY   Judgment of Michaelis
the count, for it says *"Cuius maritagium ad ipsum pertinet,"* 27 Hen VI
and does not say that he was under age at the time of the
ravishment, etc   PORTYNGTON·   Whether he be under
age or of full age, the marriage belongs to him, etc

The case has not been identified in Y B Mich 27 Hen VI, or in the Case 17
early abridgments.

(18) **In a quare impedit,** where the plaintiff counted on a gift in tail, of the manor with the advowson, made to his ancestor in tail, he should make himself heir to him who was last seised, and mention everyone who held the estate, as well as in a Formedon, etc

Case 18   Statham has no citation to this case   It has not been elsewhere identified

Note   **See as to** Count, in the title of Debt, and in the title of Bar, Paschal, 18 Hen VI, and also in the title of Detinue, and in the title of *Quare Impedit,* Trinity, 18 Hen VI

For the case in the title of Bar, see *supra* Statham, title Barre, p 33 b, case 30   The case in *Quare Impedit* has not been identified in Statham   The references to the other titles are incomplete

Hilary 2 Hen IV   (19) **In debt** upon the arrears of an account, he did not show in his count for what things the defendant should account, and it was adjudged good   But in debt upon the arrears of an account against executors, he should show for what things their testator accounted, etc   As appeared in the same year   (But yet I do not know any difference), etc

Case 19   The case has not been identified in Y B Hilary, 2 Hen IV, or in the early abridgments

Anno 11 Ed III   (20) **The demandant** counted against the tenant, for a receipt, etc   In Formedon   *Simile,* Anno 3 Hen VI

Case 20   There is no early printed year for 11 Ed III   The case has not been identified in the Rolls Series, 11–12 Ed III   The point, however, may have been concealed in the midst of a long case, and may very well have escaped the eye of the editor

Michaelis 22 Hen VI   (21) **In a quare impedit** and in a writ for an advowson, a man shall count that his clerk was admitted and instituted, and he need not say that he was inducted or installed, etc   By NEWTON and PASTON in a *Quare Impedit*

Case 21   The case has not been identified in Y B Mich 22 Hen VI, or in the early abridgments

Statham 39 a Trinity 19 Ed III   (22) **A count** in *Quo Jure* against all the tenants is good, notwithstanding every one of them had a several right, because it is in the nature of a trespass, and this in *Quo Jure*, etc.

There is no early printed Y B for Trinity, 19 Ed III   The case has not been identified in the Rolls Series for that year and Term   Case 22

(23) The count in *Contributione Facienda* shall mention as well every one holding the land, and as well everyone shall pay, and one shall answer without the other, etc   Paschal 18 Ed II

Reported in Y B Paschal, 18 Ed II, p 604, pl 5 (Contribution)   Case 23.

[23] After the title of Barre the old learning of the Count follows naturally   Heath [Maxims and Rules of Pleading, p 3] says, "There is holden a maxim in our books that *it sufficeth if a bar be good to common intent, but a count in the substance thereof must be good to every intent*"   So in the step from the bar to the count we seem to pass from the less formal to the more precise   The count also seems to have to be 'good to any intent," yet often seems miraculously to escape being declared bad   In our second case we find that the count was declared good, but the commentator does not think that it should have been so declared   He states that in a writ of dower "there is no count, but a demand"   Glanville supports the note, for he says   "The woman shall set forth her claim against her adversary in the following words, 'I demand such land, as appertaining to such Land which was named to me in dower'"   The words of Glanville are   "*Peto terram illam sicut pertinentiam illius terræ, quæ mihi nominata est in Dotem*"   [Glanville, Liber 6, Chap VIII   Beames, Glanville, p 122, Beale's ed p 101 (1812)]   Nevertheless, although the form seemed that of a demand, it appears to have been known as the count and the question is whether there was at that time any foundation for this distinction   Is the seeker for dower a demandant or a plaintiff?   In instances of the early action of Debt the active party is often put before us, not as complaining but as demanding   [P & M Hist of Eng Law, 2d ed , Vol 2, p 572   Bracton, Note Book, pl 52, 177, 325, 381, etc]

As to the count Maitland says   "It is a formal statement bristling with sacramental words, an omission of which would be fatal"   (*Ib* , p 605)   This, of course, while the pleading was in its earlier stages   Later the pleading, while still subject to criticism, was placed on a more scientific basis

The cases given in the abridgment do not show the "sacramental words" of Maitland, they do not even show a strict dependence upon form   The first case is indeed quite to the contrary, for without any exact date given, and "nothing said as to any king," the count was adjudged good   This does not look like a servile dependence upon mere words   If we go down the list of the cases here given we shall find, or so it seems, that the reason for the decision — where a decision is given —

is based not on the infinitely small, the quibble, the difference in a spelling or word, it is the reasoning that is paramount here, that is the chief matter for thought in the typical cases here presented   They are not chosen to show that the count was bad for some trivial reason, but because some underlying principle was violated   In spite of the pettiness of many of the cases it is this fact which comes to us more and more in the Year Book reading   Small people saw small things large and argued as if they were really large, the larger people saw things in a better proportion and it was the men of larger minds who seem to us to have predominated   To be sure the man who wishes to make the lesser reason seem the larger is often among the users of the lengthy and involved arguments intended to show the force of the really forceless, or the great importance of the missing word or "addition"   Yet while he gets the full benefit of his argument which may occupy a half of the folio page he is not often the man who wins in the end   There is generally some short-phrased and wise judge to state the law to him, and to do it in very brief and effective fashion   He has known what the law was all through the barren wilderness of wordy talk, and he says so without mincing words, so the law is kept on its track, and gets down to us not a matter of quibbles and chaff, but with its sound principles intact

CHAMPARTIE

<table>
<tr><td>Hilary
30 Ed III</td><td>(1) In champerty the plaintiff shall show the date of the writ in his count, and although the count be that the defendant had purchased part, etc, pending the plea, still that means the writ, etc, as well before the plea as after   And this in Champerty.</td></tr>
<tr><td>Case 1</td><td>Reported in Y B Hilary, 30 Ed III, p 3, pl 15</td></tr>
<tr><td></td><td>(2) In champerty it is no plea to justify the purchase by force of a condition or covenant made before the writ was purchased, unless he says, "without this that he purchased for Champerty" or to maintain the quarrel in any other manner   And this in Champerty</td></tr>
<tr><td>Case 2.</td><td>There is no citation for this case given in Statham   The case has not been identified in the early abridgments</td></tr>
</table>

CHARGE

<table>
<tr><td>Statham 39 b
Paschal
5 Hen V</td><td>(1) If a man leases land for a term of years, and then charges the land, and then the termor surrenders his estate,</td></tr>
</table>

whether the lessor holds the charge during the term or not was well argued

And it was said in the same plea, if I lease lands for the term of twenty years without impeachment of waste, and then I confirm his estate for the term of his life, that he shall not be impeached for waste during the term of twenty years, etc

Reported in Y B Paschal, 5 Hen V, p 8, pl 20 See also Brooke, Charge, 10   Case 1

(2) **A man** can charge a reversion, to wit by a fine or by a deed indented, for the estoppel, but not by a simple deed By THORPE in a *Scire Facias*.   Hilary 38 Ed III

Reported in Y B Hilary, 38 Ed III, p 4, pl 15   Case 2

(3) **If the tenant** of the king charges [his lands] and dies while his heir is under age and in the wardship of the king, the king shall hold charged because he claims in another's right But it is otherwise if it comes to him by escheat or forfeiture But yet other persons than the king shall hold charged for these reasons etc , for when the king has the vacancies of a bishopric or of an abbey, which was charged, etc , he who shall have such a charge from the king shall have an allowance for it, etc In the Exchequer, etc   Trinity 38 Ed III

The case has not been identified in Y. B Hilary, 38 Ed II, or in the early abridgments   Case 3

(4) **Land was** leased to a woman for a term of years, and she took a husband who granted to the plaintiff ten shillings of rent, out of this same land, to do different services for him and his wife The husband died, after whose death the woman paid the rent, and then the plaintiff brought a writ of Debt for this same rent And the opinion was that the woman should hold discharged, notwithstanding that payment, for immediately after the death of her husband the land was discharged in fact. as if a man had issue a daughter and died, and his wife is *enceinte* with a son, the daughter is charged after the son is born, and pays the rent,

this payment does not conclude them for the above reason,
etc   Like matter, Mich. 3 Hen VI, in Avowry.

And it was said in the same plea if the husband had built
a house upon the same land that the wife would be forced
to sustain it, or else she would be impeached for waste
Which was conceded, etc

Case 4   The case has not been identified as there is no citation given by
Statham

Trinity   (5) **Where one is** to charge a prebend, it is necessary
11 Hen IV.   that the ordinary confirm it, and also the dean and the
chapter of the cathedral church in which the prebend is,
for they are patrons, etc.   And of some prebends the bishop
is a patron

And see in the same plea that the plaintiff showed a
ratification made by the chapter, and the dean was not
named in it, but one who was a commissionary of the dean
in the absence of the dean was a party to the deed, and
put his seal to the deed.   And the opinion of THIRNING
and HULS was that this was good enough

And see in the same plea, if in a writ of Annuity the
patron and the ordinary are prayed in aid, and it is returned
that they were summoned and did not come, but the
annuity is received against the patron, the church will be
charged forever, etc   The law is the same where one of
them comes and the other does not, since he joins in aid
alone, in that case

Case 5   The case has not been identified in Y B Trinity, 11 Hen IV, or in
the early abridgments

Hilary   (6) **If a prior** who is presentable has a convent and a
12 Hen IV   common seal, whether such prior and convent can charge
the house in perpetuity, without the assent of their patrons
and ordinary, was well argued in a writ of Annuity

And it was said in the same plea, that if an annuity be
brought against an abbot or prior and he would levy a fine to
the plaintiff for this same annuity, or for a lesser sum,
this fine will bind his successors, for if he will admit the action
of the demandant, that will bind his successor, and con-

sequently a fine levied upon the same [land], etc See that in the first case he had been ousted of the aid. And it was also said that he shall not have a writ of right for an advowson for the tithes, nor a writ of *Juris d'Utrum*, etc. Query?

The case has not been identified in Y B Hilary, 12 Hen IV, or in Case 6 the early abridgments

(7) **If one be** disseised of an acre of land in tail, and of another acre in fee simple, and grants a rent charge out of both acres, and dies, his heir shall hold the land tailed discharged, but by the opinion of THIRNING, the land in fee simple shall be charged with all the rent, etc. Hilary 12 Hen IV

The case has not been identified in Y B Hilary, 12 Hen IV, or in Case 7 the early abridgments

(8) **Where a man** devises a rent charge with a clause of distress, it is good, and the devise shall be pleaded without showing the testament, for it does not belong to him, etc As appeared Anno 40, *Liber Assisarum*, in an office Anno 40 *Liber Assisarum*

The case has not been identified in Anno 40, *Liber Assisarum*   Case 8

(9) **In an assize for rent** the tenant pleaded "out of his fee," and the plaintiff produced a deed by which one J granted the rent issuing out of the manor of F, to wit to receive so much by the hands of one such, tenant, and so much by the hands of one such. And the opinion was that notwithstanding these words, all the manor should be charged, and every part of it, etc. Query, for he did not say how the distress was, etc. But yet that did not change the matter as to the assize, but in an avowry, etc Paschal 7 Ed III

The case has not been identified in Y B Paschal, 7 Ed III, or in the Case 9 early abridgments

CHARTRE [24]

(1) **The sheriff** returned that the garnishee was dead And without more the charter was allowed, etc Statham 40 a Hilary 40 Ed III

Reported in Y B Hilary, 40 Ed III, p 2, pl 4 and 5 See also Case I Fitzh Chartre, 3

Hilary
48 Ed III

(2) **In account** against one H, he was outlawed and had a charter of pardon and sued a *Scire Facias*, etc., to which the sheriff returned that he had nothing by which to be garnished, and then he came and prayed that he might count against the said H. FYNCHEDEN You should sue a *Sicut Alias*, for when a *Scire Facias* is awarded he cannot answer unless he comes by the process, but at the *Sicut Alias* he can because of the mischief. As in a voucher, at the summons he cannot answer, unless he be summoned, but at the *Sequatur* he can, for the mischief (etc.) But yet when one is vouched and is ready to enter before any summons is issued, he can enter into the warranty well enough, etc Then the *Sicut Alias* was awarded, etc And from this it follows that the *Sicut Alias* is peremptory, etc.

Case 2   Reported in Y B Hilary, 48 Ed III, p 1, pl 1

Hilary
48 Ed III

(3) **In debt** brought by three against three, until they were outlawed, and one of them sued a charter of pardon, and had a *Scire Facias* against the plaintiffs, etc. And the sheriff returned that one was garnished, and that the other two had nothing, etc PERCY He that was garnished did not come, wherefore we pray that he be demanded to the effect that if he does not come, that he be nonsuited, in which case the nonsuit of one of them is the nonsuit of all, as well as in the first action, etc. And then he was demanded, and appeared by attorney, wherefore a *Sicut Alias* was awarded against the two and the same day given to him, etc Query, if at the *Sicut Alias* all the three come, if they shall be received to count against him, because in the first case they could not count against him until his companions came, etc (But I believe he would have the same day, until the others had sued their charters) Query well, etc In a *Scire Facias*, etc.

Case 3   Reported in Y B Hilary, 48 Ed III, p 3, pl 7 See also Fitzh Chartre, 5

Hilary
50 Ed III

(4) **In debt,** the defendant was outlawed, and had a charter of pardon and sued a *Scire Facias*, to which the plaintiff declared, etc And the plaintiff found main-

prise, and had a day over, on which day he made default, and the plaintiff prayed that the charter be disallowed And the opinion of WILLOUGHBY was that it should be allowed, and a *capias* issued against his mainpernors, etc

Simile, in the same term, in Debt, where upon the *Scire Facias* the defendant pleaded in bar, and the plaintiff demurred in law upon the plea, and the opinion was that the charter should be allowed, etc, immediately, etc Query?

The case has not been identified in Y B Hilary, 50 Ed III, or in the early abridgments   Case 4

(5) **The husband** and his wife were outlawed. The wife had a charter of pardon, and produced it before the Court, and prayed, by NEWTON, that she might go free   THIRNING   You may well pray, yet we cannot allow it, for she cannot have a *Scire Facias* without her husband, wherefore the charter was delivered back to the woman and she was allowed to go free, etc   (It seems that she was imprisoned by a *capias utlagium* and sued this charter), etc   Trinity 11 Hen IV

Reported in Y B Trinity, 11 Hen IV. See also Brooke, Chartres de Pardon, 18   Case 5

(6) **In debt,** the husband and his wife were outlawed, and the wife had a charter of pardon, and showed it to the Court, and prayed to be dismissed, since she could not have a *Scire Facias*   HANKFORD   At the common law when one was outlawed and had a charter of pardon, the plaintiff was put [to sue] a new original, and the case is the same here, wherefore she was dismissed and the plaintiff had a *capias utlagium* against the husband and his wife. Query, if the husband had a charter afterwards, if he should have a *Scire Facias* in his own name, leaving out his wife? And it seems not, etc   Hilary 13 Hen IV

Reported in Y B Mich (not Hilary), 13 Hen IV, p 26 (1), pl 2   Case 6

(7) **In trespass,** the defendant said that the plaintiff was outlawed, and the plaintiff produced a charter of   Michaelis 32 Ed III

pardon, which was purchased pending the writ   And it was adjudged good, etc

Case 7

There is no printed year for 32 Ed III   The case has not been identified in the early abridgments.

Michaelis 11 Hen IV

(8)   **One was attainted** in an appeal, and he took to his clergy; and the plaintiff said that he was a bigamist, and a writ issued to certify it, and afterward the plaintiff died, and the defendant had a charter of pardon   And because this special matter was not related in the charter, the opinion was that it was of no value, etc

Case 8

Reported in Y B Mich 11 Hen IV, p 11, pl 24   See also Fitzh Chartre, 16   The case was continued to Hilary Term of the same year   See Hilary, 11 Hen IV, p 48, pl 23

Michaelis 9 Hen IV

(9)   **In an appeal** against two by a woman, they were outlawed at her suit, and then one of them purchased a charter of pardon, and had a *Scire Facias* against the plaintiff, who was garnished, and did not come, wherefore the charter was allowed   And then the other defendant purchased a charter of pardon and prayed that it be allowed HANKFORD   You should have a *Scire Facias*   NORTON No, sir, for the woman was garnished at the suit of my companion, and she did not come, so the original is ended HANKFORD   If it was in an action in which the plaintiff could count upon the first original, you would speak according to law, but in this case she cannot count, but shall ask you if you have anything to say why you should not be hung Wherefore it was adjudged that he should sue a *Scire Facias*, if he would   (Note this matter for various reasons, etc)

Case 9

Reported in Y B Mich 9 Hen IV, p 24 (1), pl 2   See also Brooke, Chartre de Pardon, 14   See a report of a like case in Mich 9 Hen IV, p 7, pl 21

Paschal 9 Hen IV

(10)   **In an appeal** for the death of a man, if the defendant had a charter of pardon and a *Scire Facias* against the plaintiff, and the sheriff returned that he was dead, that charter shall not be allowed until he has a *Scire Facias* against his heir, etc.   *Simile*, Mich 11 Hen IV, etc

The case has not been identified in Y B. Paschal, 9 Hen IV, or in the early abridgments The reference to Mich. 11 Hen IV, may be to the case 8, *supra*

(11) **One was** outlawed at the suit of the Dean and Chapter of Lichfield, in a writ of Debt, and he sued a charter of pardon and a *Scire Facias* against the plaintiff, and the sheriff returned that they were garnished, on which day the defendant said that after the last continuance the dean died, and he prayed that the charter be allowed, and that he be dismissed. And because the attorney of the plaintiff could not deny this, it was adjudged that the charter be allowed, etc It seems that he should have no such exception before the declaration (But yet perchance the report here is not perfect, etc)

Reported in Y B Mich. 11 Hen VI, p 1, pl 1 See also Brooke, Chartres de Pardon, 56, and Fitzh Chartre, 20 Statham has here expressed the ever-present doubt as to the correctness of the reported cases in the Year Books, or as to the reported cases anywhere It is the feeling one has constantly in reading the digest which goes under his name, but the more closely one reads the digested cases the more one feels that the reporting at least was very faithfully done

[24] This title conveys an exactly opposite idea to the modern reader to that which it conveyed to the contemporary student to whom a copy of Statham was first presented There were other charters than these presented here under this title, like and unlike those of later times, yet related to them in a greater or less degree, but the charters presented to us by Statham are of a different character It takes the second part of their full title to convey their real meaning, for they are wholly charters of pardon granted by the king, but not, as the modern mind would immediately take for granted, for criminal offences, or for offences against the State Half of the cases here collected are for debt, account, or rent "Process continued until they were outlawed" is a frequent phrase But the phrase need not convey visions of Robin Hoods and Maid Marians, these people did not take to the woods — not all of them, perhaps many did — nor did they cease to live the life of the ordinary citizen any more than does a person to-day against whose goods a judgment has been taken and execution awarded The student will find the whole process of outlawry for debt set out at length and with great clearness in Crompton's Practice [Crompton Practice Commonplaced, 3d ed 1786, Vol 2, pp 32–69]

Maitland [P & M Hist of Eng Law, 2d ed , Vol 2, 127, 143, 207–216] gives us the early history of the action of debt He says elsewhere,

"In the course of the fourteenth century the power of outlawry spreads rapidly through many of the personal actions " [P & M Hist of Eng Law, 2d ed , Vol 1, p 476–7] Process continued until he was outlawed sounds like a linkéd process long drawn out — and is so   A man had to be 'exacted' five times — that is demanded in the county courts five times — it might be that this process would take from two and a half to five years   [See Bracton, f 125, b]   But this was in Bracton's time and for felony   "Outlawry is no longer punishment, it is mere 'process' compelling the attendance of the accused "   [P & M Hist of Eng Law, 2d ed , Vol 2, p 459]   This change has come about before the writing of judicial records, even Bracton could use outlawry in debt and covenant [Bracton, f 441] and in the time of the cases in our abridgment the process was usual   How did it come about?

By the Statute of 13 Ed I, the outlawry lies in account [Boote Action at Law, p 103]   We find that it was given for debt, detinue and replevin by the Statute of 25 Ed III, c 17, and by 19 Henry VII, cap 9, it was given in an action on the case   And this process, although by the Statute of Ed III it was forbidden to anyone but the sheriff to put any outlaw to death even for felony, put the defendant beyond the protection of the king, forfeited all his goods, put him in prison and lost to him all the profits of his land   And Boote [*supra*, p 103] says that for this reason great care was taken that no person should be outlawed without sufficient notice   And therefore it was that three *capiases* should issue before there should be a process of outlawry, *i e* , "the *capias, alias* and *pluries* (words familiar to our later law)   Thus, when a *capias* issued upon a return of the original, and that *capias* was returned *non est inventus*, the *alias* issued, and upon *non est inventus* returned on the *alias*, the *pluries* issued, and upon the return thereof, process of outlawry issued "   There was much abuse of these restrictions and two statutes were made to enforce them, 6 Hen VIII, and 31 Eliz (this of course being long after our period)   But this was apparently the process spoken of so often in the Year Books, and it was then, as it was later, the method of securing judgment and execution

But so far we have gotten only to the outlawry   Having been put in this parlous position—outside the law and yet subject to its exactions— through the all too common impossibility of the payment of a debt, or even through the refusal to pay a debt which the defendant felt or knew he did not owe, though he could not prove his contention in court, it seemed that there was some way needed of getting out of the situation which the courts themselves did not provide   The simple way, in those days, was to appeal to the king's mercy, and the easiest and surest way to secure that mercy was to purchase it   A person outlawed for civil reasons was still an outlaw, and as outlaws were so frequently pardoned by the king the analogy to the criminal law, in the judgment, was carried out in the relief, and the outlaw sued his charter of pardon from the king, and when haled into court again upon the judgment, produced his charter and went quit " If he did not have it he might pay the debt and be relieved from debt, but he was still an outlaw In the *Natura Brevium* of Fitzherbert [Fitzh *Nat Brev* 247, g] the manner of securing the pardon is given "And if a man be condemned in the Common Pleas in Debt and outlawry upon the same, then, before he shall have his Pardon, he ought for to yield himself to the Prison of the Fleet, and satisfy the Party, and the Record of his Condemnation and of the Satisfaction ought to be certified by *Certiorari* unto the King in his Chancery and thereupon he shall have his Pardon, and that is by the Statute of 5 Ed III, cap 12 " [See Fitzh *Nat Brev* 8th ed , Hale, 1755, 559] So after payment and pardon the debtor could at last be restored to his status as a citizen, and ceased to be an outcast before the law To the sociologist, who seems not to have troubled the history of the law overmuch, the matter would seem to be of some interest, as well as to the historian of the law, who in his turn seems not to have troubled about the matter at all

CHALLENGE

(1) **A juror** was challenged because he was not of the hundred. The triers said that he was not of the hundred, but they said further, upon their own responsibility, that there were six hundreds which all came to one Court, and that he was within one of them. And this was held a good reply, wherefore he was sworn, etc And the inquest passed against the defendant, and the defendant who was out on bail before, was sent to prison Statham 40 b
Michaelis
2 Hen IV

Reported in Y B Mich 2 Hen IV, p 6, pl 22 See also Brooke, Challenge, 28, and Fitzh Challenge, 74 The report of the case makes the defendant fail to appear, and sends the mainpernors to prison Case 1

(2) **Where** an inquest was awarded, and the plaintiff challenged all the jurors, some of the justices said that they should be discharged But yet he was tried, for the Court, who is the third person, will see that right is done But yet, query? How shall it be tried? Hilary
2 Hen IV

Reported in Y B Hilary, 2 Hen IV, p 14, pl 13 See also Brooke, Challenge, 30 and Fitzh Challenge, 76 The case says "some" of the jurors, Brooke "many," instead of "all," as our abridgment has it Case 2

Hilary
2 Hen IV

(3) **A juror** was challenged because he was godfather of one of the children of the plaintiff, etc. And this was a peremptory challenge, and it is so the other way, to wit when the plaintiff is grandfather to one of the children of the jurors, etc

Case 3

Reported in Y B Hilary, 2 Hen IV, p 15, pl 16 See also Brooke, Challenge, 31, and Fitzh Challenge, 77 See the report of the case as to the law on the subject

Hilary
43 Ed III

(4) **The array** was quashed because the sheriff was *des robes*[1] to the plaintiff Although the bailiff of the sheriff made the array in a good manner, not knowing that his master was *des robes* to the plaintiff, etc

Case 4

Reported in Y B 44 Ed III, p 44, pl 56 See also Brooke, Challenge, 24; and Fitzh Challenge, 96

Hilary
50 Ed III

(5) **The array was challenged** because one of the hundred was put in the panel PERSHAY All the hundred is within the seignory of the plaintiff, and they are under the distraint, etc And the array was adjudged good since they were of the next hundred adjoining And it seems that this challenge does not go to the array, etc

Case 5

The case has not been identified in Y B Hilary, 50 Ed III, or in the early abridgments

Trinity
31 Ed III

(6) **If a man** pleads in bar of the assize that which is no bar, wherefore the assize is awarded, the defendant shall not have any challenge And this by the opinion of SHAR-SHULL, in Assize

Case 6

There is no printed year for 31 Ed III The case has not been identified in the early abridgments

Hilary
35 Ed III

(7) **In formedon,** the tenant and the vouchee were at issue upon the place And then the inquest came, and the tenant challenged the array and vouched also WIL-LOUGHBY That shall be quashed immediately THIRNING,

---

[1] "If the sheriff was *des robes*, as they called it, to either party, it was a cause for a challenge " Reeves, Hist. of Eng Law, vol 3, p 104.

for the demandant   We say that the tenant and the vouchee are in collusion, and they will do this "*in infinite*" to the end that we shall never have the effect of our suit And we will aver that the panel is impartial, and we pray that it be tried immediately   And the opinion of SHAR-SHULL was that it should be tried, etc

There is no printed year of 35 Ed III   Fitzh   Challenge, 156, has the case

Case 7.

(8) **See how,** in a writ of right, the parties shall have their challenge before the panel is made and not afterwards, etc *Simile*, Hilary, 39 Ed III   And this is to the knights and not to the jurors   Query, how shall it be tried?

Trinity 7 Hen IV

The case has not been identified in Y B Trinity, 7 Hen IV, or in the early abridgments

Case 8

(9) **The defendant challenged** all except one, and the plaintiff challenged him   And the justices would not allow the one challenged by both to be a trier, because it might well be that when the plaintiff challenged one of them, it was by his assent, and so it would be a fraud, but they took triers of all the others challenged, etc

Paschal 21 Hen VI

The case has not been identified in Y B Paschal, 21 Hen VI   Fitzh Challenge, 38, has a longer and somewhat different abridgment of the case

Case 9

(10) **In an appeal** against two, one as principal and the other as accessory, they pleaded not guilty, and at the *Nisi Prius* the accessory challenged the array, and the principal said nothing   And because the array was quashed at his challenge HANKFORD would not take the inquest against the other, etc

Michaelis 4 Hen IV

Reported in Y B Mich 4 Hen IV, p 5, pl 18   See also Fitzh Challenge, 157

Case 10

(11) **In an appeal,** ten were sworn and the inquest remained for default, etc   And on another day the defendant challenged one of them who was sworn before, and showed cause   And although he could have had the same chal-

Michaelis 9 Hen V

lenge on the first day, still he had the challenge then to expedite matters, etc

Case 11   The case has not been identified in Y B Mich 9 Hen V, or in the early abridgments

Michaelis 1 Hen V   **(12) In an appeal** of robbery against several, who pleaded not guilty, one of them challenged a juror, and was driven to show cause at the beginning, etc   From this it follows that if he challenged one of them, he should not challenge peremptorily afterward   And then others were sworn, and he who was challenged was sworn in, and then another of the defendants challenged him, and could not [have his challenge] because he did not say anything at the commencement, etc   And so see that in Crown law the challenges are different from those in other actions   See the plea for various reasons

Case 12   Reported in Y B Mich 1 Hen V, p 10, pl 1   See also Fitzh Challenge, 70   The "divers causes" for which the case was to be consulted were apparently too "divers" for the abridger

Michaelis 32 Ed III   **(13) One was challenged** because he was *des robes*[1] to the attorney of the plaintiff, etc   Query, is it peremptory, etc ?   And also if he is of his blood?

Case 13   There is no printed year for 32 Ed III   The case has not been identified in the early abridgments

Hilary 3 Hen VI   **(14) In trespass,** a juror was challenged because he was chosen to be an arbitrator in regard to the same trespass and because he was chosen by the plaintiff, etc   And this was adjudged a peremptory challenge   It is otherwise where an arbitrator is indifferently chosen by both parties, etc

And it was said in the same plea that if one be chosen by the plaintiff and another by the defendant, to be arbitrators indifferently, yet since each is a stranger to the election of the other, it is a good challenge, etc

Case 14   Reported in Y B Hilary, 3 Hen VI, p 24, pl 3   See also Brooke, Challenge, 7, and Fitzh Challenge, 16

[1] See case 4, *supra*

(15) **If one be challenged** because he has nothing Paschal within the hundred he shall stand by, etc , and he shall ³ Hen VI not be trier if there be four others of the hundred, and enough outside.   And also if there be many of the hundred, a man can challenge them at the commencement, to the intent that they shall not be sworn, etc   And if he has nothing within the hundred, still if he lives within the hundred and has enough outside in the same county, he shall be sworn, etc   Query, if he dwells outside of the hundred, and has enough within the hundred, shall he be sworn?   And this in Estrepement, etc   It seems not, for he cannot have so good a knowledge, etc

Reported in Y B Paschal, 3 Hen VI, p 38, pl 3   See also Brooke, Case 15 Challenge, 8, and Fitzh Challenge, 18

(16) **One was challenged** because he was tenant to the Paschal defendant   And the jurors said he was not   But they ³ Hen VI said he was enfeoffed of certain lands to the use of one such who was tenant to the defendant, and held this same land of him, etc   PASTON Then he is his [tenant]   And for this reason he was withdrawn, etc   And then the inquest remained because there were not enough of the rape [1] and the plaintiff prayed ten tales   PRISOT We say that the plaintiff is lord of the rape and we say that there are none within the rape except his tenants and within his distress, Statham 41 a. wherefore we pray that the tales be awarded in the next hundred adjoining the rape   And we pray that our distress be tried by triers immediately, and that the eleven who were taken, and the others who were challenged because they had nothing within the rape, be sworn, etc   STRANGE That cannot be tried here now, but they can come in upon the return of the sheriff   MARTYN The same case was adjudged before   HANKFORD In a *Nisi Prius* at Lewis, etc   And afterwards by advice, etc , it was adjudged that it should be tried immediately, and so it was   They said that there were enough who were not his tenants, wherefore ten tales were awarded from the rape   And this in Account, where

[1] A rape in Sussex, which is divided into six rapes, is the same as a hundred in other counties, or a wapentake

the defendant said that he had fully accounted at B, in another county, and upon this they were at issue, etc

Case 16   Reported in Y B Paschal, 3 Hen VI, p 39, pl 5   See also Brooke, Challenge, 9, and Fitzh Challenge, 19

Michaelis
11 Hen IV

(17) **One was challenged** because he was not of the hundred, and it was said that he was of a hundred next adjoining, and these two are one rape   And it was found by triers that each hundred had a leet by itself, and that no one was juror to another, wherefore the challenge was adjudged good, although both hundreds were within one rape, since there were.separate jurors to the leet, etc

Case 17   Reported in Y B Mich 11 Hen IV, p 2, pl 5   See also Brooke, Challenge, 44, and Fitzh Challenge, 86

Michaelis
11 Hen IV

(18) **In a writ of annuity**, they were at issue upon the seisin, because the seisin was alleged in another county   A jury was awarded from both counties, and the plaintiff challenged the array of one inquest, and the defendant challenged the array of the other inquest   HORTON We pray one of one inquest and one of the other inquest to try both the arrays   HANKFORD   That shall not be, for there are separate *Venire Facias* by which the justices choose two of each inquest who affirm the array, and then they cause them to be sworn, to wit   one of one county and the other of the other county, and so until six of each panel are sworn   Which note   And one panel was challenged and two triers were sworn upon it, and because they could not agree they were put in ward until the next day, and also one of the other inquest who was sworn upon the principal [matter] and also the two triers of the same inquests were put in ward until the next day, and the next day they agreed   HORTON prayed that they might have food for there was no fault in the three   HANKFORD One of them is sworn upon the principal matter, and therefore he cannot have food, but the other two can, for they are not sworn upon the principal [matter]   THIRNING In that case no default can be adjudged upon him, although

he be sworn upon the principal [matter], wherefore give
him food, etc

Reported in Y B Paschal (not Mich), 11 Hen IV, p 62, pl 14   Case 18
See also Brooke, Challenge, 46, and Fitzh Challenge, 88

(19) **The array** was challenged because the coroner who Michaelis
made the array had an action of debt pending against the 11 Hen IV
defendant, which was of an older date than the assize, etc
And it was adjudged that it was not peremptory, but
it was said that if the action had been trespass for a battery
it would have been peremptory, or if the defendant had
had an action of debt against the coroner, that that would
have been peremptory, etc   But yet, query?

Reported in Y B Mich 11 Hen IV, p 26, pl 50   See also Brooke, Case 19
Challenge, 45, and Fitzh Challenge, 87

(20) **In trespass** to the damage of twenty pounds, a Michaelis
juror was challenged for non-sufficiency   It was found 18 Hen VI
that he had a freehold to the value of one mark a year
FORTESCUE   If the damages were ten pounds, it were
necessary that the jurors should [be able to] expend ten
shillings, and now the damages are twenty pounds, in which
case he should expend twenty shillings to the hands, etc
And it was not allowed, wherefore he was sworn

The case has not been identified in Y B Mich 18 Hen VI, or in the Case 20
early abridgments

(21) **See that** no challenge to the array is peremptory Michaelis
unless on a special case, as to say that the sheriff was out 7 Hen IV
of the kingdom and there was no under sheriff, or such like
case, etc   Study well, etc

The case has not been identified in Y B Mich 7 Hen IV, or in the Case 21
early abridgments

(22) **A juror** was challenged for non-sufficiency, and the Michaelis
triers said that one H leased certain lands to the juror for 7 Hen IV
life, rendering a certain rent, and one re-entered for default
of payment   And the opinion was that he was not enabled

by such a freehold, which is defeasible, to be a juror   And this in a writ of Entry, etc.

Case 22

The case has not been identified in Y B Mich 7 Hen IV, or in the early abridgments

Michaelis
8 Hen V

(23) **The plaintiff challenged** one poll and the defendant challenged another poll. POLE (for the plaintiff)   We release our challenge   STRANGE   Then we challenge him   HILARY   To that you shall not get now, inasmuch as you did not put your challenge to him when the plaintiff challenged him, for then he had been withdrawn immediately   Wherefore he was sworn, etc

Case 23

Reported in Y B Mich 8 Hen V, p 10, pl 21   See also Fitzh Challenge, 151

Michaelis
8 Hen V

(24) **In debt** on an obligation, the plaintiff challenged because formerly it passed against the plaintiff in a writ of debt for this same debt, which was reversed afterwards by a writ of error, etc   HILARY   Where is the record?   ROLFF   In the King's Bench   HILARY   Then your challenge is not peremptory, unless you show the record   Which the Court conceded   And another day he was challenged because the plaintiff had a writ of trespass pending against him in the same place, etc   And this defendant said that this writ was of a later date than the writ of debt, and was brought by fraud between them with the design that he should not pass in this inquest   And it was inquired immediately whether it was brought by fraud or *bona fide.* And it was said by fraud of the plaintiff   And they were sworn to inquire further if he was favorable for this reason or for any other reason   They said "no"   Wherefore he was sworn, etc   But if the writ of trespass had been of an older date than was the action of debt, I think that the challenge had been a peremptory challenge, and that the other party could not have been aided by alleging such a fraud, etc   (But there could have been fraud as well in one case as in the other)

Case 24

Reported in Y B Mich 8 Hen V, p 11, pl 22   See also Fitzh Challenge, 179

(25) **In a writ of entry,** one was challenged because he
was tenant to the vouchee, and [it was not][1] allowed
Query, as to the reason?

Michaelis
7 Hen IV

Reported in Y B Mich 7 Hen IV, p 1, pl 4   See also Brooke,
Challenge, 34, and Fitzh Challenge, 84

Case 25

(26) **In formedon,** ten were challenged by the demandant
and one by the tenant   Twelve [ten?] were sworn, and
because these who were sworn could not try by themselves, it
was adjudged that one of those who was challenged by the
demandant, and another of those who was challenged by
the tenant, should be sworn to try with them   SKRENE
He who was challenged by the demandant is heir to the
demandant, etc. THIRNING   Yet you cannot challenge
for that in this case.   Which note, etc

Michaelis
7 Hen VI

The case has not been identified in Y B Mich 7 Hen VI, or in the
early abridgments

Case 26

(27) **In attaint,** four of the hundred are enough, as well
as in an inquest of twelve, etc   And so it was adjudged
in an Attaint, etc.

Hilary
9 Hen IV

There is no printed Hilary Term for 9 Hen IV   The case has not
been identified in the early abridgments

Case 27

(28) **It is a good challenge** to the array that many
villeins are empanelled   And this in an Appeal, etc

Michaelis
26 Ed III

The case has not been identified in Y B Mich 26 Ed III, or in the
early abridgments

Case 28

(29) **It is a good challenge** to the array that the sheriff
is cousin to the wife of the plaintiff   In an Assize at Exeter
Contrary, Anno 18 in the *Liber Assisarum*   Query if it
be peremptory?

Statham 41 b
Anno
12 Hen VI

The case has not been identified in Y B Anno 12 Hen VI   Fitzh
Challenge, 159, has the case, but gives no page or placitum

Case 29

(30) **It is a good challenge** to the array made by the
coroner, that the same panel which he had returned was
formerly returned by the sheriff and quashed   And this

Hilary
25 Ed III

[1] Words from the case

in Array, etc   Query, if it be a good challenge for part of the first panel empanelled?

Case 30   There is no printed Hilary Term for 25 Ed III   The case is reported in Y B Trinity, 25 Ed III, p 80, pl 1 Fitzh Challenge, 121, has the case   The report of the case has it that the challenge was not allowed

Hilary
12 Ed III
(31) **It is no challenge** to the array that the panel was made by the bailiff of the franchise of which the plaintiff is seneschal, unless he says that the seneschal removed the bailiff, etc   In an Assize, etc

Case 31   There is no early printed year for 12 Ed III   The case has not been identified in the Rolls Series for that year, or in the early abridgments

Michaelis
8 Hen VI
(32) **It is no challenge** to the array that the sheriff had put in a person favorable to one party or to the other, unless he says that the sheriff knew of it   In a note

Case 32   The case has not been identified in Y B Mich 8 Hen VI, or in the early abridgments

Anno
27 Ed III
(33) **It is no challenge** to say that the defendant is tenant to the sheriff without saying, "And so favorable" And this in an Assize, etc   In a note.

Case 33   The case has not been identified in Y B 27 Ed III, or in the early abridgments

Michaelis
12 Hen VI
Case 34
(34)   Three were triers in an Attaint
The case has not been identified in Y B Mich 12 Hen VI, or in the early abridgments

Michaelis
2 Ric II
(35) **It is no challenge** to the trier that after he was sworn he had eaten with the defendant   And this in an inquest

Case 35   There is no printed Year Book for 2 Ric II   The case has not been identified in the early abridgments

Hilary
2 Hen IV
(36) **Where the inquest** is awarded for default, and the plaintiff challenges a poll, it shall be tried   And this in a note

Case 36   The case has not been identified in Y B Hilary, 2 Hen IV, or in the early abridgments

(37) **It is a good challenge** that he holds of one J, who Michaelis
holds over of the plaintiff   And this by the opinion of the 13 Hen VI
COURT, in Debt

    The case has not been identified in Y B Mich 13 Hen VI, or in Case 37
the early abridgments

(38) **It is a good challenge** in an Attaint that one of the Michaelis
Grand Jury had married the daughter of one of the petty 12 Ed III
jury.

    There is no early printed year for 12 Ed III   The case has not Case 38
been identified in the Rolls Series for that year, or in the early abridgments

(39) **A man** shall have a challenge to the polls notwith- Anno
standing the king was a party in the Exchequer   Query 6 Ric II
if he shall have one to the array?   It seems not, unless in
special cases, etc

    There is no printed Year Book for 6 Ric II   The case has not been Case 39
identified in the early abridgments

(40) **If a man** who is outlawed for felony says that at Paschal
the time, etc , he was so sick that he could not come, and 11 Ric II
the reverse is alleged for the king, he shall have his challenge
And the law is the same where one abjures [the kingdom]
and is taken out of the high road   By the opinion, etc
Coram Rege

    There is no printed Year Book for 11 Ric II   The case has not been Case 40
identified in the early abridgments

(41) **If the party** challenges one who is the son of the Anno
plaintiff, the plaintiff may say that he is a bastard   And 26 Hen VI
the opinion was that this should be tried by the triers, etc
And this in an Assize at Southwark

    There is no printed year of 26 Hen VI   The case has not been Case 41
identified in the early abridgments

(42) **A man** can challenge thirty-five without cause, as Anno
well in an appeal of felony as in an indictment for felony, 1 Hen V
etc   *Coram Rege.*

Case 42   This case is not found in Y B Anno 1 Hen V, but it appears in Y B Trinity 9 Hen V, p 7, pl 21, where Brooke, Challenge, 50, and Fitzh Challenge, 72, put it

Michaelis 25 Ed III

(43) **If a juror** be challenged because the party had an action against him, he shall show the record if it be not in the same Court And the law is the same in outlawry.

Case 43   The case has not been identified in Y B Mich 25 Ed III, or in the early abridgments

Michaelis 7 Hen V

(44) **If the party** challenges a juror because he had a writ of Trespass pending against him before the purchase of this writ, the other party may say that this is by fraud. And that shall be tried, in Trespass

Case 44   The case has not been identified in Anno 7 Hen V, or in the early abridgments

Paschal 13 Hen IV

(45) **It is a good challenge** that he ate at the cost of the plaintiff after he was empanelled But it is otherwise if he ate lately And this in Trespass, *Coram Rege*

Case 45   The case has not been identified in Y B Anno 13 Hen IV There is no printed Paschal Term for that year The case has not been identified in the early abridgments

CONFIRMACION

Statham 42 a

Paschal 46 Ed III

(1) **In an assize,** the tenant pleaded the feoffment of the plaintiff, made to one J, whose estate he had And the deed read that the plaintiff had leased land to this J for a term of years, and the plaintiff confirmed his estate in fee And the tenant pleaded in accordance with this And the plaintiff said that at the time of the confirmation this J had nothing in the lands. FYNCHEDEN To that you shall not get, inasmuch as you have admitted the deed FYNCHEDEN That was merely a relation which does not preclude him, etc Query?

Case 1   The case has not been identified in Y B Paschal, 46 Ed III, or in the early abridgments

(2) **If one holds** an acre of land of me for twelve pence Paschal
9 Hen VI and another acre for four pence, and I confirm his estate in both, to hold for six pounds for all services, the opinion is that this confirmation is void, for then it may be that that acre which was charged with four pence is charged with six pence, which cannot be, etc Query, if the avowant bound the seisin by my hands, could I plead such a confirmation, made to such a one whose estate I have, etc , against that seisin, etc Query, if it be in the purview of the Statute?

Possibly the case reported in Y B Paschal, 9 Hen VI, p 8, pl 22 Case 2 It is given by Brooke, Confirmacion, 1, and Fitzh Confirmacion, 1 The case as there reported differs from the case in Statham in many ways

Reference to the Statute is not clear

(3) **See by** HANKFORD where my entry is legal, my con- Hilary
3 Hen IV firmation or release is good, although there is no privity between us, for in this case the confirmation or release will countervail an entry and a feoffment; and it was adjudged before by me, and this in an Assize, etc.

Reported in Y B Hilary, 3 Hen IV, p 9, pl 5 See also Fitzh Case 3 Confirmacion, 12

See of confirmation in the Assize of the Prioress of Note Clerkenwell

(4) **Confirmation** to him who is tenant, by executors, Hilary
33 Ed III is good for the reconusor And this in an Assize *Simile*, Anno 31 *Liber Assisarum*, in an Assize of rent, etc

There is no printed year for 33 Ed III The case has not been Case 4 identified in the early abridgments

(5) **Confirmation** by a joint tenant and his companion Trinity
34 Ed III is of no value By THORPE and GRENE in an Assize, etc And that his part does not pass by it, but his half is extinguished in the half of his companion and breaks the survivorship, etc

There is no printed year of 34 Ed III Fitzh Confirmacion, 15, has Case 5 the case

(6) **Confirmation** of a franchise to him "who does not Michaelis
24 Hen VI use or abuse it" is void, if there were not these words

in the charter *"licet abusus vel non usus fuerit"* By the opinion of the COURT in Trespass, *Coram Rege* It seems to me the contrary, for he is at all times seised of the franchise until the king seizes it

Case 6   There is no printed year of 24 Hen VI The case has not been identified in the early abridgments

CONTYNUELLE CLAYME

Statham 42 b
Hilary
9 Hen IV

(1) **If a man** wishes to take advantage of a continual claim he should make his claim from year to year, and not cease for three or four years And also he should come near there so that he can see the land and show it to the people, and say that he dares not approach for fear of death

And see that it was held in the same plea, that a man cannot bind a continual claim in his father and also in himself, for then it is double, for the party shall have a traverse to the continual claim, as it appeared in this plea, where the plaintiff said that the tenant made no claim in any place where he could see the land And this in an Assize, etc They should then say that he made a continual claim at all times to enter at any time, to claim, etc

Case 1   Reported in Y B Mich (not Hilary), 9 Hen IV, p 4, pl 18 See also Brooke, Continuel Claime et Non Claime, 1, and Fitzh Continuel Claime et Non Claime, 3 Both give the page as five, as that is the page where the point appears

CONDICIONS[25]

Hilary
40 Ed III

(1) **In detinue** for writings, the defendant said that the writings were delivered upon certain conditions, to wit if one A did certain things (and he showed them all in certain) that then, etc And he did not know if the said A had performed the conditions with the plaintiff And he prayed a *Scire Facias* against A, and had it And note

that he did not say that the writings were delivered by the plaintiff to this A, in which case A is a stranger to the delivery, so it seems that he should not have had a *Scire Facias*, inasmuch as no one was a party to the delivery, except he himself, etc   See the plea, etc , to wit   in the case of *Pecchy*, he should have alleged that the conditions were not performed, judgment if action, etc

Reported in Y B Hilary, 40 Ed III, p 11, pl 24   Case I

(2) **In debt** upon an obligation, the defendant showed certain conditions by an indenture, to wit   if the defendant received certain [lands] [1] by such a day, and enfeoffed the plaintiff of the same lands, before the said day, that then, etc   And he said that he received the land and would have enfeoffed the plaintiff before the same day, and the plaintiff would not take the feoffment for doubt of champerty, [but] he commanded the defendant to enfeoff one J, and he did so, judgment if action   BELKNAP   He pleads another thing which is not comprehended within the conditions of the indenture, and for this he does not show anything, wherefore judgment, etc   Wherefore the plaintiff was put to answer to that plea   Which study, etc   And it seems that it is double, etc

Michaelis 42 Ed III

Reported in Y B Mich 42 Ed III, p 23, pl 2   See also Brooke, Condicions, 24   Case 2

(3) If the plaintiff declares upon a contract without a specialty, the defendant shall say that the same contract was made upon certain conditions, without showing anything in regard to them

Michaelis 44 Ed III

Reported in Y B Mich 44 Ed III, p 27, pl 6   See also Brooke, Condicions, 28   Case 3

(4) **If a man** leases land to me for a term of years, by a deed indented, rendering a certain rent, and he brings a writ of Debt against me for the rent, I shall say that one H enfeoffed the plaintiff before the lease upon conditions which were broken on the part of the plaintiff, and that

Statham 43 a
Paschal 45 Ed III

[1] Word from the case

the feoffor had entered, before which entry nothing was in arrear, I do not show anything of the conditions, since I am a stranger to them, etc

Case 4

The case has not been identified in Y B Paschal, 45 Ed III, unless it is the case reported on p 8, pl 10, in which the matter is similar to the case abridged Brooke, Condicions, 29, abridges the case on another point

Trinity 45 Ed III

(5) **In a writ** upon the Statute of Laborers, against the servant, he said that he was retained upon certain conditions, and he had the plea without showing anything of them, since the action is not founded upon a specialty

Case 5

The case has not been identified in Y B Trinity, 45 Ed III, or in the early abridgments The Statute is that of 23 Ed III (1349) The Statute of Laborers, Stats at Large, Vol 2, p 26

(6) **In an assize,** neither the tenant nor the plaintiff can plead conditions without showing them in writing, all the same the assize can find the conditions, inasmuch as seisin can be delivered upon condition, since they can have notice But as to other conditions I think that they cannot

Case 6

There is no citation given by Statham for this case, and it has not been identified No case from 50 Ed III is abridged by Brooke or Fitzherbert under this subject

Hilary 50 Ed III

(7) **See** that the reason why, in Detinue, the defendant shall say that the writings were delivered to him by the plaintiff and another, upon certain conditions, and not show anything of them, is not because the third person is a party to them, as many say, but the reason is because the action is not founded upon a specialty. By THORPE, in Detinue, etc

Case 7

The case has not been identified in Hilary, 50 Ed III, or in the early abridgments

Michaelis 7 Hen VI

(8) **In trespass,** the defendant pleaded that he himself enfeoffed the plaintiff upon condition to re-enfeoff him, etc And he did not show anything of the conditions And it was the opinion that he should have the plea in this writ

of Trespass, because it is not to recover the freehold for which the conditions are pleaded, for in no writ where a man is to recover land can such conditions be pleaded without a deed   Query as to the difference, etc.

Reported in Y B Mich 7 Hen VI, p 7, pl 10   Case 8

(9) **Four brought** a writ of Debt as executors of one A And the will read, "I ordain and constitute such and such to be my executors, and if they refuse, then I ordain such and such"   And because all four were named, where more than two cannot be executors, for such a condition it was adjudged that the writ should abate

And see by MARTYN, in the same plea   If I am bound to a man in an obligation for twenty pounds, upon the condition that if he goes to Canterbury the said obligation shall be good.   In such a case, if he brought an action upon the obligation, he could show that he had performed the condition, in his declaration, for that is the cause of his action But I believe that such a condition avails not, unless it be in this manner, to wit   "I bind myself, A J of B, in twenty pounds, under these conditions, etc ," for if such conditions be after the obligation, or upon the back, he does not need to show them in his declaration

And see in the same plea, by MARTYN   If I enfeoff a man upon the condition that if he pays certain moneys on a certain day, etc , that he shall not have a fee if he does not pay me at the day, etc , I can re-enter, etc , although no such clause be in the deed, to wit   if not, that I can enter, etc.   See the plea because it was well argued

Reported in Y B Mich 3 Hen VI, p 6, pl 6   See also Brooke, Case 9 Condicions, 10   A long and often-cited case, containing many points of interest

(10) **If one pleads** a deed in bar simply, and the deed contains certain conditions, the plaintiff can well say that nothing passed by the deed.   By the opinion of THIRNING, in the Assize of *Pecche*, etc   Query well, etc.

Case 10

The case has not been identified unless the point is contained in the case reported in Y B Mich 11 Hen IV, p 18, pl 42   Brooke, Condicion, 39, abridges the case on another point

Paschal
19 Hen VI

(11) **One H enfeoffed** one B upon condition that he would enfeoff one A and K, his wife, in tail, the remainder to one F, in fee, before such a day, etc   And before the day the said B, by such a one, his attorney, offered a deed of feoffment to the husband according to the conditions, and he refused, etc   And now if the entry of H, the feoffor, be legal or not is the question   MARKHAM   His entry is legal, for the tender to the husband alone is not according to the conditions, wherefore, etc   FORTESCUE   The tender is good, for if he had tendered to the husband and his wife and the husband had not agreed, that is the disagreement of both   Which was conceded   And the opinion of NEWTON was that the entry of H was legal, etc   In an Assize   Well argued.   And then the parties agreed

And it was said in the same plea that if a man bind himself in a condition which is against the law, and also in a condition which is impossible to be fulfilled, such a condition is void   Query, if the obligation be endorsed with a condition which is void in law, if the obligation be single,[1] etc

Case 11

Reported in Y B Paschal, 19 Hen VI, p 67, pl 14, and in Y B Trinity, 19 Hen VI, p 73, pl 2   See also Brooke, Condicions, 55

Paschal
21 Hen VI

(12) **If I lease land** for a term of years upon condition that he will not alienate his term, that condition is good   But if I enfeoff a man upon such a condition, the condition is void, for it is contrary, etc   By NEWTON, in a note   But yet, query as to the difference   And it seems that in the first case, although the lease be by deed, that the lessor shall not have a writ of covenant [on the] conditions, etc   Then if the plaintiff cannot enter he has no remedy   Query, if the gift of a horse be upon condition, if the donor can afterwards take it back upon condition broken, although such a clause was not rehearsed?

[1] "Simple' in Brooke

Reported in Y B Hilary (not Paschal), 21 Hen VI, p 33, pl 21 Case 12
See also Brooke, Condicions, 57, and Fitzh Condicions, 4 HANK-
FORD laughs over the statements in the case

See good matter upon conditions in the title of *Audita* Note
Querela, Mich 44 Ed III, and in the title of Detinue; and
in the title of Certification, Mich 32 Ed III, and in the
title of Debt, Mich. 46 Ed III

(13) **In formedon,** the tenant showed how one such Trinity
11 Ed III
enfeoffed him upon condition, etc , and for default in the performance of the conditions he had entered pending the writ,
so the writ was abated, etc And he asked for judgment
of the writ, and he did <u>not</u> show anything of the conditions,
to wit no writing, and still he had the plea And they
took it for reasonable because the plaintiff was a stranger
to the deed, and also it might be that the deed was delivered
when he re-entered, etc (But yet I believe that is not the
law)

There is no early printed year of 11 Ed III The case is printed in Case 13
the Rolls Series, 11–12 Ed III, p 114

(14) **A man leased** land for a life term, upon condition Anno
6 Ric II
that if he granted the reversion the lessee should have a fee.
And afterwards he granted the reversion by a fine, and the
condition was adjudged void, etc In the case of *Plesyng-
ton*

There is no printed Year Book for 6 Ric II No reference is found to Case 14
the case elsewhere

(15) **If I am bound** to a man in an obligation for twenty Statham 43 b
pounds, upon condition that if I pay to him ten pounds Michaelis
36 Hen VI.
before the feast of Michaelmas next ensuing, then etc
And if, after that, and before the said feast, I see him
at a time forty days before the said feast, and after that I
cannot find him until the said feast is passed, my obligation
is forfeited, for I could at one time have paid him, when I
saw him, in which case I cannot be excused, etc. And it
was my folly to be bound in such a manner. But if I am
bound as above to pay a lesser sum, at such a place, before
such a feast, although I see him a hundred times after-

wards and before the said feast, it is sufficient for me to come to the said place, the last moment before the said feast, to tender the money   And this by the opinion of all the justices in the case of *John Johnson*.   And see the plea, for the justices were of different opinions upon the issue which was joined in that case

Case 15   Reported in Y. B Anno 36 Hen VI, p 15, pl 19   See also Brooke, Condicions, 91

[25] Estates upon condition were so well known to our law that we may expect to find many cases covering solely the law upon such conditions, but as has been said, [P & M Hist of Eng Law, 2d ed , Vol 1, p 408] "Condition also has hard work to do in our law of property and of obligations "   In the abridgment we have to do not only with the law of Estates upon Condition, but also with the law of conditions in "obligations "   No attempt is made to classify the cases into their proper species in any of the old abridgments   A condition is a condition and it makes no difference whether the law of real property or personal property is involved, any more than it concerned the law of outlawry whether the person had committed a crime or had not paid a debt   Bacon [Abridgment, title Conditions, 6th ed , p 629] observes "By the word condition is usually understood some quality annexed to real estate   also qualities annexed to personal contracts and agreements are frequently called conditions," so that we have fairly late authority for treating the different sorts of conditions under one head, as they are treated in the earlier abridgments   The cases here abridged are many of them well-known cases which have had their due share in the growth of some important questions in the law, questions of contract, debt and evidence, in particular

COVENANT [26]

Michaelis
2 Hen IV

(1)   **One brought a writ** of Covenant against the master and the brothers of M, and counted that a covenant was made between one J, predecessor of the master, and U, his ancestor, to wit   that the said master and his successors should find perpetually two chaplains to sing divine services in the chapel of T, for the said U and his heirs, and that the successors had withheld the services for a long time, etc   THIRNING   The plaintiff had demised the manor within which the chapel is, and had retaken an estate to himself and

his wife, not named, etc. SKRENE   That goes to the
action   MARKHAM   This covenant is brought as heir
and extends to the heir, and not to him who had the manor,
wherefore say something else, etc   All the same some hold
that a man shall never have a writ of Covenant, except
against him who sealed the deed, neither *é contra*   But
that is to be understood of a covenant which is merely personal   Query?

Reported in Y B Hilary, 2 Hen IV, p 6, pl 25   See also Brooke, Case 1
Covenant, 17, and Fitzh Covenant, 13

(2) **If a man be bound** in any covenant which is possible Hilary
to be performed, although by sudden events it is overthrown, 40 Ed III
he is bound to fulfill it if he can do so by any possibility, for
that is the covenant in the deed, which will be taken strictly
It is otherwise as to conditions in law, etc   Well argued,
in Covenant

Reported in Y B Hilary, 40 Ed III, p 5, pl 11   See also Brooke, Case 2
Covenant, 4, and Fitzh Covenant, 16

(3) **One brought a writ** of covenant against a prior Hilary
because his ancestor had made a covenant with the prede- 42 Ed III
cessor of the prior, to sing for him and his servants in the
chapel of K, within the manor of E, and that the successors
had withheld, and he brought action as heir, etc   CANNDISH
The plaintiff nor his servants never dwelt within the
manor, etc   But he dared not demur, but said that
there was one H living, who is a nearer heir to that ancestor,
etc   BELKNAP   And inasmuch as he does not deny that
we were seised of the manor, judgment, etc   And so to
judgment, etc

Reported in Y B Hilary, 42 Ed III, p 3, pl 14   See also Brooke, Case 3
Covenant, 5, and Fitzh Covenant, 17

(4) **In covenant** against the husband and his wife, Trinity
because the plaintiff had leased to them a manor for a term 45 Ed III
of years, rendering twenty pounds a year, and that the
defendants bound themselves to make surety to the plaintiff
before a certain day, and they had never, etc   And because

the writ was brought against them both when it should have been brought against the husband alone, the writ was abated, for it is not the same as where an action is brought against them upon the lease which is to the advantage of the woman, for this is a collateral security not arising from the land, in which case the husband alone is charged, as well as by an obligation made by them, etc

And it was said in the same plea that if I lease land to the husband and his wife, rendering a certain rent, and if the rent be in arrear, I can distrain in other lands of the woman which are not charged, etc

Case 4   Reported in Y B Mich (not Trinity), 45 Ed III, p 11, pl 7   See also Brooke, Covenant, 6, and Fitzh Covenant, 18

Hilary
46 Ed III

(5) **The writ** was that he [did not][1] hold [a] covenant of all the lands that he had of the lease in such a vill, and because he put in certain what the lands were, although they were not put in certain in the deed, yet the writ was abated, etc

Case 5   Reported in Y B Hilary, 46 Ed III, p 4, pl 13   See also Brooke, Covenant, 8

Statham 44 a
Trinity
47 Ed III

(6) **One shall have** an action of covenant against executors because their testator made a covenant with the plaintiff to send him a servant, etc   And the action was maintained

And it was said by FYNCHEDEN, in the same plea, that if the tenant in tail leases land to me for a term of years and dies, and his issue ousts me within the term, that I shall not have an action of covenant against his executor, etc

Case 6   Reported in Y B Mich (not Trinity), 47 Ed III, p 22, pl 50   See also Brooke, Covenant, 11, and Fitzh Covenant, 20

Hilary
48 Ed III

(7) **A man shall not** have an action of covenant against executors where their testator did not bind these executors by express words, no more than the heir or vouchee shall be barred where there not any words in the deed "*dedi*," etc.

---

[1] Words from the text of the case

And it was said by FYNCHEDEN, in the same plea, that if I grant the reversion of my termor, and he attorns, and then the grantee loses the land, in that case the termor shall have a writ of covenant against me, notwithstanding his attornment, for he cannot have an action against the grantee

Reported in Y B Hilary, 48 Ed III, p 1, pl 4 See also Brooke, Case 7 Covenant, 12, and Fitzh Covenant, 21

(8) **In covenant,** the plaintiff counted upon an indenture Michaelis with many covenants, and that the defendant had broken 30 Hen VI the covenants, without showing which covenants, for there was time enough for him to show them when the other offered him an issue

The case has not been identified in Y B Mich 30 Hen VI, or in the Case 8 early abridgments

(9) **A man leased lands** to another for a term of years, by a deed indented, and the lessee should repair the houses, and do other things, rendering ten shillings rent, and to fulfill all the aforesaid covenants the lessee bound himself to the lessor in twenty pounds And the lessor brought a writ of debt for the twenty pounds, and declared that the rent was in arrear and so he had broken the covenant, etc CHOKE. The deed is, "To all covenants," etc And this is not a covenant, for he could have a writ of debt for this And if I lease lands for a term of years by a deed indented, rendering a certain rent, and the rent is in arrear, I shall not have an action of covenant, but a writ of debt FORTES-CUE You say truly, but in this case he brought his action wholly on the deed, so it shall be called a covenant As if one grants a corody to me, to wit bread, meat, and ten shillings rent, and I wish to bring an action for the rent, all the same I cannot have an assize, but a writ of annuity But if I would bring an action for the whole corody, I shall have an assize, as well for the rent as for the bread and meat, etc YELVERTON I understand that a man shall have a writ of debt for things which are in covenant, for it is in certain, as is the case here. As if an indenture be made

between us by such words, to wit "So it is covenanted between us that J C shall pay to me twenty pounds at the end of Paschal, etc ," upon that I shall have an action of debt. But it is otherwise as to a covenant, which is not put in certain, for there a man cannot have any other action but a writ of covenant; and I think that this is the reason, and not the other, to wit the uncertainty, for a contract and a covenant are of much the same effect except only for this reason, for a contract is as if two persons are drawn together, and a covenant is as if two persons come together, etc And the opinion was that the action well lay, etc

Case 9   Statham fails to give a citation for this case It has not been precisely identified, so no citation is given, although there are many similar cases to be found in the Year Books

Note

See of covenant in the title of Debt, Hilary, 3 Hen IV

The citation has not been found in the title of Debt in Statham

Paschal
18 Ed III

(10) **If the father** of the tenant makes a feoffment with warranty and dies, and the lord recovers by a writ of wardship, and at the full age of the infant, the infant enters, the feoffees shall have a writ of covenant, or warranty of charter, etc See the Statute Query, if an administrator shall have an action for a covenant broken to him who died intestate?

Case 10   There is no early printed year for 18 Ed III The case has not been identified in the Rolls Series for that year

The Statute is that of 52 Hen III, cap 6 (1267), Stats at Large, Vol 1, p 59

[26] Our abridgment does not give us any early cases under this title, nevertheless we have evidence that it was one of the earliest actions In Bracton's Note Book we have at least fifteen such cases [Bracton, Note Book, see p 186 of vol 1] Most of these are actions in which a claim to land, or rents or profits from land, are involved One of the earliest actions in the Note Book was in 1225 [Brac N B 1058] upon a covenant made by the defendant to allow the plaintiff and his wife to live with him, but it adds that if they wish to go away certain lands shall be given them In 1234 the covenant was that the plaintiff keep pigs in the wood of the defendant This may seem to be claiming a profit, as Maitland says [P & M Hist of Eng Law, 2d ed , Vol 2, p 218, n 4,

where he discusses these cases], but it is not clear that the profits as arising from land have anything to do with the bringing of the action, and it would seem that it is the covenant strictly which gives the action Long before our time, our earliest case being in 40 Ed III (1366), the agreement that can be enforced has to be supported by a written and sealed document [P & M Hist of Eng Law, 2d ed, Vol 2, p 219] We have the assertion in *Birch v Weaver* [2 Keble, 225] that "debt lies on any covenant where the sum is reducible to a certainty' That the case was looked upon as authority seems clear from the fact that in a treatise on covenants published anonymously in London in 1711 it is cited without any question There can be little question also that the unknown author did not look up his citation to F N B, Law of Covenants, 1711, p 6, or he would have discovered that he could not there find the point on which he relies It appears to have been over a hundred years after our last case in the abridgment that it was declared in an action of debt upon an obligation "And the words of the obligation were I am content to give to W ten pounds at Michelmas, and ten pounds at our Lady day It was holden by the Court that it was a good obligation, and it was also holden by the Court that an Action of covenant lay upon it, as well as an action of Debt, at the Election of the Plaintiff" [3 Leon 119, 27 Eliz 1584] Covenant thus became concurrent with debt, some of the interrelations of debt, account and *assumpsit* have already been noticed in the note on the title of Accompte

The first Statute on the action is the *Statutum Walliae* [12 Ed I, 1284, Stats at Large, Vol 1, p 144], p 153 for the writ and p 160 for observations on the writ It is evident from the words of the Statute, "*quia infiniti sunt contractus conventiones*" (p 160), that at that time the infinite diversity of covenants which were enforceable was recognized, and no attempt to draw them into strict limits was felt to be possible It may well be assumed that the reason actions to enforce covenants concerning land, especially leases, were so common in the early days was that land was the one great "real thing" of permanent value, and the people all, or nearly all, were living on the land, literally getting their living from it, the greater number of actions arose in regard to that one great asset, the land, its leases, profits, transfers And also it was natural that as movable property became more common and more valuable the actions concerning such property should increase in number

Reeves gives us the process of the writ "Upon pledges *de prosequendo* being found, the defendant was to be summoned once, and, if needful, a second time If he did not come at the second summons, nor send an essoin, the *petitio* of the plaintiff was to be heard, and the thing in question, if a tenement, was to be taken into the king's hands, if a chattel, the thing or its value, and another day was given to the parties If within fifteen days he replevied the thing so taken and came at the day appointed, he was received to answer and make his defence, but if he did not appear, the claim of the plaintiff was adjudged to him by default, together with damages taxed .   and he was to be in *misericordia*   If the defendant appeared, both parties came to allegations and at length to an inquest of the country, by which the matter was determined "   [Reeves, Hist of Eng Law, Vol 26, p 263, 2d ed 1787]   The old *Natura Brevium* gives the writ and says "This wryt lyeth where covenant is made by indenture sealed betwyxt two partyes and the one of them holden at covenant, then he that feleth him grived shal have the sayd wryt "   [Old *Nat Brev* f cxxn, ed of 1528]

Why among so many cases of covenant just exactly these few cases should appear in the abridgment it is not easy to say   The use of the abridgment by the students may have been the reason for selecting some of them, if indeed we may claim that the book was intended primarily for student use   If not we may assume that they were the cases that seemed to Statham to contain some core of the law which he felt would be needed by those who should use his book, or by himself in his coming position upon the bench

CONUSANCE [27]

Statham 44 b.

Hilary
40 Ed III

(1)   **In debt,** the defendant came by the exigent, and the bailiffs of E asked conusance of the plea,[1] and were ousted, etc   And the law is the same in a *Præcipe quod Reddat* after default, for they cannot give judgment upon the default that is [recorded][1] here, and in a *Quare Impedit* he shall not have conusance   In the same plea, etc

Case 1.

Reported in Y B Hilary, 40 Ed III, p 2, pl 1   See also Brooke, Conusance, 8, and Fitzh   Conusance, 25

Hilary
40 Ed III

(2)   **In a praecipe quod reddat,** the demandant asked conusance of the plea, and by the charter, which he showed, he had conusance of all pleas   THORPE   If you do not show that it has been allowed here, or that it was granted to you by express words of the charter, to wit   that you should have conusance where you yourself are a party, you shall not have the conusance, etc   Wherefore it was adjudged that he be ousted of the conusance

Case 2.

Reported in Y B Hilary, 40 Ed III, p 10, pl 21   See also Brooke, Conusance, 9, and Fitzh   Conusance, 26

[1] Words from the report of the case in the Year Book   The abridgment is so meagerly worded that it is not comprehensible by itself

(3) **In a praecipe quod reddat** for land in Lincoln, the bailiff asked conusance, and showed a charter which King Henry had granted to the Burgesses of Lincoln, that they should not plead nor be impleaded outside the walls of their city, but that they had "Burghmanmote" THORPE What is this "Burghmanmote? BELKNAP Jurisdiction of pleas [which touch the freehold[1]] of land from week to week, and pleas personal, as in a Court of *Pié Poudré* THORPE It is not so (but he did not explain it) And because the charter did not limit it to be before any certain judges, they were ousted of the jurisdiction And the same day the Abbot of Reading asked jurisdiction, and produced a charter which the king had granted to the abbot and to the co-monks that they should have conusance of all pleas in the court of their abbey and monastery, and it did not determine before what judges, but because it was "in their court," it shall be understood before the judges of the abbey, for if the justices of the king should serve there, that would not then be the court of the abbey, wherefore they had their charter allowed, etc.

Reported in Y B Trinity, 44 Ed III, p 17, pl 8 See also Brooke, Conusance, 11, and Fitzh Conusance, 27, 28

(4) **The transcript** of a fine came into the Chancery by a *certiorari*, out of the Court of an abbot, and it was delivered into the Court by the abbot himself, and sent to the Bench by a *mittimus*, out of which issued a *Scire Facias* against the terre-tenant, to execute the fine And then the abbot came and asked jurisdiction THORPE In a writ of right which is removable out of the Court of a lord he shall not have jurisdiction And also the plea is at an end And although you have jurisdiction of all pleas you cannot levy fines for the entry of them is, such a one "*dat domino rege pro licenciam concordandi*" So the king will be disherited, wherefore it seems that the whole fine is void, etc.

Reported in Y B Mich 44 Ed III, p 28, pl 8 See also Brooke, Conusance, 12, and Fitzh Conusance, 30

[1] Words from the case

Michaelis
45 Ed III

(5) **In trespass** at the distraint, a man shall not have conusance because the Court is seised of the plea And he could have come on the first day and demanded it, since the place is comprised within the writ, as well as in a *Præcipe quod Reddat*, etc But in debt or detinue, where no place is comprised within the writ, a man comes in sufficient time to have conusance before the exigent is awarded, etc But at the distress a man shall say, in Trespass, that the place is within the bishopric of Durham, etc But this goes as far, merely, as to the jurisdiction, etc

Case 5

The case has not been identified in Y B Mich 45 Ed III, or in the early abridgments

Paschal
46 Ed III

(6) **One sued an attachment** upon a prohibition against a spiritual judgment, and counted that he was summoned to H, within the franchise of Ely, to appear at Ely, etc And after sentence was given at Cambridge, the bailiff of Ely came and asked conusance, because the summons was made there, and by the summons made [there] the party was injured as well as by the sentence FYNCHEDEN The action is entire, and the greater dignity draws to it the lesser dignity, wherefore stand ousted of the conusance

And it was said in the same plea if a writ of right be brought on a right of which part is in such a franchise and part outside, all the writ shall abate because he could have had separate writs, etc. Query, if part be in such a franchise where there is no jurisdiction except for a return of writs, shall the whole writ abate, etc ?

Case 6

Reported in Y B Paschal, 46 Ed III, p 8, pl 1 See also Brooke, Conusance, 14, and Fitzh Conusance, 34

Hilary
50 Ed III

(7) **An attaint** was brought in the King's Bench for a false oath given in the franchise of the Abbot of Ramsay, where the abbot came and showed a charter of the king, for a conusance of all pleas, and he asked for the conusance And if he should have the conusance or not was well argued, etc Query? How would the record come into the King's Bench in that case? etc And if so be that the abbot had conusance of the first action in which the attaint was sued, can

the attaint be sued in the same franchise, etc ? And it was said not, but the record came to them by a *certiorari*, etc

The case has not been identified in Y B Hilary, 50 Ed III, or in the early abridgments Case 7

(8) **The Abbot of Battle,** who had conusance in the franchise of the tenant, prayed aid of the king and had it, wherefore the plaintiff prayed a re-summons and had it, for it was said that the king would not send a *procedendo*, except to those who were his justices in his Bench, etc And then a *procedendo* came into the Bench, and the abbot prayed the conusance again and had it (which is wonderful, since they had once failed of the right belonging to the, etc) And in London, if in a bill of fresh force the tenant prays aid of the king, they will let the parole come by the equity of the Statute, etc

Michaelis 21 Ed III

Reported in Y B Mich 21 Ed III, p 38, pl 34 See also Brooke, Conusance, 24, and Fitzh Conusance, 43 The Statute is that of 4 Ed I, cap 2 (1276), Stats at Large, Vol 1, p 114

Case 8

(9) **Conusance** will not be granted where the writ is not sued And this in an Assize, etc *Simile* Hilary, 13 Hen IV, in an Assize, where the bailiff asked conusance and the tenant said, "never attached for fifteen days " And they would not grant the conusance until they had examined the bailiff, etc , for if it be found that he was not attached for fifteen days they shall not have the conusance, etc

Michaelis 13 Ed III

There is no early printed year of 13 Ed III The case has not been identified in the Rolls Series for that year, or in the early abridgments Case 9

(10) **In debt,** one asked conusance before the defendant made his defense, etc Query?

Michaelis 38 Ed III

The case has not been identified in Y B Mich 38 Ed III, or in the early abridgments Case 10

(11) **In a cessavit** against one who was under age, at the return of the Grand Cape the bailiffs of Oxford asked conusance ROLFF That cannot be, for by the awarding of the Grand Cape the Court here is seised of the plea, etc PASTON The award is void, for the demandant shall not

Michaelis 3 Hen VI

have any advantage through this default, but he shall count against the infant; consequently they shall [not] have conusance Which BABYNGTON conceded

And see in the same plea that MARTYN said if in a *Præcipe Quod Reddat* one is essoined at the summons, that on the day which he has by the essoin, they shall not have conusance, etc   (Which I do not believe, unless he is demanded at the summons, for otherwise he has gone over his time, etc)

Case 11   Reported in Y B Mich 3 Hen VI, p 10, pl 12   See also Brooke, Conusance, 1, and Fitzh Conusance, 1

Michaelis
1 Ed III
Statham 45 a
(12) **When conusance** is granted, he who asks for the conusance shall give a day to the parties, or else the justices cannot give a day to the parties   As appeared in Trespass

Case 12   Reported in Y B Mich 1 Ed III, p 23, pl 12

Hilary
25 Hen VI
(13) **When jurisdiction** is granted, the pleading in the franchise shall be according to the common law, because they are in the place of the justices, and not according to the customs of the franchise which are against the common law, etc. By NEWTON, in Trespass, etc

Case 13   There is no printed year for 25 Hen VI   The case has not been identified elsewhere

Michaelis
3 Hen VI
(14) **One arraigned** two assizes at Gloucester for tenements in the same vill, of which the bailiffs should have conusance   And an assize was awarded, and they asked conusance of the other lands, and it was challenged because they did not ask conusance of the lands for which the assize was awarded, and so at that day they had lost the advantage of their franchise   And upon this the assize adjourned, and afterwards the conusance was granted, etc

Case 14   Reported in Y B Mich 3 Hen VI, p 14, pl 19   See also Brooke, Conusance, 2, and Fitzh Conusance, 2

Hilary
3 Hen VI
(15) **In detinue for writings,** the bailiffs of Lincoln asked conusance. ROLFF   This is the second writ, where-

fore they have over past their time, besides which they desire to aver that all the vill of Lincoln is one county by itself, in which case they can have conusance of the place well enough, because the Statute says that actions of debt and detinue shall be brought in the counties where the contract is made, so that by the common usage the action is brought on a contract or detinue within the same vill, etc BABYNGTON You say well, for it is not like another county which is part in franchise and part in gildable [out of the franchise] [1] for the Statute is indifferent in respect to which vill the contract is made   And then by advice of all the justices they were ousted of the conusance for the above reason   Which note

Reported in Y B Hilary, 3 Hen VI, p 30, pl 18   See also Brooke, Case 15 Conusance, 3, and Fitz Conusance, 3

The Statute is that of 6 Ric II, cap 2 (1382), Stats at Large, Vol 2, p 253

(16) **In a writ** upon the Statute of Laborers, the bailiffs Hilary of H had conusance on the first day, notwithstanding the 11 Hen IV court was seised of the body of the defendant who was not bailable, etc   See the Statute of Laborers, if he be bailable, etc

Reported in Y B Hilary, 11 Hen IV, p 43, pl 15   See also Brooke, Case 16 Conusance, 18, and Fitzh Conusance, 20

The Statute is that of 23 Ed III (1349), Stats at Large, Vol 2, p 26

(17) **Where an accountant** in the Exchequer is sued in Hilary the Exchequer by a bill, upon his account, a man shall not 8 Hen V have the conusance because this is a private liberty out of the common law, etc   Query, if I have a bill against a man in the King's Bench, in the custody of the marshall, shall the conusance be granted?   And this in a bill, etc

Reported in Y B Hilary, 8 Hen V, p 5, pl 23   See also Fitzh Case 17 Conusance, 66 and 89

(18) **In a recordare,** the bailiff of H demanded conusance Michaelis And the opinion of the Court was that he should not have 33 Ed III

[1] Words from the case

it, because if the bailiff be named in the franchise they could not award the two deliverances, etc

Case 18   Reported in Y B Mich 38 Ed III, p 31, pl 39   See also Brooke, Conusance, 23

Hilary
5 Ed III

(19) **Conusance** shall not be granted for part, and not granted for part   (In a note)

Case 19   The case has not been identified in Y B Hilary, 5 Ed III, or in the early abridgments, unless it is the case abridged by Fitzh   Conusance, 55

Trinity
30 Ed III

(20) **Conusance** shall not be granted, by the opinion of the Court, where judgment between the same parties is given in Court, and he who demands the conusance has been reversed for error.   And this in an Assize, etc.

Case 20   The case has not been identified in Y B. Trinity, 30 Ed III, or in the early abridgments

Hilary
7 Ed III

(21) **Conusance** shall not be granted to one in a writ of right brought in his Court, and then removed into the county Court, and then into the Bench by a pone, etc

Case 21   Reported in Y B Hilary, 7 Ed III, p 2, pl 2   See also Fitzh Conusance, 49

Hilary
7 Hen VI

(22) **He who has** conusance of all pleas shall not have conusance in Attaint, etc   As was adjudged by NEWTON (at Sarum)

Case 22   The case has not been identified in Y B Hilary, 7 Hen VI, or in the early abridgments

Trinity
12 Ed III

(23) **Conusance was demanded** by a charter, by these words, "That they should have conusance of all pleas touching the Dean and the Chapter and their men"   And this word "men" was adjudged to mean their villems   And this in an Assize, etc

Case 23   There is no early printed year of 12 Ed III   The case has not been identified in the Rolls Series for that year   The case is similar to that cited by Brooke, Conusance, 34, as being in the *Liber Assisarum*, 35, where I have not been able to find it

(24) **When conusance** is granted, it belongs to the Hilary
bailiff to examine the record at his expense, and not at that 32 Ed III
of the demandant, etc. Contrary, Anno 27 *Liber Assisarum*

There is no printed Year Book for 32 Ed III The case has not Case 24
been identified in the early abridgments

(25) **Conusance was granted** in an action of covenant Michaelis
to levy a fine, etc Query? 13 Hen IV

The case has not been identified in Y B Mich 13 Hen IV, or in the Case 25
early abridgments

(26) **In an assize** of common of pasture, conusance was Trinity
denied because the land to which, etc , was out of the 16 Ed II
franchise, etc *Simile* if an advowson be made in ancient
demesne to a free tenant in gildable, etc

The case has not been identified in Y B Trinity, 16 Ed II, or in Case 26
the early abridgments

(27) **An abbot** brought a *Præcipe quod Reddat,* and he Michaelis
asked conusance of the plea, and had it, notwithstanding 4 Ed III
he himself was a party and had brought his action in the
Court of the king, for he could not have any other writ
except one returnable in the Court of the king, etc *Simile*
Hilary, 8 Ed III

The case has not been identified in Y B Mich 4 Ed III, or in the Case 27
early abridgments

(28) **Conusance was granted** in the franchise The Hilary
tenant vouched a foreigner, wherefore a re-summons was 8 Ed III
sued, and since the warranty was ended, the bailiffs asked
conusance and could not have it, for it is not the case of
the Statute of Gloucester, for they had once failed of their
right because of lack of power [in the Court],[1] etc

Reported in Y B Hilary, 8 Ed III, p 10, pl 29 See also Fitzh
Conusance, 52

The Statute is that of 6 Ed I, cap 12 (1278), Statute of Gloucester Case 28
Stats at Large, Vol 1, p 117

[1] Words from the report of the case

[27] The word Conusance has been left in the title as it stands and retained generally, but not always, in the translation It is properly to be translated jurisdiction, and yet there is a flavor and a something about it which seems to escape when we use the word jurisdiction It may be because originally the word was used for a jurisdiction that is not exactly our jurisdiction in the modern sense It is not a mere matter of procedure "It is intertwined with the law of property and the law of personal status, and this in many different ways " [P & M Hist of Eng Law, 2d ed , Vol 1, p 527] So the thing, while it is jurisdiction, and deals with the powers of courts, deals also with rights — rights as to property and also as to persons Jurisdiction itself is a right which may be the subject of litigation In our third case we have the Burgesses of Lincoln showing that they have "burghmanmote " Thorpe queries, "What is this Burghmanmote?" and Belknap answers, "Jurisdiction of pleas of land which touch the freehold from week to week, and pleas personal, as in a court of *pré poudré* " Thorpe replies, "It is not so " The reporter had evidently waited with some interest for Thorpe's reply, for there is a note of disappointment in his "But he did not explain it " This was an ancient name for the court, for we have regulations of the Burghmoot in Edgar's day [Edgar 1, 1 *Leges Regis Edwardi*, II, 5 Thorpe Ancient Laws and Institutes of England, p 609] The moots are to be held at stated times—three times a year, or if necessary more than three times But it is a weary stretch of years from Edgar to the fortieth year of Ed III The ancient terminology has gone out of use, and when the old charters are produced the words convey no meaning to those who read or hear them From the printed case one would judge that Thorpe was jealous for the jurisdiction of the king, and sought for an excuse to evade the charter

To any one interested in the old pleading many of these cases are worthy of study notably cases 4, 6, 8, 9, 13, 15, 17, 21, 24, which all "moot" interesting questions

For the only enlightening modern writing on the jurisdiction of courts we must look to Pollock & Maitland in their chapter on jurisdiction and the communities of the land [P & M Hist of Eng Law, 2d ed , Vol 1, Cap III, pp 527–532] Full of original thought, it does not only tell us what is known of the history of these things, but its light shows us, dimly, shapes not as yet wholly known, forms as yet blurred to our sight So also the few cases abridged here show the law of the time shadow-like, indistinct, for all the light that has as yet been thrown upon them How would a man — a trained legal scholar — answer the questions propounded in them? How much does he know of that old law if he cannot?

CAUSE DE REMOVER PLEE

Statham 45 b
Paschal
45 Ed III

(1) **In debt, the bailiffs** of H had conusance, and then the plaintiff sued a re-attachment, and he said that in the

franchise the bailiffs can [return][1] issues, to wit at one
time one penny, another time two pence, and so on *ad
infinitum*. FYNCHEDEN· He can have the same exceptions in the franchise, wherefore this is not to the purpose,
unless you say that it is by collusion between them   Wherefore he said it was, etc.

Reported in Y B Paschal, 45 Ed III, p 7, pl 7   See also Brooke, Case I
Cause de Remover Plee, 9, and Fitzh Cause de Remover Plee, 9

(2) **A man cannot** have any cause for removing a plea Michaelis
out of ancient demesne, except for the reason that he holds 21 Ed III
them at the common law.   And the cause shall be put in
the writ, to wit   a cause that proves the land to be a
free fee, etc   See good material for this in the title of
Ancient Demesne, etc.

Reported in Y B Mich 21 Ed III, p 32, pl 17   See also Brooke, Case 2
Cause de Remover Plee, 17, and Fitzh   Cause de Remover Plee, 18

(3) **When the plea** is removed out of ancient demesne, Paschal
nothing shall be tried here except the cause [for the removal][2] 16 Ed III.
for they cannot hold the plea without a new original   As
appeared in a Recordare, etc.   Query, if they will send it
back? etc

There is no early printed year of 16 Ed III   The case is found in Case 3
the Rolls Series, 16 Ed III, Pt 1, p 204

See of causes for removal of pleas, in the title of Resum- Note
mons

Statham, title Resummons et Reattachment, p 160 a and b, *infra*

(4) **It is no cause** for the removal of a plea to say that Michaelis
the bailiffs who have conusance are parties, etc , because 2 Hen IV
he could have had the plea when conusance was demanded
And this in Conusance

Reported in Y B Mich 2 Hen IV, p 4, pl 14   See also Brooke, Case 4
Cause de Remover Plee, 11, and Fitzh   Cause de Remover Plee, 6

(5) **It is no cause** [for removal of the plea][2] that the Hilary
bailiff in ancient demesne is a *des robes* to the plaintiff   And 12 Hen IV
this in an Assize of Fresh Force

[1] Words from the case   [2] Words from the report of the case

Case 5

Reported in Y B Hilary, 12 Hen IV, p 17, pl 14   See also Fitzh Cause de Remover Plee, 8.

Hilary
12 Hen IV.

(6) **When the plea** is removed out of the Court of the king, although the cause be not sufficient, still it shall not be remanded, etc   It is otherwise in any other Court, etc.

Case 6

Reported in Y B Hilary, 12 Hen IV, p 13, pl. 4   See also Brooke, Cause de Remover Plee, 13, and Fitzh   Cause de Remover Plee, 7

Hilary
16 Ed III

(7) **The plea shall be remanded** if the party cannot maintain the cause.   Query, how shall it be tried? etc.

Case 7

There is no early printed year of 16 Ed III   The case has not been identified in the Rolls Series for that year.   See Fitzh   Cause de Remover Plee, 13

Michaelis
12 Ed III

(8) **Two sued a writ** of right close in ancient demesne, and removed the plea for the reason that they claimed to hold at the common law   And then in the Bench one of them made default, and the plea was remanded, for it was said that one of them could not maintain the cause without the other, etc   It seems that the demandant did not show cause, etc.

Case 8

There is no early printed year of 12 Ed III   The case has not been identified in the Rolls Series for that year, or in the early abridgments

Michaelis
21 Ed III

(9) **When the plea** is removed out of ancient demesne, with a cause that is put in the writ, the plaintiff can show another cause.   As appeared in a pone where THORPE said that he could show five reasons to give the Court jurisdiction

Case 9

The case has not been identified in Y B Mich 21 Ed III, or in the early abridgments

Anno
11 Hen VI

(10) **A recordare** was sued out of ancient demesne, because the demandant was bailiff of the same court BABYNGTON   That is no reason for the removal of the plea, but if the lord were a party, or if it had been of record that the demandant was bailiff and also judge, that had been a good reason, etc.   MARTYN (To the same effect).

For he has not said that the bailiff is a judge, then the suitors of the court are judges, etc. And afterwards a *procedendo* was granted to those in ancient demesne, etc.

Reported in Y B Anno 11 Hen VI, p 10, pl 22   See also Brooke, Case 10 Cause de Remover Plee, 30, and Fitzh   Cause de Remover Plee, 2

CESSAVIT [28]

(1) **In a cessavit against three** who waged their law Statham 46 a of non-summons, and on the day two made default and the Michaelis third said that the land was held by an entire service, to 40 Ed III wit by fealty and one grain of pepper, and he offered the arrears for all three   And the opinion was that he saved the land for all, for otherwise his part would be charged for the entire service, etc.   But it is otherwise if the services are severable, etc

Reported in Y B Mich 40 Ed III, p 40, pl 20   See also Brooke, Case 1. Cessavit, 4, and Fitzh   Cessavit, 10   The latter gives a wrong citation to the case

(2) **In a cessavit, the tenant said** that he did not hold of Michaelis him, and before the inquest was taken he admitted that he 41 Ed III did hold of him, and he offered the arrears for four years, and the demandant said that he was in arrears for twenty years   And the inquest was taken to say how much he was in arrears   (But yet it seems that they could not charge the inquest on that point, *rigore juris*, for it is contrary to the Statute of Westminster the Second, which says that they shall not be jurors unless they were summoned for that at the first, and they were not summoned on that point, etc)   And they found that the rent was in arrears for nine years.   And then he offered the arrears for nine years, and it was received, etc   And they found surety, etc

Reported in Y B Mich 41 Ed III, p 29, pl 29   See also Brooke, Case 2 Cessavit, 5, and Fitzh   Cessavit, 12   The Statute is that of 13 Ed I (1285), Stat 1, cap 30, Westminster the Second, Stats at Large, Vol. 1, p 203

(3) **Where the woman** is endowed of a manor in gross she shall have the cessavit

Reported in Y B Paschal (not Hilary), 43 Ed III, p 15, pl 10, and in Mich Term, p 27, pl 7   See also Brooke, Cessavit, 7, and Fitzh Cessavit, 14

(4) **In a cessavit against an abbot** for divers services, the writ did not allege that he held of him, but yet the writ was adjudged good, etc   And the tenant said that he did not hold of him, etc   But he dared not demur, etc. See the plea, because it was well argued

And it was said in the same plea, that if before the Statute of *Quia Emptores Terrarum* one had given land to an abbot, he would hold of him by the same services that he held over, unless the gift was in free alms, etc   Query, if land be given to an abbot in free alms, and to do certain divine services, if that be free alms?

Reported in Y B Mich (not Trinity), 45 Ed III, p 15, pl 16   See also Brooke, Cessavit, 8, and Fitzh Cessavit, 15   The Statute is that of 18 Ed I, Stat 1 (1290), *Quia Emptores Terrarum*, Stats at Large, Vol 1, p 255

(5) **In a cessavit,** the tenant said that one H, whose estate you have in the seignory, enfeoffed one B, Prior of K, in the same land, in free alms, and to his successors, by this deed, etc , whose estate we have, judgment, etc. And he also produced the deed by which the prior enfeoffed him, etc (But yet he did not need to do this) FYNCHEDEN We and our ancestors have been seised of the services since the time of the limitation of the assize, and we pray seisin of the land   SKIPWITH   Since you do not answer to the deed, judgment, etc   THORPE   If I enfeoffed an abbot in free alms, who demises himself of his estate, I shall have from his feoffee such services as I held over, etc , for his feoffee, who is a layman, cannot hold in free alms no more than the feoffee of tenant in free marriage can hold in free marriage   WILLOUGHBY   He will bar you of the action if he had the first deed, etc   Wherefore it was adjudged that he be barred, etc   Query, shall he have a writ of Mesne in that case, inasmuch as he, as it seems,

shall do no services for him, etc ? It seems that he can
have a writ of *Contra Formam Collationis*, notwithstanding
it is given in pure and perpetual alms

There is no printed year of 31 Ed III Fitzh Cessavit, 22, has an Case 5
abridgment of the case

(6) **In a cessavit** by an abbot against one A, it was Hilary
alleged that the said A had no entry except by one H, 48 Ed III
who held these same tenements of the demandant by certain services which should revert to him, because this A,
against whom the writ is brought, had ceased for two
years And the writ was challenged because the entry
was alleged by H, who had not ceased, etc , for he could
have had a writ alleging that we held of him FENCOT
He has not alleged seisin by you And because the writ
seemed bad, THORPE [said] That is the reason that he has
brought this writ in the per, wherefore answer PERSHAY
demanded the view, and had it, notwithstanding it was of
his own cessor, because the demandant had no seisin by
him, etc PERSHAY Where the abbot has alleged that we
hold of him by homage and suit at his court, and twenty
shillings of rent, we tell you that one F, his predecessor,
enfeoffed the said H, by whom our entry is alleged, to hold
of him by ten shillings for all services And as to these ten
shillings, open to his distress. FYNCHEDEN This that he
pleads as to quantity of services is only protestation, and
the issue will be taken upon the distress, for when he comes
to tender the arrears it is time enough to inquire about the
quantity, etc THORPE He should answer to the quantity now, wherefore WICHINGHAM offered to aver that
as to that part he was not ousted, etc PERSHAY Now
judgment, inasmuch as he has admitted his count to
be false in part As if a man avows for ten shillings, and
the plaintiff says that he was enfeoffed to hold by five shillings, and as to that nothing in arrear, and the avowant
replies to that, and immediately his avowry is wholly
abated, so here. THORPE In neither case will it abate,
except for that portion Wherefore, as to the portion it

was adjudged that it would abate, etc   Query, if in that case the tenant could vouch out of the line, etc

Case 6   Reported in Y B Hilary, 48 Ed III, p 4, pl 8   See also Brooke, Cessavit, 10, and Fitzh   Cessavit, 16

Michaelis 11 Ed III

(7) **If my tenant** ceases for two years, and a stranger disseises him, I shall have this writ of *Præcipe quod Reddat*, to the demandant, etc   "That J of B *de eo tenuit per certa servicia et que*, etc , *reverti debent eo* J of B *in faciendo*, etc , *cessavit*, etc ," for he cannot have a writ that "he who is now tenant of this 'terret,'" because he cannot bind seisin in him, for the seisin is traversable, etc. (But it seems that the writ should be in the post, etc). Query, for it seems that the seisin is not traversable, etc

Case 7   There is no early printed year of 11 Ed III   The case is printed in the Rolls Series, 11–12 Ed III, p 297

Trinity 19 Ed III

(8) **If I give lands** to a man in tail, to hold of me, I shall not have a cessavit against him, etc , unless the remainder be over in fee   Query, if the lord who had only an estate tail shall have a cessavit?

Case 8   There is no early printed year of 19 Ed III   The case is reported in the Rolls Series, 19 Ed III, p 152   See also Fitzh   Cessavit, 30

Michaelis 29 Ed III

(9) **A cessavit was sued** against one A, and he counted how one B held of him, and that the tenements ought to revert to him because this A, against whom the writ is brought, had ceased for two years   And then the writ was adjudged good without mentioning any entry, etc

Case 9   The case has not been identified in Y B Mich 29 Ed III Brooke, Cessavit, 28, has the case

Hilary 33 Ed III

(10) **Two coparceners** had a tenant who ceased for two years and then one of them had issue and died   The opinion of WILLOUGHBY was that the other should not have the cessavit, since the action was once given to her, and to the other, who is dead, and there is no survivorship, etc   In a Cessavit, etc

Case 10   There is no printed year of 33 Ed III   Fitzh   Cessavit, 42, has the case

(11) **In a cessavit,** the tenant said that he did not hold of him And upon that they were at issue, and it was found for the demandant, and the inquest was made to say for what services; who said, by lesser services than the demandant had counted And then the tenant tendered the arrears according to the verdict SHARSHULL They should not tender them, etc , for this plea was to disprove our lordship, and at least if he tenders them he should tender them according to our count, for he could aver the quantity of services by protestation, and the inquest would not have inquired as to that, etc

Statham 46 b.
Michaelis
33 Ed III.

There is no printed year of 33 Ed III Fitzh Cessavit, 53, has an abridgment of a similar, if not the identical, case

Case 11

(12) **In a cessavit,** the demandant counted that the defendant held a chantry of him, to do certain divine services, and he and his predecessors had held the said chantry of the demandant and his ancestors by such services, for time, etc , and that the tenant had ceased, etc MARKHAM The Statute is that "an action shall lie for the donor or his heir," and he has not counted of any gift, wherefore, etc And for that reason it was adjudged that he take nothing, etc

Trinity
7 Ric II

There is no printed Year Book for 7 Ric II The case has not been identified in the early abridgments

The Statute is that of 13 Ed I (1285), cap 41, Westminster the Second, Stats at Large, Vol 1, p 218 (269)

Case 12

(13) **A man shall not have** a cessavit against an abbot or a prior for lands which are of his foundation, by THIRNING, and HANKFORD, etc., in a *Jure d'Utrum*, etc See the Statute of Ed III, Anno 9, cap 12, etc It seems that they spoke truly, for in a writ on the Statute the action is not given to the foundation, for those words, "*eodem modo,*" which give the cessavit, shall be considered as referring to the next chapter before which commences "*eodem modo,*" which gives the *Contra Formam Collationis* to the donor and not to the founder, for the first chapter gave the action to the founder, etc.

Trinity
7 Hen IV

Case 13   Reported in Y B Trinity, 7 Hen IV, p. 20, pl 30   See also Brooke, Cessavit, 13, and Fitzh Cessavit, 44

There is some error in the citation of the Statute, which is presumably that of Westminster the Second, 13 Ed I, cap 41 (1285), Stats at Large, Vol 1, p 218   The "chapters" are the paragraphs of cap 40

Hilary
12 Ric II

(14) A cessavit for rent adjudged good, etc   But yet, query?

Case 14   There is no early printed Year Book for the reign of Ric II   Fitzh Cessavit, 45, has the case, apparently copied from Statham   The case is reported in Y B Hilary, 12 Ric II, p 103, Ames Foundation, ed. Deiser   The granting of the Cessavit for rent caused the judges to "marvel "

Hilary
22 Ed III

(15) A cessavit was adjudged good for an advowson, etc But yet, query?

Case 15   The case has not been identified in Y B Hilary, 22 Ed III   Fitzh Cessavit, 46, has the case, apparently copied from Statham

Trinity
7 Hen IV

(16) A cessavit does not lie for the founder, for the lands of his foundation

Case 16   Reported in Y B Trinity, 7 Hen IV, p 20, pl 30   See *supra*, case 13

Michaelis
20 Ed III

(17) A cessavit was adjudged good which was brought against two by different *præcipes*, "that they should revert to him, since the two had ceased for two years "

Case 17   There is no early printed year of 20 Ed III   The case has not been identified in the Rolls Series for that year

Michaelis
20 Ed III

(18) In a cessavit it is no plea that the demandant was seised after the Statute. Query as to the reason   And query, if it be a plea to say that the demandant enfeoffed him?

Case 18   There is no early printed year of 20 Ed III   The case has not been identified in the Rolls Series

---

[28] "The writ of Cessavit lieth in divers ways   For one writ is where there is Lord and Tenant, and the Tenant will not pay his Rent [our case 2] nor do his Services, as Suit, etc , to his Lord as he ought to do, nor hath sufficient Goods or Chattels upon the Land to be distrained for the Rent or Services behind, but suffereth the Land to lie fresh, not occupied for two Years following together, then the Lord of whom the lands are holden may have the Writ against the Tenants.' [Fitzh *Nat.*

Brev 478, ed 1755] This is a description of the writ *Cessavit per Biennium*, given by the Statutes of Gloucester and Westminster the Second [Stat of Glou , 6 Ed I, chap 4, Stat of West II, 13 Ed I, chap 21 Stats at Large, Vol. 1, p 117 and p 163] Coke, writing upon the Statute of Gloucester [Coke, 2nd Inst 295] says, "And I reade amongst ancient Records that a cessavit was brought in the raigne of King John, but this Act is the first Statute that was made by authority of Parliament concerning the cessavit, after this came the Statutes of West II and 10 Ed I, *De Gamletto, Implacitentur de Gamletto*, which is a kind of Cessavit, for gamel or gabble or gable in one of the senses is taken for *census*, rent, etc and *gamelleium* is as much as to say, cease, or let to pay the rent [Coke, 2d Inst 402] and note that the writ framed upon this act doth recite the statute " The statute here mentioned seems to be ignored by all other writers, but Coke refers to Vet Mag Cha 122, and the statute is there found fully set forth, as well as in the later editions of the Statutes

Another writ of cessavit is given in West II, chap 41, for the cessation of services due for a religious use, as to find a chaplain to sing divine services This is the writ used in our case 12, and is in very common use in the Year Book period The statute allowed the heir to demand the land given for "a chantry, light, sustenance of poor people, or other alms, if such alms be withdrawn for the space of two years " The gift doubtless was often given in order that masses might be sung for the donor, and after his death his heir might very well look pretty sharply after the doing of the services in order to get back the land which had been given out of that which he probably regarded as his just patrimony None of the modern writers upon legal history whom I have consulted touch upon the action of cessavit further than to mention the *Cessavit per Biennium* of the Statute of Gloucester and the Statute of Westminster the Second, chapter 21 It may be that the actions of cessavit to recover lands against an abbot or other clerical holder is not now important, yet it was very important at the period covered by the histories of our early law It is important to the history of the times, since it is another of the old actions which were so intimately related to the customs and usages which had grown up around the life of the people, and illustrate so well that intimate life that history so rarely pictures, and which, therefore, leaves us cold to the very things that would most move us, could we come to a closer understanding of them

At what period did the action of cessavit, true to its name, cease to be? Shepard [Epitomé of the Law, p 707] says, "There is a writ called *Cessavit de Cantaria*, of no use at this day " "This day" being some one of the thirty-six years prior to 1656, in which as he tells us the Epitomé was in preparation We may assume, as he does not remark upon the other writs of cessavit, that they were still used Rastell, in his Book of Entries published in 1566, has much learning upon the writ, setting forth the form and the pleading and many other matters   In 1674 Brown published his *Formulæ Placitandi*, or Book of Entries, in which he omitted any title of cessavit, but in 1701 Booth in his book on Real Actions [pp 133–135] gives the writ and the process as well as cases upon it   We may therefore assume that this writ was in use as late as the year 1700, but it had become antiquated and needed to be re-cast, for in 4 George II (1731), c 28, an act was passed which was thought to have been founded upon the older action [Jacob Law Dict Tomlins' ed , 1809], but if so it clearly ends the old action of *Cessavit per Biennium*, and gives an action of ejectment after the rent has ceased to be paid for six months   [Stats at Large, Vol 16, p 253]   There are certain phrases in the new bill which upon comparison will show a sufficient likeness to warrant the belief that the new bill was founded upon the old cessavit   In 11 Geo II (1738) c 16, [Stats at Large, Vol 17, p 189, cap 19] another act of the same nature was passed, giving the landlord possession when any tenant at rack rent shall be one year's rent in arrear, and shall have deserted the premises, leaving them uncultivated   These two statutes probably provided a procedure which took the place of the *Cessavit per Biennium*   Yet it probably is for the reason that the matters which gave rise to the older writ had ceased to give occasion for litigation that the cessavit in the old form ceased to appear among the writs

CONSPIRACY [29]

Statham 47 a

Paschal
44 Ed III

(1) **A writ of conspiracy** was brought against the Abbot of S and others, because they took the plaintiff and by force compelled him to make an attorney, who brought, in his name, an assize against the same abbot, who said that we were his villein   And the attorney said "free"   And by verdict of the assize he was found the villein of the abbot   FYNCHEDEN   It seems that such an action does not lie for you until the judgment be defeated by an attaint, etc   No more than upon an indictment you should be acquitted before the hearing of such a writ, etc   See the plea because it was well argued

And it was said in the same plea, that he who comes shall answer as in Trespass, but yet the death of one abates all the writ, etc   Query, if there be more defendants than two, if the death of one will abate all the writ, since two of the defendants are living, and the writ is to inquire, to wit if they conspired together, etc   And see the beginning of this plea, Paschal, 42 Ed III

Reported in Y B Paschal, 44 Ed III, p 14, pl 32   Case 1
The case referred to as in 42 Ed III is to be found on p 14, pl 27 It is a longer and better report of the case   See for that report, Brooke, Conspiracy, 6, and Fitzh Conspiracie, 10

(2) **One brought** a writ of conspiracy because one H and F were lords of a manor to which an advowson was appendant, and of this manor they enfeoffed the plaintiff, and then the advowson became vacant and the defendants conspired [to make] a writ of presentation, in the names of the said H and F, to the bishop, by force of which their clerk was admitted and our clerk refused, wherefore we brought a *Quare Impedit* against the bishop, and against H and F, and we recovered, wherefore our clerk was admitted and their clerk ousted, so by their false alliance we lost our possession for that time, etc And the action was maintained, etc.   And it was challenged because the plaintiff did not allege possession in himself nor in him by whom he claimed, etc.   (But yet it seems that it is not necessary, for he is not to recover the advowson in this case, nor to have a writ to the bishop)

Reported in Y B Paschal, 40 Ed III, p 19, pl 10   See also Fitzh Conspiracie, 16

Paschal
40 Ed III

Case 2

(3) **In a writ of conspiracy,** it was alleged that they were to procure a man to make a false deed, etc   HANK-FORD   This man whom he alleges was procured is one of the defendants, judgment, etc.   And for this reason the writ was abated   Contrary, 42 Paschal Term, etc

Reported in Y B Trinity, 46 Ed III, p 20, pl 26   See also Brooke, Conspiracy, 7, and Fitzh Conspiracie, 17

Trinity
46 Ed III

Case 3

(4) **In a writ of conspiracy** comprising this matter Whereas he and his predecessors stood seised of the manor of B, of time, etc , there the defendants such a day, etc , before the justices of Oyer and Terminer conspired between them, so that it was presented that we had given an advowson appendant to the same manor to a chaplain of a chantry

Trinity
47 Ed III

to find a chaplain, etc., wherefore the king was seised until we should have livery in the Exchequer, and so we were put to much trouble etc   And judgment was demanded, inasmuch as he did not show the record of the presentation, and it was not allowed.   PERLE· Judgment of the writ, because he does not show that he had livery, to wit by a traverse of the office or otherwise, for in conspiracy upon an indictment the defendant should show how he was indicted, and before what justices.   FYNCHEDEN In your case he shall say before whom he was acquitted, but he shall not say how he was acquitted   For I have seen a like case where the plaintiff had replied that he was not acquitted, and he said that he took himself to his clergy, and how he was acquitted by an inquest of office, and the action was maintained , wherefore answer   And then it was said that because it appeared by the office that the king had no cause to seize, albeit the king is seised in fact, this action is not maintainable, for peradventure he had livery *cum exitibus* And it was also said that a *Scire Facias* should have been awarded against this present plaintiff at the suit of the king before the king was seised, etc.

Case 4   Reported in Y B Mich (not Trinity), 47 Ed III, p 15, pl 22 See also Brooke, Conspiracy, 10, and Fitzh   Conspiracie, 18

Trinity
47 Ed III
(5) **A man shall have** a writ of Conspiracy against the judge before whom the indictment was made, if he be not a judge by commission   *Simile, Liber Assisarum*

Case 5   Reported in Y B Mich (not Trinity), 47 Ed III, p 16, pl 30 See also Brooke, Conspiracy, 9, and Fitzh   Conspiracie, 18

Trinity
47 Ed III
(6) **Two brought** a writ of Conspiracy against one who demanded judgment of the writ brought by them in common, where the damage of the one could not be the damage of the other, or *è contra*   But yet the writ was adjudged good Contrary elsewhere

Case 6   Reported in Y B Mich 47 Ed III, p 17, pl 32   See also Brooke, Conspiracy, 10, and Fitzh   Conspiracie, 19

Michaelis
24 Ed III
(7) **In conspiracy** against two, one came and was found guilty, and the other did not come   And it was adjudged

that the plaintiff should recover against him [who came].
Which appears strange, for if the other be acquitted afterward, then the judgment is false, for he cannot conspire with himself, wherefore it seems that he should not
be put to answer in that case. And they gave as the
reason for their judgment that the plaintiff declared that by
a conspiracy between the defendants the defendant who
was found guilty had procured the plaintiff to be indicted,
so in a manner he was the principal actor THORPE said,
in the same plea, that a writ brought against one, alleging
that he conspired with others not named, is of no value
From this it follows that if two conspire and one of them
dies, my action fails, etc.

Reported in Y B Mich 24 Ed III, p 34, pl 34 See also Brooke, Case 7
Conspiracy, 21, and Fitzh Conspiracie, 20

(8) **In conspiracy** against two, one pleaded in abate- Paschal
ment of the writ upon which the plaintiff and he were at 14 Hen VI
issue, and the other pleaded in bar, upon which the plaintiff demurred in law And then the issue was found for
the plaintiff, and the other plea was adjudged against him
And the opinion was that the plaintiff should recover
against him who pleaded in abatement of the writ, albeit
the other was acquitted, for he was not acquitted by
verdict, but by the bad pleading of the plaintiff, etc
So it might happen well enough that they conspired together

Reported in Y B Anno 14 Hen VI, p 25, pl 75 See also Fitzh Case 8
Conspiracie, 1

(9) **If the defendant** justifies the felony as in self- Michaelis
defense, or otherwise, or if it be found so by verdict, he shall 10 Hen IV
never have conspiracy for it by TYRWHIT, etc.

And see in the Term, a bill of conspiracy in the King's
Bench for him who was indicted for a common trespass,
etc , adjudged good, etc

The case has not been identified in Y B Mich 10 Hen IV Fitzh Case 9
Conspiracie, 21, has a short abridgment of the case

(10) **In conspiracy** against several because they conspired on a Monday, etc   And all except one pleaded not
guilty, and he said that on a Wednesday, a long time
after the Monday, and before the indictment, at such a
place, before the justices of the peace aforesaid, to wit
before the same justices before whom the plaintiff had
counted, etc , he was sworn with others to present legally
for the king, etc , and he then swore to inform others of
his companions of the inquest that the plaintiff had done the
felony, etc   And after this information, and before the verdict, the justices of the peace, for certain reasons which they
moved, ousted us of the inquest, and we demand judgment if
action.   FORTESCUE On another day than that we have
counted, which is no answer to us, and he has not answered
us.   MARKHAM I undersatnd that I can justify on any day
before the indictment, and therefore all the precedent conspiracy is saved   NEWION The plaintiff has alleged that
you conspired with others named in the writ   And you
have justified a conspiracy with others, to wit those of
the inquest, which cannot be the same conspiracy. PAS-
TON The conspiracy with those named is not denied by
him, for the justification with the others who are indicted
on his pretence shall be the end of all   NEWTON If two
inquests are charged to inquire for the king, they cannot
well sit together, and this is the reason they are not put in
ward, but go at large to inquire of that which is done in
the county Suppose, then, that two of one inquest
exhort others of the other inquest to indict a man, and by
their information they indict him   Now those two shall
be punished by a writ of Conspiracy, and yet they were
sworn for the king.   Then there is a difference where they
give their verdict after such a conspiracy, and where not,
wherefore, etc   And, Sire, when either many or less are
sworn for the king, and one of them will not agree with his
companions the justices can discharge [him]   And we
think that this was the reason of his discharge   And then
he never agreed to indict him, and so his justification is
false, wherefore, etc   PASTON That reason is not bind-
ing, for he could disagree to the indictment of another

person and be discharged for that reason, and yet, peradventure, he had agreed to indict the plaintiff, wherefore, etc. And they adjourned.

The case has not been identified in Y B Mich 19 Hen VI, or in the early abridgments   Case 10

See as to conspiracy, in the title of Actions on the Case, etc.   Note

See Statham, Accions sur le Cas, *supra,* pp 10 b–11 b

(11) **Conspiracy** brought by two was adjudged good, etc   Hilary 47 Ed III

The case has not been identified in Y B Hilary, 47 Ed III, or in the early abridgments, unless it is the case adjudged *supra,* p 47 a, case 6   Case 11.

(12) **In conspiracy,** the defendant was received to plead not guilty, notwithstanding he had been found guilty at the suit of the king for the same conspiracy And this in the Book of Assizes   Anno 27 Ed I

Reported in Y B *Liber Assisarum,* Year 27, p 141, pl 59 See also Brooke, Conspiracy, 28   Case 12

(13) **Conspiracy** was adjudged good where the plaintiff in an appeal was nonsuited, and the defendant acquitted at the suit of the king, upon the declaration, etc   Hilary 5 Ed III

The case has not been identified in Y B Hilary, 5 Ed II Fitzh Conspiracie, 22, has the case, but does not complete the citation, evidently not having been able to identify the case   Case 13

(14) **Conspiracy** does not lie where a man admits the felony, and justifies And this in the *Liber Assisarum,* in a Presentment, etc   Anno 22 Ed III

Reported in Y B *Liber Assisarum,* p. 102, pl 77 See also Brooke, Conspiracy, 26, and Fitzh Conspiracie, 14   Case 14

(15) **Where a man** is indicted for a conspiracy at the suit of the king, and is attached, the judgment is as in an Attaint, but at the suit of the party, it is only a common judgment, etc HANKFORD said that the difference was because the indictment was by the common law, and against the party the action is given by the Statute etc. *Coram Rege.*   Michaelis 4 Hen V

There is no printed year of 4 Hen V The case has not been identified in the early abridgments For the Statute, see *Articuli super Cartas,* c. 10, Stats at Large, Vol 1, p. 297   Case 15.

[29] Again in this topic the question arises whether it was of statutory origin solely, as Maitland asserts, [P & M Hist of Eng Law, 2d ed , Vol 2, p 539] or whether it had been known at the common law, as Coke says [Coke, 2nd Inst 562] "I have read," says Coke Maitland says that Coke "relies upon the fictions in the Mirroir," and it is true that his statement is accompanied by a citation to that discredited book The Year Books, however, show that there was a general understanding that the writ had been used before the enactment of the Statute of Ed I There is a case of conspiracy in Trinity, 11 Hen VII [p 26, pl 7] in which the writ of conspiracy at the common law" is spoken of That case is also authority for the statements "For at the common law one shall not have conspiracy except upon an indictment for felony " "For at the common law they shall have a process of outlawry in conspiracy and in trespass ' We also have a case [case 14] which unfortunately is from a manuscript, as there is no printed year of 4 Hen V But Hankford is reported as saying that the indictment was by the common law, and against the party the action is given by the Statute Here are two cases to sustain Coke (granting that our case 14 has authority), showing that he did not depend wholly upon the "fables in the Mirroir " Coke's remarks also show that he knew the general arguments upon the subject, and that he did not more specifically refer to the cases which he says are found "plentifully in our books" because it was the common knowledge of his day Somehow one has a certain sense of pleasure in finding that Coke knew what he was talking about He breathed the atmosphere of the old law at all times, which we can only get as filtered down to us through the breath of others Every phrase of his paragraph on the subject shows that he had a full knowledge of the matter in hand

We have also the case of the "villaneous Judgment" cited by Coke [2nd Inst 562] which is in 24 Ed III [Y B 24, Ed III, p 34 pl 34], which he says is at the common law, "for it is given by no statute " This villainous judgment certainly deserves its name, for the party found guilty could "never more be sworn in Juries or Assizes, nor admitted to give any testimony elsewhere, and if he have to do in the King's Courts, he shall come by Attorney, and not in Person that his Lands, Goods and Chattels shall be seized in the King's hands, and estreaped if he find not the more Favor, and his Trees digged up, and his Body imprisoned " [Termes de la Ley, title Villaneous Judgment] This description is evidently taken from the case in the *Liber Assisarum* [27 *Liber Assisarum*, p 141, pl 59] which case is also cited by Coke [Coke, 2d Inst p 562] Coke has also seen our case in 4 Hen V (14), either in Statham or in the manuscript itself There is evidently a conflict of authorities, or rather the modern writers have not given sufficient attention to the matter to put themselves exactly in line with the older writers upon the subject The matter is mooted here to call the attention of those who may care to go further into it, to the fact that there is here something of interest which seems to be obscure in our present law

COLLUSION AND COVYNE [30]

(1) **In a writ of waste** by a prior, he had judgment to recover his damages and the place wasted, before the collusion was tried, but execution of the land shall tarry until the collusion is tried, etc. Query, wherefore the collusion shall not be inquired into by the same inquest which found the waste? Michaelis 40 Ed III

Reported in Y B Mich 40 Ed III, p 37, pl 10   See also Brooke, Collusion and Covyne, 7 Case 1

(2) **In a** *Præcipe quod Reddat* against one who vouched an abbot to warranty, who vouched over another, who made default, wherefore the Grand Cape *ad valenciam* issued, and he made default, wherefore the demandant had judgment to recover against the tenant, and each one over against the other, wherefore it was adjudged that the collusion be inquired into by a *quale jus* [1] before the abbot could have execution, and by the opinion of THORPE that the execution of all should cease until, etc Hilary 50 Ed III

The case has not been identified in Y B Hilary, 50 Ed III, or in the early abridgments Case 2

(3) **A scire facias** issued against the creditor in a statute merchant, because he had raised the monies which were garnished, and he made default, wherefore one J came and said that he who made default leased to him his estate, and that by covin between the plaintiff and him to make him lose his term, this action was brought, and he prayed to be received. HULS You are not in the position of the termor who has a certain estate   And you are in such a position that you could have an Assize if you were ousted, without making yourself a party, and in that Assize the covin could be tried   Wherefore let it stand over, etc Hilary 21 Ed III

Reported in Y B Hilary, 21 Ed III, p 1, pl 1 Case 3

(4) **In a writ** of dower, the tenant vouched to warranty the heir of the husband, as of full age and out of wardship Statham 48 a Trinity 24 Ed III

[1] A judicial writ for a man of religion, before execution

And at the summons, one H came and said that the heir was under age and in his wardship. And he said that this voucher, in the manner, was by covin between the demandant and the tenant to make him lose his wardship, and he prayed to be received by the equity of the Statute of Gloucester. And the opinion was that it should not be, for that recovery in value did not injure him, because he did not vouch in his wardship, etc

Case 4

The case has not been identified in Y B Trinity, 24 Ed III, or in the early abridgments

The Statute is that of 6 Ed I, cap 2 (1278), Statute of Gloucester, Stats at Large, Vol 1, p 117

Paschal
19 Ed III

(5) **If an abbot** sues execution by an *elegit*, the collusion shall be inquired into. by WILLOUGHBY, etc.

Case 5

There is no early printed year of 19 Ed III The case has not been identified in the Rolls Series for that year

Hilary
44 Ed III

(6) **In an assize** by a woman, the tenant said that the husband of the woman enfeoffed one H, with warranty, who enfeoffed us with warranty, and one J, by your covin, entered upon us and endowed you in defeasance of our warranty, upon which we entered, judgment if action BELKNAP· Inasmuch as he has admitted her title of dower to be one of an elder time, etc , judgment. And so to judgment, etc

Case 6

Reported in Y B Mich (not Hilary), 44 Ed III, p 45, pl 63 See also Brooke, Collusion and Covyne, 10

Hilary
34 Ed III

(7) **A prior** brought a writ of wardship and recovered; and the opinion of WILLOUGHBY was that the collusion should be inquired into, inasmuch as he recovered the lordship by this recovery, etc

Case 7

There is no printed year of 34 Ed III, except in the *Liber Assisarum*, where the case has not been identified It has not been identified in the early abridgments

Michaelis
9 Hen VI.

(8) **In a praecipe quod reddat,** they were at issue, and the plaintiff said that after the last continuance one A brought an Assize against him, and he pleaded in bar, on

which the plaintiff made title, and we traversed the title, and it was found for him, wherefore he recovered and sued execution Judgment of the writ. FULTHORPE That Assize was brought by covin between you, to the intent to abate our writ, besides this that you should aver that you did not disseise him BABYNGTON. I understand that I can falsify a recovery, to which I am a stranger, on the same point on which it was formerly tried, where that recovery goes in bar of my action, but not where it goes merely in abatement of the writ, as is the case here MARTYN It is all one, but it is to be seen if the plea is double, for when one recovers upon a false title, he who is a stranger can take issue upon that same title, and so falsify the recovery without pleading of any covin But when he recovers upon a good title he should show the reason for the covin, for in the common intent a man cannot falsify a recovery upon a good title without alleging the covin As if the tenant makes a feoffment pending the writ, and against his feoffment he disseises him, and the other brings an Assize and recovers; now he recovers upon a good title, and yet that recovery shall not injure me, etc But yet it seems that in that case the demandant shall not show covin, but he shall show all the matter — how the title of him who recovered commenced after the purchase of his writ But where he recovers upon a good title, the plaintiff can say that he was seised until disseised by the tenant, by covin between him and the one who recovered, to the intent to make me lose my warranty, and so the recovery was false And see such matter in the *Liber Assisarum*, Anno 22, folio 8 In an Assize, etc

Reported in Y B Mich 9 Hen VI, p 41, pl 18 Case 8

(9) **The guardian** is not in the purview of the Statute of Gloucester, which says that the termor shall aver collusion in his action on his term by THIRNING and HANKFORD, in Wardship. Paschal 7 Hen IV

The case has not been identified in Y B Paschal, 7 Hen IV, or in the early abridgments The Statute of Gloucester, 6 Ed I, cap 11 (1278), Stats at Large, Vol 1, p 117 Case 9

**Paschal
7 Hen IV**

(10) **The lord** shall have collusion against the feoffment made by his tenant by a fine. (In a note), etc *Simile* 12 of the same king, in Wardship.

Case 10

Reported (as a note) in Y B Paschal, 7 Hen IV, p 15, pl 22 See also Brooke, Collusion and Covyne, 14, and Fitzh Collusion and Covyne, 14

**Hilary
9 Hen IV**

(11) **If the tenant** of the king alienates other lands, which are not held of the king, with the intent to enfeoff his heir when he comes to his full age, in that case the king shall have collusion And yet it is not in the purview of the Statute, for the land which was aliened was not held of him By I HIRNING and HANKFORD in a *Scire Facias* Well debated, etc But yet the king shall have all in Wardship, through his prerogative

Case 11

Reported in Y B Mich (not Hilary), 9 Hen IV, p 6, pl 20 See also Brooke, Collusion and Covyne, 24, and Fitzh Collusion and Covyne, 12

Note

See of Covin in the title of Falser de Recover

Statham, title Falser de Recover, *infra*, pp 101 b and 102 a

**Hilary
16 Ed III**

(12) **If a man** of religion recovers in a writ of Annuity, the collusion shall not be inquired into As appeared in a note, etc

Case 12

There is no early printed year of 16 Ed III The case is reported in the Rolls Series, 16 Ed III, Hilary Term, Pt 1, p 67, No 17 See also Fitzh Collusion and Covyne, 41

**Michaelis
2 Ed III**

(13) **If an abbot** recovers against another abbot, the collusion shall not be inquired into As appeared in a writ of Entry

Case 13

The case has not been identified in Y B Mich 2 Ed III, or in the early abridgments

**Trinity
2 Ed III**

(14) **Collusion** shall not be inquired into in a *Juris d'Utrum*, where the issue is taken upon the right, etc.

Case 14

The case has not been identified in Y B Mich 2 Ed III, or in the early abridgments

**Michaelis
7 Ed III**

(15) **In replevin** against an abbot, he shall have a recovery without inquiring as to the collusion, because there was no judgment by that return to recover his rent, etc.

Case 15

The case has not been identified in Y B Mich 7 Ed III, or in the early abridgments

(16) **An abbot** brought a writ of entry upon a disseisin
made on his predecessor   The tenant traversed the disseisin and it was found for the abbot   And the collusion
was inquired into by the same inquest, notwithstanding
the title of the abbot was found.   And they said that in a
writ of entry on a lease made by his predecessor and found
for him, they would award seisin of the land without
inquiry as to the collusion   Query as to the difference,
etc.? *Contra* Paschal, 29 Ed III

There is no early printed year of 16 Ed III   The case is reported
in the Rolls Series 16 Ed III, 2, p 10   The case cited at the end of
the abridged case is reported in Y B Paschal, 29 Ed III, p 33, pl 53.

(17) **In trespass** against an abbot, who said that the
plaintiff was his villein regardant, etc   And they examined
the plaintiff [to find] if he did it by collusion.   But yet
that is not the case [provided for] in the Statute.

Reported in Y B Paschal, 29 Ed III, p 35, pl 60   See also Fitzh
Collusion and Covyne, 13 and 45

See as to collusion, in the title of *Quale Jus*
Statham, *infra*, p 148 b

[30] The Statute of Westminster I, cap 29, was passed to prevent the
unlawful shifts and devices cunningly contrived," by the "Sergeants,
Apprentices, Attorneys, and Clerks of the King's Courts " [Coke,
Inst 2 213] Therefore this act was made "in affirmance of the common law, only it added a greater punishment "
We find that it is decided in some of the cases that the collusion is
one which should be inquired into, in other cases it is decided that there
shall be no inquiry   At first sight the decisions seem rather arbitrary,
but on examination we find that there are certain writs in which the
collusion may be inquired into, as *Quare Impedit*, and Assize and the
like, which one corporation brings against another [Termes de la Ley,
Collusion, p 138.] In one of our cases it is a *Præcipe quod Reddat* in
which the collusion is inquired into by a *Quale Jus* — given by the Statute
[Case 2] In another case [case 5] an abbot sues execution by an *elegit*
and the collusion is inquired into   In our case 7 a prior brings a writ
of wardship and recovers   Willoughby thinks the collusion should
be inquired into   But in our case 12, the monk who recovers in a
writ of annuity is saved from the inquiry   In a *Jure d'Utrum* the
inquiry is not allowed "where the issue is taken upon the right "   [Case
14.] In cases 13 to 15 the inquiry is not allowed, apparently because
it seemed that there was no harm done by the recovery   It is granted

again in case 16, and yet they would refuse it in a similar case, and there is a "query as to the difference" Is there any one now sufficiently learned in the older law to tell us why it should have been allowed in the one case and refused in the other? Was it in the discretion of the court to inquire if one of the parties appeared to have been unjustly enriched at the expense of the other? It would almost seem so from the cases, and it is evidently a proceeding of an equitable nature Fraud and deceit are allied actions, but there is an indefinable difference Deceit furnishes a separate title to the abridgment What was the difference in the mind of the lawyer of the day between collusion, covin and deceit? Deceit, on the whole, seems to have been much more technical, as we shall see when we reach the subject If one may venture to sketch the difference very briefly, one may say that deceit was the technical legal remedy for a certain kind of deception (deception in a legal action), and collusion and covin led to a writ which was in fact an equitable remedy for almost all forms of fraud There was another writ given by the Statute of Gloucester [6 Ed I, cap 11 (1278), Stats at Large, Vol 1, p 117] This writ is referred to in cases 4 and 9, and it is more like the writ of deceit in that it is based upon a previous action in court, that is, that there was a feigned suit to make, through collusion or by fraud, the termor lose his term The interdependence of the older actions and their gradual absorption by one or the other, or a division into new forms, is a part of the history of the law which has never been fully investigated, except in the case of a few of the better known actions The whole field is one of great interest, an interest which is stimulated to a greater activity by the few selected cases such as we have in this abridgment, than it is by the more crowded collections of later days Of course these few cases are mere finger posts to point the way which we must take through the larger collections — the Year Books themselves and the other sources of the law But a finger post at the beginning of the way is an immense advantage to the traveler who must walk in unknown paths

COUNTREPLEE DE VOUCHER

Statham 48 b
Hilary
40 Ed III

(1) **He whom you vouch** nor any, etc , never had, etc , except that which the father of the vouchee holds for the term of his life of your own lease THORPE That is not a counterplea BELKNAP Of such an estate he cannot enfeoff the tenant, but it shall be called a surrender to him THORPE He has admitted such an estate in him upon which he can make a feoffment between the tenant and the demandant,

and that shall not be called a surrender. Wherefore he said to the tenant, "Let the voucher stand," etc.

Reported in Y B Hilary, 40 Ed III, p 12, pl 27 See also Brooke, Case 1. Countreplee de Voucher, 4, and Fitzh Counterplee de Voucher, 18.

(2) **The tenant** vouched one A as cousin and heir of one Hilary B, son of J, son of the said B, and because he was under 40 Ed III age, etc , the demandant said that this J was a bastard And the opinion was that he should not have such a counter-plea, because if this matter be so he can say that he who vouched, nor any of his ancestors, etc But yet it seems that the counterplea is good by the common law, etc.

Reported in Y B Paschal (not Hilary), 40 Ed III, p 22, pl 22 See Case 2. also Brooke, Countreplee de Voucher, 6

(3) **In formedon** in the descender, it was alleged that Trinity one A granted the reversion of a tenant for life to the 41 Ed III ancestor of the demandant. The tenant vouched, etc BELKNAP He who, etc., never had, etc , after the seisin of our ancestor, etc. And the opinion was that this was not a counterplea, for the vouchee could have possession after the grant, and before the seisin before which the reversion was executed, etc

Reported in Y B Trinity, 41 Ed III, p 15, pl 7 See also Brooke, Case 3 Countreplee de Voucher, 9, and Fitzh Counterplee de Voucher, 20

(4) **Where the** tenant vouches himself to save the tail, Michaelis the demandant shall have a counterplea to the cause, in 41 Ed III the same manner as the vouchee in other cases shall have to the place, etc

The case has not been identified in Y. B Mich 41 Ed III, or in the Case 4 early abridgments

(5) **"He whom you vouch,"** etc. BELKNAP To that Michaelis you shall not be received, for after the gift your ancestor 41 Ed III. enfeoffed this same vouchee by a fine, judgment, etc Query, etc.? In Formedon, etc.

Reported in Y B Mich 41 Ed III, p 29, pl 32 Case 5

(6) **In formedon** the tenant vouched, etc FENCOT He, etc , nor any, etc , except he who vouched jointly with the tenant, and others who have released all to the tenant, judgment, etc THORPE Such a plea as the above, that the other is dead, so that all accrues to the tenant by the survivorship, has been adjudged good, etc But yet the opinion was that the counterplea was not good, etc And see Trinity, 45, of the same king, in a *Præcipe quod Reddat.* The demandant said that he, etc., never had, etc , except jointly with the tenant, without saying that he was dead or that he had released, and the opinion was that he should have the plea, because he could not vouch him for such an estate, etc But yet he could release to him with warranty, in which case the possession and the release together are a cause for a voucher Query? It seems that this counterplea will abate the writ of the demandant.

Case 6

The case has not been identified in Y B Mich 44 Ed III, or in the early abridgments

(7) **In a writ of cosinage,** the tenant made default and one was received and vouched one H to warranty BELKNAP J, your father, whose heir, etc , was the first who abated, etc. FENCOT This H was disseised and leased to the tenant, who made default, and then granted the reversion to us, without this that J, our father, had anything. BELKNAP demurred upon the plea (Which see, for it was well argued)

And it was said in the same plea, that it is a good plea to say that at time of the levying of the fine "my father who levied the fine, had nothing in the lands, but I myself was seised," etc. So here, if he shows that he does not claim by him who abated, it seems that it is a good plea in avoidance of the counterplea, etc

Case 7

Reported in Y B Hilary, 46 Ed III, p 2, pl 3 See also Brooke, Countreplee de Voucher, 15, and Fitzh Counterplee de Voucher, 29

(8) **In a writ of escheat** it was alleged that one H held of him, and committed a felony The tenant vouched to warranty SPIGORNEL He, etc , never had, etc , after

the seisin of him on whose possession we demand   And the opinion of many was that he should say, "after the felony was committed," etc. See the plea for it was well debated, etc

Reported in Y B Mich (not Hilary), 48 Ed III, p 28, pl 14   See also Brooke, Countreplee de Voucher, 19, and Fitzh   Counterplee de Voucher, 32

Case 8.

(9) **"He whom** you vouch is my villein," is a good counterplea. by FYNCHEDEN in a Formedon, for otherwise the villein will be enfranchised, etc

Trinity 48 Ed III

The point is to be found in a case of Formedon in the Descender, in Y B Trinity, 48 Ed III, p 16, pl 1   (Point on p 17)   See also Brooke, Countreplee de Voucher, 18, and Fitzh   Counterplee de Voucher, 31

Case 9

(10) **"He whom you** vouch never had anything except at the will of my father," is a good counterplea, by the opinion of the COURT and this in Voucher

Hilary 50 Ed III

Reported in Y B Trinity (not Hilary), 50 Ed III, p 12, pl 2

Case 10

(11) **In a praecipe quod reddat** one of the tenants died, and therefore the writ was abated, and for *journez accompté,*[1] he purchased another writ, and the tenant vouched to warranty FYNCHEDEN He, etc , had nothing, etc , except by a demise made by one of the tenants in the first writ, after the first writ was purchased   [This is] a good counterplea, etc

Hilary 50 Ed III.

And it was said in the same plea that if the cause be put without day, at the re-summons the tenant can vouch other persons whom he did not vouch before   (But I believe that this does not mean where it is put without by a protection.)

Reported in Y B Hilary, 50 Ed III, p 2, pl 5   See also Brooke, Countreplee de Voucher, 20

Case 11

---

[1] "Journez Accompté" are called in Termes de la Ley "Journees Accounts," and explained thus   "If a writ be abated without the default of the plaintiff or demandant, he may purchase a new writ, which if it be purchased by journies accounts (that is, within as little time as he possibly can after the abatement of the first writ) then this second writ shall be as a continuance of the first, and so shall oust the tenant or defendant of his voucher '   Termes de la Ley, ed of 1721

(12) **In a praecipe quod reddat,** the tenant vouched one J as son and heir of B because he was under age. FYNCH-EDEN. B, nor any of his ancestors, never had, etc THORPE That is no counterplea by the Statute and by the common law there was no counterplea to the possession SHARSHULL· It is no counterplea for another reason, for he can bind J by the deed of another ancestor, etc Wherefore FENCOT said that B nor any of the ancestors of J ever had anything, and the plea was accepted But yet it seems that for this cause it was good enough, for he could not bind him by the deed of another ancestor when the demandant had suffered a delay, etc, no more than he could bind him by his own deed, etc But it seems that it is no plea for another reason, for if it be a plea it is by the common law to oust the delay, to wit that the vouchee may not have his age And by the common law there is no counter-plea which limits any time in certain, to wit, after the title of the writ, for by the common law the tenant shall have his voucher as well of a warranty made after the title of the writ of the demandant as before, but it is ousted by the Statute of Westminster the First, which gives the counterplea to the possession after the title of the writ of the demandant.

Case 12   Reported in Y B Hilary, 21 Ed III, p 9, pl 27 See also Brooke, Countreplee de Voucher, 29, and Fitzh Counterplee de Voucher, 85 Fitzherbert calls the writ in the case a Formedon

The Statute is that of 13 Ed I (1275), cap 40, Westminster the First, Stats at Large, Vol 1, p 74 (100), Voucher to Warranty and Counterpleading of Voucher

(13) **In a writ of wardship,** the defendant vouched one because he leased the wardship to him, etc , and he did not show a deed of the lease, etc (And so see that he should show cause), etc The plaintiff said that the defendant was the first who got the wardship after the death of the ancestor of the infant, etc And the opinion of SHARSHULL was that this was not a counterplea, for the Statute is, "Where lands and tenements are demanded," etc

Case 13   Reported in Y B Hilary, 21 Ed III, p 10, pl 34 See also Brooke, Countreplee de Voucher, 28

(14) **In a writ of dower,** the tenant vouched to warranty Paschal
the heir of the husband, under age and in the wardship of 21 Ed III
one H, for part, and for another part, in the wardship of
one F, and for another part, in the wardship of the king
FENCOT   The king never had anything in wardship
Ready as to that part.   THORPE   That is no plea, for that Statham 49 a
issue cannot be tried without the counsellor of the king
DARR   He will be inconvenienced if he has not the plea
SHARSHULL   If this plea be true the cause will be stayed
against all, see the Statute of *Bigamus*, to wit   *"De
dotibus mulierum,"* etc   And then the issue was taken
STOUFORD said that if the issue be found against the defendant, that the demandant shall have judgment to recover
all her dower, which SHARSHULL denied, and said that she
would recover only for a part, etc.

   Reported in Y B Paschal, 21 Ed III, p 53, pl 1   Case 14
   The Statute is that of 4 Ed I (1276), cap 3, the Statute of
Bigamy   Stats at Large, Vol 1, p 114 (115)

(15) **The demandant** shall not say that "he whom you Michaelis
vouched is dead," except on the first day that the tenant 21 Ed III
vouches, for on another day, during the process, he cannot,
etc , but it comes in upon the return of the sheriff [1]   And
this in a *Præcipe quod Reddat*   See the Statute which
gives this counterplea, for it gives it generally without
mentioning any time, etc

   Reported in Y B Mich 21 Ed III, p 36, pl 30   See also Brooke, Case 15
Countreplee de Voucher, 30   The Statute is that of 3 Ed I (1273),
cap 40, Westminster the First, Stats at Large, Vol 1, p 74 (100)

(16) **In a juris d'utrum** for rent, the tenant said that Hilary
he was tenant of the land of which, etc , and he vouched 18 Ed III
to warranty.   SALT   It is a rent service   Judgment if
the voucher   And the opinion of many was that this was a
good counterplea   But yet he had the voucher.   Query
as to the reason, etc.

   Reported in Y B Hilary, 18 Ed III, p 1, pl 2   Case 16

     [1] The *sicut alias*

Paschal
14 Ed II

(17) **He who,** etc , never had, etc , except by the father of the vouchee jointly with the tenant, which estate they continued all the lifetime of the same father, and then the father died, and the tenant had all by the survivorship, judgment, etc. And the opinion was that this was a good counterplea by reason of the delay, because he said that the vouchee was under age, etc   But yet it seems that the continuance of the possession cannot be counterpleaded in this case, for it amounts to no more than that he did not enfeoff him, or that he did not release him, which is a counterplea of the place   And this well debated

Case 17

The case has not been identified in Y B Paschal, 14 Ed II, or Ed III, or in the early abridgments

Michaelis
18 Ed III

(18) **In formedon,** the tenant vouched the husband and his wife. The demandant said that the wife nor any of her ancestors ever had anything, etc.   And it was adjudged no counterplea   The law is the same where the tenant vouches two, it is no plea to counterplead the possession of one   But they said in the same plea that in a writ of possession where the husband and his wife are vouched, it is a good counterplea to say that the wife was the first who abated after the death of the ancestor of whose possession, etc   *Simile*, Anno 39 Ed III

Case 18

Reported in Y B Mich 18 Ed III, p 53, pl 68

Michaelis
21 Ed III

(19) **One vouched** himself to save the tail, and showed cause, to wit   that such a one enfeoffed, etc   The demandant said that he did not enfeoff, and he could not have the counterplea, because it was a counterplea of the place, wherefore he said that he who enfeoffed was never seised, etc   (And against the law, as I believe, for where a man shows cause the demandant shall not have the same counterplea that the vouchee has   As it appeared, Mich 44 Ed III)

Case 19

Reported in Y B Mich 21 Ed III, p 37, pl 31   See also Brooke, Countreplee de Voucher, 31, and Fitzh   Counterplee de Voucher, 91

Hilary
23 Ric II

(20) **In dower,** the tenant vouched a stranger, and the demandant said that he, who, etc , was the first who

abated after the death of our husband, of whose possession, etc   And the opinion was that that was not a counterplea, because his title did not commence solely on the
death of her husband, for it might be that her husband
made a feoffment to the vouchee, and then came to the
land and died seised   Wherefore she said that he who,
etc , had nothing, etc , after the marriage   RIKHILL That
is no counterplea, for the title of the demandant could
commence after the marriage by the purchase of the husband   Then you should say, in that case, that he had
nothing after the title of the writ as your title is not
certain, for your title is the marriage, the possession
and the dying   And in any case where the title is uncertain the counterplea shall be after the title, as in a writ
of entry upon a disseisin, you shall say, "after the title
of your writ" and this shall be understood to be the possession before the disseisin. But where the title is certain
it is otherwise, as in formedon in the descender, he shall
say, "after the gift" And in a writ of escheat, "after
the felony done," and so in each case   And they adjourned.

There is no printed Year Book for 23 Ric II   The case does not **Case 20**
appear to have been abridged by Brooke or Fitzherbert

(21) **In dower,** the tenant vouched a stranger and the Michaelis
demandant said that the tenant entered by her husband. 18 Ed III
And it was adjudged no plea, etc   Contrary, *Anno Primo*
Ed II.

Reported in Y B Mich 18 Ed III, p 55, pl 75   **Case 21.**

(22) **In a quod ei deforceat,** it is a good counterplea Paschal
to say, if the demandant vouches, that he whom he vouches 33 Ed III
had nothing in the reversion, for the Statute gives to him
the voucher of him in the reversion, and of no other   By
the opinion, etc

There is no printed Year Book for 33 Ed III. The case has not **Case 22**
been identified in the early abridgments

The Statute is that of 3 Ed I (1275), cap 40, Westminster the
First, Stats at Large, Vol 1, p 74 (100)

(23) In a praecipe quod reddat, the tenant vouched to warranty, and prayed that he be summoned in another county, and the demandant said that the vouchee had assets within the same county where the writ was brought. FYNCHEDEN· That is no plea BURTON· It has been adjudged a plea in an eyre FYNCHEDEN You speak truly and the reason is because the justices in eyre cannot make a process in a foreign county, so he shall have the plea, because of the mischief And the law is the same in an Assize of Mort d'Ancestor which is brought *in pais* before justices of the Assize, for the above reason, etc.

Case 23   There is no printed Year Book for 32 Ed III   The case has not been identified in the early abridgments

(24) In a sur cui in vita out of the degrees, *nisi post dimissionem quam,* U de B, formerly her husband, etc , FYNCHEDEN vouched to warranty one H, as cousin and heir of the said U FENCOT H nor any of his ancestors, etc FYNCHEDEN To that you shall not be received, since your writ alleges that A made the demise FENCOT Although you have vouched him as heir, that does not prove that he is heir THORPE You can say that he, etc., nor any, etc , whose heir he is FENCOT That is not warranted by the Statute, to wit· "Whose heir he is " THORPE. Show how [he is] cousin FYNCHEDEN. I do not show it until the vouchee comes, and then I shall show it to him in ample time, etc Which the Court conceded, upon which FENCOT said, "We are cousin and heir to U of B, without this that H, or any of his ancestors whose heir he is, ever had anything, etc And the counterplea was received. Which note, for it is not warranted by the Statute But THORPE said that when a man cannot have the counterplea by the Statute, where it is contrary to his writ, as in the case above, he shall aid himself by special matter, which can stand with the Statute Query, if he shall say that a stranger is heir, without this (as above)?

Case 24   Reported in Y B Trinity, 38 Ed III, p. 15, pl 19. See also Brooke, Countreplee de Voucher, 24, and Fitzh Counterplee de Voucher, 11

The Statute is that of 3 Ed I (1275), cap 40, Westminster the First, Stats at Large, Vol 1, p 74 (100)

(25) **In a praecipe quod reddat,** the tenant vouched two   The demandant said that one of them was dead, and he had the plea.

Michaelis 39 Ed III

Reported in Y B Mich 39 Ed III, p 32, pl 36   See also Brooke, Countreplee de Voucher, 36, and Fitzh   Counterplee de Voucher, 16

Case 25

(26) **In a cui in vita** in the post, against one J, son of H, it was alleged that he had no entry except after the demise that one A, the mother of the demandant, made to one A and B   The tenant vouched the said A and B to warranty The demandant said that this J, who is tenant, recovered the same land by a *Cui in Vita* on a demise, etc , against the said A and B, and sued execution, and that estate continued by force of that recovery, until the day the writ was purchased, and at all times thereafter, which matter etc , without this that the said A and B, or any, etc , ever had anything in another manner   BABYNGTON   That is no counterplea by the Statute, and at the common law there was no counterplea to the possession   And it also appears by his plea that the tenant is in by title of a recovery, and he has not shown that his title is older than the title of the tenant, so this plea shall be taken the more strongly against him, to wit   that he had no cause of action, etc   And also he said, "without this that he never had any other possession, and that is contrary to the allegation of his writ, which alleges the demise to be made to them by the husband of the mother of the demandant, etc   MARTYN   That cannot be a counterplea, for the possession is the cause of the voucher, albeit he had not warranted, as if I disseise a man and then I am impleaded, I shall vouch him, etc , and it is no counterplea to say that I never had anything except by disseisin, etc   Well argued

Statham 49 b
Michaelis 9 Hen VI

Reported in Y B Mich. 9 Hen VI, p 49, pl 31   See also Brooke, Countreplee de Voucher, 2, and Fitzh   Counterplee de Voucher, 1

Case 26.

The Statute is that of 3 Ed I (1275), cap 40, Westminster the First, Stats at Large, Vol 1, p 74 (100)

Note **See** of Counterplea of Voucher, in the title of Voucher.
(See *infra*, Statham, p 182)

Hilary
21 Ed III

(27) **If the tenant** demurs in law upon a counterplea of voucher, and it is adjourned until another term, it is peremptory for him, for although the Statute says, "he shall be further compelled to answer," it is intended that he shall reply immediately, etc. *Simile* 20 Ed. III, Paschal Term, in Dower

Case 27

Reported in Y B Hilary, 21 Ed III, p 10, pl 34   See also Brooke, Countreplee de Voucher, 28, and Fitzh   Counterplee de Voucher, 89

The Statute is that of 3 Ed I (1275), cap 40, Westminster the First, Stats at Large, Vol 1, p 74 (100)   "He shall be further compelled to another answer "

Michaelis
15 Ed III
Case 28

(28) **A good counterplea** is "none such in being "

There is no early printed year of 15 Ed III   The case has not been identified in the Rolls Series for that year

Hilary
16 Ed III

(29) **A good counterplea** is, "He whom you vouch is my villein "   In a *Juris d'Utrum.*

Case 29

There is no early printed year of 16 Ed III   The case has not been identified in the Rolls Series for that year

Paschal
6 Ed III

(30) **A good counterplea** in a writ of right of the seisin of the demandant is, "He whom you vouch never had anything after the seisin of which I have counted "   And this by the opinion of the COURT, etc

Case 30

The case has not been identified in Y B Paschal, 6 Ed III, or in the early abridgments

Michaelis
10 Ed III

(31) **A counterplea** of a voucher is not peremptory in an Assize of Mort d'Ancestor although the points of the writ shall be examined

Case 31

Reported in Y B Mich 10 Ed III, p 45, pl 6½   (This paragraph should be pl 7, but is skipped in the numbering in the "vulgate "   These placita are both "notes "   In the older editions of the Year Books the placita are correctly numbered, and this note is placitum 7)

Hilary
15 Ed III

(32) **The tenant** shall not be further compelled to another answer upon a counterplea at the common law.   And this in Error

There is no early printed year of 15 Ed III   The case has not been   Case 32
identified in the Rolls Series for that year   It is very difficult to trace
these extremely small points through the cases, although I have little
doubt that if the proper amount of time could be given, nearly all these
points could be traced to their original cases

(33) **Where one is** vouched as heir to one B, who is under   Michaelis
age, it is no counterplea to say that, "this B, nor any of his   21 Ed III
ancestors "   Query, etc   In a *Præcipe quod Reddat*

The case has not been identified in Y B Mich 21 Ed III, or in the   Case 33
early abridgments

(34) **A man shall have** the counterplea against the   Hilary
vouchee, as well where he comes by process, if he vouches   9 Ed II
over, as if he entered immediately, etc   Although not by
the words of the Statute, etc   In a writ of Cosinage, etc

Reported in Y B Hilary, 9 Ed II, p 291, pl 3   Case 34
The Statute is that of 3 Ed III, cap 40 (1273), Westminster the
First, Stats at Large, Vol 1, p 74 (100)

(35) **In a mort d'ancestor** against a prior, it is a good   Anno
counterplea that the predecessor of the prior was the first   40 Ed III
who abated after the death of the ancestor, etc   *Liber
Assisarum,* etc.

Reported in Y B *Liber Assisarum,* 40 Ed III, p 238, pl 2   See   Case 35
also Brooke, Countreplee de Voucher, 43

(36) **A good counterplea** in a writ of wardship is, "He   Michaelis
who vouched had nothing," etc , after the death of the   19 Ed III
ancestor of the tenant   But yet it is not given by the
Statute, etc

There is no early printed year of 19 Ed III   The point abridged   Case 36
appears in a writ of wardship, reported in the Rolls Series, 19 Ed III,
p 280
For the Statute, see *supra*, case 34

COUNTREPLEE DE GARANTIE

(1) **In a writ of escheat,** the tenant vouched one J to   Statham 50 a
warranty, who came and demanded of him what he had   Hilary
45 Ed III

to bind him to the warranty; who showed his own deed And the vouchee said that the tenant who vouched him had nothing in the land the day the writ was purchased, etc And because he had demanded of him what he had to bind him, it was the opinion that he should not have the plea, no more than where a man demands what they have for the remainder, he shall not come in afterwards to plead anything in abatement of the writ

And it was said in the same plea that in warranty of charter it is a good plea to say that he had nothing in the land the day, etc. But yet, query, etc.?

Case 1   Reported in Y B Hilary, 45 Ed III, p 2, pl 3

Michaelis
5 Ed III   (2) **It is a good counterplea** of warranty to say that "a long time after the feoffment of our father, which you show, our father died seised, and you abated," etc. In Dower

Case 2   Reported in Y B Mich 5 Ed III, p 37, pl 18.

Trinity
14 Ed II   (3) **It is no counterplea** of warranty to say that his father never had anything in the land except in tail, as to which land he has a writ pending, etc. In Dower.

Case 3   The case has not been identified in Y B Trinity, 14 Ed II, or in the early abridgments.

COUNTREPLEE DE AYDE

Michaelis
31 Ed III   (1) **See in scire facias** two counterpleas of aid, etc Good matter in Aid

Case 1   There is no printed year of 31 Ed III. The case has no citation in the early abridgments

Michaelis
46 Ed III   (2) **In a formedon,** the tenant showed how the land had descended to him and to one F, who made partition of these acres in demand and another acre, and he prayed aid, etc. HAMOND You yourself remain seised of both acres, judgment if the aid BELKNAP· Inasmuch as you

deny the partition and do not show how your sister enfeoffed us, judgment, etc , for although we cannot recover *pro rata portione* we shall have the paramount warranty THORPE It appears that you cannot have the warranty for your part alone.   And in many cases the law is so, for if the action be brought by two coparceners, and one admits the action of the demandant, the other can vouch FYNCHEDEN It is true   The law is the same as to a livery made to them as in the case of joint tenants, etc THORPE So here, for in both cases when he shows his livery he shall aid himself by special matter, and show how his companion would not vouch, or that he had made a feoffment, and unless he shows such special matter the vouchee can drive him out of the place, etc   Wherefore, to my mind, the cases are all one, but yet the demandant cannot take advantage of that, etc.

The case has not been identified in Y B Mich 46 Ed III, p 31, pl 33, or in the early abridgments   Case 2

COUNTREPLEEZ DE RESCEIPTE

See of Counterpleas de Receipt in the title of Receipt

COSYNAGE [31]

(1) **In a writ of cosinage,** the defendant pleaded in bar by a fine, to which the demandant made title, and the tenant would have waived his bar, and have pleaded to the point of the writ, to wit   that the ancestor did not die seised   And the opinion was that he should not get to that, because it is different from an Assize of Mort d'Ancestor, and also from an Assize of Novel Disseisin, if he does not admit an ouster   Statham 50 a / Paschal 40 Ed III

Reported in Y B Paschal, 40 Ed III, p 19, pl 11   See the note which refers to Statham in the margin of the reported case   Case 1

(2) **In cosinage,** the tenant said that this same ancestor had a daughter, who was the nearest heir, etc   BELKNAP.   Michaelis 44 Ed III

She was not his daughter, Ready   FYNCHEDEN   That is no
plea, unless you estrange her from the blood, as to say
that she is a bastard, or else give her another father
Which THORPE conceded

Case 2.   Reported in Y B Mich 44 Ed III, p 43, pl 50   See also Brooke,
Cosynage Aiel or Besaiel, 2, and Fitzh   Cosynage, 3

Michaelis   (3) **A writ** of cosinage was adjudged good upon the
22 Ed III   possession of his great-grandfather, etc   Contrary, Trinity,
46 Ed III,[1] and Trinity, 7, of the same king.[2]   Query as to
this, etc

Case 3   Reported in Y B Mich 22 Ed III, p 13, pl 28   See also Fitzh
Cosynage, 7

Paschal   (4) **In a writ** of cosinage on the possession of his uncle,
2 Hen V   the opinion was that the writ should be abated, inasmuch
as he could have an Assize of Mort d'Ancestor, etc

Case 4   Reported in Y B Paschal, 2 Hen V, p 1, pl 5   See also Fitzh
Cosynage, 1

[a1] Our first case makes the statement that this writ is different from
a Mort d'Ancestor   We are also told that "There is a small family of
actions which is marked off from all others by numerous procedural
distinctions, it is the family of petty assizes   There is the closest
possible affinity between the Mort d'Ancester and the action of cosynage   If I claim the seisin of my uncle, I use the one, if I claim the
seisin of a first cousin, I use the other   But procedurally the two stand
far apart "   [P & M Hist of Eng Law, 2d ed , Vol 2, 569]
    The writ of cosinage is of the time of Henry II   The only writ of
cosinage in the Note Book appears to be of the date of 1236 [20 Hen
II   Bracton, Note Book, 1215]   Again in the "earliest years of Edward
I" [Maitland, Reg of Writs, Sel Essays in Anglo-American Law, Vol
2, p 583] we find the writ of cosinage   There are a number of cases
given in the printed Year Books of Ed II   [See Fitzh Cosynage]
    In Fitzherbert's *Natura Brevium* [221 Hale's ed 508] we find our case
3 commented on, and in the next paragraph we have the case in 66
Ed III also noted, where the principles to be deduced from both
cases are stated   Fitzherbert makes this marginal note to the case in
22 Ed III   "It is admitted that tresael is cousin '   The critic of case
3 does not seem to have been aware of this

[1] See Trinity, 46 Ed III, p 15, pl 6   [2] Trinity, 7 Ed III, p 30, pl 26

CUI IN VITA [32]

(1) **Land was given** to a woman upon condition that she should sell it, and distribute the money for the alms of the feoffor And then she took a husband and he sold the same land, and distributed the money for the alms of the feoffor, according to the conditions, and died The woman shall not have a *Cui in Vita* for any part By the opinion of SHARSHULL and WILLOUGHBY in a *sub pœna.*

Hilary
34 Ed III

There is no printed year of 34 Ed III The case has not been identified in the early abridgments under the subject *Cui in Vita*

Case 1

(2) **If the husband** and his wife and a third purchase jointly and the husband alienates the whole and dies, the woman shall not have a *Cui in Vita* for any part of that while the third lives, because they can join in a writ of right, etc But if the third dies, she shall have a *Cui in Vita* for the whole And this by THORPE But if it was of a joint purchase before the coverture, she shall not have a *Cui in Vita* except for the half, no more than in a *Cui ante Divorcium*, etc In a *Cui in Vita*, well argued

Paschal
36 Ed III

There is no early printed year of 36 Ed III The case has not been identified in the early abridgments under the title of *Cui in Vita*

Case 2

[32] The innumerable cases of this writ in the Year Books show its importance in the legal life of the period Our abridgment gives so few that they give little opportunity for comment, except to call attention to the fact that this was one of the oldest writs It is found in the earliest known register [Maitland, Register of Writs, Essays in Anglo-American Law, Vol 2, p 574, writ No 39] but its life was not as long as that of the greater number of the writs It would appear that by the Act of 32 Hen VIII [32 Hen VIII, cap 28 (1540), Sec V, Stats at Large, Vol 5, p 44] the alienation of the husband without the joinder of the wife was void, and the wife had a writ of entry, so that there was no longer any need of the *Cui in Vita*, and a writ which had been most industriously used through the period previous to the Year Books and all through their long life died, as did the books themselves, in the latter years of Henry the Eighth

CERTIFICAT

Statham 51 a
Hilary
21 Ed III

(1) **If an assize** be adjourned for a difficulty as to the verdict, where the tenant pleaded to the Assize by his bailiff, and so the judgment is given in the Bench and the record remains there, and if the tenant desires to sue a certificate, he ought to have a writ to show to the justices, to bring the record before the justices of Assize, and there he shall have his certificate   The law is the same in Attaint.

Case 1

Reported in Y B Hilary, 21 Ed III, p 3, pl 8

Michaelis
12 Hen IV

(2) **One sued a certification,** and first he had a *Certiorari* against the executors of the justice of the Assize, because he was dead.   And upon this he had a certification upon the Statute of Westminster the Second and a *Scire Facias* to the party, and a *Venire Facias* to the jurors of the Assize   And then, at the *Venire Facias*, the sheriff returned that two of the jurors were dead, and upon that they adjourned the parties to [be] before them at Westminster   And many held that this adjournment was void, for the Statute speaks only of Assizes, etc   And then, in the Bench, SKRENE [said] that the certification does not lie, inasmuch as some of the jurors are dead, for it shall be presented by the same jurors, and not by others for the writ is *"Venire Facias jurat' ejusdem assisæ "*   And when they have come, none of the parties shall have a challenge to them, unless the cause of his challenge be *"Venire ex post facto,"* for it shall be considered the same jury and in the same plea as they were in the assize   HANKFORD denied this, as far as the challenge *ex post facto*, and said that it seemed that in place of those who were dead, others should be put in the jury for them, for if an inquest be charged upon an issue, and before the verdict two of them die, then a new *Scire Facias* shall not issue, but a tales to have two to be sworn with the others   So here   THIRNING   In your case a new *Venire Facias* shall issue, but it seems here that they should

plead before you proceed to that matter, for if the defendant would deny the deed upon which this certificate is sued, and the plaintiff would estop him because the deed is enrolled or some other reason, it seems the jury shall not be taken And if in the certification all the jurors make default, still the parties shall plead, as in an Assize, etc And it seems that the certification well lies, for the writ says, "*Venire Facias jurat' Assisæ*," but it does not say all the jurors of the Assize, wherefore, etc And a man shall have attaint although all the jurors are dead but one. HANKFORD. At the common law where an Assize was taken at large, and they were not well examined, in that case, before judgment, the party can have a certification to examine them better before judgment was rendered and if one juror was dead the examination would fail, And this certification shall be of the same nature, and if all the jurors do not appear, you shall not award the tales against the others who make default, but always proceed against the entire jury, to fulfill their first verdict HILARY This certification is not like that certification at the common law, of which you speak, but it is brought after judgment upon new matter and is given by the Statute But in your case the verdict is not complete until the judgment is rendered, and then it is rendered upon an entire verdict, but in this case there shall be two judgments. And they adjourned, etc And HULS said further, if the justices did not well examine the verdict, where the Assize is taken at large, the party shall have a writ of error; which HANKFORD and THIRNING denied expressly And this well argued, etc.

Reported in Y B Mich. 12 Hen IV, p 9, pl 18 See also Brooke, Case 2 Certification d'Assize, 4, and Fitzh Certificat, 3

The Statute is that of 13 Ed I, cap 25 (1285), Westminster the Second, Stats at Large, Vol 1, p 163 (198) "Of what things an Assize shall lie, Certificate of an Assize, etc " "*Venire fecerunt jurat illius assisal*"

(3) **One had recovered in an assize** in the King's Hilary Bench, at York, in the time of King Richard   And then 9 Hen IV

the King's Bench was removed to Westminster, and the tenant sued a certification out of the same Bench to the sheriff of the County of York, before the king, etc   NOR-TON   It is to be seen where this certification should issue out of this place, or out of the Chancery.   And also whether it should be returned here, for by the Statute it shall be taken in the county where, etc   GASCOIGNE   It is the common course here to do as above, and when they are at issue then it shall be taken to the county, etc , and taken in the nature of a *Nisi Prius*   And the law is the same as to an assize taken in the King's Bench, and then remanded, etc   And then the King's Bench was removed, etc , wherefore they proceeded to the matter, etc

Case 3

The case has not been identified in Y B Hilary, 9 Hen IV, or in the early abridgments

Statute of Westminster the Second, 13 Ed I, cap 25 (1285)   Stats. at Large, Vol 1, p 163 (198)

CONSCIENCE [33]

Statham 51 b

Michaelis
31 Hen VI

(1) **In the exchequer chamber,** KIRKEBY, clerk of the Rolls, related a matter which was in the Chamber — how one had made a feoffment of trust, and declared his will to the feoffee after the feoffment, that after his decease one of his daughters should have the land. And then he came to the same feoffee and said that she who should have the land would not be married by him, nor be well governed, wherefore he said that he revoked his will, and that he wished the other daughter [to have] the said land after his decease   And then he died, and the question is which of the two daughters shall have the land? LACON When he declared his will the daughter had immediately an interest in the land, which he could not defeat afterwards, no more than where a man enfeoffs me to enfeoff another, who is a stranger to his blood, he cannot revoke it afterwards, etc   ILLINGTON   *Contra*, for he does not show that the feoffment should be made to the daughter for any cause, so that the feoffor would have a *quid pro quo*, so

there was no bargain but at his mere will, which he can conscientiously change well enough   For if that daughter will not be governed by him it is not in conscience nor reason that she should have the land.   And I put the case that after he had declared his will, he himself had been in poverty, and for that reason he would require the feoffee to re-enfeoff him, is it not in conscience that the feoffee would re-enfeoff him? (As if he said it was) PRISOT Contra, for when he has declared his will, then he is as well the feoffee of the daughter as the feoffee of the feoffor And if the daughter declares her will to him, he is bound to do it after the death of the feoffor   And I think that such a declaration of his will is as strong as a condition declared upon a livery of seisin, etc.   FORTESCUE We are not arguing the law in this case, but the conscience, and it seems to me that he can change his will for a special reason, but otherwise not   And I put the case that I have issue a daughter, and I am ill, and I enfeoff a man, and say to him that my daughter shall have my land after my decease, then I revive, and I have issue a son, now it is conscience that the son shall have the land for he is my heir, for if I had a son at the time, etc , I would not have made such a will   And the law is the same if I will that one of my sons shall have the land, and then he becomes a thief   And "conscience" comes of con and scioscis And so together they make "to know with God" to wit to know the will of God as near as one reasonably can For a man can have land by our law, and by conscience he shall be damned, etc   ARDERUN If I enfeoff a man I cannot declare my will to him afterwards   Which was denied   And they adjourned.   Query, was the rest of it in the Chancery?

The case has not been identified in Y B Mich 31 Hen VI   Case I

[13] Although we have but one case under this title of Conscience, yet that case is important because of the statement of Fortescue "We are not arguing the law in this case, but the conscience " Our case is not in the Chancery, as one might well expect a case of conscience to be, but in the Exchequer.   Yet the Exchequer in its earlier existence did

among other things, "incidental justice" [P & M Hist of Eng Law, 2d ed , Vol 1 109]

Causes were often adjourned from the other courts to the Exchequer where the barons sat to resolve the difficulties, not so much as judges of the law, but, as in this case, to decide as to the right or the "conscience" of the case I have not been able to trace this jurisdiction, although it does not seem that the task should be a difficult one There is confusion among the authorities and the cases themselves require a very careful study in order that anything definite may be gotten from them

COLOUR [14]

Statham 52 a
Paschal
40 Ed III

(1) **An assize was brought** by a woman against the Prioress of Clerkenwell, who said that she leased the same land to one B, and K, his wife, for their two lives K died, and B took this plaintiff to wife, and the prioress confirmed their estate for the term of their two lives B died, and she remained in, and the defendant ousted her And this was held sufficient color

It was said by FYNCHEDEN, in the same plea, that it is good color against a woman to say that her husband died seised, and she entered claiming dower, etc.

Case 1.

Reported in Y B Paschal, 40 Ed III, p 23, pl 24 See also Brooke, Colour, 79, and Fitzh Colour, 44

Hilary
19 Hen VI

(2) **In a writ of forcible entry,** the defendant said that one A enfeoffed one B and the defendant. B died, and the plaintiff, claiming by color of a deed, by which the said B entered, and the defendant peaceably, etc , without this, etc And the color was challenged because B died before the claim And it was not allowed And it was also challenged because the color was only as to half. And it was not allowed because B could make a feoffment for the whole. But it was said that such a plea is not good if I say that my father died seised after whose death I entered, and the plaintiff claimed, as above, because there was no color to enter upon me who was in by descent, etc Query, if it be good to say that after the death of my

father the plaintiff abated and by color of such a feoffment, and so show his possession before my possession, etc ?

Reported in Y B. Hilary, 19 Hen VI, p 49, pl 4   See also Brooke, Colour, 19, and Fitzh Colour, 9   Case 2

(3) **In trespass** for a box, the defendant said that the property of the same box, a long time before, etc , was in one B, who bailed the same box to one A, to keep   And the plaintiff took it and carried it to the place where, etc , and we, as servant of B, took it, etc   And the opinion of all the Court was that this was no plea, for they said that he did not give a tortious color to the plaintiff, no more in this writ than in an Assize   Wherefore the plaintiff pleaded as before, and that the same A gave these same goods to the plaintiff, and he as servant, etc (as above)   Paschal 21 Hen VI

Reported in Y B Paschal, 21 Hen VI, p 36, pl 3   See also Brooke, Colour, 22, and Fitzh Colour, 25   Case 3

See as to colour, in the title of Assize,[1] and in the title of Bar,[2] and in the title of Trespass.[3]   Note.

" This title of color seems to belong simply to the older and now defunct mode of pleading   Yet although colorable pleading — first mentioned in the reign of Ed III [Crabb Hist of Eng Law, p 407] was an important part of pleading in the Year Books, the giving of color as a plea survived until very recent times   The older formula is of course obsolete, but the pleading founded upon it is still a part of our modern procedure   Reeves [Hist of Eng Law, Vol 3 438] seems to think that the cases in which colorable pleading was used were few prior to the reign of Ed IV   Of course our cases are all of a prior period, but they are also very few, and not of great value   Many of those in Fitzherbert are of the period of Henry VI, so it would appear that the growth of this 'device," as Reeves calls it, was quite rapid   In explaining this matter of color, Reeves [*Ib* , Vol 3, p 25] cites our case 1, of the prioress, [40 Ed III] as a typical case

The idea of the pleading was for the tenant in an assize to plead such matter in bar as would delay the assize, so "he gives the Demandant or Plaintiff a shew at first Sight that he hath good Cause of Action, when in truth it is no just Cause, but only a Colour and Face of a

[1] Statham, *supra*, pp 14 a–16 a   [2] Statham *supra*, pp 32 b–37 b
[3] Statham, *infra*, pp 170 a–174 a

Cause And it is used to the Intent that the Determination of the Action should be by the Judges, and not by an Ignorant Jury of twelve Men " [Termes de la Ley, tit Colour]

Stephen [Pleading, App p 220 and LVIII, note 51] takes us back and out of the common law, and cites Juvenal to show the connection between the old methods of pleading and the ancient rules of logic and rhetoric He also gives a clear and detailed explanation of express and implied color, and the pleading thereon as it existed at that date After the abolition of the actions of assize and the writ of entry in the nature of an assize, the device of colorable pleading could only be used in the personal action of trespass We have one case [case 3] of the writ used in this action as far back as 21 Hen VI, so that we have an historical continuity for this writ in a personal action for nearly five hundred years It is probable, indeed, that before it had been recognized as a special form of pleading it had been gradually coming into use Reeves says, after giving some of the rules, "by which these fictitious suggestions were measured," that "provided these, and some of the others of less consequence, were adhered to, the defendant was at liberty to state whatever happened to strike his mind, colours being as various as the possible ways in which the subject in question might be transferred and possessed " [Reeves, Hist of Eng Law, Vol 3 441] It is probable that the fancy of the pleaders first introduced these colorable pleas and that the rules were introduced to curb and keep them within bounds Indeed any one reading Year Book cases will, it is probable, come to that conclusion, for the arguments in those cases in which such pleading occurs inevitably leads to the conclusion that the rules concerning these pleadings were of a slow growth, and were not over well understood by many of those using it, or else — which may also be probable — that when there was a chance of giving the plaintiff color it was taken and then, if it was not allowed, the pleading was changed, as in the case from 21 Hen VI, where Markham amended his plea, it being agreed by the justices, that he had not given sufficient color to the plaintiff

CHEMYN

Trinity
3 Ed III

(1) **The royal road** is that which leads from vill to vill, and the common road is that which leads from the vill to the fields [and] their lands And this in Trespass, etc

Case 1

The case is reported in Paschal, 6 Ed III, p 23, pl 48, where Fitzh Chemin, 2, gives it I have not been able to find such a case in Trinity, 3 Ed III That this citation was an error appears from the case below

(2) **The franchise** of the Royal Road belongs to the lord of the soil, and he shall have the purpresture As appeared Trinity, 6 Ed III, placitum 1 Trinity 6 Ed III

This is apparently a reference to the case cited in the note above (case 1) The Term is not Trinity, but Paschal Case 2

CONSULTACION

(1) **Consultation shall** not be granted for a thing done before the collector of the Pope, etc See of the power of the collector of the Pope, well argued, in the same plea And this in a Consultation Statham 52 b Michaelis 2 Hen IV

Reported in Y B Mich 2 Hen IV, p 9, pl 45 See also Brooke, Consultation, 2, and Fitzh Consultation, 3 Case 1.

(2) **If a parson** of a church sues a spoliation in the Court Christian, by which a *judicavit*, which is a prohibition, is directed to the spiritual judges, if the matter be brought into the Chancery in a libel, and it appears that the matter on which he sues the spoliation is pleadable in the King's Court, or that the patronage will come into question, upon that they will not grant a consultation As appeared in a note, Anno 44 *Liber Assisarum* Anno 44 *Liber Assisarum*

And it was said in the same plea that if one who is a parson emparsoné shall not have a *Quare Impedit*, because he cannot allege that the church was void, but he shall have a spoliation, etc But yet it was denied that he should not have a spoliation, for he could have an Assize of Novel Disseisin or a writ of Trespass, or a writ of Right of Advowson, etc. Query.

(2, part 2) **And see** Anno 38 Hen VI Such matter in the Exchequer Chamber, where it was said that where an incumbent was ousted by his patron upon a suggestion that he was created a bishop, or that he had resigned, or that he had accepted another church, where there was no plurality, so that his patron presented another clerk who was admitted, Paschal 38 Hen VI there he shall have spoliation· but where another patron claims the patronage it is different, for there the right to the advowson comes into question. And see the plea in Townesend's Book, because it is good

Case 2   Reported in Y B Mich 44 Ed III, p 23, pl 19 See also Brooke, Consultation, 1, and Fitzh Consultation, 4

Part 2   Reported in Y B Hilary, 38 Hen VI, p 19, pl 1 See also Fitzh Consultation, 1 The "Book of Townesend" must have been one of the reports then extant, of which we have no remnant now existing It seems there is little doubt that there were many manuscript 'reports" circling about among the members of the bar, which were known by the names of the reporters or owners, and were used in citing cases in the courts, but were probably of very little authority

CONTRA FORMAM COLLACIONIS

Hilary
2 Hen IV

(1) **A contra formam collationis** was brought against an abbot upon an alienation made by his predecessor And it was questioned if the action lay, because the writ which is given by the Statute[1] is *"et quod ad predictum a reverti debet per alienationem quam predictus abbatis fecit"* But yet the opinion was that the writ lay well enough, etc

Case 1   Reported in Y B Hilary, 2 Hen IV, p 16, pl 24 See also Brooke, *Contra Formam Collationis*, 1, and Fitzh *Contra Formam Collationis*, 2

Michaelis
45 Ed III

(2) **If an abbot** alienates land which is of the foundation of the king, he [the king] can enter without suing a *Contra Formam*, etc. In a *Præcipe quod Reddat.*

Case 2   Reported in Y B Trinity (not Mich), 45 Ed III, p 18, pl 14 See also Fitzh *Contra Formam Collationis*, 4

Trinity
19 Ed III

(3) **A man** shall not have a *Contra Formam Collationis*, unless the abbot alienates with the convent; by the opinion of SHARSHULL and HERLE, in a *Juris d'Utrum*, because after the death of the abbot his successor can have it without the assent of the chapter, etc Query?

[1] The Statute is that of 13 Ed. I (1285), cap 41, Westminster the Second Stats at Large, Vol 1, p 163 (218)

There is no early printed year of 19 Ed III   The case has not been Case 3
identified in the Rolls Series for that year   Fitzherbert had practically
the same abridgment of the case   See Fitzh. *Contra Formam Colla-*
tionis, 5

(4) **When a man** has judgment to recover in a *Contra* Hilary
Formam Collationis, he should have a *Scire Facias* against 23 Ed III
the tenant.   And the opinion of SHARSHULL was that he
could have traversed the action of the demandant on the
same point which was tried between the demandant and
the abbot, because he was a stranger   And this in a *Scire*
Facias, etc.

There is no printed Term of Hilary, 23 Ed III   The case appears Case 4
in Fitzh *Contra Formam Collationis*, 3

(5) **If a man** gives an advowson to an abbot in free Hilary
alms, who alienates the advowson, etc , upon the next 20 Ed III
vacancy the donor shall present, because he cannot have a
Contra Formam Collationis   By the opinion of SHARSHULL
and WILLOUGHBY, in a *Quare Impedit* brought for the king
in a like case

The case is reported in Y B Hilary 20 Ed III of the Rolls Series, Case 5
Pt 1, p 102   There is no early printed year of 20 Ed III

[34] "The method by which the king executed his ecclesiastical jurisdiction by his power of committing to commissioners of his own nomina-
tion under the great seal " [Hale Analysis of the Law, p 15] This
statement is only applicable to our second case   The Commission
before whom the finding was made in our first case was the commission
which must have been issued by his letters patent under his ordinary
jurisdiction   The limitation of their power to simply inquire into the
matters brought before them is to be noted   Commissions have always
been a favorite mode of getting behind the law, they have had their
periods of prosperity and their times of desuetude   A thorough examination into the histories of commissions in the past is desirable in view of
the great popularity of the commission in the law of our present day

CONTINUANCE

(1) **In a** *Præcipe quod Reddat* against the husband and Statham 53 a
his wife, they waged their war of non-summons   And at Paschal
40 Ed III

the day, etc , the husband was essoined by a common essoin, and afterwards for service of the king, and the wife appeared. And then on another day the wife was essoined for service of the king, and the husband made default. CANDISH prayed seisin of the land because the default of the husband is the default of the husband and his wife. FYNCHEDEN The wife was essoined, and when she comes she will be received to defend her right, wherefore it seems that we should award only the Petty Cape to continue the process, etc. Query?

Case 1   Reported in Y B Paschal, 40 Ed III, p 21, pl 17

Michaelis
8 Hen V

(2) **In trespass,** the defendant said that there are two Dales within the same county and neither of them without an addition JUVN They have had "*dies datum est,*" in which case by the Statute "*de Exceptionibus*" he shall not have any challenge to the writ, unless it is of a later time And the record was looked at, and it was "*quod defendens*" and prayed a day for imparlance, etc , which they conceded, and the same day they sent a plea to the justices saying that this continuance was to emparl, to have an answer to the writ But the Statute of Exceptions is meant [to apply] where their entry is "*dies datum est partibus,*" etc , for there the writ is affirmed to be good unless the entry is, "*salvis partibus acceptionibus suis,*" etc

Case 2   Reported in Y B Mich 8 Hen V, p 8, pl 8 The Statute is that of West II, 13 Ed I (1285), cap 31 (Stats at Large, Vol 1, p 206)

(3) **If one pleads** a release after the last continuance, upon which they are at issue, on the next day or ever after, he cannot plead a release after the last continuance, for if he could do so he could delay the plea forever Query, if he pleads matter of record? It seems not, unless he shows it "*sub pede sigilli*" for otherwise there might be the same delay if the record be traversed, etc

Case 3   Statham gives no citation for this case It has not been identified

CONTRACTE [35]

(1) **If I make a contract** with a man to marry his daugh- Statham 53 b.
ter, and that I shall have a certain sum of money, if the Michaelis
contract be without deed I shall not have an action except 45 Ed III
in the Court Christian   But if it be by a deed I shall
have an action in the King's Court   And this in Debt

    The case has not been identified in Y B Mich 45 Ed III   Fitzh Case 1
Contract, 1, has a case upon a similar point, but it is apparently not the
case abridged here

(2) **If I make** a covenant with a man to be his slaughter- Paschal
man, and to kill all his oxen and sows, etc , that is a con- 3 Hen VI
tract, and I shall have an action of debt for the salary, etc.

    Reported in Y B Paschal, 3 Hen VI, p 42, pl 13   Case 2

(3) **A man** shall have an action of debt and detinue Paschal
all in the same writ, for the essoin in detinue is [as] in a plea 22 Ed III
of debt, etc

    Not identified in 22 Ed III   The case has not been identified else- Case 3.
where

---

[35] The few cases in the abridgment upon the subject of contract do
not invite us to enter the vast field of research which unfolds before us
in the mere appearance of the word on the printed page   We really
have but two cases of contract, the third case having evidently strayed
in from some other title, or, possibly it is a mere note never intended to
figure in the abridgment at all   But the bare fact that we have but
two cases shows us how slow had been the progress in the advance of
the doctrine of contract   Bracton gives us what have been called
"meagre chapters' [P & M Hist of Eng Law, 2d ed , Vol 2 194]
on contract   The main thing that we learn from it all is that at the
end of Henry III's reign our King's Court had no general doctrine of
contract
    In our second case we seem to have an epitome of the history of the
law of contract   "Covenant," "debt," "contract," are all used in the
few words of the abridgment   The history of contract was still in the
making, and these cases have but little light to throw upon it   As yet
it was undeveloped as a law, not of the covenant, not of account, not
debt, but of contract as we know it in later times

COMMISSION ET COMMISSIONERS [36]

Michaelis
8 Hen. V

(1) **If it be found** before commissioners that land is seizable into the hand of the king, still they cannot seize it unless their commission extends to it by express words, for they have no power to execute their inquiries And this in a note

Case 1

Reported in Y B Mich 8 Hen V, p 10, pl. 15

Hilary
5 Hen V

(2) **A commission issued** for the king, etc. And they found a divorce made in another county And because the divorce so found was to the advantage of the king, the opinion was that the justices should send to the bishop to certify them if there was such a divorce or not, and this, notwithstanding it was in another county And this well argued, etc

Case 2

Reported in Y B Hilary, 5 Hen V, p 2, pl 5

CORPUS CUM CAUSA [37]

Statham 54 a

Trinity
24 Ed III

(1) **One who was imprisoned** at Newgate sued an *Audita Querela*, to wit a man [did so] for him by suggestion, wherefore he had a *Scire Facias* against the party, and a writ to have the body of him who was imprisoned, without mentioning the cause And then they were at issue in the Bench upon the fact And the sheriff of London came and showed to the Court how he was condemned, etc., and delivered to them in execution, so they are chargeable, and he prayed that he be remanded WILLOUGHBY He shall be remanded, but not before the plea is ended, etc

Case 1

Reported in Y B Trinity, 24 Ed III, p 27, pl 3 See also Fitzh *Corpus cum Causa*, 22

(2) **If a man** be impleaded in the Marshalsea, he shall Michaelis 4 Hen VI have a *Corpus cum Causa* to the steward there, if the action be pending against him in the Bench, and if he be condemned there pending an action against him in the Bench it shall be void. And yet it is held by many that the Marshalsea is the oldest Court that the king has, etc. Query, shall a man have a *Corpus cum Causa* out of the Chancery to the Steward of the Marshalsea? etc

Reported in Y B Mich 4 Hen VI, p 8, pl 22 See also Fitzh **Case 2** *Corpus cum Causa*, 1

(3) **If a man** be impleaded in the Bench and he departs Michaelis 13 Hen IV without leave of the Court, and is condemned in another and lower Court, the condemnation is good And if he comes in by a *Corpus cum Causa*, upon showing this matter he shall be remanded, or the party shall have a *procedendo*

The case has not been identified in Y B Mich 13 Hen IV, or in the **Case 3** early abridgments Fitzh *Corpus cum Causa*, 21, gives it as in Hilary, 13 Hen IV, p 1, but it does not appear there

(4) **A corpus cum causa issued** out of the Common Michaelis 9 Hen VI Bench to the sheriff of London, to have the body of one W Lucy, who was arrested there pending a suit against him in the Common Bench, at the suit of the same person who affirmed the complaint, etc And because of this the opinion of the Court was that the plaintiff should be imprisoned, and should be fined for the contempt And the complaint was affirmed meanwhile between the date of the writ pending in the Common Bench, and the return of the same, etc And one had another action pending against the said W in the Common Bench, and would have counted against him, because he was in Court, and the justices would not suffer it, for BABYNGTON said that he was in the keeping of the sheriff of London, and not their charge, until the plaintiff had appeared in his action. But if he was in the care of the Court he should answer to every action, etc And the plaintiff would have counted against him in a writ of Account, which was pending against him at the suit of this same plaintiff, and he

could not until he had appeared to the writ of Debt which the *Corpus cum Causa* had mentioned, etc. Wherefore the plaintiff was demanded on this writ of Debt, and was nonsuited, wherefore the defendant was dismissed, etc

And BABYNGTON said in the same plea that one H was imprisoned in the King's Bench and was brought here into the Common Bench to answer to an action pending against him, and was put to answer it. Query, by what process was he brought in, etc?

Case 4.

Reported in Y B Mich 9 Hen VI, p 44, pl 24 See also Fitzh *Corpus cum Causa*, 2

---

[7] A word seems necessary here because of the general idea that this writ was not in general use in the early years of the reign of Ed III Hurd, *Habeas Corpus*, p 131, states that "there is a case upon this writ as early as 48 Ed III " [See also Bouvier, Dict *Habeas Corpus*] Hurd is quoting from the "Canadian Prisoners' Case" [Hill's Report, 6] Church [*Habeas Corpus*, 4] says the writ "was familiarly in use between subject and subject in the reign of Hen VI, 1422–1461 " Our first case is in 24 Ed III

We can, of course, trace the writ back into the earlier law of England even to its foreshadowings in Magna Charta, and perhaps back of that into the Roman law, this seems not to be questioned The only matter to be cleared up here, if possible, is that of the date of the appearance of the writ in the Year Books, and the period at which it came into general use I know of no data in the case except that which we have in the Year Books, since such data as we have elsewhere appears to be based upon an error due to a failure to examine the books themselves The first case I have been able to find in the Year Books is that in Trinity, 14 Ed III [Y B Trinity, 14 Ed III, Rolls Series, p 204, case 12] It is in a suit on a statute merchant, and seems in no way to have been an unusual occurrence The writ is issued out of the Chancery and appears to be a *Corpus cum Causa*, since the writ was granted upon the condition that "he be detained for that reason (that named in the suggestions to the Chancery) and no other " This takes us ten years back of the first writ of the abridgment, and goes far to show that the writ was known and used in the early days of Ed III, and probably earlier, since there is no suggestion in either the case in 14 Ed III, or in that of 24 Ed III, that there is anything unusual or novel in the procedure The usual name for the writ at that and even a much later date was *Corpus cum Causa*, and we find it so termed in the marginal notes to the Year Books

Corpus cum Causa being only one limited kind of *habeas corpus* is necessarily circumscribed in its scope, but the point for us is Are the authorities in general correct in their assumption that the requisition of the body with the cause is a comparatively late custom? From the testimony of the earlier Year Books I do not believe it was Maitland [P & M Hist of Eng Law, 2d ed , Vol 2, p 593, note 4] speaks of "the Bractonian Process which inserts a *habeas corpus* between Attachment and Distress a little later this *habeas corpus* seems to disappear" The question to be decided is, did it disappear? If it did disappear, at what time did it re-appear? Earlier than our authorities seem to suspect, evidently, but just how early? This *habeas corpus* of Bracton [Bracton, Note Book, pl 526, 527, 1370, 1376, 1407, 1408, 1420, 1421, 1446] is not the *Corpus cum Causa*, the body is to be there, but nothing is said as to the cause In these cases the defendant is attainted for defaults of certain kinds, and after attachment, and before the distress, this writ issued to bring his body before the Court The *Corpus cum Causa* is apparently used like the modern *habeas corpus*, to bring up the body of a person detained in custody and to bring the cause of the detention before the Court, very much as it is done under the later writ of Charles II [31 Car II, chap 2] In writing the history of the writ it is usual to discuss the *habeas corpus* as if it were the *"habeas cum causa '* If we are to assume that the writers on the writ of *habeas corpus* are correct we have to assume that the *habeas corpus cum causa* was founded, as far as the statute law is concerned, on Magna Charta [See Church, *Haveas Corpus*, p 70, Amos, Eng Const p 170, etc, Hallam, Const Hist etc , etc] Crabb, however, speaks of the "common law writ of *habeas corpus*," [Crabb, Hist of Eng Law, p 513] the act of Charles II being only an extension of that writ Reeves is silent on the subject Adams [Origin of the English Constitution p 244] expresses the most modern view, probably "There is a sense in which it is not wrong to say that this broader protection was secured to us by Magna Carta, and also to say the same of the other rights once erroneously supposed to be directly intended by the charter, like the jury trial, *Habeas Corpus*, and consent to taxation " He declares that what did revive them was the steady development of constitutional government [See also p 262] Mr Jenks in his Story of the *Habeas Corpus* [18 L Q Rev 64 (1902)] tells his tale most entertainingly, and sheds much light upon his subject Yet he has to say that the older statutes refer to the writ 'as a thing well known " As we follow back the story we find the same assumption everywhere The writ is accepted as a primordial fact A few vague flourishes about ancient liberties are supposed to account for its existence It would almost seem as if it were indiscreet to inquire too closely into the origin of the sacred instrument But it would be very well if some one would seek and find the clue to the true history of the writ of *Corpus cum Causa*, it has not yet been written

CUSTUME

(1) **In trespass against an abbot,** because the plaintiff held the hundred of B at fee farm of the king, by reason of which he could make an attachment and distress for the debts of the king within the same hundred, etc And he said that for a certain debt of the king he took certain cattle of one H, and the abbot made a rescous upon him The abbot said that he was seised of the manor of H, within which manor there was such a custom, and had been time, etc , that if any distress be taken within the said manor, that it would be put in the pound of the abbot of this same manor, and not be driven out of the manor, and the distress should remain there for three days, so if the party would make satisfaction within the three days, that then he should have his cattle, etc And he said that the plaintiff would have driven the cattle out of the manor and he would not allow it Judgment, etc Upon which the plaintiff demurred in judgment, inasmuch as there would not be a profit to the abbot, but a charge for keeping another's cattle And also that the king shall not be subservient [to] nor bound by such a custom as another person would be, wherefore it was adjudged that the plaintiff should recover his damages, etc.

Reported in Y B Hilary, 21 Ed III, p 4, pl 11

(2) **See the year** 22 Ed III, the custom of Gavelkind expressed, to wit where the father is hung the son shall have the land, for their custom is, *"The father to the bough, the son to the plough"* And this is taken strictly, for if the father be outlawed for felony, or abjures the realm, the son shall never have the lands, for the above reason, etc.

The case has not been identified in Y B Hilary, 22 Ed III Brooke, Customs, 54, abridges the case, but does not give any complete citation

(3) **If a man** would entitle himself by a custom which is restrained by a Statute, he can show that the custom is conformed after that Statute, as if a man should say

that in London there is a custom that they can devise to the dead hand without a license, he should show confirmation of their customs after the Statute *"de Religiosis,"* and if he can confirm it by a deed he should show it, etc. Query, if he should produce the Statute, etc? But yet it was said that a general Statute does not defeat a custom, unless it be by express words, etc

The case has not been identified in Y B Mich 7 Hen VI, or in the early abridgments   Case 3.

Statute for the Clergy, 14 Ed III (1340), Stats at Large, Vol. 1, p 494

CORODIE

(1) **The king sent to the Abbot of B,** to receive one T, his manservant, to be supported as others had been received in the time of his progenitors, etc , and at the *sicut alias vel causam*, etc , the abbot returned that he held in pure and perpetual alms, by a deed and confirmation of the progenitors of the king And also that he who was received before to such support, was [received] at the instance of the queen, etc. And upon this a *Scire Facias* issued against the abbot to bring his deeds and confirmation into the Chancery He came and demanded hearing of the record THORPE Your return is the record by which you had notice, wherefore, etc. And he said that he did not think that in this place they would force him to answer And it was not allowed And they adjourned It seems that this return was not sufficient, for it was not denied by him, although it was of the foundation of the king And although he held in free alms, still the king shall have his corody, because it is of his foundation And although none of the serving men had been admitted before, that shall not prejudice the king, if the abbot cannot discharge himself by prescription

Statham 55 a
Hilary
18 Ed III

Reported in Y B Hilary, 18 Ed III, p 2, pl 8   Case 1

(2) **Although an abbey** be not of the foundation of the king, still if the abbey holds any lands of the king,

Michaelis
24 Ed III

and the king can bind possession of the corody in the time of his progenitors, he shall have the corody for one of his men servants, etc. By the opinion of the COURT, in Contempt, etc.

Case 2

Reported in Y B Mich 24 Ed III, p 33, pl 29 See also Brooke, Corodie, 5, and Fitzh Corodie, 6

Paschal
14 Hen VI.

(3) **The King sent** a writ to the Prior of St Bartholomew of London, to admit his manservant to the corody, etc. And at the *pluries* the prior returned that in the time of King Henry the Second the same priory was a hospital, and the same King Henry made it a priory, and the same King Henry by his letters patent, granted to one H, then our predecessor upon the said foundation, that he and his successors should hold the same priory as freely as he had his crown, without this that he would aver that the king nor any of his progenitors had ever had such a corody after time of memory WAMPAGE He shows the letters-patent of Henry the Second, which are before time, etc , and he does not show an allowance of them after time, etc. And therefore this return is not sufficient For if a man has jurisdiction of the pleas, of the the grant of the king, before time, and if he does not show an allowance of that charter after time, etc , he shall not have the jurisdiction PORTYNGTON· They cannot compel the king to write to them to admit a serving man, unless he will; then their charter cannot be allowed unless for such matter. HODY If the prior had shown a confirmation after time, etc , then it had been good, but it seems that such a general grant does not conclude the king, for at the time of the grant he had no title to have a corody. And if the king enfeoff me to hold as freely as he holds his crown, still I shall hold of him by knight's service And if I alienate without license, I shall be fined So here See the plea because it was well argued, etc And there was a difference suggested between a pension and a corody, for a corody is the sustenance of a monk, and a pension is for a clerk of the king. Query, if the pension be all in money or in sustenance, etc ? And it was said that the king shall have a pension in every abbey, although

his clerk be advanced at the time of the death of the abbot.
Query, if he be advanced, if he shall have a pension for
another clerk, of the same abbey? But a corody for a
serving man is for the whole life of the serving man, etc
In the same plea.

Reported in Y B Anno 14 Hen VI, p 11, pl 43 See also Brooke, Case 3
Corodie, 6, and Fitzh Corodie, 1

CORONE ET PLEEZ DE CORONE

(1) **A woman brought** an appeal for the death of her Statham 55 b
husband against three, and one was outlawed, and the Michaelis
other two came by the exigent, and the woman declared 43 Ed III
against the two because they received the third who was
outlawed, who killed, etc. And the receiving was alleged
[to have been] in another county, and for that reason the
writ was abated, etc Wherefore they prayed to be restored
to their goods, and could not [be], because the exigent
was properly awarded And it was challenged because
the exigent should not have been awarded against the
accessories until the principal was attainted, etc. THORPE
If the appeal had been commenced before the coroner, so
that he could make known to us who are the principals
and who are the accessories, the law would then be as you
say, but this appeal is general, wherefore, etc

Reported in Y B Paschal (not Mich), 43 Ed III, p 17, pl 21 See Case 1
also Brooke, Corone, 8, and Fitzh Corone, 93

(2) **Three approvers** sued an appeal against a man at Hilary
Windsor for robberies committed in different counties 44 Ed III
according to the Statute which provides that justices
of gaol delivery shall proceed through all England, who
was taken and led before them, and pleaded "not guilty"
And a *Venire Facias* issued to each sheriff, and the defendant was found guilty at the suit of one of the appellors by
an inquest. And it was adjudged by KNYVET that he be

hung   And the chattels of the other two appellors were forfeited since he could not be attainted at their suit.

Case 2   Reported in Y B Mich (not Hilary), 44 Ed III, p 44, pl 57   See also Brooke, Corone, 13, and Fitzh   Corone, 95

The Statute is that of 4 Ed III (1330), cap 2, Stats at Large, Vol 1, p 430

Michaelis
44 Ed III

(3) **A woman** sued an appeal of rape against one B, and against two others as accessories. B did not come but the other two came, and they were indicted for the same deed, and also for burglary and other felonies done at the same time. BELKNAP prayed that they might be arraigned for the other felonies FYNCHEDEN That cannot be, for they are now attainted [at the suit of the king] And on this account the action of the woman was lost, etc   Query?

Case 3   Reported in Y B Mich 44 Ed III, p 38, pl 35   See also Brooke, Corone, 11, and Fitzh   Corone, 97

Trinity
47 Ed III

(4) **At Newgate;** at the gaol delivery, one W. Pulton, who was an approver, had appealed three, of whom one had waged battle and the others pleaded "not guilty" And then before the issue was taken the king granted to the appellor a charter of pardon   And upon that, by the advice of all the justices of England, the defendants were delivered without more.   Query, if it had been after the issue, etc.?

Case 4   Reported in Y B Trinity, 47 Ed III, p 5, pl 10. See also Brooke, Corone, 16, and Fitzh   Corone, 103

Trinity
47 Ed III

(5) **A woman** sued an appeal for the death of her husband against one who was acquitted in her suit, and then this same person who was acquitted and another were indicted for this same death, and the woman would have sued her appeal against the other, and could not, for LUDLOW said that if the defendant be acquitted, or if she be nonsuited, she shall never have another appeal, etc.   And then the other was arraigned at the suit of the king, etc.

Case 5   Reported in Y B Mich (not Trinity), 47 Ed III, p 16, pl 27 See also Fitzh   Corone, 104

(6) **An appeal** was sued before the sheriff and the coroner, for the death of a man, upon which a writ issued to the sheriff and coroner to bring the appeal into the King's Bench, who sent the appeal, etc., upon which a *Scire Facias* issued to garnish the plaintiff, because they had no day before the sheriff, and the sheriff returned that he had nothing of which to be garnished, upon which a *Sicut Alias* issued, and the sheriff returned, as above, wherefore PERSHAY prayed that the defendant might go quit, for it is not reasonable that he remain in prison, etc   FYNCHEDEN It may be that the plaintiff had [sufficient] in another county, and if the defendant now goes quit he could recover his damages   Query, etc. And the opinion was that he should go quit   And the law is the same in a *Scire Facias* which issues against the lord upon the reversal of an out-lawry, etc   But it is otherwise in detinue, for he should be garnished, or else the process might go on forever.

Reported in Y B Mich 48 Ed III, p 22, pl 2   See also Fitzh Corone, 105

Michaelis 48 Ed III

Case 6

(7) **One approver** appealed another, who came and admitted his appeal to be true, and he would have appealed many, and could not, because his admission was an attainder of the felony, for it is not the same where a man confesses a felony before a coroner and where it is at the plea of the party, etc. Which note   And also, in an appeal, the defendant cannot become an approver, for he shall not do anything to delay the plaintiff from execution, etc

There is no early printed year of 15 Ed III   There is a "note" in the Rolls Series for that year (p 310) which may be the case abridged by Statham

Trinity 15 Ed III

Case 7

(8) **In an appeal** by one under age, the defendant said that he did not think that during his nonage, etc. And the justices were of different opinions, etc   (But see, in the case of *Bullock* about the eighth year of King Henry the Sixth, it was adjudged by CHEYNE, and all the justices of England, that he shall be made to answer the appellor,

Trinity 21 Ed III

under age. And they gave as a reason, because it was his own act, and he had lost the advantage of waging battle; just as one of full age shall not have the battle where a woman brings an appeal against him, for in both cases the issue shall be taken immediately by an inquest and not by battle. And if he be indicted for this same death, they will arraign him immediately, but they will not take the inquest until the year be past, to the intent that the party may sue his appeal. And if the appeal be pending against him, they will arraign him on the indictment, but not take the inquest, for the suit of the party will be preferred, etc. But if they arraign one within the year, and he be acquitted, he is well acquitted, and there is no error, and the appellee shall go, etc)

Case 8

Reported in Y B Trinity, 21 Ed III, p 23, pl 16   See also Fitzh Corone, 114

The portion of the case in parentheses must have been added by Statham, as it dates from a period much later than the case to which it is apparently a note

Michaelis
13 Ed III

(9) **See by Herle** where the appeal abates by matter apparent, the defendant shall not be arraigned at the suit of the king upon that, etc. From this it follows that the plaintiff shall have a new appeal in that case. And he also said that in no case where the plaintiff is barred of his appeal shall the defendant be arraigned at the suit of the king, etc   Query?

Case 9

There is no early printed year of 13 Ed III   The case appears to be that reported in the Rolls Series, 13–14, Ed III, p 12, case 10

Hilary,
1 Hen VI

(10) **If an appellor** appeals another, who joins battle, and then the approver admits his appeal to be false, the defendant shall be acquitted   But if the defendant pleads "not guilty," although the plaintiff admits the appeal to be false, still he shall be arraigned at the suit of the king, and a new *Venire Facias* shall issue, etc

Case 10

There is no printed Hilary Term of 1 Hen VI   The case has not been identified in Y B Mich Hen VI (the only printed term in 1 Hen VI), or in the early abridgments.

(11) **A man** who had abjured the country came back, Statham 56 a
and would have become an appellor, and could not, etc   Hilary
19 Ed III

There is no early printed year of 19 Ed III   The case has not been Case II
identified in the Rolls Series for that year   Fitzh   Corone, 443, has the
case

(12) **If a man** be acquitted in an appeal, or upon an Paschal
19 Ed III
indictment, although there is an error in the process, the
acquittance is good, because he was arraigned upon the
original indictment, which was good, and not upon the
process   But it is otherwise where the appeal or indictment
is not sufficient, etc. *Coram Rege,* etc
And in the same plea it was decided that where the
defendant is acquitted upon an indictment or appeal which
does not appear sufficient, he shall not recover his damages because since he was attainted upon that, the plaintiff
shall not have any judgment, etc , against him, etc

There is no early printed year of 19 Ed III   The case has not been Case 12
identified in the Rolls Series for that year, or in the early abridgments

(12a) **A clerk** [under] attaint escaped and killed a man, Hilary
17 Ed III
and for this he was arraigned   And he would have appealed
and could not, by the advice of all the justices, because he
was, in a manner, out of the law through the first attaint,
etc.

Reported in Y B Hilary, 17 Ed III, p 13, pl 47   See also Fitzh Case 12a
Corone, 112

(13) **An indictment is** of no value if one of the indictors Hilary
11 Hen IV
be outlawed   And this in an indictment, etc.

Reported in Y B Mich (not Hilary), 11 Hen IV, p 11, pl 24 Case 13
See also Fitzh   Corone, 85

(14) **It is not a sufficient** indictment that *"felonice* Anno
8 Ed III
abduxit unum equum rubeum," etc   In the Eyre of Nottingham

The case has not been identified in 8 Ed III, and we have not the Case 14.
printed Eyre   We apparently have the case, however, in Y B Hilary,
2 Ed III, p 1, pl 3

(15) **An indictment** [ran] "because one led another into the fields for the whole night, so that he died of the frost", and because it was not *"felonice,"* it was held to be null   And this in an indictment

The case has not been identified in Y B Hilary, 2 Ed III, or in the early abridgments.

(16) **"Felonice** *succidit arbores et asportavit"* is not a felony.

There is no citation to this case, which is apparently but a note, and apparently was never intended to be inserted in the abridgment

(17) **In an appeal** the writ was, *"Ad respondendum"* to the plaintiff *"secundum formam statuti,"* made the year six of King Richard, etc   *"Quare uxorem suam rapuit unde cum appellat."* STRANGE   Judgment of the writ, for he has answered the plaintiff where the Statute gives no answer to the plaintiff, for his answer was at the common law. ROLFF   The Statute provides that he shall not have battle, and so it determines the answer.   STRANGE: Still, judgment of the writ, for it is not *"felonice rapuit"* but *"rapuit"* only, etc , which shall be understood to be merely a trespass   And as to the felony, "not guilty," etc   Query, to what effect he pleaded over, for the exception is matter apparent, which is triable by the record, in which case, if the exception be good, he shall not be arraigned at the suit of the king, etc.   But it is otherwise if he pleads matter of fact which is triable by an inquest, then he pleads over to the felony, for these two pleas are only triable in one manner, etc.   But in the other case one matter is triable by the record, and the other by the inquest, etc   Query'

Reported in Y B Mich (not Hilary), 1 Hen VI, p 1, pl 1   See also Fitzh   Corone, 1

The Statute is that of 6 Ric II (1382), Stat 1, cap 6   Stats at Large, Vol 2, p 252 (255)

(18) **If an appellee** be attainted before the sheriff and the coroner in the county, if it is removed the writ shall go to the coroner and not to the sheriff, and yet the appeal is not good unless it be arraigned before the sheriff in the

county, and the sheriff is judge. But that is by the Statute, to wit· that the sheriff shall control the coroner, etc., but the coroner has the record in his keeping

And it was said in the same plea that if a man in an appeal says that the plaintiff has another appeal pending, says further that the same defendant is of Dale, and not of Sale, and prays allowance, etc , he shall not have both the pleas, because one is matter of record and triable in another manner, but he can have twenty exceptions which are of one and the same nature, and pray allowance of them, "and as to the felony, not guilty " And the law is the same in an Assize of Novel Disseisin

And in the same plea the plaintiff admitted the exception of the defendant, wherefore it was held that the writ should abate And the defendant prayed to be dismissed. GRISWOLD It should be by mainprize, for he shall be arraigned at the suit of the king, upon the declaration CHEYNE That cannot be so, for the writ is abated, and so the declaration is null, etc But on a nonsuit it is as you say Wherefore it was adjudged that he should go quit Which note well, etc Well argued, etc.

Reported in Y B Hilary (not Mich), 4 Hen VI, p 15, pl 15 See Case 18 also Fitzh Corone, 4

The Statute is that of 3 Ed I (1275), cap 10, Westminster the First Stats at Large, Vol 1, p 74 (82)

(19) **In an appeal** of mayhem, where the plaintiff counted that one of the defendants mayhemed him, and the others aided and abetted him; still all are principals, as in Trespass And yet the plaintiff declared that the defendant "feloniously mayhemed," etc _{Michaelis 21 Hen VI}

Michaelis
21 Hen VI

The case has not been identified in Y B Mich 21 Hen VI Fitzh Case 19 Corone, 11, has the case, but gives no citation to page or placitum

(20) **He in whom** the property is shall have treasure trove Query, if he dies before it be found, shall his executor have it? etc It seems he shall, for "*non competit regi nisi quando nemo sit quis abscondit thesaurum,*" etc. As appeared in a case in Ireland, etc

Michaelis
22 Hen VI

The case has not been identified in Y B Mich 22 Hen VI, or in Case 20 the early abridgments

Michaelis
7 Hen IV

(21) "He who incites a man to kill another is a principal,"
if he be present at the time the felony is done.   As appeared
in an Appeal.

Case 21

Reported in Y B Mich 7 Hen IV, p 27, pl 4.   See also Brooke,
Corone, 19, and Fitzh Corone, 80

Michaelis
21 Hen VI

(22) **In an appeal** of death against two, one as principal
and the other as accessory, the accused waged battle and the
plaintiff demurred upon the plea   CHOKE The Statute is
that the accessory shall not be bound to answer until the
principal is attainted or acquitted FORTESCUE. The Statute
has always required that the accused shall answer immediately, but the issue shall not be tried until the principal
is attainted or acquitted.   And if the principal be acquitted
the other issue shall not be tried   In which all concurred
And also if the accused will pray that inquest be taken,
and waives the advantage of the Statute, we have no power
to prevent it, etc WAMPAGE The defendant pleaded
this plea by fraud, because he would not be arraigned at the
suit of the king   And this clearly appears, for it is no plea
And if, in an Appeal, the defendant pleads a release enrolled,
bearing date while the writ is pending, still he shall be
arraigned at the suit of the king, because it was done by
fraud between them, to wit. the plaintiff and himself,
so here, etc   Query?

Case 22

The case has not been identified in Y B. Mich 21 Hen VI   Fitzh
Corone, 10, has the case
The Statute is that of 3 Ed I (1275), cap 14, Westminster the First
Stats at Large, Vol 1, p 74 (83)

Paschal
30 Hen VI

(23) **In an appeal of robbery** against a prior, he said
that the plaintiff was his villein, etc   And then the plaintiff was nonsuited   The defendant prayed to be dismissed
CHOKE He shall be arraigned at the suit of the king,
because the declaration is of record   WANGFORD That
he shall not, inasmuch as he pleaded a plea which goes to the
action, and when the plaintiff is nonsuited, the plea shall be
understood to be true, as well as if the plaintiff had demurred
in law upon him, and it had been adjudged against the

plaintiff, or tried against the plaintiff by an inquest, the Statham 56 b defendant in these cases shall not be arraigned. FORTESCUE I grant that your cases are clear, but this case is not like them, for when he is nonsuited nothing concludes him Wherefore he was arraigned, etc.

And he said in the same plea that if the defendant says, in an Appeal, that the plaintiff is a bastard, or pleads another plea in bar, which is adjudged or tried against him, still he shall not be attainted for the felony, but there shall be an inquiry into the felony as well as in an Attaint, or an Assize, where no ouster is expressly admitted, the disseisin shall be inquired into   So it shall be in an Appeal, when it is not expressly admitted, etc   And although in an Appeal the defendant pleads in bar, and does not plead over to the felony, still the felony shall be inquired into, if the bar be adjudged or found against him, as well as in an Attaint or an Assize where the defendant takes an exception, and does not say, "And if it be found," etc , still it shall be inquired into, to wit   into the indictment in an Attaint, and into the disseisin in an Assize; and so in the other cases, and even more because it expedites matters

There is only a very short printed year of 30 Hen VI Paschal Case 23 Term has only a few cases, and this case does not appear among them It has not been identified in the early abridgments

(24) **One was taken** out of the sanctuary, etc , and put in Hilary prison, since he was indicted because he killed his master. 21 Ed III And then he became an approver and appealed one J And afterwards he was nonsuited and prayed to be restored to the sanctuary SHARSHULL. That shall not be, because you have become an approver, in which case, by the law, you shall be hung immediately, unless the king prolong your life for his advantage   Whereupon it was adjudged that he be hung, but not that he be drawn, because he was nonsuited, etc. (Query, what the nonsuit had to do with it? For I do not know)

Reported in Y B Hilary, 21 Ed III, p 17, pl 21   See also Brooke, Case 24 Corone, 38, and Fitzh Corone, 447 The remark at the end of the case is one of those which go to show that Statham himself did not revise his work

**Paschal
21 Ed III**

(25) **One was** committed to prison because he was attainted for a certain trespass, and he would have become an approver and could not, because the cause of his imprisonment was only a trespass, etc   In a note   Query? For from this it follows that a man cannot become an approver unless he be indicted for felony, or put in prison upon suspicion of felony, and he who is appealed for the death of a man can become an approver, etc

Case 25

Reported in Y. B. Paschal, 21 Ed. III, p 18, pl 24   See also Brooke, Corone, 41, and Fitzh   Corone, 448

**Paschal
21 Ed III**

(26) **One was indicted** for a felony, and pleaded not guilty, and the inquest was charged, and then he would have become an approver and could not, because the inquest shall not be discharged, but the Court shall hear him and such as he accuses, and the sheriff shall indict them in his torn, etc   Query well.   In a note, etc

Case 26

Reported in Y. B. Paschal, 21 Ed. III, p 18, pl 25   See also Brooke, Corone, 42, and Fitzh   Corone, 449

**Hilary
21 Hen VI**

(27) **One became** an approver at Newgate, before Sir Richard Newton, and then a coroner was assigned to him, etc   And so see that he confessed the felony before the justices, etc.   Query, if the justices were absent if he could demand the coroner, and become an approver, etc ?   And the justices gave him three days space with the coroner And note that he shall never more appeal after that time, etc.

And on the same day another was arraigned because he had abjured the realm, and he was taken out of the high road   He said that he went out of the high road ignorantly, and as soon as he knew that he was out of the road he went to the constable and prayed him to put him on the road, and he took him and arrested him, etc.   And this matter was found, and he went quit, and he was commanded to keep the high road, nor henceforth, etc.

Case 27

The case has not been identified in Y B Hilary, 21 Hen VI, or in the early abridgments

(28) **One was arraigned** because he received one who was an attainted clerk, and the justices would not take the inquest because the clerk might be purged, etc.

The case has not been identified in Y B Hilary, 41 Ed III   Fitzh Corone, 450, has the case

(29) **One was arraigned** because he stole two sheep of the price of twenty pence   And the inquest said that he was guilty, but they said that the sheep were worth only ten pence, wherefore he was remanded to prison to do his penance, and at the next sessions he shall be delivered, etc

The case has not been identified in Y B Hilary, 41 Ed III   Fitzh Corone, 451, has the case

(30) **One was arraigned** at the suit of the king, because the appellor was an approver and was hung   The defendant said that that approver was outlawed, and he showed the record   THORPE   He is dead, and if he were alive he could, perchance, show a charter of pardon, wherefore sue in the Chancery to assure us that he had no charter, and then you will be delivered   Query? For it seems that the outlawry was nothing to the purpose, for that was the suit of the king, then if he would plead a release of the plaintiff who is dead, or a nonsuit, that would not aid him, for that release does not injure the king, no more than a release from the king shall injure the party.   In an Appeal, etc.

Reported in Y B Paschal, 21 Ed III, p 17, pl 20   See also Brooke, Corone, 37, and Fitzh   Corone, 452

(31) **An approver** was hung through the testimony of the sheriff and the coroner that he had appealed certain people whom he did not know, in order to prolong his life   And this is in a note, etc

Reported in Y B Paschal, 25 Ed III, p 85, pl 34   See also Fitzh Corone, 133

(32) **One was arraigned** for the death of one H, and it was found that he was not guilty   And they were charged

to find who killed him, etc. Wherefore they indicted another And this in a note.

Case 32   Reported in Y B Paschal, 21 Ed III, p 17, pl 22 See also Brooke, Corone, 39, and Fitzh Corone, 453

Hilary
7 Hen IV

(33) **See in a writ** of Error in the Common Bench, that it was held by THIRNING that in every case of felony, where a man is indicted as a principal and afterwards has a charter of pardon, or else he abjures the realm, the accessory, in that case, shall not be arraigned, for when the life of the principal is pardoned by the law in whatever manner it may be, that felony is extinct in his person, and consequently he is acquitted, and for the same reason the accessory is acquitted, etc Query, if the principal resorts to his clergy?

Case 33   The case has not been identified in Y B Hilary, 7 Hen IV, or in the early abridgments

Trinity
43 Ed III

(34) **If one be taken** upon suspicion of felony, and delivered to a bailiff, and he suffers him to go, and then he who escaped is indicted for the same felony, the bailiff shall be charged for an escape

Case 34   The case has not been identified in Y B Trinity, 43 Ed III Fitzh Corone, 454, has the case

Trinity
47 Ed III

(35) **If a man** who has lands in the right of his wife be attainted of felony, his lands shall be forfeited for the term of his life And HERLE said that if before the attainder he and his wife are disseised, and afterwards he is attainted and restored to the peace, still they cannot have the Assize, etc.

Case 35   The case has not been identified in Y B Trinity, 47 Ed III, or in the early abridgments

Statham 57 a
Hilary
33 Ed III.

(36) **If a man** be attainted for felony he shall forfeit all the lands that he had the day the felony was committed But it is otherwise as to his chattels, for if they are sold before the attainder the sale is good, etc. In a *Scire Facias*.

Case 36   There is no printed year of 33 Ed III. The case has not been identified elsewhere

(37) **If an exigent** of felony be adjudged against a man, and the exigent is erroneously awarded, he can have a writ of error before the outlawry is pronounced, but if the exigent be well awarded, and afterwards he is outlawed, and he reverses the outlawry, because he was imprisoned at the time the outlawry was pronounced, still his goods are forfeited forever   As appeared in the case of *Powny-ing*, where an exigent of felony was awarded against him, at which time, and also at the time the outlawry was pronounced, he was imprisoned in the Tower by the King's command   And he desired to have a writ of error, and he assigned for error that he was imprisoned at the time the outlawry was pronounced with the intention of being restored to his goods   And the opinion of the justices was that he should have the advantage of having been imprisoned at the time the exigent was awarded   But they counselled him that after the reversal of the outlawry he should sue to the king to be restored to his goods   And so note that immediately after the exigent is awarded, his goods are forfeited forever, etc   And from this it follows that he shall forfeit all the goods that he had the day the exigent was awarded; and this is contrary to the case above, to wit Anno 33, etc [1] But it is otherwise where an exigent is awarded in a personal action, for there, by the reversal of the outlawry, his goods are saved   And also if he appears the day of the return of the exigent, he will save his goods, for upon such an exigent they are not forfeited. But yet some say that the escheator can seize them, etc

Michaelis
30 Hen VI

The case has not been identified in Y B Mich 30 Hen VI, or in the early abridgments   Case 37

(38) **If one be indicted** *"super visum corporis"* before the coroner for the death of a man, and it be found that he fled, all his goods are forfeited immediately, although he be acquitted afterwards, etc   Query, as to the reason, for if one be indicted before other justices the law is otherwise. But yet, if he be indicted before other justices, and is acquitted and it be found that he fled, still he shall forfeit his goods for that contumacy. And see that before the

Michaelis
5 Hen IV

[1] Case 36, *supra*

coroner immediately upon his indictment, the vill shall be made answerable at once for his goods if it be found that he fled, and otherwise not

The case has not been identified in Y B Mich 5 Hen IV The only printed term of 5 Hen V, is that of Hilary The case has not been identified in the early abridgments

(39) **Fortescue asked** of the serjeants If a woman be indicted because she has carried away the goods of her husband, shall she be arraigned upon such an indictment? PORTYNGTON It seems to me she shall not, for the property cannot be in the wife unless it be in the husband WAMPAGE If she carries them away and gives them to another that divests the property of the husband FORTESCUE In your case it is only a trespass, and the husband shall have a writ of Trespass, for the entire tort shall be placed upon him who took the goods of the woman, and I do not know how she can be arraigned, etc.

The case has not been identified in Y B Hilary, 21 Hen VI, or in the early abridgments

See of presentment, in the title of Dower, Mich 41 Ed III

(40) **If the king** has a hundred within which I have a manor, and the king grants the view of frankpledge of my tenants of the said manor Query, if the ministers and officers of the hundred shall take presentment of the things done in my manor, etc ?

And it was said by SHARSHULL that of things presented to me when I am lord of the same manor they shall take, etc , but not of my tenants, for then they would be charged twice for one and the same thing

The case has not been identified in Y B Hilary, 21 Ed III, or in the early abridgments

(41) **Where the ordinary** accepts one to his clergy who is not a clerk, he shall forfeit his temporalities By SHARSHULL, etc From this it follows that the ordinary can accept one, although he does not know how to read In an Appeal, etc.

There is no printed year of 34 Ed III The case has not been identified in the early abridgments

(42) **One A beat one B** upon the head so that he was in despair of his life. A was arrested and delivered to two constables who had him in keeping by their assent. And afterwards they let him go. And B died, and A was indicted for his death And the opinion of many was that the constables should be held to answer to the felony, etc. Query, how and in what manner? etc , if the law is so, for it seems that it is only an escape, etc. But it is otherwise where one is indicted and delivered to the gaoler, etc Query?

The case has not been identified in Y B Mich 11 Hen IV, or in the early abridgments

(43) **One was indicted** for certain goods carried away, which belonged to the king. And because it was learned by the Court that a general pardon was granted afterwards, etc., the king counted against him in the nature of a trespass And the opinion was that he should not be held to answer to that without a new original, since the indictment was void, whereupon the defendant waived the advantage of the pardon and said that one of the indictors was outlawed at the time, etc. And for that reason the indictment was annulled Which note But yet such a general pardon is not good unless he shows a charter, etc , unless it be by authority of Parliament, etc. (That was the case of this pardon.)

The case has not been identified in Y. B Hilary, 11 Hen IV, or in the early abridgments

(44) **If a man wounds** another in one county, who dies of it in another county, the opinion of HANKFORD was that he could have his appeal in either county, etc

The case has not been identified in Y. B Paschal, 11 Hen. IV, or in the early abridgments

(45) **In the exchequer chamber,** FORTESCUE showed how an approver had appealed many in different counties, and that some were attainted by process, and against some the process was still pending, and not yet determined,

and that it seemed to them of the King's Bench that his appeal was suspicious, for they had inquired of the solid people of the country where they were appealed, who said that there are no such persons living to their knowledge. And he asked them if for this the said approver should be hung? GODEREDE The appellee has two answers, one, by battle, another, by inquest, and if the appellor be hung, he has lost one of them, to wit wager of battle PASTON So have they when the appellor is non-suited and *à fortiori* here, when it is the act of the justices And FORTESCUE showed a record of the Eyre of North[ampton] [showing]

Statham 57 b how an approver had appealed many and some of them were attainted by battle, and process was pending against the others; and because the appell[or] was suspected he was hung, etc. And also an approver was demanded when the sheriff returned that the appellee was not found, and he said that the appellee was in Flanders And because, although the appellee was outlawed, that afterwards when he came back it could be reversed for such a reason — that he was out of the realm — it was adjudged that he be hung, etc And all the justices and serjeants except GODEREDE held that he should be hung, etc

Case 45   Reported in Y B Paschal, 21 Hen VI, p 34, pl 1 See also Brooke, Corone, 49, and Fitzh Corone, 56

Hilary
9 Hen IV

(46) One was indicted before Justices of the Peace, who admitted the felony and appealed others, and his appeal was held void here in the King's Bench, because the Justices of the Peace had not power to assign a coroner to him, etc

And it was said in the same plea that Justices of the Peace have not power to inquire as to the death of a man nor of high treason, unless they have a special commission, for by their general commission they have not the power, etc.

Case 46   Reported in Y B Mich (not Hilary), 9 Hen IV, p 24, pl 1 See also Brooke, Corone, 25, and Fitzh Corone, 457

Trinity
9 Hen IV

(47) An appeal was sued by a woman against one H, who said that formerly the same woman brought an appeal for the same death before justices of gaol delivery in the county of S, against one F, who was attainted at her suit, and he prayed allowance for this, and as to the felony "not guilty," etc.   But yet in an appeal of the year 18 Ed III, the defendant said that the plaintiff was his villein, and did not answer to the felony, and he had the plea, where SHARSHULL said that the law is the same of an outlawry or excommunication, etc   But yet the opinion at this time is that he does not plead over, still if his bar be found against him they shall inquire as to the felony, etc   SKRENE· That which he pleads is not to the purpose, for the justices of gaol delivery have no power to take any appeal except against those who are in their prison, so we have no power to do otherwise except to have separate appeals   GASCOIGNE   She could have sued her appeal here against all, or else in the county, and had it removed by a writ   Wherefore it was adjudged that she take nothing

Reported in Y B Mich (not Trinity), 9 Hen IV, p 1, pl 7   See Case 47 also Fitzh Corone, 77

(48) **If one rob me** in one county and takes the goods   Hilary into other counties, I shall have my appeal in whatever   9 Hen IV county the goods come   And so it was held in this plea In an Appeal, etc

The case has not been identified in Y B 9 Hen IV   There is no   Case 48 printed Hilary Term for this reign   The case has not been identified in the early abridgments

(49) **One was arraigned** for robbery and stood mute, and   Michaelis an inquest of the servants of the Marshal was taken to   8 Hen IV inquire if he did it of malice, etc , and they found he did, etc   Query, if the robbery was in another county if the same inquest would inquire if the plaintiff made fresh suit, and if they were his goods, etc.?   And if, in such a case, the defendant shall forfeit his goods or chattels, etc ? See the plea, because it was well argued

Reported in Y B Mich 8 Hen IV, p 1, pl 2   See also Brooke,   Case 49 Corone, 21, and Fitzh Corone, 71

Michaelis
8 Hen IV

(50) **A man who had abjured** was taken, and it was asked of him if he had anything to say why he should not be hung. He said that he was taken out of sanctuary, against his will, and he prayed to be restored And the attorney of the king averred the contrary, and upon that a *Venire Facias* issued, returnable on a certain day; on which day he stood mute, and the inquest was taken, and found against the thief And the justices commanded the same inquest to inquire if he held himself mute maliciously. They said he did. But yet TYRWHIT and others said that there was no need to inquire as to that, inasmuch as he had admitted the felony before, upon which admission he should be hung Wherefore it was adjudged that he should be hung. And then he pleaded, and said that he was a clerk and had his clergy Which note, inasmuch as it was after judgment *Simile*, Anno 28 Hen VI, where one was condemned and taken away and led to the gallows, and there he said that he was a clerk, and was brought before FORTESCUE and had his clergy, etc

Case 50

Reported in Y B Mich 8 Hen IV, p 3, pl 5 See also Brooke, Corone, 22, and Fitzh Corone, 72

Hilary
8 Hen IV

(51) **It is not mayhem** to cut a man's ear, by which he loses his hearing, etc , but to knock out his teeth is mayhem, because they can be a defence to him in battle

Case 51

The case of Mayhem reported in Y B Paschal, 8 Hen IV, p 21, pl 1, does not contain the point made by Statham The MS case may have it in the argument, however Fitzh Corone, 74, has the case on a point borne out by the report

Michaelis
30 Hen VI

(52) **One J. Grant** was indicted in the King's Bench, because that at A, etc , one U beat him, etc , and twenty sacks of the price, etc., feloniously took, etc. And it was challenged because it should be "twenty sacks of this U," for he did not allege in whom the sacks were And notwithstanding that, the indictment was adjudged good, etc

Case 52

The case has not been identified in Y B Mich 30 Hen VI, or in the early abridgments.

Paschal
27 Hen VI

(53) **One J. Warren** was indicted in the King's Bench because he was reported to have made one hundred shillings

by alchemy "*ad instar pecunie domine regis* at Westminster." And he was arraigned and found guilty. And it was moved that the indictment was not sufficient, because he did not state certainly what money it was: to wit, groates or pennies ILLINGWORTH The indictment is good, for it shall be taken most favorably for the king. As if a man be indicted because he has killed a certain man unwittingly, that is good, and yet in an appeal it is of no value. And a man shall have a writ of detinue for a bag with money, sealed up, to wit one hundred pounds, and yet it is uncertain what money it is; and yet he shall recover the bag with the money. FORTESCUE In your case it is certain that such a man was killed, but it is not certain in this case, for if he made one penny he is a traitor. But in your case of the sealed bag he shall not say how much of the money was in the bag. But yet, query? For it might be that the bag and the money were lost. And then the indictment was annulled, etc.

There is no Paschal Term of 27 Hen VI, in the printed year books Case 53
The case has not been identified in the early abridgments

(54) **Where the younger**[1] brother kills his older brother, Michaelis 28 Hen VI
the youngest brother shall have the appeal, and yet he is not the heir And the law is the same where the wife kills the husband, the heir shall have the appeal And this is because of the heinousness [of the crime] And this by FORTESCUE in an Appeal

The case has not been identified in Y B Mich 28 Hen VI, or in the Case 54
early abridgments

(55) **In an appeal,** the defendant said that the plaintiff Michaelis 28 Hen VI
was a bastard, and he was certified to be legitimate, and the defendant was received to plead "not guilty" because at the beginning, when he alleged the bastardy, he could not plead over to the felony, because it shall not be tried Statham 58 a
at the same trial that the bastardy shall be tried, etc As when in an Assize the defendant says that the plaintiff is a bastard, and the bishop certifies that he is legitimate, still the Assize shall be taken, although one record is

[1] Between the oldest and the youngest

certified against him For the above reason, query, if a man pleads a plea in an Appeal which is triable in another county, shall he plead over to the felony, etc, because it demands two trials, etc?

Case 55   The case has not been identified in Y B Mich 28 Hen VI, or in the early abridgments

Michaelis 28 Hen VI   (56) **In an appeal** of robbery, can the plaintiff oust the defendant from waging battle, inasmuch as he was taken with the booty, or other sure proof of it, if it be a thing which could not be carried there? etc The defendant shall not have anything [to say] as to that By FORTESCUE, etc

Case 56   The case has not been identified in Y B Mich 28 Hen VI, or in the early abridgments

Paschal 30 Hen VI   (57) **In the exchequer chamber,** MARKHAM held that if a man be outlawed for felony he shall forfeit no lands but such lands as he had the day the outlawry was pronounced, for he is not attainted of felony, but he shall forfeit his goods and lands for the contumacy, for if the king pardons the outlawry, still he shall be arraigned for the felony, and this proves that he was not attainted of felony. FORTESCUE and all the other justices held the contrary, for they said that as soon as the principal in an appeal is outlawed, the accessory shall be made to answer, which is an attainder in law, etc And yet if the principal be dead, the accessory shall never be arraigned, etc

Case 57   The case has not been identified in Y B Paschal, 30 Hen VI, or in the early abridgments

Anno 44 Ed III   (58) **It was presented** that a Lombard had increased the price of merchandise by subtilty And it was challenged because the presentment was not sufficient KNYVET A man came to Cotteswold, and said in the country that no wools should be sold that year, with the idea of increasing the price of the wool, by which means the price was decreased through all the country. And he was taken and set before the king, and could not deny it, wherefore it was adjudged that he make a fine and ransom, so here

Wherefore the defendant pleaded "not guilty." And this
Coram Rege.

The case has not been identified in Y B Anno 44 Ed III, or in the Case 58
early abridgments

(59) **The party** shall not be restored to his goods upon Hilary
an indictment for robbery, although it be found that he 22 Ed III
made fresh suit, unless he sues an Appeal, etc. Query, if a
man shall have an appeal of felony, etc , to wit any other
felony than that of robbery, etc ? As of goods carried
away, etc , and like damage?

And see in the same plea, two were robbed who had
goods in common, and one of them sued an Appeal, etc ,
but no exception was taken to the writ Therefore, for that,
query, etc ? And one of the defendants became an approver
and appealed two men of London upon which a writ issued
to the sheriff of London to take them, who returned that
there were not any such two persons in the city And
the approver said that they were in the vill of Lincoln, and
he was not received to that, but was hung, etc

The case has not been identified in Hilary, 22 Ed III, or in the Case 59
early abridgments

(60) **A woman** was found guilty, and was a clerk, and the Hilary
ordinary demanded her as a member of the church And 22 Ed III
because she was indicted for other ordinary felonies, the
ordinary could not have her until she was arraigned for
them, etc

The case has not been identified in Y B Hilary, 22 Ed II, or in the Case 60
early abridgments

(61) **If the thief** escape and the gaoler loses sight of Hilary
him at any time, although he takes him, still it shall be 22 Ed III
judged an escape As appeared in an escape out of the
Castle of Canterbury

The case has not been identified in Y B Hilary, 22 Ed III, or in the Case 61
early abridgments

(62) **In a franchise** where they have infangthief, etc , Hilary
although a thief be taken for larceny, and he admits it 22 Ed III

before the seneschal, still he cannot proceed to judgment, unless he puts himself on the country for good and evil, etc , for it is not in the power of any Court Baron to take such jurisdiction, etc.

Case 62   The case has not been identified in Y B Hilary, 22 Ed III   See also Fitzh Corone, 237

Paschal 22 Ed III   (63) **When anyone** is feloniously killed by day, unless the felon is captured, all the vill shall be charged, etc. By SHARSHULL.   Query, if shall be called an Escape or an Amercement?

Case 63   The case has not been identified in Y B Paschal, 22 Ed III   See Fitzh Corone, 238

Paschal 22 Ed III   (64) **One who was** indicted of a felony and thereof was found guilty, said that the king took him away, and for this he produced a charter that the king led him into Gascony in the army, etc   And they said the charter should be allowed

Case 64   The case has not been identified in Y B Paschal, 22 Ed III   See Fitzh Corone, 239

Paschal 22 Ed III   (65) **A certain woman** was condemned for theft, and it was counted that she was pregnant, and she was adjudged to prison until she should be delivered, etc

Case 65   The case has not been identified in Y B Paschal, 22 Ed III   See Fitzh Corone, 240

Paschal 22 Ed III   (66) **The treasure** found belongs to my lord the king, and not to the lord of the franchise, nor is it by special words And this in a Presentment, or else in a Prescription, etc

Case 66   The case has not been identified in Y B Paschal, 22 Ed III   See Fitzh Corone, 241

Paschal 22 Ed III   (67) **A man** was in prison for larceny, and his keeper gave him leave to go to another vill and come back, and because he was found out of the boundaries of the prison it was held to be an escape, etc

Case 67   The case has not been identified in Y B Paschal, 22 Ed III   Fitzh Corone, 242, has the case

(68) **Coroners** can record a breaking of prison, and by Paschal
22 Ed III that record at the *Nisi Prius* prosecutors were hung without having had an answer. So cases of imprisonment made a felony, etc.

The case has not been identified in Y B Paschal, 22 Ed III   See Case 68 Fitzh Corone, 243

(69) **It was presented** that a certain lunatic struck him- Paschal
22 Ed III self with his knife and afterwards recovered from his infirmities, and he had a jury of the church, and he died because of his wounds, and his chattels were not forfeited

The case has not been identified in Y B Paschal, 22 Ed III   See Case 69 Fitzh Corone, 244

(70) **If a clergyman** or rector be convicted for a felony, Paschal
22 Ed III all his goods shall be confiscated, and the tithes [he has] received, if they are in the sanctuary, etc

The case has not been identified in Y B Paschal, 22 Ed III   See Case 70 Fitzh Corone, 245

(71) **If the sheriff** allows a man to have mainprise Hilary
25 Ed III where he is [not] mainpernable, it is an escape if the cause be a felony, etc   In a note

The case has not been identified in Y B Hilary, 25 Ed III   See Case 71 Fitzh Corone, 246

(72) **He who confesses** a felony, before justices, nor he Trinity
I Ed III
in a Note who is attainted at the suit of the party in an Appeal, nor he who was forsworn, shall not make their purgation, etc So it was held by all the justices, Anno 9 Hen VI   And, by the opinion of SPIGORNEL, a common thief shall not make his purgation   In the Eyre of Cornwall, folio 3

The case has not been identified in Y B Trinity, 1 Ed III   See Case 72 Fitzh Corone, 247

(73) **An escape** cannot be adjudged against he who Statham 58 b
Paschal
22 Ed III himself, etc , is committed for trespass

The case has not been identified in Y B Paschal, 22 Ed III   See Case 73 Fitzh Corone, 248

**Paschal
22 Ed III**

(74) **A certain monk** was indicted for a felony, who said that he was a clerk And he who was Abbot of B, who was present, took him as one professed. And he was admitted to do this in the place of the ordinary, etc

Case 74

The case has not been identified in Y B Paschal, 22 Ed III See Fitzh Corone, 249

**Paschal
22 Ed III**

(75) **A clerk** committed [to prison] that killed his keeper and ran away, and afterwards was retaken, and notwithstanding his clerkship he was hung, for WILLOUGHBY said that it was against the law to invoke the aid for one was legally committed.

Case 75.

The case has not been identified in Y B Paschal, 22 Ed III See Fitzh Corone, 250

**Paschal
22 Ed III**

(76) **One was taken** at the suit of the party and led toward the prison, and on the way he escaped And when the plaintiff counted against him in his Appeal, he would have waged battle, and could not because he had broken prison, etc , although they were at issue that he did not escape out of the keeping of the ministers [of justice] Query, if that shall be the end of it all?

Case 76

The case has not been identified in Y B Paschal, 22 Ed III See Fitzh Corone, 251

**Paschal
22 Ed III**

(77) **If the principal** take himself to his clergy the accessory shall not be arraigned, because it may be that the principal will be purged.

Case 77

The case has not been identified in Y B Paschal, 22 Ed III See Fitzh Corone, 252

**Trinity
22 Ed III**

(78) **A woman** was found guilty, and because she was *enceinte* she remained in prison until, etc   And afterwards she was brought to the Bar and said that she was again *enceinte* And because she lost her answer the first time, she was hung, etc

Case 78

The case has not been identified in Y B Trinity, 22 Ed III See Fitzh Corone, 253

(79) **Although a man** who is a clerk will not betake himself to his clergy, and the justices know well that he is a clerk, they will not give judgment to hang him. As happened in the case of *Lacy* Trinity
22 Ed III

The case has not been identified in Y. B Trinity, 22 Ed III See Case 79 Fitzh Corone, 254

(80) **An approver** disavowed his appellee, who said that he did it through duress And the coroner said that it was of his free will, and by the record of the coroner he was hung But yet in such cases one has such an answer. And it was inquired into by the nearest neighbors to the prison, etc Anno 13 Ed II. Trinity
22 Ed III

The case has not been identified in Y B Trinity, 22 Ed III See Case 80 Fitzh Corone, 255

(81) **One was** indicted *"eo quod felonice succidit arbores et asportavit eas "* And it was moved that this could not be called a felony, because it could not be done without taking much time, and also *"felonice succidit"* is not good, as it seems, etc Trinity
22 Ed III

The case has not been identified in Y B Trinity, 22 Ed III See Case 81 Fitzh Corone, 256

(82) **The ordinary** refused a clerk, because, before that time, he broke prison Wherefore he was hung, etc. Trinity
22 Ed III
And see, in the same plea, that if the ordinary challenges one who is no clerk, he shall lose his temporalities, etc.

The case has not been identified in Y B Trinity, 22 Ed III See Case 82 Fitzh Corone, 257

(83) **A thief killed** a merchant, and the journeymen of the merchant pursued him and killed him, and this was not held a felony, etc. Trinity
22 Ed III

The case has not been identified in Y B Trinity, 22 Ed III See Case 83 Fitzh Corone, 258

(84) **It was presented** that a man strangled himself with a cord; and it was adjudged that his goods were for- Trinity
22 Ed III

feited and his lands, because "*felo de se, non domine*," *causa patet.*

Case 84   The case has not been identified in Y B Trinity, 22 Ed III See Fitzh Corone, 259

Trinity 22 Ed. III   (85)   **A principal** had a charter of pardon, and yet the accessory was arraigned, since the principal was acquitted by grace of the king and not by course of law

Case 85   The case has not been identified in Y B. Trinity, 22 Ed III See Fitzh Corone, 260

Trinity 22 Ed III   (86)   **Where a man** justifies the death of another, as by a warrant to arrest him and he would not obey him, etc , or that he came to his house to commit a burglary, and such like matter, if the matter be so found, the justices will let him go free, without the grace of the king But it is otherwise where a man kills another by accident, etc

Case 86   The case has not been identified in Y B Trinity, 22 Ed III See Fitzh Corone, 261

Trinity 12 Ed III   (87)   **An attainted clerk** who has broken prison shall not have his clergy if the ordinary refuses it, etc. Query, if the ordinary refuses a man who knows how to read, etc ? For in Trinity, 9 Ed III, he was put to his penance in that case, etc

Case 87   There is no early printed year of 12 Ed III The case does not appear in the Rolls Series for that year.

(88)   **If the** principal be arraigned and found guilty, and then the king pardons him, shall the accessory be arraigned? Query, etc ?

Case 88   There is no citation given for this case in Statham It is probably incorrect to call it a case, for it is evidently but a note for the editor's own use

(89)   **The coroner** cannot hold Pleas of the Crown by the Statute of Magna Carta, cap. 15 But yet he can commence appeals and indict many, but not proceed, etc., for that Statute is a *supersedeas* to him, etc.

There is no citation to this case, but this is apparently an abridgment Case 89
from a reported case

The Statute of Magna Charta, Stats at Large, Vol 1, p 1   The
chapter should be 17, not 15

(90) **Two were** arraigned for the death of one A, and it was Trinity
found that they were quarrelling and arguing, and one 22 Ed III
would have thrust the other with his knife, and the other
[would have treated] him in the same manner, and this A
came between them to stop them, and between them he
was killed, wherefore they were both hung, because each
of them would have killed the other, so it cannot be said
to be an accident, etc

The case has not been identified in Y B Trinity, 22 Ed III   See Case 90
Fitzh Corone, 262

(91) **One was** indicted because he killed an infant in Michaelis
the mother's womb   And the opinion was that he should 22 Ed III.
not be arraigned upon that because there was no name of
baptism in the indictment.   (And also it is hard to know
if he did kill it, etc)

The case has not been identified in Y B Mich 22 Ed III   See Case 91
Fitzh Corone, 263

(92) **Burglars are those** who break into houses or churches Michaelis
with the intent to carry away goods, in which case, although 22 Ed III
they do not carry away anything, they shall be hung, etc

The case has not been identified in Y B Mich 22 Ed III   See Case 92
Fitzh Corone, 264

(93) **Punishment** for treasure trove taken and carried Michaelis
away, wreck of the sea and waifs, shall be by imprison- 22 Ed III
ment and fine, and not of life and of member.

Reported in Y B *Liber Assisarum*, 22 Ed III, p 107, pl 99   At the Case 93
end of an Appeal of Mayhem.   See Brooke, Corone, 96, Fitzh Corone,
265

(94) **In an appeal** for the death of a man, the defendant Hilary
was outlawed, and had a charter of pardon.   And it was the 13 Hen IV
opinion of HANKFORD that the heir of the plaintiff should
sue execution because the plaintiff was dead

Reported in Y B Mich (not Hilary), 13 Hen IV, p 6, pl 14   See also Case 94
Fitzh: Corone, 266

Hilary
13 Hen IV.

(95) See by Hankford, if one be indicted *quod clausum J B felonice fregit [ad ipsum interficiendum]* [1] that is no felony, but "*quod domum*" etc , is felony, for that is burglary But if it be "*quod domum fregit ad ipsum verberandum*" etc , that is only a trespass And it was said that if a man be indicted because he "lay in wait *ad ipsum depredandum,*" although he took no money from him, still that is a felony

Case 95

Reported in Y B Mich (not Hilary), 13 Hen IV, p 7, pl 20 See also Fitzh Corone, 229 and 267

Statham 59 a
Hilary
13 Hen IV

(96) In an appeal of robbery, if the defendant wages battle the plaintiff can bring in the booty, and oust him of the battle, then the defendant can claim property in the goods, and so they are at issue for the property Query, if it be peremptory? And see, by GASCOIGNE, in the same plea, that if the defendant wages battle the plaintiff may oust him as by saying that the defendant injured him at the time of the robbery, and show his injury to the Court

Case 96

The case has not been identified in Y B Hilary, 13 Hen IV Fitzh Corone, 230, has the case

Michaelis
10 Hen IV

(97) In an appeal, it is no plea that the plaintiff has another appeal for the same death pending in the county or in London, etc But in that case the Court will send for the appeal, etc Query, to what effect, etc ? Query, if it be a plea to say that the plaintiff was appealed of this same death in the county in which the appellee was non-suited?

Case 97

Reported in Y B Mich 10 Hen IV, p 4, pl 14 See also Fitzh Corone, 269 and 465

Michaelis
10 Hen IV

(98) The principal took himself to his clergy, and the accessory was arraigned and hung, notwithstanding the principal might make his purgation, etc

Case 98

Reported in Y B Mich 10 Hen IV, p 5, pl 18 See also Fitzh Corone, 466

---

[1] These words are not in the reported case, and evidently should be omitted in reading the abridgments

(99) **A man** who is outlawed does not forfeit his goods which he had in common with another And this in a note, etc

There is no early printed year of 15 Ed III The case has not been identified in the Rolls Series for that year, or in the early abridgments

(100) **If a gaoler** procures a prisoner [to be] an appellor it is a felony By SCROPE. And see in the same plea, it is no felony if a juror who passes upon such a felony betrays their counsel. And this by the opinion of the Court in the Eyre of Nottingham, etc

The cases cited as from the Eyres appear neither in the Year Books nor in the abridgments, although under some heads there are other cases cited as from various Eyres

(101) **One brought** an appeal of rape and counted that he ravished his wife against the form of the Statute of Richard, etc ROLFF: He has not counted that after the ravishment the woman assented to the ravishment, in which case he should have had an action upon the Statute of Westminster the Second, for otherwise his action is not warranted by the Statute of Richard, etc TYRWHIT He has concluded that he ravished her "against the form of the Statute of Richard the Second," wherefore answer, etc ROLFF. The action is brought against two, and he counts against both as principals, in which case the ravishment of the one cannot be the ravishment of the other TYRWHIT He who assisted him and aided him, is a principal in this case, wherefore answer And then she said that she was never joined in legal matrimony HANKFORD She was his wife in possession, and he shall have this action, wherefore that is no plea But the plaintiff was put to answer to that plea, against the opinion of many, etc

The case has not been identified in Y B Mich 10 Hen IV, or in the early abridgments

The Statutes are The Statute of 6 Ric II (1382), cap 6, Stats at Large, Vol 2, p 252 (255), and 13 Ed I (1275), Stats at Large, Vol 1, p 163

(102) **A daughter** shall not have an appeal for the death of her ancestor   In an Appeal, etc

The case has not been identified in Y B Hilary, 5 Ed III, or in the early abridgments

(103) **A man** was indicted before the sheriff in his tourn at Holborn in the county of Middlesex, for an encroachment made on the highway   And the indictment was sent into the King's Bench, and the distraint issued against the party, who came and said that the indictment was not sufficient inasmuch as no day was put in the indictment And HANKFORD said that a *Venire Facias* should issue against the indictors to amend this, since the indictment was taken in the same county where that place is   Which was conceded, etc.

Reported in Y B Mich 8 Hen V, p. 8, pl 4 or in the early abridgments

(104) **It was presented** that one had entered upon another with force, and he was made to answer to it. And the law is the same if it be presented that a man took my horse with force, albeit I can have an action because of the contumacy exhibited against the king, it is a good indictment   Query, then, what evil the Statute of Forcible Entry [would cure] which was made after that time, etc ?

The case has not been identified in Y B Hilary, 7 Hen VI, or in the early abridgments

The Statute is that of 8 Hen VI (1429), cap 9   Stats. at Large, Vol 3, p 121

(105) **If a man** be indicted for felony [or] treason, he answers to that has he one name or another   But it is otherwise in an appeal. Query, if it be in the baptismal name? By HANKFORD in a *Scire Facias*

Reported in Y B Paschal (not Mich), 1 Hen V, p 5, pl 8   See also Brooke, Corone, 201, and Fitzh Corone, 274

(106) **A woman** abjured the land in the Iter of Kent, etc   Query, if a man is adjudged to be hung and escapes

from the sheriff and takes sanctuary, query if he shall
have abjuration since judgment is given upon the same
felony?

There is no citation for this case given by Statham   It has not been   Case 106
identified elsewhere

(107) **In an appeal**, the defendant stood mute, and it   Paschal
was found that he could speak; therefore he was hung.   21 Ed III

The case has not been identified in Y B Paschal, 21 Ed III, or in   Case 107
the early abridgments

(108) **If a man** robs me in one county, and carries the   Paschal
goods into another county, I shall have an appeal in the   7 Hen IV
one county or the other, as in Trespass   And this in an
appeal *Coram Rege*, etc

Reported in Y. B Paschal, 7 Hen IV, p 43, pl 9   See also Fitzh·   Case 108
Corone, 79

(109) **An approver** appealed a man of Flanders, and   Paschal
therefore he was hung   1 Ed III

The case has not been identified in Y B Paschal, 1 Ed III, or in the   Case 109
early abridgments

(110) **An appeal** of robbery lies for the warden of a church   Anno
for the goods of the church   By the opinion of all the   2 Hen V
Court; and in an Iter of Kent it was adjudged good, etc

The case has not been identified in Y B Anno 2 Hen V, or in the   Case 110
early abridgments

(111) **In an appeal** for mayhem, it is a good plea to say   Paschal
"By his own consent," etc   But if he says that the   25 Ed III
plaintiff assaulted him in another place in the same county,
and the evil which he has, etc., that is no plea, but he
should agree with him as to the place, because a mayhem
is done in one place and cannot be continued as a battery,
as appeared in an appeal of Mayhem, *Coram Rege*, Anno
41 Ed III

The case has not been identified in Y B Paschal, 25 Ed III, or in   Case 111
the early abridgments

**Hilary
22 Ed III**

(112) **In an appeal** for rape after nonsuit, the defendant was arraigned at the suit of the king and acquitted. And they inquired as to the abettors, etc. *Simile*, Anno 40, *Coram Rege*

Case 112

The case has not been identified in Y B Hilary, 22 Ed III

**Hilary
22 Ed III**

(113) **In an appeal** against a monk who was acquitted, the justices would not suffer them to inquire as to the abettors, because the monk could [not] recover damages, etc And they said that the law is the same in an appeal against a married woman, etc.

Case 113

The case has not been identified in Y B Hilary, 22 Ed III, or in the early abridgments

**Hilary
7 Hen IV.**

(114) **The accessory** shall not be bound to answer to the party, notwithstanding the principal was acquitted at the suit of the king, and not at the suit of the party

Case 114

Reported in Y B Mich (not Hilary), 7 Hen IV, p 27, pl 4 See also Brooke, Corone, 19, and Fitzh Corone, 80

**Michaelis
9 Hen IV.**

(115) **Justices** of the Peace cannot take appeals nor assign coroners And this in an Appeal

Case 115

Reported in Y B Mich 9 Hen IV, p 24, (1) pl 1. See also Brooke, Corone, 25, and Fitzh Corone, 457

**Anno
11 Ed III**

(116) **In the meantime** between the charging of the inquest and the going out and their return, the defendant would have become an approver and could not In an indictment, etc Contrary at Newgate, Anno 4 Ed III [1]

Case 116

The case has not been identified in Y B Anno 11 Ed III, or in the early abridgments

Statham 59 b

**Anno
28 Hen VI**

(117) **If a man** be arraigned for a felony within the year, at the suit of the king, the appeal is gone, etc, be he acquitted or attainted, etc *Coram Rege*

Case 117.

The case has not been identified in Y B Anno 28 Hen VI, or in the early abridgments

[1] Ed IIII in the text, but it is a clear error for "Ed III"

(118) **The principal** had a charter of pardon and the Trinity 3 Ed III
accessory was arraigned, etc. But yet, query well, etc

The case has not been identified in Y B Trinity, 3 Ed III, or in the Case 118
early abridgments But see Y B Trinity, 2 Ed III, p 27, pl 17

(119) **The principal** resorts to his clergy, the accessory Trinity 5 Ed III
shall not be arraigned, because the principal might make
his purgation.

The case has not been identified in Y B Trinity, 5 Ed III, or in the Case 119
early abridgments

(120) **One was** arraigned upon an indictment for felony, Anno 13 Hen VI
notwithstanding the appeal was pending for the same
felony, by an infant under age, etc Before NEWTON at
Sarum (I believe that he was credibly informed that he
was not guilty, etc.) [1]

There is no early printed year of 13 Hen VI Case 120

(121) **Where a man** is acquitted as principal, he shall Trinity 2 Ed III
not be arraigned for the same felony as accessory afterwards And this in an indictment.

Reported in Y B Trinity, 2 Ed III, p 26, pl 14 See also Fitzh Case 121
Corone, 150

(122) **A man** was arraigned for the death of an unknown Trinity 1 Ed III
man, etc

Reported in Y B Mich (not Trinity), 1 Ed III, p 25, pl 26 Case 122

(123) **Where a man** becomes an approver and then an Anno 2 Hen V
appeal is sued against him, he shall be arraigned upon the
appeal, etc From this it follows that a man cannot
become an approver in an appeal against him

The case has not been identified in Y B Anno 2 Hen V, or in the Case 123
early abridgments

---

[1] The note is apparently put in by Statham from contemporary
authority, probably a fact known to those who were in Court when
the case was tried

Anno
32 Ed III

(124) **One was** arraigned at the suit of the king, notwithstanding an infant under age had an appeal against him for the same felony And SHARSHULL gave as a reason that it might be that he who was indicted would by fraud make an infant within the age of three or four years appeal him, and thus the suit of the king shall perish, which is not reasonable And this *Coram Rege.*

Case 124

There is no early printed year of 32 Ed III In the *Liber Assisarum,* 32 Ed III, p 196, pl 8, a like case appears

Anno
40 Ed III

(125) **In an appeal of mayhem.** KNYVET. The plaintiff brought another appeal for this same mayhem and those whom he now assigns as principals he then assigned as accessories, upon which writ he was nonsuited, judgment, etc. Wherefore it was adjudged that he take nothing. Which note And also see that he assigned principals and accessories in this appeal of mayhem, which is not legal, as I think, etc *Coram Rege.*

Case 125

Reported in Y B *Liber Assisarum,* 40 Ed III, p 238, pl 1

Anno
40 Ed III

(126) **When the principal** was attainted, the accessory was held to answer, and he found mainprise because accessories, etc In an appeal *Coram Rege,* etc Query, if he shall do so before Justices of Gaol Delivery, etc ?

Case 126

Reported in Y B *Liber Assisarum,* 40 Ed III, p 240, pl 8 See also Brooke, Corone, 117

Anno
40 Ed III

(127) **In an appeal** by a woman for the death of her husband, the defendant said that her husband was alive, and it was tried by provers, etc. *Coram Rege.* (It seems that the plea amounts to no more than "not guilty," etc)

Case 127

Reported in Y B Mich 40 Ed III, p 42, pl 24 See also Fitzh Corone, 90

Anno
41 Ed III

(128) **A man was** indicted and arraigned because he beat a man in Westminster Hall And he was found guilty, and it was adjudged that his right hand be cut off,

and his lands and chattels forfeited, etc   (Which was strange as to the lands, etc.)

The case has not been identified in Y B Anno 41 Ed III, or in the early abridgments   Case 128

(129) **In an appeal,** if the defendant breaks prison and is retaken, he will be ousted of battle for that reason   But if he have the king's charter [of pardon] for that breaking, it is otherwise   As appeared Trinity, 1 Ed III, in a note   Paschal 1 Ed III

The case has not been identified in Y B Anno 1 Ed III, or in the early abridgments.   Case 129

(130) **A presentment** that one is a common thief is not good, etc   For apparent reasons.

DAMAGES

(1) **In debt against one,** the plaintiff declared upon two obligations in different counties   The defendant admitted one, and they were at issue upon the other   And the plaintiff had to wait for the damages on the first obligation until the issue should be tried by the same inquest. All the damages shall be inquired into albeit they are in another county.   And this by the opinion of the COURT, in Debt, etc.   Statham 60 a
Hilary
41 Ed III

The case has not been identified in Y B Hilary, 41 Ed III, or in the early abridgments   Case 1

(2) **In a writ of wardship,** at the proclamation the defendant made default, and a writ issued to the sheriff to inquire if the infant was married and all the circumstances, which the inquest gave in their verdict, who returned the damages accordingly   Hilary
42 Ed III

Reported in Y B Hilary, 42 Ed III, p 1, pl 5   Case 2

(3) **In a writ of entry** upon a disseisin made on the father of the demandant, he shall not recover damages because the Statute says only that the disseisee shall   Paschal
42 Ed III

recover damages against him who is found tenant after the disseisin, etc.   And this is a writ of entry in the per, for a disseisin made on the disseisee, and not on his heir

Case 3

Reported in Y B Hilary (not Paschal), 42 Ed III, p 7, pl 30   See also Brooke, Damages, 20, and Fitzh Damages, 68

The Statute is the Statute of Gloucester, 6 Ed I (1378), cap. 1 Stats at Large, Vol 1, p 117 (119)

Paschal
42 Ed III

(4) In a writ of warranty of charter, they were at issue upon the charter, and it was found for the plaintiff The opinion was that he should recover damages for the delay.

Case 4

The case has not been identified in Y B Paschal, 42 Ed III, or in the early abridgments

Michaelis
43 Ed III

(5) If the tenant has repaired the tenements of which the disseisin was made, the damages shall be recovered according to the rate, etc   In an Assize   (But yet that was against the opinion of FORTESCUE and others, etc)

Case 5

The case has not been identified in Y B Mich 43 Ed III, or in the early abridgments

Trinity
45 Ed III

(6) In a quare impedit against two, the plaintiff and all the defendants made title to the advowson, and their titles were traversed, to wit   each one traversed the other's title, and it was found for one of the defendants, and he had a writ to the bishop, and judgment to recover his damages against the plaintiff, and against his companion named with him   But yet, query? For it seems that when the title of the plaintiff was found against him that they should not inquire further, etc

Case 6

Reported in Y B Mich (not Trinity), 45 Ed III, p 14, pl 12   See also Brooke, Damages, 173, and Fitzh Damages, 38

Michaelis
45 Ed III

(7) A man shall not recover damages against the incumbent except in the cases where he pleads a plea which proves him to be a disturber, etc   In a *Quare Impedit*

Case 7

The case has not been identified, but it is possibly the same case which is digested in case 6, *supra*

(8) **In an attaint** against two for a false oath in a *Quare Impedit*, it was found that the Petty Twelve had made a false oath, and one hundred pounds were recovered in a *Quare Impedit*. And then the Grand Jury taxed this one hundred pounds, and another hundred pounds as damages. And it was adjudged that the plaintiff should recover one hundred pounds against one of the defendants, who recovered, etc, this one hundred pounds in common against both, because the other was now tenant of the advowson, etc And this attaint was brought by a woman, where the first damages in the *Quare Impedit* were recovered against her husband and herself, and the husband died, etc (All the same some think that the action is given to the executors of the husband, and not to the wife, but FYNCHEDEN said that by the same reasoning, if she had survived her husband, the execution of the damages would be sued against the wife, and not against the executors, and by this same reasoning she shall have the attaint, and not the executors, etc)

Reported in Y B Mich 46 Ed III, p 23, pl 5 See also Brooke, Damages, 174, and Fitzh Damages, 78

Michaelis 46 Ed III

Case 8

(9) **In a writ of trespass** brought by tenants "*pro indiviso*," where one is tenant of three or four parts, and the other is tenant of only one part upon the finding of this matter their damages were severed, etc , by FYNCHEDEN in Trespass

Michaelis 46 Ed III

The case has not been identified in Y B Mich 46 Ed III, or in the early abridgments

Case 9

(10) **Damages** were [recoverable] in an Attaint at the common law By HULS in an Attaint

Paschal 3 Hen IV

Reported in Y B Paschal, 3 Hen IV, p 14 (15), pl 3 See also Brooke, Damages, 187, and Fitzh Damages, 55

Case 10

(11) **Damages** were recovered in an Attaint where there were no damages in the first action. (But I believe that these damages were only the profits in the meantime), etc.

Hilary 16 Ed III

There is no early printed year of 16 Ed III The case has not been identified in the Rolls Series for that year, or in the early abridgments

Case 11

(12) **In a writ of admeasurement** of dower, a man shall recover damages for the profits in the meantime, but in admeasurement of pasture no damages shall be recovered   As appeared in an Amercement.

There is no printed year of 34 Ed III   The case has not been identified in the early abridgments

(13) **In an appeal,** the plaintiff was nonsuited and the defendant acquitted at the suit of the king, upon a declaration, and he recovered his damages against the plaintiff, etc

There is no early printed year of 15 Ed III   The case has not been identified in the Rolls Series for that year, or in the early abridgments

(14) **A woman** who had lost her dower by a tried action, where she had vouched the heir, now had the record brought into the Chancery because she was endowed there, and she had a *Scire Facias* against the heir to be newly endowed, and was newly endowed, but she recovered no damages, for they do not award damages in the Chancery   And also there was no default in the heir, unless it be for the delay after the recovery against the woman.

Reported in Y B *Liber Assisarum*, 43 Ed III, p 274, pl 32   See also Brooke, Damages, 116

(15) **In gavelkind,** one had issue two sons, and died seised of certain lands, and they entered [the sons] against whom their mother brought a writ of dower and recovered half by the action, and twenty pounds damages   And then she married, wherefore the sons entered, because she had forfeited [her dower], by the customary law.   And her husband and herself sued execution of the damages, by a *Scire Facias*, etc., and recovered the twenty pounds notwithstanding they had forfeited the principal

The case has not been identified in Y B Hilary, 50 Ed III, or in the early abridgments

(16) **In a quare impedit,** because the defendant caused himself to be essoined after appearance, he was adjudged

a disturber   All the same he would have averred that there
was not any disturber named, and could not for the above
reason   But the plaintiff recovered damages against him

And it was said in the same plea, if in a *Quare Impedit*
the plaintiff causes himself to be essoined, and the six
months pass so that the bishop presents through the lapse,
still if the plaintiff avers that the defendant is a disturber,
he shall recover his damages   Query, why, etc ?

There is no printed year of 31 Ed II   The case has not been identi- Case 16
fied in the early abridgments

(17)   **In a cessavit** brought by the lord against the tenant,   Trinity
it is necessary to tender the arrears with the damages as   21 Ed III
well as where a Cessavit is brought for the cesser, for lands
leased in fee farm   And still the Statute of Westminster
the Second does not give damages in that case   But he
cited the Statute of Gloucester, which gives a Cessavit
for a fee farm, and says, "in the same manner," etc

Reported in Y B Trinity, 21 Ed III, p 23, pl 17   See also Brooke, Case 17
Damages, 147

Statute of Westminster the Second, 13 Ed 1 (1285)   Stats at Large,
Vol 1, p 163   Stat of Gloucester, 6 Ed I (1278), cap 4   Stats at
Large, Vol 1 p 117 (121)

(18)   **In an annuity** against an abbot, the plaintiff declared Hilary
the damage to the amount of forty pounds   The attorney   1 Ed III
of the abbot admitted the action, so he recovered the annuity and the damages were taxed at ten pounds, and not
according to his count   But it is otherwise where a man
recovers as *"non defendam,"* etc. And so see that he Statham 60 b
recovered damages in a writ of annuity, which is against
the opinion of many, etc , who say that a man shall recover
the annuity with the arrears, and not damages, etc

Reported in Y B Hilary, 1 Ed III, p 3, pl 12   Case 18

(19)   **In a writ of wardship,** at the return of the dis- Michaelis
tress, because the defendant made default at the proclama- 24 Ed III
tion, the plaintiff had a writ to inquire as to the damages.
But yet the Statute does not speak of the damages, etc.

Case 19   Reported in Y B Mich 24 Ed III, p 33, pl 21   See also Fitzh Damages, 162

Statute of Westminster the Second, 13 Ed I (1285), cap 35   Stats at Large, Vol 1, p 163 (209)

Paschal
3 Hen IV

(20) A man shall recover damages in an attaint at the common law, and in an attaint given by the Statute, and yet the Statute does not speak of damages, etc

Case 20   Reported in Y B Paschal, 3 Hen IV, p 14, pl 3   See case 10, *supra*   See also Brooke, Damages, 187, and Fitzh Damages, 55

The Statute of Westminster the First, 3 Ed I (1275), cap 38   Stats at Large, Vol 1, p 74

Paschal
14 Hen VI

(21) In trespass for a forcible entry, the party shall recover treble damages, and the costs of his suit shall also be trebled, for it is included in the damages.   And it is so in every case where a man shall have his costs, except in the case of the Statute of Gloucester, for that is given by a special form, etc

Case 21   Reported in Y B Anno 14 Hen VI, p 13, pl 44   See also Brooke, Damages, 88, and Fitzh Damages, 23

The Statute of Gloucester, 6 Ed I (1278)   Stats at Large, Vol 1, p 117

Hilary
8 Hen IV

(22) In an appeal by a woman for the death of her husband, the defendant said that she formerly brought an appeal for this same death against one H, who was hung at her suit, judgment, etc.   And she could not deny it, wherefore it was adjudged that she take nothing, etc   And the defendant prayed his damages against the plaintiff, and could not, etc

Case 22   The case has not been identified in Y B Hilary, 8 Hen IV, or in the early abridgments

Hilary
5 Ed III

(23) In an appeal, the defendant said that this same ancestor of whose death, etc , had a daughter who was his heir, judgment, etc   And for this reason the writ was abated   And yet his daughter could have had the appeal, etc   And the defendant prayed his damages and could

not have them, because she might be found guilty at the
suit of the king by an indictment

And it was said in the same plea that the defendant shall
not be arraigned at the suit of the king, albeit the plaintiff
has declared, because the plaintiff had no cause of action,
etc

The case has not been identified in Y B Hilary, 5 Ed III, or in the Case 23
early abridgments

(24) **In a quare impedit,** where the plaintiff recovered Paschal
damages for half a year, he recovered no other damages, 24 Ed III
etc

Reported in Y B Paschal, 24 Ed III, p 25, pl 13   See also Brooke, Case 24
Damages, 151, and Fitzh   Damages, 4

(25) **The patron** shall not have damages to the value Trinity
of two years, where the six months have passed, if he 39 Ed III
wishes to have a writ to the bishop, etc   In a *Quare Im-*
pedit, etc , for such damages are not given, except where
the bishop can present after the time when the other had
a writ to the bishop, as it seems, etc   Query, then can
the other, when this matter is shown, have his damages for
two years, etc ?

The case has not been identified in Y B Trinity, 39 Ed III, or in Case 25
the early abridgments

(26) **In a writ** of entry in the *per*, the tenant vouched Hilary
the disseisor, by whom his entry was alleged, and the 33 Ed III
opinion of WILLOUGHBY was that the demandant should
recover damages against him, albeit no damages were recovered against the tenant   And he gave as a reason that
because the demandant counted against the vouchee in the
quibus, and so in the purview of the Statute, because it is
of his own tort, etc

There is no printed year of 33 Ed III

The Statute is that of Marlbridge, 52 Hen III (1267), cap 29 (*de* Case 26
quibus), Stats at Large, Vol 1, p 55 (73)   See also Fitzh   Damages, 6

(27) **In waste,** the inquest found the waste to the damage Hilary
of forty pounds, where the plaintiff only declared to the 34 Ed III

value of ten pounds, and the forty were treble, etc   (And I
believe that the reason is because the Statute provides that one
shall recover treble of that which the inquest shall tax, for
in other actions he will not recover more than he counts), etc

Case 27   There is no printed year of 34 Ed III

Statute of Gloucester, 6 Ed I (1278), cap 5   Stats at Large,
Vol 1, p 117 (123)   See also Fitzh   Damages, 7

Michaelis
15 Hen VI
(28) In trespass for a close broken and certain ash trees
cut down, the defendant was found guilty, and the inquest
would have severed the damages, to wit   for the breaking
so much, and for the cutting so much, etc   PASTON   All
that is but one entire trespass, for if he answers to the
cutting he answers to the other.   Wherefore give entire
damages, etc.

Case 28   There is no printed year of 15 Hen VI   The case has not been
identified in the early abridgments

Trinity
15 Hen VI
(29) In trespass for forcible entry, the justices omitted
the damages and also the costs, and besides that the plaintiff recovered the third of that which he would have after he
had the increase, as well of the damages as of the costs, etc

Case 29   There is no printed year of 15 Hen VI   The case has not been
identified in the early abridgments

Michaelis
38 Hen VI
(30) A man shall recover damages in an *Audita Querela;*
by THORPE, etc.

Case 30   The case has not been identified in Y B Mich 38 Hen VI, or in the
early abridgments

Michaelis
8 Hen VI
(31) In detinue, the plaintiff declared to the damage
of twenty pounds   And afterwards the plaintiff and the
garnishee were at issue   And at the *Nisi Prius* the inquest
found for the plaintiff to the damage of a hundred pounds
And it was the opinion that he should recover a hundred
pounds, notwithstanding he counted for only twenty pounds
against the defendant, etc

MARTYN said in the same plea   If the lord joins his
bailiff in the avowry, the plaintiff shall recover damages

against the lord and not against the bailiff, for the bailiff is at once out of Court

Reported in Y B Mich 8 Hen VI, p 4, pl 11 See also Brooke, Damages, 18, and Fitzh Damages, 21 *Case 31*

(32) **In an appeal** against the husband and the wife, they were acquitted And it was the opinion of RIKHILL that their damages should be severed, for if the husband dies the wife shall have the damages and not the executor, and that cannot be unless they are severed, etc *Hilary 12 Ric II*

There is no early printed year for 12 Ric II The case has not been identified in the early abridgments, or in the Ames Foundation Year Book of 12 Ric II, ed by Deiser *Case 32*

(33) **A man shall** recover damages in a writ of annuity, and also in an Assize for rent. As appeared in a judgment for a writ of annuity by the tenant against the queen, etc *Michaelis 9 Hen VI*

Reported in Y B Trinity (not Mich), 9 Hen VI, p 12, pl 1 *Case 33.*

(34) **If the judges** increase or diminish the damages, the plaintiff shall never have attaint, for they will not do the one or the other except at the special prayer of the party, which shall be entered upon the record. And this by BABYNGTON, etc *Paschal 9 Hen VI*

The case has not been identified in Y B Paschal, 9 Hen VI, or in the early abridgments *Case 34*

(35) **In replevin,** the sheriff returned that the defendant had carried away the cattle, upon which the plaintiff took the cattle of the defendant in withernam[1] And then the defendant came and claimed property, upon which they were at issue. And the plaintiff waged deliverance of the cattle that he had in withernam,[1] and the defendant had a writ to have them delivered, etc To which the sheriff returned that they were carried away, wherefore he had a withernam, to which the sheriff returned that he had no goods or chattels, wherefore he had a *capias* against the plaintiff And then the issue was tried and found for the *Michaelis 11 Hen IV*

[1] Took the cattle which were distrained out of the county so that the sheriff could not replevy them

plaintiff, wherefore he prayed judgment to recover his damages   NORTON   You will not give him judgment until we have judgment of the withernam   And it was not allowed   Wherefore he had judgment and the defendant prayed an exigent against the plaintiff since the *capias pluries* was returned, and he had it   And so note that the plaintiff will be outlawed upon his own judgment, etc, and if he comes, the defendant shall recover damages against him, and each shall recover damages against the other.

Case 35

Reported in Y B Mich 11 Hen IV, p 10, pl 21   See also Brooke, Damages, 50, and Fitzh   Damages, 58

Hilary
11 Hen IV

(36) **In dower,** if the tenant says that he has been at all times ready to render dower, and still is, he shall have the plea to excuse himself from the damages, if he comes at the summons   But in a writ of Cosinage it is not so,

Statham 61 a

because the occupation of the abator is not legal, as it is in the other case by the presumption of the writ, etc

Case 36

Reported in Y B Hilary, 11 Hen IV, p 40, pl 5   See also Brooke, Damages, 52

Paschal
11 Hen IV

(37) **In trespass** for goods carried away, the defendant pleaded an arbitration in a foreign county, which was traversed, and found against the defendant   And the opinion was that those of the same inquest should tax the damages, for it is not like a foreign plea pleaded in an Assize, where an ouster is confessed, there those of the foreign county do not tax the damages, because they have no notice of them, since no damages were declared in the Assize, etc   But in this case, when the damages are declared in certain, to which the defendant has pleaded a false plea, without any protestation or anything to excuse him from the damages, they can tax them well enough By THORPE, etc *Simile*, Paschal 44 Ed III

Trinity
7 Hen IV

(38) **In an assize** of waste, in Annuity, and other such writs, a man shall recover his damages for the arrears incurred pending the writ, as well as those incurred before the writ   By THIRNING, in Annuity

Case 38

Reported in Y B Trinity, 7 Hen IV, p 16, pl 4   See also Brooke, Damages, 43.

(39) **If in an appeal** the principal is acquitted, the accessory shall not recover damages against the abettors, because they have never put his life in jeopardy, etc

There is no citation for this case given by Statham   The case has not been identified   Case 39

(40) **One J sued a praemunire facias against three,** against one as principal, and against the others as accessories, who pleaded "not guilty", and were found guilty, and the plaintiff had a general judgment for his damages against all three, etc   And the law is the same in an appeal of mayhem, where it is sued against the principal and accessories, etc

And it was said in the same plea, that the plaintiff can sue execution against which of them he will   Query, if the principal dies, pending the writ, if the writ shall abate? etc   And so see if he can have a *Præmunire Facias* against the accessory?   And see similar material, Mich 30 Hen VI, in the case of *Thwaites*, etc

Reported in Y B Mich 8 Hen IV, p 6, pl 9   See also Brooke, Damages, 46, and Fitzh   Damages, 56   The statements in the abridgments and in the reported case itself contradict Statham   Case 40

Michaelis 8 Hen IV

(41) **If my tenant for a term of years** be ousted by a stranger, against whom I recover by an action, and the termor afterwards brings a writ of *ejectione fermae*, etc, against the stranger, he recovers no damages, for he barred himself by the recovery in the Assize, but he can enter upon me and have a writ of Trespass, and in that way he can get to his damages, etc   (It seems that he can have an *ejectione fermae*, and recover all his damages, etc)

Statham and Fitzherbert (Damages, 8) cite this case as in Mich 12 Hen VI   Fitzherbert gives it as on p 4 of the Y B for that year, but I have not been able to identify the case   Case 41

Michaelis 12 Hen VI

(42) **In detinue for charters,** the garnishee was garnished and did not come, wherefore it was adjudged that the plaintiff should recover the writings but not the damages, because the defendant had done what in him lay,

Michaelis 27 Hen VI

etc   And so see that the defendant can save himself from the damages, etc , although the plaintiff delivered the writings to him alone, for the plaintiff shall have no answer to that matter, etc   Query?

Case 42

Reported in Y B Mich 27 Hen VI, p 4, pl 27, and p 2, pl 11 See also Brooke, Damages, 11 and 191, and Fitzh Damages, 27, 28

(43) **One disseises me** and dies seised, his heir being under age   The lord seises the wardship; then I bring a writ of entry, shall I recover for the time that he was in wardship, since his possession was legal? etc

Case 43

Statham gives no citation for this case, it has not been identified

Paschal 27 Hen VI

(44) **In a quare impedit,** the plaintiff can have judgment to recover his damages, to wit   the value of the church for two years   And he prayed the costs of his suit and could not have them   And that is against those who say that in every case where the woman recovers her damages she shall recover the costs of her suit, etc.   It seems that he should recover his costs when he recovers only for the disturbance, etc

Case 44

Reported in Y B Trinity (not Paschal, there being no printed Paschal Term for this year), 27 Hen VI, p 10, pl 7   See also Fitzh Damages, 29

Note

See as to damages, in the title of Actions on the Statutes, Hilary, 30 Ed III

The case in 30 Ed III is abridged by Statham under the title Accions sur lez Estatutz, *supra,* p 10 a, case 4

Michaelis 34 Hen VI

(45) **In an assize** for rent, it was found that the tenant of the lands made a rescue with force and with a multitude of people, and the plaintiff prayed treble damages, by the Statute of the year 8   And the opinion of all the justices was that he should not have them because it was not in the purview of the Statute, for the Statute is, "If the tenant enter and disseise him with force," or, "enter peaceably and detain with force," so it is necessary that there shall be an entry in any case, and a man cannot enter in rent when he is tenant of the land, to make a rescue, wherefore, etc

Case 45

Reported in Y B Hilary (not Mich), 34 Hen VI, p 26, pl 4

The Statute is that of 8 Hen VI (1429), cap 9, Stats at Large, Vol 3, p 111 (121). See also the Statute of 5 Ric II (1381), cap 7, Stats at Large, Vol 2, p 234 (240).

(46) **In debt** by executors, on an obligation made to their testator, the release of the testator was pleaded in bar, which was found false, and the damages were inquired into, as well for the time of their testator as after, because they represented the estate of their testator, and they recovered to the use of the testator and not to their own use, etc
Anno 19 Ed III

There is no early printed Y B for 19 Ed III The case has not been identified in the Rolls Series for that year *Case 46*

(47) **In detinue,** the defendant said that he was at all times ready to deliver and still is And the plaintiff would have undertaken to aver that he was not, but could not because the defendant came on the first day, etc
Trinity 12 Ed III

There is no early printed year of 12 Ed III The case appears in the Rolls Series, 11 & 12 Ed III, p 641 *Case 47*

DEFAUTE

(1) **The default of the husband** was adjudged the default of himself and his wife In Dower, etc Contrary elsewhere, etc.
Statham 61 b. Michaelis 41 Ed III

The case has not been identified Brooke, Defaut et Appearance, 5, gives the citation as Mich 41 Ed III, p 24 There is no case of dower to be found there, and no question of default arises there, nor does the point appear in any case reported in Y B 41 Ed III, so far as I have been able to ascertain *Case 1*

(2) **The demandant** cannot waive the default of the tenant unless he will agree to it.
Paschal 42 Ed III.

Reported in Y B Hilary (not Paschal), 42 Ed III, p 8, pl 36 See also Fitzh Defaut, 14 *Case 2.*

(3) **If an infant** under age makes default at the summons upon the return of the Grand Cape, the demandant shall
Trinity 32 Ed III

have no advantage because of that default, but shall count against him, etc

Case 3

There is no printed year of 32 Ed III The case has not been identified in the early abridgments

Michaelis
12 Ric II

(4) **In a cessavit** against the bishop, the dean, and the chapter of B, the chapter answered by attorney, and the dean made default HANKFORD We pray seisin of the land, for the default of the dean is the default of them all, etc And they adjourned Query, to what intent was the bishop named? etc

Case 4

There is no early Year Book for the reign of Ric II The case appears in the Y B of the Ames Foundation, ed by Deiser, 12 Ric II, Hilary (not Mich), p 128 It shows a nonsuit at the end

Note

See as to default, in the title of Process, and also in the title of Saver de Defaute, etc. Many matters

See Statham, title of Process, *infra*, pp 138 b–141 a, and also in the title of Saver de Defaute, *infra*, pp 166 b–167 a

DEFENCE

Hilary
44 Ed III

(1) **If a man pleads** a plea which goes to the jurisdiction of the Court, he cannot make a full defence, but shall say this, to wit to defend the tort and the force and demand judgment if the Court will take jurisdiction for, etc , and plead this plea, etc   Query, if he shall do so when he pleads to the disablement of any person through profession or villeinage? And it seems he can, for if he makes a full defence he cannot disable the person but he can plead the same matter to the action, after a full defence, etc

Case I

The case has not been identified in Y B Hilary, 44 Ed III, or in the early abridgments

Michaelis
12 Ric II

(2) **In trespass against one H,** who made a full defence, and said he was a professed monk, and his abbot was not named, and he demanded judgment of the writ CROSSE He has made a defence, wherefore, etc WADE He is the defendant, wherefore he does well, wherefore it is necessary to answer him

There is no early printed Year Book for the reign of Ric II   The Case 2
case has not been identified in the early abridgments, or in the Y B
12 Ric II, Ames Foundation, ed Deiser

See how a man shall defend himself in a writ of right, Note
in the title of Right

See Statham, *infra*, title of Droit, pp 73 b–74 a

DECIES TANTUM

(1) **An inquest was taken** by *Nisi Prius in pais*, in a Statham 62 a
Quare Impedit before which justices a bill was shown Trinity
[which showed], that the jurors had taken [bribes] from both 41 Ed III
parties.   And it was immediately inquired into according
to the Statute, and it was found that they had taken [bribes],
wherefore the jurors were adjudged to prison, and given a
day in the Bench   And then it was challenged because
the justices of *Nisi Prius* sent the jurors to prison before
judgment   THORPE   For that sue a writ of error if you
will, for we award that the king and the party shall recover
And they tendered the half to the party   FYNCHEDEN. The
king shall be first served   THORPE   No, sir, for that which
the king shall have is only in the way of a fine, in which
case the parties shall be always first served   And so it
was   And for that which belonged to the king they found
sureties, etc   And a *Venire Facias* was awarded against the
embracers, because they were not in the bill, etc   This
Statute does not give a *Decies Tantum* only, but a bill against
the jurors or the parties, and that the party shall recover
his damages   And the party shall have a fine, etc   And
if another than the party sues for the king he shall have half
of the fine, etc   (And the Statute was made in the year 34 of
Ed III, cap 7   And the *Decies Tantum* was given in the
year 38 of the same king, and the year 8 of Henry the Sixth,
etc   But that was only for a certain time, which is past), etc.

Reported in Y B Paschal (not Trinity), 41 Ed III, p 9, pl 3   See
also Brooke, *Decies Tantum*, 5, where he says that the case is badly
reported, but does not improve upon it, and Fitzh *Decies Tantum*, 9 Case 1.

The Statutes are those of 34 Ed III, cap 8 (1360), Stats at Large,
Vol 2, p 134 (139), and 38 Ed III, cap 12 (1363), Stats at Large,
Vol 2, p 169 (172), and not 8, but 18 Hen VI, cap 14 (1439), Stats
at Large, Vol 3, p 218 (236)   The words I have placed in paren-

theses were evidently added by the editor, as the date of the last statute is later than the case

Trinity 44 Ed III

(2) **In a decies tantum,** the sheriff returned to the distraint that they had nothing, etc And the plaintiff prayed, for the king, that he might have a distress against him for the lands that he had on the day the inquest passed, and he could not have it except for the lands that he had on the day of the purchase of the writ, etc.

Case 2

Reported in Y B Paschal (not Trinity), 44 Ed III, p 12, pl. 18 See also Brooke, *Decies Tantum*, 7

Michaelis 44 Ed III

(3) **If he who** is attainted in a *Decies Tantum* offers the money, they shall not take the part of the king, but put it in the receipts with the penalties, with a writ, etc ; or else they will command the serjeant of the king to go with them and he shall be delivered from the Fleet

Case 3

Reported in Y B Mich 44 Ed III, p 36, pl 28 See also Brooke, *Decies Tantum*, 8

Paschal 21 Hen VI

(4) **A man shall not have** a *Decies Tantum* against one who is empanelled unless he be sworn, although he took money, etc By the opinion of NEWTON. Query, if he shall have the *Decies Tantum* before verdict passes, etc ?

And see in the same plea, that a man can sue a *Decies Tantum* in whatever county he will

Case 4

Reported in Y B Paschal, 21 Hen VI, p 54, pl 9

Note

See as to decies tantum, in the title of Actions on the Statutes, etc

See Statham, *supra,* title of Accions sur lez Estatutz, p 10 a

Michaelis 50 Ed III

(5) **A decies tantum** was adjudged good where the writ alleged that the juror took [bribes] And yet it seems that the receipt of one juror cannot be the receipt of the others. The Statute which gives the *Decies Tantum* says that he shall be sued by a bill, etc , and that it shall not be inquired into by an inquiry brought by the king, etc.

Case 5

The case has not been identified in Y B Mich 50 Ed III, or in the early abridgments

Statutes of 34 Ed III, cap 7 (1360), Stats at Large, Vol 2, p 134 (139) and also 18 Hen VI, cap 14 (1439), Stats at Large, Vol 3, p 218 (236).

DISCLAYMER [38]

(1) **One vouched a bishop to warranty,** and bound Statham 62 b him for the reason that his predecessor enfeoffed him in the Trinity tail; so by reason of that reversion he bound him   And the 40 Ed III bishop would have disclaimed and could not, because his predecessor gave it with the assent of the dean and chapter, in which case it shall be prejudicial to the chapter and to his successors

And it was said by FYNCHEDEN in the same plea, that if the tenant in tail brought a writ of mesne against him who was in the reversion that he cannot disclaim   (And it seems that none in the reversion can disclaim, for I do not know in whom it would vest)

Reported in Y B Trinity, 40 Ed III, p 27, pl 4   See also Brooke, Case 1 Disclaimer, 7, and Fitzh Disclaimer, 10

(2) **In replevin** brought by one who was tenant for a Paschal term of years, the defendant avowed upon a woman 45 Ed III who was the lessor of the plaintiff, for rent, etc   KYRTON Sir, you have here the woman who is tenant of the freehold, who is ready to join the party who is her lessee, and they both disclaim   BELKNAP She cannot join, for she is not injured, for the joinder shall be in place of an acquittance, and the termor cannot have a writ of mesne, etc   FYNCH- EDEN   He can have a writ of covenant, and discharge himself of the damages, which are so much in value, etc   And therefore the joinder was admitted   And because the termor put his term in jeopardy, as well as the lessor, they were admitted to disclaim together, etc.   And the termor, who was plaintiff, had judgment to recover his damages immediately, etc

And it was said in the same plea, that in an Assize against the tenant of the freehold and the termor, that if the tenant of the freehold pleads to the Assize, that the termor may plead the release of the plaintiff of all actions   Query, if he can plead the release of all the right, etc ?   For it was said he shall plead no other plea, unless he be a tenant by a Statute Merchant or *Elegit*. See the Statute of Gloucester, etc   Query, how shall the writ of right upon a disclaimer be brought in that case, and against whom, etc ?

Case 2   Reported in Y B Paschal, 45 Ed III, p 7, pl 9   See also Brooke, Disclaimer, 10, and Fitzh   Disclaimer, 12

Statute of Gloucester, 6 Ed III (1278), Stats at Large, Vol 1, p 117

Trinity 47 Ed III (3) **A man** cannot disclaim in a writ of recaption, where the defendant avows for other causes, but he should maintain his writ, etc

Case 3   Reported in Y B Mich (not Trinity), 47 Ed III, p 7, pl 3   See also Fitzh   Disclaimer, 20

Trinity 31 Ed III (4) **In a formedon** against three, one said that he disclaimed in the lands, saving that the reversion was in him Query? For it seems that he should not disclaim unless he devested all his right   (But it seems that his plea was only a nontenure) But yet he had the plea, and then by the default of the others he was received to defend his right, etc.

Case 4   There is no printed year of 31 Ed III   The case has not been identified in the early abridgments

Michaelis 13 Ed III (5) **In an assize** against two, one disclaimed in the freehold, the other pleaded jointly with him who disclaimed And the plaintiff was forced to answer that, for his disclaimer was not to the purpose, for it could not vest in his companion, as in a *Præcipe quod Reddat*   Query as to the reason, etc ?

Case 5   There is no early printed year of 13 Ed III   The case has not been identified in the Rolls Series, or in the early abridgments

Hilary 4 Ed III (6) **If a præcipe quod reddat** be brought against one he cannot disclaim, for it cannot vest in no one, etc , wherefore he shall plead nontenure, etc

Case 6   The case has not been identified in Y B Hilary, 4 Ed III, or in the early abridgments

(7) **In a praecipe quod reddat** against one who vouched two to warranty, and bound them by reason of the reversion, because they leased the lands to him for the term of his life And one of them disclaimed And the Court was in doubt whether the reversion by this disclaimer would vest in the other in the reversion, or in the tenant for life, etc But yet, query, if the disclaimer lies in that case, etc ? Hilary 33 Ed III

And it was moved in the same plea, if a writ be brought against two, where one had only a term for life, the reversion to a stranger, and he disclaimed, will it vest in the stranger who had the reversion, or in his companion?

There is no printed year of 33 Ed III Fitzh Disclaimer, 21, has the case *Case 7*

(8) **See in a formedon** against several, and one of them disclaimed, and he showed how he had the wardship of the land, because he was bound to him, and, saving to him his seignory, be disclaimed in the tenancy And so to this effect he showed this matter, but if he had disclaimed generally he had lost his seignory, etc Trinity 15 Hen VI

There is no printed year of 15 Hen VI The case has not been identified in the early abridgments *Case 8*

(9) **If the avowry** be made upon the mesne, and he joins himself to the plaintiff who is tenant, and they disclaim, the lord shall have a writ of right upon the disclaimer against the tenant of the land By FYNCHEDEN, in Replevin, etc (But yet it seems that he shall not have such an action in that case, etc) Hilary 35 Ed III

There is no printed year of 35 Ed III The case has not been identified in the early abridgments *Case 9*

(10) **See by** SHARSHULL, the reason why, when one disclaims, it shall vest in his companion For the law looks upon them as joint tenants by the feoffment, then if one of them takes seisin for both, the tenancy is in the one who was not there as well as in the other, until he has dissented in a court of record Then when an action is brought against them, and he disclaims having anything Hilary 35 Ed III

in the land, then the land shall vest in his companion, and this by force of the feoffment, etc. And each of them shall be estopped from afterwards saying the contrary And yet the suit shall not abate, for the plaintiff cannot have another writ, inasmuch as both were tenants until one disclaimed in a court of record And he said further that they could not disclaim unless they were joint tenants by a feoffment, for if they were joint tenants by descent or by a fine, the demandant could show it and extort a disclaimer from him, because, if the case be so, he cannot disclaim (But yet it seems that the law is the other way, for a man can waive a descent if he sees that he will be charged, or else that he had no title, etc And so, as to the descent, it seems that the law is not so, for the writ lies against them, although they did not enter in fact. But yet it seems that it does not vest in the other in that case, although the demandant shall have seisin of the land upon a *"nihil dicit,"* etc. Query, if they are joint tenants by a disseisin, etc ? Study well In a *Scire Facias*.)

Case 10   There is no printed year of 35 Ed III Fitzh Disclaimer, 23, has the case The evident bewilderment of the maker of the notes will be shared by the student, for the law is left in a confused state

Trinity
15 Hen VI

(11) See of disclaimer in the title of Dower, where one, upon whom the avowry was not made, disclaimed. And yet the avowry is not made upon any person, but upon the lands charged, etc. Hilary, 15 Hen VI

Case 11   There is no printed year of 15 Hen VI The case has not been identified in the early abridgments

Trinity
34 Ed III

(12) Where my tenant disclaims in an avowry, I shall have a writ of right of Wardship, and a writ of right of Customs and Services, for by this disclaimer my lordship is not gone in law, unless at my will, but the possession of my lordship is gone through it, for I cannot make an avowry nor have an Assize, etc. And SHARSHULL and WILLOUGHBY said that all my lordship was gone, and I must be put to my action for the lands, etc Well argued, in an Avowry. It seems that the disclaimer is no bar in a writ of Wardship, nor in an Escheat, because no judgment is given upon that disclaimer, etc

There is no printed year of 34 Ed III Fitzh Disclaimer, 24, has Case 12 the case

(13) **See by** GRENE, that the husband cannot disclaim Hilary for his wife, for if he could, the judgment that the plaintiff 32 Ed III shall have will be of no force, for after death of the husband Statham 63 a the woman can enter or have the assize, for it is not reasonable that she shall be disinherited where she has not been examined, etc And also, if the disclaimer be admitted, she cannot be received after the default of her husband, for by this disclaimer she is out of Court. And this well argued in a *Præcipe quod Reddat*, etc

There is no printed year of 32 Ed III Fitzh Disclaimer, 25, has Case 13 the case

(14) **In a per que servicia,** the tenant would have dis- Trinity claimed and could not, etc 11 Hen IV

Reported in Y B Trinity, 11 Hen IV, p 72, pl 10 See also Brooke, Case 14 Disclaimer, 12, and Fitzh Disclaimer, 8

(15) **If one vouches** another to warranty and binds him Paschal by reason of the reversion, he can disclaim as to the reversion 20 Hen VI and then the tenant has lost his lands, for he has failed of his voucher, etc And they said that such a disclaimer lies in every case where the tenant binds him by reason of the reversion, in case the tenant is in by the lease of him who is vouched And yet many say that if that lease be without a deed that he may disclaim well enough And they said that where the reversion had been granted by a fine that he has been received to disclaim in the reversion, etc Query, as to that sort of disclaimer, for it cannot vest in any person, but it remains in him who granted the reversion, etc Query? For the reversion was out of his person and in the grantee until he disclaimed, and consequently it vested, through the disclaimer, in the grantor of the reversion, etc.

The case has not been identified in Y B Paschal, 20 Hen VI, or in Case 15 the early abridgments

(16) **In replevin,** the defendant avowed upon the plaintiff, and he disclaimed ROLFF To that you shall not be received for you have made a feoffment of the land, etc , so there is no power to have a writ of right upon a disclaimer against you And this was held a good plea to oust him of the disclaimer Wherefore the plaintiff said that he was seised of the land in fee, without this that he had made a demise, etc Query, if he could get to plead anew, *rigore juris*, inasmuch as the other had forced him to disclaim, etc But I believe that he should say that his feoffor had given notice to the avowant, etc

Case 16

Reported in Y B Hilary, 8 Hen V, p 2, pl 4 See also Fitzh Disclaimer, 26

(17) **In a formedon** against two, one disclaimed, the other vouched to warranty DANBY (for the demandant) We pray seisin of the land, as to which he has disclaimed, for as to that the other has not undertaken the tenancy POLE He has no need to, for it is vested in him immediately by the disclaimer PRISOT That is not so, for you can choose whether you will plead in bar of the whole or of the half, wherefore POLE took upon himself the tenancy of the whole, and vouched to warranty, which note, etc.

And see, in the same Term, that he who is in the reversion cannot disclaim where the tenant by the curtesy or in dower vouches him, and binds [him] by reason of the reversion And this by PORTYNGTON and ASSHETON in a Formedon, etc

Case 17

Apparently the case reported in Y B Anno 36 Hen VI, p 28, pl 30 Brooke, Disclaimer, 17, has the case, and Fitzh Disclaimer, 9, has it, although he calls it a *Præcipe quod Reddat*

Note

One avows upon two, one disclaims Query, What shall be done?

(18) **In a writ of entry** *de quibus*, on a disseisivit of the demandant or his ancestors one of the tenants would have disclaimed, and could not because he was in of his own wrong, etc

And it was said in the same plea that in a *Præcipe quod Reddat* against two, where one disclaims and the other cannot disclaim also, because it could not vest in anyone, but he can plead specially and say that he never agreed to the feoffment, etc Or, if he be in by descent, he can say that he waived the possession And this by HALS, etc

There is no printed Hilary Term for 4 Hen V Brooke, Disclaimer, Case 18 36, has the case

(19) **A man cannot** disclaim in a *Per que Servicia*. Trinity As appeared in a note 11 Hen IV

Reported in Y B Trinity, 11 Hen IV, p 72, pl 10 See also Brooke, Case 19 Disclaimer, 12 and Fitzh Disclaimer, 8 See *supra*, case 14.

(20) **An infant under age** cannot disclaim in a *Nuper* Paschal *Obiit*, etc (The contrary seems true, etc) 9 Ed III

Reported in Y B Paschal, 9 Ed III, p 14, pl 21 Case 20

(21) **After a day** taken for a *Prece Partium*, the tenant Trinity cannot disclaim And this in a *Cui in Vita* 14 Ed III

There is no early printed year of 14 Ed III The case has not been Case 21 identified in the Rolls Series, or in the early abridgments

(22) **The tenant** disclaimed in a *quo jure*, and the justices Paschal said that his common was extinguished by this. And 12 Ed II this in the Eyre of Nottingham

And in the same Eyre one brought a *quo jure* for estovers, and it was adjudged good Query as to the reason why a man shall not have a *quo jure* for rent? etc.

The case has not been identified in Y B Paschal, 12 Ed II, or in Case 22 the early abridgments

---

[38] This is a plea known to Britton [Britton, 107, 120, b, 128, b, 173, b, 175, b) Coke tells us of it in quaint language Where the lord has received homage he is not free to disclaim when vouched by the tenant, for "he has accepted his humble and reverent acknowledgment to become his man of life and member and terrene honour " [Coke, 1st Inst , sec. 145, b] There are various sorts of disclaimers, Coke tells us, mostly disclaimers in the tenancy in the "bloud" and in the seignory Most of our cases are disclaimers in the tenancy Again we have a subject of which the Year Books are full Litigants and persons vouched are always disclaiming It was a matter to be handled carefully, because there was danger — as in our case 2 — that the termor

might put his term in jeopardy.   The facts as to just how and when one could disclaim are vague and puzzling to the modern reader   These cases of the abridgment do little more than suggest the subject, yet they do suggest it, and few as they are they serve to show that the pleading of this plea raised many important points   Our case 10 is an interesting example of the arguments used in the cases, and the manner of carrying on such arguments   Case 15 shows where the tenant stands to lose his lands if his voucher disclaims, and again we have an argument showing that the law did not appear to be well settled even in the twentieth year of Henry VI

DENZINE [39]

Michaelis
14 Hen IV

(1) **Although an alien** be sworn in a Leet or Sessions to be loyal to the king, still he is not thereby made competent to purchase lands nor to be put in a jury, unless he be made capable by the letters of the king   And this in a Challenge, etc

Case 1

Reported in Y B Hilary (not Mich), 14 Hen IV, p 19, pl 23 See also Brooke, Denzine and Alien, 2 and 11

[39] The alien could not hold lands, but there was a way of making him something less than a citizen and yet to give him more powers than were given to the alien   This was by way of letters patent from the king, making him capable of purchasing lands, as in our sole case, or to acquire them by gift   He cannot inherit lands, however [Coke, 1st Inst , sec 198, p 129, and P & M Hist of Eng Law, 2d ed , Vol 1 460], in case a child was born, except by act of parliament

Apparently a denizen, by these letters, acquired all the other rights of citizens, including as a matter of course, the right to "be put on a jury " [Coke, *supra*, § 198, p 129]

DISCONTINUANZ DIVERSEZ

Statham 63 b
Michaelis
40 Ed III

(1) **The tenant vouched** himself to save the tail, and process issued against him as vouchee, and because the charter was omitted in the process, the tenant prayed that it be discontinued   And because it was his own suit he was not received to allege a discontinuance, wherefore the vouchee pleaded in bar, etc

Case 1

Reported in Y B Mich 40 Ed III, p 36, pl 7   See also Brooke, Discontinuance de Process, 46 and Fitzh Discontinuances Diverses, 42

(2) **In an oyer and terminer,** one was outlawed and sued
a charter of pardon, and had a *Scire Facias* against the
plaintiff, who came and counted upon the first original   And
then the defendant alleged a discontinuance in the process
of the first original, and the opinion of WILLOUGHBY was that
he should not get to that inasmuch as he had sued a charter
of pardon where he could have had a writ of error, etc

The case has not been identified in Y B Paschal, 24 Ed III, or in
the early abridgments

(3) **In a praecipe quod reddat,** the tenant vouched
to warranty   Process was continued until the *sequatur*,
on which day the sheriff did not return the writ, wherefore
the demandant prayed seisin of the land   MARKHAM
To judgment you should not go, for the case is this·
To the summons *ad warrantizandum* the sheriff returned
"*mandavi ballivo libertatis de B, qui mihi nullum
dedit responsum,*" upon which a *non omittas* issued, to
which he returned "*nihil habet nec est inventus,*" upon
which a *pluries* issued; on which day the sheriff returned
as before, so the *alias* was omitted, and the process discontinued   For in a writ of debt where the sheriff returns
to the *capias,* as above, whereupon a *non omittas* is awarded,
that first *capias* cannot be counted, wherefore, etc
STRANGE From that it follows (by your reasoning) that a
new *sequatur* shall issue where the sheriff has not served
any of the other writs, and returns the *sequatur*, to wit
the mandamus, as above   WAMPAGE It has been seen
that two *sequaturs* have been awarded, as, if the tenant
vouches one who is under age, and the demandant says
he is of full age, then process shall issue against him to wit
Summon another *pluries* and a *sequatur*, and if he comes
at the *sequatur*, and is adjudged to be of full age, a new
process shall issue against him, for the other process could
not be seen   GODEREDE It seems that the process is
discontinued, for the *non omittas* does not say *præcepimus
tibi sicut alias*, etc , wherefore after the *non omittas*, the
sicut alias and *pluries* shall issue. JUYN The tenant
is out of Court, because he cannot allege that matter.

HODY He can plead a release after the last continuance, or that the demandant has entered, etc And consequently he can allege a discontinuance in the process against the vouchee, for this is the suit of the demandant, etc TRES-HAM There is a difference between a case of debt and the case here, for in the case here, if four writs be awarded, although one of them be served, the land is lost, but the exigent does not issue until one writ is first served, etc And they adjourned, etc

Case 3 Reported in Y B Anno 14 Hen VI, p 19, pl 60

Michaelis (4) **If a protection** be put forward after issue all is dis-
15 Hen VI continued, as well as where it is put without day by the death of the king, for in the case here at the *Venire Facias* the tenant made default, upon which the Petty Cape issued, on which day the tenant produced a protection, and after the year the demandant was resummoned, and was forced to count anew, for all was discontinued, etc But if he had sued a special resummons, reciting the whole case, peradventure it had been otherwise

Case 4 There is no printed year of 15 Hen VI The case has not been identified in the early abridgments

Hilary (5) **See a like case** in a Formedon, Michaelmas, 1st Hen
1 Hen V V, well argued, where they made a distinction, where the process is discontinued until it be put without day, by a protestation, or by the death of the king For if it is properly continued and a *Venire Facias* issues, on which day it is put without day by the death of the king, at the resummons the demandant shall sue a *Habeas Corpus* against the jurors, etc (But I believe this cannot be unless the resummons specially recites the whole case, etc)

Case 5 Reported in Y B Hilary, 1 Hen V, p 2, pl 3

Trinity (6) **In a formedon** they were at issue, and on the return
18 Hen VI of the *Venire Facias* the tenant made default, upon which a petty cape issued, on which day the plea was put without day by a protection And then the demandant was re-summoned, and the tenant made default, upon which the

Great Cape issued, and the demandant released the defendant from the Great Cape, and prayed that the tenant save the default of the petty cape   NEWTON That is reasonable, for the resummons says that he shall be in the same position in which he was on the day that the protection was thrown, and on that day the default was not saved, consequently, etc   FORTESCUE That cannot be, for, if on the return of the Great Cape the demandant be essoined, the tenant shall never save his default, for he had no day on which to do it   And the law is the same where the tenant essoins himself for service of the king, and he fails of his record, etc   And if one pleads to the assize, and it remains for lack of jurors, and a general reattachment is sued, the tenant shall plead in bar, for the default is discontinued, and all that is dependent upon it   ASCOUGH   To the same effect.   For by the default the issue is discontinued and the default is gone through the protection.   And this is clearly proved, for now a Great Cape is awarded at the resummons, and that proves clearly that the first default does not remain of record, for a man cannot have the Great Cape after the petty cape, unless the petty cape is discontinued   And also the resummons runs *"ad audiendum record'"*   And this default was never recorded   And also it was wholly discontinued before the protection was thrown, wherefore, etc.   Well argued

Reported in Y B Trinity, 18 Hen VI, p 14, pl 3   Case 6

(7) **In a quare impedit** against two   STRANGE Process   Michaelis
is discontinued, for the pone was served against one, and not   9 Hen VI
against the other   HANKFORD   Although in a writ of Trespass the pone be served against one, and not against the other, yet he who appears shall be forced to answer, and that in an action of the same nature, wherefore answer, etc

The case has not been identified in Y B Mich 9 Hen VI, or in the   Case 7
early abridgments

(8) **A man** shall not get to allege a discontinuance in   Hilary
the process after he has made his defence and emparled,   38 Ed III
etc , but before the imparlance and after the defence, he

can, etc. By THORPE, in Trespass   (But yet it seems
for anything that appeared, that a man shall get to allege
a discontinuance at any time, etc)

Case 8   The case has not been identified in Y B Hilary, 38 Ed III, or in
the early abridgments

Michaelis 7 Hen VI   (9) **In trespass** against two, a discontinuance against
one is a discontinuance against both. And the law is the
same in Debt by several *præcipes*, because it is only an
original writ, which cannot be discontinued in part, and
stand good for the remainder, etc   For it cannot stand good
in part unless the process be determined against the other,
etc   Contrary above, and also below in the next plea, etc

Case 9   Reported in Y B Paschal (not Mich), 7 Hen VI, p 21, pl 1   See
also Brooke, Discontinuance de Process, 19

Statham 64 a   (10) **In trespass** against two who pleaded not guilty.
Hilary 7 Hen VI   And on the return of the *Venire Facias* one came and said
that the other was dead, and prayed that the writ should
abate   MARTYN   It seems that the writ should abate,
for they have become joint defendants by their plea, for
by the issue of their joint *Venire Facias* the discontinuance
against one of them is a discontinuance against both.   It
is otherwise if they had had a separate *Venire Facias*, for
then a protection thrown by one shall serve only for himself
But upon a joint *Venire Facias* the plea is put without
day for all. STRANGE   There is a difference between
your cases, for where a protection is thrown for one,
and the inquest shall be taken for the other, he shall be
discharged. And afterward, when the year has passed,
they shall come back to give their verdict between the
plaintiff and the other defendant, and so they will be
harassed   But when one is dead they can give their
verdict and be discharged forever, and so it seems that
the writ is good.   GODEREDE   And so it seems to me that
a *Venire Facias* shall issue, for this *Venire Facias* is discontinued   And it was said in the same plea that a man
cannot relinquish his suit in such a case, where a protection

is thrown by one, because a man cannot relinquish his suit before it has been adjudged, etc   Query, etc.?

Reported in Y B Paschal (not Hilary), 7 Hen VI, p 21, pl 1 See Case 10 also Brooke, Discontinuance de Process, 19   See *supra*, case 9

(11) **See by** MARTYN, in a *Quare Impedit,* [that there Michaelis is a] difference where judgment is given upon process, and 3 Hen VI where it is given upon the verdict, as if a man be outlawed in Debt, where there were only two *capias* awarded or where a Grand Cape is awarded instead of a petty cape and the demandant recovers by default, in all such cases the tenant or defendant can have error, or allege a discontinuance, if he had a day in court, etc   But it is otherwise where the defendant comes upon such process wrongly awarded, and pleads, and the plaintiff and he are at issue and it is found for the plaintiff, the defendant shall not have any advantage for that, because he has passed the step, in that he has admitted the process to be good when he appeared and pleaded, etc   But yet, query as to that, for it seems, for anything that appeared, that the defendant should have all the said advantage of the discontinuance, or else have a writ of Error, etc

Reported in Y B Mich 3 Hen IV, p 8, pl 9 See also Brooke, Case 11 Discontinuance de Process, 1

(12) **In a recordare,** the defendant said that the plea Hilary was discontinued in the county   MARTYN   What is that 3 Hen VI to the purpose?   For when we plead, it shall be answered as if it had been here [first]   Which the Court conceded

Reported in Y B Hilary, 3 Hen VI, p 30, pl 17   Case 12

(13) **Although the processes** in the judicial writs are Hilary badly awarded, and the defendant appears upon them, 11 Hen IV he shall be forced to answer, for the original is good, and the other shall be amended   And this in Trespass.

Reported in Y B Hilary, 11 Hen IV, p 40, pl 3   Case 13

(14) **At the nisi prius** the inquest passed against the Hilary defendant, and then he came and said that he who appeared 11 Hen IV. as attorney for him never had any warrant of attorney,

wherefore you should not go to judgment HANKFORD
It has been held in such cases that the demandant shall
recover, and the defendant shall have a writ of Error.
THIRNING That he cannot, as his own act. But to my
mind, if he be ousted by such a judgment, he shall have
the assize, for he is not a party to that   Query well, etc
In Trespass, etc   It seems that there is no other remedy
in a personal plea, except a writ of deceit, and no more is
there in a plea of land, etc

Case 14.   Reported in Y B Hilary, 11 Hen IV, p 44, pl 16

Michaelis
18 Hen VI.   (15) **In a writ of debt,** the defendant as to part waged
his law, and as to the remainder they were at issue, and
he had a day to make his law   And the *Venire Facias*
was returned on the same day, on which day his attorney
was essoined, and the essoin was awarded, and they adjourned until now, and [had] a *habeas corpus* returnable the
same day   And now the plaintiff showed how the attorney
of the defendant was essoined where the defendant himself
should have been essoined, and he prayed his debt, for which
he [had] waged his law   PORTYNGTON The process is discontinued against him as to that part, and consequently as to
all since it is upon one and the same original, etc.   MARK-
HAM It is only mis-continued, no more than in a *Scire
Facias* where the tenant is essoined when an essoin does not
lie, and yet it is not a discontinuance, inasmuch as he has
had a day for that, but it is mis-continued and shall be
amended   NEWTON It is not the same, for in your case
a day is given between the parties, but in this case not any
on the part of the defendant, for the attorney in this case
is only the same as a stranger, because he should have
appeared always in his own person   BROWN As to that
which is pleaded to the country, the process is not discontinued, for when the *habeas corpus* issued, the entry
was "*juratores prosunt in respectu*," which shall be understood to refer to the acts of the parties, etc.   Which NEW-
TON conceded, etc.

Case 15   The case has not been identified in Y B Mich 18 Hen VI, or in
the early abridgments

See of discontinuance, in the title of Entry Congeable, ^{Note} etc And see how rent can be discontinued, Mich 48 Ed III, in the title of *Per que Servicia*, etc

Statham, title of Entre Congeable, *infra,* pp 84 a, b Statham, title of *Per que Servicia, infra,* p 142 b

(16) **If the tenant in tail** leases for life and dies, and ^{Anno 5 Hen VI} his heir releases all his right and dies, it was said that this is a discontinuance, because by the lease a new reversion of the fee was reserved, which descended to the heir, and although the estate tail had descended in law, yet it is discontinued, by the opinion of many In an Assize But it was not adjudged, etc

There is no printed year of 5 Hen VI The case has not been iden- ^{Case 16} tified in the early abridgments

DETTE [40]

(1) **A man brought** an action of debt against executors ^{Statham 64 b} because he was retained by their testator for the term of ^{Hilary 2 Hen IV} his life to take one hundred shillings a year in peace and war, and that his salary was in arrear for two years, amounting, etc And it was held that he should not take anything by his writ

Reported in Y B Hilary, 2 Hen IV, p 14, pl 12 See also Brooke, ^{Case I} Dette, 53

(2) **In debt** against two upon a joint contract, if one be ^{Paschal 40 Ed III} outlawed and the other appears, he shall answer for the whole debt, and for that he shall be charged, etc

And see, in the same plea, that he who appeared said that the other was dead before the outlawry was pronounced and for that reason the writ was abated, etc.

Reported in Y B Trinity (not Paschal), 40 Ed III, p 26, pl 1 ^{Case 2}

(3) **In debt** against two upon a joint contract, they ^{Michaelis 40 Ed III} waged their law in common, and on the day, etc, one made

his law, and the other made default, and the plaintiff prayed his debt against him who made default. FYNCH-EDEN You abated your writ by the acceptance of the law of one of them, wherefore you take nothing, etc Query, if he had held him to the default, if the default of one would be the default of both? etc

Case 3

Reported in Y B Mich 40 Ed III, p 35, pl 4

Michaelis
40 Ed III

(4) **In debt,** the plaintiff counted partly upon an obligation and partly upon a contract The defendant admitted the obligation, and as to the contract "nothing owing him " Ready by the country, etc , wherefore he had judgment for that which was admitted, but not for the damages, until the issue should be tried, because the same inquest shall tax all And at the *Nisi Prius* the plaintiff did not come, and then, in the Bench, he prayed judgment for the damages admitted, etc THORPE You are nonsuited, wherefore, etc And also it was your folly at first, for you could have released your damages for that portion But yet it was held that he should have a writ to inquire as to the damages, etc Which note

Case 4

The case has not been identified in Y B Mich 40 Ed III, or in the early abridgments

Hilary
41 Ed III

(5) **In debt** against the Prior of St Johns, the plaintiff counted on a loan to the prior by the hands of one J, his *confrère,* besides this that he would aver that the monies came to the use of the house, etc And the count was held good.

Case 5

The case has not been identified in Y B Hilary, 41 Ed III, or in the early abridgments

Hilary
41 Ed III

(6) **In debt** upon arrears in an account, the defendant said that by a deed indented, which he produced, the plaintiff had agreed to take, for the same sum, the manor of D, judgment if action And the opinion was that this was no plea, without answering to the *debet.*

Case 6

Reported in Y B Hilary, 41 Ed III, p 7, pl 11 See also Fitzh Dette, 120

Paschal
41 Ed III

(7) **In debt** against several by separate *præcipes,* all acknowledged the debt, and the plaintiff had judgment

to recover the entire debt against each of them, but he did not have execution, except against one of them at his election.

Reported in Y B Paschal, 41 Ed III, p 9, pl 1 See also Brooke, Dette, 30 The report of the case states that he recovered against "all in common" Case 7

(8) **"Assets descended** to him after the death of his ancestor," is no plea in debt against the heir, unless he says, "Assets by descent the day the writ was purchased," for by the alienation before the writ was purchased, that descent would not injure him, because he could not have execution on that, and other execution he shall not have But it is otherwise if he waives the possession, for the law throws the possession on him, etc But in a Formedon the plea is good that assets descended to him after the death of his ancestor, without saying more, etc

Paschal 42 Ed III

Reported in Y B Paschal, 42 Ed III, p 10, pl 12 Case 8

(9) **Debt is not** maintainable against executors of a warden who allowed a condemned prisoner to escape, as appears in a note *Coram Rege*, etc But yet, query? For an action of debt lies against the warden at the common law And by the Statute an action is given against the warden of the Fleet if he allows a condemned prisoner to go on bail, or on security, etc And in that case if the warden of the Fleet dies, it seems that the action of debt lies against his executors, and so it seems in the other case Query? For there is no specialty, nor record that the prisoner has gone, etc

Anno 40 Ed III

The case has not been identified in Y B 40 Ed III, or in the early abridgments Case 9

The Statute is that of Westminster the Second, 13 Ed I (1285), cap 11 Stats at Large, Vol 1, p 163 (188), pl 8

(10) **A man shall** have a writ of Debt for the damages recovered in a writ of Waste, for damages recovered in a writ of Aiel, Cosinage, Mort d'Ancestor, and Assize. And in a writ of Entry, but not for the arrears of rent recovered, etc Well argued.

Hilary 45 Ed III

The case has not been identified in Y B Hilary, 45 Ed III, or in the early abridgments Case 10

Hilary
46 Ed III

(11) **In debt,** the plaintiff counted that he sold a horse to the defendant for forty shillings, etc. The defendant said that he did not admit the contract to have been for so much as he alleged, but he said that it was for only four shillings, which he had been at all times ready to pay, and still is, etc And as to the forty shillings, "nothing owing him" And the other demanded judgment, inasmuch as he had admitted the contract, in a manner, in which case he shall not get to his law in another plea, without showing an acquittance FYNCHEDEN If he had paid all except four shillings, he cannot plead otherwise, for if he does not confess the contract with you, he shall not allege payment without showing an acquittance, wherefore, to my mind, he pleads wisely, etc Query?

Case 11

Reported in Y B Hilary, 46 Ed III, p 6, pl 16

Trinity
47 Ed III

(12) **In debt** against the husband and his wife, damages were recovered against the wife before the coverture, and the writ was "*debet et detinet,*" and it was held good

Case 12

Reported in Y B Mich (not Trinity), 47 Ed III, p 23, pl 56 See also Brooke, Dette, 44

Trinity
47 Ed III

(13) **The Prior of** B brought a writ of debt upon an obligation made to one J, his predecessor, and the obligation was not to him and to his successors, but to the prior solely And still the action was maintained And also the writ was "*debet,*" etc Query, if he showed in his count that it was made for goods or duties due to his house

Case 13

Reported in Y B Mich (not Trinity), 47 Ed III, p 23, pl 57 See also Brooke, Dette, 45, and Fitzh Dette, 134

Michaelis
10 Ed III

(14) **If a man** has nothing by descent, except in Gavelkind, a writ of debt shall be brought against him and his co-heirs, and specially counted Query, if he alleges in his declaration that the defendant had nothing by descent except there, etc ?

Case 14

The case has not been identified in Y B Mich 10 Ed III, or in the early abridgments

(15) **In debt** against two by one *præcipe*, one came and the other came not, and the plaintiff declared against him who came, upon an obligation by which each was bound, "*pro toto et insolido*" And because he had but one *præcipe*, it was adjudged that one should not answer without the other, but the same day was given, etc. Hilary 48 Ed III

Reported in Y B Hilary, 48 Ed III, p 1, pl 2 See also Brooke, Dette, 197 Case 15

(16) **In debt** upon an obligation, if the plaintiff declares for a lesser sum than is comprised within the obligation, he should acknowledge that he is satisfied as to the remainder Hilary 48 Ed III

And see in the same plea, where the obligation was endorsed upon conditions, the defendant alleged a payment without showing an acquittance

Reported in Y B Trinity (not Hilary), 48 Ed III, p 18, pl 3 Case 16

(17) **In debt** upon an obligation for twenty pounds, the defendant said, "not his deed," Ready and the other alleged the contrary And it was found that the defendant[1] borrowed ten pounds of the plaintiff, and that he made this obligation, and it was delivered to the defendant for ten pounds and the defendant sealed it, and so not his deed And upon this they were adjourned. (And whether he recovered the whole, or ten pounds, or nothing, I do not know) Statham 65 a Hilary 50 Ed III

The case has not been identified in Y B Hilary, 50 Ed III, or in the early abridgments Case 17

(18) **In debt,** the plaintiff counted that he leased land to the defendant for the term of his life, rendering a certain rent, and if the rent was in arrears that he could enter and retain it until satisfaction should be made with him for the arrears And he showed how the rent was in arrear for a year, wherefore he entered and brought this action for the arrears NEWTON The deed says that he shall retain it until, etc , wherefore he has no other remedy but to retain it until, etc And the action was maintained, etc. Paschal 24 Ed III

The case has not been identified in Y B Paschal, 24 Ed III, or in the early abridgments Case 18

[1] "Plaintiff" in the text, but a patent error

Michaelis
18 Ed III
(19) **In debt** against the warden of a prison because he had allowed a prisoner to go, who was delivered to him by reason of a Statute Merchant   He was not named warden in the writ, and yet the writ was held good, for the Statute does not say that he shall be named warden, etc

Case 19   Reported in Y B Mich 18 Ed III, p 35, pl 18   The Statute is that of Westminster the Second, 13 Ed I (1285), cap 11, Stats at Large, Vol 1, p 163 (188)

Michaelis
46 Ed III
(20) **In debt,** the plaintiff declared upon an obligation for two hundred pounds   The defendant said that the obligation was endorsed that if the defendant would pay twenty pounds to the plaintiff before the feast of Easter, etc , that then, etc., and we have paid him the twenty pounds, etc   FYNCHEDEN   You do not say that you paid him before the day, wherefore your plea shall be more strongly against you, to wit   that you paid him after the day, which cannot be in performance of the conditions, since the conditions are at an end,   so your plea amounts to no more than that you have paid him twenty pounds, and for that you do not show any acquittance   Wherefore it was adjudged that the plaintiff should recover two hundred pounds and his damages, etc.   And so see that it is not the same as where a man alleges payment in another place than that which plaintiff has alleged, and that the plaintiff received them, for that is good, if it be paid before the day of payment, but after the day the conditions have expired, etc   But if the defendant had pleaded wisely, in that case he could have barred the plaintiff by that matter, etc   (But yet it were not easy to do it, etc)

Case 20   The case has not been identified in Y B Mich 46 Ed III, or in the early abridgments

Paschal
3 Hen IV
(21) **In debt** upon a contract, the defendant said that the plaintiff had an obligation for the same debt, etc.   And the plaintiff said that the obligation was made for another cause.   And he was forced to say for what cause, etc

Case 21.   Reported in Y B Paschal, 3 Hen IV, p 15, pl 14   See also Brooke, Dette 57

(22) **Where my father** leases lands for a term of years, rendering a certain rent, and dies, I shall have a writ of debt for the arrears which accrued after the death of my father And this by PASTON, etc.

The case has not been identified in Y B Anno 14 Hen VI, or in the early abridgments

(23) **In debt** against the warden of Newgate, because he allowed a condemned prisoner to go at large, he was not named warden in his writ but in his count, and it was held good

There is no early printed year of 11 Ed III The case has not been identified in the Rolls Series for that year See *supra*, case 19, for a similar case

(24) **In debt** in the Common Bench, the defendant said that the plaintiff had a bill for the same debt pending against him in the Exchequer, and it was not allowed, etc

There is no printed year for 34 Ed III The case does not appear in the early abridgments

(25) **The tenant** in dower leased land for a term of years, rendering a certain rent, and died, and he who was in the reversion agreed to the lease, and for rent in arrear afterwards he brought a writ of debt And it was the opinion of many that it was not maintainable because there was no privity, etc. Query, how could he declare in that case?

There is no printed year of 15 Hen VI The case has not been identified in the early abridgments

(26) **If an obligation** be made to the husband and his wife, and the husband makes the same woman his executrix and dies, she can choose to bring the action on the obligation as executrix, or else in her own name, by the opinion of PASTON, etc. Query, if she made a release after the death of her husband, in her own name, omitting the name of executrix, would that bar her when she brought an action as executrix?

Reported in Y B Mich 4 Hen VI, p 5, pl 15 See also Fitzh Dette, 24

Paschal
4 Hen VI

(27) **In debt,** [if] the plaintiff declares upon a lease for a term of years, without a deed, it is a good plea to say that the plaintiff had a deed indented for the same lease, in which case he should count upon the lease, etc

Case 27

Reported in Y B Paschal, 4 Hen VI, p 17, pl 1

Hilary
35 Ed III

(28) **In debt** upon a contract, it is no plea to say that the plaintiff had an obligation from a stranger for the same duty, etc But to say that he had an obligation from the defendant for the same duty is good· by SHARSHULL, etc

Case 28

There is no printed year of 35 Ed III Fitzh Dette, 83, has the case

Michaelis 16,
Paschal
21 Ed III

(29) **In debt** against the heir, the writ was challenged because he was not named heir, and also because the writ was *"debet et detinet,"* whereas it should be *"detinet"* as against executors And it was adjudged good as a whole.

Case 29

The case has not been identified in Y B Paschal, 21 Ed III, or in the Rolls Series, 16 Ed III, for Michaelmas Term

Paschal
18 Hen VI

(30) **In debt,** the plaintiff counted that he leased certain lands to the defendant to hold at will, rendering ten shillings a year, and for so much in arrear, etc MARKHAM. Judgment of the count, for you have not counted that we occupied for that time, etc , and if we did not occupy you shall not have an action, for such a lease is as well at the will of the defendant as at the will of the plaintiff PORTYNGTON (agreeing) For if you make me your bailiff, etc , pledging by the year, etc , and I bring an action of debt for my salary, I shall count that I occupied, etc FORTESCUE In your case it is reasonable, for you are by way of an action, but here the action is brought against the occupier, wherefore, if he would have the advantage of that, he is bound to show it PASTON If the law is as MARKHAM says, that the lease shall be at the will of both, the case had been colorable, but I understand it to be at will of the lessor solely then if the defendant did not occupy, it is his folly, for he could have an action against a stranger as well as the tenant for a term of years, etc

Case 30

Reported in Y B Paschal, 18 Hen VI, p 1, pl 1

(31) **If a man** grants a rent charge to another for the term of his life, and then the grantor alienates the land to another, then the rent is in arrear, the grantee dies, the tenant aliens over. Now it was asked of HANKFORD, against whom the executors of the grantee would have a rent of debt for the arrears? It seems against the tenant of the land, which THIRNING denied, and said that the action fails. And this in a note, etc. Trinity 11 Hen IV

The case has not been identified in Y B Trinity, 11 Hen IV, or in the early abridgments Case 31

(32) **In debt** against the heir, he was not named heir in the writ, but in the count. And the writ was held good. And the writ was *"debet,"* etc. Paschal 32 Ed III

There is no printed year of 32 Ed III. The case has not been identified in the early abridgments, it seems identical with our case 29 Case 32

(33) **In debt** upon the arrears of a lease for a term of years, the defendant said that "your wife was tenant in dower of these same lands by the inheritance, etc, and you yourself leased them to us for a year, within which year your wife died, and this same person in the reversion entered, wherefore your estate is ended," judgment, etc. FYNCHEDEN. To that we say that you yourself sowed the land in the lifetime of our wife, and had the land all the year for which you sowed, so you have the profit and occupation of the land, etc. But he did not say, "without this that he who had the reversion entered," and for this reason it does not seem a plea, etc. THORPE. If my father leased to you for a term of years, and died, I shall have the rent incurred in the lifetime of my father, because I cannot oust you, for the executor of my father cannot have it, because the rent descends to me in the reversion. FYNCHEDEN. In your case no one would have it, because it is a rent service, and his wife is dowable of that, but in this case it seems that the lessor shall have the rent, for the heir of the woman shall not have it, nor her executor, nor can the woman make a devise of it, etc. Statham 65 b Michaelis 22 Ed III

Case 33   There is no printed year of 32 Ed III See also Fitzh Dette, 9, where he has abridged a case which may be this case or one very like it

Michaelis
8 Hen VI

(34) In debt upon the arrears of an account The plaintiff was examined and it was found by the examination that it did not lie in account, wherefore it was said to him that he should amend his count, and so he did and he counted upon a contract, etc , which note, for it seems that the writ should abate See the Statute, which gives an examination in that case, etc Query, if the defendant wages his law and prays that the plaintiff might be examined, and it is found that it lies in account, shall the defendant plead in bar, etc ?

Case 34   Reported in Y B Mich 8 Hen VI, p 10, pl 25, and see also more of the case on p 15, pl 36 See also Brooke, Dette, 89

    The Statute is that of Westminster the Second, 13 Ed I (1285), cap 11 Stats at Large, Vol 1, p 163 (188)

Paschal
12 Ric II

(35) In debt upon an amercement imposed by a presentment in a Court Baron, it is no plea to say that no such presentation, etc But yet, query? For if he cannot wage his law, the plea is good (but he can wage his law), as it seems, etc

Case 35   There is no early printed Year Book for the reign of Ric II The case is reported in Y B Paschal, 12 Ric II, p 180 Ames Foundation, ed Deiser

Trinity
22 Hen VI

(36) Where the judgment was given, etc Query, if he removes the record, etc ? But on a recognizance a writ is well brought in each county Query, if the jurisdiction be special, to wit. "*et nisi fecerit quod de catallis suis in London*'," etc.

Case 36   The case has not been identified in Y B Trinity, 22 Hen VI, or in the early abridgments

Michaelis
7 Hen VI

(37) One recovered a debt in the Exchequer and the defendant was put in prison for the fine to the king, at the prayer of the attorney of the king upon the said facts, and the warden let him go at large because he had made a fine And the plaintiff brought an action of debt against him, and it was questioned if such an action lay, because the Statute of Richard gives an action of debt against the warden if he lets a prisoner go at large on "bail or by baston " But [some say that] where he lets a prisoner go at large it was at the common law, and some held that this was not in debt, but upon the case But yet the action was held good, etc Then, inasmuch as the plaintiff did not pray execution, some held that he should not have this action, and some held the contrary, because it shall not be ended until the party is satisfied, and at least that he shall not let him go until the party is satisfied, etc And they adjourned *Simile*, Anno 28 Hen. VI, in the case of the *Lord Cromwell* against *Tallboys*.

Reported in Y B Mich 7 Hen VI, p 5, pl 9 See also Fitzh Case 37 Dette, 26 The Statute of I Ric II (1377), cap 12, Stats at Large, Vol 2, p 204 (211)

(38) **If one lease** land to another for a term of years, Trinity rendering a certain rent, and then ousts him and enfeoffs me, 9 Hen VI and the termor re-enters and claims his term, I can then distrain for my rent, but I shall not afterwards have an action of debt for that, because there is no privity between us

But yet it was said in the same plea that I shall have an action of waste, etc.

And it was said in the same plea, that if the lord ousts his tenant and enfeoffs a stranger, the lordship is extinct Query, in that case, if the tenant when he has re-entered shall have a writ of Mesne against him who has thus extinguished his lordship, for otherwise he is injured, etc

Reported in Y B Trinity, 9 Hen VI, p 16, pl 7 See also Fitzh Case 38 Dette, 31.

(39) **If I recover** a debt against one who is condemned, Michaelis and his body is in execution on the suit of another, if the 11 Hen IV warden lets him go I shall have a writ of debt against him by HANKFORD, notwithstanding he was not in execution at my suit

The case has not been identified in Y B Mich 11 Hen IV, or in the Case 39 early abridgments

Paschal
11 Hen IV (40) **Where a man** had judgment to recover against executors for the goods of the deceased, he shall not have an action of debt against them upon that recovery, but he shall sue the execution accordant to the [judgment]   For if he should have such an action of debt, he would have a general judgment against them, which is contrary to the first receipt   And this in Debt

Case 40   Reported in Y B Mich (not Paschal), 11 Hen IV, p 5, pl 11

Paschal
11 Hen IV. (41) **In debt,** the plaintiff counted for part of the arrears on a lease, and part upon a contract, and part upon another contract   HORTON   As to the first plea, he did not lease, and as to it he waged his law   And as to the other contract, he has been at all times ready, and still is, etc   NORTON. As to the first plea, we leased, etc   Ready. And as to the second plea, as to which you waged your law, we have no more to do with that   And as to the remainder, we pray delivery of the money.   HANKFORD   You have admitted your writ to be false in part, and so you have abated all your writ   And notwithstanding this the issue was taken upon the lease, and as to that which he admitted, he had judgment to recover, and as to that with which he would have no more to do, it was adjudged that he take nothing but be in mercy   (And if the issue be found against him I think he will be again amerced, etc)

Case 41   The case has not been identified in Y B Paschal, 11 Hen IV, or in the early abridgments

Paschal
11 Hen IV (42) **In debt,** the defendant said that he had been at all times ready, etc   HORTON   This is the second distress, wherefore to that you shall not be received, etc   SKRENE It is not like dower, for there the demand is certain, but here he might owe money upon different contracts   THIRN-ING   So he could say in dower that he did not acknowledge the lands, etc   And they adjourned

Case 42   The case has not been identified in Y B Paschal, 11 Hen IV, or in the early abridgments

(43) **Debt** is maintainable against a man on an attachment made by his servant, if the goods came to his use,
notwithstanding the servant had no warrant from his
master to do that, if so be he be known as his servant
By the opinion of the COURT, in Debt, etc   Query, if he
shall count thus? etc.

   There is no printed Year Book for 11 Ric II   The case has not been
identified in the early abridgments

(44) **Debt was brought** against two executors, and it
was counted that their testator was found in arrears before
the assigned auditors   NORTON prayed that the plaintiff
be examined. HANKFORD   To what effect? For they
cannot wage their law upon the contract of another   THIRN-
ING   It seems that the action does not lie against them,
for this is neither on a specialty nor record. But if their
testator had been committed to the prison, and had sued
ex parte talis and it had been found against him, then it
had been of record, and otherwise not   HANKFORD
If my tenant for life dies, I shall have an action of debt
against his executors for the arrears   THIRNING   I doubt
it   But against the executors of your tenant for years
you shall have it, because they represent his estate, etc.
HANKFORD   I think that in all cases where their testator
could not wage his law, that the action is plainly maintainable against his executors, without a specialty, etc
And they adjourned, etc

   Reported in Y B Paschal, 11 Hen IV, p 64, pl 17, and continued in
Trinity Term, p 91, pl 48   See also Brooke, Dette, 67

(45) **If a parson** of a church grants an annuity by the
assent of the patron and of the ordinary, to a man in fee,
and grants further that if the rent be in arrear for one
month after the feast when the payment, etc , that he shall
lose one hundred shillings in the name of a penalty *totiens
quotiens*, etc , and the rent is in arrear for one month,
the grantee shall not have an action of debt for the penal
sum, because it is inheritable, and of the same nature that

the annuity was, but he shall have a writ of Annuity for it, etc   By HANKFORD and HULS

And it was said in the same plea that if a man grants to me a rent charge in fee, with distress, and if the rent be in arrear, as above, that he shall pay a hundred shillings in the name of a penalty, and that I shall distrain for the hundred shillings, albeit no distress is given to me for the said hundred, which is the penalty, for the above reason, because the accessory follows the principal

Case 45   Reported in Y B Trinity, 11 Hen IV, p 84, pl 34

Michaelis 18 Hen VI

(46) **If one** leases land to a man for a term of years, rendering ten pounds rent by the year, and he leases the same term to his lessor, rendering to him ten marks, the opinion of NEWTON was that the surplus is extinguished But he said that he should have a writ of Debt for that which was in arrear before he retook the estate, etc Which PASTON denied, and said that he should not have an action, etc   From this it follows that if my tenant for years surrenders to me, to which I agree, that I shall not have an action of debt for that which was in arrear before the surrender, etc   Query?

Case 46   The case has not been identified in Y B Mich 18 Hen VI, or in the early abridgments

Trinity 19 Hen VI

(47) **If a parson** of a church, who has an annuity from me in fee, to him and to his successors, makes an exchange of his church, he shall have a writ of Debt for the arrears of the annuity accruing before the change, and yet the freehold is continued, that is to say, in his alienee, who is his successor By the opinion of NEWTON, etc.

And he also said that if I grant the reversion of my tenant for life, where a rent is reserved upon the reversion, and the tenant attorns, still I shall have a writ of Debt for the arrears accruing before the grant, and the law is the same if I grant the services of my tenant, and he attorns, and yet the fee and the freehold are continued in both parties And he also said that if I disseise a man of a manor, which is part in mesne and part in service, and

I continue the possession "years and days," and then he
brings an Assize against me and recovers, I shall have an
action of debt against the tenant, for the arrears for which
I have paid the damages (But yet all the case were
refused him), etc   But it was said that when the freehold
is ended that then the action well lies, as for executors
against executors, and also for me myself, where I lease
lands for the term of another's life, and he for whose life
[I leased] is dead, etc   And in every case where the freehold is continued; as if I recover by a writ of Waste against
my tenant for life, I shall have a writ of Debt for the arrears
before the recovery, and yet his estate is continued in law,
etc

Reported in Y B Mich (not Trinity), 19 Hen VI, p 41, pl 85   Case 47

(48) **In debt** against an abbot, the plaintiff counted by _{Hilary 20 Hen VI}

PORTYNGTON, that on such a day the plaintiff loaned to
one B, his predecessor, twenty pounds, for which debt the
said predecessor bound himself by the deed (which he produced), without this that he would aver that the said sum
was converted to the use of the house MARKHAM.
Your count is double, one, the contract, the other, the
obligation. NEWTON: We cannot do otherwise, for if we
committed ourselves to the contract, you would say that
we had an obligation for this same debt, and if we counted
upon the obligation, that would not bind you who are his
successor, unless we showed, as above, etc. YELVERTON
When you took the obligation by that fact you discharged
him from the contract, and so your action is gone by your
own folly MARKHAM It is no plea to say that the plaintiff had an obligation for the same sum, unless for him who
is a party to the contract, and he who is a party to the
contract shall not say that the plaintiff had sued [on] an
obligation for the same sum for another person, but for
himself it is a good plea, etc   He could have counted
upon the contract and shown that the sum had come to the
house, as where a man sells a horse to a married woman
which comes to her husband, he shall have an action of debt
against the husband. NEWTON Yes, sir, if the horse was

sold to the use of the husband, and otherwise not ASCOUGH It seems to me that the contract is not defeated by the obligation, for if a man be bound to me and then he enters into religion, now then his community shall be charged against me, etc, and then he dies, now the abbot is discharged, and his executor or his heir are charged so here, although the abbot was charged for his life on the obligation, still by the death of the abbot the obligation is ended, and the house charged by reason of the contract, etc YELVERTON The executor of him who enters into religion is charged, and not the abbot ASCOUGH Lord, no! No more than where a woman is bound to me and then takes a husband, now the husband is charged, then the husband dies, now the woman is charged, and the heir and the executor of the woman, and not the executors of the husband And if a woman commits a trespass on me and enters into religion, now the abbot is charged as to me, and if the monk dies the abbot is discharged, etc And they adjourned. Query, etc.?

Case 48   Reported in Y B Hilary, 20 Hen VI, p 21, pl 19 See also Fitzh Debt, 1

Paschal 20 Hen VI   (49) **Debt was sued** by the Dean and Chapter of Saint Stephen's Chapel of Westminster And it was counted that they leased to the defendant a wallhouse, rendering to them twelve pence by the week so long as they occupied it, and he showed exactly how long he had occupied it, which amounted to the sum in demand And the action **Statham 66 b** was maintained, etc NEWTON said that such a tenant at will shall have fealty, which the Court conceded.

Case 49   Reported in Y B Paschal, 20 Hen VI, p 26, pl 15

Paschal 8 Hen V   (50) **A man** brought a writ of Debt in the Exchequer "*quo minus,*" etc, and he counted upon an obligation as executor, etc And it was said that since his writ alleged that he could not pay the king unless he was paid by the defendant, and by the intendment of the law he cannot satisfy the king with such money as she received as executor, wherefore it was adjudged that he take nothing by his writ,

etc   And so see that if a man be accounting in the
Exchequer, that this is a good way to get his debt, for the
defendant cannot wage his law in this action, albeit he
declares upon a simple contract, and this is to the advantage of the king, etc

There is no Paschal Term in the printed year of 8 Hen V   The Case 50
case is reported in Y B Mich 8 Hen V, p 10, pl 19

(51) **An executor** brought a writ of Debt against an abbot, Hilary
and he counted that the abbot had granted a corody to his 12 Hen IV
testator for the term of his life, and that his testator had
granted his estate in the corody to the said abbot, rendering
to him ten shillings a year   And for rent in arrear for four
years in the life of his testator he brought action   SKRENE
The grant of the corody cannot be without a deed, nor,
consequently, is the reservation of the rent without a deed
to the purpose, wherefore, inasmuch as he shows no
deed, judgment, etc   As if I lease a common to a man for
a term of years, without a deed, rendering a certain rent,
that is of no value, etc.

Reported in Y B Hilary, 12 Hen IV, p 17, pl 13 See also Fitzh Case 51
Dette, 116

(52) **In debt,** the plaintiff declared upon a contract for Michaelis
forty shillings   The defendant said that the contract was 28 Hen VI
for twenty shillings, which he is ready, etc , and as to the
remainder he waged his law   DANBY The contract was for
forty shillings, as we have counted, and since he has admitted
the contract, judgment, etc.   PORTYNGTON You can pray
judgment for that which he has admitted, for he shall have
his law for the remainder, since you cannot have the plea
as you have pleaded it   Which ASSHETON conceded, etc

The case has not been identified in Y B Mich 28 Hen VI, or in the Case 52
early abridgments

See as to debt on the arrears of an annuity, in the title Note
of Annuity, etc

See Statham, *supra*, title of Annuite, pp 12 a–12 b

(53) **One had** recovered a debt against another in the Trinity
Cinque Ports, and had his body in execution, and then the 30 Hen VI

warden to whom he was committed in the Cinque Ports let him go at large in Middlesex, wherefore the plaintiff brought an action of debt against this same warden, and the writ was brought in Middlesex, and he declared upon this matter, and he did not show the record. MOILE He can have an action within the Cinque Ports upon the record there, wherefore the action is not maintainable here. PRISOT The writ is that he permitted him to go at large at D, within the county of Middlesex, and that action thus conceived cannot be tried within the Cinque Ports He shall have a *Quare Impedit* for it [churches in Wales][1] in this Court, etc. And all the justices held that the action was maintainable, etc

Case 53   Reported in Y B Trinity, 30 Hen VI, p 6, pl 5 See also Fitzh Dette, 53

Michaelis 19 Hen III   (54) **In debt** against one as heir, he says that he had nothing by descent, and it is found that he had one acre, the plaintiff shall have execution of all his goods for his false plea *Simile*, Hilary, 5 Ed III, and in Trinity, 7 Ed. II, in Debt The contrary was held by FORTESCUE, etc

Case 54   There is no early printed year of 19 Ed III The case has not been identified in the Rolls Series for that year

Trinity 7 Ed III   (55) **Debt was brought** against an abbot upon an obligation made by the prior in a time of vacancy And it was adjudged good because it was for a thing which came to the use of the house, etc

Case 55   The case has not been identified in Y B Trinity, 7 Ed III, or in the early abridgments

Michaelis 22 Hen VI   (56) **Where an abbot** and the convent make an obligation, and the abbot is made bishop, he is not charged by that obligation, but his successor who is abbot shall be charged And this in Debt

Case 56   Reported in Y B Mich 22 Hen VI, p 4, pl 6 See also Fitzh Dette, 46

---

[1] Words from the case

(57) **Debt** was adjudged good against a man notwithstanding another was jointly bound with him, who was alive, but he was under age, etc. Michaelis 14 Hen IV

The case has not been identified in Y B Mich 14 Hen IV, or in the early abridgments Case 57

(58) **Debt** upon an obligation made to one as executor, was in the "*debet*" and was adjudged good, etc Paschal 25 Ed III

The case has not been identified in Y B Paschal, 25 Ed III, or in the early abridgments Case 58

(59) **In debt,** it is a good plea that another was bound with him, and the plaintiff had broken the seal of the other, so his debt was extinguished, etc *Simile*, Anno 7 Hen VI, in Debt Michaelis 33 Ed III

There is no printed Year Book of 33 Ed III Fitzh Dette, 84, has the case Case 59

(60) **Debt** was brought in the name of an executor upon an obligation made to the plaintiff "as executor of my will," etc. And notwithstanding the defendant by his deed called the plaintiff "executor," the plaintiff was forced to show the testament Paschal 25 Ed III

The case has not been identified in Y B Paschal, 25 Ed III, or in the early abridgments Case 60

(61) **Debt** against a gaoler because he suffered the condemned prisoner to go "Nothing owing him" is no plea, but he should show an acquittance And this in Debt, etc Paschal 2 Ric II

There is no printed Year Book for 2 Ric II The case has not been identified in the early abridgments Case 61

(62) **Debt** brought for tithes sold was abated because it belonged to the Court Christian Paschal 19 Ed III

There is no early printed year of 19 Ed III The case has not been identified in the Rolls Series Case 62

(63) **In debt** upon a sealed tally, "Nothing owing him" is a good plea. But yet, query? etc. Trinity 2 Ric II

⁴⁰ A note on the action of debt could be of no value unless it were much more than a note   The subject of debt has been so widely and deeply discussed that it would be useless to take it up here

There are one or two matters, however, directly brought up by the abridged cases themselves which may call for very brief mention   Our first case is an action against an executor   It is in the second year of Hen IV   By that time the action of debt has already had a long history, and is working itself out   Bracton says that "Actions cannot be bequeathed." [Bracton, f 107, b, P & M Hist of Eng Law, 2d ed , Vol 2 346]   The struggle between the ecclesiastical courts and the secular courts was still going on in the time of Edward I, but "A change as momentous as any statute could make was made without statute very quietly   Early in Edward I's reign the Chancery had framed and the King's Court had upheld a writ of debt for executors and a writ of debt against executors "   [P & M Hist of Eng Law, Vol 2 347, 2d ed., 341]   We have seen in a note upon account [*supra*, p 20] that the Statute of West II, cap 23, had given the action of account to the executor   Before the fourteen hundreds the executor is often sued and often sues, he has not fully come into his own, in fact in the division of rights between the heir and the executor the early custom has survived in our law to the present time   The reason for it may have vanished long since but the thing itself has been most tenacious of life   In a reported case in the Year Books, HANKFORD waxes indignant that this servant of the law is put in no better position than "a common laborer "   A good deal earlier, in Edward I's reign it is possible that the plaintiff might have recovered without a sealed writing or "specialty" if the cases reported in Y B 21 and 22 Ed I [Rolls Series p 456] and in Y B 30, 31 Ed I [R S p 238] may be thought strong enough to prove this   Holdsworth [Hist of Eng Law, Vol 3 455] seems to think them sufficient to support the proposition, but it seems at best somewhat doubtful   Apparently, without a specialty, the executor was not liable at this period or for some time to come   This state of the law was very unsatisfactory, but this dissatisfaction probably gave rise to the general custom, still very common in wills, of directing a payment of all the debts of the deceased   The ecclesiastical courts did sometimes enforce these obligations, but it is quite a different thing to have a court with the power to coerce persons to do a thing, and to have that power in the person's own hand   The action of *Assumpsit*, founded upon an equitable doctrine, finally came to the relief of the claimants

Our case 50 is a writ of *Quo Minus*   The commentator says, "And so see that if a man be accounting in the Exchequer, that this is a good way to have his debt "   However, in our case, he took nothing by his writ   The case explains that he was indebted to the king by his own deed, therefore the king could not have execution of the money he had as executor   Thus this case is no argument against the use of the *Quo*

Minus to recover debts from an executor, the theory of this action which is that the king would be injured if the debt was not paid would in this case, as in others, make for the granting of the writ

DETENU [41]

(1) **In detinue,** the garnishee showed other conditions than those which the defendant showed   And the opinion was that he should not be received to do that, for he was not injured   For if the defendant had showed false conditions he had charged himself against the plaintiff, and also against the garnishee, etc   But he need not have shown the conditions when he prayed for the *Scire Facias*, but he should have said that the writings were delivered to him by the plaintiff and another, etc , and not have expressed the conditions, etc

Statham 67 a
Hilary
40 Ed III

Reported in Y B Hilary, 40 Ed III, p 11, pl 24

Case 1

(2) **In detinue,** the plaintiff counted that the defendant detained from him an obligation in which he was bound to one H, upon certain conditions which were performed The defendant said that this same H had another writ for this same obligation returnable on this day, and he is ready to deliver to whom, etc   Whereupon H was demanded and did not come, wherefore it was adjudged that he be nonsuited, and the plaintiff prayed delivery of the obligation   THORPE   That you cannot have, but the Court awards a *Scire Facias* against H because the obligation was made to him, in which case, if it was delivered to the plaintiff and the conditions were not performed, H is without recovery, but although it had been delivered to H, if he had appeared and this plaintiff had been nonsuited, still he who is now plaintiff could be aided by way of a plea when H brought an action upon the obligation, etc   Wherefore a *Scire Facias* was awarded against H

Michaelis
41 Ed III

The case has not been identified in Y B Mich 41 Ed III, or in the early abridgments

Case 2.

(3) **In detinue** for certain chattels, the defendant said that the plaintiff was indebted to him for his table, in a certain sum of money, and that the plaintiff bailed to him the chattels in pledge for the same debt, at London, etc KYRTON Our action is brought in Surrey. And he shows a bailment in pledge, etc, at London, which cannot be understood to be the same bailment upon which our action is founded, etc. THORPE That is not denied by him, and if you have delivered it to him afterwards this plea is good FYNCHEDEN He should admit the bailment to the plaintiff and show that after that bailment he bailed it to the defendant in pledge at London, or else plead over, as above, "without this that he bailed it in Surrey, etc." And then the plaintiff said that he did not bail them in pledge, Ready, etc And the other alleged the contrary Query? etc

Reported in Y B Mich 46 Ed III, p 30, pl 29

(4) **Detinue** was brought against executors, and he counted as heir to one H And the writ did not mention the heir, but it was adjudged good And the writ was brought against executors, showing that a chest of muniments came to their possession after the death of their testator And he said that there were several executors not named And it was not allowed because the possession charged them individually, etc, in which case there was no need to have named them executors in the writ, etc

There is no printed year of 31 Ed III Fitzh Detinue, 50, has the case

(5) **Where the custom** is that the heir shall have the principalities[1] after the death of his father, he shall have a writ of Detinue for the same principalities if he be deforced of them, and count upon the custom, and how, after the death of his father, they came into the hands of the defendant as executor Query, if a stranger took them, how should he declare, etc ?

Reported in Y B Hilary, 30 Ed III, p 2, pl 9 See also Fitzh Detinue, 51

[1] The "principalities" were in the chamber the best bed, in the hall the better table with trestles, basin and pitcher, in the kitchen the best pot, etc

(6) **In debt,** the plaintiff declared upon a bailment made to the defendant of an obligation made by this same defendant to the plaintiff. MARTYN It seems that the action does not lie between those who are parties. ROLFF Be it of what value it may, that is my case, etc.

Reported in Y B Mich 4 Hen VI, p 5, pl 11 See also Fitzh Detinue, 2

Michaelis 4 Hen VI

Case 6

(7) **In detinue.** YELVERTON Judgment of the writ, for he has counted as to three tallies, and the writ is "goods and chattels" where it should be "*præcipe quod reddat* three tallies," etc., as upon an obligation, etc ASCOUGH Both are good enough in both cases, wherefore answer. YELVERTON He has declared the value of the tallies, and he does not recover the value, because he can receive them back in the Exchequer NEWTON Answer. Wherefore he waged his law, etc

Reported in Y B Hilary, 21 Hen VI, p 29, pl 13 See also Brooke, Detinue, 24.

Hilary 21 Hen VI

Case 7

(8) **In detinue** for charters, the plaintiff counted how he himself and one T delivered the charters to the defendant into his own hand, upon certain conditions between the plaintiff and the said T, to re-deliver to him who performed the conditions, etc (Query if this declaration is good?) The defendant said that he did not know if the conditions were performed, and said that T was dead, and had issue one J, to whom certain lands, which the said charters concerned, had descended, and he prayed a *Scire Facias*, and had it, notwithstanding the death of T was not returned, etc

Reported in Y B Mich 21 Ed III, p 41, pl 44

Michaelis 21 Ed III

Case 8

(9) **In detinue,** where they are at issue upon the detinue, the justices of *Nisi Prius*, it being found that he detained them, shall inquire if it was burned, or else the plaintiff shall not have judgment in the Bench, unless a new inquiry, etc. Contrary elsewhere, etc

The cases cited in this way are rarely to be distinguished in the Year Books Some of the Iters are being published by the Selden Society

Iter of Norfolk Anno 7 Ed III

Case 9.

Paschal
30 Ed III

(10) **In detinue** for a writing, the defendant said that the plaintiff, by the same deed that he demanded, had released to one T, who was a party to the bailment, and many others And he prayed a *Scire Facias* against all, and could not have it, except against T, because a man shall not have a *Scire Facias* against any except against him who was a party to the bailment, or his heirs or executors, etc

Case 10

There is no printed Paschal Term for the year 30 Ed III   The case has not been identified in the early abridgments

Note

See garnishee, in the title of Excommunication, etc , Paschal, 3 Hen VI

See *infra*, Statham, title Excommengement, p 79 b

Hilary
38 Ed III

(11) **In detinue** against a husband and his wife, for a bailment made to them after the coverture, the writ was abated because it should have been brought against the husband alone, for no bailment during the coverture shall charge the wife   Query, if the husband dies, against whom shall I have an action? etc

Case 11

Reported in Y B Hilary, 38 Ed III, p 1, pl 1   See also Brooke, Detinue, 22, and Fitzh Detinue, 36

Michaelis
7 Hen VI

(12) **If I bail** a deed to one to rebail to me, and he is enfeoffed by the same deed, by a stranger, so that the deed belongs to him by feoffment, or by descent, he can bar me in a writ of Detinue   As appeared in Detinue, etc.

Case 12

The case has not been identified in Y B Mich 7 Hen VI, or in the early abridgments

Hilary
9 Hen VI

(13) **In detinue,** the plaintiff counted that his father, whose heir he is, bailed the deed to one B, to re-bail to him and to his heirs, etc   And how the same deed came into the possession of the defendant, as executor of B, etc And the opinion was that the declaration was of no value because he had not commenced the title to the land to

Statham 67 b

which the deed was a covenant, to him as heir, etc , for otherwise the deed belonged to the executors of his father, because the property was in his father as a chattel   But where a man bails a deed to bail to a stranger, the stranger shall have an action of detinue, because the property is out of him who bailed it ROLFF If the declaration had been good, and the heir had recovered, then the executors shall be twice charged, for they are charged against the executors of his father. MARTYN: It is not so, for no bailment was made to the defendant, so he is not chargeable, except against him who had the right As if one A bails to me a deed concerning land and I lose it, and one B finds it and delivers it to the said A, it is clear that I shall not have an action against B But if I deliver the deed to B, to re-bail to me, and he bails it to A, now by his own deed he has discharged himself against both of us, etc.

Reported in Y B Hilary, 9 Hen VI, p 58, pl 4 See also Brooke, Detinue, 7, and Fitzh Detinue, 7   Case 13

(14) **In detinue** against two, for a bag with one hundred pounds contained in the same FORTESCUE Judgment of the writ, which does not allege that the bag was sealed, in which case he should have had a writ of Debt PASTON How shall a man have a writ of Debt when the property is in him? FORTESCUE If you borrow money from me, the property is in you, and yet you shall have an action of debt So here ASCOUGH You shall not have the bag by a writ of Debt NEWTON, to FORTESCUE Answer FORTESCUE, for one, said that he did not detain, and a like plea was pleaded for the others MARKHAM Inasmuch as the action is conceived against them jointly, to such several pleas, no law, etc And so to judgment, etc   Trinity 18 Hen VI

Reported in Y B Mich (not Trinity), 18 Hen VI, p 20, pl 5 See also Fitzh Detinue, 13   Case 14

(15) **In detinue,** the defendant said that the obligation was delivered to him and one B, who is still living, not named, judgment of the writ RIKHILL Inasmuch as you do not deny that you detained it, judgment, etc. And then it was adjudged that the writ should stand. And this was against the opinion of THIRNING. Query, as to the cause, etc   Michaelis 7 Hen IV

Reported in Y B Mich 7 Hen IV, p 6, pl 37 See also Brooke, Detinue, 16   Case 15

(16) **In detinue** for a box, sealed, with charters, where the defendant had a *Scire Facias* against certain persons, they were at cross purposes as to a deed within the box The Court opened the box, for it would be in vain to take issue upon the deeds if there were no such deeds within the box And this in Detinue, etc

Case 16 Reported in Y B Hilary, 7 Hen IV, p 7, pl 4

(17) **If two bail writings** to a man, to re-bail to them, or to one of them, one of them cannot have an action without the other By the opinion of THIRNING, etc. For if they could, each of them could bring an action, and the Court could not know to whom the delivery should be [made], etc

Case 17 Reported in Y B Hilary (not Paschal), 12 Hen IV, p 18, pl 19 See also Brooke, Detinue, 20

(18) **In detinue,** if the plaintiff entitles himself to a deed concerning tailed land, and the defendant entitles himself to the land, he shall have a traverse to the gift, by HANK-FORD, and THIRNING said that he should answer to the Detinue, etc.

Case 18 The case has not been identified in Y B Paschal, 7 Hen IV, or in the early abridgments

(19) **See by** ASCOUGH, that a man shall have a traverse to the bailment, by special matter, as to say that the plaintiff gave him the deeds, without this that he bailed them to him to re-bail, etc , or that the plaintiff bailed them to him to re-bail to himself, and that he delivered them to one B, without this that he bailed them to re-bail to him, etc And so of similar things, etc In Detinue

Case 19 The case has not been identified in Y B Paschal, 28 Hen VI, or in the early abridgments

Note **See as to detinue,** in the title of Law, M 3 Hen VI, and in the title of Count, M 18 Hen. VI, and in the title of Counterpleader, M 18 Hen VI, and in the title of Attorney, Hilary, 8 Hen VI, and in the title of Conditions, in

different places, and also in the title of Garnishee and
Garnishment, which will be made here [1]

See Statham, title of Ley, *infra*, p 118 b, case 14   Statham, title
Connte, *supra*, p 38 b, case 11   Statham, title of Attourney, *supra*,
p 18 b, case 10

(20) **If in detinue** the plaintiff entitles himself to the charters as heir, it is a good plea to say that he is a bastard, etc

Michaelis
18 Ed III

The case has not been identified in Y B Mich 18 Ed III, or in the
early abridgments

Case 20

(21) **In detinue** for charters, it is no plea to say that the
house to which, etc , is in ancient demesne   In the Iter
of Northampton, etc

Anno
13 Ed III

We have no early printed year of 13 Ed III   The cases printed in
the Rolls Series are from the regular Year Books

Case 21

(22) **A plea of detinue** was removed out of Chester
because the defendant said that the charters were delivered
to him by the plaintiff and another, who was out of the
jurisdiction of Chester, and the Court held that they could
not proceed, etc   Query, when a man pleads such a plea
shall he show the deed to the Court before the garnishee
comes, etc ?   Query, if the plea shall be removed upon such
a plea in London? etc

Statham gives no citation for this case, and it has not been identified.

Case 22

(23) **If one bails** a deed to a man to re-bail to himself,
which deed comes to another and not to him, and he to
whom the bailment was made dies, so that the deed comes
to his executors, he shall not have an action of detinue
against them, without a specialty   By HANKFORD, in
Detinue, etc   (But yet the contrary would appear, because
the detinue is the cause of the action, and the other is only
a continuance, etc   But for charters it is clear that a man
shall have a writ of Detinue, without a specialty, because
the testator cannot wage his law, etc)

Hilary
11 Hen IV

Reported in Y B Hilary, 11 Hen IV, p 45, pl 20   See also Brooke,
Detinue, 19

Case 23

[1] Evidently referring to titles which were to appear in the Digest,
but which were still in the making   The note was evidently not
intended to appear in the finished work

(24) **In detinue,** the defendant asked judgment of the count because he counted on a chest with charters and muniments, and he did not say that it was either sealed or locked PRISOT Did he not declare for any certain deed? MOILE No, sir, but they are concerning a manor of which he is seised, etc PRISOT Then the count is worth nothing at all, which PORTYNGTON conceded, for if it was not sealed he might have had notice, but if it be sealed he could choose, etc But yet, although it be sealed, they usually count of a writing in special, concerning certain lands, for otherwise he could wage his law, etc

Case 24

The case has not been identified in Y B Mich 31 Hen VI, or in the early abridgments

41 The two subjects of debt and detinue are so closely related that to speak of one is almost of necessity to speak of the other, so far as their early development is concerned Of course by the time our Year Book cases are being reported, the distinction is plain enough Debt has separated from detinue, and the latter action has become common Possibly in the beginning the action was given only against the bailee [Holmes Common Law, 169, P & M Hist of Eng Law, 2d ed , Vol 2 175], although this is a proposition not so firmly established that a deeper search may not prove its undoing Holdsworth [Vol 3 275, n 2, and the cases cited by him on pp 276–7] argues that the action of detinue very naturally took the place of the old action for *res adiratae* Our own cases do not cover sufficient ground for us to take up the question here, but it seems best to note that it is not safe, in spite of good authority to the contrary, to settle down upon the statement that the action of detinue was only given against bailees, or one who had temporarily parted with the goods A careful search through the cases, in the light of the advantage given such a search by the cases cited by Holdsworth, might very probably show that the action of detinue was given against everyone to whose hands the property had come So far as it is revealed by our cases, the argument that the action cannot be maintained because no bailment is shown is merely the argument pointed out by Holdsworth, that there was a bailment claimed and that the claim being on the bailment, and no privity shown in the defendant, the case must fall

One interesting point about the actions of debt and detinue is that the "special peculiarity" of these two actions is the wager of law There have been numerous guesses at the reason for this peculiarity, but that of Maitland appears the most reasonable He says "The simple truth is that they are old actions, older than trial by jury " [P & M Hist of

Eng Law, 2d ed , Vol 2 634] The cases in Bracton's Note Book are numerous [Bracton, Note Book, 7, 143, 396, and Bracton, fo 366] They are trying to get beyond the wager of law in our period, only one of the abridged cases ends with a wager of law [case 7] To get away from the wager of law is a thing so desirable, even necessary if justice is to be done, that it is interesting to trace through all these old actions the attempts to discover some action which is free from this evil

DISCEIPTE

(1) **In deceit,** the plaintiff was restored to his lands, with the issues in the meantime, etc

Statham 68 a
Hilary
41 Ed III

Reported in Y B Hilary, 41 Ed III, p 2, pl 4 See also Brooke, Deceit, 8

Case 1

(2) **In deceit,** upon examination it was found that the bailiff of the sheriff held the plea on the day that the tenant was garnished, and not the garnishor, wherefore it was awarded that the tenant be restored, etc

Paschal
42 Ed III

The case has not been identified in Y B Paschal, 42 Ed III, or in the early abridgments But it appears in Mich 43 Ed III, p 31, pl 27 Fitzh Deceit, 27, has the case

Case 2

(3) **A man** recovered damages in a writ of Deceit, where he was impleaded for certain lands through malice of the defendant, although he who impleaded him was nonsuited See [this case] for it was well argued.

Michaelis
43 Ed III

Reported in Y B Trinity (not Mich), 43 Ed III, p 20, pl 6 See also Brooke, Deceit, 9, and Fitzh Deceit, 28

Case 3

(4) **In deceit** it was found that he was summoned by only one summons, and for this reason he was restored to the lands, but not to the issues in the meantime, etc

Hilary
50 Ed III

Reported in Y B Trinity (not Hilary), 50 Ed III, p 16, pl 9

Case 4

Paschal
18 Ed III

(5) **One brought a writ** of deceit because the defendant had put the plea without a day by a protection *"quia profecturus est,"* whereas he remained at all times thereafter in England, in such a place, etc And the action was maintained.

Case 5

There is no early printed year of 18 Ed III The case is printed in the Rolls Series, 18 Ed III, p 12, No 6

Michaelis
3 Hen IV

(6) **In deceit,** the plaintiff counted that the defendant was seneschal of the manor of D, and that a covenant was made between the defendant and the plaintiff at B, in the county of M, that the defendant should arrange that the plaintiff should have certain acres of land to hold at will of the said manor, to fulfill which covenant he received from the plaintiff five shillings at the same place And then the defendant got the lord of the manor to enfeoff one L of the same lands, in deceit of the plaintiff, wrongfully, and to the damage, etc And the writ was brought in another county than that where the land was, and it was the opinion that it was good, etc

Case 6

Reported in Y B Mich 3 Hen IV, p 3, pl 12

Michaelis
9 Hen VI

(7) **In deceit,** the plaintiff counted that he bought a pipe of romany of the defendant, and the same defendant, knowing it to be spoiled and decayed, etc, warranted it to be useful, etc And the opinion was that the action had been maintainable without any warranty And the defendant said that he sold to the plaintiff by one who was his servant, without this that he sold it in any other manner And upon that they demurred in law And the action was taken against the defendant and not this B, etc Query?

Case 7

Reported in Y B Mich 9 Hen VI, p 53, pl 37

Trinity
20 Hen VI

(8) **One brought** an action upon the case because the plaintiff and the defendant bargained that the defendant should enfeoff the plaintiff of a manor before such a day, for which the plaintiff should pay him one hundred pounds in his hands, and that the defendant before the said day had enfeoffed one J of the same manor in fee, so he had

disabled himself from keeping our covenant   And the
opinion of many was that the action did not lie because
the action sounded in covenant, of which covenant nothing
is fulfilled, etc , in which case he cannot be deceived in
fulfilling the covenant, inasmuch as no part of it is fulfilled

And PASTON said, in the same plea, that a man shall have
an action of deceit where there was not any covenant, as
if a man sell me a horse without saying that he warranted
it, still I shall have an action of deceit against him, since
he sold me a horse knowing him to be unsound

Reported in Y B Trinity, 20 Hen VI, p 34, pl 4   See also Brooke, Case 8
Deceit, 2, and Fitzh Deceit, 14

(9) **In a quare impedit** against an abbot, who held the Hilary
church to his own use, he made default at the distress, 27 Hen VI
wherefore the plaintiff had a writ to the bishop, and then
the abbot brought a writ of Deceit against thes heriff, and
the summoners and mainpernors.   And the sheriff returned
that one of the summoners was dead, and that the others
were summoned   And so many of the summoners appeared
and were examined, and said that the abbot was not summoned   And now the case is Shall the abbot be restored
or not?   DANBY· It seems to me that he shall be restored
for the process in this writ is, by summons, attachment and
distress at the common law, in which case he should be
summoned, attached and distrained before the writ was
awarded to the bishop for his default   As in a writ of Wardship, the Statute is that he shall be summoned, attached
and distrained, and if he be not summoned then there shall
never be a distraint, for if the sheriff returns "nihil" to the
summons, the plaintiff shall never have any other process
but the summons until he be summoned   And this is
clearly proved in a writ of Debt, where, if the sheriff returns
"nihil" to the summons, a *Capias* shall issue immediately
and not the distress, then in this case when he was not
summoned, the attachment and the distress were erroneously
awarded, etc   ASCOUGH Then he would have alleged
this matter when he was distrained, in which case he would
have saved his advowson, for that which is error cannot be

reversed by a writ of Deceit   And a writ of Deceit does not lie in this action, which is personal, for it does not lie except where it can save the default of the summons, so that upon that default the judgment is given   But in this case the judgment was not given upon the whole process   And in this *Quare Impedit* the plaintiff does not recover the advowson, but the possession, to which the defendant cannot be restored. PORTYNGTON   If he was not summoned attached, nor distrained, then it is reasonable that he have this writ   Then when it is found upon examination that he was not summoned, we do not need to inquire further, for it appears to us that the attachment and the distraint were wrongfully awarded   And also the abbot held the same church to his own use, in which case he cannot have another action to recover the advowson, except a writ of right   And although the plaintiff recovers only the possession still the defendant loses the advowson, for he is out of possession by this recovery, and that is the fault of the sheriff, wherefore, etc   ASSHETON   In a *Præcipe quod Reddat*, if it be found upon examination of those first summoned that the tenant was not summoned, the justices shall not inquire further, because upon that first summons the land was lost.   But in this case the advowson is lost on all three writs, and so it is not the same   FULTHORPE· Although this action be mixed in the personalty, still it is not like a personal action, for in no action which is merely personal can a man recover by default before appearance   But in this *Quare Impedit* he can recover by default before appearance   And also the abbot holds to his own use, which is yet stronger, etc   And also we have found upon examination that he was never summoned, attached or distrained, wherefore the Court awards that the abbot be restored to the church, to hold to his own use, as he held it before the judgment, and that he recover his damages that he lost in the *Quare Impedit*, and that he have a writ to the bishop to oust the clerk of him who recovered in the *Quare Impedit*, etc   Query, what writ he would have to recover his damages, etc ?   I believe that it would be a *Fieri Facias*, or an *Elegit*, or a *Capias*, etc   Well argued, etc

The case has not been identified in Y B Hilary, 27 Hen VI, or in Case 9
the early abridgments   The Statute is Marlbridge, 52 Hen III (1267),
cap 2, Stats at Large, Vol 1, p 55 (60)

See as to deceit, in the title of Action on the Case Note
Many matters, etc

Statham, *supra*, title of Accions sur le Cas, pp 10 b–11 b   Statham 68 b

(10)   **In deceit,** the plaintiff was restored to the land and Michaelis
to the issues, and he also recovered his damages, etc.   18 Hen VI

The case has not been identified in Y B Mich 18 Hen VI, or in the Case 10
early abridgments

(11)   **The tenant** by his warranty had a writ of Deceit Michaelis
against the demandant, who recovered against the tenant, 3 Ed III
upon his warranty, in a writ of Dower, because he had
assets in the same county, and he was not summoned,
etc   Query, if the vouchee brings a writ of Deceit against
the tenant, or against the demandant? etc.

The case has not been identified in Y B Mich 3 Ed III, or in the Case 11
early abridgments

(12)   **In deceit** the one who was summoned made default, Trinity
and the other appeared and was examined, and the exam- 18 Hen VI
ination was [held] good   Query, if one were dead? etc

The case has not been identified in Y B Trinity, 18 Hen VI, or in Case 12
the early abridgments

(13)   **In deceit,** if the defendant pleads joint tenure in a Paschal
plea which is tried against him, he will lose his land without 18 Ric II
any examination   And this by the opinion of the COURT
And they also said that the writ is well brought against
him who recovers, although he is not a tenant, as in
a writ of Error

There is no printed year for 18 Ric II   Fitzh   Deceit, 49, has the Case 13
case

(14)   **The heir** of him who lost by default had a writ of Michaelis
Deceit   And it was adjudged good.   18 Ric II

There is no printed Year Book for 18 Ric II   Fitzh   Deceit, 50, Case 14
has the case

Michaelis 16
and Hilary
17 Ed III
(15) **One sued** a *Scire Facias* upon a recognizance, and
had an execution by default, and he sued a writ of Deceit,
and was restored to that which he lost, with the issues, etc
Which note, since no freehold was lost, or put in execution,
etc

And it was said in the same plea, that although the sheriff
returned at the petty cape that the tenant was summoned,
when he was not summoned, that the tenant shall not have
a writ of Deceit, although the lands be lost, etc

Case 15   There are no early printed years of 16 or 17 Ed III   The case is
found in the Rolls Series, 16 Ed III, p 292, Pt 2, No 9, and in the
same series, 17 Ed III, p 204, No 44   See also Fitzh   Deceit, 36

Paschal
17 Ed III
(16) **In deceit** by the lord of ancient demesne, to annul
a fine levied of lands which were held of the manor, which
fine was annulled   And the opinion of the justices was
that notwithstanding the annulment the fine was good
between the parties, and the party could take advantage
of the fine, etc   But yet, query?

Case 16   There is no early printed year of 17 Ed III   The case is found in the
Rolls Series, 17 Ed III, p 444, No 35   See also Fitzh   Deceit, 37

Trinity
19 Ed III
(17) **Where a writ issued** to the sheriff to inquire as
to waste, the defendant had an action of deceit, and said that
he was not summoned nor attached, etc   *Simile*, 19 Ed. II

Case 17   There is no early printed year of 19 Ed III   The case is found in the
Rolls Series, 19 Ed III, p 146, No 8

Paschal
29 Ed III
(18) **In deceit,** the first summoners came, and the viewers
and pernors, and the second summoners made default,
and the first summoners were examined, and they said
that no summons was made, wherefore the tenant was
restored, etc. Although if he had said that he was summoned, then it seems that they should have awarded process
against the others, to wit   the second summoners, etc
Query? etc.

Case 18   Reported in Y B Trinity (not Paschal), 29 Ed III, p 42, pl 33
See also Fitzh   Deceit, 59

DISTRESSE

(1) **A man cannot** distrain for corn in sheaves, while Statham 69 a they are in the field or in the grange, for the sheriff cannot Hilary replevy them, because he cannot notice one sheaf or any 18 Ed III other any more than a man can distrain for silver in pennies, etc   And also in the carriage of the sheaves he may lose part of the grain, in which case he cannot restore them in as a good condition as they were when he took them, etc   In rescous, etc

The case has not been identified in Y B Hilary, 18 Ed III, or in Case 1 the early abridgments

(2) **If the king gives** or sells his wardship to a man, Hilary or leases a manor or castle to him, to hold for life or a term 12 Ric II of years in fee, he cannot distrain out of his fee, as the king could when it was in his hand, etc

There is no early printed Year Book for the reign of Ric II   The Case 2 case has not been identified in the early abridgments.   The case has not been identified in Y B 12 Ric II, Ames Foundation, ed Deiser

(3) **A writ** issued out of the Exchequer to return certain Trinity goods which were the property of one H, who was attainted 12 Ric II of treason, who said that he leased certain lands to the said H for the term of his life, rendering a certain rent, and for so much in arrears before the attainder and before the treason done, he took the goods, judgment, etc WADE Inasmuch as you have admitted the property to be in him at the time, judgment, etc   And so to judgment   Query, if he need say "before the treason," etc ?

There is no early printed Year Book of Ric II   The case is printed Case 3 in the Y B of 12 Ric II, Ames Foundation, ed Deiser, p 3

(4) **The sheriff** can distrain for an amercement in his Trinity torn for all the county, and this in an avowry   But the 2 Hen IV lord of a leet cannot distrain out of his precinct   And this by HANKFORD, etc   Query?

Reported in Y B Trinity, 2 Hen IV, p 24, pl 17   See also Brooke, Case 4 Distress, 13, and Fitzh Distress, 10

Hilary
33 Ed III

(5) **Distress** does not lie against the heir of the mesne who has acknowledged the acquittance, in a *Scire Facias*, etc. And distress against him who acknowledges, etc. By HERLE, in a *Scire Facias*, etc

Case 5

There is no printed Hilary Term of 33 Ed III The case has not been elsewhere identified

Hilary
8 Hen V

(6) **On the day** for the pleadings in Trespass, if the defendant makes default, distress *"ad audiendum judicium"* shall issue. And if he makes default then, there shall issue a writ to inquire as to the damages But in debt he shall have judgment to recover immediately Which the Court conceded, etc.

Case 6

The case has not been identified in Y B Hilary, 8 Hen V, or in the early abridgments

Michaelis
3 Ed III

(7) **Distress** *ad audiendum judicium* issues when the defendant makes default on the next day after issue, etc Query, if he does not come at that distress?

Case 7

The case has not been identified in Y B Mich 3 Ed III, or in the early abridgments

DISCENT

Paschal
49 Ed III

(1) **If a man** purchases land in fee, and dies without heirs *de parte paterna*, the land shall descend to his heir *de parte materna* But if the land came to him by descent on the part of his father, it shall never go to the heirs on the part of the mother, nor *è contra*, but it shall rather escheat, etc And so it was decided in an Assize, etc And a man can be heir to his son by a mesne, as if the son dies without issue, then his uncle on his father's side shall be his heir And if the uncle dies without issue, his brother, who is father to the son, is heir to his brother, and so by this mesne he shall be heir to his son, etc And my uncle may well be my heir, for I have not come from him, for the issue of one brother does not come from the other brother, nor *è contra* And that is the reason that they can inter-

marry within certain degrees, etc But all have come from
the stock and he cannot be heir to any of them, and therefore my father cannot be my heir, as can my brothers,
uncle, nephew and the like, for I did not descend from any
of them, but my father, grandfather and great-grandfather,
nor my mother's grandfather or great-grandfather shall
never be my heir, because I lineally descended from them, etc.

Reported in Y B Paschal, 49 Ed III, p 11, pl 5 See also Brooke'
Discent, 7, and Fitzh Discent, 7

DEUX PLEEZ LOU UNE VA A TOUT

(1) **In a writ of dower,** the tenant as to part pleaded Statham 69 b.
a joint tenancy, and as to the remainder, "never married," Trinity
etc. And the opinion was that he should have both 40 Ed III
the pleas, although one went to all Well argued, etc
Michaelis, 43, in Formedon, etc

Reported in Y B Trinity, 40 Ed III, p 31, pl 13 See also Brooke, Case 1
Deuz Pleez, 7

(2) **In a resummons** upon a writ of Wardship against Hilary
the heir, the defendant pleaded, as to the body, non-tenure; 18 Ed III
and as to the land, that he did not hold of him, and he had
both the pleas, notwithstanding the last plea went to all,
etc

The case is reported at length in Y B Hilary, 18 Ed III, p 4, pl 15 Case 2
The point is to be found on p 16, near the end of the case

(3) **In trespass for a horse** taken and killed POLE Michaelis
As to the taking of the horse, we found him doing damage 30 Hen VI
in our several soil And as to the killing, "not guilty"
DANBY Your last plea goes to all, for our action is founded
upon the killing MOILE No sir, for although he did
not kill the horse, still, if he took the horse without cause,
he did you a wrong, wherefore he shall have both the pleas.
Which NEWTON and PASTON conceded

The case has not been identified in Y B Mich 30 Hen VI, or in the Case 3
early abridgments

(4) **In account,** it was alleged that the defendant was his bailiff of his house and had the care and administration of certain goods   The defendant said as to the house, "never his bailiff," and as to the goods of the plaintiff he said that the plaintiff was indebted to him in twenty pounds, and assigned the same goods, etc   HANKFORD   The first plea goes to all   Which the Court conceded   And also the last plea is no plea, for he could have had it upon the account, etc   Wherefore the issue was taken whether he was his bailiff or not   And it was said that the law is otherwise now, to wit   that this plea does not go to all, for if he had the care of my goods, as wine to sell, and things of that sort, I cannot have any other writ except as above

The citation to 40 Hen IV is palpably an error, as Henry IV reigned only fourteen years   The case can be found in Y B Hilary, 14 Hen , IV, p 20, pl 25

(5) **In replevin for cattle** taken in P, in the vill of B, against one F and others   ROLFF said (for F) P is in the view of T, and not in B , Ready, etc   And upon the return he avowed the taking in B for damage feasant   And for the others he said that the property in them was in one A at the time of the taking, and not in the plaintiff   COTTES-MORE   The first plea is no plea, for the place is not traversable any more than in battery   MARTYN   Not the same, for a man cannot justify a battery   And in trespass for battery the freehold cannot come into question, but here it can, wherefore, etc   COTTESMORE   P is the in vill of B, and not in T, Ready   And the other alleged the contrary   And as to the cattle the property was in the plaintiff at the time, etc.   And the others alleged the contrary, etc

The case has not been identified in Y B Trinity, 2 Hen VI, or in the early abridgments

(6) **In dower** against two, one said that he had assigned to her ten shillings in allowance for all her dower, to which she agreed   The other said that he is and has been at all times ready, etc   To which the demandant, as to the first plea said, that she did not agree, and alleged the

contrary   And she prayed judgment against the other
MARTYN   The first plea goes to all, and if it be found
against you, you will be barred; as if in a Formedon against
two, one says that the demandant is a bastard, and the
other admits the action, the demandant shall not have
judgment against him who admits the action until the other
is tried   (Query? For it seems the contrary, for each
can plead and lose his portion, for it is not like a joint action
of debt, etc)

The case has not been identified in Y B Mich 7 Hen VI, or in the   Case 6
early abridgments

(7) **In wardship of the body** and of land, against   Michaelis
one F, who said, as to the body, that one H leased to him   7 Hen VI
etc , and he vouched him to warranty.   And as to the lands
he pleaded joint tenancy   COTTESMORE   The last plea
goes to all   As in a writ of Cosinage the tenant, as to part,
vouched to warranty, and as to another part, he said that
the demandant was a bastard, and he did not have both
the pleas   MARTYN   He pleaded no plea as to the body,
but he thinks to put the plea on another vouchee   And
as to the land, he shows such matter as he has, and that
is the case where a man pleads non-tenure as to part, and
"never married" to the remainder for no other purpose
except to excuse himself as to the damages, because he
pleaded non-tenure   So here, by his plea, he is to charge
the vouchee with the damages   And the opinion of the
Court was that he should have both the pleas, etc

Reported in Y B Mich 7 Hen VI, p 14, pl 23   See also Brooke,   Case 7
Deuz Pleez, 13

DROIT [42]

(1) **In a writ of right** after the battle is waged or the   Statham 70 a
plea joined, the demandant or his attorney should come on   Paschal
the first day after with his champion and offer himself, and   42 Ed III
repeat the words upon which the battle is joined   And if
he does not come, judgment shall be given for the demand-

ant on the fourth day, and not before   And if the demandant does not do (as above) on the first day, the justices will award a nonsuit on the fourth day, etc

Case 1

Reported in Y B Paschal, 42 Ed III, p 15, pl 28   See also Brooke, Droit, 3, and Fitzh Droit, 9

Michaelis
44 Ed III

(2) **See in a writ of right** against the husband and his wife, if they would make a surrender the woman shall be examined By THORPE   Query?

And in the same plea [the woman] was received upon the default of her husband and oyer of the count, but there was no declaration against her, because she was a party to the first declaration

Case 2

The case has not been identified in Y B Mich 44 Ed III, or in the early abridgments

Michaelis
30 Ed III

(3) **In a writ of right,** the tenant made a defeasance under this form, "You have here H, etc , who defends, etc ," and whereas G demands against him the manor of B, and he counted that this was his right, and he repeated all the count, defending the tort and force and the right of G outright, and the seisin, etc , word for word according to the count, and this his freeman, R by name, who is here, is ready to defend with his body, and so if this R, whom God defend, does not come, he is ready to defend by another who can, etc   And he took the champion by the right hand, and then he went out and came back with the champion, with but one glove upon the hand of the champion and under his fingers a penny, repeating all, and making defence to all, as above   And he waged battle, to wit each champion gave his glove to the other as a gage of battle, and then a day was given them, and they were commanded that the champions should not go into fair or tavern, etc , and that they should offer the money in five different places, in honor of the five wounds of God, etc.

Case 3

Reported in Y B Mich 30 Ed III, p 19, pl 23   See also Fitzh Droit, 13   The account of the manner of waging battle is fuller and more accurate in the case itself, as well as much more dramatic, than it is in the abridgment   Fitzherbert's account is also full and good

(4) **The king** brought a writ of right and recovered by Hilary
34 Ed III. default, etc. And so note, etc

There is no printed year of 34 Ed III The case has not been iden- Case 4 tified in the early abridgments

(5) **In a writ of right,** it is a good bar to say that formerly Paschal
34 Ed III one brought an action against him who now demands, and this present tenant, and you disclaim in this same land, judgment if you should have this action And not to rely upon the right, for by his disclaimer his right is gone And the law is the same as to a release of the plaintiff, etc By WILLOUGHBY But SHARSHULL said the opposite, for he said that the nature of this writ of right is to have the right tried, and a final judgment, then when the plea of the tenant proves that he has the right, he shall say thus "and so he has the better right," etc But where it appears by his plea that he has no right, but his plea is a bar by reason of a covenant, as of a collateral warranty, there he shall not conclude upon the right, for he has no more right by reason of that, in which case, if he relies upon the right, it will be found against him, and so because of the hardship for the tenant he shall have the plea, without concluding to the right: For by the same reason that if he was impleaded by a stranger he could vouch him and recover in value, for the same reason he could plead the same warranty in bar, etc And the law is the same as to a lineal warranty, or a warranty by the plaintiff himself, if he relies upon the warranty, since he cannot get to the warranty without pleading the feoffment or release, etc. And it may be that he had no right to the land, and still he could bar the demandant by reason of the warranty, which is a real covenant by which the demandant is bound, etc

And it was said in the same plea that a fine upon a conusance of right is a good bar without relying on the right, because it has extinguished his right by matter of record (But yet this is contrary to the reason given above, etc)

There is no printed year of 34 Ed III See Fitzh Droit, 29 Case 5

Paschal
35 Ed III

(6) **The lord of the court,** when the parties are joined at the Great Assize, cannot do anything, for he cannot have a process against the four knights who make the array, by which it shall be removed But if he wages battle it shall be determined before the lord himself, etc. In Droit, etc

And it was said in the same plea, that the demandant should count for all who possibly could hold an estate

And it was said in the same plea, that where a man enters, where his entry is not legal, but is defeated afterwards by entry or by a recovery, still he shall have a writ of right on his possession, if he had a right before, and yet if he had not entered he had been without a remedy

And it was said in the same plea, that it is a plea for the tenant to say that he in whom the demandant found seisin was never seised And if it be found he had no right, etc (But I believe that that is not law, to wit to say, "And if it be found," etc.)

Case 6

There is no printed year of 35 Ed III Fitzh Droit, 30, has the case

Trinity
34 Hen VI

(7) **In a writ of right,** the tenant vouched one A to warranty, who entered into the warranty and said that he had a better right, etc , without making any title in himself And the tenant could say the same, to wit that he had a better right, without making title in himself, etc

Case 7

The case has not been identified in Y B Trinity, 34 Hen VI, or in the early abridgments

Hilary
1 Hen VI

(8) **See a writ of right** against the Count of Northumberland, where there is good matter and all the form of the trial by battle, etc

And in the same plea, when the battle was joined, the parties were commanded to find sureties for their champions to do battle, and so they did, to wit each of them two pledges And I believe that this was for the amercement, for if the tenant makes default after battle, he shall be amerced, etc.

And it was said in the same plea, that it is a good plea to

say that the champion is a villein, etc   Query, if he shall
say that he is an outlaw, or excommunicated?

And they were clothed in red leather and had long
staves, but the staves had no knobs upon the end, as the
staff of an appellor, nor their heads shorn like that of an
approver

And it was said in the same plea, that it is a good plea
to say that the demandant leased him the same lands for
the term of his life, judgment if action, for he has admitted
that the plaintiff had the right by reason of the reversion,
so he shall say, "and so he had more right to hold the land
for the term of his life by force of the lease," etc   And
although the lease be made by indenture, that does not
change the case, for an estoppel is no bar in this writ of right,
etc

Reported in Y B Mich (not Hilary), 1 Hen VI, p 6, pl 29, where Case 8
the ceremony of the wager of battle is very fully set forth   See also
Brooke, Droit, 20, and Fitzh Droit, 1

(9) **In [a writ of right]** the writ was, "who claims to hold Trinity
of the king *in capite*" KYRTON   The land is held of one 38 Ed III
R, and not of the king, judgment of the writ   FYNCHEDEN
That is nothing to you, for it does you no harm, because
you can be saved by protestation   But if the lord of the
Court was here, he could demand his Court   (Query as
to this?) Wherefore he passed over, etc

Reported in Y B Trinity, 38 Ed III, p 13, pl 10   See also Brooke, Case 9
Droit, 9, and Fitzh Droit, 5

(10) **If a man recovers** a rent service against me by Statham 70 b.
a tried action, and I bring the *ne injuste vexes* against him, Trinity
and he pleads that recovery, I cannot join the plea against 38 Ed III
that recovery, but it shall bar me   By GRENE, etc   In
the *Scire Facias* of the Abbot of [Lincoln], etc

And see the title *Ne Injuste Vexes*, for the lord against
whom the writ was brought made a defence, and besides
that he entitled himself to the rent, and bound seisin, etc
And then the demandant made a defeasance to him and had
become tenant, etc. And these are the two negatives

of which the *Natura Brevium* speaks, etc. As appears in the title

Case 10

The case has not been identified in Y B Trinity, 38 Ed III, or in the early abridgments

The title of *Ne Injuste Vexes* in the old *Natura Brevium* is supposed to be referred to There is no such title in Statham, and the later *Natura Brevium*, known as Fitzherbert's, was not then printed

Anno
4 Ed III

(11) A man shall not have a writ of right for a rent charge, nor for rent seck, nor or of any rent except a rent service By HERLE, in the Eyre of Nottingham, etc

And see in the same plea that he held clearly that in a writ of right it is a good bar to plead a fine upon a conusance of the right of the demandant, or his ancestor, because the judgment in such a fine is final, etc Query? And also he held clearly in the same plea that in a writ of right it is a good bar to plead a recovery against the demandant or his ancestor by a writ of *Cessavit* by default, for when he recovers by default in a *Cessavit*, the judgment is final by the Statute, which says that the land incurs the remedy, etc. But if he pleads the recovery in the *Cessavit* by a tried action, it is no bar, but he shall conclude to the right, etc

Case 11

The case has not been identified in Y B Anno 4 Ed III, or in the early abridgments

The Statute is that of West II, 13 Ed I (1285), cap 41, Stats at Large, Vol 1, p 163

Paschal
3 Ed II

(12) Where a man grants to me the services of his tenant, by a fine upon a conusance of the right, I shall have a writ of customs and services, notwithstanding the tenant did not attorn, etc But I cannot avow, etc But it seems hard to maintain this writ of customs and services, for he should bind possession in himself, or in his ancestor. And in that case there was no possession in fact, as it seems, etc In Replevin By the opinion of the COURT, etc

Case 12

There is no Paschal Term in the printed year book of 3 Ed II (the Maynard) Fitzh Droit, 33, has the case

(13) **In a writ,** the tenant vouched to warranty, and the demandant counted against him, and he emparled, and then went away in despite of the Court, and final judgment was given against him Michaelis 9 Hen VI

The case has not been identified in Y B Mich 9 Hen VI, or in the early abridgments Case 13

(14) **If the tenant** makes default in a writ of right, at the return of the Grand Cape, final judgment will not be given And so see that no final judgment shall be given unless the pleas are joined upon the right, except in the case where the tenant departs in despite of the Court, as in the above case, etc Hilary 3 Ed III

The case has not been identified in Y B Hilary, 3 Ed III, or in the early abridgments Case 14

(15) **In [a writ of] right** against the husband and his wife, who joined the plea, and the demandant emparled until another day, on which day defendants made default, and the demandant had a final judgment, notwithstanding the pleas were never entirely joined, etc Query, if the demandant could be nonsuited inasmuch as the offer of the pleas comes entirely from the part of the tenants, etc ? And they paid no attention in this case [to the fact that] the woman tenant was a married woman Paschal 11 Ed III

There is no early printed year of 11 Ed III The case is found in the Rolls Series of 11 Ed III, p 5 An allusion is made in the case to the facts that the tenant was a married woman Case 15

(16) **In a writ of right,** the tenant held to the right, for it is the point of the writ, to wit "He holds full right," etc As in a writ of Entry upon a Disseisin, the point of the writ is the disseisin, which shall be answered, and yet he declares on the possession, as in a writ of right, etc And if it be a *præcipe in capite*, it is "which he claims to be his right," which is the point, etc

There is no citation given by Statham for this case, and it has not been identified It seems more like a general note than an abridgment of any specific case Case 16

⁴² This is, of course, the writ of right, named from the words of the writ
"*Quod sine dilatione plenum rectum teneas*" [Coke, 1st Inst 115, a]
The writs of right are The writ of right patent, the *præcipe in capite*,
and the little writ of right [Holdsworth, Hist of Eng Law, Vol 3 3]
It seems to have been "the highest real action" [Booth Real Actions,
p 84] Booth [*Ib*, p 87] says, "it is called in the Books 'Droit' because
it hath the greatest respect, and the most assured judgment" For
all interested in this action, Booth in his book upon Real Actions
gives every part of the action in full

The writ of right close was peculiar to tenants in ancient demesne,
and we frequently meet with it in "the books" We have one case of a
ne injuste vexes [case 10] This was an old common-law writ given to
the tenant against the lord [Booth Real Actions, 125, 126] to restrain
the lord that he "unjustly vex not, or permit to be vexed," his tenant,
by a demand for services which the tenant did not owe, or was not used
to do

DONNE ⁴³

Statham 71 a

Hilary
42 Ed III

(1) **A man cannot give land** to himself by way of a
reservation, for he cannot reserve a lesser estate, etc,
consequently his heir shall not have a Formedon for such
a reservation, etc As appeared in a *Scire Facias*. Well
argued, etc

Case 1

Reported in Y B Hilary, 42 Ed III, p 5, pl 17, at the end of the
case See also Brooke, Formedon, 9

Hilary
50 Ed III

(2) **If lands** be given to two men in tail, he who survives
shall have it by the survivorship, although he dies without
issue, and the other has issue, that issue shall not have it,
but he should preferably re-enter, etc

Case 2

The case has not been identified in Y B Hilary, 50 Ed III, or in the
early abridgments, unless it is the case in Y B Hilary, 50 Ed III,
p 50, pl 3

Trinity
50 Ed III

(3) **A man** was seised of lands, the remainder to his right
heirs, and the tail was to him and his wife and to their heirs
male, etc And he had issue a son and a daughter, and a
son by another wife, and died, so that the reversion of the
fee descended to the elder son And then the elder son
died without issue, and the opinion of THORPE was that

the sister should have the land, because the fee was in her brother, etc   But the possession of the fee was not in him, etc.

The case has not been identified in Y B Trinity, 50 Ed III, or in the Case 3 early abridgments

(4) **A gift** to the sacristan of such a house is good. Hilary FYNCHEDEN And by such a gift the house shall inherit, 49 Ed III as well as where land is given to the house and to the convent, without naming any certain person.   And this in a *Scire Facias*   But yet, in the first case, although the gift be good, it seems that he had only a life term, etc.

The case has not been identified in Y B Hilary, 49 Ed III, or in Case 4 the early abridgments

(5) **In a formedon,** a deed was produced which read, "I Paschal give, etc , to R, and K, his wife, and their heirs and to the 5 Hen V other heirs of the aforesaid R, if the said heirs of the said R and K die without heirs by them begotten " And this was adjudged a good tail, etc   Well argued, etc.

Reported in Y B Hilary 5 Hen V, p 6, pl 13   The only printed Case 5 term for that year is Hilary Term

See of gift in the title of Free Marriage, and in the title Note of Feoffment, and in the title of Devise

See Statham, title of Frank Marriage, *infra*, p 96 b , Statham, title Feoffments et Faitz, *infra*, p 96 b, and Statham, title of Devise, *infra*, 71 b and 72 a

(6) **If lands be given** to a man in tail, the remainder to Paschal the right heirs of one J, who is living, if J dies while the 32 Hen VI donor is living, the remainder is good, and otherwise not By the whole COURT in an Avowry

There is no printed Paschal Term for the year 32 Hen VI   The Case 6 case has not been identified in the early abridgments

(7) **Where land** is given to a man, and to her who shall Michaelis be his first wife, in tail, although he had no wife at the time 11 Hen IV of the gift, yet it is a good tail By the opinion of THIRNING. In a note, etc.

The case has not been identified in Y. B Mich 11 Hen IV, or in the Case 7 early abridgments

Trinity
11 Hen IV

(8) **If lands be given** to an abbot and to the convent, and there is no mention of their successors, still they shall have the lands by an impropriation· By HANKFORD   And this in Debt, etc.

Case 8

Reported in Y B Trinity, 11 Hen IV, p 84, pl 34

[There has been much difficulty in tracing the citations under this title, as the writs are not given, though they may presumably be writs of Formedon, and points are apparently taken from cases not brought upon the gift, or upon writs related to the Formedon   The points are very probably to be found somewhere in the printed Year Books, but time is lacking to trace them through all their mazes]

[43] The gift, as we have it in these cases in the abridgment, is solely the gift of land, which is a very ancient form of alienation   Bracton treats of it in his Second Book [Bracton, Book 2, *De Acquirendo Rerum Dominio*]   Reeves gives us a great deal of learning upon it [Reeves, Hist of Eng Law, Vol 2 289–303]   It has been said [P & M Hist of Eng Law, 2d ed , Vol 1 12] "In the thirteenth century every sort and kind of alienation (that word being used here in its very largest sense) is a gift, and yet it is a gift which always, or nearly always, leaves some rights in the giver "   And again, "The mediæval 'gift' is almost as wide as our modern 'assurance' ' " [P & M Hist of Eng Law, 2d ed , Vol 2 13, note 1]   The subject naturally runs into that of the form of the gift, the "Formedon," and some of our cases in the abridgment may be taken from cases in which that writ was brought, one we know, however, to be a writ of *Scire Facias* [case 1]   It is most probable that had these cases come up in a Formedon they would have been placed under that subject, yet our case 5 is a Formedon, so we have no means of judging by the cases themselves why they were thus separated and part placed under Gift, part under Formedon

The common form of the gift of land is given by Britton [99, b , Nicholl's edition, Vol 1, p 252]   "In single gifts it is sufficient to say this, 'Know all men present and to come that I, John, have given to Peter so much land with the appurtenances in such a town', and it is proper to specify between what boundaries "

DEVISE

Statham 71 b
Michaelis
44 Ed III

(1) **In an assize,** the tenant pleaded in bar, by force of a devise made by the father of the plaintiff, and the plaintiff entitled himself as heir, etc   The plaintiff said that his father, after the devise, made a feoffment to defeat the

devise, and retook an estate and died seised, after whose
death, etc   THORPE   Inasmuch as you do not deny the
testament, and that this was his last will, judgment, etc.
WILLOUGHBY (to the plaintiff)   You should show as special
matter that he did not agree, etc   And so he did.

Reported in Y B Mich 44 Ed III, p 33, pl 18   See also Brooke, Case 1
Devise, 8, and Fitzh Devise, 16.

(2)   **If I lease lands** for the term of another's life, which Trinity
are devisable, and my lessee devises them in fee, and dies, 33 Ed ̧III
living him for whose life [etc], and the devisee enters, the
opinion of WILLOUGHBY was that I cannot enter, because
my reversion was not discontinued by that devise, inasmuch
as he died in possession   And this in a *Præcipe quod Reddat*
(But I believe that the law is the other way   But if my
tenant for life devisees in fee, I cannot enter in his lifetime
because he can disagree to that and it does not take effect
until he is dead), etc

There is no printed year of 33 Ed III   Fitzh Devise, 21, has the Case 2
case

(3)   **Land was devised** for a term of life, the remainder Trinity
to John, son of one R, and to his heirs male of his body 9 Hen VI
begotten; and in default of issue, the remainder to the next
heirs male of the said R, and to the heirs male of their bodies
begotten   R died, the first devisee for a term of life
entered, John, the son, died without issue male in the life
of the tenant for life   The tenant for life died, and one
Alice, cousin and heir of the said R, entered and enfeoffed
one H in fee.   And the said Alice had issue male and died
The opinion was that this issue should not have the land,
because at one time the remainder was void, living the
tenant for life, because no issue male was living who was
heir to R, and also the remainder was to the right heirs of
R, and not "of his body begotten "   Then it seems that
these words "to the right heirs male" are void, for the heirs
female would inherit as well by these words as the heirs
male.   Then if it be not tailed to the right heirs male of
R, it cannot be tailed to the heirs of their heirs   As if I

give land to a man and to his heirs male, he has a fee
Then, although I say further, "and to the heirs of the
body of his heirs male begotten," that cannot be a tail in
the issue, since their father had a fee, etc. So here. See
the plea, because it was finely argued.

And see in the same plea, that by the custom of London
a man can devise that his executors sell his lands; and
in that case they can give a man a fee, and still they have
no fee nor freehold, but they give it as attorneys, in a
manner, etc

And see in the same plea, by PASTON If a man devises
as above, that his executors sell his lands, and dies seised,
his heir is in by descent still by the sale of the executors
he will be ousted, and in the same manner his heir after
him But if a man devises his lands to his executors,
so that the freehold passes to them by the devise, and then
the heir of the devisor abates, and dies seised, and his heir
is in by descent, in that case the executors cannot oust
the heir who is in by descent, etc

And it was said in the same plea, by GODEREDE, that
if a man devises to a man for the term of his life, who is
not a person who is capable of taking, as a monk, or who
is not in being, the remainder over in fee, the remainder
is good. And I believe that the reason is because it re-
quires no livery of seisin, so at whatever time the remainder
falls in he can enter, etc   Query?

Case 3

Reported in Y B Trinity, 9 Hen VI, p 23, pl 19, and Mich 11
Hen VI, p 12, pl 28 See also Brooke, Devise, 5 and 32, and Fitzh
Devise, 2

Trinity
3 Hen VI

(4) **If a man** devises land to his son and heir in tail, the
remainder over in fee, and dies, his son cannot disagree
to the devise, and this is because of the remainder By
the opinion of PASTON in a *Cui in Vita*

Case 4

Reported in Y B Trinity, 3 Hen VI, p 46, pl 1   See also Brooke,
Devise, 4   Paston does not appear in the report of the case, nor does
it stand strongly for the point in question, the report only going as far
as the joinder of issue   Brooke's report differs greatly from that of
Statham

(5) **Where the land** is devisable, if a man devises the reversion of his tenant for life, to be sold by his executor, and dies, and the executor sells the reversion, that is good enough without a deed, and without attornment of the tenant, for if the testator himself devised the reversion to a stranger and died, immediately after his death the reversion is out of his heir, and that is without deed   And when he devises that it shall be sold by his executors and they sell it, it passes by that contract, for they have not the reversion but their power is limited, etc   And since the sale, which is only a personal thing, is good without a deed, consequently there is no need of attornment   But yet it seems that the grantee cannot avow without an attornment, any more than where the reversion is granted by a fine, etc , for that devise is executory, by an *"ex gravi querela,"* as well as in a fine by a *Scire Facias*, etc   Well argued. Michaelis
18 Hen VI

The case has not been identified in Y B Mich 18 Hen VI, or in the early abridgments Case 5

(6) **If a man** devises a horse to me, or a robe, after the death of the devisor I can take it out of the possession of the executors, but if a stranger takes it before I take it, I cannot have an action of Trespass, for it is not like a gift which is immediately executed, etc   But if a man devises "the third part or the fourth part" of his goods, I cannot take them because it is not certain, but I should sue in the Court Christian Paschal
27 Hen VI

Reported in Y B Hilary (there is no printed Paschal Term), 27 Hen VI, p 8, pl 6   The facts differ somewhat from those in the abridgment but on the whole the law appears to be to the same effect   See also Brooke, Devise, 6, where he queries the sweeping statement as to the executor Case 6

(7) **See of devise** in the title of Waste, and in the title of Issue, etc Michaelis
49 Ed III

See Statham, Waste, pp 179 b–181 b, and Statham, Issue, pp 115 b– 117 b, *infra*

(8) **In the exchequer chamber,** ILLYNGWORTH told how a citizen of London, by his testament enrolled in the hust- Trinity
30 Hen VI

ings of London, had devised certain tenements within the
same city to his son, and to three others in fee, and his will
was, by this same testament, that one of the three should
have all the profits of the said lands during his whole life
And then, because he who should have the profits was dead,
the heir, who was another of the feoffees, brought a bill
in the Chancery, comprehending this matter, and that
the said devise was in trust, etc , and prayed that the others
should release to him, etc   WANGFORD   When by his

Statham 72 a testament he devised the land to all the four in fee, and
by the same devise it was his will that one of them should
have all for life, it appears clearly that after the death of
him who was to have the profits, that the others shall have
the fee   And they shall not release to the heir, for it is not
like a feoffment in which no will is expressed   But when
his will is expressed it shall be considered wholly his will,
in which case they hold to their own use, etc   FORTESCUE
I can see no difference between a feoffment and a devise
as to the intent, wherefore if you will not deny it, to wit
that it was a trust, it is reasonable that you release to the
heir, etc   Which all the justices conceded, etc

Case 8   The case has not been identified in Y B Trinity, 30 Hen VI, or in
the early abridgments

Anno
10 Ed III   (9) **"Devised"** and "not devised" shall be tried by a
jury, notwithstanding the testament be shown, etc   But
yet it seems that he shall answer to the testament, etc.
In the Iter of Northampton

Case 9   This is one of the unidentified cases from the Iter of Northampton

Michaelis
22 Ed III   (10) **If lands** be devised to a man, he has only an estate
for life, [but if] be to have to him "forever," although
no mention be made of his heirs, still he shall have a fee,
etc   The law is the same as to a devise to a man and his
assigns, etc

Case 10   Reported in Y B Mich 22 Ed III, p 16, pl 59   See also Brooke,
Devise, 33, and Fitzh Devise, 20

Michaelis
25 Hen VI   (11) **If a man** devises lands of which he is not seised,
and afterwards he purchases these same lands and dies

seised, the devise is good   Query, if the law will be the same
in regard to a fine? etc

There is no printed year of 25 Hen VI   The case has not been iden- Case 11
tified in the early abridgments

(12) **If lands** be devised to a man and his heirs male of Trinity
his body, etc , and he has issue a daughter, who has issue 28 Hen VI
a son, this son shall inherit   And yet of a gift in the tail
the law is otherwise   And this by the opinion of all the
justices in the Exchequer Chamber

The case has not been identified in Y B Trinity, 28 Hen VI   Fitzh Case 12
Devise, 18, has the case in almost the same words as Statham

(13) **If goods be** devised to the king, he shall have a writ Anno
of Debt, or he shall have upon suggestion a *Venire Facias* 40 *Liber*
Assisarum,
or a *Scire Facias* according to the form of the Exchequer in a *Scire*
and upon that a *Fieri Facias*, etc , notwithstanding that *Facias*
for other persons it belongs to the law of the Church, etc

Reported in the *Liber Assisarum*, p 24, pl 35, Anno 40   The case Case 13
does not give the details as given by the abridgment   See also Brooke,
Devise, 44, and Fitzh Devise, 19   Fitzherbert differs from the other
abridgments and from the case

(14) **If a man** entitles himself to land by a devise, he shall Anno
say that the vill in which the land is, is an ancient borough, 40 *Liber*
Assisarum
for if it be an "uplandish vill" [1] it will have no such custom, etc
for such lands devisable are pleadable in the same borough,
so he shall say it is a borough or else ancient demesne
By the opinion of the COURT in an Assize

Reported in Y B *Liber Assisarum*, 40 Ed III, p 250, pl 41   See Case 14
also Brooke, Devise, 20

DOUBLE PLEE

(1) **A prior brought** a *Quare Impedit* and counted Statham 72 b
that his predecessor was seised, etc , and presented   And Hilary
then the king seised the temporalities by reason of war 40 Ed III

[1] The vill of Uplands according to the report of the case   This case
is interesting historically

and presented. And afterward we had restitution by reason of an accord between the kings, and the church is now vacant   And the title was held sufficiently single, etc.

Reported in Y B Hilary, 40 Ed III, p 10, pl 22   See also Brooke, Double Plee, 122, and Fitzh   Double Plee, 72

(2) **In a resummons,** the demandant assigned certain points in which the Court of his franchise had failed to do right, and the bailiffs offered to aver the contrary upon all the points, and because the king was in a manner a party, to wit   to maintain the jurisdiction of his Court, the issue was taken upon all the points, etc

Reported in Y B Hilary, 40 Ed III, p 11, pl 23   See also Brooke, Double Plee, 119, and Fitzh   Double Plee, 73   The latter has much the longest and best digest of the case, which has some important points upon jurisdiction

(3) **In replevin,** the defendant avowed upon the plaintiff because the father of the plaintiff held of him, etc., by homage, fealty, and ten shillings of rent, and for the homage after the death of his father he avowed, etc   CANN-DISH   We hold by fealty and all services, Ready   And as to the homage and rent, our father was not of age, etc And by excessive distress you were seised by the hands of [your] father, etc   BELKNAP   That plea is double   FYNCH-EDEN   Answer both, etc   But it seems he did not need to speak of the excessive distress, and also that he was not of age, for one of them is sufficient reason to render the seisin void, etc

Reported in Y B Mich 42 Ed III, p 26, pl 11

(4) **In trespass** for goods carried away, the defendant said that the plaintiff was indebted to him in twenty shillings, and that the same plaintiff delivered to him the said goods in satisfaction of the twenty shillings, and then he delivered the same goods to the plaintiff to keep, and then took the same goods out of his possession, for which taking he has brought this action   And the opinion clearly was that it was no plea, because of the doubleness.

The case has not been identified in the printed Y B Mich 30 Hen Case 4 VI, which is a very short report, consisting of only eight short placita, none of them cases of Trespass

(5) **W and K,** his wife, brought a *Scire Facias* out of a Trinity 38 Ed III fine by which the said K, before the marriage, had given the same lands to one M, saving the reversion, and that M died without issue, etc And the writ was challenged because it was that it ought to revert to the wife and not to the husband [1] FYNCHEDEN It is good here, but it is otherwise in regard to a remainder, etc. FYNCHEDEN We tell you that W and K were seised after the death of H, and enfeoffed one H, whose estate, etc WILLOUGHBY We say that formerly we brought a *Scire Facias* against you for the same land, and recovered by default, and made the feoffment to H, upon condition, etc , which conditions were broken and we entered, and then you brought a writ of Deceit against us, because you were never garnished, and it was found for you, wherefore you were restored to the lands, and we pray execution, etc (Query, if he need to show the deed in that case?) etc FYNCHEDEN The plea is double. THORPE He cannot do otherwise, for if the feoffment had been simple, he could never have execution, because by the feoffment his right is gone, wherefore the plea is good. UFFLETE The feoffment was simple, without this, Ready And the other alleged the contrary, etc

Reported in Y B, Trinity, 38 Ed III, p 16, pl 21 Case 5

(6) **In a praecipe quod reddat** or other action, if the Trinity 9 Hen VI defendant shall plead a sufficient plea in bar, and he also traverses the point of the writ, that is not double, for the bar is not to the purpose, but the plea which traversed the point or title of the writ shall be taken By PASTON, and this in a note, etc

Reported in Y B Trinity, 9 Hen VI, p 26, pl 23 See also Brooke, Case 6 Double Plee, 11, and Fitzh Double Plee, 40 Statham gives much the best abridgment of the case

[1] The case has it that the proper form should have been that the land should revert to the wife, not to the husband

Michaelis
3 Hen VI

(7) **In debt against executors** who said, "Nothing in their hands and fully administered the day the writ was purchased " And the opinion was that this was not a double plea, since they are both of one substance, and one plea answers both Wherefore the plaintiff said, "Assets in their hands " And it was adjudged that the issue was good, etc

And it was said in the same plea, that if the defendant pleaded a double plea, and the plaintiff rejoined only to one matter, and upon that the issue was taken, it was well taken, and the other matter was waived And it was also said if the plaintiff answers all, and all are found for him, that he shall recover Which was conceded, etc.

Case 7

Reported in Y B Mich 3 Hen VI, p 3, pl 4. The point as to the double plea does not come until the middle of p 4 See also Brooke, Double Plee, 3

Hilary
3 Hen VI

(8) **See by Martyn,** in Dower, that if a man pleads two or three matters, and relies upon one of them, that the plea is single enough, for then that upon which he relies is his plea, and the other but a convenience, and if it be not a convenience it will not be entered

Case 8

Reported in Y B Hilary, 3 Hen VI, p 28, pl 11 See also Brooke, Double Plee, 4 He is correct in making it an Avowry, not Dower

Michaelis
11 Hen IV

(9) **In detinue,** the garnishee showed certain conditions, to wit. that the plaintiff came on such a day to Westminster, after a reasonable warning, and levied a fine, etc , to the costs, etc , [of J E, and if he did not come] [1] And he showed how he sued a writ of Covenant, and the sheriff returned that he was garnished and that he did not come, and also we notified him on such a day, etc., fifteen days before, etc And the opinion was that the plea was not double, for the return of the sheriff was only to show that he could come by course of law to levy the fine Query, if the garnishment of the sheriff is a good plea if the plaintiff is distrained, since he was not summoned, etc.?

Case 9

Reported in Y B 11 Hen IV, p 18, pl. 42 Brooke, Double Plee, 127, comes to a different conclusion from Statham, *i e ,* that the plea

[1] Words from the case

was declared to be double   The case is not over clear, but a careful reading seems to show that Statham is correct, and that Brooke took an argument of counsel for the decision

See as to double plee, in the title of Escheat, Michael- Note mas 11 Hen IV, and in the title of *Audita Querela*, Michaelmas, 44 Ed III.

Statham, Escheat, *infra*, p 80 a, has no citation to Mich 11 Hen IV   Statham, title *Audita Querela*, *supra*, p 20 a

(10) **In account,** the defendant said that at the time of Paschal the receipt he was under age and still is, and they said that 16 Ed III this plea was double because it demanded two trials, to wit. that he is still under age is triable by the judges by their inspection, and that he was under age at the time is triable by the jury   (But yet the last mentioned goes to all), etc

There is no early printed year of 16 Ed III   The point has not been Case 10 identified in the Rolls Series for that year

I have taken this citation to 16 Ed III to be for this case, as the case beside which it appears is evidently a note, and would naturally have no citation

(11) **In trespass for cutting wood,** the defendant jus- Anno tified because he was seised of a house in the same vill, 11 Hen VI to which there was common of estovers in the same wood, appendant to the said house, and that he and all those whose estate [he had] had been accustomed, time, etc , to cut underbrush in the same wood, to burn on their hearths in the same house, and how he cut, etc , as well he might And the opinion was that the plea was double, to wit one, the appendancy, and the other, that he and all those whose estate [he had], etc , for it might be that he could have the estovers there, time, etc , of one who was tenant of the house, and that he and all the tenants by force of that grant had used the estovers, still this did not prove them to be appendant, then each of them is a good plea for him, wherefore, etc.   (But yet it seems that if such a grant is beyond time of memory, it shall be understood to be appendant)

Reported in Y B Mich 11 Hen VI, p 11, pl 27   See also Brooke, Case 11 Double Plee, 115

DOWER "

Statham 73 a

Michaelis
2 Hen IV
(1) **The Lady of M** was in the Chancery to be endowed of certain lands of which her husband died seised, as appeared by a *diem clausit extremum* returned there, etc And because the king had allowed and committed the guardianship of the heir of her husband and of his lands to this same lady during the nonage of the heir, it was adjudged that she should not be endowed until the coming of age of the infant

Case 1

Reported in Y B Mich 2 Hen IV, p 7, pl 30 See also Brooke, Dower, 27, and Fitzh Dower, 23

Michaelis
2 Hen IV
(2) **In dower** against one who vouched the heir of the husband to warranty At the *sequatur sicut alias* [1] he did not come, wherefore it was adjudged that the woman should recover her dower against the vouchee, if he had [assets] in the same county, and that the tenant should hold in peace And if he had not, then that she should recover against the tenant, and he over, etc

Case 2

Reported in Y B Mich 2 Hen IV, p 7, pl 35 (The placitum was skipped in the numbering of the Year Book) See also Brooke, Dower, 28

Paschal
40 Ed III
(3) **A woman shall not be endowed** unless the fee and the freehold be united in her husband in fact Well argued, etc In Dower

Case 3

Reported in Y B Paschal, 40 Ed III, p 15, pl 2 See also Brooke, Dower, 6, and Fitzh Dower, 37 Both give fuller and better digests than Statham, yet his point is the clearer for its brevity

Paschal
41 Ed III
(4) **In dower** against the heir, who said that she detained certain muniments, etc The woman said that she was great with child with one who should be the heir if God, etc. And the tenant is brother to our husband, etc. And this was adjudged a good plea BELKNAP She is not *enceinte*

---

[1] *Sequatur sub suo periculo sicut alias* Brooke notes the examination by the court as to the facts, before judgment

by her husband, Ready THORPE. You shall have no
such issue to bastardize the child, etc Wherefore he said
she was not *enceinte* the day her husband died Ready.
And the others alleged the contrary Query? How shall
this be tried — by women or otherwise?

Reported in Y B Paschal, 41 Ed III, p 11, pl 9 The text of Case 4
the case differs from Statham in some points, but the law is the same
See also Brooke, Dower, 8, and Fitzh Dower, 47 The latter ignores
the plea as to the child

(5) **Where the heir** is bound by his own deed and does Paschal
not know how to bar the demandant of her dower, she shall 19 Ed III
recover against the wife and not against the heir, although
he had assets in the same county. But it is otherwise if
he is bound by the deed of his father, etc. Query, as to
the difference?

And see in the same plea, when she shall have judgment
to recover her dower against the heir, she shall change her
demand, for even if it be so that it agrees with the writ
since it is general, to wit reasonable dower of the freehold,
etc, still the demand is special, and that can be changed
before judgment, as well as abridged By THORPE and
SHARSHULL. (And study this well)

And see in the same plea that if she vouches a stranger
who is not the heir, even if the vouchee had assets within
the same county, still she shall not recover against the
vouchee, and this is against the reasoning of some who say
that the reason that the woman recovers her dower against
the heir who is vouchee is because the recovery in value of
the land is uncertain since it is of the third part, etc.

There is no early printed year of 19 Ed III The case has not been Case 5.
identified in the Rolls Series for that year The case is confused but
there is no printed case by which to correct it

(6) **Where the husband** is enfeoffed upon a condition Trinity
which is fulfilled in his lifetime on the part of the feoffor, 34 Ed III.
so that the feoffor enters and defeats his estate, still the wife
of the feoffee shall be endowed By SHARSHULL And the
law is the same if I enfeoff a man upon condition that he
shall enfeoff another before such a day, and before that day

he makes the feoffment, still his wife shall be endowed, etc. (But yet the first case is not law, etc)

Case 6

There is no printed Year Book for 34 Ed III Fitzh Dower, 127, has the case   He makes the same remark that the first statement is not law, probably copying from Statham   He gives the *Liber Assisarum* as authority for his remark

Michaelis 44 Ed III

(7) **If the tenant** for life leases his estate in reversion for the term of his life, rendering a certain rent, and for default of payment one re-enters, shall the wife of the reversioner be endowed of this possession or not was well argued in Dower, etc   See the adjudication, to wit   that she shall be endowed   A like case was adjudged in Trinity, 45, in Dower, but there no entry was reserved for default of payment, etc

Case 7

Reported in Y B Mich 44 Ed III, p 31, pl 12   See also Fitzh Dower, 44

Paschal 19 Ed III

(8) **If in dower** against the committee of the king he prays aid, he shall not have aid for he is ousted by the Statute of Bigamies.

Case 8

There is no early printed year of 19 Ed III   The case has not been identified in the Rolls Series for that year

The Statute of "*Bigamus*," 4 Ed I (1276), cap 3, Stats at Large, Vol 1, p 114 (115)

Trinity 46 Ed III

(9) **If the tenant** vouches one in the wardship of the king, in Dower, for which a day is given *ad interloquendum cum Rege*, and then a *procedendo in loquela* comes, they shall proceed to judgment without a *procedendo ad judicium* well enough, because the matter will be examined in the Chancery before any *procedendo* issues   In Dower, etc   In all other writs the law is the other way

Case 9

Reported in Y B Trinity, 46 Ed III, p 19 pl 23   See also Brooke, Dower, 20

Michaelis 5 Ed III

(10) **Out of the fee** of the husband is no plea in a writ of Dower for rent, for it does not belong to the wife to show title, etc

The case has not been identified in Y B Mich 5 Ed III, or in the early abridgments

(11) **If the tenant** in a writ of Dower vouches one in the wardship of the king for part, and for another part, in the wardship of another; against the king a day shall be given *ad interloquendum cum Rege*, and against the other the common process. And although a writ of *Procedendo* does not come, still the plea shall be continued all the time against the stranger   But yet, query?   For it seems when the aid is granted that it is discontinued against the other guardian, etc   Query?   And if the heir be vouched in wardship, and is under age, even though the demandant recovers against the tenant, still he shall not have judgment in value against the heir until he is of full age, for it is not the same as where a writ of Dower is brought against the guardian, for there, even if the guardian renders dower of that of which she is not dowable, the heir shall have an Assize of Mort d'Ancestor at his full age   But if the tenant should recover in value against him, he could not, at his full age, have an Assize of Mort d'Ancestor, wherefore it shall be saved to him by way of answer in a *Scire Facias*, etc   For in no case will process issue against the infant where he is vouched in wardship, etc

Reported in Y B Trinity, 46 Ed III, p 19, pl 23   A second digest of case 9   See also Brooke, Dower, 20

(12) Tenant in tail alienated, and retook an estate to himself and to his wife in tail, and had issue   Shall the second wife be endowed or not was well argued, and the opinion was that she should not be endowed, for the heir can choose to claim which estate he will   But if land be given to a man and to his wife in tail, and for default of issue the remainder to the right heirs of the husband, and the wife dies, and their issue dies, the second wife of the husband shall be endowed against the collateral heirs of the husband, for after the death of his issue he had a fee simple, and no other estate   (But yet in the first case it seems that "to their issue" is a general tail, etc)

Reported in Y B Trinity (not Mich), 46 Ed III, p 16, pl 11

Hilary
50 Ed III

(13) **In a scire facias** against a woman, who said that she was tenant in dower of the inheritance of one J, and prayed aid of him   And she was driven to show upon whose assignment she was endowed, for to that the demandant shall have an answer   Wherefore she said that it was on the assignment of one H, who was guardian, and she showed how, etc

Case 13

The case has not been identified in Y B Hilary, 50 Ed III, or in the early abridgments

Paschal
31 Ed III

(14) **In dower,** the tenant said that the land was given to the husband and his first wife, in tail   FYNCHEDEN

Statham 73 b   Seised so that he could endow her, etc   And he could not have the plea without answering the special matter, etc

Case 14

There is no printed Year Book of 31 Ed III   The case has not been identified in the early abridgments

Michaelis
31 Ed III

(15) **If a woman** be endowed in the Chancery, be it legally or tortiously, a man cannot defeat it by way of answer, but he should sue in the Chancery to defeat it, etc In a *Quare Impedit.*

Case 15

There is no printed year of 31 Ed III   Fitzh   Dower, 128, has the case

Trinity
5 Ed III

(16) **If land** be recovered [in value] against the husband by reason of a warranty made by his ancestor before the marriage, still his wife after his death shall be endowed, for her husband could have alienated the lands before he was vouched, and then it shall not be rendered to the value, consequently the title of the woman is the elder, for the title of him who vouches does not commence till the day of the voucher.   And that in Dower.

Case 16.

The case has not been identified in Y B Trinity, 5 Ed III   Fitzh Dower, 129, has the case   Perkins Prof Book, has a case of Dower in this year and term, which is contrary to this   Perkins Prof Book, p 61

Hilary
21 Ed III.

(17) **In dower** against the heir, he said that she held certain muniments, etc.   And she could say that she had

delivered them to him, and not answer to the detinue, as in a writ of Detinue, etc

And see in the same plea, that if there are two heirs who have made partition, and she delivers the deeds to one of them, that is good enough   Query? etc

Reported in Y B Hilary, 21 Ed III, p 8, pl 24   Case 17

(18) **A woman** brought a writ of Dower against one T, Hilary 48 Ed III who vouched to warranty the heir of the husband, as of full age and out of wardship, as to one part, and produced a deed to that effect; and as to the other part, he vouched the heir under age and in the wardship of one F, who had part of the lands with the body   And he prayed that he be summoned in the same county, and also that the heir be summoned in the same county, because he was vouched as of full age.   And he vouched the same heir in the wardship of one H, who had the wardship of other lands, and prayed that he be summoned in another county   And process was made against the guardians to that effect, etc , until now, when the guardian who was vouched in the foreign county came, and the other guardian made default   And the heir, as of full age, was essoined, because he who came said that the lands were held of the king, who granted to us the wardship of the body and of the lands by his letters patent, and we do not think that of this part without the counsel of the king, etc   BELKNAP   It is necessary that you have the same days until the other guardians come   FYNCHEDEN   It seems that he shall enter into the warranty for his portion, for the voucher is severed, and each one answers for his portion, etc   But yet if he who appears be sufficient, peradventure he will render in value for all. THORPE   No, sir, only for his portion   no more than in a Statute Merchant.   And then the Great Cape *ad Valenciam* was awarded against each for his portion, and a writ to the sheriff to extend the lands.   But the Great Cape did not issue until after the extent was returned   And the same day was given to the lessor, and they would be advised if the same day should be given to that guardian who appeared, or should he answer immediately?   Query?

For it was said before, that execution shall not be made in value until the full age of the heir, and that is contrary to the reasoning of FYNCHEDEN, etc.

Case 18 Reported in Y B Hilary, 48 Ed III, p 5, pl 9 See also Brooke, Dower, 98, but the digest of Brooke is of little value

Trinity 31 Ed III

(19) **In dower,** the tenant vouched the heir in the wardship of one H, and of one F, and at the summons they said that they had nothing in wardship. And it was found that one had so much, and the other nothing, and against him who had, he had judgment to recover in value, and against the other, nothing, etc. But yet it seems that he had failed of his voucher

Case 19 There is no printed year of 31 Ed III The case has not been identified in the early abridgments

Trinity 24 Ed III

(20) **In dower,** the tenant showed how his predecessor granted the rent to the husband of the demandant, and to his heirs, upon condition that when any of his heirs should be under age that the rent should cease until his age, And he said that "the heir of your husband is under age," wherefore, etc. And it was adjudged that she should recover her dower, but execution should cease until the full age of the heir, etc. And it was said that should she recover her dower, and then another heir was under age, that her dower should cease for the time of his nonage Query, etc ?

Case 20 Reported in Y B Trinity, 24 Ed III, p 29, pl 18 This is but a *"residuum,"* however The principal case is reported in Y B Mich 22 Ed III, p 19, pl 86

Michaelis 21 Ed III

(21) **In dower,** the tenant vouched to warranty the heir of the husband, in the wardship of the demandant by reason of nurture, and he produced a deed, etc BURTON For the same reason he could plead in bar. And he did so, and said that she was guardian in socage, and could endow herself of the best, etc

And it was said in the same plea, that the heir shall be vouched in the wardship of the guardian, as in the wardship of another, but yet it seems that it is not so, for a writ of Dower does not lie against a guardian in socage, consequently, etc   And if it were so, query if the process shall issue against the guardian in socage? etc

Reported in Y B Mich 21 Ed III, p 28, pl 2   See also Fitzh Case 21 Dower, 84   Fitzherbert apparently had access to a different report of the case from that given in the printed Year Books

(22) **Lands were given** to H, and M, his wife, in tail, Trinity who had issue F. And H died, and M leased the same 24 Ed III lands to F for a term of years, and then released to him all her right, etc ; and then F had issue S, and died, while M was living, and then M died, and S died without issue, wherefore G, who was brother to the said F, entered, against whom one K, who was the wife of F, brought a writ of Dower, and recovered her dower against the opinion of many, for the estate tail cannot commence in F, living M, his mother, then he had only an estate for the term of another's life, for it is not like a surrender to him who has a fee in the reversion, etc

Reported in Y B Trinity, 24 Ed III, p 28, pl 14   See a further Case 22 report of the case on pp 58, 59, pl 47   See also Brooke, Dower, 50, and Fitzh Dower, 98   The Court said that the reason for the grant of dower was that the mother had such an estate that by the release she could make a fee to F   Brooke disagrees with this

(23) **If the heir enters** after the death of his father, and Michaelis takes a wife, and then endows his mother, his wife shall be 23 Ed III endowed of that part of which his mother was endowed, because he was seised of the same lands at one time in fee, and the woman who was his mother only demanded a freehold against him, so the fee continued at all times, etc.

And it was said in the same plea, that if the lord purchases the demesne, and then the tenant dies, and his wife brings a writ of Dower, and recovers her dower, that she shall not pay the third part of the rent, for by the purchase of the lord her rent was extinct, etc   And although she recovers her dower, still she cannot avow for her rent, for there was no tenant in dower

And WILLOUGHBY said in the same plea, that if a man takes land in exchange and dies, his wife shall be endowed of both, etc.

Case 23   The case has not been identified in Y B Mich 23 Ed III, or in the early abridgments   Perkins Prof Book, p 83, states a like case

Statham 74 a.   (24) **If the tenant** in Dower recovers against the heir
Trinity   of the husband, her entry shall be alleged [as] by her husband
36 Hen VI   to wit   in the per   And if she recovers against a stranger
who disseised the husband, the heir shall allege his entry in the post   And this by FORTESCUE in the Assize of Baildon, etc   Query, if another stranger has title to the lands, how he shall allege his entry, etc ?

Case 24   The case has not been identified in Y B Trinity, 36 Hen VI, Fitzh Dower, 30, has a very short digest of the case

Hilary   (25) **Lord, mesne and tenant:** The tenant held of the
22 Ed III   mesne by one penny, and the mesne over for twenty pence
The mesne released to the tenant all the right that he had in the lands, and the tenant dying, his wife is endowed of the lands   now she shall attorn to the heir for the third part of the penny, and not for the third part of the twenty pence, for she shall be endowed of the better possessions of her husband   And it was said in the same plea, if I give land to a man before the Statute, or on that day, in the tail, to hold of me by a penny of rent, and then, after his decease, his heir shall pay me twenty shillings forever; he dies and his wife is endowed of the lands, she shall attorn to the heir for the third part of the twenty shillings, for it is all one rent, and for the same rent the land is charged by the conditions in the deed, etc   And she cannot have an acquittance from the heir, because the land is charged by the deed of his father, of whose possession she claims dower, etc

And it was said in the same plea that if the tenant fore-judges the mesne, still the wife of the mesne shall have a writ of Dower for the rent that the mesne had from the tenant, and she shall hold of the tenant, because between her and the tenant the services are revived.   But

yet, query as to this, for then she does not hold in the same
course in which her husband held, etc.   In Dower

The case has not been identified in Y B Hilary, 22 Ed III, Fitzh   Case 25
Dower, 131, has the case   See also Perkins Prof Book, pp 64 and 83

Statute of Westminster the Second, 13 Ed I (1285), cap IV, Stats
at Large, Vol 1, p 163 (171)

(26) **In dower,** the tenant pleaded "never married," etc   Trinity
And the bishop certified "married," on which day the   18 Ed III
tenant made default, and it was adjudged that the demandant should have seisin of the land, without awarding any
petty cape, for that contradicts the verdict, for in an
Assize after such a verdict the wife has been ousted of the
receipt, etc

The case has not been identified in Y B Trinity, 18 Ed III, or in the   Case 26
early abridgments

(27) **The husband and wife** acknowledged by a pone   Hilary
the tenements which were in the husband to be the right   25 Ed III
of a stranger, and bound themselves and the heirs of the
woman to warrant the same lands, to the intent that the
wife should not afterwards have her dower   And after
the death of her husband she brought a writ of Dower, and
upon this matter shown she had judgment to recover her
dower, because the Court was deceived at the time the fine
was levied, for if they had perceived that the land was
the right of the husband, they would not have taken warranty of the woman for other lands, etc

The case has not been identified in Y B Hilary, 25 Ed III   Fitzh   Case 27
Dower, 132, has the case

(28) **If a woman** be endowed against the common law   Michaelis
as of a manor in gross, and so of other like things, etc ,   26 Ed III
she shall take the land so charged, etc   In Dower, etc

The case has not been identified in Y B Mich 26 Ed III   Fitzh   Case 28
Dower, 133, has the case

(29) **In a writ** of Dower *ex assensu patris*, the tenant said   Michaelis
that one H was the son and heir of his father, and your   29 Ed III

husband was the younger son, etc   And it was adjudged
a good plea   From this it follows that a man cannot endow
his wife *ex assensu* of another ancestor than his father, for
his wife shall not have a writ of Dower "*ex assensu con-
sanguinii*," etc.   Wherefore the woman said that H was a
bastard   But yet, query if she could have that plea,
for her husband could not have said that he was a bastard
generally, where he had admitted the marriage. But
peradventure the woman could, for she was not privy in
blood, etc

Case 29   The case has not been identified in Y B Mich 29 Ed III   Fitzh
Dower, 134, has the case   See also Perkins Prof Book, p 85

Hilary
13 Ed III

(30) **If my villein** purchase lands, and I am seised, the
wife of the villein shall be endowed.   And this by HERLE,
in Dower, etc

Case 30   There is no early printed year of 13 Ed III   The case has not
been identified in the Rolls Series, 12 and 13 Ed III

(31) **In dower,** the tenant said that the husband of the
woman took other lands in exchange, in the Bishopric of
Durham, in the vill of H, of which the wife had her dower,
judgment, etc. STOUFORD   Inasmuch as the writ of the
king does not run there, judgment, etc   And it was not
allowed, for HERLE said that it had been a good plea to say
that her husband took lands in exchange in Ireland, of which
she was endowed, etc   (From this it would follow that
an exchange for lands in another county is good) The
woman said that she had never recovered her dower, Ready,
etc.   And it was tried by people of Northumberland, which
was next adjoining, etc   And it was said by HERLE, in the
same plea, that where a woman is endowed against the
abator, and then the heir brings a writ for the two parts
and recovers, that the reversion of the third part of which
the wife is endowed is in him, which SETON denied, and said
that he could claim the reversion in a Court of record, as
to bring an action of waste against the woman, and if she

said that he has nothing in the reversion and he shows this matter, then the Court will award that she should attorn to him, to wit· from that day forward And in this same manner one can claim the reversion which his villein had, etc

Statham gives no citation for this case It has not been identified Case 31

(32) **If I enfeoff** a man to enfeoff another, and he performs the conditions, [the wife of] the feoffee of my feoffee shall be endowed, but if he does not make the feoffment, so that I or my heir enters for conditions broken, then she shall not be endowed As was adjudged in the *Liber Assisarum* Michaelis 27 Ed III

The case has not been indentified in Y B Mich *Liber Assisarum* Case 32 The *Liber Assisarum* is not divided into terms Fitzh Dower, 135, has the case

(33) **If a man** before the espousals makes a feoffment in tail, rendering a certain rent, and for default of payment one re-enters, and then takes a wife, and he is seised of the rent and dies, and the heir enters because the rent is in arrear, the wife in that case shall not be endowed of the rent or of the lands either By FYNCHEDEN and THORPE in Dower, etc Michaelis 44 Ed III

The case has not been identified in Y B Mich 44 Ed III, unless it is Case 33 in a case on p 25, pl 1, in a point made in the long argument there reported Brooke, Dower, 14, and Fitzh Dower, 43, have the case here cited but not the point made by Statham

(34) **In dower** against the guardian, who said that the demandant was guardian in socage of the other lands, and could endow herself of the very best And because she could not deny it, it was adjudged by the Court that she should take the lands of the heir into her custody, being to the value of the third part with the appurtenances, to hold in the name of dower for her aforesaid third part, for which she prays Query? For she had no right to hold, as above, until the age of the heir, to wit fourteen years And from this it follows that she shall not be newly endowed at the Hilary 16 Ed III

Statham 74 b — age of the heir, which is contrary to law, as they said, and so the whole charge will fall upon the husband, etc , as in other cases, to wit where my very tenant makes a lease for a term of years, and dies, his heir under age, and I am seised of the wardship, I shall oust the termor Still when the heir comes to his age, the termor shall have his entire term, etc

Case 34 — There is no early printed year of 16 Ed III The case has not been identified in the Rolls Series for that year, or in the early abridgments Coke (Dower, 1st Inst 39) refers to this case, but has no complete reference

Michaelis 16 Ed III — (35) **In dower,** the tenant vouched to warranty the heir of the husband of the demandant, in the wardship of the demandant. And the justices were in doubt what should be done, for process could not issue against her, because she was the demandant who could not plead with herself But I believe that the demandant should recover her dower, and that the tenant should demur upon the warranty until the coming of age of the infant, for it is no plea to say that she can endow herself of the very best, inasmuch as she is guardian in Chancery, for she holds it in her own right, etc See the matter below in this same title, etc

Case 35 — There is no early printed year of 16 Ed III The case has not been identified in the Rolls Series, or in the early abridgments

Paschal 28 Ed III — (36) **In dower** as to part, one vouched the heir of the husband as of full age, and prayed process against him, and for another part he vouched him under age and in the guardianship of one H, within the same county, and he had process against the guardian And for another part he vouched him in the wardship of one F, in another county, and prayed process against the guardian And from this it follows that it is in the election of the tenant to vouch the heir in wardship or out of wardship, for if the heir has lands which are not in wardship he shall have execution of them, and where they are in wardship he shall have execution against the guardian By SHARSHULL and WILLOUGHBY, that judgment in value against the guardian will bind the heir as well as where the demandant recovers her dower against the guardian, for the one depends upon the other, and when

one estate is determined, the other is determined   Then
if the demandant has more upon her dower against the
tenant than she should have, and he has as much in value
against the heir, by the conusance of the guardian the heir
is injured, for he cannot have a writ of Admeasurement,
etc   But I believe that the heir can have an assize of Mort
d'Ancestor, as well as where the guardian endows the
wife of lands of which she is not dowable, in that case the
heir shall have, at the common law, an Assize of Mort
d'Ancestor   Query? (And examine this case, for the
summons which issued against the guardian provided that
he should bring the heir with him   And from this it follows
that the heir shall plead, and if so, then the tenant may
show the place of his ancestor, and he shall be made to
answer, and that under age, which cannot be, for WIL-
LOUGHBY said clearly, that the guardian shall have an
answer to the place and not the heir)

And see in the same plea, that as to this that he vouched
the heir in wardship within the same county, the judgment
was that she should recover against the guardian if he had
sufficient lands from the same father, and that the tenant
should hold in peace, and if not that he should recover
against the tenant   And if the guardian has but a part, that
the demandant shall recover that part against the guardian,
and the remainder against the tenant.   And still the guardian in whose wardship the heir was vouched entered into
the warranty as he who never had anything in the wardship
of the same father   And with that judgment the Register
agrees, and a writ, to wit *Habere Facias Seisinam*,[1] etc.
Query, if by this writ of *Habere Facias Seisinam* the sheriff
shall have the extent of the lands of the heir, and if he
delivers more than the value, what remedy, etc ?   And as
to this that he was vouched in a foreign county, the demandant recovered against the tenant and he over against

[1] The writ of *Habere Facias Seisinam* is "a judicial writ which lies
where one has recovered certain lands in the King's Court, then he
shall have the said writ directed to the sheriff, commanding him to
give him seisin of the land "   Termes de la Ley, 1721   See also
Cowell, Interpreter, ed 1672

the guardian   And for that for which the heir was vouched as of full age within the same county, that the demandant should recover against the heir, and that the tenant should hold in peace, etc

Case 36.   The case has not been identified in Y B Paschal, 28 Ed III, or in the early abridgments, which is much to be regretted, as some of the points in the case are rendered obscure by the brevity of the language used

Hilary 20 Ed III

(37) **In dower,** the tenant vouched one who vouched the heir of the husband within the same county   in that case she shall not have judgment against the heir but against the tenant, and he over, etc , for HERLE and SETON said that she shall not have judgment against the heir, except in that case where he is vouched by the tenant in demesne, etc

Case 37   There is no early printed year of 20 Ed III   The case has not been identified in the Rolls Series for that year, or in the early abridgments

Michaelis 18 Ed III

(38) **In dower,** the tenant vouched the heir of the husband in the same county and in another county, and yet the judgment was given against the heir, and that the tenant should hold in peace, etc   But yet it seems that that is not warranted by the writ, as to that which is in another county, etc

Case 38   A report of a like case appears in Y B Mich 18 Ed III, p 55, pl 74, but in the case the demandant is given a judgment against the heir, and if he has not sufficient in that county, against the tenant

Trinity 18 Ed III

(39) **In dower,** the tenant vouched the heir of the husband in the same county, who came and demanded judgment of the voucher, for he said that the day of the voucher he was in the guardianship of one H, who was his guardian in chivalry, in which case he should have been vouched in his wardship, etc   The tenant said that he was out of wardship, and upon that they were at issue, etc   Query, if the tenant could not have said, "enough of other lands out of the wardship to give him in value, etc."   And the demandant prayed judgment immediately against the heir, and could not have it before the issue was tried, for HERLE said that if the issue be found for the heir, that then she

should have her judgment against the tenant, and the tenant had failed of his voucher   And if it be found against the heir, then she would have her judgment against the heir, and so it was uncertain   But it is otherwise when the heir is vouched in a foreign county, who comes and he and the tenant are at issue as to the place   In that case the demandant shall recover her dower immediately, for even if the issue be found for the tenant or against the tenant, it is certain that the judgment will be given against the tenant, and PERLE(?) said that when the heir is vouched in a foreign county, that the demandant shall have judgment immediately, which HERLE and WILLOUGHBY denied expressly, and said that she should not have judgment before the vouchee came, because the vouchee could bar her, etc   But if they are at issue (as above) then as above. The reason appears, etc

The case has not been identified in Y B Trinity, 18 Ed III, or in the early abridgments Case 39

(40) **In dower,** the tenant vouched the heir of the husband within the same county, who entered into the warranty as he who had nothing by descent   And the tenant said that he had [assets] by descent. And because the heir had admitted the warranty, the demandant had judgment to recover against the heir immediately, for the judgment is conditional, to wit   that if the heir had [assets] by descent, then she would recover against him, and if not, against the tenant   And a writ accordingly issued to the sheriff to extend the lands of the heir, if, etc , and deliver them to the demandant, and if not, etc , to extend the lands of the tenant, so, etc , and deliver them to the demandant, etc   But yet, query to what purpose he would extend the lands of the tenant? For it might be extended upon the *Habere Facias ad Valenciam* against the heir, etc   And note that this extent, so made by the sheriff, does not conclude the parties or their issue, etc

Hilary 16 Ed III.

Statham 75 a

There is no early printed year of 16 Ed III   The Rolls Series, 16 Ed III, Pt 1, p 16, has a similar case, but there are enough differences to prevent identification from being complete   It seems that the author of the query misunderstood the decision in the case Case 40

(41) **In dower,** the tenant said that he himself brought a writ of right against the husband of the demandant, of whose seisin, etc, "and your husband vouched himself to warranty, because his father gave the same lands to himself in tail, etc. To which we said that he did not give them, and it was found against your husband, wherefore we recovered judgment, etc" BELKNAP Answer, etc. THORPE It seems that she shall recover her dower, for although the tenant recovered against her husband by a tried action, still that trial was not to the point of her action, but upon something which was dilatory, which shall be taken as the act of the husband And the possession which the husband had was not put to trial, but it can stand well enough with that which was tried, wherefore, etc

Case 41   Reported in Y B Trinity, 49 Ed III, p 23, pl 9 The case has some unlikenesses with the abridged case, but cites both Statham and Brooke, Dower, 24, in the margin

(42) **In a writ of dower** upon separate *præcipes*, the demandant made several demands

Case 42   The case has not been identified in Y B Trinity, 1 Ed III, or in the early abridgments

(43) **And see** like matter as above in Hilary, 15 Ed III, in which a *Præcipe quod Reddat* was brought against the husband, who pleaded joint tenure or some other dilatory plea, which was found against him, wherefore the demandant recovered, still his wife shall be endowed, etc

Case 43   There is no early printed year of 15 Ed III The case has not been identified in the Rolls Series for that year

(44) **If a woman** be endowed of a rent service in gross, and the tenant of the land dies, his heir being under age, she shall have a writ of Wardship, but if the tenant dies without an heir, she shall not have a writ of Escheat, no more than any other tenant for a term of life, etc, but she shall have the rent as a rent seck, etc. Query? For it was not decided, etc. In a writ of Escheat

Case 44   There is no printed year of 33 Ed III The case has not been identified in the early abridgments

(45) **If a woman** is endowed by the guardian, she shall Paschal 33 Ed III
be held to the guardian for the third part of the services
which he holds over in right of the heir, etc   And if the
guardian dies, she shall hold to his executors during the
nonage of the infant   And when he comes of age she shall
hold to him, etc

There is no printed year of 33 Ed III   Fitzh Dower, 138, has Case 45
the case

(46) **In dower,** the demand was for rent   TILLESLEY Trinity 11 Hen IV
Who could endow her? HORTON One F granted the rent
to our husband in fee, by a deed, and before any day of
payment our husband died, and we pray our dower,
because the rent was in him, etc   HANKFORD It is better
for you to say generally, "Seised so he could endow her,"
and put this matter in evidence. HORTON It is matter
in law THIRNING What has that [to do with it]? Wherefore Horton said, "Seised, etc." Ready. And the other
alleged the contrary. And THIRNING said that she should
be endowed Query? etc

Reported in Y B Trinity, 11 Hen IV, p 88, pl 39 The report Case 46
has verbal differences from the digest See also Brooke, Dower, 35,
and Fitzh Dower, 29, where the digests differ also

(47) **In dower,** if the tenant vouches in a foreign county, Hilary 13 Hen IV
the demandant shall have judgment to recover her dower
immediately And the reason is because the judgment
cannot be otherwise, for she cannot recover her dower
except in the same county, but she shall not sue execution
until the voucher be determined By NORTON and HANK-
FORD, etc   But yet, query? For the same reason could
be given in a *Præcipe quod Reddat*, etc

The case has not been identified in Y B Hilary, 13 Hen IV, or in the Case 47
early abridgments

(48) **In dower,** if I show that her husband never had Paschal 2 Hen V
anything except for life, it is sufficient for him to say,
"Seised so that he could endow her" But if I show an
estate of inheritance in her husband, to wit   that the

lands were given to him and to his first wife in tail, then she should answer the special matter, for that is matter in law, which does not lie in the notice of lay people, etc

Case 48

The case has not been identified in Y B Paschal, 2 Hen V, or in the early abridgments

(49) **In dower,** if I show that her husband had only a term for life, etc.   As above

Case 49

There is no citation to this case   It has not been identified

Paschal
2 Hen V

(50) **A woman** shall be endowed as well of the villeins in gross as of the villeins appendant   By MARTYN, etc

Case 50

The case has not been identified in Y B Paschal, 2 Hen V, or in the early abridgments   There are one or two like cases, but they do not appear identical

Michaelis
3 Hen VI

(51) **In dower,** the tenant vouched to warranty the heir of the husband of the demandant in the wardship of the king   BROUN   When you vouch the king in wardship, you should show cause   Which the Court conceded   Query, if he should show cause when he vouches him in the wardship of other persons, etc ?

Case 51

Reported in Y B Mich 3 Hen VI, p 17, pl 24   See also Brooke, Dower, 2, and Fitzh   Dower, 19

Paschal
10 Ed II

(52) **Assignment** of dower is good for the husband alone, who holds jointly with his wife, etc   In Dower   But where one holds jointly with another person, it is otherwise   By CHANNTEREL and others, etc , Mich 18 Hen VI

Case 52

The case has not been identified in Y B Paschal, 10 Ed II, in Mich 18 Hen VI, or the early abridgments

Michaelis
16 Ed II

(53) **If the husband** enfeoffs me and dies, and one disseises me and endows his wife, and I bring an Assize against the disseisor and the woman, I shall recover against the woman   By the opinion of HERLE, for otherwise I have lost my warranty, and then she would recover her dower against me, etc   And I recover damages against her if the disseisor be not sufficient, etc.   Query, if she should

recover her dower against the disseisor, would that change the case? etc   Michaelmas, 16 Ed II   (All the same I think that the law is not so, etc , but that the endowment by the disseisor is good, etc)

There is no printed Michaelmas Term of 16 Ed II   The case has not been elsewhere identified   **Case 53**

(54)   **If land** be given to a man and to the heirs begotten of the body of such a one, formerly his wife, and at the time of the gift that wife is dead, and the second wife of the donee brings a writ of Dower against the issue of the husband, who was begotten upon the first wife before the gift [was the question]   And it was the opinion of many that she should not be endowed   And yet she was not in the case of the Statute, for no gift was made to the first wife, but it shall be taken upon the equities, etc   In Dower, etc   **Michaelis 12 Hen IV.**

Reported in Y B Michaelis, 12 Hen IV, p 1, pl 3   See also Brooke, Dower, 36   **Case 54**

The Statute is that of Westminster the Second, 13 Ed I (1285), cap 1, Stats at Large, Vol 1, p 163   The case is long and interesting

See of dower at the church door, in the title of Trial, Mich 40 Ed III and in the writ of Engettement of Wardship, in the same term, and in the title of *Scire Facias*, Paschal, 45 Ed III, and in the title of Remitter, Mich 21 Ed III [1]   Good matter, etc   **Note**

(55)   **In dower,** the tenant vouched one J to warranty, who entered into the warranty and vouched the heir of the husband of the demandant, who was under age and in the wardship of the demandant and her husband, now demanding, who entered into the warranty and answered to the action themselves, wherefore it was adjudged that they should have, of the lands of the heir in wardship, what would amount to the value, etc., and that they should have execution of that to the value, and that the tenant should hold in peace, and if they had not that which amounted, etc ,   **Hilary 29 Ed III**

[1] Statham in these various titles does not give cases with these citations

then against the tenant, etc , and he over in value against
J, and he over in value against the heir, etc., and if he had
not to the value of the part as demanded, then so much
to that part, and so much of the remainder against the
tenant, as above, etc   And see a writ in the judicial
Register in accordance with that judgment   Query, in
that case, if the tenant shall sue execution against the heir
of the lands descending to him afterwards by the same
ancestor, before he comes to his full age?   For the Register
made no mention as to that, but said that he should recover
in value against the heir, when summoned, etc

And see in the same plea, that she shall not recover her
dower against the heir who is vouched, in any case, except
for lands that he had by descent by her husband, and this
the writ of execution shall mention.

Statham 75 b *(margin)*

Case 55 *(margin)* The case has not been identified in Y B Hilary, 29 Ed III, or in the
early abridgments

Michaelis 17 Ed II *(margin)*

(56) **In dower** *ex assensu patris*, the tenant shall have
the averment that the father did not assent, notwithstanding
that the deed of the father giving the assent was shown
And it was tried by process, etc

Case 56 *(margin)* Reported in Y B Mich 17 Ed II, p 507   This is one of the very
few of Bereford's decisions we get in Statham   The phrase, "his cousins
and his aunts," seems to have been in common use before Gilbert made
it his own   See the report of the case

Michaelis 23 Ed III *(margin)*

(57) **Writ of dower** for free tenements   And she counted
a count, etc.   It seems that she could have made demand,
etc   It seems that she should have a writ of Dower of
common, as well as an Assize of common   All the same they
are not alike, for in an Assize nothing is demanded, and one
has never seen a *Præcipe quod Reddat* for a common, etc

Case 57 *(margin)* The case has not been identified in Y B Mich 23 Ed III, or in the
early abridgments

(58) **If a man** takes his tenant to wife and dies, query
if she shall be endowed? etc

Case 58 *(margin)* The case has not been identified as there is no citation for it in Statham
It seems much more like a note than a case

(59) **Dower was brought** against the tenant by *elegit*, Hilary
and it was abated   And a difference was noted between I Ed III
this case and that where a writ of Dower is brought against
the guardian, for there the *Præcipe* is "*Præcipe* such a one,
in the custody," etc.   So the heir is named, etc

> Reported in Y B Hilary, 1 Ed III, p 2, pl 7   Case 59

(60) **It is a good plea** in Dower against the guardian Michaelis 8,
that she detains the heir, etc   Paschal 2
Ed III

> Reported in Y B Mich 8 Ed III, p 71, pl 39   There is no early Case 60
> printed year of 11 Ed III, and the case has not been identified in the
> Rolls Series for that year, although there are a number of cases of dower
> in the volume

(61) **In a writ of dower,** the heir of the woman's husband Michaelis 8,
was vouched and entered into the warranty, and said that Trinity 16,
Ed III
she withheld certain charters concerning his inheritance
of these same lands, etc , and he could not have the plea
unless the action were brought against him, no more than
a strange tenant, etc.   And the law is the same when the
heir is received to defend his right, etc

> Reported in Y B Mich 8 Ed III, p 55, pl 3   There is no early Case 61
> printed year of 16 Ed III   The case has not been identified in the Rolls
> Series for that year and term

" There is ample knowledge of the law of Dower, but one feels like
saying with Perkins of the Profitable Book, "But yet by the grace of
God something should be said here concerning dower " [Perkins Prof
Book, p 60, b] Our old friend Britton says that "it is expedient that
married women should be endowed, in order to give women the better
disposition to love matrimony " [Britton, 246, b , Nich ed , p 236]
The fear of an indisposition toward matrimony is not often urged in the
utterances of the writers upon the common law, yet a sentence like this
of Britton's sometimes comes to the surface, indicating, it might seem,
an undercurrent of suspicion in the minds of the time that the law laid
its hand a little heavily on the married woman and that if that weight
were felt too much there might come a breaking point — in other words,
the average woman might fall out of love with matrimony
     In all the writings upon the law of dower which I have been able to
consult, I have never found the faintest suggestion of the real underlying fact which made some sort of dower an absolute necessity in the
life of a community which had become sufficiently settled to acquire

any sort of capital, and which had emerged from that family life in which the married woman had a right to the support of the family upon the inability, defection, or death of her husband   Where the property was family property, the family, of necessity and of right, took upon itself the support of the woman no longer supported by the labor or capital of her husband   In such communities the case was usually no hardship, for the woman, if young and active, was a commercial asset, she earned her own living whether married or unmarried If old it was the duty of all, except in the least advanced communities, to care for the aged, be they men or women   But when society emerged from that stage we find everywhere some provision made for the support of the woman who has made the bearing and rearing of the children of a marriage, their care and education, and the care of the home in which they are reared, her work in life   When the husband dies, society has not left it in the discretion of the husband to leave the wife to freeze or starve or become a burden upon that society   It has provided in one way or another that the husband shall provide for the wife, after his support is withdrawn, some modicum at least of comfort, whether he has desired to do so or not   Not, indeed, in spite of Britton, to make the woman love matrimony the more, but in order that the social economy might not be upset   The true reason for dower in all its forms is an economic reason   A society fashions its laws, and naturally a society protects itself   In community life it protects itself by making the kin responsible, in capitalistic communities it protects that capital by seizing — if one may so phrase it — a part of the capital of the husband and using it for the support of the widow who would otherwise be thrown upon that community and its capital for support   The same idea is now breaking through our law of master and servant   The master must use some of his capital for the support of his injured servant, not because of any delict upon his part, not because it is necessary to make the laborer more in love with labor, not for any humanitarian idea or any sentiment whatever, but simply because the community refuses any longer to be financially responsible for the support of a man who has given his life or his earning power to the support of his employer, and who for generations had been thrown back by the employer upon the community for that support which he alone owed to that workman   The community, upon realizing this situation, placed the burden where it thought it belonged   That community which does not afford to certain members some way of making a provision for its own support must, and usually does, more or less wisely and liberally, provide some means for that support beyond that of public or private charity   No society which has passed the community stage desires to take upon itself the support of all widows who may be left without means of support through the carelessness or the whim of the husband Imagine for a moment the condition in which a widow would have been left in these Year Book days which we have under consideration without the endowment *ad ostia ecclesia* It has been stated that the reason for the endowment at the church door was because of the publicity of such endowment [P & M Hist of Eng Law, 2d ed , Vol 2 375] This is doubtless true, but there is an underlying idea in all these endowments on the morning of the marriage—morning gifts to the wife from the husband, all settlements of this kind—that the woman is giving up her life to a certain kind of employment, which is going necessarily to exclude her from all other gainful labor by which she might support herself In those days, however rich she might be, she theoretically — it was not wholly so in fact — enriched her husband with all her worldly goods, though the words of the marriage service may have inverted the phrase This left her at the mercy of her husband, economically speaking The family of the bride and the sense of the community coincided in the view that the best time to make a good bargain for the wife was on the marriage day and at the church door, where all the friends of both parties were sure to be, where both parties would be proud of a proper provision, and where all the kin of both sides would be witnesses to the fact

This economic tendency to make the beneficiary of labor, be it the workman's or the wife's, responsible for those who produce the capital without sharing in the accumulation of it, and without having any power over that accumulation, remained apparently quiescent for some centuries During those centuries the people have very largely ceased to be tenants of lands They are no longer set in families which secure their living from the land they live on When the lord died, in those Year Book days, his widow had her residence secured to her, and her dower, that is, she had supposedly support adequate to her situation When the yeoman died it was the same, the support may have been less adequate, but it was in the same proportion to the previous circumstances of the persons concerned Always there has been the class which made its living somehow while it lived, and dying left nothing but the burden of the burial to the survivors In the earlier days the lord was supposed to look after all such poor dependents The Church sometimes helped out, in some of the worst cases, when the lord was blind to the need In the other such cases parish charity, or some parish machinery, supplied grudgingly the absolutely necessary food and shelter

To-day there is slowly growing up an economic sense that the law is bound to provide for such individuals as are made helpless through the economic conditions which are forced upon them by the power of the majority This is the case of the woman who, having elected the supposedly honorable and desirable vocation of wife and mother, finds herself a widow with several children, without means of support for herself or her children According to all the law and the prophets she has chosen that calling which by nature she is best fitted for, for which, by all the traditions which she knows, of time past and present, she should have the greatest desire, in which, by all the teachings of Church and State, she should find happiness, protection and support   But suddenly between the ages of thirty and forty, very probably, she finds she has neither support nor protection   The Church says, "Marry and bring up children " She has done so, but the Church has for her only a very cold charity, which at best puts her children in a home, while she works elsewhere The State says, "Marry and bring up children for my continuance and protection " She has done so, but the laws of the State allow her to be evicted from her home, thrown out into the streets, and while, if she continues to obstruct the street long enough, it will remove her to a poorhouse, it will not let her stay there with her children if she is capable of any labor   It will not provide labor, however, she must go out and get it, and the children can remain paupers if she does not get labor sufficiently remunerative to provide for them   This would have been the position of most women of all the centuries if there had not been some form of dower, and it is a position which the civic sense is beginning to feel quite out of harmony with the desire of the State to bring up carefully and well, and in the best surroundings, those children who are to make the citizenship of the State   The condition is now found to be intolerable, and the earliest development of the feeling for the need of a public support — not charity — for the widow is that of the widow's pension The helpless woman who has fulfilled the demand made of her by both Church and State, and thereby made herself incapable of earning a proper support for herself and for the children to whose care she has devoted herself, is now in many communities endowed by the State with that support which the husband could not give in the shape of accumulated capital when he died, and the community in its shortsighted selfishness refused to supply   "It is all one,' as the lawyers of the Year Books used to say—the support of the widow through the law of the State, which enforced the dower under one or another name, and the support of the widow through the endowment by the State   Dimly through all the centuries the minds of men have felt that somehow the injustice of training women to one vocation, and then leaving them helpless if a single misfortune befalls them, would work against the "disposition of women to love matrimony,' and furthermore, and still more dimly, since apparently it has here first been exposed, have they felt the economic necessity of providing for the person who, under the conditions they had thus created for her, would be a burden on the community unless thus provided for

The authorities upon which this general note upon the law of Dower is founded

Bracton Note Book, pl 4, 7, 9, 18, 91, 96, 109, 148, 150, 191, 203, 204, 220, 253, 261, 265, 279, 345, 365, 377, 380, 459, 475, 500, 547, 571, 577, 591, 622, 632, 642, 695, 721, 737, 767, 794, 814, 878, 891, 941, 944, 953, 965, 970, 972, 977, 1007, 1008, 1017, 1026, 1083, 1098, 1102, 1193, 1246, 1334, 1335, 1338, 1390, 1413, 1516, 1525, 1531, 1576, 1592, 1644, 1668, 1683, 1824, 1843, 1873, 1902, 1919

Britton   Vol 2, Nich ed , Book 5, ff 246, b, 264

Glanville   Book VI   Of Dower

Fleta   Lib 5, cap 23, 24, 25, 26, 27, 28, 29, 30, 31, 32, 33, 34

Horne   Mirroir of Justices, 11, 12

Liber de Antiquis Legibus   Camden Soc 56, Preface, lv, lvii

Natura Brevium (Old), ff 4, 5, 6, 7, 8, 9, 10, 11

Grand Coutumier de Normandie, cap 101, ff 124–25

Fitzherbert   Natura Brevium, 7–10, 147–151

Perkins   Prof Book, 60–88

Coke   1st Inst , Liber 1, cap v, §§ 36–55

Laws of Canute, Wilkins ed , 144, cap 71, p 144

Magna Charta, cap 7

Stat 27 Hen VIII, cap 10

Bacon   Abridgment, title Dower

Leges Edm , cap 2   Wilkins ed , p 75

Leges Hen I, cap 70, pp 266, 267

Skene   Regiam Majestatem, Lib 2, cap 16 Of Dower, cap 17

Crabb   History of English Law, pp 79–83, 185

Watkins   Principles of Conveyancing, chap on Dower, pp 41–63

Park   Dower

Gilbert   Uses, 148, Bar of Dower

Reeves   History of English Law, eg Vol 1, pp 100–104, 144–147, 241–243, 261, 312–313, 384–386   Vol 3, pp 332–334

Cameron   Dower   Canada, 1882

Scribner   Dower   Phila , 1883

Barrington   Obs on the Statutes, 7–9

Lambert   Dower   N Y , 1834.

Kent   Commentaries (Vol 4), pp 35–73

Wright   Tenures, 192, 1768

Thomson   Charters, 68, 69, 108, 109, 121, 134, 148, 172, 173, 403

Pollock & Maitland   History of English Law, Vol 2, pp 147, 374, 375, 394, 404, 420–427

Holdsworth   History of English Law, Vol 2, pp 77, 435, Vol 3, pp 15, 16, 157, 161–65

DURESSE

(1) **In debt,** the defendant said that he was imprisoned at the suit of one B, by procurement of the plaintiff, at the time, etc , and he then made the obligation   And the opinion was that that was a good plea, etc.   Statham 76 a   Hilary 43 Ed III

Case 1

Reported in Y B Hilary, 43 Ed III, p 6, pl 15 See also Brooke, Duress et Manass, 20, and Fitzh Duress, 10 The margin of the report gives this case as "Statham 2" — palpably an error, as the next case on page 10 of the report is again, and properly, "Statham 2"

Hilary
43 Ed III

(2) **If the defendant** be imprisoned at the suit of the plaintiff legally, and there makes an obligation, that cannot be declared void for duress, etc. In Debt

Case 2

Reported in Y B Hilary, 43 Ed III, p 10, pl 32 See also Brooke, Duress et Manass 4, and Fitzh Duress, 11

Paschal
9 Hen VI

(3) **In debt,** if the plaintiff declares that the obligation was delivered to B, the defendant can say that it was made by duress in another county, and not reply to the delivery alleged by the plaintiff And the law is the same if the defendant pleads a release of the plaintiff, bearing date at B. The plaintiff can say that it was made by duress at C, in another county, and so it seems that the place in that case is not material And this in Laborers, etc

Case 3

Reported in Y B Paschal, 9 Hen VI, p 10, pl 28 A writ of Trespass on the Statute of Laborers The case is reported under other heads in the early abridgments, but not under the title of Duress

Michaelis
4 Hen IV

(4) **In debt** upon an obligation against the parson of a church, who said that the plaintiff on such a day called the defendant before him at B, etc., and demanded of him why he sued the tenants, inasmuch as the plaintiff had a Court in which they could be corrected The defendant said that he sued them in the Court Christian for tithes, of which your Court cannot take jurisdiction. And the plaintiff said that unless the defendant would make him an obligation to stand at the command of one F, that otherwise the defendant should be taken in his own house and beaten, etc And the defendant, by reason of this menace and for fear of greater evil, made the said obligation And it was adjudged a good plea And so note that he was in no fear of death and yet the plea was good.

Case 4

Reported in Y B Mich 4 Hen IV, p 2, pl 6 The question as to whether it was necessary to be in fear of death was "well debated" in the case, the conclusion seeming to be that such a plea had generally been held necessary   The threat, as reported in the case, however, was to "beat him so that he should never recover"   See also Fitzh   Duress, 19

(5)   **Christopher Watres** brought a writ of Debt against J Streilley, and counted upon an obligation made in London, in such a ward and parish, etc   POLE   Action, etc , for a long time [prior] to the making of this obligation, to wit   such a day, etc , the said plaintiff by one J Cliston and others of his securing, at D, in the county of Nottingham, menaced the said defendant that he would beat him and imprison him, and keep him in prison unless he would pay to the plaintiff the said sum, or else make an obligation to him as security for the said sum   And the defendant, because of such threats and for fear of the imprisonment aforesaid, came to London and made the obligation in the ward and parish aforesaid, etc   DANBY   That is no plea for three reasons   First. It appears by his plea that the obligation was made one half year after the said threats, in which case he could have had a remedy for the said threats by the law, etc   Another reason is that he said that the plaintiff by one J C, and others of his securing, menaced, etc , and he did not say that the said J C threatened him by the command of the plaintiff, and that should be considered of his own tort   Another reason is that he said for dread of those threats he made the obligation, which cannot be tried, because man cannot know his mind, whether he did it for dread or not   But if a man wishes to avoid a deed he must allege matter of fact, as to say that he was imprisoned, and for such duress he made it, etc   POLE   As for the first reason, because the obligation was made a half year after the threats, that does not change the case, whether the obligation be made immediately or afterwards. And as to the second reason, it is good enough, for in Account I can allege that you are my receiver by other hands because he who does it by others, etc   And as to this that he made it for dread, that is good and can be tried as well as a continual claim, etc. PORTYNGTON   It seems to me that the plea is good

Michaelis 26 Hen VI

And to this that he says, that he threatened him by another, and that he for dread of that made an obligation, the plaintiff can have his choice of two answers, and say that he made it of his free will, without this that the plaintiff threatened him by the said J C, or else as above, without this that he did it for dread of his threats   And the opinion of the justices was that the plea was good, wherefore DANBY, seeing the opinion of the Court, waived his demurrer and took issue with him

Case 5

The case has not been identified in Y B Mich 27 Hen VI, or in the early abridgments

DARREIN PRESENTMENT

Statham 76 b
Paschal
20 Ed III

(1) **If the ordinary,** through a lapse, makes a collation at the next vacancy, if I be disturbed I shall have a Darrein Presentment, showing a presentment in me, or in my ancestor, and the last presentation by the ordinary in my right   And the law is the same where the guardian presents in the right of the heir, etc   And it suffices for the defendant in that case to void the first presentation, without replying to the presentation of the ordinary   And in that Assize of Darrein Presentment the plaintiff shall have title against (etc)   And this in a Darrein Presentment   See the *Registrum*

Case I

There is no early printed year of 20 Ed III   The Rolls Series, 20 Ed III, Easter Term, p 210, No 26, has a case which, while differing in some points, is probably the case digested here   See also Fitzh Darrein Presentment, 12

Michaelis
45 Ed III

(2) **In an assize** of Darrein Presentment, the plaintiff in making his title showed how the manor to which, etc , was given to his ancestor in tail, etc   And the writ was brought against a prior, who said that he held the church to his own use, and that it was filled by him, and was so filled years and days before the writ was purchased. And it was appropriated in the life of his ancestor judgment of the writ   BELKNAP   The plea is double.

THORPE He relies upon the plenity BELKNAP Show what you have for the appropriation SHARSHULL So I will — to the Court — but not to you. FYNCHEDEN He cannot have another action, and although he does not put his claim within the [six months] still it seems that the action lies, since the church is appropriated, for it is not like another presentation to a separate person, and so it seems to me that he can make his claim when he will, and have an Assize of Darrein Presentment, or a *Quare Impedit*, for such a plenity by way of appropriation is not a plenity, for he is patron, wherefore, etc THORPE But I will not grant your reasoning And they adjourned Query, if the incumbent shall be named? And if so, if he shall plead any such plea as he shall in a *Quare Impedit?* etc

The case has not been identified in Y B Mich 45 Ed III, Fitzh Case 2 Darrein Presentment, 8, has a fuller and clearer digest of the case

(3) **If a man** has a *Quare Impedit* and an Assize of Dar- Hilary rein Presentment for one and the same advowson pending 10 Ed III at the same time, the Darrein Presentment shall abate, and the *Quare Impedit* shall stand, because it is of a higher nature By HANKFORD and HILARY, in a *Quare Impedit*

The case has not been identified in Y B Hilary, 10 Ed III, or in Case 3 the early abridgments

(4) **In a darrein presentment,** it is a good plea to say Michaelis that the church is filled by the presentment of the plaintiff 7 Ed III

The case has not been identified in Y B Mich 7 Ed III Fitzh Case 4 Darrein Presentment, 3, has a longer digest of the case

(5) **In a darrein presentment,** if the plaintiff be non- Paschal suited, still the Assize shall be taken to inquire as to the 8 Ed III title of the defendant, and if it be found for him he shall have a writ to the bishop, as well as in a *Quare Impedit*, etc

Reported in Y B Paschal, 8 Ed III, p 18, pl 2 Case 5

ESSOIN [45]

Statham 77 a
Michaelis
2 Hen IV

(1) **In annuity,** one was prayed in aid, and he was essoined, and on the day, etc , the defendant was essoined, and [the essoin] was awarded, for it was said that in this writ a man shall be essoined after every appearance.

Case 1

Reported in Y B Mich 2 Hen IV, p 4, pl 10 See also Brooke, Essone, 31, and Fitzh Essone, 131

Hilary
41 Ed III

(2) **In a praecipe quod reddat,** the Grand Cape *ad valenciam* was served against the vouchee, on which day the tenant would have been essoined and could not, but the demandant had judgment to recover seisin of the land. Contrary elsewhere, etc

Case 2

The case has not been identified in Y B Hilary, 41 Ed III Fitzh Essone, 152, has the case

Michaelis
41 Ed III

(3) **Where a venire facias** issued against an infant under age, in order that he might be viewed, he should not be essoined, no more than where the guardian is told to bring the infant, etc By the opinion of THORPE, in a *Præcipe quod Reddat*

Case 3

Reported in Y B Mich 41 Ed III, p 29, pl 27 See also Brooke, Essone, 20, and Fitzh Essone, 146

Paschal
42 Ed III

(4) **In a writ of nuisance** which was removed out of the county by a pone, the defendant was essoined, because there was a summons, etc.

Case 4

The case has not been identified in Y B Paschal, 42 Ed III, or in the early abridgments

Michaelis
43 Ed III

(5) **In a praecipe quod reddat,** the demandant was essoined, and the tenant produced a protection And the protection was allowed, and the essoin was awarded, but not adjourned

Case 5

The case has not been identified in Y B Mich 43 Ed III Fitzh Essone, 147, has the case

(6) **In an assize,** the tenant pleaded in bar, and process Hilary issued against witnesses to come to the next session, on 43 Ed III which day the justices did not come, and then a reattachment was sued, and the plaintiff was essoined, and the essoin was awarded and adjourned Which note.

Reported in Y B Hilary, 44 (not 43) Ed III, p 5, pl 21 See also Case 6 Brooke, Essone, 24, and Fitzh Essone, 149

(7) **In debt,** the defendant came in charge of the sheriff Paschal and waged his law, and on the day, etc , an essoin was 44 Ed III thrown for him, and not allowed, but the plaintiff recovered. Query, if he had come in the keeping, etc ?

Reported in Y B Paschal, 44 Ed III, p 12 pl 19 See also Brooke, Case 7 Essone, 25 (he gives his reason for the decision), and Fitzh Essone, 150

(8) **In a praecipe quod reddat** on the return of the Michaelis Grand Cape, the tenant waged his law and had a day, on 44 Ed III which day he was essoined, and on the day of the essoin the tenant would have been essoined, and the opinion was that he should not be, etc.

Reported in Y B Mich 44 Ed III, p 38, pl 33 Statham leaves Case 8 out the essoin of the demandant which is necessary to the decision of the case See also Brooke, Essone, 26, and Fitzh Essone, 151

(9) **In debt,** the defendant came by the exigent and the Trinity plaintiff was essoined FENCOT (for the defendant) Sir, 45 Ed III we took a day until an Eyre, by the Statute FYNCHEDEN. The Statute applies only in writs where attachment and distress lie, and that is meant where the first writ is an attachment, as in Trespass, wherefore, etc , the defendant shall go without mainprise THORPE If the defendant does not come on the day of the essoin the plaintiff shall not have any other process but distress *infinite,* etc

Reported in Y B Mich (not Trinity), 45 Ed III, p 10, pl 3 See Case 9 also Brooke, Essone, 27, and Fitzh Essone, 155

The Statute is the Statute of Gloucester, 6 Ed I, cap 8, Stats at Large, Vol I, p 117 (123)

Hilary
25 Ed III

(10) **Avowry was made** upon the husband and his wife, as in right of the wife, and he prayed aid of his wife and had it, and he was told to bring his wife on the next day, on which day he appeared and his wife was essoined, and the essoin was awarded and adjourned, although no process issued against her, etc

Case 10

The case has not been identified in Y B Hilary, 25 Ed III Fitzh Essone, 71, gives the case in exactly the same words He, of course, has no complete citation to the case, or it could be identified

In Iter of
Northumber-
land, Anno
4 Ed III

(11) **Essoin for service** of the king does not lie in Dower, *Quare Impedit*, Assize of Novel Disseisin or the like, where protection does not lie. And this by HERLE, in Dower

And it was said in the same plea that essoin *de malo lecti* does not lie in a writ of right, after appearance, unless it be thrown by the party himself who is ill, etc   (But after the plea is joined, no essoin lies, as I believe, etc)

Case 11

The cases in these Eyres have not usually been identified

Trinity
5 Ed III

(12) **In debt,** the defendant waged his law, and on the day, etc , the plaintiff was essoined and the defendant appeared and had the same day, on which day the defendant was essoined, and it was awarded notwithstanding it was not the second day after issue, etc   Query, if the plaintiff shall be essoined on another day, etc ? And so on for eternity and beyond?

Case 12

Reported in Y B Trinity, 5 Ed III, p 20, pl 3   Statham's remark (if indeed it is his) seems justified by the case, where it is stated that there can be an essoin after every appearance

Michaelis
21 Ed III

(13) **An essoin** for service of the king was challenged because the essoinor was under age, and it was not allowed etc

Case 13

Reported in Y B Mich 21 Ed III, p 33, pl 21   The case is as brief as the digest   See also Brooke, Essone, 133

Michaelis
21 Ed III.

(14) **In a praecipe quod reddat** against three by several *præcipes*, the demandant was essoined against one of them

And the opinion was that he could not be essoined against one and appear against the others, no more than he could be nonsuited against one of them, etc

The case has not been identified in Y B Mich 21 Ed III, or in the early abridgments   Case 14

(15) **Essoin for service** of the king was quashed for him who was prayed in aid, etc   Query as to the cause, etc ?   Hilary 18 Ed III

Reported in Y B Hilary, 18 Ed III, p 9, pl 30   It is merely a short note   Case 15

(16) **In a resummons** on a writ of Wardship against executors of the defendant, the plaintiff would have been essoined at the *Nisi Prius*, and could not because the original was ended, etc.   Paschal 18 Ed III

The case has not been identified in Y B Paschal, 18 Ed III, or in the early abridgments   Case 16

(17) **In a praecipe quod reddat** against the husband and his wife who made default, on the return of the petty cape the husband was essoined for service of the king, and had a day to bring his warrant, and the wife was essoined for the service of the king, "for she was nurse, etc " And it was awarded   Which note, for the husband had lost the lands and she did not come to be received But it was said that that essoin was given to him by the common law, etc   Query, shall she have her defence at the day of the essoin, and shall a resummons be sued upon that essoin, or shall another day be given upon that?   Michaelis 30 Ed III

Reported in Y B Mich 30 Ed III, p 19, pl 30   Case 17

(18) **In a quare impedit** at the *Venire Facias*, the defendant was essoined by a common essoin, although the action was brought for the king.   Paschal 3 Hen IV

Reported in Y B Paschal, 3 Hen IV, p 15, pl 6   See also Brooke, Essone, 33, and Fitzh Essone, 133   Case 18

Paschal
14 Hen VI

(19) **Essoin** for service of the king is not allowed in the Exchequer By the opinion of PASTON Query as to the reason, etc ?

Case 19

The case has not been identified in Y B Anno 14 Hen VI, or in the early abridgments The year 14 Hen VI is not divided into terms

Trinity
14 Hen VI

(20) **The Abbot of Waltham** brought a writ of Debt against one J, and they were at issue, and at the *Habeas Corpus* the abbot was essoined NEWTON The essoin does not lie, because this is the second day, and the Statute is general, to wit "*Postquam aliquis posuerit se*," etc , which is meant as much for the plaintiff as for the defendant PASTON *Contra* For at the common law the plaintiff shall be essoined on every writ after issue, until the process has been ended Then the Statute of Marlborough is "*Postquam aliquis posuerit se*," etc "After any one hath put himself, etc , which must pass, etc , he shall have but one essoin, or one default, so that if he come not at the day given to him by the essoin, or make default the second day, then the inquest shall be taken by his default," which shall be understood wholly on the part of the defendant, for the inquest cannot be taken by default of the plaintiff, but a non-suit shall be awarded, etc And the Statute of Westminster the Second is to the same effect, which says "But all the other days following, the taking of the inquest

Statham 77 b shall not be delayed by the essoin," which cannot be understood on the part of the plaintiff, because the inquest cannot be taken for his default And also the Statute is in restraint of the common law , so that it must be construed strictly NEWTON The Statute cannot be taken so strictly, for in a real plea, on the second day after issue, the inquest shall not be taken for default of the tenant, but the Petty Cape shall be awarded, etc PASTON It is true, and then the land is lost if he cannot save the default by saying that he could not come by reason of the rising of the waters And then by advice it was held that the abbot be amerced because it counterbalanced a nonsuit. And this well argued, etc

Case 20

Reported in Y B 14 Hen VI, p 19, pl 59 See also Brooke, Essone, 80, and Fitzh Essone, 100

The Statute of Marlborough, 52 Hen III (1267), cap 13, Stats at Large, Vol 1, p 55 (66), and Statute of Westminster the Second, 13 Ed I (1285), cap 27, Stats at Large, Vol 1, p 163 (202)

The digest gives but a very inadequate idea of the case, for it was "well argued"

(21) **In a writ of entry** in the nature of an Assize, the tenant was essoined, and it was awarded, etc

Trinity
14 Hen VI

Reported in Y B Trinity, 14 Hen VI, p 22, pl 65   See also Brooke, Essone, 81, and Fitzh   Essone, 102

Case 21

(22) **In a writ of dower,** the demandant was essoined, and the tenant made default, wherefore the essoinor prayed the Grand Cape   HERLE   You cannot have the Grand Cape before a demand be made, for it is uncertain, etc , and you cannot make a demand because you have no warrant to do that   And so it seems that by the essoin the process is discontinued

Paschal
16 Ed III

And it was said in the same plea, that the essoiner cannot pray seisin of the land, for the above reason

There is no early printed year of 16 Ed III   There is a case in the Rolls Series which is interesting as being on the legal points involved in the digested case, but it is not, apparently, the same case   Rolls Series, 16 Ed III, Pt 1, p 242, case 39

Case 22

(23) **He who prays** to be received cannot be essoined, as appeared in a *Præcipe quod Reddat*, etc

Michaelis
15 Ed III

There is no early printed year of 15 Ed III   The case has not been identified in the Rolls Series for that year, or in the early abridgments

Case 23

(24) **In a quid juris clamat,** the tenant was ousted of the essoin   And the law is the same in a *Pereq que Servicia,* and a *Quem Redditum Reddit,* by the equity of the Statute, to wit   *"De his que recordata sunt,"* which ousts the essoin in a *Scire Facias,* etc.

Paschal
16 Ed III

There is no early printed year of 16 Ed III   The case has not been identified in the Rolls Series for that year and term, or in the early abridgments

Case 24

The Statute is that of West II, 13 Ed I (1285), cap 45, Stats at Large, Vol 1, p 163 (224)

**Hilary
33 Ed III**

(25) **Essoin does not lie** in an Assize of Novel Disseisin, for the plaintiff, but it is otherwise in an Assize of Mort d'Ancestor

Case 25

There is no printed year of 33 Ed III   Fitzh   Essone, 72, has the same short digest of the case

**Paschal
33 Ed III**

(26) **If the tenant** wages his law of non-summons by attorney, on the day, etc , he himself shall be essoined, and not the attorney.   And the law is the same in Debt, because he shall make his law in his own person, etc

Case 26

There is no early printed year of 33 Ed III   Fitzh   Essone, 73, follows the case in Statham exactly

(27) **Essoin for service** of the king does not lie in Attaint By WILLOUGHBY, etc

Case 27

There is no citation for this short case   Possibly it may have been meant for a note to case 26   The law seems to be correctly stated See Viner, Abr , Essoin, p 176

**Hilary
1 Hen VI**

(28) **In trespass,** the defendant said that such a one was seised, and enfeoffed him for a term of years, and he gave color to the plaintiff, as was necessary, because he justified in his own right.   CANNDISH   It is the freehold of the plaintiff, Ready   And the other alleged the contrary. (But yet I believe that that is no plea, without showing how it is his freehold, since the defendant had pleaded a special matter in bar, etc)   Query, if the defendant prayed in aid and it was granted, and on the return of the summons the plaintiff was essoined, and on the day of the essoin he came and joined himself to the defendant, wherefore a *Venire Facias* issued, returnable now, and the party was essoined another time?   CANNDISH   The essoin does not lie for him, for the Statute is, "After any has put himself, etc."   And in this case the issue is not joined for him, etc.   HANKFORD   But yet he may lose his freehold by this issue, wherefore we will be advised   And so note that a *Venire Facias* will not issue until the parties have joined in aid, etc.

Case 28

Reported in Y B Mich (this is the only term reported for this year in the printed year books), 1 Hen VI, p 3, pl 11   See also Fitzh   Essone, 89

The Statute is that of Marlbridge, 52 Hen III (1267), cap 13, Stats at Large, Vol 1, p 55 (66)

(29) **In formedon** they were at issue, and at the *Nisi* Hilary 1 Hen VI *Prius* the tenant made default, and before the day in the King's Bench the king died, and then at the resummons the tenant threw an essoin And the opinion of many was that it did not lie But yet it seems that if the resummons is general, that the essoin well lies, etc

Reported in Y B Mich (see case 28, *supra*), 1 Hen VI, p. 6, pl 24 Case 29 The case does not very well support the digest The "opinion of many" changes into the "opinion of the Court" See also Fitzh Essone, 90

(30) **The prayer in aid,** after he has joined himself to Michaelis 9 Ed III the defendant, shall not be essoined because he is only a party in aid, etc. But at the summons in aid he shall be essoined. And this in a *Præcipe quod Reddat.*

The case has not been identified in Y B Mich 9 Ed III, or in the Case 30 early abridgments

(31) **In a praecipe quod reddat** against the husband Paschal 40 Ed III and his wife, they waged their law of non-summons And on the day, etc , the husband was essoined, as on the service of the king, and on the day that he had to bring his warrant he made default, and his wife was essoined, as on the service of the king And the demandant prayed seisin of the land, because the default of the husband shall be taken to be the default of the husband and his wife FYNCHEDEN It seems that the petty cape should issue, upon which day, if he makes default, the wife can be received, etc (Query, if the petty cape shall issue for the half or the whole?) THORPE· Upon this essoin the plea shall be without day against both FYNCHEDEN Still, shall there be any process against the husband until the wife has her warrant? For otherwise the whole is discontinued (Query, if such a case could occur in an Assize of Mort d'Ancestor?) etc Study this well, etc

Reported in Y B Paschal, 40 Ed III, p 21, pl 17 See also Brooke, Case 31 Essone, 128, for a very poor digest It is a very slight case to "study well," as it appears in the printed books   The manuscript case might be better

(32) In a praecipe quod reddat, the husband and his wife prayed to be received for default of their tenant   And the demandant said that they had nothing in the reversion, and upon that they were at issue   And on the day of the *Venire Facias* the husband was essoined for service of the king, and the essoin was quashed   And the wife prayed to be received, and was received, etc

Reported in Y B Hilary (not Trinity), 5 Hen V, p 11, pl 29   See also Brooke, Essone, 48, and Fitzh Essone, 128   Statham has the best digest

(33) Two brought an assize and were essoined, and on the day of the essoin one of them made default, wherefore a *summoneas ad sequendum simul* issued against him, on which day he was essoined, and the essoin was adjudged, etc   And so note two essoins before appearance, etc   But they were for different reasons, etc

The case has not been identified in Y B Mich 45 Ed III, or in the early abridgments

(34) In formedon, the tenant was essoined   SKRENE There was an attorney of record who should be essoined HULS It may be that he was removed, wherefore put your challenge upon the essoin and it shall be adjourned *sub calumnia*, etc. (Wherefore he put the blame upon the essoin)

Reported in Y B Paschal, 2 Hen V, p 2, pl 8   See also Brooke, Essone, 118, and Fitzh Essone, 127

(35) In debt, the defendant waged his law, and on the day, etc., the plaintiff was essoined for service of the king MARTYN The essoin does not lie, for then he could delay us *in infinito* HULS After a common essoin another common essoin does not lie   Wherefore it was adjudged that the defendant go free without making his law, because the plea was delayed upon the essoin   Study this, because error was assigned upon this in the following year

Reported in Y B Paschal (not Mich), 9 Hen V, p 5, pl 16, if this Case 35
is indeed the case   The digest has the plaintiff essoined for service
of the king, the case has a common essoin   This alters the case, for
though a common essoin might not lie on a common essoin, essoin for
the king's service was different   See also Brooke, Essone, 49, and
Fitzh   Essone, 129

(36)   **In a writ** *Dum non fuit compos mentis*, on the return Michaelis
of the *Venire Facias*, because it was not returned [1] a *Sicut* 9 Hen V
Alias issued, on which day the tenant was essoined, and
it was quashed, etc

Reported in Y B Mich 9 Hen V, p 12, pl 12   See also Brooke, Case 36.
Essone, 51, and Fitzh   Essone, 130   Both give much fuller digests
than Statham

(37)   **In a writ of annuity,** the sheriff returned that he Statham 78 a
was a clerk, wherefore a *Venire Facias* issued to the bishop, Michaelis
on which day the clerk was essoined   FYNCHEDEN Essoin 38 Ed III
does not lie, no more than where a writ issues to the
guardian to cause the infant to come, the infant shall be
essoined, so here   And it was awarded, etc

Reported in Y B Mich 38 Ed III, p 21, pl 8   There is nothing Case 37
in the case like the latter part of the case in the abridgment   See also
Brooke, Essone, 52, and Fitzh   Essone, 143

(38)   **In a praecipe quod reddat,** the tenant was essoined Paschal
and then vouched to warranty, and at the *summoneas ad* 39 Ed III
warrantium [2] he was essoined again and it was awarded, etc

Reported in Y B Paschal, 39 Ed III, p 8, pl 8   See also Brooke, Case 38
Essone, 77, and Fitzh   Essone, 143

(39)   **In a praecipe quod reddat** at the *sequatur*, the sheriff Michaelis
returned the writ *"tarde,"* and the vouchee was essoined 39 Ed III
THORPE   Unless he appears the land will be lost, for this
essoin is ousted by the Statute, which says, "It lieth not
where the summons is not returned, or the party not
attached, or because the sheriff hath returned that he was
not found," etc.

[1] Word from the case
[2] "Grand Cape *ad valenciam*," in the report of the case, and in
Brooke and Fitzherbert

Case 39   The case has not been identified in Y B Mich 39 Ed III, or in the early abridgments

The Statute is that of Essoins, 12 Ed II (1318), Stats at Large, Vol 1, p 357

Trinity
24 Ed III

(40) **In replevin,** the plaintiff prayed in aid, and the party was essoined for service of the king, and on the day, etc , he failed of his warrant although he did not lose twenty shillings, etc , because the Statute is, "When the defendant has himself essoined," etc

Case 40   The case has not been identified in Y. B Trinity, 24 Ed III, or in the early abridgments

The Statute of Gloucester, 6 Ed I (1278), cap 8, Stats at Large Vol 1, p 117 (123, 124)

Paschal
48 Ed III

(41) **In London** the tenant pleaded the release of the ancestor demandant with [assets by] descent in a foreign county, wherefore the plea was sent to the Bench and a *Venire Facias* awarded, on which day the tenant was essoined, and still it was the second day after issue joined But yet it was the first day after the *Venire Facias* was awarded   And this in a Formedon

Case 41   Reported in Y B Trinity (not Paschal), 48 Ed III, p 21, pl 9 See also Brooke, Essone, 30, and Fitzh Essone, 157

Michaelis
13 Ric II

(42) **Where the defendant** comes in wardship and pleads to the issue, he shall not have an essoin afterward, etc.

Case 42   There is no printed Year Book for 13 Ric II   The case has not been identified elsewhere

Trinity
2 Ric II

(43) **In formedon,** the parties were at issue. Process issued against the jurors until the distress, on which day the demandant was essoined   RIKHILL That is the third writ after issue, wherefore the essoin does not lie, etc. CHARLETON The Statute is meant for the defendant and not for the plaintiff. And so it was held Anno 20 Ed III To which the Court agreed

Case 43   There is no printed Year Book for 2 Ric II   The case has not been identified elsewhere

The Statute is that of Marlbridge, 52 Hen III (1267), cap 13, Stats at Large, Vol 1, p 55 (66)

(44) **When a man** has found mainprise, he shall not have a common essoin, nor an essoin for service of the king afterwards, and yet he can throw a protection Query, as to the reason, etc ?

Reported in Y B Hilary, 9 Hen VI, p 58, pl 3 See also Brooke, Essone, 4, and Fitzh Essone, 95 The reason as given in the case seems sufficient to answer Statham's query

(45) **In a writ of annuity,** the essoin is in a *placito* *terræ*, because he demands an inheritance, etc

Reported in Y B Hilary, 11 Hen IV p 43, pl 14 See also Brooke Essone, 37.

(46) **In a praecipe quod reddat,** the tenant as to part vouched to warranty, and as to the remainder he pleaded non-tenure And upon the non-tenure they were at issue And process issued against the vouchee until the *Sequatur*, on which day the writ was not served, and as to that part the tenant was essoined SKRENE He had appeared on the day, and when his appearance is of record he cannot be essoined. HANKFORD He was essoined for the other part, wherefore, etc And they adjourned It seems that the essoin well lies, for if the tenant had made default as to that on which they were at issue, then the petty cape would issue And as to the other part he could well be essoined, and still his default would be of record, etc And consequently he can be essoined when his appearance is of record, when it is for another thing, notwithstanding it is upon one and the same original, etc.

Reported in Y B 11 Hen IV p 82, pl 26 See also Brooke, Essone, 40, and Fitzh Essone, 136

(47) **Where an essoin** is challenged because he was seen in Court, it shall be tried the same day, and shall not be adjourned, etc In a writ of Entry, etc. Query, how shall it be tried, etc ?

The case has not been identified in Y B Trinity, 18 Hen VI, or in the early abridgments

(48) **In a formedon,** the husband and his wife were vouched and entered into the warranty, and then made default, wherefore the petty cape issued in a *terra petita,* on which day the husband was essoined for service of the king, and the wife appeared by attorney PORTYNGTON It appears that the husband had an attorney in the plea who was not removed, and he is not essoined, wherefore we pray seisin of the land FORTESCUE Such an essoin does not lie for the attorney, no more than a protection NEWTON A protection does not lie for the plaintiff, and yet such an essoin for the service of the king lies for him, and it might be that the attorney was on the service of the king PORTYNGTON The essoinor has not sworn that his master was on the service of the king And they demanded of the essoiner if he would swear Who said that he would swear that he was the carver of the king, but he could not say more, wherefore the essoin was disallowed, and the woman was received to defend her right, etc See the Statute of Marlbridge, cap 25, which says that neither in a hundred nor in a Court Baron, in the county, or elsewhere, is it necessary for any to warrant his essoin, etc Query well how this is meant, etc For it seems that it is not meant for an essoin thrown in the Bench, and if it be, still it is not meant except as to a common essoin, and not as to an essoin for the service of the king, etc Query?

Reported in Y B Hilary, 19 Hen VI, p 51, pl 10 See also Brooke, Essone, 64, and Fitzh Essone, 103

The Statute of Marlbridge, 52 Hen III (1267), cap 19 (not 25), Stats at Large, Vol 1, p 55 (66) The words of the writ are, "Touching essoins, it is provided, That in Counties, Hundreds, or in Courts Barons, or in other Courts, none shall need to swear to warrant his Essoin "

(49) **In replevin** they were at issue, and at the *Habeas Corpora* the plaintiff had thrown an essoin for service of the king MARKHAM This is not the first writ after issue, wherefore, etc. NEWTON The Statute means only a common essoin when it says— Which was conceded, etc

Reported in Y B Hilary, 19 Hen VI, p 51, pl 10   (See *supra* Case 49
case 48)   See also Brooke, Essone, 65, and Fitzh Essone, 104

Statute of Marlbridge, 52 Hen III (1267), cap 13, Stats at Large,
Vol 1, p 55 (66)

(50) **Essoin de malo lecti** shall be thrown for the tenant, Hilary
although there was an attorney in the plea   And so it seems 19 Hen VI
that it shall be for every essoin, except a common essoin,
etc.

The case has not been identified in Y B Hilary, 19 Hen VI, or in the Case 50
early abridgments

(51) **In a writ of entry** on the return of the petty cape, Hilary
the plea was put without day by a protection, and then at 19 Hen VI
the resummons the tenant sued to be essoined   POR-
TYNGTON   The essoin does not lie, for at the petty cape
no essoin lies for him, and the resummons is that he shall
be in the degree he was when he was put without day, etc.
FORTESCUE   If the tenant now makes default, a Grand
Cape shall issue, so the first default is waived, wherefore, etc   And the opinion was that the essoin lay, etc
Query?

The case has not been identified in Y B Hilary, 19 Hen VI, or in the Case 51
early abridgments

(52) **In a praecipe quod reddat,** at the summons the Hilary
12 Hen IV
tenant was essoined for service of the king, and he had a
day to bring his warrant, on which day he made default,
wherefore the Grand Cape issued, on which day he would Statham 78 b
have waged his law of non-summons   And it was the
opinion of all the Court that he could not   But yet after
a common essoin he shall wage his law, wherefore, query
as to the difference?

And it was said in the same plea, that a man shall not
have essoin for service of the king after another essoin for
being on the service of the king

And it was said in the same plea that where one who is
essoined for service of the king does not bring his warrant
on the day, etc , that a *Capias* shall issue against the essoinor

and also against the tenant, to answer to the contempt, for deceit, etc.

Case 52

It is difficult to identify this case   In some points it resembles the case reported in Y B Hilary, 12 Hen IV, p 14, pl 7, in others it is quite unlike   The remarks regarding essoin for service of the king are found there   The case is digested by Brooke, Essone 42, and Fitzh Essone 138

Michaelis 12 Hen VI

(53) **In a scire facias,** the plaintiff was essoined, and because the Statute ousts delays in a *Scire Facias*, although in other cases the plaintiff can delay himself, it was adjudged that the essoin be quashed, etc   Query as to an essoin *ad sectam terram* for serving for so much time, etc   And of essoin *de malo villæ*, and of essoin *de malo lecti*, and of essoin *de ultra mare*, and of essoin *de gesyn*

Case 53

The case has not been identified in Y B Mich 12 Hen VI, or in the early abridgments

The Statute is that of Westminster the Second, 13 Ed I (1285), cap 28, Stats at Large, Vol 1, p 163 (202)   The various essoins here mentioned are   1   Sick in town   2   Sick in bed   3   Beyond the sea   4   For burying

Note

See of essoin, in the title of Protection, Mich 4 Hen VI

See Statham, title of Proteccion, *infra,* p 134 b, case 15

Paschal 6 Ed III

(54) **Essoin** was not allowed in a resummons at the *Jure d'Utrum*   And this in a note

Case 54

Reported in Y B Paschal, 6 Ed III, p 25, pl 55   See also Fitzh Essone, 56

Michaelis 9 Ed III

(55) **The prayer** in aid shall not be essoined after he has joined, and this by opinion, etc   In a note

Case 55

This may be the case reported in Y B Mich 9 Ed III, p 26, pl 1, but it is not clear

Trinity 29 Ed II

(56) **Essoin does not lie** for the defendant in an Oyer and Terminer, etc   In Southwark.

Case 56

The date 29 Ed II is obviously incorrect, as Edward the Second's reign only covered a period of twenty years   The case has not been elsewhere identified

(57) **Essoin does not lie** in a *Scire Facias* after issue, nor before.
Hilary 25 Ed III.

The case has not been identified in Y B Hilary, 25 Ed III, or in the early abridgments
Case 57

(58) **The plaintiff** in replevin prayed in aid, and the party was essoined at the summons, etc
Paschal 6 Ric II

There is no printed Year Book for 6 Ric II The case has not been identified elsewhere
Case 58

(59) **Essoin does not lie** for the vouchee at the *Sequatur*
Michaelis 29 Ed III

The case has not been identified in Y B Mich 29 Ed III, or in the early abridgments
Case 59

Query, if the essoiner of the plaintiff in an Assize can pray the Assize?
Note

(60) **At the distraint** against the jury, the demandant was essoined And this in a Formedon, etc
Trinity 2 Ric II

There is no printed Year Book for 2 Ric II The case has not been identified in the early abridgments
Case 60

(61) **Upon the** return of the *Venire Facias* the defendant shall not be essoined if it be by mainprise, etc , or if it be by the exigent, so that he is a prisoner, etc
Michaelis 32 Ed. III

There is no printed Year Book for 32 Ed III The case has not been identified in the early abridgments
Case 61

See as to essoin on service of the king, which was adjourned for a year and a day, and the defendant kept that day without a resummons As appeared in a resummons, Michaelis 27 Hen VI.
Note

See Statham, title Resummons and Reattachment, *infra*, p 160 b, case 18 The term there, however, is given as Paschal

(62) **If essoin for service** of the king be disallowed, the essoinor shall be imprisoned, etc In a writ of Entry
Hilary 5 Ed III

The case has not been identified in Y B Hilary, 5 Ed III, or in the early abridgments
Case 62

Anno
20 Ed II

(63) **Essoin for service** of the king shall be adjourned to the common day, etc   (See the last paragraph)

Case 63

The case has not been identified in Y B Anno 20 Ed II, or in the early abridgments

Michaelis
7 Hen. IV

(64) **Essoin for service** of the king can be warranted by a protection   And this in a *Præcipe quod Reddat*

Case 64

The case has not been identified in Y B Mich 7 Hen IV, or in the early abridgments

Trinity
4 Ed III

(65) **Essoin for service** of the king was allowed for the tenant after appearance   In an Attaint

Case 65

Reported in Y B Trinity, 4 Ed III, p 34, pl 21   See also Fitzh Essone, 52

Michaelis
22 Ed III

(66) **A man can be essoined** for service of the king notwithstanding he has surety, etc   In Account.

Case 66

The case has not been identified in Y B Mich 22 Ed III, or in the early abridgments

Hilary
44 Ed III

(67) **Essoin for service** of the king does not lie in Dower And this in a writ of Dower

Case 67

Reported in Y B Hilary, 44 Ed III, p 5, pl 19   See also Brooke, Essone, 24, and Fitzh   Essone, 148

Michaelis
27 Ed III

(68) **Essoin for service** of the king because of nurture where it is not good for the woman unless she is his guardian (in fact)

Case 68

The case has not been identified in Y B Mich 27 Ed III, or in the early abridgments

Hilary
5 Ed III

(69) **Essoin for service** of the king was quashed by command of the king, etc   In a writ of Entry, etc

Case 69

The case has not been identified in Y B Hilary, 5 Ed III   Fitzh Essone, 53, has the case in a slightly different form

Hilary
9 Ed II

(70) **Essoin for service** of the king was allowed on the return of the Grand Cape   And this in a *Præcipe quod Reddat*

Case 70

The case has not been identified in the very brief Paschal Term 9 Ed II   There is no case of a *Præcipe quod Reddat* in the report of the term

(71) **On the return** of the petty cape the wife was Trinity essoined for service of the king, and the husband appeared, and on the day which she had by the essoin the husband was essoined for service of the king, and the woman appeared and she did not show any warrant for the essoin, wherefore the demandant prayed seisin of the land and could not [have it], for they said that the wife shall never produce a warrant in the absence of her husband, but it was in time enough on the day that her husband had, etc Wherefore a day was given for the essoin, and the same day was given to the woman, etc

There is no early printed year of 12 Ed III The case has not been Case 71 identified in the Rolls Series for that year

[45] The law of Essoin, while it is peculiar to the older period of the law, is too well known to make it necessary here to put forth any extended commentary upon this "bulkiest chapter of our old law " [P & M Hist of Eng Law, 2d ed , Vol 2 562] It has been called "an excuse" for not coming to court when summoned To the court it must have been rather a reason than an excuse, as we use the latter term to-day, yet that it was used as a mere excuse we cannot doubt There were so many reasons why a person could not go to court, and so many more why it was impossible to reach the court after having really taken the road for the place where the court was sitting, that it was very easy to give one of these reasons without the court being able to secure evidence that it was a mere subterfuge to save the litigant from leaving his comfortable fireside to face the very real rigors which were the fate of a plaintiff or defendant in many cases

While this matter of essoins may very properly be called a bulky chapter in our law, our abridgment gives us but seventy-one cases upon it On the whole the law, while using a different terminology, a terminology which seems to set it apart as something archaic, rested upon very much the same principles that it does at the present time The convenience of the litigant had to be considered, but not, if possible to prevent it, to the delaying of justice But as such principles soon crystallized into rules, and the rules became too rigid, and then stood in the way of that justice they were designed to protect, it became necessary, time after time, to appeal to the legislature to amend these rules Thus we begin to reach statutory enactment on the subject of essoins very early in our legal history In the fifty-second year of Henry the Third, in the thirteenth chapter of the Statute of Marlbridge, it was provided that when a man had put himself upon any inquest he should have but one essoin, and if he came not at the day given him by the essoin, he should lose

by default of such appearance Coke [2d Inst 126] says that "the
mischief before this statute was, for the great delay that might come
to the plaintiff in any personal action" (there being no inquest by
default in a real action) In chapter 19 of the same statute it was provided that no one was to be obliged to swear to the truth of an essoin
This latter provision, however, was taken to "be understood of one of
the essoins and that is of the common essoin *de malo veniendi*, so that
in the other essoins the oath was required as before " As Coke puts it,
the reasons were that the essoin *de service de Roy*, the delay granted—
a year and a day — was so great that it needed "particular proof"
[Coke, 2d Inst , p 137] and that the "other essoins were very rare "
It is apparent that the justices felt it best to ignore the law when it
occasioned an "inconvenience " Eight years later (1275), in the
Statute of Westminster the First, cap 42, it was provided that "after
the tenant hath once appeared in the Court, he shall be no more essoined",
and in the next chapter (43) it is furthermore provided "Forasmuch as
the Demandants be oftentimes delayed of their Right, by reason that
many Parceners be Tenants, of which none may be compelled to answer
without the other, or there may be many jointly enfeoffed (where none
knoweth his several) and such Tenants oftentimes vouch [fourch] by
Essoin, so that every of them hath a several Essoin, .   such
Tenants shall not have Essoin but at one Day,   so they shall no
more vouch [fourch] but only shall have one Essoin " The ingenuity
of those who sought delay seemed to be inextinguishable. the fourcher
or dividing of the essoins is but one example, though an ingenious one
The essoin *de ultra mare* was used by the persons who, perchance, had
never passed beyond seas at all, but "indeed were within the realm"
the day of the summons Chapter forty-four of Westminster the First
ordained that this essoin be not always allowed, but it might be, if the
tenant challenged it, the demandant might aver that he was in England
the day of the summons, and the case was then adjourned for the demandant to prove his assertion, and if he did so the essoin was turned into
a default The Statute of Gloucester took up the matter, and in its
chapter ten forbade husband and wife to "fourch" by essoin (that is, to
"fork" or divide the essoin into two parts) In chapter eight of the same
statute, if plaintiffs in trespass caused themselves to be essoined after
the first appearance, a day was to be given until the coming of the justices, meanwhile the defendant should be in peace And furthermore,
in actions where there was process of attachment and distress and the
defendant essoined himself *de servitio Regis*, and did not produce his
warrant on the day, he must give the plaintiff twenty shillings, these
being in the way of damages for his long journey, and he was to be
amerced In 1285 the essoin *de malo lecti* was attacked in Westminster
the Second, chapter 17 It had been the custom to ascertain the truth
of this excuse by the writ of *faciando videre*, by which the fact of the bed-
sickness was established by eye witnesses Now it was allowed to the

demandant to except that the tenant was not sick and the exception could be admitted, and they could try this by the inquest, and the essoin was turned into a default "And such an essoin shall not lie in a Writ of Right between two claiming by one Descent" [*Ib*, cap 17] Chapter 27 of the statute cured a defect in the Statute of Westminster the First, which, as we have seen, allowed only one essoin, the time when the essoin could be had was not precisely stated, so that advantage was taken of this, and much inconvenience was caused, so now the essoin was allowed only on the next day after the inquest This, again, was considered to relate only to personal actions [Reeves, Vol 2 185] Neither was any essoin allowed after a day given in *prece partium* [Cap 27] In Chapter 28, the essoin denied to the tenants in Westminster the First is also denied to the demandant

In 1318 [12 Ed II] we have the Statute of Essoins Reeves says [Reeves Hist of Eng Law, Vol 2 303] this statute "seems to be mostly a declaration of the common law," although some of its provisions were contrary to the common law It declared that an essoin "does not lie where the land is taken into the king's hands, nor where the party is distrained by his land, nor where judgment was given thereupon, if the jurors came, nor where the party was seen in the court The essoin of *ultra mare* was declared not to lie where another time the party hath been essoined *de malo veniendi* It did not lie where the party had essoined himself another day, nor where the sheriff was commanded to make the party appear The essoin *de servitio Regis* would not lie where the party was a woman unless she were a nurse, a midwife, or commanded by a writ *ad ventrum inspiciendum*, it did not lie in a writ of dower — the cases show why better than the words of the act — nor because a plaintiff had not found pledges to prosecute his suit It did not lie when the attorney was essoined, nor when the party had an attorney in his suit, nor where the essoignor confessed that he was not in the king's service, nor where the summons was not returned, or the party not attached because the sheriff had returned *non est inventus,* nor where the party had already been essoigned *de servitio Regis*, and had not put in his warrant It did not lie where one was resummoned in an Assize of Mort d'Ancestor or Darrein Presentment, or "because such a one is not named in the writ", or where the sheriff had a precept to distrain the party to come, by his lands and his goods, or where the bishop was commanded to cause the party to appear, or because the term was passed And it was to be noted that an essoin *de servitio domini Regis* was to be allowed after the Grand Cape, petty cape, and after distress taken upon the land and goods This seems to be a pretty extensive summary, and that more should not be needed, yet there is still another "fragment of old law" entitled *Statutum de visu terræ* [Stats at Large, Vol 1, p 399] in which it is provided that *"Essonium de servitio domini Regis"* should not lie in a writ of Novel Disseisin, a writ of Dower *unde nihil habet,* nor in an appeal for the death of a man

In 1335 [9 Ed III, St 1, cap 3] we have an enactment forbidding executors to fourch by essoin, showing that men were still claiming double rights by virtue of a combination of interests It seems very natural in these days They were forbidden by this statute to have more than one essoin before appearance, and but one after appearance, that is, no more than their testator would have had

Essoins continued to be allowed and were a part of the practice of the courts for over four centuries By the act of 2 Geo IV & 1 Will, cap 70, par 6, the practice was greatly modified

A modern example of an argument upon essoins after the act of George IV is to be found in 1 Dowling's Practice Reports 448 (1832) The courts now sit exclusively on the days of the term, or on such days as are fixed for sittings in banc, and the old term "essoin" is no longer heard, although as much cannot be said for the word delay, for justice still moves slowly, and litigants still seek to defer a final judgment

ESTRAY

Statham 79 a.

Hilary
31 Ed III

(1) **A man cannot entitle** himself to an estray until the year and the day be passed without a claim upon the part of anyone For he in whom the property is can take it within the year Yet, query, if he should make satisfaction for his waif first, etc.?

Case 1

There is no printed year of 31 Ed III Fitzh Estray et Wayff, 4, has the case

ESTREPEMENT

Hilary
21 Ed III

(1) **One showed how another** recovered lands by a verdict of the Assize. And after the verdict the tenant had cut wood, and he who had recovered prayed a writ of Estrepement. SHARSHULL· For all damage that the defendant has done to you, since the verdict and before judgment, you shall have a writ to the sheriff to inquire [as to the waste], and to that the defendant shall have no answer, but to a writ of Estrepement he shall have an answer, so the other is the better remedy, wherefore sue such a writ, etc.

Case 1

Reported in Y B Hilary (additional), 21 Ed III, p 51, pl 4 See also Fitzh Estrepement, 8

(2) **In formedon,** pending the issue the demandant sued Michaelis
an estrepement, etc   And pending the issue the defendant 32 Ed III
committed waste, wherefore he was in contempt.   FYNCH-
EDEN   You cannot have this action until the issue is tried,
for it may be found against you, and the king can sue for
the contempt, wherefore take nothing, etc

There is no printed year of 32 Ed III   Fitzh   Estrepement, 7, has Case 2
the case in a longer digest than that of Statham

(3) **In a writ of estrepement,** the defendant told how Michaelis
the land was held in socage, and that one Alice, his mother, 3 Hen VI
seised the land as next friend, and made the waste, without
this that we have made waste or estrepement   And it
was the opinion of the Court that this was a good plea,
since there was no default in him   Query, what remedy
there is for the plaintiff?

Reported in Y B Mich 3 Hen VI, p 16, pl 22   (The point Case 3
is digested on p 17)   See also Brooke, Estrepement, 3, and Fitzh
Estrepement, 4

EXCOMMENGEMENT

(1) **Where an action** is brought by a commonalty Statham 79 b
where outlawry is alleged in one of them, the whole writ Michaelis
shall abate   By the opinion of WILLOUGHBY   And this in a 30 Ed III
Rescous

Reported in Y B Mich 30 Ed III, p 15, pl 16   See also Fitzh Case 1
Excommengement, 7, who goes directly to the point, which is the
excommunication, which, being alleged as to one of the community,
was not proved as to that one or any of them

(2) **In annuity,** the defendant said that the plaintiff was Michaelis
excommunicated and he showed the letters of the commis- 19 Hen VI
sary of the Bishop of S   FORTESCUE   No letters are of
record here, except the letters of the bishop himself, for the
letters of the pope shall not serve you here, wherefore it
was adjudged that the letters should not be allowed

No case of excommunication has been identified in Y B Mich 19 Case 2
Hen VI, but a like case is found in Y B 20 Hen VI, p 1, pl 1

(3) **In detinue,** the garnishee came and said that the plaintiff was excommunicated, and he had the plea. But yet, query, for it has been held that the vouchee shall not say that the demandant is excommunicated, for the tenant has admitted him to be able So it seems here But the vouchee can say that the tenant was excommunicated, etc. Query?

Reported in Y B Paschal, 3 Hen VI, p 39, pl 6 The beginning of this case is reported in Y B Hilary Term of the same year, p 35, pl 31 See also Brooke, Excommengement, 1

(4) **When the defendant** says that the plaintiff is excommunicated, and produces the letters of the bishop, the judgment is that the defendant shall go to God, and then when the plaintiff is assoiled he shall have a resummons or attachment, to wit whatever the process was at the time, etc , for the writ does not abate, and so he cannot bring a new writ, but process shall issue upon the same writ, etc

There is no printed Year Book for 11 Ric II Fitzh Excommengement, 25, has the case

(5) **In trespass,** the defendant said that after the last continuance the plaintiff was excommunicated at the suit of the Archbishop of C, for various contumacies which he committed in his Court, upon which the said archbishop had signified to the king in his Chancery, by these same letters, praying power to make the excommunication And he produced these same letters that the archbishop wrote to the king, witnessing the excommunication, etc MARKHAM These letters are good to secure a writ to the Chancery to take him, but not here, unless the bishop writes to you, etc   And also he does not make the date of the excommunication certain, for if the excommunication be before the last continuance he has passed that step And this was the opinion, etc   Wherefore, upon another day the defendant brought the letters of the bishop directed to the same justices, witnessing as above And the day of the excommunication was made certain MARKHAM showed how he was excommunicated for his non-

appearance where he, as a matter of fact, had appeared, wherefore he sued an appeal within ten days, according to the law, etc , to the Court of Rome, etc   And he carried the appeal into the Chancery, upon which the king ceased [the process to take him] make execution   And he showed the same appeal to the Court, and prayed that the defendant should answer him, etc   NEWTON If a man be outlawed, and sues a writ of Error, still it need not be replied to until it be reversed in fact, because it may be that the judgment will be affirmed, etc   So here   PASTON But the law of holy church is not so, for when he has sued the appeal he can immediately celebrate mass, and although the sentence of excommunication be affirmed, still it shall only relate to the time of the affirmance, etc   NEWTON We will confer with the doctors   And they adjourned, etc

Reported in Y B Paschal, 20 Hen VI, p 25, pl 12   See also Brooke, Excommengement, 3, and Fitzh Excommengement, 12

(6) **In an assize,** the tenant showed that the plaintiff was excommunicated and he produced the letters of the Bishop of B, who was named with him in the writ, which letters told how the plaintiff was excommunicated for his contumacy at the instance of him who answered as tenant And because the action was brought against them, they were obliged to answer over   And so see that if the bishop be named, he can sue, notwithstanding, etc.   And for that reason he named the bishop in the writ, etc.

Reported in Y B Mich 8 Ed III, p 69, pl 37   See also Fitzh Excommengement, 2

(7) **In an attachment** upon a prohibition the defendant showed letters of the bishop proving the excommunication of the plaintiff   The plaintiff showed that he sued an appeal to the Court of Rome, and the whole cause was reversed, etc   And he produced the letters of the Pope proving this   But it was not allowed because the letters of the Pope are not of record here   And they said that he should have made the Pope write to the Metro-

Michaelis
8 Ed III

Case 5

Case 6

Paschal
12 Ed III

politan to assoil him, and thus be aided by the absolution of the archbishop, etc.

Case 7   There is no early printed year of 12 Ed III   The case has not been identified in the Rolls Series for that year, or elsewhere

Trinity 19 Ed III   (8) **In trespass** after the *Nisi Prius*, on the day in the King's Bench, the defendant alleged the excommunication of the plaintiff   And this was received, notwithstanding he had no day, etc   (But I believe the excommunication was after the *Nisi Prius*)

Case 8   There is no early printed year of 19 Ed III   The case has not been identified in the Rolls Series for that year, or elsewhere

ESCHETE

Statham 80 a
Hilary 46 Ed III   (1) **If a man gives** a rent service in tail [to one] who dies without issue, and the tenant of the lands dies without issue, or heir, the donor shall not have a Formedon in the Reverter for the lands, but a writ of Escheat   But if the tenant in tail had been seised as in his escheat, by way of entry, then the donor could have had a Formedon. And this in *Whitby's* case

Case 1   Reported in Y B Hilary, 46 Ed III, p 4, pl 11   See also Brooke, Eschete, 2   Statham abridges the case in such a way as to leave out some of the steps in the case, so that it is scarcely intelligible without the case itself

Trinity 47 Ed III   (2) **In a quare impedit,** it was said by FYNCHEDEN, that if land which is held of an honor which is in the hand of the king comes to the king by escheat, and he makes a feoffment of it, and does not express by what services it should he held, he shall hold as the tenant held, to wit of the king as of the honor, etc , and by the same services   But if they come to the king by forfeiture, and the king makes a feoffment, as above, he shall hold of the king as of his crown   But yet, query, if he shall hold by a rent as it was held before, for he held it by knight's service, as the other held it, but not for the same rent, as it seems, etc

Case 2.   Reported in Y B Mich (not Trinity), 47 Ed III, p 21, pl 47   (See the end of the case) See also Fitzh Eschete, 11

(3) **If a rent service** be given in the tail, and the tenant attorns, and the grantee grants over the services in fee, and the tenant attorns and dies without an heir, so that the lands escheat to the second grantee, and the first grantee dies without issue, the donor shall have a writ of Escheat, and not a Formedon in the Reverter (But yet it seems that he shall not have any action, because the seignory, and the reversion also, were out of him at the time of the death of the tenant of the land, etc)

There is no printed year of 33 Ed III Fitzh Eschete, 9, has the case, which agrees word for word with the abridgment of Statham

(4) **In a writ of escheat,** it was alleged that one D held of him and died without an heir. NORTON D had issue A, who entered after the death of D and endowed M, his mother, of the lands now in demand, in the name, etc , and M leased to us her estate in the possession of the said A, by this deed and this release, etc Judgment if action. HANKFORD: The plea is double, one, that D had issue who survived him, which had been a good plea by itself in abatement of the writ, for the writ shall be brought on the possession of him who was last seised Another is the release, etc THIRNING He means that by the endowment of M the possession of A was annulled, so the writ is good, for if my tenant had issue who survived his father, and died before any possession, I shall not mention him in my writ of Escheat, because he had no estate, and the case is the same here then the release is his plea, and the other only a convenience [to show] the estate of him who made the release, etc. And the opinion was that the plea was double, because he relied upon the fact that D had issue A, who survived him, as above, and then that A survived him, judgment if action, etc HORTON He died without an heir, without this that he had any such son And so note that the "without this" came from the part of the plaintiff And yet it seems that the tenant should answer to his writ, which alleged that his tenant died without an heir, to wit to say, as before, "without this that he died without an heir" Query? etc

And it was said in the same plea, if the son be attainted of felony in the life of his father, and then the father dies, the lord shall not have a writ of Escheat, but I can enter, etc

Case 4   This case, unfortunately, has no citation in Statham   It has not been identified

Hilary
34 Ed III

(5) **If my tenant** be arraigned for felony and holds himself mute so that he is dead by torture, I shall not have a writ of Escheat, for no such writ is given to me, nor in that case will he forfeit the lands, etc   Query, if my tenant has judgment to be hung, and then is delivered to the ordinary, shall I then have a writ of Escheat, etc ?

Case 5   There is no printed year of 34 Ed III   Fitzh Eschete, 10, has the case

Note

See as to escheat, in the title of Warranty, Michaelmas, 30 Ed III, etc

Statham, title of Garrantie, *infra*, p 104 b, case 7

(6) **A man seised** of an advowson in gross dies without an heir, who shall have it? etc   The same question [arose] as to a villein in gross, etc   And it seems he is free   The same question arose as to a common, and as to a rent charge   (But in those two cases the land is discharged, as it seems, etc)

Case 6   There is no citation for this case in Statham   It has not been identified

Anno
16 Ed III

(7) **Escheat for rent** was adjudged good, etc   (But yet he demanded lands and rent)

Case 7   There is no early printed year of 16 Ed III   The case is given in the Rolls Series, 16 Ed III, Pt 1, p 62, case 13   See Fitzh Eschete, 5

Michaelis
22 Hen VI

(8) **If the son** is attainted for felony in the lifetime of his father, and purchases a charter of pardon, the writ of Escheat shall be that his father died without an heir   By NEWTON, in the Exchequer Chamber

Case 8   Reported in Y B Hilary (not Mich), 22 Hen VI, p 38, pl 5   See also Brooke, Eschete, 8

(9) **In escheat,** it is no plea to say that the same tenant whom he alleged died without an heir, enfeoffed the tenant, unless he says "without this," etc   But yet, query?

Hilary
16 Ed III

There is no early printed year of 16 Ed III   The point has not been identified in the case of escheat in the Rolls Series for that year

Case 9

(10) **If a man** dies seised of a manor which is part in service, one can have a writ of Escheat to demand the land and the rent which is part of the manor, etc   But a rent which is for land held in villeinage he cannot demand, for the freehold of the lands of which, etc , is in the lord, so he is tenant of the lands, etc   (But it seems that in such cases the writ is good for a manor with the appurtenances But yet it may be that it is not a manor, wherefore, query?)

Hilary
16 Ed III

There is no early printed year of 16 Ed III   The point has not been identified in the Rolls Series for that year

Case 10

(11) **In a writ of escheat** it is [not] a good plea to say that the tenant did not hold of the demandant the day the felony was committed, unless he says, "nor ever afterward," for if he comes to the tenancy after the felony it escheats, etc   Query, if the lands descended to him after the felony was committed? etc

Michaelis
14 Ed III

There is no early printed year of 14 Ed III   The case is reported in the Rolls Series, 14 and 15 Ed III, p 32, case 9

Case 11

(12) **The elder son** is attainted for felony while his father is living, the lands escheat, and the younger son shall have them

Trinity
13 Ed II

The case has not been identified in Y B Trinity, 13 Ed II, or in the early abridgments

Case 12

(13) **If a man** be attainted for heresy and burned, to wit if his lands shall escheat, and if so, if to the king or to the chief lord, since it is a sort of treason? But yet, judgment, for that is not in our law, etc   Query as to men decapitated on the field for treason And see the *Statutum Templariorum,* where it was said that it was clearly meant at the time that the lands of the Templers

should escheat because of their heresy, etc   Query, if an abbot be attainted for treason, he shall forfeit the lands of the house, as it is said he will forfeit the goods, etc ? Query, if he is deposed pending the suit or after the commission of the treason? And if he is, how shall he be attainted, and the whole escheat, as it was said of the Templers?

Case 13

There is no citation given for this case in Statham, and it has not been identified

The Statute is the *Statutum de Terris Templariorum*, 17 Ed II, (1324), Stats at Large, Vol 1, p 385

ESCHANNGE

Statham 80 b

Michaelis 45 Ed III.

(1) **If either of the parties** die before the exchange is fully executed on both sides, the exchange is void   As appeared in a *Quare Impedit*, etc

Case 1

The case has not been identified in Y B Mich 45 Ed III   It may be the case digested by Fitzh   Exchange, 10

Michaelis 45 Ed III

(2) **See good matter** as to Exchange, Michaelis 45, in an Assize, where it seems clearly that an exchange can be made without a deed, for if any words be in the deed, to wit "*dedi*" or "*concessi*," that is no exchange but a feoffment. For if he vouches to warranty and shows a deed of the ancestor for the exchange which contains "*dedi*" and "*concessi*" he has failed of his voucher, etc   Query, if a man cannot reserve a rent upon an exchange without a deed to the other parceners, etc , (in the same plea)   For the law will not force them to make an exchange, etc   A man cannot exchange lands for rent (in the same plea) because they are of diverse natures. And also he cannot have that rent except by the act of another person, to wit   the attornment of the tenant, etc   (In the same plea)   A man cannot exchange lands for lands in another county, etc   And (in the same plea) if a man exchanges lands for lands, and one is not of so great a value as the other, he can give rent which amounts to the value, etc , but he ought

to have a deed for the rent   Query, then, if it is an exchange? And query, if a man can exchange rent for rent, etc ?

And it was said in the same plea, when a man makes an exchange of lands in the right of his wife, that she shall have a *Cui in Vita*, since that is a discontinuance. And in the same manner the issue in the tail can have a Formedon and although assets by descent be pleaded in bar, he can waive the assets, and have judgment to recover the other lands tailed   As appeared Hilary, 14 Hen VI

The case has not been identified in Y B Mich 45 Ed III   Fitzh Case 2 Exchange, 1, appears to have the case

See as to exchange, in the title of Dower, Hilary, 10 Note Ed III

The case in Hilary, 10 Ed III, does not appear in that title in Statham

(3) **In a cui in vita,** the tenant said that the demandant Trinity and her husband made an exchange of this land and other 10 Ed II lands of which the demandant was seised   And notwithstanding they were equal in value, yet it was adjudged a good bar   In a writ of Entry

Reported in Y B Trinity, 10 Ed II, p 318, pl 10   See also Fitzh Case 3 Exchange, 13

(4) **Exchange** was adjudged a good plea in bar, in a writ Trinity of Right, without concluding to the right. 16 Ed I

There is no early printed Year Book of 17 Ed I   The case has not Case 4 been identified elsewhere

ENCUMBENT

(1) **The incumbent** shall be charged for damages where Michaelis he answers to the title of the plaintiff 45 Ed III

See, in the same plea, in what cases the incumbent shall plead

The case has not been identified in Y B Mich 45 Ed III, or in the Case I early abridgments

Paschal
50 Ed III
(2) **The statute of Edward,** Anno 25, cap 7, says that in every writ where the right of the queen [king] shall be tried, the incumbent shall have an answer to the title of the king, and this applies as well in a *Scire Facias* out of a judgment given in a *Quare Impedit* as in a *Quare Impedit*, etc.

And it was said in the same plea, that the *Scire Facias* is brought against the incumbent leaving out the patron, because the issue in a *Quare Impedit* is between the king and the incumbent, for default of a patron, etc   Which see

Case 2   The case has not been identified in Y B Paschal, 50 Ed III   See Fitzh Encumbent, 10

A Statute for the Clergy, 25 Ed III (1350), cap 7, Stats at Large, Vol 2, p 38 (42)

Michaelis
1 Hen V
(3) **In a scire facias** brought by the king against one H, out of a recovery in a *Quare Impedit*, to have execution, etc   CHEYNE Judgment of the writ, for this H is the incumbent, and there is no patron named, etc   NORTON From the fact that the king had judgment to recover, he was the patron, etc   Wherefore answer, etc

Case 3   Reported in Y B Trinity (not Mich), 1 Hen V, p 7, pl 2   See also Fitzh Encumbent, 9

Note   **See as to incumbent,** in the title of *Quare Impedit,* and also in the title of Darrein Presentment

See Statham, title of *Quare Impedit, infra,* pp 146 a–148 b, and Statham, title of Darrein Presentment, *supra,* p 76 b

ENQUESTE [46]

Statham 81 a
Hilary
33 Ed III
(1) **Where the defendant** by his plea admits the action and the demandant avoids it, as if he pleads the release of the plaintiff, or an arbitration, or something of that sort, and the defendant makes default, in all these cases the plaintiff shall have judgment to recover, without taking the inquest, because the action is admitted, etc , and he cannot maintain the issue   But where he traverses the action upon which they are at issue, and then he makes

default, he shall only have the inquest for his default, as if
in debt upon an obligation, he says that it is not his deed,
etc *Simile*, Hilary, **42**, and Trinity, **45** Ed III

There is no printed year of 33 Ed III   The case has not been iden- Case 1
tified in the early abridgments

(2) **In dower** where they were at issue [upon] "Out of his Paschal
fee," etc , and on the day of the *Venire Facias* the avowant 20 Ed III
did not come, the inquest was taken for his default, albeit
after the avowry he had become an actor, etc

There is no early printed year of 20 Ed III   The case has not been Case 2
identified in the Rolls Series for that year   Brooke, Enquest, 71, and
Fitzh Enquest, 11, have the case

(3) **If the parties** were agreed, after all the jurors had Michaelis
come, and before they were sworn, still the justices will 4 Hen VI
take the inquest for the advantage of the king
    And it was said in the same plea, that if the inquest
remains for default of jurors, that the whole inquest shall
be amerced, as well those who appear as those who make
default   (Which is not reasonable, etc)

Reported in Y B Mich 4 Hen VI, p 6, pl 19   See also Brooke, Case 3
Enquest, 58   The case is a very interesting one to the student of trial
by jury   One of the jurors was finally withdrawn so that they could
adjourn the inquest

(4) **In a writ of entry** against two, who traversed the Michaelis
action of the demandant, upon which they were at issue, 12 Hen VI
at the *Nisi Prius* one of them made default   PASTON
You cannot take the inquest, for you should record the
default   And upon this, in the Bench there was issued a
petty *capias* against him who made default, and when he
came at the petty cape and saved his default the whole
writ abated   And if the demandant releases his default, all
the writ abates   And also both tenants are parties to the
issue, so they cannot take the inquest   In which BABYNG-
TON concurred

Reported in Y B Hilary (not Mich), 12 Hen VI, p 6, pl 5   See Case 4
also Brooke, Enquest, 78, and Fitzh Enquest, 56

(5) **When the inquest** was sworn, the plaintiff commanded Michaelis
his servant to guard them, and the defendant commanded 26 Hen VI

his servants to guard them, and they did this in an Assize at Southwark, etc, where it was held that where an inquest comes from two or three franchises, or hundreds, that two in one franchise or hundred are sufficient, so that there are four from both, etc Query?

Case 5   There is no printed year of 26 Hen VI The case has not been identified in the early abridgments

Note   **See as to inquest,** in the title of Repeal — good matter — Hilary, 14 Hen VI, and in the title of *Scire Facias*, Mich 12 Hen VI And also in the title of Challenge, etc

See Statham, title of Repelle, *infra*, p 163 a, case 1 Title of *Scire Facias*, *infra*, p 161 b, case 19 And title of Challenge, *supra*, pp 40 b–41 b

Trinity 16 Ed III   (6) **In an appeal,** the defendant pleaded not guilty, and was allowed mainprise, and on the day, etc, he made default But the inquest was not taken for the default,[1] but a *capias* and *exigent*, etc Query, what the process shall be against his mainpernors? etc

Case 6   There is no early printed year of 16 Ed III The case is printed in the Rolls Series, 16 Ed III, Pt 2, p 216, case 64

Michaelis 20, & Hilary 15, Ed III   (7) **In account,** the defendant said that he had fully accounted, upon which they were at issue And at the *Venire Facias* the defendant made default, wherefore a *Capias ad Computandum* was awarded, without taking the inquest upon his default, etc Query as to this? For it seems by the Statute which gives him "one essoin or one default" that process should have issued, and he should not have been condemned for the first default, etc And it was also wrong to condemn him without taking the inquest, unless the action be founded upon a specialty, etc

Case 7   There are no early printed years for either of these terms The case has not been identified in the Rolls Series, 15 Ed III, but is reported in the Rolls Series, 20 Ed III, Pt 2, p 498 The case says, "Because, on his first plea he had confessed the receipt of moneye, inasmuch as he said that he had fully accounted, and he did not pursue that issue, therefore a *capias*," etc

[1] Because the judgment affected life and limb

The Statute is that of Marlbridge, 52 Hen III (1267), cap 13, Stats at Large, Vol 1, p 55 (66)

(8) **Justices of gaol delivery** can take a panel of the sheriff without making a precept on him, but justices of Oyer and Terminer cannot, etc. And the difference is because the general command is made to the sheriff by the justices of gaol delivery to make the jury come, against their coming, etc But if they have a special commission it is otherwise, etc In the Exchequer Chamber, by HANKFORD

Anno 4 Hen V

There is no printed year of 4 Hen V Fitzh Enquest, 55, has the case

Case 8

(9) **Where process** was awarded against the first jurors upon an issue, to wit "Not comprised" When the first jurors come they will not be part of the number of twelve, but will be joined to the inquest, in the same manner as witnesses will be If some come and some do not, those who come shall be joined to the inquest, and if the sheriff returns that all are dead, the inquest shall be taken without doing more And all these cases were decided before SKRENE at Exeter, at the Assizes

Anno 5 Hen V

The case has not been identified in Y B Anno 5 Hen. V Fitzh Enquest, 54, has the case

Case 9

[46] In the Enquest, or Inquest, as we now usually have it, we seem to find, or it is generally conceded that we find, the outgrowth of the Frankish *inquisitio* [P & M Hist of Eng Law, 2d ed , Vol 1 140–141] This being accepted as a fact, we have to concede, as Maitland says, that this "palladium of our liberties," the jury, has grown up out of French, not English, soil It is not so difficult for Americans to accept this fact, we can realize better, perhaps, than any other people how much good can spring from imported seed If there had not been much that was fine in the French law and custom, much less that was destined to grow and flourish would have sprung up in alien soil, it is only strong and vigorous seed that can germinate in new soils, under new suns, in new conditions

When we find the title of Enquest in Statham and no title of Jury, we are reminded that we have gotten pretty well back into the beginnings Yet, of course, the jury was a well established fact in our earliest Year Books It is only that when one was preparing titles in the later fourteen-hundreds one naturally included the inquest and left out the jury, because the inquest was the more familiar fact

"From the beginning of the thirteenth century the inquisition, mainly dying slowly out in France, began its peculiar, astonishing development in England" [Thayer Evidence, p 50] Glanville and Bracton know both inquest and jury (See especially Bracton Note Book, Inquest, 83, 130, 359, 414, 478, 632, 718, 1135, and Jury, eighty or more cases) "There come to be four actions in which a plaintiff may obtain a royal writ which will direct that there shall be an inquest to reply to the question of the writ These are the four petty assizes The Assize Utrum, Novel Disseisin, Mort d'Ancestor, Darrein Presentment" [P & M Hist of Eng Law, 2d ed, Vol 1 149] The assize frequently turns into a jury [Ib] The jury grows faster than the assize, slowly the inquest yields ground, yet never wholly loses, our inquest of to-day connects us lineally with the old procedure

The cases in our abridgment are too few to give us much light on this development, we might take each case as typical and as a text for the development of that part of the subject A slight text can be made to support a long and heavy sermon Further, it would seem that with Thayer's great book on Evidence to enlighten us, with the Germans to plod and plough for us, the matter of the inquest should all stand clearly before us Yet it is not wholly so, the history of the inquest as it developed into the jury may be clear, the history of the inquest as it continued side by side with the jury does not seem clear That it is not so small a matter as to be made clear in a note to our title is apparent We have in this abridgment the title of inquest, the inquest, although the forerunner of the jury, is not the jury even though at times they apparently amalgamate Always there is the subtle difference, and ultimately, differentiation This is the reason why the title is of interest to the student of legal history, one of the oldest and supposedly most widely-known subjects has not yet had its full working out

ESTOPPELL

Statham 81 b
Paschal
40 Ed III
(1) **In a scire facias** out of a fine, it was alleged that the land was given to one J, and K, his wife, in tail, the remainder to the plaintiff, and that J and K were dead, etc The tenant said that he was their issue, etc And the demandant said that he was a bastard And the opinion was that he should be estopped from saying generally that he was a bastard, without showing special matter, inasmuch as he had admitted the marriage, etc

Case 1   Reported in Y B Paschal, 40 Ed III, p 16, pl 6

(2) **In a writ of cosinage** of the seisin of one U, his grandfather, the tenant estopped him from saying that he died seised, because the reversion was found between the father of the tenant and the grandfather of the demandant, in an Assize, although the demandant did not claim the land as of the possession of his grandfather, etc Michaelis 40 Ed III

Reported in Y B Mich 40 Ed III, p 38, pl 14 See also Brooke, Estoppel, 27, and Fitzh Estoppel, 1 Case 2

(3) **In a scire facias,** the tenant pleaded the release of the demandant, etc , who said that it was made by duress of imprisonment at D, etc , and afterwards he was nonsuited And in another *Scire Facias* he said that it was made by duress at F And it was the opinion that he should not have the plea, etc Contrary, Hilary, 4 Hen IV, in Debt, etc But he shall not say in the second writ, "Not his deed," etc Query as to this matter, for there seems a distinction where the plea comes from the part of the plaintiff and where from the part of the defendant, for the nonsuit is made on the plaintiff, etc , in which case he shall be estopped, etc Hilary 45 Ed III

Reported in Y B Hilary 45 Ed III, p 2, pl 4 See also Brooke, Estoppel, 39, and Fitzh Estoppel, 197 Case 3

(4) **In a quare impedit,** the plaintiff made his title by grant from the defendant of the next vacancy, etc The tenant said that at the time, etc , he was under age HAM To that you shall not be received, for on such a day you sued livery out of the Chancery, as of full age (And he showed the record) And after that time you made the deed, judgment, etc And it was the opinion that this was an estoppel, etc For various reasons Hilary 46 Ed III

The case has not been identified in Y B Hilary, 46 Ed III, or in the early abridgments Case 4

(5) **A woman** brought a *Scire Facias* to have execution on a recovery in a writ of Dower SKIPWITH Execution you should not have, for this very person against whom you recovered, after the recovery assigned to you the manor Paschal 31 Ed III

of H, in allowance, etc , to which you agreed, judgment, etc. BIRTON Since you do not show anything for the agreement, judgment, etc , for your feoffor could not estop you without a specialty, against this matter of record, nor consequently, you, etc   And the opinion was so, etc

Case 5

There is no printed year of 31 Ed III   The case has not been identified in the early abridgments

Trinity
31 Ed III

(6) **In a formedon** brought by two sisters against one H, who pleaded that he did not give, and at the *Nisi Prius* he pleaded that one of the demandants had married since the last continuance   Ready. And the other said the contrary, to wit   that she was single. And on the return of the *Venire Facias* he made default, wherefore the petty cape issued for the entirety, on which day he cast a protection   And then the demandants sued a resummons, on which day he made default, wherefore the petty cape issued, on which day he came   And then that demandant, who the tenant alleged had married, said that she would release her default, and prayed process against the jury PERSHAY That you shall not have, for after the last continuance you brought a writ of Trespass against one F, and you named the woman F, and at the *Capias* the sheriff returned that F could not be found, and that he had taken your body, on which day a protection was produced by your husband, and it was allowed, and inasmuch as you suffered the protection to be allowed, and the plea was put without day for both, where if you had not been his wife it would not have been put without day, except for himself, and you could then have abated our writ, and you did not, judgment, etc   And it was debated whether that estoppel would estop both the plaintiffs or not   And then THORPE said that the process was badly awarded   For, first, the petty cape should have been awarded only for half, and then, in accordance with that, the resummons should have been several, to wit   each of them resummoned for the half, for if it had been found against the tenant, to wit the last issue, he would lose only the half   And then it seems that the first issue would be between the other

demandant and the tenant, for if the last issue had been
found against the demandant, the writ would not abate,
except as to him, no more than as if she had been nonsuited, etc   And the opinion was that the resummons was
badly sued, etc , wherefore THORPE said that it was well
to begin now where the mistake began, that is, at the petty
cape   (But that could not be, for all that which was
before the resummons was discontinued, etc)

There is no early printed year of 31 Ed III   The case has not been Case 6
identified in the early abridgments   The language of the case is very
condensed, but it conveys the sense, and I have not thought it best to
extend it in many cases

(7) **An assize** was brought for tenements in Danby, and Hilary
the tenant said that the fine was levied between the father 6 Ed III
of the plaintiff and one A, by which fine your father alleged
the same tenements to be in Dauley, judgment, etc   And
because it might be that it was known by both names, the
writ was adjudged good   (But it seems that the plea is
good, and that the plaintiff shall say that it is known by
both names, and thus the writ shall be good, etc)

The case has not been identified in Y B Hilary, 6 Ed III, unless it is Case 7
the case reported in that year and term, p 1, pl 2   It is an Assize of
Novel Disseisin, with a misnomer of Clovebure, Clanbery, or Clambery
But the point as digested is not clearly made in the reported case

(8) **In a praecipe quod reddat,** the tenant alleged joint Michaelis
tenure, by a deed   The demandant said that as to that 8 Ed III
he should not be received, for formerly we brought a *Præcipe
quod Reddat* against the same person who is now tenant,
and his wife   And the wife made default after default,
and he who is now tenant said that he was tenant of the
entirety, without this, etc   And we maintained our writ,
and pending the issue the wife died, wherefore the writ
abated, and we have now freshly brought this writ, judgment, etc   And it was the opinion that it was a good plea,
etc

The case has not been identified in Y B Mich 8 Ed III, or in the Case 8
early abridgments

Michaelis
19 Ed III
(9) **In cosinage,** the tenant demanded judgment of the writ, for formerly the demandant brought another such writ against our father and named him J, son of H, and now he names him J, son of M   And our father traversed his action and died, wherefore the writ was abated, judgment, etc   And the writ was adjudged good, etc

Case 9
There is no early printed year of 19 Ed III   The case has not been identified in the Rolls Series for that year, although there is a curious case printed in that volume (p 332), which in part resembles this case

Michaelis
19 Ed III
(10) **One brought formedon** as son of H SETON Your father levied a fine by the name of F, to one D, whose estate, etc , judgment if against, etc   And the plaintiff averred that he was named H, and this was received because he demanded only the fee-tail, in which case he did not claim by him, etc

Case 10
There is no early printed year of 19 Ed III   The case has not been identified in the Rolls Series for that year, or in the early abridgments

Hilary
18 Ed III
(11) **In formedon** in the Reverter against one A for a gift made by U, the grandfather of the demandant   SHARSHULL   One F was seised and enfeoffed the said U, your grandfather, and K his wife, in fee, which U gave, etc , and Statham 82 a after the death of U, K brought a *Cui in Vita qua clamat eius jus et hereditate sua* against one who vouched to warranty this same person who now demands, as heir of U, under age. Wherefore by the Statute which says, "*Expectet emptor,*" etc , it was adjudged that she should recover immediately, wherefore she entered and enfeoffed one H, whose estate we have; judgment if action, etc   GAYNE: This same K had only a life term, and we do not think that by that recovery you shall oust us from claiming the estate of our grandfather by the tail, etc   KELSHULL To that you shall not be received against the recovery of your ancestor whose heir you are, by which she recovered a fee simple. And it was not allowed, because he could not claim anything by the said K, but by another ancestor, etc

There is no early printed year of 18 Ed III The case is printed Case 11 in the Rolls Series, 17 & 18 Ed III, p 574, case 31 There are minor differences, but on the whole the case and the abridgment agree

Statute of Westminster the Second 13 Ed I (1285), cap 40, Stats. at Large, Vol 1, p 163 (218)

(12) **One sued a scire facias** upon a recognizance in the Michaelis Chancery against one who pleaded the release of the 24 Ed III plaintiff made after the recognizance And the plaintiff said, "Not his deed", upon which they were at issue And the record was sent to the King's Bench for trial, and at the *Venire Facias* the plaintiff was nonsuited, and then be brought another *Scire Facias* in the King's Bench, because the record was there And then the plaintiff said that the deed was not a sufficient answer to that, because it was erased NORTON To that you shall not be received, for when you said, "Not your deed," you affirmed the deed to be sufficient, etc But yet he was received to that And because it appeared to the justices that the deed was erased, they committed him to prison, just as where a man denies his deed, etc And see that it is reasonable that there be no estoppel in that case, for the matter appeared in the deed, etc.

The case has not been identified in Y B Mich 24 Ed III, or in the Case 12 early abridgments

(13) **See by Grene,** in a writ of Mesne, that if a man Michaelis pleads a plea which is traversed and found against him, 30 Ed III that all the circumstances of the deed, and everything comprised within the same deed which is in his plea, shall be held to be admitted by him, notwithstanding the issue was only taken upon one point, as if I plead the feoffment of your ancestor, with warranty, and assets by descent, and you say, "Nothing by descent," and it is found against you, all shall be held as admitted by you And if it be found for you, nothing shall be held as admitted by you All the same these matters are to be distinguished

Reported in Y B Mich 30 Ed III, p 21, pl 38 The latter part Case 13 of the digest is merely spoken in the course of the argument by Grene, and makes no part of the case

Michaelis
30 Ed III

(14) **In a praecipe quod reddat,** the tenant vouched one J to warranty SETON. He whom you vouch, etc FYNCHEDEN To that you shall not be received, for you yourself previously brought such a writ against our father for the same lands, who vouched the same father, and you accepted him, and then our father died, judgment if, etc THORPE You cannot estop him from having the counter-plea, wherefore say something else, etc

Case 14   Reported in Y B Mich 30 Ed III, p 24, pl 49   See also Fitzh Estoppel, 159

Michaelis
3 Hen IV

(15) **In a writ of dower** the tenant said, "Your husband was never seised so that he could endow her" MARK-HAM To that you shall not be received, for our husband by his deed indented, which is here, leased the same lands to you for the term of your life, judgment if against, etc HORTON Inasmuch as you are a stranger to the deed, judg-ment, etc. And suppose that my tenant for life leases his lands for the life of the lessee, although my reversion be discontinued, still my tenant for life shall not have such an estate as that his wife shall be endowed; and it may be that your husband had merely a life term, etc

Case 15   Reported in Y B Mich 3 Hen IV, p 6, pl 27   The digest mixes up the observations in the latter part of the case, but the result seems clear enough   See also Brooke, Estoppel, 51, and Fitzh Estoppel, 93

Michaelis
14 Hen VI

(16) **In trespass,** the defendant said that one H was seised and leased to the father of the plaintiff, by his deed, for a term of twenty years. And after the term was ended this same H entered, and we came in aid of him and gave color to the plaintiff as heir, etc. CHAUNT Our father died seised in fee. Ready. NEWTON You are estopped from claiming any other estate than by the release, for your father was estopped, etc PASTON You who came in aid of the said H cannot estop him, for you are a stranger to the deed Which the Court conceded, etc. But yet, query?

Case 16   The case has not been identified in Y B Mich 14 Hen VI, or in the early abridgments

(17) **In waste** against one J, it was alleged that he held for a term of life of the heritage of the plaintiff, by the assignment of U, son and heir of H   J said that one F was son and heir of H and not of U   Ready   PRISOT. To that you shall not be received, for by this deed indented, which is here, you recited that whereas U, son and heir of H, granted to us your reversion, and by the same deed attorned to us, judgment, etc.   BELKNAP That recital or the attornment will not oust you of the averment, no more than if I recite that one H was seised of lands and I released to him, yet afterwards I shall say that at the time, etc , he had nothing in the lands, etc.   And they adjourned, etc

Michaelis 49 Ed III

Reported in Y B Paschal (not Mich), 49 Ed III, p 14, pl 8   See also Fitzh   Estoppel, 207

Case 17

(18) **In some cases** a man who is a stranger to a record shall estop the plaintiff, as where he certifies "bastard," etc., at the suit of a stranger, etc   And also when the defendant pleads that the plaintiff is named H and not J, and it is found against the plaintiff, every stranger can estop him, wherefore, etc   But in some other cases it is wrong to estop him, unless he is a party or a privy, etc   As appeared in a Cassation   Well argued

Paschal 33 Ed III

There is no early printed year of 33 Ed III   The case has not been identified elsewhere   It may be that these are merely notes, not meant to have citations attached

Case 18

(19) **In a cui in vita** brought, etc   "Your husband and you gave these same lands to us in tail, rendering two shillings per year   And after the death of your husband you came to us and demanded the rent, and we paid you," judgment, etc   YELVERTON   For anything, etc   And so to judgment.   PORTYNGTON   By her own acceptance she shall be barred   As, if my tenant be disseised, and I accept the rent from the disseisor, he can force me to avow upon him   PASTON   That is not so, for rent can be paid by the hands of others, but if you accepted the fealty or the homage, then he can force you, etc   But in this case, although the woman was a party to the demise, still it is

Hilary 21 Hen VI

only the demise of her husband, in law, and that is clearly proved for the writ alleges everywhere that the husband made it, and not the husband and the wife, etc   And if the husband alone had made the demise, the woman could not have had the rent.   And it seems to me that it is all one   And if the issue in the tail accept the rent which was reserved upon the continuance, that does not conclude him, for immediately upon the death of the father, the rent was extinct, so here   NEWTON *Contra*   To this that is said that the demise is wholly the demise of the husband, and so is the writ, still if she and her husband made the demise, and after the death of her husband she got the rent, the tenant cannot bar her of the rent, for it is in her election to have one or the other   And when she brought the *Cui in Vita* she disagreed to the rent, but she came too late to disagree to the rent inasmuch as she had received it   And if she had received the rent in a Court of record she would be concluded   And she would as well be so when it is not denied by her that she had received it, etc   And if your tenant disclaims in a Court of record, and then you accept the rent, you will be barred in a writ of right upon a disclaimer.   Which PASTON denied, etc   And they adjourned, etc

Statham 82 b *(margin)*

Case 19   Reported in Y B Hilary, 21 Hen VI, p 24, pl 5

Trinity 12 Ed III *(margin)*

(20) **The husband** pleaded joint tenure with his wife, wherefore the writ was abated, and in the second writ they pleaded a misnomer of the vill, and the plaintiff would have estopped them inasmuch as the husband pleaded joint tenure in the first writ, and it was not allowed because the wife was not a party to the first writ, etc

Case 20   There is no early printed year of 12 Ed III   The case has not been identified in the Rolls Series for that year, or in the early abridgments

Michaelis 9 Hen VI *(margin)*

(21) **If a man** binds himself by the name of J F of Sale, it is no plea to say that he is of Dale, because he is bound by the name itself.   And this in Debt, etc.

The case has not been identified in Y B Mich 9 Hen VI   There Case 21
is a case reported in Y B Mich 10 Hen VI, p 8, pl 26, which is much
like the case abridged here   See also Brooke, Estoppel, 214, and Fitzh
Estoppel, 27

(22) **In formedon,** the defendant counterpleaded the Trinity
vouchee   RIKHILL   To that you shall not get, for formerly 12 Ric II
you yourself brought formedon for the same land, and the
same gift, and we vouched the same father himself and you
said nothing but suffered process to be sued against him
until all was discontinued by the death of the king, judgment, etc   And this was held a good estoppel, etc   Contrary elsewhere, etc

There is no printed Year Book for the reign of Ric II   There is a Case 22
longer digest of the case in Fitzh   Estoppel, 212

(23) **In formedon** against two, both of them pleaded Trinity
a several tenancy   WADE   To that you shall not be re- 12 Ric II
ceived, for you have taken a day by *prece parhum* in the
last term, as tenants in common, wherefore, etc   CHARLE-
TON   They cannot now allege non-tenure, or joint tenancy,
or several tenancy   MARKHAM   That is not so   And
they adjourned, etc

There is no early printed Year Book for the reign of Ric II   Fitzh: Case 23
Estoppel, 213, prints the case as does Statham, but reports that the
case came up again after the adjournment, and that then it was adjudged
that this was a good estoppel   The case has not been identified in the
Y B 12 Ric II, Ames Foundation, ed Deiser

(24) **In debt** upon an obligation, the defendant voided Hilary
it because he was a layman,[1] etc   WESTON   To that you 9 Hen VI
shall not be received, for formerly you brought a writ of
Detinue for these same writings, against one B, who said
that it was delivered to him by me and you, on certain
conditions, and you came by a *Scire Facias*, and you and
we were at issue upon other conditions, which were found
against you, wherefore, judgment if you shall be received,
etc   PASTON   That is not an estoppel, for the plea that

[1] The man was not a clerk and could not read the conditions, which
were said to be different from those of the writ.

he pleads now in avoidance of the deed can stand with the plea that he pleaded in the action of Detinue, for the action was taken upon the condition, and not upon the deed, etc. BABYNGTON He could have taken it by protestation, and he cannot say, "Not his deed" generally PASTON It is true, but he can plead to the special matter, as to the deed, etc And this was the opinion, etc.

And it was said in the same plea, that if a man be indicted for trespass, and makes a fine to the king, and then the party brings a writ of Trespass against him for the same trespass, he can plead "not guilty," etc. But yet BABYNGTON said that if the entry be "that he admits the trespass," then he shall be estopped from pleading not guilty. But if the entry be "that he puts himself on the mercy of our Lord the King," it shall not be so, no more than when one is indicted for a felony and has a charter of pardon Still in an appeal he can plead not guilty, etc. But it seems that this should be qualified when the entry is that he shall not be estopped, because he that would estop him is a stranger to that, etc And see that as to that BABYNGTON said that he could have made a protestation in the action of detinue PASTON said that the protestation is not to the purpose, because it is contrary to his plea. And he also said that although it were not, yet when an issue was taken upon the plea and found against him, he shall never have any advantage of the protestation As if a man says by protestation that the plaintiff is his villein, and pleads over a plea which is found against him, the protestation is void, etc Query? And see like matter in the *Liber Assisarum*, Anno 33, in an Assize

Case 24   Reported in Y B Hilary, 9 Hen VI, p 59, pl 8 See also Fitzh Estoppel, 23 There is a further report of the case in Mich 11 Hen VI, p 6, pl 11, in an Assize But the point of the estoppel is not brought up

Hilary
9 Hen VI

(25) **In trespass,** the defendant said that the plaintiff was villein regardant to his manor of Dale. ROLFF This same plaintiff formerly brought a writ of Trespass against one A, then seised of the said manor, who pleaded that we were his villein, as above, and we said "free," etc And

it was found for us, and then the said A brought an Attaint, and the first verdict was affirmed, which estate in the said manor you have, etc Judgment, etc. NEWTON He does not show that we were privy in blood to the said A, wherefore, etc PASTON It is reasonable, to my mind, that every one who had the manor shall be estopped, wherefore, etc And then the defendant of his free will passed over and said that A had nothing at the time, etc

Reported in Y B Hilary, 9 Hen VI, p 67, pl 12 See also Fitzh Case 25
Estoppel, 25

(26) **In debt** against administrators ROLFF Judgment of the writ, for the plaintiff has another writ pending against two others as executors, which is older than this, to which they have not appeared, etc MARTYN That is a mere allegation, and also you are a stranger to that, etc. And also you shall not have that advantage, unless you show he had recovered against them, so that it took effect, wherefore answer, etc.

Michaelis
3 Hen VI

Reported in Y B Mich 3 Hen VI, p 14, pl 17 See also Fitzh Case 26
Estoppel, 15

(27) **In trespass** for trees cut, the defendant said that it was his freehold The plaintiff said that the ancestor of the defendant leased this same land to the ancestor of the plaintiff for life, and then released, etc TROM To that you shall not be received, for formerly you brought a writ of Trespass, to which we said that our ancestor leased to your ancestor for life, and your ancestor died, and you, alleging that he was seised of his estate in fee, entered, upon which, etc To which you said that he died seised in fee, without this that anything passed by the deed, upon which we were at issue, and then you were nonsuited And inasmuch as at that time you voided that same deed, judgment, etc THIRNING Although he mistook the issue at that time, since it was not tried it will not estop him, no more than it will estop you, for at that time you said that it passed by the deed, still you can say the contrary now, for the above reason, and yet your meaning now is

Michaelis
11 Hen IV

Statham 83 a

contrary to that which you took issue on before, etc   And
that was the opinion, wherefore he passed over, etc

Case 27   Reported in Y B Mich 11 Hen IV, p 30, pl 56   See also Brooke,
Estoppel, 62, and Fitzh   Estoppel, 99

Hilary
20 Hen VI

(28) **In a writ of waste** against the tenant in dower of
the inheritance of the plaintiff   MARKHAM   Your father
whose heir, etc , was seised of the same lands in fee, and
enfeoffed one B with warranty, which B leased to us for
the term of our life   Judgment if, against the warranty,
etc , you shall be received to say that we were tenant in
dower of your inheritance, without showing how   (But
see that that was no plea to any intent, unless he showed
the deed of the feoffment with warranty, etc) PORT-
YNGTON   That is no plea, for neither she nor he was made
privy to the deed, for a man shall never estop one by his
deed unless he be a party or a privy, to wit   heir of the
party, and especially when it is by way of defence   But
peradventure he may estop the plaintiff by a deed to which
the plaintiff is neither party nor privy, to wit   when the
plaintiff entitles himself by one who may be estopped
Query as to this distinction, etc   And also, although his
warranty may be pleaded in this action of waste, it is
double to my thinking, etc   NEWTON   The warranty can
be pleaded well enough, as in Trespass the defendant says
that the place where, etc , was his freehold, I can show
how his father enfeoffed me with warranty, judgment if
against, etc , he shall be received to say that it is his freehold   YELVERTON   There you are a party to the deed, etc
And in an Assize of Mort d'Ancestor the feoffment of the
said ancestor with warranty is no bar, because the title of
the plaintiff is after the warranty   So here, the writ is that
the defendant has made waste of lands which she holds in
dower of his inheritance, so it should be taken that his
father died seised and that he endowed her, for otherwise
he shall have no action of waste, for otherwise we think
that by the dying seised the heir has a new title   NEWTON
The new title in the case of a Mort d'Ancestor is no reason
that he be not barred, but the contrary is the case, for it

is merely contrary to the writ, for the writ is to inquire if he died seised and the plea is that he made a feoffment with warranty, so it seems the warranty in fee, being the point of the writ, shall not be questioned YELVERTON Then in the Mort d'Ancestor such a warranty is no bar, and *à fortiori* that is no plea here, for our estoppel should be good to all common intent, and it may be that the father made such a feoffment, and retook an estate and died seised MARKHAM dared not demur, but pleaded as before, without this that she was endowed by the plaintiff or any of his ancestors NEWTON That is but an argument, by which he says, "without this that she held in dower of his inheritance" Ready. And the others alleged the contrary.

Reported in Y B Hilary, 20 Hen VI, p 19, pl 14 See also Brooke, Case 28 Estoppel, 9, and Fitzh Estoppel, 36 Statham gives a fuller digest than the other abridgments

(29) **A scire facias** was sued by the Abbot of Battle Michaelis against one W, parson of a church without a chapel at 27 Hen VI Maxey, out of a judgment tailed against the predecessor of the said parson, in a writ of Annuity PRISOT Judgment of the writ, for the said W is parson of the church of N, and Maxey is a chapel within the said parish, without this that he is parson of M in another manner MOILE That is no plea, for it is doubtful how these words ' in another manner" should be taken, and an issue should be certain PORTYNGTON He can say — as above — without this that he is parson of M ASSHETON That cannot be, for he has said that M is within the parish of N, and he is parson of everything within his parish, wherefore, etc PRISOT If we cannot have the plea we are injured, for it may be that we were presented by such a name as we have pleaded, then, if we have not the plea, we cannot have aid from the patron, etc And it may be that a consolidation was made of the two churches, and sometimes the name of the two churches was used, and sometimes the name of one of them, wherefore, etc PORTYNGTON If the case be so, you can show it MOILE Sir, we have matter to estop him, and we say that formerly the predecessor of the abbot sued a writ of Annuity

against the predecessor of the said parson by the same name
which is contained in the *Scire Facias*, and he appeared by
that same name, and prayed aid of the patron and of the
ordinary, who were summoned and made default, wherefore
the abbot had judgment to recover the annuity. Judgment,
etc PRISOT· That cannot bind us, since the patron and
the ordinary made default. NEWTON It is not so. PRISOT·
We say — as above — within which parish the said chapel
was founded by the devotion of the common people, after
time of memory, without this that the said chapel is, or
was at the time the writ of Annuity was brought, a parochial
church, and without this that the said predecessor of the
defendant was parson of the church of Maxey at the time
of the suing of the said writ of Annuity, except as parson
of the parochial church of N, within which parish the said
chapel is, and we demand judgment if, upon such a record,
etc MOILE For anything that he has said, etc And
so to judgment And then it was adjudged that the plaintiff should recover the annuity because the defendant was
estopped from saying that his predecessor was parson,
without this that he was in by succession, and he cannot
say the contrary of that which he has admitted, no more
than where my ancestor levies a fine, I cannot void the
fine, unless I claim by another man — no more here, for
although he is in by presentation, still he is privy to him
And this is clearly proved, for he shall have a writ of Error
or Attaint, etc And also he has admitted that the said
chapel is within the parish of N, wherefore, etc But note,
that that case was more clear than it is here, for the defendant was named in the *Scire Facias* "W of F, Chancellor
of the Cathedral Church of Chichester, parson of the church
without a chapel of Maxey," and the recovery in the
Annuity was by the same name, and he pleaded by the same
name, to wit that he was chancellor — as above — and
parson of the church of N, which is annexed to his Chan-
cellery, without this — as above — which is a true succession But if he put it only "parson of N," the case had
been good, etc.

Case 29   The case has not been identified in Y B Mich 27 Hen VI, or in the
early abridgments

(30) **In a quare impedit,** where the incumbent pleaded Michaelis
a plea, the plaintiff estopped him by a matter which was 39 Ed III
between the plaintiff and the patron, as to the same incumbent, because the incumbent claimed by the patron, etc

And it was said in the same plea by THORPE, that where
one is named son and heir to one, whereas he has no need
to be named heir, that will not estop him afterwards from
saying that he is not heir, etc   Query?

Reported in Y B Mich 39 Ed III, p 24, pl 17   See also Brooke, Case 30
Estoppel, 103, and Fitzh   Estoppel, 115

(31) **In replevin,** the defendant said that the plaintiff Michaelis
was his villein   To which the defendant said   to that you 3 & 5 Ed III
shall not be received, because you have suffered us to Statham 83 b
have a replevin, and also you have made an attorney
against us, so you have affirmed us to be answerable, etc
And notwithstanding that, the plaintiff was made to answer
to the villeinage, etc

Reported in Y B Mich 3 Ed III, p 38, pl 14   Case 31

(32) **An assize** was brought against one P, who said that Hilary
an Assize there should not be, for he said that one J was 7 Hen VI
seised, etc , and died seised, and the lands descended to
him as son and heir.   And the plaintiff, claiming, etc ,
said that this J had nothing except by a disseisin made
on him, upon which he made a continual claim all his life,
and after the death of the said J we entered and were seised,
until, etc   The tenant said that, to that you shall not be
received, for formerly we brought a writ of Trespass against
you for the entry on these same lands, and you said that you
leased these same lands for the term of your life, by force of
which, etc   To which we said that this same J died seised,
and you abated and made the trespass   And you said that
he leased — as above — without this that he died seised
Upon which we were at issue.   And it was found for us
that he died seised, wherefore we recovered our damages,
judgment if you shall be received to say the contrary, etc
And because the plea which is pleaded now is not contrary
to the first plea, but they can stand together — for the

first issue was upon dying seised in fact, and the matter which he alleges now is that he died seised in law, the opinion of many was that it was not an estoppel, etc. Well debated, etc.

Case 32

Reported in Y B Mich (not Hilary), 7 Hen VI, p 8, pl 14 See also Brooke, Estoppel, 77, and Fitzh Estoppel, 20 The case is continued in the same year, in Hilary Term, p 20, pl 3, but it is merely an extension of the argument

Paschal
9 Ed III

(33) **He who** has the estate of another cannot estop the plaintiff, for he should be a party or privy in blood As appeared in an Assize, etc

Case 33

The case has not been identified in Y B Paschal, 9 Ed III, or in the early abridgments

Michaelis
31 Hen VI

(34) **If the demandant** shows matter to estop the tenant, and he cannot deny it, can he plead another matter in bar? etc It seems not, *rigore juris*.

Case 34

The case has not been identified in Y B Mich 31 Hen VI, or in the early abridgments

(35) **If a man** be bound to keep the peace, and then a *Scire Facias* issues against him, because he beat one, who comes and is found guilty, and then he brings a writ of Trespass against him for this same battery, and he pleads not guilty, he shall estop him by the matter found at the suit of the king, notwithstanding he is a stranger to that By the opinion of FORTESCUE and YELVERTON, in Trespass *Coram Rege*, etc And I believe that the reason was that the action was brought for the same thing for which he was attainted As if my servant be beaten and I bring an action and recover, and then my servant brings an action for the same battery, and he pleads not guilty, he shall estop him for the above reason, etc But yet he can say that it was with his own consent, etc, for that can stand with the first trial, as appeared in the case of *Sir Robert Wingfield*, Trinity, 26 Hen VI, by the opinion of NEWTON and PORTYNGTON, etc *Simile*, Michaelis 20 Ric II, where one was indicted for Trespass and made a fine and then the party brought a writ of Trespass — as above And

the opinion clearly was that he should be estopped from pleading not guilty, etc.

There appears to be no citation for this case, the citation given to the Case 35 case above (34) may be meant for this case, but as it has not been identified in the Year Book or in the early abridgments, it is impossible to say with certainty that it is meant for one or the other

(36) **False imprisonment** against two, one said the Michaelis plaintiff was his villein, and they were at issue, and the 37 Hen VI other justified as servant to his master, and they were at issue And separate *Venire Facias'* were awarded, etc MARKHAM said that if the issue were found against the master, that would not conclude the servant, for he could not have an Attaint, etc Then if it be found for the servant by the other inquest, to wit that the plaintiff was the villein of his master, then afterwards the servant can take the villein, and justify it as being the command of his master, and still the master cannot take the villein, for he is estopped against the servant from saying the contrary, although he is a villein, and still his master cannot take him nor command another person to take him, except the said servant who was a party to the trial, etc And so note that a man can command a thing which he cannot do himself, etc. But yet it seems that he can have an action for false imprisonment against the master, because of his command, for he is the principal actor in it, but against the servant the action does not lie, for the above reason

The case has not been identified in Y B Mich 37 Hen VI, or in the Case 36 early abridgments

ENTRE CONGEABLE

(1) **If a vicar** alienates or exchanges land in the right of Statham 84 a his vicary and dies, his successor can enter It is otherwise Michaelis as to a dean or master of a college, who have a convent 2 Hen IV and a common seal, etc Query, as to a parson of a church?

Reported in Y B 2 Hen IV, p 5, pl 18 See also Fitzh Entre Case 1 Congeable, 23, *"Dictum fuit pro lege"* The case is merely a note

Michaelis
2 Hen IV

(2) **It was found** by the verdict of the Assize that one J, who was the husband of the present woman tenant, enfeoffed one H upon certain conditions, to wit to enfeoff the said J and his wife in tail, and for default of issue, the remainder to the right heirs of J J died without heirs of his body, and the woman took another husband, and the said H enfeoffed the second husband and the woman for the term of the life of the woman, the remainder to the right heirs of the first husband, and the heir of the first husband entered because of the broken conditions And it was adjudged that his entry was not legal, for although the feoffment was not wholly accordant to the conditions, still there was no disadvantage to him, wherefore, etc Query?

Case 2   Reported in Y B Mich 2 Hen IV, p 5, pl 20

Paschal
40 Ed III

(3) **After the death** of the father, because the elder son [had passed beyond the sea, he] [1] was ousted, the mother of the younger son entered and continued possession until the fourth in descent, and the issue of the elder brother who was the fifth in degree, etc, entered upon the tenant who was in by descent And because it had always been continued in the blood the opinion of FYNCHEDEN was that his entry was legal on account of the privity, etc

Case 3   Reported in Y B Paschal, 40 Ed III, p 24, pl 26 See also Brooke, Entre Congeable, 6, and Fitzh Entre Congeable, 24

Paschal
42 Ed. III

(4) **If a woman** makes a feoffment while under age, and is married while under age, and upon coming of age she suffers her feoffee to continue "years and days," her entry is not lawful, by the opinion of THIRNING, although she is able by her husband, etc

And it was said in the same plea that the entry of the heir of the disseisee is legal, upon the disseisor and his alienee, etc

And it was said in the same plea, that if the husband leases lands in the right of his wife for a term of years and dies, she can enter, for that is not a discontinuance.

Case 4   Reported in Y B Paschal, 42 Ed III, p 12, pl 18

[1] Words from the case The reported case refers to Littleton, cap. Discentes, fol 83, b, which is probably an error for 93

(5) **If I lease** lands for a term of years, or in fee, rendering Trinity
47 Ed III a certain rent, and for default in payment one re-enters, and the rent is in arrear, it is necessary for me to demand the rent before I enter   And this in Covenant

Reported in Y B Mich (not Trinity), 47 Ed III, p 12, pl 11   Case 5 See also Brooke, Entre Congeable, 14

(6) **Where one enters** claiming for himself and another, Paschal
34 Ed III or to the use of another, where his entry is not lawful, that does not give possession to the others without an agreement, etc.   It is otherwise where it is lawful   (But yet it can be distinguished)

There is no printed year of 34 Ed III   Fitzh Entre Congeable, 50,   Case 6 has the case.

(7) **The tenant in tail** died seised, after whose death Hilary
3 Hen IV his son entered and endowed his mother, who leased the same lands for the term of the life of the lessee, and the son confirmed the estate of the lessee in fee, with warranty The lessee died and his heir entered, upon whom one H, who was issue of the son who made the confirmation, entered   And the opinion was that his entry was not legal, for, although his father, who made the confirmation, had nothing except in tail, still he could enter because that alienation by his tenant in dower was to his disinheritance, then his confirmation was of as much avail as if he had entered and made a feoffment, and so a discontinuance   But yet, query? For if my father who is tenant in tail leases for the term of another's life and dies, and I release or confirm in fee, and I die, still after the death of him in whose life my heir could enter, and if I die without issue, the donor can enter, for by the confirmation the estate of the lessee was not aided   But HANKFORD made a distinction [as to the case] where his entry was lawful at the time of the confirmation, and where not, etc Well argued

Reported in Y B. Hilary, 3 Hen IV, p 9, pl 5   See also Brooke, Case 7 Entre Congeable, 19   He refers to the title of Warranty in Littleton

(8) **If my tenant** who is under age alienates in fee, and dies without an heir, I can enter And if my tenant be disseised and dies without an heir I can enter, for I cannot have a writ of escheat And if the tenant in tail alienates and dies without issue, the donor cannot enter, because his reversion is discontinued In the same plea, etc

Case 8

There is no early printed year of 16 Ed III The case has not been identified in the Rolls Series for that year, or in the early abridgments Being a series of small points these may very naturally have been taken out of the body of a case decided upon very different matters

(9) **If I recover lands** against a man, I can enter upon him after the year But if he makes a feoffment I cannot enter upon the feoffee after the year By THORPE, etc And the law is the same if the man against whom I recover dies and his heir is in by descent, I can enter upon the issue, but not upon the issue of a stranger, within the year, nor after the year

Case 9

Reported in Y B Trinity, 49 Ed III, p 23, pl 10 See also Fitzh Entre Congeable, 35

(10) **If one marries a woman** and enters into religion, and his wife alienates land which is in her own right, and then she deraigns [1] her husband, the entry of the husband is lawful By THORPE, in an Assize, etc (It seems that she could take [hold] her husband by the [deed] poll in that case, without any other deraignment)

Case 10

There is no printed year of 33 Ed III The case is given by Fitzh Entre Congeable, 52

(11) **If I recover** against the tenant in tail, and he dies before execution is sued, still I can enter upon his issue who is in by descent But it is otherwise where one grants and renders land to me by a fine, and dies before I enter, etc

Case 11

There is no printed year of 33 Ed III Fitzh Entre Congeable, 51, has the case in the exact words of Statham

[1] The word is used in various senses In this case it is apparently as Coke uses it (Coke, 1st Inst § 292, p 136 b) "When a monk is deraigned he is degraded and turned out of his order of religion, and become a lay-man "

(12) **A man** was seised of lands in the right of his wife, Michaelis
4 Hen VI
and enfeoffed one H, upon condition that he should enfeoff
him and his wife and the heirs of the husband   The husband died, H enfeoffed the woman to her and to her heirs [1]
And because of conditions broken the heir of the husband
entered, and the woman ousted him   And the opinion of
the COURT was that the entry of the woman was lawful, for
by the entry of the heir the discontinuance was annulled, for
if his father had entered because of conditions broken, and
had died, the entry of the woman upon the heir had been
lawful, and no other right could descend except such as his
father could have had by reason of the conditions broken.
Consequence, etc   (But it seems that she could not enter
upon him, since he was in by descent, etc   But yet no
possession descended to him, etc)   Well argued, in [a writ
of] Error.

Reported in Y B Mich 3 Hen VI, p 2, pl 5   See also Brooke, Case 12
Entre Congeable, 38, and Fitzh   Entre Congeable, 1

(13) **The tenant in tail** gave lands to a man for life, Michaelis
21 Hen VI
and then granted the reversion to another in fee, and the
tenant attorned and then surrendered his estate to the
grantee, then the tenant in tail died; the tenant for life
died, the issue in tail entered, the other brought an Assize
and this matter was found   NEWTON   It seems to me
that he shall be barred, that the entry of the issue in tail
is lawful, and the surrender does not change the case, for
he holds charged for the whole life of the tenant for life,
if the tenant for life was charged   FORTESCUE *Contra*
If a man had issue by two wives and leased lands for life,
and died, the issue of the first wife died without issue,
now the issue of the second wife shall not have the lands
Yet if the tenant for life had surrendered his estate to the
issue of the first wife, the issue of the second wife shall
never have the lands, but rather shall they escheat Statham 84 b
And thus the surrender made to him in the reversion or

[1] The case says that this was done by mistake, the tail should have
been to the heirs of the husband

remainder changes the case   And then the plaintiff had judgment to recover   Which note well, etc

Case 13   Reported in Y B Trinity (not Mich), 21 Hen VI, p 52, pl 8   See also Fitzh Entre Congeable, 7

Paschal 44 Ed III

(14) **The abbot of York** brought an Assize against a man who said that he had nothing except in right of his wife, and if it be found, etc   The Assize was taken, which said that the defendant alienated the lands which were in the right of his wife to one J, in fee, upon condition to enfeoff one A, son of the defendant, and one E, his wife in tail, and for failure of issue the remainder to the right heirs of the defendant   And they said that E, the wife of A, who should have been enfeoffed, died, and the abbot brought an *"ad terminum qui præterut"* against J, on a lease made to one A, by his predecessor, and he recovered by default; and the right of the abbot was found by a *Quale Jus*, and they said further that the land was the right of the abbot, but they said that the lease was made to one G, and not to A, as was found by the *Quale Jus* And they said that after the recovery the defendant ousted the said J, claiming his first estate, and then the abbot entered by force of the recovery and the defendant re-ousted him, and he prayed the discretion of the judges FYNCHEDEN If the entry of the defendant was lawful, then he is in his first estate, as in right of his wife, and so it seems, for no day as to the conditions was definitely limited in certain, in which case he was bound to make the feoffment immediately   And since the remainder should be to his right heirs it is [clear] that it should have been made to him, so he could enter without a demand, which THORPE denied And it is also proved by his recovery against the said J that he could have traversed the action of the abbot, which was false, and he did not, in which case he had disabled himself from making the feoffment   And although the abbot entered upon the tenant, that does not change the case, for that was by the default of the said J, for if I enfeoff one to enfeoff me again, and one feigns a false action against him and has judgment to recover, and then he

enfeoffs me, the other who recovered enters upon my re-entry, so here   And to that which they have found, that this is the right of the abbot, that does not lie in their jurisdiction, nor in their voucher at present, etc   And they adjourned   See this plea because it was well argued, etc.

Reported in Y B Paschal, 44 Ed III, p 8, pl 10   See also Fitzh Case 14 Entre Congeable, 33   It is necessary to go to the case for a full under-standing of the facts, or the reasoning in such long cases as this   A link in the chain of facts not absolutely necessary to the legal reasoning and therefore left out in the digest frequently clears up the case, which seems obscure in the digest   It is impossible to note all these omissions as space would fail us before we had reached a quarter of the abridg-ment   The digest given by Fitzherbert is very long

(15) **It was found** by verdict of the Assize that one N Michaelis was seised, etc , and had issue two daughters, to wit   K 21 Ed III and A, to wit   K before marriage and A afterwards   And after his death they entered and made partition between them   And K married one H, and had issue, and K died, and he remained in by the curtesy, and was seised until disseised by A   And it was adjudged that he should re-cover, although K was a bastard, still, inasmuch as she con-tinued in possession all her life without any reclaim (in which case the entry of A had been lawful) upon the issue [of] K, nor consequently upon the tenant by the curtesy And the issue also could have estopped him from bastar-dizing her, inasmuch as they made the partition, etc   (But yet that was the better judgment, etc)

Reported in Y B Mich 21 Ed III, p 34, pl 25   See also Brooke, Case 15 Entre Congeable, 31

(16) **The lord** and the tenant were disseised   The dis- Hilary seisor enfeoffed another in fee   The tenant died without 2 Ric II heir   The lord entered upon the feoffee of his tenant   And it was the opinion of all the COURT that his entry was not lawful because he had a tenant who was in by title, in the life of his tenant, upon whom he could make an avowry And so it was adjudged, etc.   But yet it is wrong unless

the feoffee had given him notice, etc And still he could choose to avow upon him, notwithstanding he gave him notice, as it seems, etc

Case 16   There is no printed Year Book for the reign of Ric II The case has not been identified elsewhere

Paschal 20 Hen VI **(17) If a woman** be disseised, and then she takes husband, and the disseisor dies, and his heir is in by descent during the coverture, that descent shall toll the entry of the woman notwithstanding the coverture, because it was her own act to take an husband And this by the opinion of NEWTON, etc

Case 17   Reported in Y B Paschal, 20 Hen VI, p 28, pl 22 See also Fitzh Entre Congeable, 5 According to this case a woman who marries an unwise husband should lose her land for making so foolish a choice

Paschal 21 Hen VI **(18) If I lease** lands at will and die, and then my lessee sows the land, and [my heir] ousts him, he shall have the emblements, for by my death his estate is ended. But it is otherwise if he had shown the land in my lifetime, etc By NEWTON, in Trespass

Case 18   The case has not been identified in Y B Paschal, 21 Hen VI, or in the early abridgments

Anno 4 Ed III

Iter de Not

(19) If an infant under age alienates and dies under age, his heir can enter because his father could have entered at all times But it is otherwise where a man who is not of sane memory alienates, for he himself could [not] enter, nor, consequently, his heir And this in a Formedon, etc

Case 19   There are no printed years in which we can trace the cases thus given

Trinity 7 Hen IV **(20) If a man** recovers land by default or surrender, against my father who is in tail, and my father dies before execution is sued, and then I enter, and he who recovered ousts me by force of the recovery, my entry upon him is legal, and if he ousts me I shall have the Assize to falsify the recovery But when he sues execution while my father is living, I cannot enter, but I am forced to bring a Formedon, etc   In a note, etc

The case has not been identified in Y B Trinity, 7 Hen IV, or in the Case 20 early abridgments

(21) **In the Assize of Wenlock** the tenant showed a Michaelis remainder tailed to the ancestor of the plaintiff, by one who 30 Hen VI disseised the tenant, and that the plaintiff, as heir to the ancestor, entered, etc   From this it follows that although the plaintiff be in by descent, if he be the first in whom the remainder was executed, so that no possession descended to him, that the tenant could enter upon him, etc   Query?

The case has not been identified in the very short printed term of Case 21 Mich 30 Hen VI, or in the early abridgments

(22) **If a man** enfeoffs another, rendering a certain rent, Trinity and for default of payment one re-enters, and the rent is 12 Hen IV in arrear, and then the feoffor dies, his heir cannot enter By the opinion of the COURT in an Ejectment from a Wardship   Query, if the father, in that case, could have entered upon the heir of the tenant who was in by descent, after the rent was in arrear? etc

The case has not been identified in Y B Trinity, 12 Hen IV, or in the Case 22 early abridgments

(23) **Where the king** had cause to seise by the forfeiture Michaelis of a tenant for life, and did not seise, but the tenant died, 23 Hen VI the entry of the reversioner was lawful. And this by the opinion of NEWTON, in an Assize, etc.

There is no printed year of 23 Hen VI   Fitzh Entre Congeable, Case 23 53, has the case much as it stands here

(24) **If the husband** and his wife and a third purchase Michaelis jointly — the husband alienates the whole and dies and the 31 Hen VI third enters, the entry of the woman upon him is lawful, by the opinion, etc , in a *Præcipe quod Reddat*, for his entry gives possession to the woman jointly with him, according to his title   (But yet it seems that it is severed

by the entry of the third. But yet he did not acknowledge his part and their title in law is joint, wherefore query?)

Case 24   The case has not been identified in Y B Mich 31 Hen VI Fitzh Entre Congeable, 54, has the case

ENTRE[47]

Statham 85 a
Hilary
14 Hen VI

(1) **In a writ upon** the Statute of Forcible Entries, it was alleged that the defendant disseised him by the strong hand And the tenant said that his father died seised, after whose death the plaintiff abated, and he entered upon him peaceably, without this that he entered by the strong hand, or detained by the strong hand NEWTON That is no plea for two reasons one, he does not reply to the point of our writ, to wit the disseisin, for he shall say, "without this that he disseised us by force," and not that he entered with force, for that is only an argument. And he also says, "without this that he detained by force" And although the Statute says that "if a man enter by force and detains by force," that is a disjunctive, and our action is conceived upon the disseisin, and not upon the detainer, so he answers to a thing that is not alleged by our action And the opinion agreed with this And see also that this is a strange color, to wit for abatement All the same if the action be merely in the nature of a Trespass it is good enough Query, etc ? And if he shall recover the land in that case? etc

Case 1   Reported in Y B Anno 14 Hen VI, p 21, pl 3 See also Fitzh Entre, 16 Statute of Forcible Entries, 15 Ric II (1391), cap 2, Stats. at Large, Vol 2, p 338 (339)

Paschal
14 Hen VI

(2) **In trespass** upon the same Statute, the writ was "*de terris prædictis et tenementis manu forti expulserunt, et disseisiverunt et sic seisiti de prædictis terris extra tenent*" PASTON I understand that the Statute is in the disjunctive, wherefore the writ is not good (But yet the writ was adjudged good, therefore see the Statute, etc) NEWTON Action, etc., for at the time of the alleged trespass the

freehold was in one J, and we, by his command entered peaceably, without this, etc   PASTON You cannot plead in this writ, which is a writ upon the case, as you can in a general writ of Trespass, for it is to recover the freehold, and in an Assize such a plea is of no value   Wherefore the defendant said that the said J was seised and enfeoffed him, etc

Reported in Y B Anno 14 Hen VI, p 16, pl 53   It is a further report of the case above (case 1, *supra*)   The Statute is the Statute of Forcible Entries, see *supra*, case 1   The words of the writ are as given in the printed case Case 2

(3)   **In a writ of entry** upon a disseisin for rent, the tenant of the lands pleaded "out of his fee" and he could not have the plea. (But the law is the other way, etc) Hilary 40 Ed III

Reported in Y B Hilary, 40 Ed III, p 13, pl 28   The case does not seem clear enough upon the law to warrant Statham's comment Case 3

(4)   **In a writ of entry** upon a disseisin, for rent, it was alleged that the tenant had no entry except by one S, who disseised the ancestor of the demandant   BELKNAP S never had anything in the lands of which, etc , except as husband to one A, which A is dead, and we are in as heir of A, and not as heir of S   Judgment of the writ.   CHELERY It may agree with my writ that he is in the lands as heir of A, and in the rent as heir of S, for it may be that S was his father, and purchased the rent, and then took to wife A, a tenant of the land   FYNCHEDEN. If your matter be such, show it, for then he has said enough *prima facie*, etc   (Study this well, etc) Hilary 43 Ed III

Reported in Y B Hilary, 43 Ed III, p 9, pl 28   See also Brooke, Entre in le Per, Cui et Post, 2 Case 4

(5)   **He who was** in the remainder brought a writ of Entry *in consimili casu*, and the writ was abated, because it was not in a like case, etc   (I believe that that is not the law) Paschal 7 Ed III

Reported in Y B Paschal, 7 Ed III, p 17, pl 19   The reasoning in the reported case seems sufficient to sustain the verdict in spite of Statham's remark Case 5

Hilary
21 Ed III
(6) **Entry in consimili casu** was maintained because he, who, etc , had only an estate tail in the reversion, etc (I believe that he himself was the lessor, and not the heir to the lessor, for tenant in tail can have a writ *de quibus* of a disseisin made on himself, but not on the disseisin made on his ancestor, etc   So it seems that a tenant for life shall have a writ *de quibus*.

Case 6
Reported in a short note in Y B Hilary, 21 Ed III, p 11, pl 36 See also Fitzh   Entre, 10, where Statham's statement is repeated verbatim

Hilary
30 Ed III
(7) **If lands be leased** to a man for life, the remainder to the husband and to his wife in tail, and for failure of issue the remainder to the right heirs of the husband, after the death of the tenant for life, and after the death of the husband and his wife and their issue, the entry of the collateral heir to the husband shall be adjudged to be for the donor and not the husband, etc   In a *Scire Facias*

And it was said in the same plea, that the release of the husband in that case without a warranty made to the tenant for life shall be a bar against the collateral heir of the husband

Case 7
Reported in Y B Hilary, 30 Ed III, p 4, pl 17. See also Fitzh Entre, 58, where he differs from the law in the case

Michaelis
7 Ed III
(8) **In a writ of entry** for rent, it was alleged that he had no entry except by one H who disseised his father   DAREL Our father died seised of the lands of which, etc , without this that H had anything in the rent, etc   And it was not allowed, unless he said that he did not enter into the rent, etc , or showed who was taker of the rent, etc

Case 8
The case has not been identified in Y B Mich 7 Ed III, or in the early abridgments

Michaelis
9 Ed III
(9) **In a writ of entry,** it was alleged that the tenant had no entry except by one R, to whom T demised it, who disseised the ancestor of the demandant, etc   The tenant said that R did not enter by T   Ready. The demandant

said that he should not be received to falsify any entry
except his own entry.   And it was not allowed, because he
could vouch as assignee to him; wherefore the demandant
said that that was no plea, unless he said that he entered,
etc   But yet the plea was adjudged good, because by that
exception he gave him a writ of Error in the *post*, etc

Case 9   The case has not been identified in Y B Mich 9 Ed III, or in the
early abridgments

(10) **In a writ of entry** in the *post*, to wit   "Except   Paschal
after the disseisin made on his brother," the tenant said that   2 Hen IV
the same brother enfeoffed one J, whose estate he had
And it was adjudged a good plea, etc
    The same plea is good in every writ of Entry, if he says
that he enfeoffed one by whom his entry is not alleged,
as well as in an Assize he shall say that the plaintiff enfeoffed
such a one whose estate he has, etc , for it is not contrary
to the writ
    And in a writ of Entry in the *per*, *cui*, or *post*, it is a good
plea to say that the plaintiff, or the ancestor of the plaintiff,
if the disseisin was made on him, enfeoffed the tenant,
judgment if action, etc

Case 10   Reported in Y B Paschal, 2 Hen IV, p 19, pl 10   See also Fitzh
Entre, 47   The latter part of the statement is Statham's   It is
not in the case

(11) **In a writ of entry** against an abbot, it was alleged   Trinity
that he had no entry except by the disseisin that one J,   10 Ed III
formerly abbot of that same place, etc   The tenant
demanded judgment because he did not name him his predecessor   And it was not allowed, for HERLE said that in
this writ he shall not [name him] heir or successor, etc

Case 11   Reported in Y B. Trinity, 10 Ed III, p 34, pl 20 The language in
both the reported case and in the digest is obscure and apparently
corrupt.

(12) **In a writ of entry** in the *post*, if the tenant can   Michaelis
show that the demandant can have a writ within the   34 Ed III
degrees, the writ shall abate, for at the common law there

Statham 85b was no writ in the *post* And the Statute is *"quod si alienationes ille, de quibus breve de ingressu dari consuevit per tot gradus fiant,* etc , *tunc habeat conquerens breve, sine mencione gradum,* ' to wit, to him who is opposed, and otherwise not And so it is outside of the Statute, etc

Case 12 There is no printed year of 34 Ed III The Statute is that of Marlbridge, 52 Hen III (1267), cap 29, Stats at Large, Vol 1, p 55 (73) "That if those alienations (whereupon a writ of entry was wont to be granted), hap to be made in so many degrees, that by reason thereof the same writ cannot be made in the form beforetime used, the plaintiffs shall have a writ to recover their seisin without making mention of the degrees "

Michaelis 39 Ed III (13) **Entry against a man** and his wife, in which the woman had no entry except by one R, who, etc CANNDISH This writ is within the degrees, and he has not alleged the entry of the husband, and the freehold is in him, etc , in which case the writ should be in the post, judgment, etc THORPE The writ is good, wherefore answer, etc. (Study this well, etc)

Case 13 Reported in Y B Mich 39 Ed III, p 25, pl 20 See also Brooke, Entre in the Per, Cui et Post, 25

Trinity 9 Hen VI (14) **In a writ of forcible entry,** the writ recited the statute, and said that the defendant entered into certain lands and tenements by the strong hand, and with a multitude of people had entered *"illicite "* And because he did not say, "Where this entry not given by law," the writ was abated, for although the writ be illegal, that shall relate to the strong hand, which cannot be lawful, but albeit he entered by the strong hand, and his entry were lawful, the plaintiff cannot recover anything upon that Statute, etc But there is another Statute Anno 5 Ric., which says that a man shall not enter by force, but his entry shall be lawful, and if he brings his action upon that Statute, then he shall recover (But the best Statute on such entries is Anno 8 King Hen. VI)

Case 14 Reported in Y B Trinity, 9 Hen VI, p 19, pl 12 See also Fitzh Entre, 15, Statute of 8 Hen VI (1429), cap 9, Stats at Large, Vol 3, p 111 (121) And 5 Ric II (1381), cap 7, Stats at Large, Vol 2, p 232 (240) Also 15 Ric II (1391), cap 2, Stats at Large, Vol 2, p 388 (339) The case is continued in 14 Hen VI, p 16, pl 53

(15) **If one disseises me,** who is disseised, and the first disseisor dies, and his issue is enfeoffed, I shall not have a writ of Entry against him in the *per*, for no one will be adjudged as continuing the first disseisin against me except the disseisor himself. Which all the Court conceded And this in a writ of Entry in the *post*, etc.

Reported in Y B Paschal (not Mich.) 3 Hen VI, p 38, pl 2   See also Brooke, Entre in le Per, Cui et Post, 1   The statement of facts differs, but the law is in agreement with Statham's case

(16) **In a writ of forcible entry** because the defendant should have entry into a house and ten shillings rent. FOR-TESCUE How can a man enter into a rent? PASTON A man can distrain with force for rent, and a man shall have a writ of Entry for rent, alleging that you have no entry in the rent except by, etc., and consequently this writ And they adjourned, etc

The case has not been identified in Y B Hilary, 19 Hen VI, or the early abridgments

(17) **If a woman** seignoress of a rent takes a husband who disseises the tenant of the land, and alienates the land and dies, the woman shall have a writ of Entry, to wit a *Cui in Vita* for the rent in the *per*,[1] and yet the writ is false And if my tenant makes a rescous of my rent and alienates the land, I shall have a writ of Entry for the rent against the alienee, and still it is not an entry in the rent by him, but into the lands, etc.

And it was said by THIRNING, in the same plea, that if a woman be enfeoffed and then takes a husband, and a writ of Entry is brought against them, the entry of the husband shall not be alleged to be by anyone   But it is otherwise when a woman is enfeoffed when she is covert, for there

[1] The case says, "in the *per* or in the *post*" and gives interesting reasons for the writ being "faux'   "If it be in the post it is necessary to suppose that the tenant had not entered until after the demise that the tenant of the land made to a stranger, which is false, because it was made by her husband, and to suppose the entry of the rent by the husband is false also, because the husband made a demise of the land "

she cannot enter unless the husband enters, for by the entry of the woman the freehold vests in the husband, "*simul et semel,*" etc. And also in a writ of Entry in the *post* the entry of the husband shall be alleged, etc

Case 17   Reported in Y B Trinity, 7 Hen IV, p 17, pl 11 See also Brooke, Entre in le Per, Cui et Post, 11.

Paschal
27 Hen VI   (18) **In a writ of entry** in the *per* and *cui* for rent, the tenant vouched to warranty him by whom his entry was alleged generally, who entered into the warranty and said that he entered on the lands from which the rent is issuing by one H, and by him whom the writ alleges DANBY That is no plea, for you alleged that you entered into the rent and not into the lands. and if in a *Præcipe quod Reddat* for rent the tenant vouches for the lands, he should show cause, for otherwise it is contrary to the writ. And also he has entered generally into the warranty, wherefore he cannot allege the contrary to that which the tenant has admitted, etc. And they adjourned, etc.

Case 18   The case has not been identified in Y B Paschal, 27 Hen VI There is no Paschal Term for that year in the printed Year Books Fitzh Entre in le Per, Cui et Post, 23, has the case

Note   **See as to entry in the post,** in the title of Receipt, Trinity, 31 Ed III, and also in the title of Bar, various matters, etc

Statham, title of Resceipte, *infra*, p 154 a, and Statham, title Barre, *supra*, pp 32 b to 37 b

Michaelis
20 Ed II   (19) **In a writ** *Dum Fuit infra Ætatem* on the lease of the demandant, the tenant pleaded the release of the demandant And because he did not say that the demandant was of full age at the time of the making of the release, it was the opinion that it was not a bar (But yet it seems good, etc)

Case 19   There is no printed year of 20 Ed II, and there is no early printed year of 20 Ed III, for which the citation might have been intended The case has not been identified in the Rolls Series for that year and term

(20) **If a man** enfeoffs the king, who enfeoffs another, etc., a writ of Entry in the *per* does not lie, because his entry shall not be alleged by the king, but he can have a writ of Entry in the *post*, etc. By SHARSHULL in an Assize, etc But if the king disseises me and enfeoffs another, I cannot have any writ, because I cannot allege that the king is a disseisor, etc Hilary 23 Ed III

The very short printed year of 23 Ed III does not give the case Fitzh Entre, 11, gives the case much as Statham does, and refers to 23 Ed III, without page or placitum, and also gives Paschal, 23 Ed III, p 7, pl 27 This is only a very short note, not giving any support to the first part of the case, the second part, however, appears Case 20

See that a man cannot enter with force into a rent, in Damages, Mich. 33, Hen VI Note

Statham, title of Damages, *supra*, p 60 a, case 43 An assize for rent

[47] The writ of Entry is one of the most common of all the writs in the Year Books Maitland takes issue with Blackstone as to the age of these writs Blackstone had said [Comm 3 184] that the writ of Entry was older than the Assizes Maitland [Forms of Action, pp 339–40] claims that "it is nonsense to suppose that our Saxon ancestors knew anything about writs of Entry Glanville gives no writ of Entry The Registers of the early years of Henry III give two such writs, the writ of entry *ad terminum qui præteriit* and the writ *cui in vita*, and on a Patent Roll of 1205 there is a writ of entry *sur disseisin*, a writ for the disseisee against the heir of the disseisor, followed by a writ which directs that this henceforward shall be a writ of course [Rot Pat 1 32] Before the middle of the century we find almost all the writs of entry in use, except those which were afterwards given by Statute The truth is that the writs of entry presuppose the Assizes I have been compelled to insist on this point because Blackstone's theory turns the whole history of seisin upside down " [p 340] It is as a guide-post to the student, who even yet is not too freely told that he is not to follow his Blackstone, that this quotation is made Maitland had spoken of writs of entry in the History of English Law [Vol 2 62–75] and in a note to that History [p 80] he had very largely incorporated this remark as to Blackstone Still it is but a note, and might well be overlooked Maitland of course bases his arguments upon well-founded proof We have that of Bracton [Treatise, pp 219, 219, b , 220 Note Book, pl 713] Reeves had noticed these cases in Bracton, and says it is probable that they — writs of entry — were introduced not long after Glanville's time [Reeves, Hist of Eng Law,

Vol 1 341] He also notices the matter of the conversion of a writ of entry into a writ of right [*Ib*, pp 386–390] And further, as to the different species of the writs of entry and the procedure thereupon, Reeves [Vol 1 388–397] and P & M Hist of Eng Law [2d ed , Vol 2, 62–75, and note to p 65] The influence of these writs upon the development of our law is sufficient to make a clear understanding of such development of much moment

EXAMINACIONE

Statham 86 a
Hilary
9 Hen VI

(1) **In debt** upon the arrears of an account brought by executors, they shall not be examined, because their account was before their testator, etc , Query, if the account had been had before themselves for a receipt had by their testator? etc.

Case 1

Reported in Y B Paschal (not Hilary), 9 Hen VI, p 8, pl 19 See also Brooke, Examination, 6, and Fithz Examinacion, 8

Michaelis
3 Hen VI

(2) **In detinue** against executors for a bailment made to their testator, they prayed that the plaintiff be examined, and so he was, etc Query, if *rigore juris*, etc ? And they admitted that the bailment was made where they declared, etc , and that their testator died in another county PASTON Judgment of the writ, then, for the action should have been brought where he died, for their charge begins there, etc. And the opinion of the Court was against him

Case 2

Reported in Y B Paschal (not Mich), 3 Hen VI, p 38, pl 1 See also Brooke, Examination, 3, and Fitzh Examinacion, 5 The case gives no decision for or against him

Trinity
3 Hen VI

(3) **In debt** upon the arrears of an account, if the attorney of the plaintiff be examined, and then the plaintiff appears, they will examine him, for he had better notice, etc And so see that an attorney shall be examined, and yet an executor, who is in a manner like an attorney to his testator, shall not be examined, etc

Case 3

So far as it has been identified, the case appears in Y B Trinity, 3 Hen VI, p 46, pl 2, where the point is made in the course of an argument on a writ of debt upon an account. See also Brooke, Examination, 5

See as to examination, in the title of Executors, in Note the title of Fines, and in the title of Deceit

Statham, title of Executours, *infra*, pp 87 a to 88 b, Statham, title of Fynez, *infra*, pp 96 a and 96 b , Statham, title Disceipte, *supra*, pp 68 a to 68 b

(4) **In debt** upon the arrears of an account, when the Trinity 28 Hen VI defendant prayed that the plaintiff should be examined, he proffered his law immediately, to wit "Nothing owing him, Ready to wage his law," and prayed that he be examined, etc

The case has not been identified in Y B Trinity, 28 Hen VI, or in Case 4 the early abridgments

ENTRE PLEDER

(1) **In detinue** by two against one H, who said that the Hilary 2 Hen IV writings were delivered to him by the plaintiff and three others, and he prayed a *Scire Facias*, and had it, on which day the sheriff returned that the writ was served And one of the garnishees did not come, but yet the two who came pleaded with the plaintiff   And yet if one of the plaintiffs was non-suited, that would be a nonsuit for both of them, etc

Reported in Y B Hilary, 2 Hen IV, p 16, pl 22 See also 3 Hen IV, Case 1 p 7, pl. 31, and Fitzh Entrepleader, 12

(2) **In a writ of wardship,** the defendant said that she Paschal 31 Ed III did not claim anything in the said body, except by reason of sustenance, and she said that one H had another writ pending against him for the same wardship, and she prayed that they might interplead SKIPWITH   This H was essoined, so it appears that he has made his own delay, wherefore it is not reasonable that we shall be delayed by that, etc   And it was not allowed, wherefore it was said to their attorneys that they should sue separate *Scire Facias'* against their masters to interplead, etc. And so it was done, wherefore they came by the *Scire Facias*, and then the defendant said that while these writs were pending

one F had brought a writ against him for the same wardship, and prayed that he be notified to interplead, and it was granted Which note, etc THORPE gave as his reason that the demandant would recover his damages against each one in accordance with the delay they had caused him, etc Query as to this matter? For it is wrong for them to interplead unless all the writs are returnable on the same day, etc

Case 2   There is no printed year of 31 Ed III Fitzh Entrepleader, 15, has the case, of which he gives a long digest

Hilary 14 Hen VI   (3) **Two brought** separate writs of Detinue on the same obligation, and each of them counted upon a bailment made to the defendant.   And the writs were returned on the same day, and the defendant prayed that they might interplead, and they could not, because he had charged himself against both by his own act [1] The law is the same where one declares upon a bailment, and the other upon another cause, as it seems, etc   But where they both declare upon any other cause than upon a bailment, then they shall interplead, etc , for then the defendant is not obliged to deliver the deed, except to him who had the right, etc. Query, if he delivers the deed to him who had no title, etc , shall he who had title have his action against him, or against him who had the possession, etc ?

Case 3   Reported in Y B Anno 14 Hen VI, p 2, pl 6   See also Brooke, Entrepleader 14, and Fitzh Entrepleader, 6

Statham 86 b
Trinity 15 Hen VI   (4) **Where an action** is brought against one, and he said that the plaintiff and another delivered it to him upon conditions, and prayed a *Scire Facias* against the other, who came and showed other conditions, the plaintiff shall have judgment to recover the writings immediately, for in no case where the garnishee varies from the conditions that the defendant has shown can they interplead.   By the opinion of the COURT, etc   For in that case the garnisher will not be injured, for if what he has said is true, the defend-

[1] "Because they had declared on several bailments," is the reason given in the report of the case

ant is charged against him in Detinue, and they cannot interplead, for the defendant is out of Court, etc

(5) **In detinue** against one J, the plaintiff counted on a bailment, and another brought a writ for the same writing, returnable on the same day, and counted that they were concerning lands, etc. The defendant said that he was ready, etc , and prayed that they might interplead, and the opinion was that they should not be forced to do this, because the defendant, by his own deed, had charged himself against them both But yet STRANGE said that if one of them who had a right to the deed recovered against him, that he could plead this recovery in bar against the other, who bailed to him; as well as in debt upon a lease for a term of years I shall show how one who had a right to the lands entered upon me, etc. Study well.

Trinity
9 Hen VI

Reported in Y B Trinity, 9 Hen VI, p 17, pl 9 See also Brooke, Entrepleader, 5, and Fitzh Entrepleader, 5 Statham may well say, "Study well," for the question is argued at length and skillfully

Case 5

(6) **The Lord of Cromwell** brought a writ of Detinue against J, and, demanded delivery of an obligation for a thousand pounds, which one G delivered to the defendant to deliver to the plaintiff And this same G brought a writ of Detinue for the same obligation, against the same person, who counted that he bailed it to him for him to rebail And the writs were returnable upon the same day. And it was debated if they should interplead, inasmuch as the defendant had admitted no privity nor any conditions between the plaintiffs in regard to the bailment, so it is chargeable against both, for he did not say anything [as to being] he was ready to deliver them, to whom, etc And then it was adjudged that they should interplead

Paschal
3 Hen VI

And it was said in the same plea, that if I declare upon a bailment where in truth the defendant found the deed, [I shall say] without this that I bailed, etc , for otherwise he is chargeable against him who had the right, etc.

And it was said in the same plea that in replevin against two for an ox, and each of them makes a separate avowry in his own right, they shall not interplead, but the whole shall abate, for both cannot have a return of one and the same ox, etc.

Case 6

Reported in Y B Mich (not Paschal), 3 Hen VI, p 20, pl 32 See also Brooke, Entrepleader, 2, and Fitzh Entrepleader, 1 The remarks quoted by Statham are not in the printed report of the case

Michaelis 18 Hen VI

(7) Two brought separate writs of Detinue returnable on the same day, and each of them declared upon a bailment MARKHAM The deed was delivered to us by both the plaintiffs, upon certain conditions, and we do not know, etc., and we pray that you interplead. PORTYNGTON Imparle Query, if this be a plea, for it goes to the abatement of both their writs.

Case 7

Reported in Y B Mich 19 (not 18), Hen VI, p 3, pl 6 This is assumed to be the case, as it corresponds in matter of fact and law to the digest Brooke, Entrepleader, 11, raises the question, brought up in several cases of interpleader, as to which of the parties to the interpleader shall be plaintiff

Michaelis 7 Hen IV

(8) **If three or four** were to have a livery out of the Chancery, where each of them is found heir to the same ancestor by different offices, the opinion of THIRNING was that they should interplead, etc

Case 8

Reported in Y B Mich 7 Hen IV, p 4, pl 25

Note

See as to interpleader, in the title of Detinue, Hilary, 36 Hen VI

Statham gives no such citation in his title of Detenu, *supra*, pp 67 a and 67 b

(9) **Query, if two** *Præcipe*'s *quod Reddat* are brought against a man for the same lands on the same day, and the tenant says that his father died seised, and because it was understood that his father had no title to the land, they would not waive the possession between them; and as they did not understand to which of the demandants the land belonged, they prayed that they might interplead, etc

And in that case they should interplead, because the defendant did not claim anything in the lands, no more than in
the cases above, for that is the cause for the interpleader,
when the defendant has a legal occupation in the thing
demanded, and does not claim anything, etc

There is no citation given in Statham for this case, and it may well **Case 9**
be a number of notes jotted down for private use and not intended
for publication   The wording is awkward, and evidently needed
revision

EXECUTOURS [48]

(1) **In debt against** two executors, one came at the   Statham 87 a
Pluries Capias, and a *distringas* issued against the others   Hilary
And the opinion was that he should be required to answer,   40 Ed III
albeit the *distringas* was never awarded against him, etc

Reported in Y B Hilary, 40 Ed III, p 1, pl 2   See also Brooke, **Case 1**
Executors, 25

(2) **In debt against executors** who pleaded fully admin-   Paschal
istered, and it was found that they had, etc   And the   40 Ed III
opinion was that the inquest should make the sum certain,
for they will not be charged except according to the finding
of the inquest, etc

Reported in Y B Paschal, 40 Ed III, p 15, pl 1   See also Brooke, **Case 2**
Executors, 141, who seems to have seen a different report of the case

(3) **See a writ of debt** brought by [against] executors of   Trinity
executors   41 Ed III

Reported in Y B Trinity, 41 Ed III, p 13, pl 3   See also Brooke, **Case 3**
Executors, 26, and Fitzh Executours, 64   Debt on a contract They
showed no obligation and took nothing by their writ

(4) **An executor brought** a writ of Debt, and he pro-   Michaelis
duced a will which proved that [there was another executor] [1]   41 Ed III
etc   The defendant said that he was alive   The plaintiff
said that he was discharged from the administration before

[1] Words from the report of the case   The remarks in the digest are
not in the case

the ordinary, and that he never administered, etc   And
because he could administer when he would, it was adjudged
that he take nothing, etc   But it is otherwise on the part
of the defendant, for the plaintiff shall not be forced to bring
his action, except against those who administer, because
he is a stranger to the will, etc.   See here that the plaintiff
did not count that his companion was dead.   It seems that
he should, because he was named in the will, etc   Query?

Case 4

Reported in Y B Mich 41 Ed III, p 22, pl 10   See also Brooke,
Executors 27, and Fitzh   Executours, 63

**Michaelis
10 Ed III**

(5) **Where [an action** is brought against][1] executors by
way of demand and one of them who has administered is
dead, his executor shall not be joined in an action with the
others, because they are strangers to the first will, but
vice versa the law is otherwise, as appeared in Mich. 41,
in a note, etc

Case 5

The case has not been identified in Y B Mich 10 Ed III, or in
Mich 41 Ed III

**Paschal
42 Ed III**

(6) **Two executors** brought an action   The defendant
showed that one of them was outlawed.   And the Court
held that the other could continue the process as well as if
one was nonsuited   And this in Debt, etc

Case 6

Reported in Y B Paschal, 42 Ed III, p 13, pl 21   See also Brooke,
Executors, 30

**Paschal
46 Ed III**

(7) **In debt** against three executors, etc   Two said,
"never executor", the third said that he had fully administered, and upon that they were at issue   And it was
found that one of those who pleaded, "never," etc., was
never, etc, and that the other was, and that the third
had four pounds in his hands.   And it was adjudged that
the plaintiff should recover the amount which was in
the hands, etc., of the goods of the deceased, etc, and
the remainder of the goods from him who was found to be

---

[1] The case seems unintelligible without these additional words, or
some emendation of the text   These words, however, do not appear in
the text of Statham

an executor [1] and that he be amerced against the third, etc
And the same judgment was given on that same day,
where an action was brought against an executor, who said,
etc   And it was found that he was, etc , and that he had
ten pounds in his hands   And the plaintiff recovered the
ten pounds of the goods [of the deceased], and the remainder
of the goods against this same, etc   Query, where such a
judgment is given wholly against himself, etc , for his false
pleas, and then he pays it to him who recovered the goods of
the deceased, shall that be called an administration against
another man, against whom he is charged as executor? etc.

Reported in Y B Paschal, 46 Ed III, p 9, pl 6   See also Brooke, Case 7
Executors, 34, and Fitzh   Executours, 72

(8) **In covenant** against executors, one cannot answer   Michaelis
without the other, because they are out of the purview   47 Ed III
of the Statute, etc   But in detinue it is different, etc
(But yet, query?)

Reported in Y B Mich 47 Ed III, p 22, pl 50   See also Brooke, Case 8
Executors, 36

The Statute is that of 25 Ed III (1350), cap 17, Stats at Large,
Vol 2, p 49 (59)

(9) **In account** by two executors, one was severed, and   Paschal
the defendant was adjudged to account   And a *Capias*   48 Ed III
ad Computandum issued against him, and upon that the
exigent, until he was outlawed   And then he sued a charter
of pardon, and came and showed an acquittance to the
Court from him who was severed; and he prayed a *Scire
Facias* against him   And then came the other executor,
who was the wife of the testator, and told how their testator
had devised all his goods to her, and the debts which were
due to him, in which case it is not reasonable that the
acquittance of our companion should injure us, and
especially after he was severed, etc   And she prayed that
no *Scire Facias* should issue against her   FYNCHEDEN If
it be his deed you are without a remedy, unless it be before
the ordinary for an account against your companion.

[1] Because of his false plea.

THORPE It seems that a *Scire Facias* should not issue against him who was severed, for the other was adjudged to sue alone FYNCHEDEN If an executor wishes to refuse to administer in a Court of record, or before the ordinary, then it is not reasonable that his acquittance shall be a bar, or that a *Scire Facias* shall issue against him, but it is different here, etc And then THORPE awarded a *Scire Facias* against the woman, leaving out the other Which note, because the contrary [has often been adjudged] elsewhere, etc But yet the acquittance of the other shall be a good bar against the woman, whether he be garnished or not, wherefore the award of the *Scire Facias* does not change the case as it seems, etc

Case 9   Reported in Y B Paschal, 48 Ed III, p 14, pl 8 See also Brooke, Executors, 37

(10) **Executors** paid twenty pounds for restitution of a wrong done by their testator, to wit a trespass Query, if that shall be called an administration against one to whom their testator was indebted upon an obligation, since they were not chargeable by the law to pay it, but in conscience they were, etc

Case 10   The case has no citation in Statham, and has not been identified The point taken is interesting

Paschal 21 Ed III   (11) **In debt** against executors, who pleaded "fully administered," the plaintiff said that he brought another such a writ against them, which was abated for a variance in the names, and that he had purchased this writ of *"Journees accomptes,"* without this that he would aver that he had assets the day the first writ was purchased THORPE Although there is a writ pending against them, they shall not omit to make an administration, etc And that was also the opinion of the Court, etc

Case 11   The case has not been identified in Y B Paschal, 21 Ed III, or in the early abridgments

Paschal 3 Hen IV   (12) **Two executors** brought a writ of Debt against one H, until he was outlawed, and then he had a charter of pardon, and a *Scire Facias* And the sheriff returned that they had notice [1] and one came and the other did not, and he who came counted against the defendant, and was received to do so   But yet it is different as to other persons, where the nonsuit of one is the nonsuit of both, and this was also a severance in fact, etc.

Reported in Y B Hilary (not Paschal), 3 Hen IV, p 10, pl 9   See Case 12. also Brooke, Executors, 44

(13)   **In debt** against two executors, the defendant showed that they were outlawed   But yet it was adjudged that they should answer, since it was only to another's use, as an Attorney, etc

Paschal 14 Hen VI

Reported in Y B Anno 14 Hen VI, p 14, pl 50   See also Fitzh Executours, 11

Case 13

(14)   **Although** the ordinary discharges one from the executorship, still the other cannot have an action without naming him, for he can administer when he wishes   And this by THORPE, in a *Scire Facias.*

Paschal 49 Ed III Statham 87 b.

(15)   **Debt was brought** against executors, and [by] executors against executors, and the writ was adjudged good, etc   And if one administers of his own tort with executors, I shall have an action against them as executors, but *vice versa* the action does not lie, etc , for the second executors are strangers to the first will, etc

Trinity 15 Hen. VI

And it was said in the same plea, if the first executors take the goods out of the possession of the second executors, they shall not have an action against them, for their testator could not have had an action if they had taken them out of his possession, etc   But if the second executors take the goods out of the possession of the first executors, they shall have a good action, etc   And it seems that if one of the first executors makes his executors and dies, and his executors take such goods as were in the possession of their testator, that the first executor shall have an action of trespass against them, for the property remains in him

[1] The case has it that one had notice, and the other had not   Brooke states the case correctly

by the survivorship, and consequently the action, since they were taken (as above), for the possession was in him as well as in the other   And also the executor who survives shall have an action for the debts of the first testator by the survivorship, consequently, etc   Query?

Case 15

There is no printed year of 15 Hen VI   Fitzh Executours, 12, has the case

Michaelis 4 Hen VI

(16) **In debt** against executors, who pleaded "fully administered," and it was found for them, wherefore it was adjudged that the plaintiff take nothing   And then the plaintiff came and showed how, after that time, they had goods, and he prayed a *Scire Facias* against them.   MARTYN   Their original suit is ended, wherefore, etc , and you can have a writ of Debt as a new original, etc   Which was conceded, etc.

Case 16

Reported in Y B Mich 4 Hen VI, p 4, pl 8   See also Brooke, Executors, 85

Michaelis 11 Hen IV

(17) **Executors** shall have a writ of Ravishment of Wardship, where the ward was taken out of the possession of their testator, etc

Case 17

Reported in Y B Hilary (not Mich), 11 Hen IV, p 54, pl 36   See also Brooke, Executors, 53, and Fitzh   Executours, 52

Paschal 9 Hen VI

(18) **Executors** can enter into the lands which their testator had in fee, or for life, after his death, and take his goods, and so can a stranger by their command   By the opinion of the COURT, in Trespass, etc

Case 18

The case has not been identified in Y B Paschal, 9 Hen VI, or in the early abridgments

Hilary 4 Hen VI

(19) **In debt against executors,** the sheriff returned "*nihil habet*" at the summons, upon which a *Capias* issued, returnable now, and one of them came and was made to answer without the other, for BABYNGTON said that the Statute was made in favor of the plaintiff, and a *distringas* cannot be awarded after one "*nihil*" returned, etc   But at the *Pluries Capias* it has in fact often been adjudged

that one shall answer without the other, because it is the third writ, and in a manner in the place of a *distringas*, etc

Reported in Y B Hilary, 4 Hen VI, p 14, pl 11 [12]   See also Brooke, Executors, 86   *Case 19*

The Statute is that of 4 Ed III (1330), cap 7, Stats at Large, Vol 1, p 430 (434)

(20) **If a man** dies intestate, and one takes his goods wrongfully, and keeps them by him, a man shall [not] have an action against him as executor, but if he sells them and pays any debt of the deceased, then an action lies against him, for then he administers as executor, etc.   By PRISOT.   Query well, etc.   *Michaelis 30 Hen VI*

The case has not been identified in Y B Mich 30 Hen VI, or in the early abridgments   *Case 20*

(21) **Executors** shall have a writ of *ejectione firmae* where their testator was ejected   By the opinion of the COURT, etc   *Hilary 7 Hen IV*

Reported in Y B Hilary, 7 Hen IV, p 6, pl 1   See also Brooke, Executors, 45, and Fitzh Executours, 53   *Case 21*

(22) **In detinue** against executors, he who first came by distress was made to answer without his companion, but yet the Statute says that the debt, etc   *Michaelis 14 Hen IV*
And it was said in the same plea, if executors bring a writ of Trespass for the goods of their testator which have been carried away, they shall be severed   And if one will not sue, yet if the writ be general, it is otherwise, etc , for there is no need to name them executors, etc.

Reported in Y B Hilary (not Mich), 14 Hen IV, p 23, pl 30, where it would appear that the conclusion was contrary to that reported by Statham   But the case appears again on p 97 of the same year and term, pl 37, where it is argued at very great length, and the three executors are made to answer for the detinue, without the fourth The case, as it appears on p 37, is an excellent example of the method and skill in pleading of the time   See also Brooke, Executors, 64   *Case 22*

The Statute is that of 4 Ed III (1330), cap 7, Stats at Large, Vol 1, p 430 (434)

Michaelis
39 Ed III

(23) **One brought** a writ of debt against one K on a contract between them, and she pleaded a release from the plaintiff of all actions, and in the deed the plaintiff was named executrix, etc CANNDISH This deed in the name of an executor will not bar us, except where we bring an action as executor and we are named as executor, etc , and here we are not named executor, judgment, etc And it was the opinion that she should be barred, etc

Case 23

Reported in Y B Mich 39 Ed III, p 26, pl 21

Michaelis
2 Hen VI

(24) **If a man** has judgment to recover the goods of the deceased against executors, and he sues execution accordingly, and the sheriff returns that they have wasted the goods, the plaintiff shall have a *Capias* to take their body and have execution of their own goods, etc

Case 24

Reported in Y B Trinity (not Mich) 2 Hen VI, p 12, pl 4 See also Brooke, Executors, 8

Michaelis
9 Hen VI

(25) **In debt,** the defendant said that there was a co-executor, not named, etc , and it was found against him And the plaintiff prayed a general judgment, and could have it only for the goods of the deceased, etc.

Case 25

Reported in Y B Mich 9 Hen VI, p 44, pl 26 See also Brooke, Executors, 13, who has either mistaken the point or has another report of the case

Paschal
9 Hen VI

(26) **In debt** against administrators, it was counted that one H died intestate at B, and that the ordinary committed the administration to them. CHAUNT. He made his will at F, etc , and by the same will he made us his executors, by force of which we administered, in which case we shall be named executors and not, etc., judgment of the writ PASTON That is no plea, for you should say that the will was approved before the ordinary, and also "without this that he died intestate," and also "without this that the ordinary committed the administration to you, etc." And they adjourned, etc

Case 26

Reported in Y B Paschal, 9 Hen VI, p 7, pl 17 See also Fitzh Executours, 8 Statham has put several remarks into his digest which are not found in the printed case He also makes the Court adjourn, where the case makes the parties imparl Fitzherbert follows the printed report of the case

(27) **Where a woman** is made executrix and marries, the release or acquittance of the woman during the coverture cannot be good, but the release or acquittance of her husband is good in his own name, etc. PASTON in Debt, etc But that acquittance should especially set forth the matter, as I believe, etc. Hilary 14 Hen VI

The case has not been identified in Y B Anno 14 Hen VI, or in the early abridgments Case 27

(28) **In debt,** the defendant can give his goods where it pleases him, pending the writ, and they shall not be put in execution unless the plaintiff recovers, because his person is charged But it is otherwise against executors, for the charge runs upon the goods of the deceased, if it be not for their mispleading, etc But yet if, pending a writ against them, another recovers and sues execution, they shall be discharged And if the execution be sued against them after judgment, so that they cannot plead it, they shall have an *Audita Querela*, etc. But it is otherwise where they have administered by their own authority, etc Paschal 9 Hen VI

Reported in Y B Paschal, 9 Hen VI, p 9, pl 25 See also Brooke, Executors, 11, and Fitzh Executours, 9 If this is indeed the case, for there is ground for doubt, Statham again has matter outside the case in his first statement Case 28

(29) **In debt** against executors, who pleaded "fully administered," and it was found against them. HANKFORD (to Wakefield, the prothonotary) Enter the judgment of the debt for the goods of the deceased, and for the damages on a general judgment And the plaintiff prayed a *Capias ad Satisfaciendum*, and had it for the damages, which note And see that in every other case when executors plead any plea in bar, except the aforesaid, to wit "fully administered," and the plea is found against them, the plaintiff shall have a general judgment against them for the debt because of their false plea; and their own goods shall be Statham 88 a. Michaelis 11 Hen IV

charged   But in the case of "fully administered," the judgment shall not be general, for if it be found against the plaintiff, still he is not barred, except as to that time, for if goods came to their hands afterwards, he shall have a new action, so he is not barred forever as in other cases, etc   (But yet some say that he shall never have such a general judgment of debt, except for the damages, etc)   Query?

Case 29   Reported in Y B Mich 11 Hen IV, p 5, pl 11   All the latter part of the digest is in Statham's own words   See also Brooke, Executors, 51

Michaelis   (30) **In debt** against executors, who said that their
18 Hen VI   testator made another his executor, to administer with them, etc   FORTESCUE   He did not administer before the purchase of the writ. Ready. And it was adjudged a good plea

Case 30   Reported in Y B Hilary (not Mich), 18 Hen VI, p 29, pl 1

Hilary   (31) **One had a fieri facias** against executors for the
19 Hen VI   goods of the deceased   And the sheriff returned that they had wasted the goods, upon which the plaintiff had a *Scire Facias* against them to say why he should not have execution against them on their own goods   And the writ was challenged because it ran *"Cum [un tiel] recuperasset,"* etc , and did not show by what writ   And the writ was adjudged good, etc   And so it seems that upon such a return (as above) they shall not have a *Capias* against them without suing a *Scire Facias*, etc

Case 31   Reported in Y B Hilary, 19 Hen VI, p 49, pl 6   See also Brooke, Executors, 71

Paschal   (32) **If a man** take goods out of the possession of executors
19 Hen VI   which are the goods of their testator, one of them cannot have an action without his companions   By the opinion of the COURT, in Trespass, etc.

Case 32   Reported in Y B Paschal, 19 Hen VI, p 65, pl 3   See also Fitzh Executours, 14

(33) **Executors** shall have a writ of Ravishment of Ward- Michaelis 11 Hen IV
ship [for the ward] who was taken out of the possession of
their testator   And this by the equity of the Statute
of Edward III, "*De Bonis Asportatis*," etc

Reported in Y B Hilary (not Mich), 11 Hen IV, p 54, pl 36 See Case 33
also Brooke, Executors, 53, and Fitzh Executours, 52

The Statute is that of 4 Ed III (1330), cap 7, Stats at Large, Vol 1,
p 430 (434)

(34) **In detinue** against executors, he who first came by Hilary 17 Ed III
the distress was forced [to answer, etc].

Reported in Y B Hilary, 17 Ed III, p 9, pl 29   Case 34

(35) **In detinue** for charters against executors, one came Michaelis 21 Hen VI
at the distress, and the other did not   Now, the question
is, should he answer or not? PORTYNGTON Although the
action be brought against them as executors, still it lies
against them without naming them executors, for their
possession is the cause of the action   And this is clearly
proved, for "never executor" is no plea   MARKHAM
Although "never executor" is no plea, still they shall have
no pleas as executors, for they say that their testator bailed
the charters to the plaintiff in another county, and they also
pleaded a release of all actions which the plaintiff made to
their testator. NEWTON I deny both your reasons, for
the executors had nothing to do with the charters, albeit
the possession came to them   And although the plaintiff
released all actions to the testator, still he could take the
writings, and consequently have an action against another
who came to the possession as executor   But, peradventure, a release of all the right that he had in the charters
might be a bar, and no judgment shall be given against them
in that case, of the goods of the deceased, nor damages
for the detinue by their testator. MARKHAM Executors
will be charged for the damage that their testator did
when their testator detained my debt   NEWTON Not
the same   MARKHAM I shall have replevin against
executors for a taking made by their testator and recover
damages against them for the taking NEWTON. That

cannot be, for your writ is false. MARKHAM I shall have a special writ against them, as well as executors shall have replevin for the cattle taken from their testator NEWTON. That is another matter, but I think that the Statute does not extend to any cases except where damages are recoverable against them for the goods of the deceased. And they adjourned, etc

And to that which was said, that the essoin in that writ was [as] in a plea of Debt, still it is another sort of action, etc And they adjourned Similar matter, 11 Hen IV Well argued

And it was said in the same plea, if I find charters, and one who has no right to them recovers against me, I am discharged as to him who had a right [to them], for I was not obliged to know who had a right in that case, but he shall be driven to take his action against him who had possession, and particularly when my possession is defeated by course of law But where a bailment is made to me the law is otherwise, unless I am able to show that he who recovered had the right, and not the plaintiff.

Case 35

Reported in Y B Mich 21 Hen VI, p 1, pl 1 In the latter part of the printed case we are told of a like case decided afterward, in which the executor was obliged to answer

The Statute is that of 9 Ed III (1335), cap 3, Stats at Large, Vol 1, p 449 (454)

Paschal 7 Hen IV

(36) **In debt** against two executors, one came at the distress and pleaded a plea in bar, to which the plaintiff replied, and they were at issue And process issued against the other executor, who came on another day and pleaded in abatement of the writ, upon which they were at issue And it was the opinion of the COURT that the plaintiff had discharged himself of the first issue, inasmuch as he had replied to the second plea, for they said that the plaintiff shall answer to only one plea against executors. For in debt against several executors, where one pleads one plea and another another plea, and so on severally, the plaintiff shall answer to only one of those pleas, and they shall be forced to keep to only one plea — that which is more

favorable to their testator, at the discretion of the judges, etc. And this is understood to apply when every plea goes in bar of the whole action, etc   Query?

The case has not been identified in Y B Paschal, 7 Hen IV, or in the early abridgments   Case 36

(37) **In an audita querela** against two executors, at the distress, one came and was made to answer without his companion, etc   Trinity 7 Hen IV

Reported in Y B Trinity, 7 Hen IV, p 16, pl 6   See also Brooke, Executors, 48   *Contra, infra*, case 39   Case 37

(38) **If I make a man** who is my debtor my executor with others, and die, the other executors shall have an action of debt against him in all their names, and they shall be summoned and severed, for it is not reasonable, when one is indebted to me, that that debt shall be extinguished   But it is otherwise when their testator is indebted to me, and he makes me and others his executors, and dies, for then he can retain as much as the debt amounted to, etc   And this was held by all the Court in a *Scire Facias*, etc.   Trinity 27 Hen. VI

Statham 88 b

The case has not been identified in Y B Trinity, 27 Hen VI, or in the early abridgments   Case 38

See as to executors, in the title of Issue, etc   Note

Statham, title of Issue, *infra*, pp 115 b to 117 b

(39) **In a writ of covenant** against executors one could not answer without the other, etc   Paschal 47 Ed III

Reported in Y B Mich (not Paschal), 47 Ed III, p 22, pl 50   See also *supra*, case 8, and Brooke, Executors, 36, on another point   Case 39

(40) **In debt against executors,** upon an obligation made by their testator, they said, "Not the deed of their testator," and it was found against them, wherefore the plaintiff prayed a general judgment, but could not have it, but he had judgment for the goods of the deceased, and as to the damages, a general judgment for so much as he   Michaelis 34 Hen VI

was damaged, after the death of the testator, and of the remainder of the goods of the deceased, etc And so see that there is a difference where they plead a plea which comes from their testator (as above) and where they plead a plea which comes from themselves, and of which they themselves had full notice, as "never executor," etc

And it was said in the same plea, that if in debt against executors they plead, "Fully administered except so much," and it is found to be so, the plaintiff shall have judgment to recover all his debt, but he shall not have execution for more than is found in their hands And afterwards when other goods of the deceased come to their hands, he shall have a *Scire Facias* against them, to have execution of the remainder But if they plead, "Fully administered" generally, and it is found for them, there the plaintiff shall not have any judgment, but afterwards, when goods come to their hands, he shall have an action against them, as it seems

Case 40   Reported at very great length in Y B Mich 34 Hen VI, pp 22–24, pl 42 See also Brooke, Executors, 22, where he notes an error in the case which was noticed by Fitzherbert and others "in the Year 23 Hen VIII," as the record was different Brooke says, "Judgment was given that the plaintiff should recover the goods of the deceased, but the books at large report further in these words, 'and if there were none, of their own goods, but these words were not in the record' And they were commanded to correct the books " This apparently was not done, as the words remain in the printed Year Books

[48] It has been said that "in the Saxon period there is no law of executors " [Holdsworth, Hist of Eng Law, Vol 2 84] On the other hand we are told after an examination of wills and deathbed gifts of the Anglo-Saxon period, "The germ of executorship seems to be here " [P & M Hist of Eng Law, 2d ed , Vol 2 319] Both authorities agree that the curthe or cuithe was also a forerunner of the executor Always and everywhere, under some name or form, it has been necessary for the dying person to give into the hands of some living person the goods which, however reluctantly, he is leaving behind, and to direct that person to a certain carrying out of wishes no longer to be controlled by the dying person, who is passing away from all worldly things

The executor, however, had become a very important person by the time of the third Edward We have, in the abridgment, some forty cases in which he is considered from the viewpoint of a court of law

We have had something to say about debt against executors under the title of Dette [*supra*, pp 492, 493] and debt forms the subject of our first few cases   Our third case shows the further extension of an action of debt to an executor of executors   "In Bracton's day it is the heir, not the executor, who sues for the debts that were due to the dead man " [P & M Hist of Eng Law, 2d ed , Vol 2 346]   In the time of Edward I, the action was being upheld in cases of debt by executors   [Y B (R S) 20 Ed I, 375, 21–22 Ed I, 258, 598, 33–35 Ed I, 62, 294   Debt against Executors, 30 and 31 Ed I, p 238]   This third case of ours was covered by the Act of 25 Ed III, St 5, cap 5 (1350), which ordained that executors of executors should have an action of debt accompt and goods carried away of the first testator   [Stats at Large, Vol 2, p 54] The case is of a date only sixteen years after the passage of the act, and the law had not been very long settled

The story of the disability of the executor to bring an account, and the right given to him to bring the writ by the Statute of Westminster II, has been partially told in the note to the title of Accompte [*Supra*, p 20]   In our case 9 the executors bring an action of Account

The administrator was for many years constantly being confused with the executor, in fact the terms were interchangeable, as we have seen in the note to the title of Administratours   [*Supra*, p 39]

ERROUR

(1) **In a writ of error** on a judgment rendered in Oxford, Hilary
50 Ed III where the protestation was in the nature of an Assize, and it was assigned for error that whereas the *habeas corpus* should have been awarded against the jurors after the return of the summons, they awarded a *distringas*, etc And another was because the Assize was for rent, and albeit the writ was *"quod vendant tenementum illud,"* still the entry shall be [*"ten' unde reddit provenit,"* etc] because by the complaint they have certified, etc   And another, that whereas the Assize was brought against the mesne and the tenant, because the tenant made the rescous, the tenant pleaded in bar, and for this reason the plaintiff prayed the Assize, upon which the Assize was taken, and they did not inquire as to the bar, in that there was error WILLOUGHBY· As to the first point, although the Assize had been taken without any process, that had been good

enough   And as to the second point, it shall be understood that the land was put in view for a rent cannot be viewed; at the same time it had been better form, as you say.   But as to the third point, it seems to us that they should have inquired as to the bar, wherefore we reverse the judgment, and the defendant shall be restored, etc   And he said to the plaintiff that he could elect to bring a new Assize or to plead anew upon this judgment, and when they were at the Assize that it could be tried at the *Nisi Prius*.   Query as to the reason they did not hold that the plaintiff should be barred?

Case 1

Reported in Y B Hilary, 50 Ed III, p 18, pl 12   It is given in the margin as "Statham, Error, 3," which is incorrect, as the short case which Statham has under this title (*infra*, case 3) is one of Account   The first part of the case as here given, however, is not found in the report of the case   See also Brooke, Error, 30

Michaelis
31 Ed III

(2)   **Error was sued** on a judgment rendered in a Formedon where the tenant appeared by attorney, and the bailiff of the Abbot of F asked jurisdiction and had it, etc   And then in the Franchise the tenant threw an essoin, and the demandant challenged it, because he appeared by attorney in the Common Bench, in which case the attorney should be essoined   And his challenge was entered, and the demandant also, in the meantime, had sent for the record out of the Common Bench, to the Chancery, and from

Statham 89 a   there to the Franchise   And notwithstanding this, because he had not an attorney before them in the Franchise, they adjudged, on the day given by the essoin, that the demandant should not take anything, whereas they should have awarded seisin of the land to him, because the tenant did not save his default, etc   And in that there was error FYNCHEDEN   It seems that they did well, for if the parole had been resummoned, the same warrant of attorney would have served, so it remains at all times here, then he shall have no attorney in the Franchise, for that which goes into the Franchise is but a transcript of the original THORPE   But when the demandant brought the record in, there it was affirmed clearly enough.   Wherefore they erred, for this same warrant which was in the Common Bench shall serve in the Franchise well enough, in which case the essoin shall be cast by the attorney, wherefore, etc PULTON You have here E of F, who tells you that the tenant who was essoined in the Franchise (which essoin you liken to a default) — he says that the same tenant had nothing but a term for life by his lease, and he prays to be received to defend his right FYNCHEDEN We have nothing to do with this matter here, except to redress that which was badly done before, wherefore, etc And also, if you would be received you should have a process to be received in the Chancery THORPE We are now to give seisin of the land to the demandant, and in the Franchise he cannot be received, for no default was enrolled, and although the day in the Franchise and this day are all one and the same day, still he came before judgment was rendered, wherefore the Court awards that the judgment be wholly annulled, and he be put in the same condition that he was in before, etc And that you, E, be received, etc And it was adjudged that the demandant count against him immediately, etc And so note this plea well, etc

There is no printed year of 31 Ed III The case has not been iden- *Case 2* tified in the early abridgments There is a very modern atmosphere about the pleading in the allegation of error

(3) **A man** shall not have a writ of Error where he is *Hilary* adjudged to account, before he has accounted. As *21 Ed III* appeared in the title of Account, etc

Reported in Y B Paschal, 21 Ed III, p 9, pl 25 See also Brooke, *Case 3* Error, 58

(4) **The master** of the scholars of Merton sued a bill *Michaelis* of fresh force against the Prior of E and certain of his *21 Ed III* *confrères*, where the prior answered as tenant, and said that the king was seised, etc, and gave to him and to his successors, etc And the plaintiff alleged the same land to be held of him and alienated in mortmain, and then he entered upon us, and we ousted him, judgment if an Assize? (Query if that be a plea? For by the seisin of the king the

seignory of the plaintiff was gone, and so the color not
sufficient) And the plaintiff said that he sued a writ out of
the Chancery to inquire of whom the tenements were held,
directed to the Mayor and Bailiffs of Oxford, and it was
found that they were held of us, wherefore we sued in the
Parliament alleging that this purchase of the king was to
defraud us of our seignory And it was adjudged in the
Parliament that we should be received to sue at the common
law, against the same prior, to recover the lands And we
entered upon him because no other recovery is given to us
And we said, when the Assize was held, that the usage of
the vill was such, etc , that if a man be seised of the land
for forty weeks, be it wrongfully or rightfully, it is not
allowed to anyone to oust him without a judgment, and
we were seised for forty weeks after, etc , judgment, etc
The prior said that the usage was not such, Ready, and
alleged the contrary, upon which the action was taken,
and such a usage was found, wherefore the plaintiff
recovered And then the prior sued a writ of Error and
assigned for error that inasmuch as by the charter of the
king these lands were pleadable at the common law, and
not by bill, in this there was error Another [was] that
the master pleaded in destruction of the bar, and he also
had made his title by the Assize, which was contradictory,
and was error And the third [was that] an issue was
taken upon the usage, which should have been tried by
their customary [law] which is their record, and not by the
Assize, like the customs in ancient demesne, etc , and in
this there was error WILLOUGHBY As to the first point,
although the tenements were pleadable at the common
law by the charter, etc , still, when the charter was annulled
by Parliament, they were of the same nature as before, etc
And as to the second point, to wit that he pleaded in
destruction of the bar, that was only a protestation
And as to the third point, inasmuch as the prior, by his own
motion, himself put in issue that which was to his own
advantage (for he could have had another issue), that was
his own act, as if in an Assize a man pleaded a foreign
matter, and relied [upon it] "Ready by the Assize " And

the plaintiff did likewise, that was well tried by the Assize And then the judgment was affirmed, etc

Reported in Y B Hilary (not Mich), 21 Ed III, p 46, pl 65   Case 4

(5) **If a man** sues a writ of Error on a judgment rendered in London, the Mayor shall have forty days to be advised, to have the record come. And then he shall send the record as vouched for by the Recorder then holding, etc. And if afterwards the party desires to [allege] diminution of the record he shall not be received, as in case where the record comes in by a writ, etc   *Hilary 18 Ed III*

The case has not been identified in Y B Hilary, 18 Ed III, or in the early abridgments The language of the text has had to be slightly extended, but it is thought not sufficiently to change the meaning of the original.   Case 5

(6) **He who was** in the reversion brought a writ of Error on a judgment tailed against his tenant for life, and assigned for error that, whereas in the Assize the sheriff sent to the Bailiff of the Franchise to secure the whole panel, where one vill was within the Franchise, and the other gildable, the sheriff should have secured the panel from that which was gildable, so error HANKFORD Your tenant for life shall never have error in that case, because he could have had an exception before the Assize was taken,[1] and as to that nothing appears, wherefore, etc , and no more shall you be received, etc Wherefore the judgment was affirmed, etc   *Michaelis 3 Hen IV*

Reported in Y B Mich 3 Hen IV, p 6, pl 30 See also Brooke, Error, 34, and Fitzh Error, 58   Case 6

(7) **One brought** a writ of Error as heir to his grandfather, to wit son of E, daughter, etc The tenant said that "your grandfather had issue one J, who is living," etc The plaintiff showed that the land was given to the grandfather and to his wife in tail, who had issue the said E, mother of the plaintiff, and that J was issue by another wife HANKFORD. Now, judgment of the writ, for he should have   *Trinity 3 Hen IV*

[1] He could have challenged the array

had a special writ. THIRNING. He cannot have another writ, wherefore answer, etc

Reported in Y B Trinity, 3 Hen IV, p 19, pl 4   See also Brooke, Error, 35, and Fitzh Error, 59   Brooke cites 9 Hen VII, folio 24, *contra*   Statham, of course, had not this later case

(8) **If one who** is outlawed be taken by a *Capias Utlagium,* he can say that at the time, etc , he was living in another vill, and so reverse the outlawry by way of answer, without suing a writ of Error, etc   But it is otherwise where he is not taken (as above) but comes in freely on the day of the return of the exigent, etc   But yet he cannot have another plea which goes in reversal of the judgment, as to say that at the time, etc , he was imprisoned in such a place, for that goes to the reversal of the judgment; but the other plea is nothing but a misnomer, to wit   that he was dwelling in another vill at the time, etc , for if he be called J of B at Dale, and he says that he was living at Sale; in that case J of B at Dale is outlawed, so that plea does not go to the reversal of the judgment, but he shall be understood to be another person, wherefore, etc   But on an error in fact or in the process, he is put to his writ of Error, etc   *Simile* 18 Hen VI, in Debt

There is no printed year of 15 Hen VI   Fitzh   Error, 23, has the case with citation to later cases

(9) **In debt,** where an exigent is awarded where no *Plures Capias* issued, and the defendant comes at the exigent and pleads and is condemned, he shall not proceed by way of error, because he has admitted the process to be good by his pleading. But it is otherwise if the original is bad, because that cannot be amended   And although he has pleaded with the plaintiff, still afterward he shall have the advantage of that by way of error, or by allegations before judgment   And a man shall not have any advantage of an error in fact if he could have had it before by way of answer, etc

There is no printed year of 36 Ed III   Fitzh   Error, 82, has the case He replaces the negative left out by Statham   He also cites 19 Ed III as being *contra*

(10) **One T brought** a writ of error against one W, who assigned for error that whereas the said W brought a *Præcipe quod Reddat* against him, and on the return of the Grand Cape waged his law by attorney, when he had not any warrant of attorney, and then on the day that he had to make his law he made default, wherefore seisin of the land was awarded SKRENE When a day was given over, where he had no warrant, the plea was discontinued NORTON He had made default after default, and the judgment was given on the default HULS When he gave a day over, the default was not of record, wherefore it was an error, etc.

Trinity 11 Hen IV

Reported in Y B Trinity, 11 Hen IV, p 88, pl 42 The case was adjourned without any decision having been given

Case 10

(11) **See in a writ of error** in the King's Bench, on a judgment given in Ireland in a writ of Error, which was sued out of the Common Bench in Ireland And there it was said that there is a difference between a writ of Error sued out of the Common Bench, and a writ of Error sued out of Ireland, or ancient demesne, for out of the Common Bench all the record will be sent, but out of Ireland or ancient demesne no more shall be certified than the transcript, etc Query as to other Courts which have jurisdiction of pleas, etc ?

Paschal 33 Ed III

There is no printed year of 33 Ed III Fitzh Error, 83, has the case

Case 11

(12) **One sued a writ of error** to reverse an outlawry because he was in the service of the king at the time, etc And he had a *Scire Facias* against the plaintiff, and after the reversal of the outlawry he counted against him on the original, etc Which note. But it is otherwise where it is reversed for matter apparent, etc [1] Query well, etc.

Michaelis 10 Hen IV.

Reported in Y B Hilary (not Mich), 10 Hen IV, p 7, pl 4 See also Fitzh Error, 84.

See Case 12.

[1] For an error apparent in the record

Michaelis
10 Hen IV
(13) **One who was** attainted of the disseisin in an Assize [1] assigned error by an attorney But it is otherwise if he should be attainted of a disseisin by force. By the opinion of HANKFORD, etc

Case 13
Reported in Y B Hilary (not Mich), 10 Hen IV, p 9, pl 8 See also Fitzh Error, 85

Michaelis
9 Hen V
(14) **If a man** be indicted and there is an error in the process, still if the defendant shall be arraigned it is no error, because he is arraigned upon the indictment and not upon the process The law is the same in an Appeal, as was adjudged here, and on the same appeal the defendant came at the exigent and pleaded "not guilty" and was acquitted, but he did not recover damages, because there was error in the exigent But yet they said that he shall not [?] be arraigned at the suit of the king, because the original was good (But I think that it is not so, for if so he puts his life in jeopardy upon the arraignment, and consequently he should recover damages, etc) Query?

Case 14
The case has not been identified in Y B Mich 9 Hen V, or in the early abridgments

Michaelis
9 Hen V
(15) **Error was assigned** because a writ of Trespass was brought against two, and one came and pleaded and was found guilty, to the damage, etc And a *Capias* was issued against the other, and an exigent also, where no *Pluries Capias* was awarded. And upon that he was outlawed, and he who was thus outlawed assigned error, and prayed that the entire judgment be reversed HULS It shall not be reversed except against him, for when the other and he were severed in pleading, it is as if separate writs had been brought Still the judgment is entire since it cannot be severed into parts, etc And they adjourned, etc.

Case 15
Reported in Y B Mich 9 Hen V, p 9, pl 5 See also Brooke, Error, 54 Hankford afterwards sent for the record, and found that a *Capias Pluries* was returned, so the allegation of error in the process would fail

[1] Without force and arms

(16) **The Baron of Dudley** brought a writ of Error against one J, son and heir of H, and he had a *Scire Facias* against one F as tenant of the half. And upon that the said J showed how his ancestor held certain lands of the king, and died, and the king seised him as his ward, and he prayed aid of him, and because he was under age he prayed that the plea be delayed And all the justices were agreed that he should have his age, etc (Query? For it seems that that plea is double, etc) NEWTON It appeared by the *Scire Facias* sued against the stranger that he is tenant of half of the lands, and this J tenant of the other half, as has been alleged, so the writ of Error is brought against J, because he is privy, in which case it is not reasonable that he have his age, for if he has nothing in the lands he shall not have his age, etc ROLFF Although he be not tenant of the lands, still he shall have his age, but in this case there is nothing else to be done, but to proceed to the examination of the errors against the terre-tenant CHEYNE It may be that at his majority he can bar the demandant as to the whole, as by a release, or bastardy, or such like And also if the judgment be reversed against the terre-tenant, the heir, on his majority, cannot say anything, because the error is assigned in the original, which is entire and cannot be severed into parts JUYN The terre-tenant can plead any plea now that the heir can plead at his majority, and yet the heir at his majority can plead also FORTESCUE A judgment can be reversed in part As if lands be given to a man and to his second wife in tail, and he had issue before by the first wife, and the lands of both are recovered against him by an erroneous judgment, and he dies the eldest son shall have a writ of Error for that, because it belongeth to him in fee simple, and he shall reverse the judgment And peradventure the second son shall be barred in that writ of Error And the law is the same as to the heirs in gavelkind And also a patent can be reversed in part, etc. The law is the same where two parceners are in by descent, and then make partition, and separate writs are brought against them, etc

And it was said in the same plea, that if the demandant

in a writ of Error is barred by a release, the judgment shall not be affirmed, but disaffirmed   And see that the *Scire Facias* which issued against the terre-tenant is upon two points . one, because the judgment shall not be reversed, the other, because he shall not be restored   RADFORD   How can they proceed to the errors when he who is a party is out of Court?   For by his nonage he is out of Court   And if he were dead you could not proceed   And also the land is prejudiced, for if the heir had a release of all actions of error the tenant could not plead that.   And if the release of all actions of error be made to himself, he cannot plead it, because he is a stranger to the record   But yet he can plead a release of all his right, because he is a tenant to the land   PASTON   The disseisor in an Assize can plead a release of all actions   So here   RADFORD   He cannot plead a release of all actions made to the heir, whose estate he has, for it does not extend to any lands, and such a release made to the heir, although he has lands, is good, wherefore, etc.   CHEYNE   He can plead as PASTON said, because it goes to the action, etc   Query?

And it was said in the same plea, that a protection cast by one of them shall not put the plea without day, except for himself, no more than in a *Præcipe quod Reddat*

And it was said in the same plea, that when a man reverses a judgment he can enter upon the heir, although he be in by descent   Well argued, etc

Case 16   Reported in Y B Mich 9 Hen VI, p 46, pl 30   See also Fitzh Error, 20   It might be well to repeat here Statham's frequent admonition, "Study well," as this case was very well argued and at great length

Statham 90 a

Michaelis 7 Hen VI

(17)   A man can have a writ of Error in the King's Bench for a judgment given in the same place, and assign error in the process, or in the return of the sheriff, or like things which are not the act of the judges   and this by the opinion of many in the case of *Gilhbrond Halywell,* well argued, etc   And the writ ran *"In redditione judicii,"* [1] etc., for there is no other writ   Which see, for it was well argued, etc

---

[1] *"Quia error in recordo, processu, aut redditione judicii,"* as it stands in the report of the case

And see in the same plea, that after judgment they can amend the process, if it be in the same term, albeit it is entered on the roll, because through the term the record is in them and not in the roll And although a writ of Error comes to them in such a case they will not put it upon the record, but will amend it, etc.[1]

Reported in Y B Paschal (not Mich), 7 Hen. VI, p 28, pl 22 See also Brooke, Error, 68, and Fitzh Error, 16

Case 17.

(18) **If a record** comes into the King's Bench by a writ of Error, and the record is not good, they will hold that the record shall remain in the Common Bench, as appeared in the case of *Fancone*,[2] where he had recovered a debt against a woman executrix, one D, and the writ ran in the record that it was between the woman and her testator, whereas it was between the woman and the said Fancone, wherefore they would do nothing. Wherefore the defendant came into the Common Bench and prayed his judgment PASTON The roll here mentions that the record has been sent to the King's Bench, wherefore, etc Query well

Paschal
9 Hen VI

Reported in Y B Paschal, 9 Hen VI, p 4, pl 8 See also Brooke, Error, 5, and Fitzh Error, 21

Case 18

(19) **One had recovered** a debt against one A, which A sued a writ of Error, and the record was sent into the King's Bench And the said A suffered the record to lie in the King's Bench without suing a *Scire Facias* against the plaintiff, or without doing anything. wherefore the plaintiff came into the King's Bench and showed all this matter, and prayed execution CHEYNE You ought to sue a *Scire Facias* against him before you have execution, albeit it is within the year And he did so, to which the sheriff returned *"nihil habet,"* wherefore he had a *sicut alias* and

Trinity
9 Hen VI

---

[1] Will amend the roll but not the record, according to the printed case This case of *Gilibrand Halywell*, or *Hillabrand Hallywell*, according to the different spellings in the reported cases, is most interesting, and well merits the commendation of Statham, and the earnest attention of the student of the procedure of the period

[2] John Franken, citizen of London, the case calls him.

the sheriff returned as before And because he was exacted and did not come, the Court awarded execution for the plaintiff, upon which he had a *Capias ad Satisfaciendum* against him, and on that the exigent And then the defendant came and showed all the matter to the Court, and how he was on the point of being outlawed, and he offered the money to the Court, and prayed a *Supersedeas* to the sheriff. and further he prayed a *Scire Facias* to the plaintiff to hear the errors, etc. NEWTON You cannot have a *Scire Facias* for you are nonsuited, wherefore you ought to satisfy the party and then sue a new original, etc. WAMPAGE He can pay the money to the Court, and if he will not sue to an end the party shall have the money, and if he sues and recovers the judgment, then he shall receive it back, etc And to that which you say as to his being nonsuited, it is not so, for he was exacted upon the *Scire Facias* to have execution, and not upon the writ of Error, for no *Scire Facias* was sued upon the writ of Error NEWTON If a man be outlawed, and sues a charter of pardon and a *Scire Facias* against the plaintiff, who does not come, he shall be nonsuited CHEYNE Not the same, for in your case the *Scire Facias* has the effect of an interpleader upon the first original, but this *Scire Facias* is only to have execution, etc, wherefore, inasmuch as he had not sued this writ of Error to the end, we will hear the assignment of errors before he has a *Supersedeas*, and if we see that they are clearly errors we will grant him a *Supersedeas*, and otherwise not. Wherefore he assigned the errors, and then he had a *Supersedeas* and a *Scire Facias* to the plaintiff to hear the errors And this in a writ of Annuity, well argued, etc

Case 19   Reported in Y B Trinity, 9 Hen VI, p 13, pl 2 See also Brooke, Error, 6, and Fitzh Error, 22 Fitzherbert says, "And so it appears a nonsuit was not adjudged here, but if the plaintiff had assigned those errors, and then had a *Scire Facias* and then would not sue, would it have been a nonsuit? Query, what would be done?"

Michaelis   (20) **J de P brought** a writ of Error against one R, upon
11 Hen IV.   a judgment given against him for the said R, in a writ of

Redisseisin, and on an outlawry pronounced on him in a writ of Debt, for the damages in the same redisseisin And he assigned for error that the sheriff took the inquest in the vill, and not upon the land, etc And for another error because the sheriff took a precept to the bailiff of the franchise, which he returned, and the sheriff took the inquest by others who were not returned by the bailiff HANKFORD: As to the first error, if the justices had a view of the land they could go to the vill and take the inquest well enough And as to the other point, the sheriff could vary from the return of the bailiff, inasmuch as he was a mediate official [1] SKRENE If he had not made the precept and the return of the bailiff a part of the record, it would be as you say ROLFF You will not be received to assign errors, for now, etc , by this deed you have released to us all the right, etc , and all actions GASCOIGNE Notwithstanding that he can assign errors in the outlawry, for no one is a party except the king ROLFF He has not assigned any errors in the original of the outlawry, to wit in the writ of Debt HANKFORD If there be error in the redisseisin, the outlawry will be reversed, because he has assigned enough (Which note, since there were two originals, etc) SKRENE He did not release HANKFORD You cannot give an answer to the release before the outlawry is reversed, which was conceded And then the outlawry was reversed But yet he will not be restored to the lands, because of the release And the law is the same where an error appears in the record, although the defendant has a release from the plaintiff, the Court will reverse the judgment, and yet the party will not be restored

And it was said in the same plea, that where one is out- Statham 90 b lawed and sues a writ of Error, he shall not have a *Scire Facias* against the party (But I believe that that is where he assigns error in the process, and not error in fact, to which the party shall have an answer for the king, etc All the same the party is not a party to the outlawry, but the king himself, etc)

[1] Inasmuch as he is the same person who made the array.

And see in this plea, that they would not grant a *Scire Facias* before he assigned an error; and if he assigned an error in fact, never afterwards He cannot assign many in fact, but he can errors which are apparent, M[ich], etc

Case 20

Reported in Y B Mich 11 Hen IV, p 6, pl 14 See also Brooke, Error, 47, and Fitzh Error, 64 And see the "residuum' on page 94 of the same year and term, pl 57

Hilary
11 Hen IV

(21) **An assize** was arrayed, etc , and the tenant said that the sheriff was out of the kingdom the day the writ was purchased and ever since, and that there was no under-sheriff nor other officer to serve the writ, and he prayed that they would not proceed, and notwithstanding that they took the Assize And the tenant took a bill of exceptions to that, and the justices sealed it, and then he sued a writ of Error and had the above record, and a *Scire Facias* against the party, upon certain assigned errors And then, after that, one of the justices before whom the Assize was arrayed came, bringing with him the bill of exceptions, sealed, and delivered it here as part of the record NORTON That bill came here without any warrant, for the bill should be brought here by the party when the record comes here, and upon that we should have awarded a *Scire Facias* against the justices to admit or deny their seals according to the Statute, or else, if the bill remained with the justices of Assize, they should have sent it here as part of the record, and if they did not send it, then the tenant could allege a diminution, etc HORTON Justices of Assize do not place it here with the record, as part of the record, for this bill was never part of the record, nor ever will be until it is brought here When they have put the record here, the power of the justices is ended as to bringing in this bill as part of the record And also no diminution can be alleged from this bill, for one never alleges diminution except of a thing which is part of the record, this bill was never part of the record until it came here, wherefore, etc., for it is not like a warrant of attorney, or things of that sort, which remain with the justices as part of the record,

wherefore it cannot come here unless by the party himself according to the Statute   And then as to that the justices were agreed that it had come in well enough by the hands of the justices   NORTON then assigned for error that they would not allow the exceptions, etc   HORTON Then it is necessary that a new *Scire Facias* issue against the tenant, for he was never notified to hear this error, for at the time the *Scire Facias* was awarded it was not part of the record   GASCOIGNE   Now [we] adjudge that it is a part and has always been a part [of the record] and so it relates, etc , wherefore it is not necessary to award a new *Scire Facias*, for it is but one record, etc.   Which the Court conceded.   HORTON (for the plaintiff)   Then we tell you that such a one who made the return in the Assize, as under-sheriff, was examined, and it was found by the examination that he was under-sheriff, so the bill of exceptions was diminished, and we pray a writ to the justices of Assize to certify it   GASCOIGNE   Diminution is never alleged in a bill   HANKFORD   Then he is injured, for the under-sheriff was examined, and that is left out in the bill and changes the case   And although the defendant himself, who made the bill, cannot allege diminution, still the plaintiff who was a party to the making of it can perfectly well allege the diminution   GASCOIGNE   That is the fault of the justices who sealed it, for they [should] not seal the bill unless the exception was heard   And also if a man alleges a diminution, which is certified, then he shall not allege diminution in that which is certified, in which the diminution was alleged before   TYRWHIT   Sir, he said he had never had a time before   NORTON   You are estopped to allege diminution, inasmuch as you demurred in law before, to wit   that that could not be part of the record   GASCOIGNE   That will not estop him   And then they agreed that he should not allege diminution , wherefore they went on to the examination of the errors   TYRWHIT   It seems that this is not error, for when the writ was found and the Assize arrayed, if it was not by the sheriff, the party can have an action of deceit against him who sued the writ   GASCOIGNE   It was not error; wherefore we reverse the judgment, and let the party be restored to the lands, and to the issues in the meantime Query, if the tenant had paid the damages, if he would get them back, etc ? (It seems not, for it was his own folly to pay them before he sued the writ of Error, etc)

Case 21

Reported in Y B Hilary, 11 Hen IV, p 52, pl 31, and the residuum on p 65, Paschal Term of the same year See also Brooke, Error, 50, and Fitzh Error, 66 Fitzherbert takes the case through 11 Hen IV, 51, 11 Hen IV, 65 and 11 Hen IV, 29, with a very long digest The case went through several terms before coming up on the points of error

The Statute is that of Westminster the Second, 13 Ed I (1285), cap 31, Stats at Large, Vol 1, p 163 (206) "An exception to a plea shall be sealed by the justices "

29 Hen VI

(22) **See such matter** Anno 29 Hen VI, in the Assize of Clyderhowe, where he sued a writ of error against the Lord of Clynton, who came at the *Scire Facias* when the plaintiff had assigned his errors, and said that in the record and process aforesaid there was no error And the plaintiff said the contrary And at the next term afterward the plaintiff assigned as error that omission was made of a replication to one of the titles in the Assize And the defendant said that the record was diminished because of that and prayed a writ to certify it, to which the plaintiff said, "to that you shall not be received, inasmuch as he has admitted his record, which is here, to be a full record" when he said, "in the aforesaid record and process," etc And this was argued a long time And the opinion of FORTESCUE was that he should get to allege the diminution well enough, inasmuch as the record which is here, and the record which remained with the justices of Assize, in which diminution is alleged, are all one record, so that his demurrer, when he said "in the aforesaid record and process," shall relate as well to that which is before the justices of Assize as to that which is here, inasmuch as it is all one record. And this can be clearly proved, for after the certification of such diminution the plaintiff shall not have a new *Scire Facias* as has been heretofore adjudged, and this clearly proves that it is all one record And also, when the party comes by the *Scire Facias*, he shall not have hearing of the record,

inasmuch as he is a party, and yet the writ of *Scire Facias* is to have hearing of the record and process, etc. But those are only formal words, as in the writ of warranty of charter, to wit *"unde chartam habet,"* etc Then he shall not have oyer of the record at the beginning And such error is assigned after he alleges diminution, because he has never admitted that before At the same time it was adjudged that he should not allege diminution, because he Statham 91 a was estopped, for the above reason, etc Well argued

There is no printed year of 29 Hen VI The case has not been Case 22 identified in the early abridgments

(23) **One G sued a writ of error,** and reversed an outlawry Hilary of felony pronounced upon him, because he was in prison 11 Hen IV at the time, etc And he had a *Scire Facias* against the terre-tenants and against the lords, mediate and immediate, who came, and one, who was a terre-tenant, said that the king by his letters patent (which he produced) leased him these same lands for the term of his life, and he prayed aid of him and had it And then at the *procedendo* he came and said that G was at large, etc And it was found that he was in prison, wherefore he prayed that the outlawry be reversed, and that he be restored to the land HANKFORD You shall not be restored to the land without a new *Scire Facias*, for that *Scire Facias* was but to inquire if he knew anything to say wherefore the outlawry should be reversed, and not repeal the letters patent THIRNING Wherefore, then, had he the aid? HANKFORD: Truly the aid was wrongly granted And then the outlawry was reversed, but whether he should be restored to the lands without a new *Scire Facias* to repeal the letters patent or not, they took under consideration, etc

The case has not been identified in Y B Hilary, 11 Hen IV, or in the Case 23 early abridgments

(24) **Executors** brought a writ of Error upon an out- Paschal lawry pronounced on their testator, and the action was 11 Hen IV maintained, etc Query, if the outlawry be for a felony? etc

Reported in Y B Paschal, 11 Hen IV, p 65, pl 22 See also Case 24 Brooke, Error, 51, and Fitzh Error, 65

(25) **In the exchequer chamber,** HODY related how Richard Wingfield was found a disseisor with force, in a special Assize in the County of Norfolk, to the damage of six hundred marks   And the justices of Assize sent the record into the Common Bench, and from there a *Capias pro Rege pro fine* was awarded,[1] upon which he was taken and his body [imprisoned] in the Fleet, upon which one of his friends came into the Chancery, relating all the matter, and that there were errors in the record, and prayed for a writ of Error and had it.   And then in the Chancery sureties were found that they would sue *cum effectu*, and also that he would satisfy the king as to his fine, and the party for his damages, if the judgment should be affirmed   Upon which they had a special writ reciting all the case, commanding the justices of the Common Bench that if they for this reason and no other detained him in prison, they should free him without delay and also that they should certify the writ of Error in the King's Bench.   And so it was done   upon which he appeared in the King's Bench, by attorney, and assigned certain errors, and prayed a *Scire Facias* against the plaintiff in the Assize   And because the errors which he assigned were not clearly errors, they would not grant him a *Scire Facias*   And then the plaintiff in the Assize prayed a *Capias ad Satisfaciendum pro Rege*   HAYDON   It seems to me that the *Capias* should issue, for in a writ of Error the plaintiff in the first [writ] came by a *Scire Facias* and pleaded a release of all actions for error, and the other could not deny it   Notwithstanding such a surety, the plaintiff, if he be present in Court, can pray an execution of his body, and consequently he shall have a *Capias ad Satisfaciendum* when he is there by attorney   FORTESCUE   The party in that case could not have a *Capias ad Satisfaciendum*, because no *Capias* lies on the first original, but he can have a *Capias pro Rege* and then it does not issue until the party is satisfied.   At the same time it seems to me that he shall not have a *Capias pro Rege* here, for the king has sufficient security, and could have a *Scire Facias* or a *Fieri Facias* out of that, for security was found

[1] "*Ad satisfaciendum Dominis Regi de fine*"   See also Fitzh Error, 24

for the king in the Chancery, and also to the party, which is a recognizance. And if he had put a caution in Court to the value of the damages, the party would have execution of the caution and not of his body. And this security countervails a caution, etc And by such security all other execution is waived HODY It has always been the habit of the King's Bench that such security shall be found in the King's Bench, and that those of the Chancery will take no security, except to sue *cum effectu*, which security is only for the nonsuit, etc And then in the King's Bench he found security by a recognizance to satisfy the party or to deliver his body to prison, if the judgment was affirmed, or else to put the money into Court, etc And upon that they awarded a writ to the wardens of the Fleet for the body of the condemned, and that he should assign errors in his own person, and not by attorney, because it seems that the justices of the Common Bench erred when they took his body by such a writ out of the Chancery, which cannot be redressed now except by a *Capias* PORTYNGTON If the security had been found in the King's Bench, I should be willing that he should assign errors in his own person, but that is a collateral security, which is clearly sufficient And they have power in the Chancery as well to take such security as they can in time of vacation upon an exigent or a *Capias* awarded in the Common Bench They can take security and award a *Supersedeas* to the sheriff; and if they can do that in term time it is well done, and it is a sufficient security there, and it is of record, and if they will they can send it to the Bench by a *mittimus*, etc GENEY A *Capias ad Satisfaciendum* issues out of the Common Pleas for one who has been condemned, and then the condemned buys a *Supersedeas* out of the Chancery [and] the sheriff shall not avow because such a condemned person is not bailable. So here the justices of the Common Bench should not obey the writ, for they have no power to take the security, for no security shall be found until the condemned party comes into the King's Bench, wherefore to adjudge it now is only an escape, in which case a *Capias* will issue for the king.

And also the security is void for it is "if the judgment be affirmed," and those of the King's Bench cannot affirm the judgment where no *Scire Facias* is awarded, for one party is not in Court, etc GODEREDE Inasmuch as they cannot grant a *Scire Facias* because no error is assigned, to my thinking they should affirm the judgment, etc And if the judgment is affirmed, he shall not have a *Capias* but execution of the security which was found And they adjourned, etc *Usque in profundum maris*

Case 25

Reported in Y B Mich (not Trinity) 18 Hen VI, p 17, pl 2

Michaelis
18 Hen VI

(26) **Error was sued** by the Baron of Dudley against one J, and a *Scire Facias* against one F, who was tenant of part J said that he was under age and heir to him who recovered, and he prayed his age and had it And whether the other

Statham 91 b

should answer to the error or not was well argued And it was adjudged that he should answer, wherefore he said that he who recovered recovered the half of the third part of a manor, as appeared by the record And he showed how one A, who was the ancestor of the plaintiff, against whom this recovery was made, was seised at the time of the recovery of the other half, so that the ancestor of the plaintiff and this J, who recovered, were tenants *pro indiviso*. And then they made a partition between them and others who were tenants *pro indiviso* of the same manor And he showed that holdings from these acres were allotted to the plaintiff, and holdings to J, whose estate he who is now tenant has, and holdings to the others, and he demanded judgment if against this division the action, etc. FORTESCUE He means that by that partition our action is gone, inasmuch as we have agreed to the record, and also that we were not tenant of the half as our ancestor was at the time, etc, but had one part in certain, but that plea is not sufficient, for he has pleaded a partition without a deed, so that the partition is void, for joint tenants or tenants in common cannot make a partition without a deed. And if one coparcener recovers against another by a *nuper obiit*, if there be error the other shall have a writ of Error, notwithstanding they have made the partition NEWTON It may well be there, because in that case the law

forces them to make partition, but in the other case not so.
But when a partition is made between tenants *pro indiviso*,
it is good, to my mind, without a deed, wherefore, etc.
And they adjourned, etc Query?

The case does not appear in Y B Mich 18 Hen VI, or, indeed, in Case 26
that year, but it does appear in Y B Mich 20 Hen VI, p 4, pl 13
See also Brooke, Error, 10, who says that the writ was allowed, but it
would not appear so from the printed case

(27) **One sued a scire facias** to have execution out of Michaelis
a fine which was served, and the demandant prayed 19 Hen VI
execution PORTYNGTON (for the tenant) Secure a writ
of Error to remove the record into the King's Bench
FORTESCUE That writ comes too late, for execution was
awarded immediately after the *Scire Facias* was awarded,
albeit the tenant had answered, as if you awarded a *Capias
ad Satisfaciendum* and the sheriff took the body, a writ
of Error would come too late NEWTON We will take
counsel (But yet it seems that the cases are not alike, for
in the case of the *Capias* it is executed in fact, etc)

The case has not been identified in Y B Mich 19 Hen VI, or in the Case 27
early abridgments

(27 a) **See by** NEWTON If one be outlawed, and the Paschal
exigent is returned, then he who was outlawed can come on 21 Hen VI
the day of the exigent and say that he was living in another
vill, etc And upon that he shall have a *Scire Facias*
against the plaintiff, for the plaintiff is not demandable
after the outlawry (Query, if he could come on another
day? etc) But it is hard for him to have any other plea
except the plea aforesaid, etc , for that plea does not reverse
any judgment, for the judgment is a good enough one, for
he who comes now will be understood to be another person

The case has not been identified in Y B Paschal, 21 Hen VI, or in Case 27 a
the early abridgments

(28) **One was outlawed** who sued a writ of Error and
had a *Scire Facias* against him on whose suit, etc. And
the sheriff returned that he was dead, wherefore the defendant prayed a *Scire Facias* against his executors, and because

his executors could not take advantage of that outlawry, it was reversed without awarding a *Scire Facias* Which note, etc.

Case 28

There is no citation for this case in Statham and it has not been identified

(29) **Four men** sued a writ of Error against a woman for an outlawry pronounced on them in an appeal by the said woman in Ireland, for the death of her husband And they had the record here, and the woman was garnished and came; and two appeared and the other two made default. NORTON Two have defaulted, wherefore we pray that the judgment be affirmed, for the nonsuit of one of them is the nonsuit of all SKRENE They can be severed HANK-FORD Certainly not It is your own folly, for you could have brought a writ in your own names, leaving out the others, but yet, query as to that, etc And the law is the same in a writ of Deceit, etc. But where error is brought on a judgment given in a real plea, the law is the other way, for there it should be brought accordingly, for other-wise they could not be restored to the lands according to the pleadings, etc And if one makes default, they shall be severed as they are in the first original, etc And the law is the same in Deceit, because a man shall be restored to the lands, etc.

Query, if two or three be condemned in a personal plea, shall one have a writ of Error without the other, since they cannot be severed, etc? And if it be brought in all their names, shall the nonsuit be the nonsuit of all? Which would be injurious, for perchance he lies in prison or is outlawed, etc

Case 29

This case has no citation in Statham, and has not been identified

Paschal
30 Hen VI

(30) **There is a difference** between a writ of Error and Attaint An Attaint lies against the tenant of the lands if the party be dead, but during all the life of him who recovered, the Attaint lies against him, although he be not tenant, but after his death it lies against the terre-tenant, and not against the heir, unless he is tenant in fact, but a writ of Error does not lie except against the party or his

heir, and a *Scire Facias* against the terre-tenant   And see, in a resummons, the difference, put by FORTESCUE, for they said that in an Attaint, to wit   the false oath cannot be assigned except for something which is of record, to wit   for a false oath which appears on the record, of which everyone who is tenant of the lands can have notice well enough   But errors can be assigned upon matters of fact, of which by force of law no one could have knowledge except one who is party or privy, and because of this a *Scire Facias* shall issue first against him who is a party or privy, and then a *Scire Facias* against the terre-tenant   And note this, etc.

The case has not been identified in Y B Paschal, 30 Hen VI, or in Case 30 the early abridgments

(31) **A vouchee brought** a writ of Error against the demandant, and had a *Scire Facias* against him. And the tenant brought another writ of Error against the same demandant and had a *Scire Facias* also And both are maintainable, for it may be that one of them had released to the demandant, which would not injure the other Query, if there be error between the tenant and the vouchee upon the place, shall the vouchee have a writ of Error against the tenant or the demandant? And if by that error between the tenant and the vouchee shall the whole be reversed? Or else no more than that which was between the tenant and himself? etc   Query well And error was assigned because the attorney for the tenant had no warrant of attorney at the time the inquest was taken, but he came to the justice before the inquest was taken and asked him to receive him as attorney, and delivered a bill to him   And the justice said that he would speak with his master, "and if it be his will to have you for his attorney I will admit you" And then he took the inquest, at which time no warrant was of record   And then afterwards the king died, and in the time of the king who now Statham 92 a is the justices recorded the warrant and not before, which cannot be sufficient, because by the death of the king their power was ended. Then, although they had a new commission from the king who now is, still he cannot bring

in the warrant without a writ, no more than when the power of a judge is ended by the death of that same judge, his executors can bring in the record without a writ GASCOIGNE The record of that warrant shall relate to the day which was [given] him, for when the parole was resummoned that would be called all one and the same record To what end shall he write to himself to bring in the record? For he could quite well bring it in without a writ

And it was said in the same plea, that if the tenant in that case died without an heir, and the lord entered as in his escheat, and then the vouchee reversed the judgment and was restored to the land which the lord had, in that case the lord could enter on the lands which the [tenant] lost,[1] still no judgment could be given for him, etc But HANKFORD held in that case that the vouchee could not assign error between the demandant and the tenant, because the tenant could not be restored But yet, query as to that, for it seems that the demandant should retain, etc

And it was said in the same plea, that in a writ of Dower, where the heir of the tenant vouched the heir of the husband, in the same county, and the demandant had judgment against the vouchee, and that the tenant should hold in peace, in that case the tenant can have a writ of Error, and still nothing was recovered against him, etc

And it was said in the same plea, when the vouchee has entered into the warranty he can allege that there was error in the same process, between the demandant and the tenant, and if it be found, they will not proceed further unless it can be amended

Case 31

There is no citation to this case in Statham but it appears to be the case reported in Y B Mich 8 Hen IV, p 3, pl 6 See also Brooke, Error, 39, and Fitzh Error, 61 See further, Y B Hilary, 8 Hen IV, p 21, pl 9

Michaelis
8 Hen IV

(32) **Error was assigned** because at the time of the taking of the Assize the sheriff nor the under-sheriff were present,

---

[1] The case says, "because the lord shall not be restored to the land against the tenant " There is an evident confusion in the text in Statham.

etc Query? And see the writ of Assize, which says that
the sheriff shall attend, etc

The point is found in the case printed in Y B Mich 8 Hen IV, p 14, Case 32
pl 14, in a long case which is further digested in the next case, *infra*,
case 33

(33) **In an assize,** the tenant said that the king enfeoffed Michaelis 8 Hen IV
[him] in fee, judgment if without the counsel of the king,
etc And he was ousted of the aid, and upon that error
was assigned, Item etc Wherefore the tenant said for the
other part, that the tenements were seised into the hand
of the king, and he did not show for what reason he was
ousted of the aid and on that he assigned error Item
Because another said that the tenements were seised, as
above And because another who was named had pleaded
in bar for the same tenements, they would not grant the
aid. And error was assigned for that, and they were
adjourned Query, etc?

Reported in Y B Mich 8 Hen VI, p 14, pl 14 See also Brooke' Case 33
Error, 41 However, the case as digested by Statham has some unlikenesses to the printed case, and the identification may be questioned

(34) **A writ of error** was brought against the heir, and a Michaelis 8 Hen IV
Scire Facias against the terre-tenants The heir died,
whereupon a writ issued to garnish the heir of the heir
And the sheriff returned that he had nothing of which
to be garnished, nor was he found, etc SKRENE He
should have attached him on those same lands HANKFORD
That is not so, but he could have an attachment for his
person if he had been found, but now, inasmuch as he was
not found, he should go to the examination of the errors
NORTON He lives in London, and we pray a *Scire Facias*
there And he had it, etc

And it was said in the same plea, that if the heir pleads
a plea, and the terre-tenant another plea, the plea of the
terre-tenant shall be taken, because he is in danger of losing,
etc.

The case has not been identified in Y B Mich 8 Hen IV, or in the Case 34
early abridgments

Note

See as to error, in the title of Replevin, Mich 3 Hen VI, in the title of Nonsuit, Hilary, 20 Hen VI, and in the title of Corone, Mich 30 Hen VI, and good matter in the case of *Pownying*, etc

Statham, title of Replegiare, *infra*, p 161 a, case 1 Statham, title of Nonnsute, *infra*, p 129 a, case 9, and Statham, title of Corone, *supra*, p 57 a, case 37

Paschal
50 Ed III

(35) **It is a good plea** in a writ of Error on a real action to say that the plaintiff himself is seised of the land And this by the opinion of THORPE, in Error, etc. (But it is not so)

Case 35

There is no printed Paschal Term for the year 50 Ed III The case has not been elsewhere identified

Note

See as to error, in the title of False Judgment, and also in the title of Outlawry

Statham, title of Faux Jugement, *infra*, p 98 b, and Statham, title of Utlary, *infra*, pp 188 b and 189 a

Note

Query, if the king recovers by an erroneous judgment against one, how shall that be reversed? And how shall error in the Chancery be reversed?

Michaelis
23 Ed III

(36) **Error,** where the king recovers, cannot be reversed without special leave, as appeared in a writ of Error And *simile* Paschal, 22 Ed III

Case 36

Probably the case reported in Y B Mich 23 Ed III, p 21, pl 3, although the point made by Statham is not clearly shown in the printed report The reference to Paschal, 22 Ed III, has not been traced successfully

Anno
7 Hen IV

(37) **Error was assigned** because the judge delivered the obligation to the plaintiff, and gave judgment upon the same obligation, etc Query, if the judge delivered the obligation to the plaintiff after judgment, is that Error, etc?

Case 37

The case has not been identified in Y B Anno 7 Hen IV, or in the early abridgments

Hilary
36 Ed III

(38) **One came in** by a *Cepi Corpus* and made an attorney The opinion of FYNCHEDEN was that error should not be

assigned for that, etc   FORTESCUE held the same opinion
Anno 20 Hen VI

> There is no printed year of 36 Ed III   Fitzh   Error, 86, has the Case 38
> case

(39) **Error can be assigned** although all the plaintiffs Michaelis
do not come, and this *Coram Rege*, etc   9 Hen V

> Reported in Y B Mich 9 Hen V, p 9, pl 5   Case 39

(40) **Error assigned** in law discharges an error in fact Anno
By the opinion of WILLOUGHBY, etc   24 Ed III

> The case has not been identified in Y B Anno 24 Ed III   Fitzh Case 40
> Error, 87, has the case

(41) **If a man sues** error in the Parliament, and he has Michaelis
a *Scire Facias* out of the Parliament to the party, it shall 8 Hen V
return to the next Parliament, for the common day in a
Scire Facias is forty days, and it is not certain when the
Parliament will be dissolved   And that by the opinion
of HANKFORD, in Error, etc

> The case has not been identified in Y B Mich 8 Hen V Fitzh Case 41
> Error, 88, has the case, and adds a comment to it   See *supra*, case 42.

(42) **As to error** sued in Parliament out of the King's
Bench, it was said that the record should remain with the
justices and that they shall show the record to the Parliament, or send a transcript there, etc   Query?

> This case appears as a separate case here   Fitzh   Error, 88, append[8] Case 42
> it to the case above, *supra*, case 41

EXECUCION

(1) **If a man** has his warrant *pro loco et tempore* by a writ Statham 92 b
of Warranty of Charters, he shall have execution of the lands Hilary
that the defendant had the day the judgment was given, 2 Hen IV
in whosesoever hands it comes   by THIRNING, etc   A man
shall have execution in a writ of Debt in the same manner,
etc   A man shall have execution of chattels that the

defendant had the day the execution was sued, and of no others by THIRNING and HANKFORD, in the same plea, etc

Case 1   Reported in Y B Hilary, 2 Hen. IV, p 14, pl. 5   See also Brooke, Execution, 23, and Fitzh Execucion, 122

Paschal
42 Ed III

(2) **A man shall have** execution of the lands which the defendant had the day the judgment was given, and not of the lands that he had on the day of the purchase of the writ   And that in Trespass against a common innkeeper.

Case 2   Reported in Y B Paschal, 42 Ed III, p 11, pl 13   See also Brooke, Execution, 16, and Fitzh Execucion, 34

Michaelis
44 Ed III

(3) **The Prior of B's** alienee was seised by reason of war, and leased it back rendering a certain rent   And then, in the Exchequer, upon the account, the prior showed how an abbot ought to pay him a pension which was in arrears for twenty years, and he prayed a writ against him for the king to bring him in to answer, so that the king could have execution of the arrears, and it was granted, etc   And this was called a *"quo minus"* But it seems that the king shall not have execution until the party has judgment to recover   Query, if it be so when this Court has no jurisdiction of the pension, but it belongs to the Court Christian shall the king then have execution?

Case 3   The case has not been identified in Y B Mich 44 Ed III, or in the early abridgments

Trinity
47 Ed III

(4) **In a fieri facias,** the sheriff returned that he had nothing but twenty shillings   And by the award the plaintiff had an *elegit* in different counties.   And the *elegit* issued after the year, without suing a *Scire Facias,* since the *Fieri Facias* was issued within the year   Which note, etc

Case 4   The case has not been identified in Y B Trinity, 47 Ed III   Fitzh Execucion, 123, has the case

Hilary
50 Ed III

(5) **A man shall have** an *habere facias seisinam* out of a fine, upon a grant and render, be it of lands or rent, and that within the year, as well as upon a recovery

Case 5   The case has not been identified in Y B Hilary, 50 Ed III   Fitzh Execucion, 124, has the case.

(6) **In debt** against one as heir to his father, who said Hilary
that he had nothing by descent. And it was found that 21 Ed III
he had an acre by descent   And the plaintiff prayed
execution of his lands and chattels, by an *elegit*, and had
it and THORPE, gave as a reason that he had pleaded
a false plea, which was found against him, as in the case
where executors plead "never executors" etc   And he said
the law is the same in Formedon   (But yet I believe
it is not, etc)

Reported in Y B Hilary, 21 Ed III, p 9, pl 28   Case 6

(7) **A man shall** not have execution by *elegit* against Hilary
the abbot nor the prior for damages recovered, etc   As 21 Ed. III
appeared in an Attachment upon a Prohibition, where he
recovered damages against a prior, etc   Query as to
the reason, and distinguish [the cases] for they are dis-
tinguishable, etc

Reported in Y B Hilary, 21 Ed III, p 11, pl 35   See also Fitzh: Case 7
Execucion, 125

(8) **If a man** makes a recognizance to me I shall have a Trinity
Fieri Facias within a year after the recognizance is made, 21 Ed III
and not within the year after the day of the payment
Query, then, if the day of payment be after the year,
I shall not have execution by *Fieri Facias* nor *elegit* before
I have sued a *Scire Facias* etc   Query?

And see in the same plea, that if one makes a recognizance with a statute merchant with a condition, that
I cannot have execution within the year, until I have sued
a *Scire Facias*, that is because of the conditions, etc

Reported in Y B Trinity, 21 Ed III, p 22, pl 14   The latter por- Case 8
tions of the digest are remarks by the digester, they are not a part of the
case

(9) **When a man** has execution by an *elegit*, and he in Trinity
whom the freehold is comes into Court and tenders the 21 Ed III
money, he shall have a *Scire Facias*, and not a *Venire Facias*
ad Computandum   But when he has cut trees, or has raised
the money in some such manner, the tenant of the freehold

shall have a *Venir Facias ad Computandum.* And in that writ the cutting and such things comes into question, and not in a *Scire Facias*, etc

Case 9

The case has not been identified in Y B Trinity, 21 Ed III, or in the early abridgments

Trinity 21 Ed III

(10) **One sued** a certification upon a statute merchant, and had a *Capias*, and the sheriff returned *"non est inventus,"* wherefore execution was awarded, and before he sued execution he died, whereupon his executors came into Court and showed the will, and prayed a *Scire Facias*, etc THORPE You shall have a new *Capias* KELSAY That cannot be, for they will not grant execution out of the certification more than once, etc WILLOUGHBY Sue then a writ upon the case to us, for we cannot know if the execution was sued or not, inasmuch as execution was awarded and no writ returned here which witnesses the death, etc Query?

Case 10

The case has not been identified in Y B Trinity, 21 Ed III, or in the early abridgments

Paschal 18 Ed III

(11) **If a man** be vouched and enters into the warranty and dies, and his heir renounces, the tenant shall have execution of the land that his father had at the time he entered into the warranty, into whatever hands it may come By THORPE, in a note

Case 11

The case has not been identified in Y B 18 Ed III, or in the early abridgments

(12) **The tenant** sued to have execution in value, and the sheriff returned that he was dead, wherefore he had a *Scire Facias* against the heir, and the sheriff returned that he had nothing, etc, whereupon a *Sicut Alias* and *Pluries* issued, and the sheriff returned as before, wherefore THORPE prayed execution at his peril WILLOUGHBY That cannot be before the garnishment be witnessed But yet execution was awarded In a note, etc

Case 12

There is no citation for this case in Statham, and it has not been identified elsewhere

(13) **The king** brought a *Scire Facias* against an abbot, to have execution out of a judgment tailed for him in a *Quare Impedit*, etc. The abbot said that after the judgment the king had seised the said advowson, together with other lands of the same abbot, because of war, etc, and had leased them back to him for a term of years, and he did not think that during the term, etc THORPE He shall not have execution NORTON We pray that our term be saved THORPE We will enter it[1] and you should sue the king, etc

Hilary
24 Ed III

Reported in Y B Hilary, 24 Ed III, p 39, pl 17   Case 13

(14) **One prayed execution** by *elegit*, and had it, to which the sheriff returned that he had nothing, etc , wherefore he prayed a *Capias*, and could not have it, but it was said to him that he could have a *Sicut Alias* if the tenant came to the lands or goods afterwards, etc But he should never have a *Capias* or a *Fieri Facias* And THORPE took for a reason that the entry is that "such a one came and *elegit executionem suam de medietate*, etc ," which is a higher sort of execution, etc.

Hilary
30 Ed III

Reported in Y B Mich 30 Ed III, p 24, pl 48 See also Fitzh Execucion, 126   Case 14

(15) **If a villein** makes a statute merchant to me, and before the days are past his lord enters, I shall not have execution against him By the opinion of WILLOUGHBY, in a statute merchant, etc

Hilary
18 Ed III

The case has not been identified in Y B Hilary, 18 Ed III, or in the early abridgments   Case 15

(16) **In the exchequer chamber,** HODY asked a question, to wit One had recovered ten pounds against two, in Trespass, and after the year he sued a *Scire Facias* to which the sheriff returned "*nihil habet*" And upon a *testatum est* he had a *Scire Facias* in another county, upon which the sheriff returned that one was garnished, who then appeared, and that the other had nothing, and the plaintiff

Statham 93 a
Trinity
18 Hen VI

---

[1] So that all be entered

prayed execution against him who had nothing   And our
doubt is if the *Scire Facias* which issued in another county
upon the *testatum* is offset by a *Sicut Alias*, for it is clear
if the sheriff returns *"nihil"* to the *Sicut Alias* that he shall
have execution   To which the Court agreed   ASCOUGH
In a *Scire Facias* in a writ of Detinue against the garnishee
it is otherwise   HODY   It is true, for in your case the
plaintiff never has any livery until he is garnished, for if
the plaintiff had livery the garnishee would be without a
remedy,   but in that case the defendant would not be hurt,
for if he had a release from the plaintiff he could have an
Audita Querela   And the law is the same in a *Scire Facias*
upon a charter of pardon, if the sheriff returns *"nihil habet"*
twice the charter will be allowed, for the plaintiff is not
hurt, because he can commence his first action, etc   Query
as to this matter, for although the *Scire Facias* offsets a
Sicut Alias, still it seems that he who appeared could bar
the plaintiff of all by a release, in which case it is not
reasonable that he have execution before the other has
pleaded with him, etc

Case 16   Reported in Y B Mich (not Trinity), 18 Hen VI, p 17, pl 2   See also Fitzh Execucion, 3

Hilary
12 Hen IV

(17) **In debt** against two upon a *præcipe*, the process
was ended against one by an outlawry,   the other came
and was condemned, and his body put in execution for the
said debt, then the other had a charter of pardon and a
Scire Facias against the plaintiff, and the plaintiff had
judgment against him, and had him in execution for the
same debt until it was satisfied by one of them   And if
one of them paid him, then the other could have a *Scire
Facias* against him to be dismissed   But in Debt by
several *præcipe*'s the law is otherwise, for it cannot be
warranted by the original, etc   By HANKFORD

Case 17   The case has not been identified in Y B Hilary, 12 Hen IV, or in the early abridgments

Paschal
7 Ed III

(18) **Where a writ** issues to the sheriff to inquire as to
waste, the plaintiff shall have execution for the damage

to the lands that the defendant had on the day the inquest
was taken, notwithstanding they were alienated before
the judgment was rendered in the Bench, etc   And the
same thing was done where the defendant alienated in mesne
between the *Nisi Prius* and the day in the Bench, etc
Simile Mich. 17, and Paschal, 18 Ed III

The case has not been identified in Y B Paschal, 7 Ed III, or in Case 18
the early abridgments

(19) **If one has** my land in execution, if I will tender him   Trinity
the monies, it should be tendered in the Court where he had   47 Ed III
execution by statute merchant or *elegit*, and upon that he
shall not have a *Scire Facias*, etc   And if the sheriff returns
that he was garnished and he does not come, the party
shall be restored without more, etc

The case has not been identified in Y B Trinity, 47 Ed III, or in Case 19
the early abridgments

(20) **If a man** be bound to me in a statute merchant and   Paschal
alienates a part of his lands, I can sue execution against   23 Ed III
him for that which remains, and he cannot force me to
sue against the other. But if I sue against the other, he
shall have an *Audita Querela* against me, and force me to
sue against all in common   And in that case the judgment shall be that he be restored to the issues in the meantime, and that the plaintiff shall have a new execution
against all in common   And that in an *Audita Querela*,
etc

There is no Paschal Term in the printed year of 23 Ed III   There Case 20
is no case of *Audita Querela* in the two short printed terms for that year

(21) **A man shall have** execution upon a statute mer-   Hilary
chant to the constables and wardens of the Cinque Ports,   18 Ed III
because the sheriff cannot make an execution there, etc

The case has not been identified in Y B Hilary, 18 Ed III, or in the Case 21
early abridgments

(22) **In a statute merchant,** the recognizee prayed that   Hilary
the land might be delivered to the extenders, because they   2 Hen IV

extended too much, and that they should answer immediately as to the debt HANKFORD The Statute of Acton Burnel is that they shall answer immediately, but that does not mean they shall pay immediately, but that they shall hold the lands and pay on the rent-days And it was so decided Which note, for in Paschal, 40 Ed III, in a Statute Merchant, the recognizee, in such a case, had a *Fieri Facias* against the extenders immediately, "*quod vide,*" etc (But I believe that that cannot be, for the land could be discharged by the entry of the issue in tail, etc.)

Case 22   The case has not been identified in Y B Hilary, 2 Hen IV, or in the early abridgments

Statute of Acton Burnel, or Statute *De Mercatoribus*, 11 or 13 Ed I (1283 or 1285), Stats at Large, Vol 1, p 141

Hilary
44 Ed III

(23) **If a man** wishes to pray that lands be delivered to the extenders he should come on the day of the return of the extent, or immediately thereafter, for if he delays until another term they will not do it, and the law is the same if the lands be once delivered to him, etc

Case 23   Reported in Y. B Hilary, 44 Ed III, p 2, pl 5

Michaelis
7 Hen VI

(24) **Two have goods** in common, and one recovers a debt or damages against one of them, who dies before execution, the plaintiff shall not have execution of those goods out of the possession of the other who had the goods by the survivorship By CHAUNT   Query, if he shall have execution in his lifetime, etc ? And it seems he may, for the other cannot have the action in his own name against him, etc. But yet he can take them and put the plaintiff to his action In an Avowry etc   Query?

Case 24   The point is found on p 2, of the Y B of Mich 7 Hen VI   The case begins on p 1, pl 6, but the point comes in merely as a part of the argument

Michaelis
26 Hen VI

(25) **If a man** recovers a debt or damages against a community, he shall not have execution of other goods than of those which they hold in common   And this by NEWTON and ASCOUGH, Mich 26 Hen. VI, in Debt, etc

There is no printed year of 26 Hen VI   The case has not been Case 25
identified in the early abridgments

(26) **If a man** brings a writ of Warranty of Charters, Paschal 16 Ed III
and counts that he was impleaded and the defendant admits
the warranty, he shall not have execution except of the
lands that he had on the day of the recognizance, to wit
the day of the judgment, and not the day on which the
writ was purchased, etc   But it is otherwise where he is
vouched to warranty, for there he shall have execution of
the lands that he had the day of the voucher, etc.

There is no early printed year of 16 Ed III   The case is to be found Case 26
in the Rolls Series, 16 Ed III, p 206

(27) **If three are** bound to me in a statute merchant, Hilary 34 Ed III
and each of them is equally bound, I can sue execution
against one of them alone, and against all at my will
But if I sue execution against two of them, they shall have
an *Audita Querela*, for I should sue all jointly, or else one for
all   And the law is the same upon an obligation made by
three who are equally, etc   I can have an entire *præcipe*
against all, or else separate *præcipe*'s, for the words are
"*Obligamus nos et quælibet nostrum*," etc   And if I bring
but one *præcipe* I shall have execution against all, and if Statham 93 t
several *præcipe*'s then only against one of them, but it is
not customary to have a joint *præcipe* in that case, because
they can fourch [and so delay], etc   But I cannot have
one *præcipe* against two, leaving out the third, no more
than in the case above, etc

There is no printed year of 34 Ed III   Fitzh   Execucion, 129, has Case 27
the case

(28) **A statute merchant** should be sealed by the parties, Trinity 6 Ric II
or else it is of no value   And this in a Replevin

There is no printed year for 6 Ric II   Fitzh   Execucion, 131, has Case 28
the case

(29) **Execution** was awarded against all the executors Michaelis 14 Hen IV
where one admitted the action   And this in a note

Reported in Y B Mich 14 Hen IV, p 12, pl 13   Case 29

Trinity
14 Hen IV

(30) **In a false judgment** out of ancient demesne, the justices of the Common Bench affirmed the judgment, and awarded execution.

Case 30

Reported in Y B Trinity, 12 Hen IV, p 23, pl 5 See also Brooke, Execution, 112

Paschal
20 Ed II

(31) **If a capias ad satisfaciendum** be awarded, although it be not found, the plaintiff cannot have another execution. *Simile* Anno 22 Ed III, *Liber Assisarum.*

Case 31

There is no printed year for the short period of 20 Ed II Fitzh Execucion, 132, has the case

Hilary
27 Ed III

(32) **Execution** shall be awarded upon the Statute of the Staple, notwithstanding the recognizee had released all the right that he had, etc In a *Scire Facias* By the opinion of the COURT, etc

Case 32

There is no printed Hilary Term of 27 Ed III Fitzh Execucion, 130, has the case

The Statute is that of 27 Ed III (1353), Stat 2, Statute of the Staple, Stats at Large, Vol 2, p 78

Michaelis
22 Ed III

(33) **If a man** sues a statute merchant for part of the lands in the name of all, he shall not have another execution And this in a statute merchant

Case 33

Reported in Y B Mich 22 Ed III, p 14, pl 42 See also Fitzh. Execucion, 86 and 134

Hilary
17 Ed II

(34) **Execution** ceases, in debt upon an obligation made by many, where one has admitted the deed, if the plaintiff will not suffer the obligation to be canceled, etc. (But yet this may be distinguished)

Case 34

The case has not been identified in Y B Hilary, 17 Ed II, or in the early abridgments

Trinity
10 Ed II

(35) **Execution** [was] awarded for executors of the executors on a judgment given by the first testator And yet they cannot have an action in that case, etc In a *Scire Facias*, etc.

Case 35

There is no case of a *Scire Facias* printed in Trinity, 19 Ed II The case has not been identified elsewhere

(36) **A man** shall not have execution upon a judgment [Paschal 20 Ed II] affirmed in a writ of Error, without suing a *Scire Facias*, although it be within the year, etc. In an Assize, etc (But yet, query?)

There is no printed Y B for 20 Ed II The case has not been identified [Case 36]

(37) **It is not allowable** for a bailiff in a Court Baron [Michaelis 11 Ed II] to sell goods upon an execution, but to retain them as distress until, etc *Simile* An 22 *Lib Assisarum*, in Trespass

The case has not been identified in Y B Mich 11 Ed II, or in the early abridgments The Book of Assizes has no cases for year 22 [Case 37]

(38) **In an assize** against two, where a judgment is [Trinity 1 Ed III] given against them generally, if one is not sufficient the other shall answer for all the damages, etc In a note, etc

The case has not been identified in Y B Trinity, 1 Ed III, or in the early abridgments [Case 38]

(39) **If I recover** against a clerk, and at the *Fieri Facias* [Hilary 16 Ed III] the sheriff returns that he has no chattels, I shall have a writ to the bishop to sequester his goods spiritual, and if the bishop will not serve it, I shall have a writ against him to answer for the contempt, directed to the sheriff, to attach him, as appeared in a *Scire Facias*, etc.

There is no early printed year of 16 Ed III The case has not been identified in the Rolls Series for that year and term [Case 39]

(40) **If a man** has lands in execution by force of a statute [Michaelis 18 Ed III] merchant, made at a later time, he can have an Assize of Novel Disseisin or a *Scire Facias* at his election, etc. Query?

The case has not been identified in Y B Mich 18 Ed III, or in the early abridgments [Case 40]

EXEMPCION

(1) **The Archbishop of Canterbury,** in his provincial [Statham 94 a, Michaelis 19 Hen VI] convocation, granted a tenth to the king in the Chancery, of which grant he notified the king, upon which the king wrote to the said archbishop to deliver the said tithes, on which the archbishop wrote his letters-patent to the Prior of Ledes to

have this same grant collected, and to pay it to the king in the Exchequer, on the octaves of St. Michael, etc On which day the prior came into the Exchequer, and showed the letters-patent of the king, by which he was exempt from such a collection during his life And the letters-patent bore a date before the grant of the tithes PORTYNGTON. It seems that they shall not be allowed, for the prior is one of the clergy who granted the tithes, and the grant is as follows "Provided that no privileged person be discharged from the collection of these same tithes," in which case he has renounced the benefit of the letters-patent ASCOUGH (to the same effect) For he should have shown his letters to the clerks, and prayed to be discharged NEWTON That cannot be, for they cannot allow it, no more than if I have a charter of exemption that I shall not be put on the jury, and I show it to the sheriff, he will not allow me [not] to be impaneled, for he has no power to allow it But when I come before the justices who have power to allow it, then I shall have the benefit from them, etc So here FORTESCUE It seems that the king cannot grant such an exemption as in the case here, for the archbishop had power over his subjects to compel them to collect such tithes And for any such exemption the archbishop himself will be forced to collect them, etc., which is not reasonable As if a man hold of me to collect my rent, the king cannot exempt him from that, because that would be prejudicial to me, so here, etc And they adjourned, etc

Case 1   Reported in Y B Paschal (not Mich), 19 Hen VI, p 62, pl 1 An enormously long case, adjourned without a decision upon the lengthily argued points

Michaelis   (2) **A man shall** not be exempt where the king is a
25 Hen VI party to the inquest, unless his charter says, *"licet ad nobis pertinet,"* etc. And it was the opinion of many that the charter [should be] *"licet nous parties sumus,"* etc And this was the opinion of FORTESCUE at St Martyns, in the year 26 of Henry the Sixth, in a *Nisi Prius*, etc

Case 2   There is no printed year of 25 or 26 Hen VI Fitzh Exemption, 5, has the case